The Gendered Society Reader

The Gendered Society Reader

Sixth Edition

Michael Kimmel

STONY BROOK UNIVERSITY, STATE UNIVERSITY
OF NEW YORK

Amy Aronson

FORDHAM UNIVERSITY

New York   Oxford
OXFORD UNIVERSITY PRESS

Oxford University Press is a department of the University of Oxford.
It furthers the University's objective of excellence in research,
scholarship, and education by publishing worldwide. Oxford
is a registered trade mark of Oxford University Press in the UK
and certain other countries.

Published in the United States of America by Oxford University Press
198 Madison Avenue, New York, NY 10016, United States of America.

Library of Congress Cataloging-in-Publication Data

Names: Kimmel, Michael S., editor. | Aronson, Amy, editor.
Title: The gendered society reader / [edited by] Michael Kimmel, Stony Brook
    University, State University of New York, Amy Aronson, Fordham University.
Description: Sixth edition. | New York : Fordham University, [2017] |
    Includes bibliographical references.
Identifiers: LCCN 2016019362 | ISBN 9780190260378 (pbk. : alk. paper)
Subjects: LCSH: Sex role. | Sex differences (Psychology) | Gender identity. |
    Sex discrimination.
Classification: LCC HQ1075 .G4672 2017 | DDC 305.3—dc23
LC record available at https://lccn.loc.gov/2016019362

ISBN: 978-0-19-026037-8

9 8 7 6 5 4 3 2 1

Printed by R.R. Donnelley, United States of America

For Jimmie Briggs
and Gary Barker

CONTENTS

*An asterisk indicates new to the sixth edition.

Introduction

AMY ARONSON AND MICHAEL KIMMEL

Every day there's another story about how women and men are different. They say we come from different planets—women from Venus, men from Mars. They say we have different brain chemistries, different brain organization, different hormones. Different bodies, different selves. They say we have different ways of knowing, listen to different moral voices, have different ways of speaking and hearing each other.

You'd think we were different species. In his best-selling book, the pop psychologist John Gray informs us that not only do women and men communicate differently, "but they think, feel, perceive, react, respond, love, need, and appreciate differently" (Gray 1995, 5). It's a miracle of cosmic proportions that we ever understand one another!

Yet here we all are, together, in the same classes, eating in the same dining halls, walking on the same campus, reading the same books, being subject to the same criteria for grading. We live in the same houses, eat the same meals, read the same newspapers, and watch the same TV shows. What gives?

One thing that seems to be happening is that we are increasingly aware of the centrality of gender in our lives. In the past four decades, the pioneering work of feminist scholars, both in traditional disciplines and in women's studies, has made us increasingly aware of the centrality of gender in shaping social life. We now know that gender is one of the central organizing principles around which social life revolves.

This wasn't always the case. Four decades ago, social scientists would have only listed social class and race as the master statuses that defined and proscribed social life. If you wanted to study gender in the 1960s in social science, for example, you would have found one course to meet your needs—"Marriage and the Family"—which was sort of the "Ladies Auxiliary" of the social sciences. There were no courses on gender. But today, gender has joined race and class in our understanding of the foundations of an individual's identity. Gender, we now know, is one of the axes around which social life is organized and through which we understand our own experiences.

While much of our cultural preoccupation seems to be about the differences between women and men, there are two near-universal phenomena that define the experiences of women and men in virtually every culture we have ever known. First: *Why is it that virtually every single society differentiates people on the basis of gender?* Why are women and men perceived as different in every known society? What are the differences that are perceived? Why is gender at least one—if not the central—basis for the division of labor? And, second: *Why is it that virtually every known society is also based on male domination?* Why does virtually every society divide social, political, and economic resources unequally between the genders? Why is a gendered division of labor also an unequal division of labor? Why are women's tasks and men's tasks valued differently?

Of course, there are dramatic differences among societies regarding the type of gender differences, the levels of gender inequality, and the amount of violence (implied or real) that is necessary to maintain both systems of difference and domination. But the basic facts remain: *Virtually every society known to us is founded upon assumptions of gender difference and the politics of gender inequality.*

Most of the arguments about gender difference begin, as does this book, with biology. Women and men *are* biologically different, after all. Our reproductive anatomies are different, as are our reproductive destinies. Our brain structures differ, our brain chemistries differ. Our musculature is different. We have different levels of different hormones circulating through our different bodies. Surely, these add up to fundamental, intractable, and universal differences, and these differences provide the foundation for male domination, don't they?

In these models, biological "sex"—by which we mean the chromosomal, chemical, anatomical apparatuses that make us either male or female—leads inevitably to "gender," by which we mean the cultural and social meanings, experiences, and institutional structures that are defined as appropriate for those males and females. "Sex" is male and female; "gender" refers to cultural definitions of masculinity and femininity—the meanings of maleness or femaleness.

Biological models of sex difference occupy the "nature" side of the age-old question about whether it is nature or nurture that determines our personalities. Of course, most sensible people recognize that both nature *and* nurture are necessary for gender development. Our biological sex provides the raw material for our development—and all that evolution, different chromosomes, and hormones have to have some effect on who we are and who we become.

But biological sex varies very little, and yet the cultural definitions of gender vary enormously. And it has been the task of the social and behavioral sciences to explore the variations in definitions of gender. Launched originally as critiques of biological universalism, the social and behavioral sciences—anthropology, history, psychology, sociology—have all had an important role to play in our understanding of gender.

What they suggest is that what it means to be a man or a woman will vary in four significant ways. First, the meanings of gender vary from one society to another. What it means to be a man or a woman among aboriginal peoples in the Australian outback or in the Yukon territories is probably very different from what it means to be a man or a woman in Norway or Ireland. It has been the task of anthropologists to specify some of those differences, to explore the different meanings that gender has in different cultures. Some cultures, like our own, encourage men to be stoic and to prove their masculinity, and men in other cultures seem even more preoccupied with demonstrating sexual prowess than American men seem to be. Other cultures prescribe a more relaxed definition of masculinity, based on civic participation, emotional responsiveness, and the collective provision for the community's needs. Some cultures encourage women to be decisive and competitive; others insist that women are naturally passive, helpless, and dependent.

Second, the meanings of masculinity and femininity vary within any one culture over time. What it meant to be a man or a woman in seventeenth-century France is probably very different from what it might mean today. My own research has suggested that the meanings of manhood have changed dramatically from the founding of America in 1776 to the present (see Kimmel 2011). (Although for reasons of space I do not include any historical material in this volume, inquiries into the changing definitions of gender have become an area of increasing visibility.)

Third, the meaning of masculinity and femininity will change as any individual person grows. Following Freudian ideas that individuals face different developmental tasks as they grow and develop, psychologists have examined the ways in which the meanings of masculinity and femininity change over the course of a person's life. The issues confronting a man about proving himself, feeling successful, and the social institutions in which he will attempt to enact those experiences will change, as will the meanings of femininity for prepubescent women, women in child-bearing years, and post-menopausal women, or for women entering the labor market and those retiring from it.

Finally, the meanings of gender will vary *among* different groups of women and men within any particular culture at any particular time. Simply put, not all American men and women are the same. Our experiences are also structured by class, race, ethnicity, age, sexuality, and region of the country. Each of these axes modifies the others. Just because we make gender visible doesn't mean that we make these other organizing principles of social life invisible. Imagine, for example, an older, black, gay man in Chicago and a young, white, heterosexual farm boy in Iowa. Wouldn't they have different definitions of masculinity? Or imagine a twenty-two-year-old heterosexual poor Asian American woman in San Francisco and a wealthy white Irish Catholic lesbian in Boston. Wouldn't their ideas about what it means to be a woman be somewhat different? The interplanetary theory of gender differences collapses all such differences and focuses *only* on gender. One of the important elements of a sociological approach is to explore the differences *among* men and *among* women, since, as it turns out, these are often more decisive than the differences between women and men.

If gender varies across cultures, over historical time, among men and women within any one culture, and over the life course, that means we really cannot speak of masculinity or femininity as though they were constant, universal essences, common to all women and to all men. Rather, gender is an ever-changing, fluid assemblage of meanings and behaviors. In that sense, we must speak of *masculinities* and *femininities,* in recognition of the different definitions of masculinity and femininity that we construct. By pluralizing the terms, we acknowledge that masculinity and femininity mean different things to different groups of people at different times.

At the same time, we can't forget that all masculinities and femininities are not created equal. American men and women must also contend with a dominant definition, a culturally preferred version that is held up as the model against which we are expected to measure ourselves. We thus come to know what it means to be a man or a woman in our culture by setting our definitions in opposition to a set of "others"—racial minorities, sexual minorities. For men, the classic "other" is, of course, women. It often feels imperative that men make it clear—eternally, compulsively, decidedly—that they are not "like" women.

For both women and men, this is the "hegemonic" definition—the one that is held up as the model for all of us. The hegemonic definition of masculinity is "constructed in relation to various subordinated masculinities as well as in relation to women," writes sociologist R. W. Connell (1987, 183). The sociologist Erving Goffman once described this hegemonic definition of masculinity like this:

> In an important sense there is only one complete unblushing male in America: a young, married, white, urban, northern, heterosexual, Protestant, father, of college education, fully employed, of good complexion, weight, and height, and a recent record in sports.... Any male who fails to qualify in any one of these ways is likely to view himself—during moments at least—as unworthy, incomplete, and inferior. (Goffman 1963, 128)

Women also must contend with such an exaggerated ideal of femininity. Connell calls it "emphasized femininity." Emphasized femininity is organized around compliance with gender inequality and is "oriented to accommodating the interests and desires of men." One sees emphasized femininity in "the display of sociability rather than technical competence, fragility in mating scenes, compliance with men's desire for titillation and ego-stroking in office relationships, acceptance of marriage and child care as a response to labor-market discrimination against women" (Connell 1987, 183, 188, 187). Emphasized femininity exaggerates gender difference as a strategy of "adaptation to men's power" stressing empathy and nurturance; "real" womanhood is described as "fascinating" and women are advised that they can wrap men around their fingers by knowing and playing by "the rules."

The essays in the first four sections of this book recapitulate these disciplinary concerns and also present the development of the sociological argument chronologically. Following Darwin and others, biological evidence was employed in the nineteenth century to assert the primacy of sex differences, and the section on biological differences presents some evidence of distinct and categorical biological differences, as well as a couple of critiques of that research from a neurobiologist and a psychologist, respectively. Cross-cultural research by anthropologists, among them Margaret Mead, perhaps the nation's most historically celebrated cultural anthropologist, offered a way to critique the claims of biological inevitability and universality lodged in those biological arguments. The selections in this section demonstrate how anthropologists have observed those cross-cultural differences and have used such specific cultural rituals as initiation ceremonies or the prevalence of rape in a culture to assess different definitions of gender.

Psychological research also challenged biological inevitability, locating the process of *acquiring* gender within the tasks of the child in his or her family. Achieving successful gender identity was a perilous process, fraught with danger of gender "inversion" (homosexuality) as the early and renowned social psychologist Lewis Terman saw it in his treatise on *Sex and Personality* in 1936. Subsequent psychological research has refined our understanding of how individuals acquire the "sex roles" that society has mapped out for them.

And it falls to the sociologist to explore the variations *among* different groups of women and men, and also to specify the ways in which some versions of masculinity or femininity are held up as the hegemonic models against which all others are arrayed and measured. Sociologists are concerned less with the specification of sex roles and more with the understanding of *gender relations*—the social and political dynamics that shape our conceptions of "appropriate" sex roles. Thus, sociologists are interested not only in gendered individuals—the ways in which we acquire our gendered identities—but also in gendered institutions—the ways in which those gendered individuals interact with one another in the institutions of our lives that shape, reproduce, and reconstitute gender.

Sociologists argue that male domination is reproduced not only by socializing women and men differently, but also by placing them in organizations and institutions in which specifically gendered norms and values predominate and by which both women and men are then evaluated and judged. Gendered individuals do not inhabit gender-neutral social situations; both individuals and institutions bear the mark of gender.

The six central, institutional sections of this book explore how the fundamental institutions of family, education, religion, politics, media, and the workplace express and normalize gender difference and, in so doing, reproduce relations of inequality between women and men. In each of these arenas, the debates about gender differences and inequality have been intense, from the questions about the division of household labor, sexual orientation of parents, effect of religion on gender identity, comparable worth, workplace discrimination, and a variety of other critical policy debates. The essays in these sections will enable the reader to make better sense of these debates and understand the ways in which gender is performed and elaborated within social institutions.

Finally, we turn to our intimate lives, our bodies, and our experiences of friendship, love, and sex. Here, differences between women and men do emerge. Men and women have different ways of loving, of caring, and of having sex. And it turns out that this is true whether the women and men are heterosexual or homosexual—that is, gay men and heterosexual men are more similar to each other than they are different; and, equally, lesbians and heterosexual women have more in common than either does with men. On the other hand, the differences between women and men seem to have as much to do with the shifting definitions of love and intimacy, and the social arenas in which we express (or suppress) our emotions, as they do with the differences in our personalities. And there is significant evidence that the gender gap in love and sex and friendship is shrinking as women claim greater degrees of sexual agency and men find their emotional lives (with lovers, children, and friends) impoverished by adherence to hegemonic definitions of masculinity. Men and women do express some differences in our intimate lives, but these differences are hardly of interplanetary cosmic significance. It appears that women and men are not from different planets—not opposite sexes, but neighboring sexes. And we are moving closer and closer to each other.

This may be the most startling finding that runs through many of these essays. What we find consistently is that the differences between women and men do not account for very much of the different experiences that men and women have. Differences *between* women and men are not nearly as great as the differences *among* women or *among* men—differences based on class, race, ethnicity, sexuality, age, and other variables. Women and men enter the workplace for similar reasons, though what they find there often reproduces the differences that "predicted" they would have different motivations. Boys and girls are far more similar to each other in the classroom, from elementary school through college, although everything in the school—from their textbooks, their teachers, their experiences in the playground, the social expectations of their aptitudes and abilities—pushes them to move farther and farther apart.

The most startling conclusion that one reaches from examining the evidence on gender difference is that women and men are not from different planets at all. In the end, we're all Earthlings!

References

Connell, R. W. *Gender and Power.* Stanford, CA: Stanford University Press, 1987.

Goffman, Erving. *Stigma.* Englewood Cliffs, NJ: Prentice-Hall, 1963.

Gray, John. *Men Are from Mars, Women Are from Venus.* New York: Harper Collins, 1995.

Kimmel, Michael. *Manhood in America: A Cultural History*, 3rd edition. New York: Oxford University Press, 2011.

Terman, Lewis and Catherine Cox Miles. *Sex and Personality.* New York: McGraw-Hill, 1936.

Changes to the Sixth Edition

- Twenty-seven new essays, including three new pieces on The Gendered Media (Part 10) and new coverage of:
  - Transgender individuals
  - Female genital mutilation
  - The masculine overcompensation thesis
  - Conservative religious communities
  - High-achieving women

Acknowledgments

The editors wish to thank the following reviewers for their feedback on the fifth edition:

Nancy L. Bishop, University of North Carolina–Charlotte

Robert B. Jenkot, Coastal Carolina University

Margaret Crowdes, California State University–San Marcos

Amanda Czerniawski, Temple University

Abbe Depretis, Temple University

Helen Emmitt, Centre College

Kathleen Farrell, Colby-Sawyer College

Karen L. Frederick, Saint Anselm College

Katrina C. Hoop, Saint Joseph's College of Maine

Harmony Newman, University of Northern Colorado

Brenda A. Riemer, Eastern Michigan University

The Gendered Society
Reader

Anatomy and Destiny

BIOLOGICAL ARGUMENTS ABOUT GENDER DIFFERENCE

Anatomy, many of us believe, is destiny; our constitution of our bodies determines our social and psychological disposition. Biological sex decides our gendered experiences. Sex is temperament. Biological explanations offer perhaps the tidiest and most coherent explanations for both gender difference and gender inequality. The observable differences between males and females derive from different anatomical organizations, which make us different as men and women, and those anatomical differences are the origin of gender inequality. These differences, as one biologist put it, are "innate, biologically determined, and relatively resistant to change through the influences of culture."

Biologists rely on three different sets of evidence. Evolutionists, such as sociobiologists and evolutionary psychologists, argue that sex differences derive from the differences in our reproductive anatomies—which compel different reproductive "strategies." Because a female must invest much energy and time in ensuring the survival of one baby, her "natural" evolutionary instinct is toward high sexual selectivity and monogamy; females are naturally modest and monogamous. Males, by contrast, are naturally promiscuous, since their reproductive success depends upon fertilizing as many eggs as possible without emotional constraint. Males who are reproductively unsuccessful by seduction, biologists tell us, may resort to rape as a way to ensure that their reproductive material is successfully transmitted to their offspring.

A second source of evidence of biological difference comes from some differences in brain function and brain chemistry. In the late nineteenth century, studies showed definitively that men's brains were heavier or more complex than women's, and thus that women ought not to seek higher education or vote. (Similar studies also "proved" that the brains of white people were heavier and more complex than those of black people.) Today, such studies are largely discredited, but we still may read about how males and females use different halves of their brains, or that they use them differently, or that the two halves are differently connected.

Finally, some biologists rely on the ways in which the hormonal differences that produce secondary sex characteristics determine the dramatically divergent paths that males and females take from puberty onward. Testosterone causes aggression, and since males have far more testosterone than females, male aggression—and social, political, and economic dominance—is explained.

To the social scientist, though, this evidence obscures as much as it reveals, telling us more about our own cultural needs to find these differences than about the differences themselves. Biological explanations collapse all other sources of difference—race, ethnicity, age—into one single, dichotomous variable that exaggerates the differences between women and men, and also minimizes the similarities between them. "Believing is seeing," notes sociologist Judith Lorber, and seeing these differences as decisive is often used as a justification for gender inequality.

The readings in this section offer critiques of these biological arguments. Anne Fausto-Sterling uses biological evidence to undermine simplistic pop biological claims about binary difference. Martha McCaughey weighs the empirical evidence from evolutionary psychology and finds it somewhat lighter than the extensive media coverage it has received. Mixing a critique of the biology and that media coverage, McCaughey exposes evolutionary psychology as a "useful fiction," answering cultural needs even if it cannot answer scientific questions. Neuroscientist Lise Eliot reviews the research on brain differences—and critiques the pop psychology that makes far more of that literature than any serious scientist ever would. And neuroscientist Robert M. Sapolsky suggests that the research on hormonal differences does not make a convincing case. Together, these essays reveal that recourse to biology exclusively may justify existing inequalities by reference to observed differences and ignoring observed similarities. It's more than bad politics: it's also bad science.

Where Does Gender Come From?

ANNE FAUSTO-STERLING

Baby showers are often color-coded events. If the new arrival is a boy, then the purchase of a blue onesie featuring a truck is in order. For a girl, perhaps a pretty pink, flowered, lacy blanket.

Many people assume that this blue and pink color code represents not only a set of cultural norms, but also the innate preferences of the child. By the time a female becomes a toddler, the fact that she prefers pink dresses and toys seems like nature just taking its course. But is biology really the reason many modern girls like pink and modern boys like blue, even before they can speak the words for these colors?

A closer look at human development suggests that the truth is more complex. Rather than defaulting to explanations rooted in biology and genetics, sex-related preferences should be an invitation to ask broader questions about gender norms and cultural expectations.[1] For example: What is the source of the pleasure that girls and boys get from certain colors? Is it the pleasure for things that are familiar to them? Or perhaps it is the positive feedback children receive for liking "gender appropriate" colors?

Preferences for certain colors, toys (trucks or dolls), or types of play (physically active versus social) are sometimes assumed to be inherent because they typically appear when a child is as young as three or four years of age. Psychologists and biologists often point to hormones, genes, and other biological factors as the underlying causes.

But these arguments do little to explain the mechanisms or processes by which preferences emerge and solidify. To more thoroughly understand the root of sex-related differences, we need to rigorously examine how potentially relevant biological and environmental factors influence development (and influence one another) over time. For example, I have been studying the development of sex-related differences through extensive video recording and analysis of infant and caretaker behavior under naturalistic conditions in the home.[2]

My research shows that, even at a young age, "nature" and "nurture" already interact.[3] The first three years of a child's life mark a period of extraordinary brain development and synapse growth. Like a sponge, the child absorbs everything around it, etching a record of its sensory experiences in its developing neurons. Social and cultural cues children experience during this period can influence their physiological development, establishing bodily patterns that set the stage for later phases of development.

One of my studies focuses on the belief that boy infants are more physically active than girl infants.[4] While the babies in the study show no sex-related differences in their own spontaneous activity, we discovered through detailed observation that the mothers interact with the boys in a more physically active way. They move boy infants, help them sit up, and touch them more often than they do girls.

The impact of the mothers' behavior may go much deeper than just setting cultural expectations—it could actually have biological consequences. While more testing is needed to understand these biological effects, it is possible that the sensory, motor, and neuromuscular systems of boys develop differently than those of girls, at least partly in response to different patterns of maternal handling.

If biological development is influenced by a child's environment in this way, "nature" and "nurture" are no longer distinct. They are a developmental unit, two sides of the same coin. Rather than talking about nature versus nurture, we should ask: How is nature being affected by certain kinds of nurturing events? And instead of viewing gender as something inherent and fixed, we should understand it as a developmental process involving the ongoing interaction of genes, hormones, social cues, cultural norms, and other factors.[5]

Moving beyond the nature versus nurture dichotomy allows us to have a more nuanced, accurate understanding of gender. For those who want to move beyond the pink and blue split, perhaps a first step is to purchase something green for the next baby shower.

Notes

1. For a thorough exploration of questions about the role of cultural, environmental, and social factors in the development of sex-related differences, see Anne Fausto-Sterling (2012) *Sex/Gender: Biology in a Social World*, New York: Routledge.
2. For examples of studies using this methodology, see: Richard Evan Ahl, Anne Fausto-Sterling, Cynthia García-Coll, Ronald Seifer (2013) "Gender and discipline in 5–12-month-old infants: A longitudinal study," *Infant Behavior and Development*, 36(2): 199–209; and Jihyun Sung, Anne Fausto-Sterling, Cynthia García-Coll, and Ronald Seifer (2013) "The Dynamics of Age and Sex in the Development of Mother-Infant Vocal Communication Between 3 and 11 Months." *Infancy* 18(6): 1135–1158.
3. Anne Fausto-Sterling, Cynthia García-Coll, and Meaghan Lamarre (2012) "Sexing the baby: Part 1—What do we really know about sex differentiation during the first three years of life?" *Social Science and Medicine*, 74(11): 1684–1692.
4. This work is currently in draft manuscript form. Readers can contact Anne Fausto-Sterling for further information.
5. Anne Fausto Sterling, Cynthia García Coll, and Meaghan Lamarre (2012) "Sexing the baby: Part 2—Applying dynamic systems theory to the emergences of sex-related differences in infants and toddlers," *Social Science and Medicine*, 74(11): 1693–1702.

Caveman Masculinity: Finding Manhood in Evolutionary Science[1]

MARTHA McCAUGHEY

The Caveman as Retrosexuality

Most of us can call up some image of prehistoric man and his treatment of women. He's a shaggy, well-muscled caveman, whose name is Thor, and we might picture him, club in hand, approaching a scrawny but curvaceous woman, whom he bangs over the head and drags by the hair into a cave to mate. I'm sure the majority of readers recognize this imagery. Indeed, today an image of modern men as guided by such prehistoric tendencies is even celebrated on T-shirts sold to American men on web sites that allow people to post and sell their own designs. One such image for sale on the Cafe Press web site features a version of Thor, wearing a fur pelt and holding a club, accompanied by the slogan "ME FIND WOMAN!" Another image available for T-shirts, boxer shorts, baseball caps, and coffee mugs features a man dressed in a one-shoulder fur pelt, with his club, smiling behind a cavewoman who is wearing a fur bikini outfit and cooking a skinned animal on a spit, with the saying "MENS PRIORITYS [sic] : 10,000 YEARS LATER AND STILL ON THE HUNT FOR FOOD AND SEX!" Another image features only the club, with the saying, "caveman: primitive pimpin'."

Everywhere we look we can find applications of an increasingly fashionable academic exercise—the invocation of evolutionary theory to explain human male behaviors, particularly deplorable behaviors such as sexual harassment, rape, and aggression more generally. The familiar portrayals of sex differences based in evolution popularize and legitimize an academic version of evolutionary thought known increasingly as evolutionary psychology, a field referred to as the "science of the mind."[2] The combination of scholarly and popular attention to evolution and human male sexuality has increasingly lodged American manhood in an evolutionary logic. The discourse of evolutionary science—however watered down or distorted the "science" becomes as it flows through popular culture—has become part of popular consciousness, a sort of cultural consensus about who men are.

The evolutionary theory is that our human male ancestors were in constant competition with one another for sexual access to fertile women, who were picky about their mate choices given the high level of parental investment required of the human female for reproduction—months of gestation, giving birth, and then years of lactation and care for a dependent child. The human male's low level of parental investment required for reproduction, we are told, resulted in the unique boorishness of the hairier sex: He is sexually promiscuous, he

places an enormous emphasis on women's youth and beauty, which he ogles every chance he gets, he either cheats on his wife or wants to, and he can be sexually aggressive to the point of criminality.

We find references to man's evolutionary heritage not only on T-shirts but in new science textbooks, pop psychology books on relationships, men's magazines, and Broadway shows. There are caveman fitness plans and caveman diets. *Saturday Night Live's* hilarious "Unfrozen Caveman Lawyer" and the affronted caveman of the Geico car insurance ads joke about the ubiquity of caveman narratives. More disturbingly, the Darwinian discourse also crops up when men need an excuse for antisocial behavior. One man, who was caught on amateur video participating in the Central Park group sexual assaults in the summer of 2000, can be heard on video telling his sobbing victim, "Welcome back to the caveman times." How does a man come to think of himself as a caveman when he attacks a woman? What made so many American men decide that it's the DNA, rather than the devil, that makes them do it?

Using the late sociologist Pierre Bourdieu's theory of habitus, or the account of how cultural ideas are taken up in the form of bodily habits and tastes that reinforce behavioral norms and social inequality, I suggest that scientific theories find their way into both popular culture and men's corporeal habits and attitudes. Evolution has become popular culture, where popular culture is more than just media representations but refers to the institutions of everyday life: family, marriage, school, work—all sites where gender and racial knowledges are performed according to images people have available to them in actionable repertoires, scripts, and narratives. As popular culture, evolutionary narratives offer men a way to think of, and embody, male sexuality.

That an evolutionary account of heterosexual male desire has captured the popular imagination is obvious from *Muscle and Fitness* magazine's

Based on Martha McCaughey, *The Caveman Mystique: Pop-Darwinism and the Debates over Sex, Violence, and Science* (New York: Routledge, 2008). Reprinted by permission of Martha McCaughey.

article on "Man the Visual Animal," which explains why men leer at women. Using a theory of the evolved difference between human male and female sexual psychologies developed by leading evolutionary psychologist Donald Symons, the article offers the following explanation under the subheading "Evolution Happens":

> Not much has changed in human sexuality since the Pleistocene. In his landmark book *The Evolution of Human Sexuality* (Oxford University Press, 1979), Symons hypothesizes that the male's sexual response to visual cues has been so rewarded by evolution that it's become innate.[3]

Such stories provide a means by which heterosexual male readers can experience their sexuality as acultural, primal: "The desire to ogle is your biological destiny."[4]

Evolution may happen (or may have happened), but these stories do not just happen. Their appeal seems to lie precisely in the sense of security provided by the imagined inevitability of heterosexual manhood. In a marketplace of masculine identities the caveman ethos is served up as Viagra for the masculine soul. Just as the 1950s women suffering what Betty Friedan famously called the "feminine mystique" were supposed to seek satisfaction in their Tupperware collections and their feminine figures, men today have been offered a way to think of their masculinity as powerful, productive, even aggressive—in a new economic and political climate where real opportunities to be rewarded for such traits have slipped away.[5]

It's hardly that most men today find themselves raising children at home while female partners bring home the bacon. But, like the 1950s housewife, more men must now find satisfaction despite working below their potential (given that their job skills have lost their position to technology or other labor sources) in a postindustrial service economy that is less rewarding both materially and morally. As journalist Susan Faludi puts it in her book *Stiffed*:

> The fifties housewife, stripped of her connections to a wider world and invited to fill the void with shopping and the ornamental display of her ultrafemininity, could be said to have morphed into the nineties man, stripped of his connections

to a wider world and invited to fill the void with consumption and a gym-bred display of his ultra-masculinity.[6]

On top of the economic changes affecting men, during the 1990s a growing anti-rape movement also challenged men, taking them to task for the problem of violence against women. More state and federal dollars supported efforts to stop such violence, and men increasingly feared complaints and repercussions for those complaints. The rape trials of Mike Tyson and William Kennedy Smith, Jr., the increasingly common school shootings (executed overwhelmingly by boys), the sexual harassment of women by men at the Citadel, the media attention given to the notorious Spurr Posse (a gang of guys who sought sex for "points" at almost all costs), the local sexual assault trials of countless high school and college athletic stars, the sexual harassment allegations against Supreme Court Justice nominee Clarence Thomas, and the White House sex scandals involving Bill Clinton meant more men lost ground. Indeed, the 1990s saw relentless—though not necessarily ill-founded—criticism of men's sexual violence and other forms of aggression.

Right-wing leaders were as upset with men as were feminists and other progressives. Those opposing abortion rights argued that sexual intercourse without procreation was undermining male responsibility, and those opposing women's equal-rights legislation argued that women's liberation would only allow men to relinquish their economic obligations to their families, sending women and children into divorce-induced poverty. Considering that critics of men came from both liberal and conservative camps, and from among men as well as women, it seems fair to say that in turn-of-the-century America moral disdain for men, whatever their age, race, or economic rank, had reached an all-time high.

For some men, the response was to cultivate a rude-dude attitude—popularized by Howard Stern, *The Man Show*, and MTV's endless shows about college spring-break vacations. For some others, the response was to face, with a sense of responsibility and urgency, men's animal natures and either accept or reform their caveman ways. While some men were embracing the role of consumers and becoming creatures of ornamentation—the "metrosexuals"—other men revolted against metrosexuality, embracing a can-do virility that Sara Stewart in *The New York Post* referred to as "retrosexuality," or that "cringe-inducing backlash of beers and leers."[7] Caveman masculinity is a form of retrosexuality that seems to carry the authority of objective science.

The popular understanding of men's sexuality as naturally vigorous and irrepressibly heterosexual helps fuel a culture Michael Kimmel[8] labeled "guyland" in his book by that name. Guyland is a social space in addition to a life stage, in which young single men act rough, gruff, sexually aggressive, and anti-gay, and do lewd, rude-dude things—resenting anything intellectual, politically correct, or smacking of either responsibility or women's authority. According to Kimmel, the five main markers of adulthood—leaving home, completing one's education, starting work, getting married, and becoming a parent—no longer happen all at once and so have left young men without a clear social marker of manhood.[9] In this context, the caveman discourse offers guys a *biological* marker of manhood.

Interestingly, feminist philosopher Sandra Lee Bartky made an argument about women's changing status impacting women's bodily comportment, saying that modern Western women began to restrict and constrict their bodies more as they gained institutional and social freedoms.[10] Bartky writes:

> As modern industrial societies change and as women themselves offer resistance to patriarchy, older forms of domination are eroded. But new forms arise, spread, and become consolidated. Women are no longer required to be chaste or modest, to restrict their sphere of activity to the home, or even to realize their properly feminine destiny in maternity: normative femininity is coming more and more to be centered on a woman's body—not its duties and obligations...[but] its presumed heterosexuality and its appearance.[11]

While women are now expected to restrict themselves in a tightly controlled, carefully managed feminine bodily comportment to compensate for their increased freedoms, I would suggest, appropriating Bartky, that we now see men finding their freedom and power in a bodily comportment just the opposite of Bartky's modern feminine woman: Men are boozing and belching their way to a lack of restrictions—to combat the increased restrictions they find in life and law.

Evolutionary theorists offer their ideas not to promote the caveman identity or fuel men's aggression, but in part because they believe the scientific facts about men's nature could help society address, and remedy, the violence and other problems so many have been blaming on men. What these scholars didn't predict is that so many average Joes would take up their ideas for slightly different reasons, namely as a move to feel powerful and domineering in a world squeezing men's resources and demanding that they be civil. Because of the ways caveman discourse appeals to many guys, it's important to consider the caveman story not simply as it is told by evolutionary scholars but as it is taken up throughout popular culture.

The Caveman as Popular Scientific Story

Popular culture is a political Petri dish for Darwinian ideas about sex. Average American guys don't read academic evolutionary science, but many do read about science in popular magazines and in bestselling books about the significance of the latest scientific ideas. As such, it is worth examining—even when magazine writers and television producers intentionally "dumb down" relatively sophisticated academic claims. In this section, I look at the way some popular texts make sense of evolutionary claims about men. Later I suggest that the caveman ideology, much of which centers on men's aggressive heterosexuality, gets embodied and thereby reproduced.[12]

In September of 1999, *Men's Health* magazine featured a caveman fitness program. Readers are shown an exercise routine that corresponds to the physical movements their ancestors would have engaged in: throwing a spear, hauling an animal carcass, honing a stone. A nice-looking, clean-shaven young man is shown exercising, his physical posture mirrored by a scruffy animal-skin-clad caveman behind him in the photo. Each day of the week-long routine is labeled according to the caveman mystique: building the cave home; the hunt; the chase; the kill; the long trek home; prepare for the feast; and rest. That an exercise plan is modeled after man-as-caveman reveals the common assumption that being a caveman is good for a man, a healthy existence.

Another issue of *Men's Health* magazine explains "the sex science facts" to male readers interested in "the biology of attraction." We follow the steps of a mating dance, but don't quite understand that's what we're doing. Indeed, we must learn the evolutionary history of sex to see why men feel the way they do when they notice a beautiful woman walking down the street:

> Of course, out there in the street, you have no thoughts about genetic compatibility or child-bearing. Probably the farthest thing from your mind is having a child with that beautiful woman. But that doesn't matter. What you think counts for almost nothing. In the environment that crafted your brain and body, an environment in which you might be dead within minutes of spotting this beauty, the only thing that counted was that your clever neocortex—your seat of higher reason—be turned off so that you could quickly select a suitable mate, impregnate her, and succeed in passing on your genes to the next generation.[13]

The article proceeds to identify the signals of fertility that attract men: youth, beauty, big breasts, and a small waistline. Focusing on the desire for youth in women, the article tells men that "the reason men of any age continue to like young girls is that we were designed to get them pregnant and dominate their fertile years by keeping them that way. . . . When your first wife has lost the overt signals of reproductive viability, you desire a younger woman who still has them all."[14] And, of course, male readers are reminded that "your genes don't care about your wife or girlfriend or what the neighbors will say."[15]

Amy Alkon's *Winston-Salem Journal* advice column, "The Advice Goddess," uses an evolutionary theory of men's innate loutishness to comfort poor "Feeling Cheated On," who sent a letter complaining that her boyfriend fantasizes about other women during their lovemaking. The Advice Goddess cited a study by Bruce J. Ellis and Donald Symons (whose work was also mentioned in *Muscle & Fitness*) to conclude that "male sexuality is all about variety. Men are hard-wired to want you, the entire girls' dorm next door, and the entire girls' dorm next to that."[16]

Popular magazines tell men that they have a biological propensity to favor women with the faces of 11½-year-old girls (where the eyes and chin are close together) and a waist-to-hip ratio of .7 (where the waist measures 70% of the hips). Men are told that their sexist double standard concerning appearance is evolutionary. Some of this research is very speculative—for instance, in some studies, men are simply shown photos of women with specific waist-to-hip ratios and then asked, "Would you like to spend the rest of your life with this woman?"—as though such staged answers reveal something about the individuals' real-life choices (or genes). But the results of this research make great copy.

Men's Health magazine in 1999 offered an article called "The Mysteries of Sex . . . Explained!" and relied on evolutionary theory, quoting several professors in the field, to explain "why most women won't sleep with you." The article elucidates:

> Stop blaming your wife. The fault lies with Mother Nature, the pit boss of procreation. Neil M. Malamuth, Ph.D., professor of psychology at UCLA, explains. "You're in Las Vegas with 10 grand. Your gambling strategy will depend on which form your money takes. With 10 chips worth $1,000 each, you'd weigh each decision cautiously. With 10,000 $1 chips, you'd throw them around." That's reproductive strategy in a nutshell.[17]

Popular magazine articles like this follow a standard formula. They quote the scientists, reporting on the evolutionary theorists' research, and offer funny anecdotes about male sexuality to illustrate the research findings. This *Men's Health* article continues to account for men's having fetishes:

> Men are highly sexed creatures, less interested in relationship but highly hooked on visuals, says David Givens, Ph.D., an anthropologist. "Because

sex carries fewer consequences for men, it's easier for us to use objects as surrogate sexual partners." Me? I've got my eye on a Zenith, model 39990.[18]

It's not just these popular and often humorous accounts of men that are based in some version of evolutionary theory. Even serious academic arguments rely on evolutionary theories of human behavior. For example, Steven Rhoads, a member of the University of Virginia faculty in public policy, has written *Taking Sex Differences Seriously* (2004), a book telling us why gender equity in the home and the workplace is a feminist pipe dream. Rhoads argues that women are wrong to expect men to take better care of children, do more housework, and make a place for them as equals at work because, he states, "men and women still have different natures and, generally speaking, different preferences, talents and interests."[19] He substantiates much of his argument about the divergent psychological predispositions in men and women with countless references to studies done by evolutionary scholars.

News magazines and television programs have also spent quite a bit of time popularizing evolutionary science and its implications for understanding human sex differences. The ABC News program *Day One* reported in 1995 on evolutionary psychologist David Buss's book, *The Evolution of Desire*.[20] Buss appeared on the show, which elaborated his theory by presenting us with supermodel Cindy Crawford and Barbie (the doll), presumably as representations of what men are wired to find desirable. As Buss explained in the interview, our evolutionary forebrothers who did not prefer women with high cheekbones, big eyes, lustrous hair, and full lips did not reproduce. As Buss put it, those men who happened to like someone who was older, sicker, or infertile "are not our ancestors. We are all the descendants of those men who preferred young healthy women and so as offspring, as descendants of those men, we carry with us their desires."[21] On that same television show, *Penthouse* magazine publisher Bob Guccione was interviewed and explained that men are simply biologically designed to enjoy looking at sexy women: "This may be very politically incorrect but that's the way it is. . . . It's all part of our

ancestral conditioning."[22] Evolutionary narratives clearly work for publishers of pornography marketed to men.

Newsweek's 1996 cover story, "The Biology of Beauty: What Science Has Discovered About Sex Appeal," argues that the beautylust humans exhibit "is often better suited to the Stone Age than to the Information Age; the qualities we find alluring may be powerful emblems of health, fertility and resistance to disease. . . ."[23] Though "beauty isn't all that matters in life," the article asserts, "our weakness for 'biological quality' is the cause of endless pain and injustice."[24]

Sometimes the magazines and TV shows covering the biological basis of sexual desire give a nod to the critics. The aforementioned *Newsweek* article, for instance, quotes feminist writer Katha Pollitt, who insists that "human beings cannot be reduced to DNA packets."[25] And then, as if to affirm Pollitt's claim, homosexuality is invoked as an example of the countless non-adaptive delights we desire: "Homosexuality is hard to explain as a biological adaptation. So is stamp collecting. . . . We pursue countless passions that have no direct bearing on survival."[26] So when there is a nod to ways humans are not hardwired, homosexual desires are framed as oddities having no basis in nature, while heterosexual attraction along the lines of stereotypical heterosexual male fantasy is framed as biological. Heterosexual desire enjoys a *biologically correct* status.

Zoologist Desmond Morris explains how evolutionary theory applies to humans in his 1999 six-part television series, *Desmond Morris' The Human Animal: A Personal View of the Human Species*.[27] The first show in the series draws from his book, *The Naked Ape*, explaining that humans are relatively hairless with little to protect themselves besides their big brains.[28] This is stated as we watch two naked people, one male and one female, walk through a public place where everyone else is dressed in modern-day clothing. Both are white, both are probably 25 to 30 years old, both look like models (the man with well chiseled muscles, a suntan, and no chest hair; the woman thin, yet shapely with larger than average breasts, shaved legs, and a manicured pubic region). This presentation of man and woman in today's aesthetically ideal form as the image of what all of us were once like is *de rigueur* for any popular representation of evolutionary theory applied to human sexuality. No woman is flabby, flat chested, or has body hair; no man has pimples or back hair. These culturally mandated ideal body types are presented as the image of what our human ancestors naturally looked like and desired. In this way and others, such shows posit modern aesthetic standards as states of nature.

Time magazine's 1994 cover story on "Our Cheating Hearts" reports that "the emerging field known as evolutionary psychology" gives us "fresh detail about the feelings and thoughts that draw us into marriage—or push us out." [29] After explaining the basics about men being less discriminating about their sexual partners than women, the article moves on to discuss why people divorce, anticipating resistance to the evolutionary explanation:

> Objections to this sort of analysis are predictable: "But people leave marriages for emotional reasons. They don't add up their offspring and pull out their calculators." But emotions are just evolution's executioners. Beneath the thoughts and feelings and temperamental differences marriage counselors spend their time sensitively assessing are the stratagems of the genes—cold, hard equations composed of simple variables: social status, age of spouse, number of children, their ages, outside romantic opportunities and so on. Is the wife really duller and more nagging than she was 20 years ago? Maybe, but maybe the husband's tolerance for nagging has dropped now that she is 45 and has no reproductive future. [30]

In case *Time* readers react to the new evolutionary psychology as part of a plot to destroy the cherished nuclear family, they are told that "progress will also depend on people using the explosive insight of evolutionary psychology in a morally responsible way. . . . We are potentially moral animals—which is more than any other animal can say—but we are not naturally moral animals. The first step to being moral is to realize how thoroughly we aren't." [31]

While many accounts of evolution's significance for male sexuality seem simply to rationalize sexist double standards and wallow in men's loutishness, a number of pop-Darwinist claims have the moral purpose of liberating men from being controlled by their caveman natures. Their message: men can become enlightened cavemen. These stories make an attempt to liberate men by getting them to see themselves differently. They tell men that they are cavemen with potential. They either make fun of men's putatively natural shortcomings or encourage them to cage the caveman within through a kind of scientific consciousness-raising.

For example, Jeff Hood's book *The Silverback Gorilla Syndrome* uses the logic of let's-face-that-we're-cavemen to get men to become more compassionate and peaceful. [32] Hood, an organizational consultant and nature lover, recognizes the common problems of contemporary Western masculinity: fierce competition in the workplace; a lack of introspection and authentic relationships; and a reliance on cunning and bluffery to maintain one's self-image or position of power. This form of masculinity is an exhausting, life-threatening charade, which costs men their marriages and their health, and threatens the entire planet due to the destruction men wreak on the environment and on other people.

Hood's introduction explains:

> In the course of emerging from the jungles of our primate ancestors, we have stumbled onto, some would say earned, a thing called awareness. This faculty has spawned a body of knowledge leading to science, industry, technology—and ultimately increased comfort and longer lives. But it has also sparked an illusion of separation from the rest of the animal kingdom. Forging ahead in the quest for control over our destiny and our planet, we act as if the laws of nature do not apply to us. We are blind to the many ways in which the dominant attitudes and competitive behavior we have inherited threaten to push us dangerously out of balance with our world. Our saving grace may be to use our awareness instead for tempering the silverback gorilla syndrome that has brought us success at such great cost. This book is an attempt to increase that awareness. [33]

Hood wants to turn men into responsible, compassionate creatures, insisting that awareness of the caveman within—an inner gorilla whom Hood playfully calls "Big G"—is the only way out.

Even well-meaning applications of evolutionary theory like Hood's book, however, fail to question the idea of men's heterosexual, aggressive inner core or evolved psychology. As such, they have a limited ability to move beyond the assumptions that lead so many others to use the same basic theory to rationalize being boorish. Men reformed via an evolutionary consciousness are still going to see themselves as different from, and even superior to, women.

The Caveman as Embodied Ethos

In a culture so attached to scientific authority and explication, it is worth examining the popular appeal of evolutionary theory and its impact on masculine embodiment. The popularity of the scientific story of men's evolved desires—however watered down or distorted the science becomes as enthusiasts popularize it—can tell us something about the appeal and influence of that story.

If the evolutionary stories appeal to many men, and it seems they do indeed, it's because they ring true. Many men feel like their bodies are aggressive. They feel urges, at a physical level, in line with evolutionary theoretical predictions. The men who feel like cavemen do not see their identity as a fiction; it is their bodily reality and seems to be backed by the authority of science.

The work of Pierre Bourdieu provides a tool for understanding how power is organized at the level of unconscious embodiment of cultural forces. I suggest that popular manifestations of scientific evolutionary narratives about men's sexuality have a real material effect on many men. Bourdieu's theory of practice develops the concepts of *habitus* and *field* to describe a reciprocally constitutive relationship between bodily dispositions and dominant power structures. Bourdieu concerned himself primarily with the ways in which socioeconomic class is incorporated at the level of the body, including class-based ways of speaking, postures, lifestyles, attitudes, and tastes.

Significant for Bourdieu is that people acquire tastes that mark them as members of particular social groups and particular social levels.[34] Membership in a particular social class produces and reproduces a class sensibility, what Bourdieu called "practical sense."[35] Habitus is "a somatized social relationship, a social law converted into an embodied law."[36] The process of becoming competent in the everyday life of a society or group constitutes habitus. Bourdieu's notion of embodiment can be extended to suggest that habitus, as embodied field, amounts to "the pleasurable and ultimately erotic constitution of [the individual's] social imaginary."[37]

Concerning the circulation of evolutionary narratives, we can see men taking erotic pleasure in the formation of male identity and the performance of accepted norms of heterosexual masculinity using precisely these tools of popular evolutionary science. Put differently, pop-Darwinism is a discourse that finds its way into men's bones and boners. The caveman story can become a man's practical sense of who he is and what he desires. This is so because masculinity is a dimension of embodied and performative practical sensibility—because men carry themselves with a bodily comportment suggestive of their position as the dominant gender, and they invest themselves in particular lifestyle practices, consumption patterns, attire, and bodily comportment. Evolutionary narratives thus enter the so-called habitus, and an aestheticized discourse and image of the caveman circulates through popular culture becoming part of natural perception, and consequently is reproduced by those embodying it.

In his study of the overwhelmingly white and male workspace of the Options Exchange floor, sociologist Richard Widick uses Bourdieu's theory to explain the traders' physical and psychical engagement with their work. Widick holds that "the traders' inhabitation and practical mastery of the trading floor achieves the bio-physical psychosocial state of a natural identity."[38] Hence the traders describe their manner as a "trading instinct." In a similar way, American men with what we might call a caveman instinct can be said to have acquired a "pre-reflexive practical sense" of themselves as heterosexually driven.[39]

Bourdieu gives the name "symbolic violence" to that process by which we come to accept and embody power relations without ever accepting them in the conscious sense of knowing them and choosing them. We hold beliefs that don't need to be thought—the effects of which can be "durably and deeply embedded in the body in the form of dispositions."[40] From this perspective, the durable dispositions of evolutionary discourse are apparent in our rape culture, for example, when a member of the group sexual assault in New York tells the woman he's attacking, "Welcome back to the caveman times." Embodying the ideology of irrepressible heterosexual desire makes such aggression appear to be natural.

Bourdieu's theory allows us to see that both cultural and material forces reveal themselves in the lived reality of social relations.[41] We can see on men's bodies the effects of their struggle with slipping economic privilege and a sense of entitlement to superiority over women. If men live out power struggles in their everyday experiences, then caveman masculinity can be seen as an imagined compensation for men's growing sense of powerlessness.[42] To be sure, some men have more social and economic capital than others. Those with less might invest even more in their bodies and appearances.[43]

Sociologist R. W. Connell discusses the significance of naturalizing male power. She states:

The physical sense of maleness is not a simple thing. It involves size and shape, habits of posture and movement, particular physical skills and the lack of others, the image of one's own body, the way it is presented to other people and the ways they respond to it, the way it operates at work and in sexual relations. In no sense is all this a consequence of XY chromosomes, or even of the possession on which discussions of masculinity have so lovingly dwelt, the penis. The physical sense of maleness grows through a personal history of social practice, a life-history-in-society.[44]

We see and believe that men's power over women is the order of nature because "power is translated not only into mental body-images and fantasies, but into muscle tensions, posture, the feel and texture of the body."[45] Scientific discourse constitutes the field for some men in the constructed figure of the caveman, enabling those men to internalize such an identity. The caveman thus becomes an imaginative projection that is experienced and lived as real biological truth.

In his book, *Cultural Boundaries of Science*, Thomas Gieryn comments on the cultural authority of science, suggesting that "if 'science' says so, we are more often than not inclined to believe it or act on it—and to prefer it to claims lacking this epistemic seal of approval."[46] To his observation I would add that we are also more likely to *live* it. Ideas that count as scientific, regardless of their truth value, become lived ideologies. It's how modern American men have become cavemen and how the caveman ethos enjoys reproductive success.

Cultural anthropologist Paul Rabinow gives the name "biosociality" to the formation of new group and individual identities and practices that emerge from the scientific study of human life.[47] Rabinow offers the example of neurofibromatosis groups whose members have formed to discuss their experiences, educate their children, lobby for their disease, and "understand" their fate. And in the future, he points out, " . . . [i]t is not hard to imagine groups formed around the chromosome 17, locus 16,256, site 654,376 allele variant with a guanine substitution."[48] Rabinow's concept of biosociality is instructive here, for the discourse of the caveman offers this form of biosociality. The caveman constitutes an identity based on new scientific "facts" about one's biology.

Of course, evolutionary psychologists might insist that men's desires are, in some final instance, biological properties of an internal psyche or sexual psychology. I am suggesting, in line with Bourdieu, that men's desires are always performed in relation to the dominant discourses in circulation within their cultural lifeworlds, either for or against the representations that permeate those lifeworlds. We can see that a significant number of men are putting the pop-Darwinian rhetoric to good use in social interactions. The scientific discourse of the caveman (however unscientific we might regard it by the time it gets to everyday guys reading magazines and watching TV) is corporealized, quite literally incorporated into living identities, deeply shaping these men's experiences of being men.

The Caveman as Ethnicity

I recognize the lure of the caveman narrative. After all, it provides an explanation for patterns we do see and for how men do feel in contemporary society, tells men that they are beings who are the way they are for a specific reason, offers them an answer about what motivates them, and carries the authority of scientific investigation about their biological makeup. Evolutionary theory offers an origin story. Plus, it's fun: thinking of the reasons you might feel a certain way because such feelings might have been necessary for your ancestors to survive a hostile environment back in the Pleistocene can be a satisfying intellectual exercise.

In telling men a story about who they are, naturally, pop-Darwinism has the normalizing, disciplinary effect of forging a common, biological identity among men. Embodying ideology allows men to feel morally exonerated while they reproduce that very ideology. The discourse of male biological unity suppresses many significant differences among men, and of course many ways in which men would otherwise identify with women's tastes and behaviors. The evolutionary explanation of men's sexual behavior is an all-encompassing narrative enabling men to frame their own thoughts and experiences through it. As such it's a *grand narrative,* a totalizing theory explaining men's experiences as though all men act and feel the same ways, and as though the ideas of Western science provide a universal truth about those actions and feelings.

I'm skeptical of this kind of totalizing narrative about male sexuality because evolution applied to human beings does not offer that sort of truth. The application of evolutionary theory to human behavior is not as straightforwardly scientific as it might seem, even for those of us who believe in the theory of evolution by natural selection. It is a partial, political discourse that authorizes certain prevalent masculine behaviors and a problematic acceptance of those behaviors. I think there are better—less totalizing, and differently

consequential—discourses out there that describe and explain those same behaviors. I'm also skeptical of men's use of the evolutionary narrative because, at its best, it can only create "soft patriarchs"—kinder, gentler cavemen who resist the putative urges of which evolutionary science makes them aware.[49]

Because evolutionary stories ultimately affirm a vision of men as naturally like one another, and naturally unlike women, caveman masculinity lends itself to becoming an "ethnic option," a way of identifying and living one's manhood. Sociologist Mary C. Waters explains that ethnic identity is actually not "the automatic labeling of a primordial characteristic" but instead is a complex, socially created identity.[50] The caveman as an ethnicity reveals an embrace of biology as a reaction to social constructionist understandings of masculinity, feminist demands on men, and the changing roles of men at work and in families. As an ethnicity, caveman masculinity is seen as not only impossible but undesirable to change.[51]

Did scholars in evolutionary psychology intend to present modern men with such an ethnic option? Of course not. To repeat: Darwinian ideas are often spread by enthusiasts—secondary school teachers, science editors of various newspapers and magazines, and educational television show producers—who take up evolutionary theorists' ideas and convey them to mass audiences. Evolutionary thinking has become popular in part because it speaks to a publicly recognized predicament of men. Changing economic patterns have propelled men's flight from marriage and breadwinning, in conjunction with women's increased (albeit significantly less prosperous) independence. If a man today wants multiple partners with as little commitment as possible, evolutionary rhetoric answers why this is so.

Evolutionary discourse doesn't offer a flattering story about men. But, more significantly, many people don't understand that it's *a story.* Evolution has become not only a grand narrative but a lived ideology. Maleness and femaleness, like heterosexuality and homosexuality, are not simply identities but *systems of knowledge.*[52] And those systems of knowledge inform thinking and acting.

Bourdieu's concept of habitus explains the ways in which culture and knowledge, including evolutionary knowledge, implant themselves at the level of the body, becoming a set of attitudes, tastes, perceptions, actions, and reactions. The status of science as objective, neutral knowledge helps make evolution a lived ideology because it feels truthful, natural, real.

Taking the historical and cultural changes affecting men seriously and embracing the diversity among men demand new understandings of masculinity, identity, and science. In gaining such a sociological perspective, men might resist making gender a new ethnicity and instead take a great leap forward to become new kinds of men.

Notes

1. A version of this essay also appears in the new edition of *Men's Lives,* edited by Michael Kimmel and Michael Messner.

2. For defenses of the study of the popularization of scientific discourse, and exemplary studies of the popularization of Darwinian discourse in different eras, see Alfred Kelly, *The Descent of Darwin: The Popularization of Darwinism in Germany, 1860–1914* (Chapel Hill: University of North Carolina Press, 1981) and Alvar Ellegard, *Darwin and the General Reader: The Reception of Darwin's Theory of Evolution in the British Press, 1859–1872* (Chicago: University of Chicago Press, 1990).

3. Mary Ellen Strote, "Man the Visual Animal," *Muscle and Fitness* (February 1994): 166.

4. Ibid., 166.

5. Betty Friedan, *The Feminine Mystique* (New York: Dell Publishing Company, Inc., 1963).

6. Susan Faludi, *Stiffed: The Betrayal of the American Man* (New York: HarperCollins, 1999), 40.

7. Sara Stewart, "Beasty Boys—'Retrosexuals' Call for Return of Manly Men; Retrosexuals Rising," *The New York Post,* July 18, 2006.

8. Michael Kimmel, *Guyland: The Perilous World Where Boys Become Men* (New York: HarperCollins, 2008).

9. Ibid., 24–25.

10. Sandra Lee Bartky, "Foucault, Femininity, and the Modernization of Patriarchal Power," in *The Politics of Women's Bodies*, ed. Rose Weitz (New York: Oxford University Press, 1998), 25–45.

11. Ibid., 41–42.

12. My argument here parallels a study of the pervasive iconography of the gene in popular culture. In *The DNA Mystique: The Gene as a Cultural Icon* (New York: W. H. Freeman, 1995), Dorothy Nelkin and M. Susan Lindee explain that popular culture provides "narratives of meaning" (p. 11). Those narratives filter complex ideas, provide guidance, and influence how people see themselves and evaluate other people, ideas, and policies. In this way, Nelkin and Lindee argue, DNA works as an ideology to justify boundaries of identity and legal rights, as well as to explain criminality, addiction, and personality. Of course, addict genes and criminal genes are misnomers—the definitions of what counts as an addict and what counts as a crime have shifted throughout history. Understanding DNA stories as ideological clarifies why, for example, people made sense of Elvis's talents and shortcomings by referring to his genetic stock (Ibid., 79–80). To call narratives of DNA ideological, then, is *not* to resist the scientific argument that deoxyribonucleic acid is a double-helix structure carrying information forming living cells and tissues, but to look at the way people make sense of DNA and use DNA to make sense of people and events in their daily lives.

13. Laurence Gonzales, "The Biology of Attraction," *Men's Health* 20.7 (2005): 186–93.

14. Ibid., 192.

15. Ibid., 193.

16. Amy Alkon, "Many Men Fantasize During Sex, But It Isn't a Talking Point," *Winston-Salem Journal,* 29 September 2005, p. 34.

17. Greg Gutfeld, "The Mysteries of Sex . . . Explained!," *Men's Health* April (1999): 76.

18. Ibid., 76.

19. Steven R. Rhoads, *Taking Sex Differences Seriously* (San Francisco: Encounter Books, 2004), 4.

20. David M. Buss, *The Evolution of Desire: Strategies of Human Mating* (New York: Basic Books, 1994).

21. David M. Buss, interview by *Day One*, ABC News.

22. Ibid.

23. Geoffrey Cowley, "The Biology of Beauty," *Newsweek* 127 (1996): 62.

24. Ibid., 64.

25. Ibid., 66.

26. Ibid.

27. *Desmond Morris' The Human Animal: A Personal View of the Human Species* ["Beyond Survival"] directed by Clive Bromhall (Discovery Communication/TLC Video, 1999).

28. Desmond Morris, *The Naked Ape* (New York: Dell Publishing Company, Inc., 1967).

29. Robert Wright, *The Moral Animal: Evolutionary Psychology and Everyday Life* (New York: Pantheon Books, 1994), 45.

30. Ibid., 50.

31. Ibid., 52.

32. Jeff Hood, *The Silverback Gorilla Syndrome: Transforming Primitive Man* (Santa Fe, NM: Adventures in Spirit Publications, 1999).

33. Ibid., 1.

34. Pierre Bourdieu, *Distinction: A Social Critique of the Judgment of Taste* (Cambridge: Harvard University Press, 1984).

35. Pierre Bourdieu, *The Logic of Practice* (Stanford: Stanford University Press, 1990).

36. Pierre Bourdieu, *Masculine Domination* (Stanford: Stanford University Press, 2001).

37. Richard Widick, "Flesh and the Free Market: (On Taking Bourdieu to the Options Exchange)," *Theory and Society* 32 (2003): 679–723, 716.

38. Ibid., 701.

39. Ibid.

40. Bourdieu, *Masculine*, 39.

41. Lois McNay, "Agency and Experience: Gender as a Lived Relation," in *Feminism After Bourdieu,* ed. Lisa Adkins and Bev Skeggs (Oxford: Blackwell Publishing, 2004), 177.

42. See McNay, 175–90, for a discussion of emotional compensation and lived experience.

43. See Beverley Skeggs, *Formations of Class and Gender: Becoming Respectable* (London: Sage Publications, 1997), for a study pointing this out about working class women.

44. R. W. Connell, *Gender and Power: Society, the Person and Sexual Politics* (Cambridge: Polity Press, 1987), 84.

45. Ibid., 85.

46. Thomas F. Gieryn, *Cultural Boundaries of Science: Credibility on the Line* (Chicago: The University of Chicago Press, 1999), 1.

47. Paul Rabinow, *Making PCR, A Story of Biotechnology* (Chicago: University of Chicago Press, 1996), 101–2.

48. Ibid., 102.

49. I am appropriating W. Bradford Wilcox's term, from his book *Soft Patriarchs, New Men: How Christianity Shapes Fathers and Husbands* (Chicago: University of Chicago Press, 2004). Wilcox argues that the Christian men's movement known as the Promise Keepers encourages men to spend more time with their wives and children without ever challenging the fundamental patriarchal family structure that places men at the top.

50. Mary C. Waters, *Ethnic Options: Choosing Identities in America* (Berkeley: University of California Press, 1990), 16.

51. See Michael S. Kimmel, *Manhood in America: A Cultural History* (New York: Free Press, 1996), 127–37.

52. Steven Seidman, *Difference Troubles: Queering Social Theory and Sexual Politics* (Cambridge, UK: Cambridge University Press, 1997), 93.

The Truth About Boys and Girls

LISE ELIOT

Parents anticipate sex differences from the first prenatal ultrasound but then seem amazed when their son goes gaga over trucks or their daughter will wear nothing but pink. Boys and girls are obviously different, and in many cases the gaps between them seem stark. But stereotypes do not always hold up to scientific scrutiny. Are boys really more aggressive and girls really more empathetic— or do we just see what we expect in them? Where true sex differences exist, are those gaps inborn, as our current Mars-Venus obsession implies, or shaped by environment—that is, by us?

A natural place to look for answers is in the brain. If there is a neurological disparity between the genders, it could explain important behavioral differences. But surprisingly, researchers have found very few notable differences between boys' and girls' brains, and even some of the widely-claimed differences between adult men's and women's brains—such as the idea that women have stronger connections between left and right hemispheres— have not held up to rigorous research. Yes, males have larger brains (and heads) than females—from birth through old age. And girls' brains finish growing earlier than boys'. But neither of these findings explains why boys are more active and girls more verbal or reveals a plausible basis for the consistent gaps in their reading, writing and science test scores that have parents and teachers up in arms.

Brain differences are indisputably biological, but they are not necessarily hardwired. The crucial, often overlooked fact is that experience itself changes brain structure and function. Neuroscientists call this shaping plasticity, and it is the basis of all learning and much of children's mental development. Even something as simple as the act of seeing depends on normal visual experience in early life, without which a baby's visual brain fails to wire up properly and his or her vision is permanently impaired.

Does growing up as a boy or as a girl also wire the brain in a particular way? Obviously, girls and boys are not identical at birth: genetic and hormonal differences must launch the male and female brain down somewhat different developmental pathways. But early experience, we now know, permanently alters the chemistry and function of the genes inside cells, leading to significant effects on behavior. Neuroscientist Michael J. Meaney and his colleagues at McGill University, among others, have found that the quality of maternal care is associated with a host of neural and psychological consequences—from the production of new brain cells to altered stress responses and memory function. The different ways parents raise boys and girls may similarly leave its stamp on their developing brains.

Most sex differences start out small—as mere biases in temperament and play style—but are amplified as children's pink- or blue-tinted brains meet our gender-infused culture, including all the tea parties, wrestling matches, playground capers and cafeteria dramas that dominate boys' or girls' existence. Through better understanding of these environmental influences, we can break down some of the gaps between boys and girls—in school achievement, risk taking, self-control, competitiveness, empathy and assertiveness.

The Kickoff

Boys are more physically active than girls, in infancy and throughout childhood. They kick, swing their arms and race around the house noticeably more than girls do, as many exhausted parents can testify. The difference may emerge before birth, although not every ultrasound study finds a sex difference in fetal movement. Nevertheless, the disparity is clear during the first year and expands through childhood, according to a 1986 analysis of more than 100 studies by psychologist Warren Eaton and his colleagues at the University of Manitoba in Canada, which reveals that the average boy is more active than about 69 percent of girls.

That gap is statistically moderate, larger than differences in verbal and math skills but small enough to permit many exceptions to the rule, notably the 31 percent of girls who are *more* active than the average boy. Sex hormones—in particular, a relative abundance of testosterone in the womb—appear to trigger boys' fidgetiness. And yet the sex difference in physical activity continues to widen during childhood, despite the fact that sex hormone levels do *not* differ between boys and girls from six months of age to puberty. Parenting is likely one factor amplifying the disparity. Mothers discourage physical risk taking more in daughters than in sons, suggest studies in the laboratory and on playgrounds. (Fathers encourage more risk taking in children than mothers do . . . but no one has tested the likely hypothesis that dads pressure sons more than daughters in this respect.) Peers also push conformity: in their preferred all-boy groups, energetic boys feed off one another, whereas energetic girls tend to settle down in clusters of more docile friends. In organized sports, girls start playing at a later age, quit earlier and join fewer teams overall than boys—differences that are influenced by parents and peers.

As many schools eliminate recess or cut back on physical education, both genders are paying the price with higher rates of obesity and attention-deficit hyperactivity diagnoses. Boys especially need more frequent physical breaks to satisfy their higher activity levels, and both sexes need the mental recharging that exercise confers during a long school day. Exercise is also important for maintaining a positive body image, which turns out to be the biggest risk factor for depression in adolescent girls.

Trucks and Dolls

Yes, boys like trucks and girls like dolls. Given a choice of Power Rangers, Tonka, Bratz and a Barbie beauty set, preschool-age boys and girls strongly prefer the gender-obvious picks. In fact, children's gendered toy choice is one of the largest sex differences in behavior, second only to sexual preference itself! But this preference is not nearly so clear in infancy, when boys, in many studies, have been found to like dolls as much as girls do. (All babies are strongly attracted to faces, for obvious survival reasons.) Rather, toy preference emerges toward the end of infancy, grows stronger through the preschool years and then declines somewhat because of a complex interaction of nature and nurture.

Toddlers' toy preference is shaped, in part, by prenatal testosterone: girls with a genetic disorder that exposes them to high levels of testosterone and other androgens before birth are more interested in toy trucks and cars than typical girls are. Even male and female monkeys prefer gender-stereotyped toys, telling us there is something about vehicles, balls and moving parts that resonates with boys' hormonal priming, drawing them away from their initial face preference and toward toys they can interact with more physically.

Starting from this innate bias, children's toy preferences grow more extreme through social shaping. Parents reinforce play that is considered gender-appropriate, especially in boys, and beginning at age three, peers perpetuate gender norms even more than adults do. In one example of peer influence, psychologists Karin Frey of the University of Washington and Diane Ruble of New York University reported in 1992 that elementary school-age boys and girls both opted for a less desirable toy (a kaleidoscope) over a slick Fisher-Price movie viewer after watching a commercial of a same-sex child choosing the kaleidoscope and an opposite-sex child choosing the movie viewer. By age five, girls show greater latitude, choosing "boy" toys and "girl" toys equally. Boys, however, rarely do this crossover—a divergence that reflects different societal norms. Girls today are allowed—and even encouraged—to play sports, wear pants and build with Legos much more than boys are pressed to don dresses and play house.

The different play preferences of boys and girls are important in shaping many mental circuits and later abilities. Sporting gear, vehicles and building toys exercise physical and spatial skills, whereas dolls, coloring books and dress-up clothes stimulate verbal, social and fine-motor circuits. Parents and preschool teachers can expand both sets of skills by encouraging girls to play with puzzles, building blocks, throwing games and even video games, while enticing boys to sew, paint, and play as caregivers using props for doctor, Daddy, zookeeper, EMT, and the like.

Sticks and Stones

Boys are more physically aggressive than girls, according to many studies, including a 2004 analysis by psychologist John Archer of the University of Central Lancashire in England. That difference is linked to prenatal testosterone but not, surprisingly, to the resurgence in boys' testosterone level in adolescence, because boys do not suddenly become more aggressive when they go through puberty, as Archer's work also indicates. Nor is this sex difference absolute. Two- and three-year-old girls, for instance, frequently kick, bite and hit other people—not quite as much as toddler boys but about three times more than either sex does later in childhood. In addition, girls fight with indirect, or relational, aggression. Through gossip, ostracism, whispers and, most recently, harassing text messages, girls leave more scars on competitors' psyches than on their bodies.

Thus, both sexes compete and both sexes fight; what differs is the degree to which such behavior is overt or hidden. Because physical aggression is a greater taboo for girls than boys, they learn, even early in elementary school, to keep it below the surface, in the eye rolling and best-friend wars that teachers rarely notice and are harder to police.

But by admitting that competitive feelings are natural for all children, we can find ways to channel them into healthier pursuits. In recent years educators have tended to take competition out of the classroom, reasoning that the opposite style of interaction—cooperation—is more important in a civil society. But competition can be highly motivating, especially for boys, and girls need to develop greater comfort with open competition, which remains essential to success in our free-market society. One solution is team competitions, where groups of students work together to try to beat others at solving math, vocabulary, history and science problems.

I Know How You Feel

Aggression and empathy are inversely related. It is hard to attack someone if you are acutely aware of what he or she is feeling. So whereas men and boys score higher on measures of physical and verbal aggression, girls and women score higher on most measures of empathy, or the awareness and sharing of other people's emotions, conclude psychologist Nancy Eisenberg of Arizona State University and her colleagues in studies dating back to the 1980s.

And yet the sex difference in empathy is smaller than most people realize and also strongly dependent on how it is measured. When men and women are asked to self-report their empathetic tendencies, women are much likelier than men to endorse statements such as "I am good at knowing how others will feel" or "I enjoy caring for other people." When tested using more objective measures, however, such as recognizing the emotions in a series of photographed faces, the difference between men and women is much smaller, about four tenths of a standard deviation, meaning the average woman is more accurate than just 66 percent of men.

In children, the difference is tinier still, less than half that found in adults, reported psychologist

Erin McClure of Emory University in 2000 after analyzing more than 100 studies of sex differences in facial emotion processing in infants, children and adolescents. So although girls do start out a bit more sensitive to other people's faces and emotions, their advantage grows larger with age, no doubt because of their stronger communication skills, more practice at role playing with dolls and more intimate friendships as compared with boys.

Little is known about the neural basis for the sex difference in empathy, although a grape-size region on each side of the brain called the amygdala is likely to be involved. The amygdala is highly activated by faces. According to a 2002 analysis of several studies, the amygdala is larger in men than in women, a fact that seemingly belies men's lesser ability to recognize facial emotions. Other studies reveal an imbalance in the activation of the right and left amygdala in men and women, however. When they are recalling highly charged emotional scenes—the kind that trigger empathetic responses—women's left amygdala is more strongly activated than their right amygdala, whereas the right amygdala is more strongly activated than the left in men, as indicated by both a study in 2004 led by neurobiologist Larry Cahill of the University of California, Irvine, and a report in 2002 by psychologist Turhan Canli, then at Stanford University, and his colleagues.

It is not yet known if this left-right difference in amygdala activation is related to empathy per se or if the same neural sex difference is present in children. Indeed, when it comes to emotionality, boys and girls differ much less in early life; if anything, baby boys are known to cry and fuss *more* than baby girls. As boys grow, they—much more than girls—are taught to hide their expressions of fear, sadness and tenderness. Scientists agree that social learning largely shapes the male-female gap in emotional responding. Boys are toughened up in a way girls rarely are, making them less expressive but also less attuned to others' feelings. This training almost certainly leaves its imprint on the amygdala, one of the more plastic structures in the brain. Teaching girls to be more resilient and boys to be more sensitive is possible and beneficial for both genders.

Girl Talk

First, let us dispense with the urban legend that "women speak three times more words every day than men." The real numbers: 16,215 for women and 15,669 for men, according to a 2007 study of nearly 400 college students fitted with digital recorders, led by psychologist Matthias Mehl of the University of Arizona. Females do outscore males on most measures of speaking, reading, writing and spelling from early childhood and throughout life, but the gaps are generally small and change with age.

Language differences emerge early in development. As infants, girls begin talking about one month earlier than boys and are some 12 percent ahead of boys in reading skills when kindergarten begins. Girls' advantage in reading and writing continues to grow through school, until by 12th grade, an alarming 47 percent more girls than boys graduate as proficient readers, with an even larger gap for writing, a conclusion drawn from several decades of data collected by the U.S. Department of Education.

These gaps appear to shrink in adulthood, however. The average woman scores higher than just 54 percent of men on a combined measure of all verbal skills, indicates a 1988 analysis by psychologist Janet Hyde and her colleagues at the University of Wisconsin–Madison. That the difference is so tiny may explain why the neural bases for language or literacy differences have yet to be uncovered. In 2008 neuroscientist Iris Sommer and her colleagues at University Medical Center Utrecht in the Netherlands dispelled one popular theory—that women use both sides of the brain to process language, whereas men use mainly the left. In their analysis of 20 functional MRI studies, the researchers detected no difference in the degree of language lateralization between men and women.

Similarly, there is scant proof that girls and women are better neurologically wired for reading. If anything correlates with reading skill, it is quite simply the amount of reading children do for pleasure outside school. Girls read more than boys, and this additional exposure makes a difference in their academic performance.

Beginning at birth, a child's language exposure is the single most important determinant of his or her later verbal abilities. Large studies in several different countries demonstrate that gender accounts for at most 3 percent of the variance in toddlers' verbal ability, compared with at least 50 percent determined by a child's environment and language exposure. Thus, the more parents can immerse their sons in conversation, books, songs and stories, the better are boys' chances of getting off to the right start in language and literacy skills. ABC and rhyming books are great for teaching phonemic awareness—the link between sounds and letters that is the first hurdle in learning to read. Boys often select different genres than girls do—especially nonfiction, comedy and action stories—so getting boys to read may be largely a matter of finding books and magazines that appeal to them. Schools with strong reading programs have managed to eliminate the difference between boys' and girls' scores, proving that this worrisome gap is more a matter of education and practice than inborn literacy potential.

Thinking in 3-D

If girls have the advantage in verbal skills, boys have it in the spatial domain—the ability to visualize and manipulate objects and trajectories in time and three-dimensional space. Sex differences in spatial skills are among the largest of the cognitive gaps. The average man can perform mental rotation—that is, he can imagine how a complex object would look when turned around—better than up to 80 percent of women.

In 2008 two research groups reported a sex difference in mental rotation in babies as young as three months of age, and other evidence suggests that this skill is influenced by prenatal testosterone. Yet the actual size of the skill gap is much smaller in children than in adults: among four-year-olds, the average boy outperforms just 60 percent of girls. So it seems likely that the skill improves in boys thanks to the wide range of visuospatial interests—targeting, building, throwing and navigating through innumerable driving and shooting games—that they pursue far more than girls. In support of this idea, neurobiologist Karin Kucian and her colleagues at University Children's Hospital in Zurich reported in a 2007 study that boys' and girls' brains display similar MRI patterns of neural activity while performing a mental rotation task that evokes different responses in the brains of adult men and women. So it appears that boys' and girls' brains diverge in spatial processing as they grow and practice different skills.

Spatial skills are important for success in several areas of science and higher math, including calculus, trigonometry, physics and engineering. Research by educational psychologist Beth Casey of Boston College shows that the spatial skill gap between boys and girls largely accounts for the consistent male advantage on the math SAT exam, an obvious hurdle for admission to engineering and other technical degree programs.

As important as they are, spatial skills are not something we deliberately teach in school. But many studies have shown they can improve with training, including playing video games! If boys naturally get more such practice in their extracurricular pursuits, girls may benefit from greater exposure to three-dimensional puzzles, fast-paced driving and targeting games, and sports such as baseball, softball and tennis.

Gender, Culture and the Brain

Boys and girls are different, but most psychological sex differences are not especially large. For example, gaps in verbal skills, math performance, empathy and even most types of aggression are generally much smaller than the disparity in adult height, in which the average five-foot, 10-inch man is taller than 99 percent of women. When it comes to mental abilities, males and females overlap much more than they stand apart.

Furthermore, few of these sex differences are as fixed, or hardwired, as popular accounts have lately portrayed. Genes and hormones light the spark for most boy-girl differences, but the flame is fanned by the essentially separate cultures in which boys and girls grow up. Appreciating *how* sex differences emerge can reduce dangerous stereotyping and give parents and teachers ideas for cross-training boys' and girls' minds, to minimize their more troubling discrepancies and enable all children to more fully develop their diverse talents.

Testosterone Rules

ROBERT M. SAPOLSKY

Face it, we all do it—we all believe in stereotypes about minorities. These stereotypes are typically pejorative and false, but every now and then they have a core of truth. I know, because I belong to a minority that lives up to its reputation. I have a genetic abnormality generally considered to be associated with high rates of certain socially abhorrent behaviors: I am male. Thanks to an array of genes that produce some hormone-synthesizing enzymes, my testes churn out a corrosive chemical and dump the stuff into my bloodstream, and this probably has behavioral consequences. We males account for less than 50 percent of the population, yet we generate a huge proportion of the violence. Whether it is something as primal as having an ax fight in a rain forest clearing or as detached as using computer-guided aircraft to strafe a village, something as condemned as assaulting a cripple or as glorified as killing someone wearing the wrong uniform, if it is violent, we males excel at it.

Why should this be? We all think we know the answer: something to do with those genes being expressed down in the testes. A dozen millennia ago or so, an adventurous soul managed to lop off a surly bull's testicles, thus inventing behavioral endocrinology. It is unclear from the historical records whether the experiment resulted in grants and tenure, but it certainly generated an influential finding: that the testes do something or other to make males aggressive pains in the ass.

That something or other is synthesizing the infamous corrosive chemical, testosterone (or rather, a family of related androgen hormones that I'll call testosterone for the sake of simplicity, hoping the androgen specialists won't take it the wrong way). Testosterone bulks up muscle cells—including those in the larynx, giving rise to operatic basses. It makes hair sprout here and there, undermines the health of blood vessels, alters biochemical events in the liver too dizzying to contemplate, and has a profound impact, no doubt, on the workings of cells in big toes. And it seeps into the brain, where it influences behavior in a way highly relevant to understanding aggression.

Genes are the hand behind the scene, directing testosterone's actions. They specify whether steroidal building blocks are turned into testosterone or estrogen, how much of each, and how quickly. They regulate how fast the liver breaks down circulating testosterone, thereby determining how long an androgenic signal remains in the bloodstream. They direct the synthesis of testosterone receptors—specialized proteins that catch hold of testosterone and allow it to have its characteristic effects on target cells. And genes specify how many such receptors the body has, and how sensitive they are. Insofar as testosterone alters brain function and produces aggression, and genes regulate how much testosterone is made and how effectively it works, this should be the archetypal case for studying how genes can control our behavior. Instead, however, it's the archetypal case for learning how little genes actually do so.

Some pretty obvious evidence links testosterone with aggression. Males tend to have higher

Robert M. Sapolsky. "Testosterone Rules," *Discover* (March 1997). Reprinted with the permission of the author.

testosterone levels in their circulation than do females, and to be more aggressive. Times of life when males are swimming in testosterone—for example, after reaching puberty—correspond to when aggression peaks. Among many species, testes are mothballed most of the year, kicking into action and pouring out testosterone only during a very circumscribed mating season—precisely the time when male–male aggression soars.

Impressive though they seem, these data are only correlative—testosterone found on the scene repeatedly with no alibi when some aggression has occurred. The proof comes with the knife, the performance of what is euphemistically known as a subtraction experiment. Remove the source of testosterone in species after species, and levels of aggression typically plummet. Reinstate normal testosterone levels afterward with injections of synthetic testosterone, and aggression returns.

The subtraction and replacement paradigm represents pretty damning proof that this hormone, with its synthesis and efficacy under genetic control, is involved in aggression. "Normal testosterone levels appear to be a prerequisite for normative levels of aggressive behavior" is the sort of catchy, hummable phrase the textbooks would use. That probably explains why you shouldn't mess with a bull moose during rutting season. But it's not why a lot of people want to understand this sliver of science. Does the action of testosterone tell us anything about individual differences in levels of aggression, anything about why some males—some human males—are exceptionally violent? Among an array of males, are the highest testosterone levels found in the most aggressive individuals?

Generate some extreme differences and that is precisely what you see. Castrate some of the well-paid study subjects, inject others with enough testosterone to quadruple the normal human levels, and the high-testosterone males are overwhelmingly likely to be the more aggressive ones. Obviously, extreme conditions don't tell us much about the real world, but studies of the normative variability in testosterone—in other words, seeing what everyone's natural levels are like without manipulating anything—also suggest that high levels of testosterone and high levels of aggression tend to go together. This would seem to seal the case that interindividual differences in levels of aggression among normal individuals are probably driven by differences in levels of testosterone. But that conclusion turns out to be wrong.

Here's why. Suppose you note a correlation between levels of aggression and levels of testosterone among normal males. It could be because (*a*) testosterone elevates aggression; (*b*) aggression elevates testosterone secretion; or (*c*) neither causes the other. There's a huge bias to assume option a, while b is the answer. Study after study has shown that if you examine testosterone levels when males are first placed together in the social group, testosterone levels predict nothing about who is going to be aggressive. The subsequent behavioral differences drive the hormonal changes, rather than the other way around.

Because of a strong bias among certain scientists, it has taken forever to convince them of this point. Suppose you're studying what behavior and hormones have to do with each other. How do you study the behavioral part? You get yourself a notebook, a stopwatch, a pair of binoculars. How do you measure the hormones and analyze the genes that regulate them? You need some gazillion-dollar machines; you muck around with radiation and chemicals, wear a lab coat, maybe even goggles—the whole nine yards. Which toys would you rather get for Christmas? Which facet of science are you going to believe in more? The higher the technology, goes the formula, the more scientific the discipline. Hormones seem to many to be more substantive than behavior, so when a correlation occurs, it must be because hormones regulate behavior, not the other way around.

This is a classic case of what is often called physics envy, a disease that causes behavioral biologists to fear their discipline lacks the rigor of physiology, physiologists to wish for the techniques of biochemists, biochemists to covet the clarity of the answers revealed by molecular geneticists, all the way down until you get to the physicists who confer only with God. Recently, a zoologist friend had obtained blood samples from the carnivores he studies and wanted some hormones in the samples tested in my lab. Although inexperienced with the technique, he offered to help in any way possible. I felt hesitant asking him to do anything tedious, but since he had offered, I tentatively said, "Well, if you don't mind some unspeakable drudgery, you could number about a thousand assay vials." And this scientist, whose superb work has graced the most prestigious science journals in the world, cheerfully answered, "That's okay. How often do I get to do real science, working with test tubes?"

Difficult though scientists with physics envy find it to believe, interindividual differences in testosterone levels don't predict subsequent differences in aggressive behavior among individuals. Similarly, fluctuations in testosterone levels within one individual over time don't predict subsequent changes in the levels of aggression in that one individual—get a hiccup in testosterone secretion one afternoon and that's not when the guy goes postal.

Look at our confusing state: normal levels of testosterone are a prerequisite for normal levels of aggression. Yet if one male's genetic makeup predisposes him to higher levels of testosterone than the next guy, he isn't necessarily going to be more aggressive. Like clockwork, that statement makes the students suddenly start coming to office hours in a panic, asking whether they missed something in their lecture notes.

Yes, it's going to be on the final, and it's one of the more subtle points in endocrinology—what's referred to as a hormone having a "permissive effect." Remove someone's testes and, as noted, the frequency of aggressive behavior is likely to plummet. Reinstate pre-castration levels of testosterone by injecting the hormone, and pre-castration levels of aggression typically return. Fair enough. Now, this time, castrate an individual and restore testosterone levels to only 20 percent of normal. Amazingly, normal pre-castration levels of aggression come back. Castrate and now introduce twice the testosterone levels from before castration, and the same level of aggressive behavior returns. You need some testosterone around for normal aggressive behavior. Zero levels after castration, and down it usually goes; quadruple levels (the sort of range generated in weight lifters abusing anabolic steroids), and aggression typically increases. But anywhere from roughly 20 percent of normal to twice normal and it's all the same. The brain can't distinguish among this wide range of basically normal values.

If you knew a great deal about the genetic makeup of a bunch of males, enough to understand how much testosterone they secreted into their bloodstream, you still couldn't predict levels of aggression among those individuals. Nevertheless, the subtraction and reinstatement data seem to indicate that, in a broad sort of way, testosterone causes aggressive behavior. But that turns out not to be true either, and the implications of this are lost on most people the first thirty times they hear about it. Those implications are important, however—so important that it's worth saying thirty-one times.

Round up some male monkeys. Put them in a group together and give them plenty of time to sort out where they stand with each other—grudges, affiliative friendships. Give them enough time to form a dominance hierarchy, the sort of linear ranking in which number 3, for example, can pass his day throwing around his weight with numbers 4 and 5, ripping off their monkey chow, forcing them to relinquish the best spots to sit in, but numbers 1 and 2 still expect and receive from him the most obsequious brownnosing.

Hierarchy in place, it's time to do your experiment. Take that third-ranking monkey and give him some testosterone. None of this within-the-normal-range stuff. Inject a ton of it, way higher than what you normally see in rhesus monkeys, give him enough testosterone to grow antlers and a beard on every neuron in his brain. And, no surprise, when you check the behavioral data, he will probably be participating in more aggressive interactions than before.

So even though small fluctuations in the levels of the hormone don't seem to matter much, testosterone still causes aggression, right? Wrong. Check out number 3 more closely. Is he raining aggressive terror on everyone in the group, frothing with indiscriminate violence? Not at all. He's still judiciously kowtowing to numbers 1 and 2 but has become a total bastard to numbers 4 and 5.

Testosterone isn't causing aggression, it's exaggerating the aggression that's already there.

Another example, just to show we're serious. There's a part of your brain that probably has lots to do with aggression, a region called the amygdala. Sitting near it is the Grand Central Station of emotion-related activity in your brain, the hypothalamus. The amygdala communicates with the hypothalamus by way of a cable of neuronal connections called the stria terminalis. (No more jargon, I promise.) The amygdala influences aggression via that pathway, sending bursts of electrical excitation that ripple down the stria terminalis to the hypothalamus and put it in a pissy mood.

Once again, do your hormonal intervention: flood the area with testosterone. You can inject the hormone into the bloodstream, where it eventually makes its way to the amygdala. You can surgically microinject the stuff directly into the area. In a few years, you may even be able to construct animals with extra copies of the genes that direct testosterone synthesis, producing extra hormone that way. Six of one, half a dozen of the other. The key thing is what doesn't happen next. Does testosterone make waves of electrical excitation surge down the stria terminalis? Does it turn on that pathway? Not at all. If and only if the amygdala is already sending an excited volley down the stria terminalis, testosterone increases the rate of such activity by shortening the resting time between bouts. It's not turning on the pathway, it's increasing the volume of signaling if it is already turned on. It's not causing aggression, it's exaggerating the preexisting pattern of it, exaggerating the response to environmental triggers of aggression.

In every generation, it is the duty of behavioral biologists to try to teach this critical point, one that seems a maddening cliché once you get it. You take that hoary old dichotomy between nature and nurture, between intrinsic factors and extrinsic ones, between genes and environment, and regardless of which behavior and underlying biology you're studying, the dichotomy is a sham. No genes. No environment. Just the interaction between the two.

Do you want to know how important environment and experience are in understanding testosterone and aggression? Look back at how the effects of castration are discussed earlier. There were statements like "Remove the source of testosterone in species after species and levels of aggression typically plummet." Not "Remove the source . . . and aggression always goes to zero." On the average it declines, but rarely to zero, and not at all in some individuals. And the more social experience an individual had being aggressive prior to castration, the more likely that behavior persists sans cojones. In the right context, social conditioning can more than make up for the complete absence of the hormone.

A case in point: the spotted hyena. These animals are fast becoming the darlings of endocrinologists, sociobiologists, gynecologists, and tabloid writers because of their wild sex reversal system. Females are more muscular and more aggressive than males, and are socially dominant to them, rare traits in the mammalian world. And get this: females secrete more of certain testosterone-related hormones than the males do, producing muscles, aggression, and masculinized private parts that make it supremely difficult to tell the sex of a hyena. So high androgen levels would seem, again, to cause aggression and social dominance. But that's not the whole answer.

High in the hills above the University of California at Berkeley is the world's largest colony of spotted hyenas, massive bone-crunching beasts who fight each other for the chance to have their ears scratched by Laurence Frank, the zoologist who brought them over as infants from Kenya. Various scientists are studying their sex reversal system. The female hyenas are bigger and more muscular than the males and have the same weirdo genitals and elevated androgen levels as their female cousins back in the savanna. Everything is just as it is in the wild—except the social system. As those hyenas grew up, there was a very significant delay in the time it took for the females to begin socially dominating the males, even though the females were stoked on androgens. They had to grow up without the established social system to learn from.

When people first realize that genes have a great deal to do with behavior—even subtle, complex, human behavior—they are often struck with an initial evangelical enthusiasm, placing a convert's faith in the genetic components of the story. This enthusiasm is typically reductive—because of physics envy, because reductionism is so impressive, because it would be so nice if there were a single gene (or hormone or neurotransmitter or part of the brain) responsible for everything. But even if you completely understood how genes regulate all the important physical factors involved in aggression—testosterone synthesis and secretion, the brain's testosterone receptors, the amygdala neurons and their levels of transmitters, the favorite color of the hypothalamus—you still wouldn't be able to predict levels of aggression accurately in a group of normal individuals.

This is no mere academic subject. We are a fine species with some potential, yet we are racked by sickening amounts of violence. Unless we are hermits, we feel the threat of it, often every day, and should our leaders push the button, we will all be lost in a final global violence. But as we try to understand this feature of our sociality, it is critical to remember the limits of the biology. Knowing the genome, the complete DNA sequence, of some suburban teenager is never going to tell us why that kid, in his after-school chess club, has developed a particularly aggressive style with his bishops. And it certainly isn't going to tell us much about the teenager in some inner city hellhole who has taken to mugging people. "Testosterone equals aggression" is inadequate for those who would offer a simple biological solution to the violent male. And "testosterone equals aggression" is certainly inadequate for those who would offer the simple excuse that boys will be boys. Violence is more complex than a single hormone, and it is supremely rare that any of our behaviors can be reduced to genetic destiny. This is science for the bleeding-heart liberal: the genetics of behavior is usually meaningless outside the context of the social factors and environment in which it occurs.

Cultural Constructions
of Gender

Biological evidence helps explain the ubiquity of gender difference and gender inequality, but social scientific evidence modifies both the universality and the inevitability implicit in biological claims. Cross-cultural research suggests that gender and sexuality are far more fluid, far more variable, than biological models would have predicted. If biological sex alone produced observed sex differences, Margaret Mead asked in the 1920s and 1930s, why did it produce such *different* definitions of masculinity and femininity in different cultures? In her path-breaking study, *Sex and Temperament in Three Primitive Societies*, Mead began an anthropological tradition of exploring and often celebrating the dramatically rich and varied cultural constructions of gender.

Anthropologists are more likely to locate the origins of gender difference and gender inequality in a sex-based division of labor, the near-universality of and the variations in the ways in which societies organize the basic provision and distribution of material goods. They've found that when women's and men's spheres are most distinctly divided—where women and men do different things in different places—women's status tends to be lower than when men and women share both work and workplaces.

Some researchers have posed challenging questions about the near-universality of gender inequality. For example, Judith Lorber asks what happens when women or men "cross over" and adopt the cultural presentation of the other sex.

And some researchers have explored the function of various cultural rituals and representations in creating the symbolic justification for gender differences and inequality based on this sex-based division of labor. For example, Gilbert Herdt describes a variety of "coming out" processes in a variety of cultures, thus demonstrating (1) the connections between sexual identity and gender identity and (2) the dramatic variation among those identities. And Thomas von der Osten-Sacken and Thomas Uwer de-couple religion from cultural practices to suggest that while rituals may use religion as a pretense, the answer lies deeper in our cultural heritage.

Men as Women and Women as Men: Disrupting Gender

JUDITH LORBER

This thing here, you call this a person? There is no such thing as a person who is half male half female.
            Meira Weiss

The French writer Colette felt that she was a "mental hermaphrodite" but had "a sturdy and perfectly female body" (Lydon 1991, 28). When she offered to travel with a noted womanizer, he said that he traveled only with women: "Thus when Damien declares that he travels only with women, implying that a woman is what Colette is not, the only linguistically possible conclusion is that she must be a man. But she and we know this not to be the case, despite her willingness to admit to a certain 'virility.' What then, can Colette legitimately call herself?" (29).[1] Cool and rational androgynous women are social men, one step removed from the "mannish lesbian" (Newton 1984). Men who use a highly emotionally charged vocabulary may be judged romantic geniuses, but their masculinity may be somewhat suspect, as was Byron's (Battersby 1989).

The history of a nineteenth-century French hermaphrodite illustrates the impossibility of living socially as both a woman and a man even if it is physiologically possible (Butler 1990, 93–106). Herculine Barbin, who was raised in convents as a girl, after puberty, fell in love with a young woman and had sexual relations with her. At the age of twenty-two, Herculine (usually called Alexina) confessed the homosexuality to a bishop, and after examination by two doctors, was legally recategorized as a man and given a man's name. But Herculine's genitals, as described in two doctors'

reports, were ambiguous: a one-and-a-half-inch-long penis, partly descended testicles, and a urethral opening (Foucault 1980, 125–28). One doctor reasoned as follows:

> Is Alexina a woman? She has a vulva, labia majora, and a feminine urethra, independent of a sort of imperforate penis, which might be a monstrously developed clitoris. She has a vagina . . . . These are completely feminine attributes. Yet, but Alexina has never menstruated; the whole outer part of her body is that of a man, and my explorations do not enable me to find a womb. Her tastes, her inclinations, draw her toward women. At night she has voluptuous sensations that are followed by a discharge of sperm; her linen is stained and starched with it. Finally, to sum up the matter, ovoid bodies and spermatic cords are found by touch in a divided scrotum. These are the real proofs of sex. . . . Alexina is a man, hermaphroditic, no doubt, but with an obvious predominance of masculine sexual characteristics. (127–28)

But Barbin, now called Abel, did not feel he was fully a man socially because he did not think any woman would marry him, and at the age of thirty he ended a "double and bizarre existence" via suicide. The doctor who performed the autopsy felt that the external genitalia could just as well have been classified as female, and that, with a penis-clitoris capable of erection and a vagina, Barbin was physiologically capable of bisexuality (128–44). But there was no social status of man-woman.

What would have become of Herculine Barbin one hundred years later? Surgery to remove the

---

testicles, enlarge the vagina, and make the penis smaller? Then hormones to produce breasts and reduce body hair? Or closure of the vaginal opening, release of the testes, cosmetic surgery to enlarge the penis, and administration of testosterone? Having been brought up as a girl, but loving a woman, would Barbin have identified as a "man," a "lesbian," or a "bisexual"? Would the woman who loved him as a woman accept him as a husband? Without surgery or gender reassignment, would Herculine and Sara have been accepted as a lesbian couple today? Without surgery, but with gender reassignment, would Abel and Sara have been accepted as a heterosexual couple? Would Barbin have used a gender-neutral name, dressed in a gender-neutral way? What sex would be on her or his official documents? What kind of work would he or she have done?[2]

One possibility was documented in 1937. A hermaphrodite named Emma, who had a penis-like clitoris as well as a vagina, was raised as a girl. Emma had sexual relationships with a number of girls (heterosexual sex), married a man with whom she also had heterosexual sex, but continued to have women lovers (Fausto-Sterling 1993). She refused to have vaginal closure and live as a man because it would have meant a divorce and having to go to work. Emma was quite content to be a physiological bisexual, possibly because her gender identity was clearly that of a woman.

Anne Fausto-Sterling says that "no classification scheme could more than suggest the variety of sexual anatomy encountered in clinical practice" (1993). In 1992, a thirty-year-old Ethiopian Israeli whose social identity was a man was discovered at his Army physical to have a very small penis and a very small vagina. Exploratory surgery revealed vestigial ovaries and vestigial testicles, a uterus, and fallopian tubes. He was XY, but when he was classified a male at birth it was on the basis of how the external genitalia looked, and the penis took precedence. Because he had been brought up as a man and wanted to have this identity supported physiologically, his penis was enlarged and reconstructed, and the vagina was closed and made into a scrotum. Testosterone was administered to increase his sexual desire for women.[3]

"Penis and Eggs"

When physiological anomalies occur today in places with sophisticated medical technology, the diagnosis, sex assignment, and surgical reconstruction of the genitalia are done as quickly as possible in order to minimize the intense uncertainty that a genderless child produces in our society (Kessler 1990). Other cultures, however, are more accepting of sex and gender ambiguity.

In the Dominican Republic, there has been a genetic phenomenon in which children who looked female at birth and were brought up as girls produced male hormones at puberty and virilized. Their genitalia masculinized, their voices deepened, and they developed a male physical appearance (Imperato-McGinley et al. 1974, 1979). They are called *guevedoces* (penis at 12) or *machihembra* (first woman, then man) or *guevotes* (penis and eggs). According to one set of reports, sixteen of nineteen who were raised as girls gradually changed to men's social roles— working outside the home, marrying, and becoming heads of households (Imperato-McGinley et al. 1979). One, now elderly, who emigrated to the United States, felt like a man, but under family pressure lived as a woman. One, still in the Dominican Republic, had married as a woman at sixteen, had been deserted after a year, continued to live as a woman, and wanted surgery to be a "normal" woman. Not all those who lived as men had fully functioning genitalia, and all were sterile.

The physicians who studied thirty-three of these male pseudohermaphrodites (biologically male with ambiguous-appearing genitalia at birth) claim that the nineteen who decided without medical intervention that they would adopt men's identities and social roles despite having been raised as girls "appear to challenge both the theory of the immutability of gender identity after three or four years of age and the sex of rearing as the major factor in determining male-gender identity" (Imperato-McGinley et al. 1979, 1236). Their report stresses the effects of the hormonal input and secondary male sex characteristics at puberty, despite the mixture of reactions and gradualness of the gender changeover.

Another physician (Baker 1980) questions whether the pseudohermaphrodites were reared unambiguously as girls, given their somewhat abnormal genitalia at birth, and an anthropologist (Herdt 1990) claims that culturally, the community recognized a third sex category, since they had names for it. Although the medical researchers described the parents' reactions during the course of the virilization as "amazement, confusion, and finally, acceptance rather than hostility" (Imperato-McGinley et al. 1979, 1235–36), their interviews with the pseudohermaphrodites revealed that as children, they had always suffered embarrassment because of their genitalia, and they worried about future harassment whether they chose to live as women or as men. That is, they were never unambiguously girls socially, and their appearance and sterility undercut their claims to be men. Nonetheless, most chose to live as men. Virilization was not total, but it provided the opportunity for the choice of the more attractive social role.[4] According to the medical researchers: "In a domestic setting, the women take care of the household activities, while the affected subjects work as farmers, miners or woodsmen, as do the normal males in the town. They enjoy their role as head of the household" (Imperato-McGinley et al. 1979, 1234).

In Papua New Guinea, where the same recessive genetic condition and marriage to close relatives produces similar male pseudohermaphrodites, the culture does have an intergender category (*kwolu-aatmwol*). Many of these children were identified by experienced midwives at birth and reared anticipatorily as boys (Herdt 1990; Herdt and Davidson 1988). Although the *kwolu-aatmwols* went through boys' rituals as they grew up, their adult status as men was incomplete ritually, and therefore socially, because they were sterile and also because they were embarrassed by the small size of their penises. They rarely allowed themselves to be fellated by adolescent boys, a mark of honor for adult men, although some, as teenagers, in an effort to become more masculine, frequently fellated older men. In their behavior and attitudes, they were masculine. Their identity as adult men was stigmatized, however, because they did not participate in what in Western societies would be homosexual (and stigmatized) sex practices, but in that culture made them fully men (Herdt 1981).

The pseudohermaphrodites who were reared as girls, either because they were not identified or their genital anomalies were hidden, did not switch to living as men when they virilized. Rather, they tried very hard to live as women, but were rejected by the men they married. Only at that point did they switch to men's dress, but they were even more ostracized socially, since they did not undergo any men's rituals. According to Gilbert Herdt and Julian Davidson: "Once exposed, they had no place to hide and no public in which to continue to pose as 'female.' It was only this that precipitated gender role change. Yet this is not change to the male role, because the natives know the subjects are not male; rather they changed from sex-assigned female to turnim-men, male-identified kwolu-aatmwol" (1988, 53).

Thus, neither childhood socialization nor pubescent virilization nor individual preferences was definitive in the adult gender placement of these male pseudohermaphrodites. Their assigned status was problematic men; away from their home villages, they could pass as more or less normal men. One was married, but to a prostitute; he had been "ostentatiously masculine" as an adolescent, was a good provider, and was known as "a fearless womanizer" (Herdt and Davidson 1988).

Switching Genders

Transsexuals have normal genitalia, but identify with the members of the opposite gender. Since there is no mixed or intermediate gender for people with male genitalia who want to live as women or people with female genitalia who want to live as men, transsexuals end up surgically altering their genitalia to fit their gender identity. They also undergo hormone treatment to alter their body shape and hair distribution and to develop secondary sex characteristics, such as breasts or beards. Transsexuals do not change their sex completely (Stoller 1985, 163). Their chromosomes remain the same, and no man-to-woman transsexual has a uterus implant, nor do any women-to-men transsexuals produce sperm. They change gender; thus, the accurate terms are *man-to-woman* and *woman-to-man*, not *male-to-female* and *female-to-male*.

Discussing only men-to-women transsexuals, Richard Docter sees the process as one in which more and more frequent cross-dressing reinforces the desire to completely switch genders:

> The cross-gender identity seems to grow stronger with practice and with social reinforcements of the pseudowoman. In unusual cases, the end result is a kind of revolution within the self system. The balance of power shifts in favor of the cross-gender identity with consequent disorganization and conflict within the self system. One result can be a quest to resolve the tension through sexual reassignment procedures or hormonal feminization. (1988, 3)

Transsexuals, however, have also indicated a sense from an early age of being in the wrong body (Morris 1975). Sexologists and psychiatrists have debated whether this anomalous gender identity is the result of biology, parenting, or retrospective reconstruction.[5]

The social task for transsexuals is to construct a gender identity without an appropriately gendered biography.[6] To create a feminized self, men-to-women transsexuals use the male transvestite's "strategies and rituals" of passing as a woman—clothing, makeup, hair styling, manicures, gestures, ways of walking, voice pitch, and "the more subtle gestures such as the difference in ways men and women smoke cigarettes" and the vocabulary women use (Bolin 1988, 131–41). Creating a new gender identity means creating a paper trail of bank, social security, educational, and job history records; drivers' licenses, passports, and credit cards all have to be changed once the new name becomes legal (145–46). Then significant others have to be persuaded to act their parts, too. Discussing men-to-women transsexuals, Anne Bolin notes:

> The family is the source of transsexuals' birth and nurturance as males and symbolically can be a source of their birth and nurturance as females. Thus, when their families accept them as females, refer to them by their female names, and use

feminine gender references, it is a profound event in the transsexuals' lives, one in which their gender identity as females is given a retroactive credence. . . . The family is a significant battleground on which a symbolic identity war is waged. . . . Because an individual can only be a son or daughter [in Western societies], conferral of daughterhood by a mother is a statement of the death of a son. (1988, 94)

The final rite of passage is not only passing as a visibly and legally identifiable gendered person with a bona fide kinship status but passing as a *sexual* person. For Bolin's men-to-women transsexuals, "the most desirable condition for the first passing adventure is at night with a 'genetic girlfriend' in a heterosexual bar" (140).

Some transsexuals become gay or lesbian. In Anne Bolin's study population of seventeen men-to-women transsexuals, only one was exclusively heterosexual in orientation (1988, Fig. 1, 62). Nine were bisexual, and six were exclusively lesbian, including two transsexuals who held a wedding ceremony in a gay church.[7] Justifying the identification as lesbian by a preoperative man-to-woman transsexual who had extensive hormone therapy and had developed female secondary sexual characteristics, Deborah Heller Feinbloom and her co-authors argue that someone "living full-time in a female role must be called a woman, albeit a woman with male genitalia (and without female genitalia)," although potential lovers might not agree (1976, 69).[8] If genitalia, sexuality, and gender identity are seen as a package, then it is paradoxical for someone to change their anatomy in order to make love with someone they could easily have had a sexual relationship with "normally." But gender identity (being a member of a group, women or men) and gender status (living the life of a woman or a man) are quite distinct from sexual desire for a woman or man. It is Western culture's preoccupation with genitalia as the markers of both sexuality and gender and the concept of these social statuses as fixed for life that produces the problem and the surgical solution for those who cannot tolerate the personal ambiguities Western cultures deny.[9]

Gender Masquerades

Transvestites change genders by cross-dressing, masquerading as a person of a different gender for erotic, pragmatic, or rebellious reasons. Since they can put on and take off gender by changing clothes, they disrupt the conventional conflation of sex, sexuality, and gender in Western cultures much more than transsexuals do.

François Timoléon de Choisy was a seventeenth-century courtier, historian, ambassador, and priest who was "indefatigably heterosexual" but a constant cross-dresser. The Abbé de Choisy married women twice, once as a woman, once as a man, and both spouses had children by him. He survived the turmoil of gender ambiguity by going to live in another community or country when the censure got too vociferous (Garber 1992, 255–59). The Chevalier (sometimes Chevalière) d'Eon de Beaumont, a famous cross-dresser who lived in the eighteenth century, seems to have been celibate. Because d'Eon did not have any sexual relationships, English and French bookmakers took serious bets on whether d'Eon was a man or a woman. Physically, he was a male, according to his birth and death certificates, and he lived forty-nine years as a man (259–66). He also lived thirty-four years as a woman, many of them with a woman companion who "was astounded to learn that she was a man" (265). Garber asks: "Does the fact that he was born a male infant and died 'with the male organs perfectly formed' mean that he was, in the years between, a man? A 'very man'" (255)? A man in what sense—physical, sexual, or gendered?

Some men who pass as women and women who pass as men by cross-dressing say they do so because they want privileges or opportunities the other gender has, but they may also be fighting to alter their society's expectations for their own gender. One of her biographers says of George Sand:

> While still a child she lost her father, tried to fill his place with a mother whom she adored, and, consequently, developed a masculine attitude strengthened by the boyish upbringing which she received at the hands of a somewhat eccentric tutor who encouraged her to wear a man's clothes . . . . For the rest of her life she strove, unconsciously, to recreate the free paradise of her childhood, with the result that she could never submit to a master . . . . Impatient of all masculine authority, she fought a battle for the emancipation of women, and sought to win for them the right to dispose freely of their bodies and their hearts. (Maurois 1955, 13)[10]

Natalie Davis calls these defiers of the social order disorderly women. Their outrage and ridicule produce a double message; they ask for a restoration of the social order purified of excesses of gender disadvantage, and their own gender inversion also suggests possibilities for change (1975, 124–51).[11]

During the English Renaissance, open cross-dressing on the street and in the theater defied accepted gender categories.[12] In early modern England, the state enforced class and gender boundaries through sumptuary laws that dictated who could wear certain colors, fabrics, and furs. Cross-dressing and wearing clothes "above one's station" (servants and masters trading places, also a theatrical convention) thus were important symbolic subverters of social hierarchies at a time of changing modes of production and a rising middle class (Howard 1988). Since seventeenth-century cross-dressing up-ended concepts of appropriate sexuality, the fashion was accused of feminizing men and masculinizing women: "When women took men's clothes, they symbolically left their subordinate positions. They became masterless women, and this threatened overthrow of hierarchy was discursively read as the eruption of uncontrolled sexuality" (Howard 1988, 424).

The way the gender order got critiqued and then restored can be seen in a famous Renaissance play about a cross-dressing character called the "roaring girl." *The Roaring Girl*, by Thomas Middleton and Thomas Dekker, written in 1608–1611, was based on a real-life woman, Mary Frith, who dressed in men's clothes and was "notorious as a bully, whore, bawd, pickpurse, fortune-teller, receiver [of stolen goods], and forger" (Bullen 1935, 4). She also smoked and drank like a man and was in prison for a time. She lived to the age of seventy-four. In Middleton and Dekker's play, this roaring girl, called Moll Cutpurse, becomes a model of morality. She remains chaste, and thus free of men sexually and economically, unlike most poor women, as she herself points out:

> Distressed needlewomen and trade-fallen wives,
> Fish that must needs bite or themselves be
>   bitten,
> Such hungry things as these may soon be took
> With a worm fastened on a golden hook. (III, i,
>   96–97)

Her cross-dressing allows her to observe and question the ways of thieves and pickpockets not to learn to be a criminal but to protect herself. She can protect any man who marries her:

> You may pass where you list, through crowd
>   most thick,
> And come off bravely with your purse unpick'd.
> You do not know the benefits I bring with me;
> No cheat dares work upon you with thumb or
>   knife,
> While you've a roaring girl to your son's wife.
>   (V, ii, 159–63)

But she feels she is too independent to be a traditional wife:

> I have no humour to marry; I love to lie a' both sides a' the bed myself: and again, a' th' other side, a wife, you know, ought to be obedient, but I fear me I am too headstrong to obey; therefore I'll ne'er go about it. (II, ii, 37–41)

Her other reason for not marrying is that men cheat, lie, and treat women badly. If they changed, "next day following I'll be married," to which another character in the play responds: "This sounds like doomsday" (V, ii, 226–27), not likely to happen soon.

Despite her gloomy views on men and marriage, Moll helps a young couple marry by pretending to be wooed by the man. His father, who has withheld his consent for his son's original choice, is so outraged that the son is thinking of marrying Moll Cutpurse that he willingly consents to his son's marriage to the woman he had loved all along. Thus, rather poignantly, Moll's independence and street smarts are invidious traits when compared to those of a "good woman."

Her cross-dressing is not a defiance of the gender order, but rather places her outside it:

> 'tis woman more than man,
> Man more than woman; and, which to none
>   can hap
> The sun gives her two shadows to one shape;
> Nay, more, let this strange thing walk, stand,
>   or sit,
> No blazing star draws more eyes after it. (I, i,
>   251–55)

Moll Cutpurse's social isolation means that the gender order does not have to change to incorporate her independence as a woman: "a politics of despair . . . affirms a seemingly inevitable exclusion of marginal genders from the territory of the natural and the real" (Butler 1990, 146).

Affirming Gender

In most societies with only two gender statuses— "women" and "men"—those who live in the status not meant for them usually do not challenge the social institution of gender. In many ways, they reinforce it. Joan of Arc, says Marina Warner (1982) in discussing her transvestism, "needed a framework of virtue, and so she borrowed the apparel of men, who held a monopoly on virtue, on reason and courage, while eschewing the weakness of women, who were allotted to the negative pole, where virtue meant meekness and humility, and nature meant carnality" (147). A masculine woman may be an abomination to tradition, but from a feminist point of view, she is not a successful rebel, for she reinforces dominant men's standards of the good: "The male trappings were used as armor—defensive and aggressive. It . . . attacked men by aping their appearance in order to usurp their functions. On the personal level, it defied men and declared them useless; on the social level, it affirmed male supremacy, by needing to borrow the appurtenances to assert personal needs and desires . . . ; men remain the touchstone and equality a process of imitation" (Warner 1982, 155).[13]

Joan of Arc said she donned armor not to pass as a man, but to be beyond sexuality, beyond gender. She called herself *pucelle*, a maid, but socially, she was neither woman nor man. She was an "ideal androgyne": "She could thereby transcend her sex; she could set herself apart and usurp the privileges of the male and his claims to superiority. At the same time, by never pretending to be other than a woman and a maid, she was usurping a man's function but shaking off the trammels of his sex altogether to occupy a different, third order, neither male nor female, but unearthly, like the angels" (Warner 1982, 145–46).

When Joan was on trial, she was denuded of her knightly armor and accused of female carnality, and then she was burned at the stake—as a woman and a witch. Twenty-five years later, at her rehabilitation trial, and in 1920, when she was declared a saint, she was presented as a sexless virgin, amenorrheic and possibly anorectic.

As a heroine today, Joan of Arc is more likely to be a symbolic Amazon, a woman warrior, than an ideal androgyne, sexless and saintly. The ambiguity of her gender representation was corroborated by one of the first women to enter West Point to be trained with men as an army officer. On her first day in the dining hall, Carol Barkalow "was startled to find among the depictions of history's greatest warriors the muralist's interpretation of Joan of Arc. There she stood in silver armor, alongside Richard the Lion Hearted and William the Conqueror, sword uplifted in one hand, helmet clasped in the other, red hair falling to her shoulders, with six knights kneeling in homage at her feet" (1990, 27). As Barkalow found later, the warrior maid had set little precedent for the acceptance of women as military leaders. The mixed-gender message of the portrait was prescient, for the main problem at West Point seemed to be one of categorization—women army officers were suspect as women when they looked and acted too much like men, but they were a puzzlement as soldiers when they looked and acted like women.

Other Genders

There are non-Western societies that have third and fourth genders that link genitalia, sexual orientation, and gender status in ways quite different from Western cultures. These statuses demonstrate how physical sex, sexuality, and gender interweave, but are separate elements conferring different levels of prestige and stigma.

The Native American berdache is an institutionalized cross-gendered role that legitimates males doing women's work. The berdache can also be a sacred role, and if a boy's dreaming indicates a pull toward the berdache status, parents would not think of dissenting. Although it would seem logical that societies that put a high emphasis on aggressive masculinity, like the Plains Indians, would offer the berdache status as a legitimate way out for boys reluctant to engage in violent play and warfare, berdaches do not occur in all warlike tribes and do occur in some that are not warlike (Williams 1986, 47–49).[14]

Berdaches educate children, sing and dance at tribal events, tend the ill, carry provisions for war parties, and have special ritual functions (Whitehead 1981, 89; Williams 1986, 54–61). Among the Navahos, berdaches not only do women's craft work, but also farm and raise sheep, which are ordinarily men's work: "Beyond this, because they are believed to be lucky in amassing wealth they usually act as the head of their family and have control of the disposal of all the family's property" (Williams 1986, 61).

Berdaches are legitimately homosexual:

Homosexual behavior may occur between non-berdache males, but the cultures emphasize the berdache as the usual person a man would go to for male sex. With the role thus institutionalized, the berdache serves the sexual needs of many men without competing against the institution of heterosexual marriage. Men are not required to make a choice between being heterosexual or being homosexual, since they can accommodate both desires. Nevertheless, for that minority of men who do wish to make such a choice, a number of cultures allow them the option of becoming the husband to a berdache. (Williams 1986, 108–9)

Since homosexual relationships do not make a man into a berdache, Walter Williams makes a distinction between homosexuality, as sexual relations between two men, and heterogendered sexual relations, between a man and a berdache: "The berdache and his male partner do not occupy the same recognized gender status" (96). Two berdaches do not have sexual relations with each other, nor do they marry. In some cultures, the berdache's husband loses no prestige; in others, he does, coming in for kidding for having an unusual sexual relationship, like a young man married to an older woman (Williams 1986, 113). Sometimes the joking is because the berdache is a particularly good provider. The berdache's husband is not labeled a homosexual, and if a divorce occurs, he can easily make a heterosexual marriage.

The berdache is not the equivalent of the Western male homosexual (Callender and Kochems 1985). The berdache's social status is defined by work and dress and sometimes a sacred calling; the social status of modern Western homosexual men is defined by sexual orientation and preference for men as sexual partners (Whitehead 1981, 97–98). The berdache's gender status is not that of a man but of a woman, so their homosexual relationships are heterogendered; homosexual couples in Western society are homogendered.

The Plains Indians had a tradition of *warrior women*, but a cross-gender status for younger women was not institutionalized in most Native American tribes (Blackwood 1984, 37). Harriet Whitehead argues that because men were considered superior in these cultures, it was harder for women to breach the gender boundaries upward than it was for men to breach them downward (1981, 86). Walter Williams speculates that every woman was needed to have children (1986, 244). The tribes that did allow women to cross gender boundaries restricted the privilege to women who claimed they never menstruated (Whitehead 1981, 92). Young women could become men in societies that were egalitarian and tolerant of cross-gendered work activities (Blackwood 1984). Among the Mohave, a girl's refusal to learn women's tasks could lead to her being taught the same skills boys learned and to ritual renaming, nose piercing, and hair styling as a man. At that point, her status as a man allowed her to marry a woman and to do men's work of hunting, trapping, growing crops, and fighting. She was also expected to perform a man's ritual obligations. Because divorce was frequent and children went with the mother,

cross-gendered women could rear children. Adoptions were also common. Sexually, cross-gendered women were homosexual, but, like berdaches, their marriages were always heterogendered— they did not marry or have sexual relationships with each other.[15] Among less egalitarian Native American societies, a legitimate cross-gender status, *manly hearted woman*, was available for post-menopausal women who acquired wealth (Whitehead 1981, 90–93). In some African cultures today, a wealthy woman can marry a woman and adopt her children as a father (Amadiume 1987).

Lesbians in Western societies differ from cross-gendered women in Native American and African societies in that they do not form heterogendered couples. Both women in a lesbian couple continue to be identified socially as women; neither becomes a "husband." If they have children, neither becomes a "father," both are mothers to the children (Weston 1991).

Hijras are a group in northern India who consider themselves intersexed men who have become women; many, but not all, undergo ritualistic castration (Nanda 1990). They serve both a legitimate cultural function as ritual performers, and an illegitimate sexual function, as homosexual prostitutes. Sometimes they are considered women, sometimes men, but they are deviant in either status not because of their sexuality but because they don't have children. Hijras are required to dress as women, but they do not imitate or try to pass as ordinary women; rather, they are as deviant as women as they are as men:

> Their female dress and mannerisms are exaggerated to the point of caricature, expressing sexual overtones that would be considered inappropriate for ordinary women in their roles as daughters, wives, and mothers. Hijra performances are burlesques of female behavior. Much of the comedy of their behavior derives from the incongruities between their behavior and that of traditional women. They use coarse and abusive speech and gestures in opposition to the Hindu ideal of demure and restrained femininity. Further, it is not at all uncommon to see hijras in female clothing sporting several days growth of beard, or exposing hairy, muscular arms. The ultimate sanction

of hijras to an abusive or unresponsive public is to lift their skirts and expose the mutilated genitals. The implicit threat of this shameless, and thoroughly unfeminine, behavior is enough to make most people give them a few cents so they will go away. (Nanda 1986, 38)

Hijras live separately in their own communal households, relating to each other as fictive mothers, daughters, sisters, grandmothers, and aunts. Occupationally, they sing and dance at weddings and births, run bathhouses, work as cooks and servants, and engage in prostitution with men; or they are set up in households by men in long-term sexual relationships. The hijras who Serena Nanda interviewed came from lower class, middle-caste families in small cities and said they had wanted to dress and act as women from early childhood. They left home because of parental disapproval and to protect their siblings' chances for marriage (65).

Hijras worship Bahuchara Mata, a mother-goddess. Shiva is also sometimes worshiped by hijras, for his manifestation in half-man, half-woman form. In the great Indian legend, the *Mahabharata,* one of the heroes, Arjuna, lives for a year in exile as a woman, doing menial work and teaching singing and dancing. Those who were not men and not women were blessed by Ram in the Hindu epic, *Ramayana.* In addition to these Hindu religious connections, Islam is also involved in hijra culture. The founders of the original seven hijra communal "houses," or subgroups, were said to be Muslim, and in keeping with this tradition, modern houses also have Muslim gurus. This religious legitimation and their performance of cultural rituals integrate hijras into Indian society, as does the Indian tradition of creative asceticism. Young, sexually active hijras, however, are seen by the elders as compromising the ascetic sources of their legitimacy.

Hijras seem to resemble transvestite performers (female impersonators or "drag queens") in modern Western society. But transvestite performers do not have roots in Western religious tradition, nor are they castrated. Castrated hijras do not have the same social status as men-to-women transsexuals

in Western societies, since transsexuals act as normal women, and hijras do not. In some respects, hijras resemble the castrati of European operatic tradition.

In the seventeenth century, because the Roman Catholic church forbade women to sing in public, women's parts were sung by castrati, boys whose testicles were removed in adolescence so their voices would remain soprano. Throughout the eighteenth century, castrati and women singers both appeared on the operatic stage, often in competition, although the castrati had the advantages of far superior training, respectability, church support, and fame. There was constant gender reversal in casting and plot. Women contraltos sang men's roles in men's clothes (now called "trouser roles"); soprano castrati sang the "leading ladies" in women's costumes (*en travesti*); and both masqueraded in plots of mistaken or hidden identity in the clothes of the role's opposite but their actual gender.

Casanova, in his memoirs, tells of being sexually attracted to a supposed castrato, Bellino, in the early 1740s. This attraction totally confounded his notorious ability to "smell" a woman in his presence, so he was much relieved, when he seduced Bellino (in anticipation of homosexual sex), to find out that Bellino was a woman soprano posing as a eunuch in order to sing in Rome. Of course, she sang women's roles. She had heterosexual sex with Casanova, although this womanizer was just as ready to make love with a man (Ellison 1992).[16]

A third type of institutionalized intermediate gender role are the xaniths of Oman, a strictly gender-segregated Islamic society in which women's sexual purity is guarded by their wearing long, black robes and black face masks when in public and by not mingling with men other than close relatives at home (Wikan 1982, 168–86). Xaniths are homosexual prostitutes who dress in men's clothes but in pastel colors rather than white, wear their hair in neither a masculine nor a feminine style, and have feminine mannerisms. They sing and eat with the women at weddings, mingle freely with women, but they maintain men's legal status. (Women are lifelong minors; they must have a male guardian.) They are not considered full-fledged women because they are prostitutes, and women, in Oman ideology, may engage in sexual acts only with their husbands. The xaniths' social role is to serve as sexual outlets for unmarried or separated men, and thus they protect the sexual purity of women. The men who use them as sexual outlets are not considered homosexual, because supposedly they always take the active role.

Xaniths live alone and take care of their own households, doing both men's work—the marketing—and women's work—food preparation. Being a xanith seems to be a family tradition, in that several brothers will become xaniths. They move in and out of the gender status fairly easily, reverting to manhood when they marry and successfully deflower their brides. To be considered a man, a groom must show bloody evidence of defloration or accuse his bride of not having been a virgin. A xanith, therefore, who shows he has successfully deflowered a virgin bride becomes a man. Just as a female in Oman culture is not a woman until she has intercourse, a male is not a man until he successfully consummates his marriage. A woman, though, can never revert to the virgin state of girlhood, but a man can revert to xanithhood by singing with the women at the next wedding.

In the sense that passive homosexual sex rather than heterogendered behavior is the defining criteria of status, the xanith is closest to the feminized homosexual prostitute in Western culture, but not, according to Wikan, to homosexual men in other Middle Eastern cultures:

> Homosexual practice is a common and recognized phenomenon in many Middle Eastern cultures, often in the form of an institutionalized practice whereby older men seek sexual satisfaction with younger boys. But this homosexual relationship generally has two qualities that make it fundamentally different from that practiced in Oman. First, it is part of a deep friendship or love relationship between two men, which has qualities, it is often claimed, of being purer and more beautiful than love between man and woman .... Second, both parties play both the active and the passive sexual role—either simultaneously or through time. (1982, 177)

One or the Other, Never Both

Michel Foucault, in the introduction to Barbin's memoirs, says of the concept of "one true sex": Biological theories of sexuality, juridical conceptions of the individual, forms of administrative control in modern nations, led little by little to rejecting the idea of a mixture of the two sexes in a single body, and consequently to limiting the free choice of indeterminate individuals. Henceforth, everybody was to have one and only one sex. Everybody was to have his or her primary, profound, determined and determining sexual identity; as for the elements of the other sex that might appear, they could only be accidental, superficial, or even quite simply illusory. (1980, viii)

Yet, in Western societies, despite our firm belief that each person has one sex, one sexuality, and one gender, congruent with each other and fixed for life, and that these categories are one of only two sexes, two sexualities, and two genders, hermaphrodites, pseudohermaphrodites, transsexuals, transvestites, and bisexuals exhibit a dizzying fluidity of bodies, desires, and social statuses. According to Annie Woodhouse, "punters" are men "who don't want to go to bed with a man, but don't want to go to bed with a real woman either." So they go to bed with men dressed as women (1989, 31). The ambiguous appearance of the women Holly Devor (1989) interviewed was typed as "mannish," and so they had difficulty being considered "opposite" enough for heterosexual relationships. As lesbians, their appearance was not only acceptable, but they could, and did, sexually excite other women when passing as men, as did Deborah Sampson, the woman who fought in the American Revolution in a man's uniform, and Nadezhda Durova, the Russian "cavalry maiden" in the Napoleonic Wars (Durova 1989; Freeman and Bond 1992). Marjorie Garber writes of Yvonne Cook, a man who dresses as a woman, considers herself a lesbian and has a woman lover who dresses as a man (1992, 4).

All these components can change and shift back and forth over days, weeks, months, and years. With unisex clothing, gender can change in minutes, depending on the context and the response of others to gender cues. Bisexuals have long-term serial relationships with women and men, but may define themselves as either heterosexual or homosexual. Transvestites consciously play with sexual and gender categories. Gay men, lesbians, and bisexuals cross Western culture's sexual boundaries but do not always challenge gender norms. Transsexuals, in their quest for "normality," often reaffirm them. Through their "subversive bodily acts," all demonstrate the social constructedness of sex, sexuality, and gender (Butler 1990, 79–141). But they have not disrupted the deep genderedness of the modern Western world. And to maintain genderedness, to uphold gender boundaries, the "impulses toward, or fear of, turning into someone of the opposite sex" that many ordinary, normal people feel, have to be suppressed (Stoller 1985, 152).

The norms, expectations, and evaluation of women and men may be converging, but we have no social place for a person who is neither woman nor man. A man who passes as a woman or a woman as a man still violates strong social boundaries, and when transsexuals change gender, they still cross a great divide. In this sense, Western culture resembles the intensely gendered world of Islam, where all the rules of marriage, kinship, inheritance, purity, modesty, ritual, and even burial are challenged by people of ambiguous sex (Sanders 1991). Rather than allowing the resultant social ambiguity to continue, medieval Islamic jurists developed a set of rules for gendering hermaphrodites: "A person with ambiguous genitalia or with no apparent sex might have been a biological reality, but it had no gender and, therefore, no point of entry into the social world: it was unsocialized" (Sanders 1991, 88). As in modern Western society, a person who was neither woman nor man had no social place and could have no social relationships without disturbing the social order: "What was at stake for medieval Muslims in gendering one ungendered body was, by implication, gendering the most important body: the social body" (89). The social body in modern Western society, both for the individual and the group, is, above all, gendered.

Notes

1. The passage as Colette wrote it is: "At a time when I was, when at least I believed I was insensitive to Damien, I suggested to him that he and I would make a pair of ideal traveling companions, both courteously selfish, easy to please, and fond of long silences. . . .

   'I like to travel only with women,' he answered.

   The sweet tone of his voice scarcely softened the brutality of his words . . . He was afraid he had hurt my feelings and tried to make up, with something even worse.

   'A woman? You? I know you would like to be one . . .'" (1933, 75; ellipses in the original).

2. After reclassification, Barbin, who had been a certified and competent schoolteacher, had to look for men's work. Bolin (1988, 156–57) notes a similar problem for men-to-women transsexuals who worked in fields dominated by men.

3. Richard Sadove M.D., personal communication. Dr. Sadove did the reconstructive surgery.

4. Fausto-Sterling 1985, 87–88; Herdt 1990, 437–38.

5. Most of the research is on men-to-women transsexuals. For reviews, see Bolin 1987; Docter 1988. For a scathing critique of transsexual research and practice, see Stoller 1985, 152–70. For a critique of the medical construction of transsexualism as a fixed core identity, see Billings and Urban 1982.

6. See Garfinkel 1967, 116–85, for a detailed account of how Bill-Agnes managed the practical details of passing while constructing a new gendered identity. Raymond (1979) is critical of men-to-women's gender identity because they have not had the previous experience of women's oppression.

7. Bolin's data on five transsexuals' postoperative sexual relationships indicated that three were bisexual and one was lesbian (181).

8. There have also been relationships between women-to-men and men-to-women transsexuals; these, however, are heterosexual and heterogendered (Money 1988, 93).

9. Actually, the mark of gender identity in Western culture is the penis—the person who has one of adequate size is male and a man; the person who does not, is not-male, not a man. Femaleness and

womanhood seem to be more problematic and need more "work" to construct. For an opposite view about masculinity, see Gilmore 1990.

10. Also see Heilbrun 1988, 32–36; L. J. Kaplan 1991, 492–500.

11. Also see Smith-Rosenberg 1985.

12. Dollimore 1986; Greenblatt 1987, 66–93; Howard 1988; Lavine 1986. On the fluidity of representations of bodily sex during the Renaissance, see Laqueur 1990a, 114–34. On the "semiotics of dress" in modern life, see E. Wilson 1985.

13. Also see Wheelwright 1989, 9–15.

14. Bolin lists seventy North and South American Indian tribes that have berdaches (1987, 61n).

15. By the end of the nineteenth century, the adoption of Western sexual and gender mores led to the delegitimation of the female cross-gender status (Blackwood 1984, 39–40), but not the male, according to W. L. Williams (1986).

16. The last known castrato, Alessandro Moreschi (1858–1922), made a series of recordings in 1902 and 1903, the year Pope Pius X formally banned castrati from the papal chapel, but he sang in the Sistine Chapel choir until 1913 (Ellison 1992, 37).

Coming of Age and Coming Out Ceremonies Across Cultures

GILBERT HERDT

Coming of age and being socialized into the sexual lifeways of the culture through ceremonies and initiation rites are common in many cultures of the world. These traditions help to incorporate the individual—previously a child, possibly outside of the moral rules and sexual roles of the adult group—into the public institutions and practices that bring full citizenship. We have seen in prior chapters many examples of these transitions and ceremonial practices, and we are certainly justified in thinking of them as basic elements in the human condition. Coming of age or "puberty" ceremonies around the world are commonly assumed to introduce the young person to sexual life as a heterosexual. In both traditional and modern

societies, ritual plays a role in the emergence of sexuality and the support of desires and relationships expected in later life.

Yet not all of this is seamless continuity, and in the study of homosexuality across cultures we must be aware of the gaps and barriers that exist between what is experienced in childhood or adolescence and the roles and customs in adulthood that may negate or oppose these experiences. Ruth Benedict (1938) stresses how development in a society may create cultural discontinuities in this sexual and gender cycle of identities and roles, necessitating rituals. She hints that homosexuality in particular may cause discontinuity of this kind, and the life stories of many gays and lesbians in western society reveal this problem. But in all societies, there is an issue of connecting childhood with adulthood, with the transition from sexual or biological immaturity to sexual maturity. In short, these transitions may create a "life crisis" that requires a social solution—and this is the aim of initiation ceremonies and rites of transition. Rituals may provide for the individual the necessary means to achieve difficult changes in sexual and gender status. Particularly in deeply emotional rituals, the energy of the person can be fully invested or bonded to the newfound group. This may create incredible attachments of the kind we have observed among the ancient Greeks, the feudal Japanese, and the Sambia of New Guinea, wherein the younger boy is erotically involved or partnered with an older male. In the conditions of a warrior society, homoerotic partnerships are particularly powerful when they are geared to the survival of the group.

The transition out of presumptive heterosexuality and secrecy and into the active process of self-identifying as gay or lesbian in the western tradition bears close comparison with these rites of passage. In the process of "coming out"—the current western concept of ritual passage—as gay or lesbian, a person undergoes emotional changes and a transformation in sexuality and gender that are remarkable and perhaps equal in their social drama to the initiation rites of small societies in New Guinea and Africa. Thus, the collective aspirations and desires of the adolescent or child going through the ritual to belong, participate in, and make commitments to communities of his or her own kind take on a new and broader scope.

Coming out is an implicit rite of passage for people who are in a crisis of identity that finds them "betwixt and between" being presumed to be heterosexual and living a totally secret and hidden life as a homosexual. Not until they enter into the gay or lesbian lifeway or the sexual culture of the gay and lesbian community will they begin to learn and be socialized into the rules, knowledge, and social roles and relationships of the new cultures. For many people, this experience is liberating; it is a highly charged, emotional, and dramatic process that changes them into adult gays or lesbians in all areas of their lives—with biological families, with

coworkers, with friends or schoolmates, and with a sexual and romantic partner of the same gender, possibly for the rest of their lives.

This transformation in the self and in social relations brings much that is new and sometimes frightening. An alternative moral system is opened up by the rituals. Why people who desire the same gender require a ritual when others in our society do not is painfully clear. Ritual is necessary because of the negative images, stigma, and intense social contamination that continue to exist in the stereotypes and antihomosexual laws of our society. To be homosexual is to be discredited as a full person in society; it is to have a spoiled identity—as a homosexual in society or as a frightened closet homosexual who may be disliked by openly gay and lesbian friends. But perhaps of greatest importance are the repression and social censorship involved: to have one's desires suppressed, to even experience the inner or "true" self as a secret.

It is hard to break through this taboo alone or without the support of a community because doing so exposes the person to all sorts of risk, requires considerable personal resources, and precipitates an emotional vulnerability that for many is very difficult to bear. But that is not all. For some people in our society, homosexuality is a danger and a source of pollution. Once the person's homosexuality is revealed, the stigma can also spread to the family, bringing the pollution of shame and dishonor to father and mother, clan and community. This is the old mask of the evil of homosexuality. . . . And this is what we have found in a study of these matters in Chicago (Herdt and Boxer 1996).

It is very typical to see an intense and negative reaction of family members to the declaration of same-sex desires by adolescents, even this late in the twentieth century. Society changes slowly and its myths even more slowly. For many people, homosexuality is an evil as frightening to the imagination as the monsters of bad Hollywood movies. Many people find it extremely difficult to deal with homosexuality and may exert strong pressures on their young to hide and suppress their feelings. Consequently, young people may feel that by declaring their same-sex desires, they will betray their families or the traditions of their sexual culture and its lifeways, which privilege marriage and the carrying on of the family name. And the younger person who desires the same gender may be afraid to come out for fear of dishonoring his or her ethnic community in the same way. To prevent these reactions, many people—closet homosexuals in the last century and many who fear the effects today—hide their basic feelings and all of their desires from their friends and families.

Here is where we may learn a lesson from other cultures. The mechanism of ritual helps to teach about the trials and ordeals of passages in other times and places, which in itself is a comfort, for it signals something basic in the human condition. To come out is to openly challenge sexual chauvinism, homophobia, and bias—refusing to continue the stigma and pollution of the past and opening new support and positive role models where before there were none. Through examples from New Guinea, the Mojave, and the Chicago gay and lesbian group, I examine these ideas in the following pages.

Many cultures around the world celebrate coming of age with a variety of events and rituals that introduce the person to sexual life. Indeed, initiation can be an introduction to sexual development and erotic life (Hart 1963). In Aboriginal Australia and New Guinea wherever the precolonial secret societies of the region flourished, the nature of all sexual interaction was generally withheld from prepubertal boys and girls until initiation. It often began their sense of sexual being, even if they had not achieved sexual puberty, since maturation often occurred late in these societies. Many of the Pacific societies actually disapproved of childhood sexual play, for this was felt to disrupt marriage and social regulation of premarital social relations. The Sambia are no different, having delayed sexual education until the initiation of boys and girls in different secret contexts for each. The stories of Sambia boys are clear in associating the awakening of their sexuality in late childhood with their initiation rites and fellatio debut with adolescent bachelor partners. The definition of social reality was thus opened up to same-gender sexuality.

Sambia Boys' Ritual Initiation

The Sambia are a tribe numbering more than two thousand people in the Eastern Highlands of Papua New Guinea. Most elements of culture and social organization are constructed around the nagging destructive presence of warfare in the area. Descent is patrilineal and residence is patrilocal to maximize the cohesion of the local group as a warriorhood. Hamlets are composed of tiny exogamous patriclans that facilitate marriage within the group and exchange with other hamlets, again based on the local politics of warfare. Traditionally, all marriage was arranged; courtship is unknown, and social relationships between the sexes are not only ritually polarized but also often hostile. Like other Highlands societies of New Guinea, these groups are associated with a men's secret society that ideologically disparages women as dangerous creatures who can pollute men and deplete them of their masculine substance. The means of creating and maintaining the village-based secret society is primarily through the ritual initiation of boys beginning at ages seven through ten and continuing until their arranged and consummated marriages, many years later. The warriorhood is guaranteed by collective ritual initiations connecting neighboring hamlets. Within a hamlet, this warriorhood is locally identified with the men's clubhouse, wherein all initiated bachelors reside. Married men frequent the clubhouse constantly; and on occasion (during fight times, rituals, or their wives' menstrual periods) they sleep there. An account of Sambia culture and society has been published elsewhere and need not be repeated here (Herdt 1981).

Sambia sexual culture, which operates on the basis of a strongly essentializing model of sexual development, also incorporates many ideas of social support and cultural creation of the sexual; these ideas derive from the role of ritual and supporting structures of gendered ontologies throughout the life course of men and women. Sexual development, according to the cultural ideals of the Sambia life plan, is fundamentally distinct for men and women. Biological femaleness is considered "naturally" competent and innately complete; maleness, in contrast, is considered more problematic since males are believed incapable of achieving adult reproductive manliness without ritual treatment. Girls are born with female genitalia, a birth canal, a womb, and, behind that, a functional menstrual-blood organ, or *tingu*. Feminine behaviors such as gardening and mothering are thought to be by-products of women's natural *tingu* functioning. As the *tingu* and womb become engorged with blood, puberty and menarche occur; the menses regularly follow, and they are linked with women's child-bearing capacities. According to the canonical male view, all women then need is a penis (i.e., semen) in facilitating adult procreation by bestowing breast milk (transformed from semen), which prepares a woman for nursing her newborn. According to the women's point of view, however, women are biologically competent and can produce their own breast milk—a point of conflict between the two gendered ontologies. This gives rise to a notion that women have a greater internal resilience and health than males and an almost inexhaustible sexual appetite. By comparison, males are not competent biologically until they achieve manhood, and thus they require constant interventions of ritual to facilitate maturation.

The Sambia believe that boys will not "naturally" achieve adult competence without the interventions of ritual, an idea that may seem strange but is actually common throughout New Guinea, even in societies that do not practice boy-inseminating rites (Herdt 1993). Among the Sambia, the practice of age-structured homoerotic relations is a transition into adulthood. The insemination of boys ideally ends when a man marries and fathers a child. In fact, the vast majority of males—more than 90 percent—terminate their sexual relations with boys at that time. Almost all the men do so because of the taboos and, to a lesser degree, because they have "matured" to a new level of having exclusive sexual access to one or more wives, with genital sexual pleasure being conceived of as a greater privilege.

The sexual culture of the Sambia men instills definite and customary lifeways that involves a formula for the life course. Once initiated (before age ten), the boys undergo ordeals to have their "female" traces (left over from birth and from living with their mothers) removed; these ordeals involve painful rites, such as nose-bleedings, that are intended to promote masculinity and aggression. The boys are then in a ritually "clean" state that enables the treatment of their bodies and minds in new ways. These boys are regarded as "pure" sexual virgins, which is important for their insemination. The men believe that the boys are unspoiled because they have not been exposed to the sexual pollution of women, which the men greatly fear. It is thus through oral intercourse that the men receive a special kind of pleasure, unfettered by pollution, and the boys are thought to acquire semen for growth, becoming strong and fertile. All the younger males are thus inseminated by older bachelors, who were once themselves semen recipients.

The younger initiates are semen recipients until their third-stage "puberty" ceremony, around age fifteen. Afterward, they become semen donors to the younger boys. According to the men's sacred lore and the dogmas of their secret society, the bachelors are "married" to the younger recipient males—as symbolized by secret ritual flutes, made of bamboo and believed to be empowered by female spirits that are said to be hostile to women. During this time, the older adolescents are "bisexuals" who may inseminate their wives orally, in addition to the secret insemination of the boys. Eventually these youths have marriages arranged for them. After they become new fathers, they in turn stop sexual relations with boys. The men's family duties would be compromised by boy relations, the Sambia men say.

The growth of males is believed to be slower and more difficult than that of females. Men say that boys lack an endogenous means for creating manliness. Males do possess a *tingu* (menstrual blood) organ, but it is believed to be "dry" and nonfunctional. They reiterate that a mother's womb, menstrual blood, and vaginal fluids—all containing pollution—impede masculine growth for the boy until he is separated by initiation from mother and the women's world. Males also possess a semen organ (*keriku-keriku*), but unlike the female menstrual blood organ, it is intrinsically small, hard, and empty, containing no semen of its own. Although semen is believed to be the spark of human life and, moreover, the sole precipitant of biological maleness (strong bones and muscles and, later, male secondary-sex traits: a flat abdomen, a hairy body, a mature glans penis), the Sambia hold that the human body cannot naturally produce semen; it must be externally introduced. The purpose of ritual insemination through fellatio is to fill up the *keriku-keriku* (which then stores semen for adult use) and thereby masculinize the boy's body as well as his phallus. Biological maleness is therefore distinct from the mere possession of male genitalia, and only repeated inseminations begun at an early age and regularly continued for years confer the reproductive competence that culminates in sexual development and manliness.

There are four functions of semen exchange: (1) the cultural purpose of "growing" boys through insemination, which is thought to substitute for mother's milk; (2) the "masculinizing" of boys' bodies, again through insemination, but also through ritual ordeals meant to prepare them for warrior life; (3) the provision of "sexual play" or pleasure for the older youths, who have no other sexual outlet prior to marriage; and (4) the transmission of semen and soul substance from one generation of clansmen to the next, which is vital for spiritual and ritual power to achieve its rightful ends (Herdt 1984b). These elements of institutionalized boy-inseminating practices are the object of the most vital and secret ritual teachings in first-stage initiation, which occurs before puberty. The novices are expected to be orally inseminated during the rituals and to continue the practice on a regular basis for years to come. The semen transactions are, however, rigidly structured homoerotically: Novices may act only as fellators in private sexual interactions with older bachelors, who are typically seen as dominant and in control of the same-sex contacts. The adolescent youth is the erotically active party during fellatio, for his erection and ejaculation are necessary for intercourse, and a boy's oral insemination is the socially prescribed outcome of the encounter. Boys must never reverse roles with the older partners or take younger partners before the proper ritual initiations.

The violation of such rules is a moral wrong that is sanctioned by a variety of punishments. Boy-inseminating, then, is a matter of sexual relations between unrelated kin and must be seen in the same light as the semen exchanges of delayed sister exchange marriage: Hamlets of potential enemies exchange women and participate in semen exchange of boys, which is necessary for the production of children and the maturation of new warriors.

Ritual initiation for boys is conducted every three or four years for a whole group of boys as an age-set from neighboring villages. This event lasts several months and consists of many ordeals and transitions, some of them frightening and unpleasant, but overall welcomed as the entry into honorable masculinity and access to social power. It culminates in the boys' entry into the men's clubhouse, which is forbidden to women and children. The boys change their identities and roles and live on their own away from their parents until they are grown up and married. The men's house thus becomes their permanent dormitory and secret place of gender segregation.

Sambia girls do not experience initiation until many years later, when they undergo a formal marriage ceremony. Based on what is known, it seems doubtful that the girls undergo a sexual period of same-gender relations like those of the boys, but I cannot be sure because I was not permitted to enter the menstrual hut, where the initiations of girls were conducted. Males begin their ritual careers and the change in their sexual lives early because the transformation expected of the boys is so great. Girls live on with their parents until they are married and achieve their first menstruation, which occurs very late, age nineteen on average for the Sambia and their neighbors. A secret initiation is performed for the girls in the menstrual hut. Only then can they begin to have sexual relations with their husbands and live with them in a new house built by husband and wife.

The first-stage initiation ceremonies begin the events of life crisis and change in identities for the boys. They are young. After a period of time they are removed to the forest, where the most critical rituals begin to introduce them to the secrets of the men's house and the secret society of the men's warriorhood. The key events involve blood-letting rituals and penis-and-flute rites, which we study here from observations of the initiation conducted in 1975 (Herdt 1982). Here the boys experience the revelation of sexuality and the basic elements of their transition into age-structured homoerotic relations.

On the first morning of the secret rituals in the forest, the boys have fierce and painful nosebleeding rituals performed on them. This is believed to remove the pollution of their mothers and the women's world that is identified with the boys' bodies. But it is also a testing ground to see how brave they are and the degree to which their fathers, older brothers, and the war leaders of the village can rely on the boys not to run and hide in times of war. Afterward, the boys are prepared by their ritual guardian, who is referred to as their "mother's brother," a kind of "male mother," for the main secret teaching that is to follow. They are dressed in the finest warrior decorations, which they have earned the right to wear through the initiation ordeals. And this begins their preparation for the rites of insemination that will follow. Now that their insides have been "cleansed" to receive the magical gift of manhood—semen—they are taken into the sacred chamber of a forest setting, and there they see for the first time the magical flutes, believed to be animated by the female spirit of the flute, which protects the men and the secrecy of the clubhouse and is thought to be hostile to women.

The key ceremony here is the penis-and-flutes ritual. It focuses on a secret teaching about boy insemination and is regarded by the men and boys alike as the most dramatic and awesome of all Sambia rituals. It begins with the older bachelors, the youths with whom the boys will engage in sexual relations later, who enter the chamber dressed up as the "female spirits of the flutes." The flute players appear, and in their presence, to the accompaniment of the wailing flutes, some powerful secrets of the men's cult are revealed. The setting is awesome: a great crowd waiting in silence as the mysterious sounds are first revealed; boys obediently lining up for threatening review

by elders; and boys being told that secret fellatio exists and being taught how to engage in it. Throughout the ritual boys hear at close range the flute sounds associated since childhood with collective masculine power and mystery and pride. The flutes are unequivocally treated as phallic—as symbols of the penis and the power of men to openly flaunt their sexuality. The intent of the flutes' revelation is threatening to the boys as they begin to guess its meaning.

I have observed this flute ceremony during two different initiations, and although my western experience differs greatly from that of Sambia, one thing was intuitively striking to me: The men were revealing the *homoerotic meanings* of the sexual culture. This includes a great preoccupation with the penis and with semen but also with the mouth of the boy and penile erection, sexual impulses, homoerotic activities in particular, and the commencement of sexuality in its broadest sense for the boys. If there is a homoerotic core to the secret society of the Sambia, then this is surely where it begins. These revelations come as boys are enjoined to become fellators, made the sharers of ritual secrets, and threatened with death if they tell women or children what they have learned. They have to keep the secret forever.

Over the course of many years I collected the stories of the boys' experiences as they went through these rituals. The boys' comments indicated that they perceived several different social values bound up with the expression of homoerotic instruction in the flute ceremony. A good place to begin is with childhood training regarding shame about one's genitals. Here is Kambo, a boy who was initiated, talking about his own experience: "I thought—not good that they [elders] are lying or just playing a trick. That's [the penis] not for eating. . . . When I was a child our fathers said, 'This [penis] is not for handling; if you hold it you'll become lazy.' And because of that [at first in the cult house] I felt—it's not for sucking." Childhood experience is a contributing source of shame about fellatio: Children are taught to avoid handling their own genitals. In a wider sense Kambo's remark pertains to the taboo on masturbation, the sexual naïveté of children, and the boys' prior lack of knowledge about their fathers' homosexual activities.

Another key ritual story concerns the nutritive and "growth" values of semen. A primary source of this idea is men's ritual equation of semen with mother's breast milk, as noted before. The initiates take up this idea quickly in their own subjective orientations toward fellatio. (Pandanus nuts, like coconut, are regarded as another equivalent of semen.) The following remark by Moondi is a typical example of such semen identifications in the teachings of the flute ceremony: "The 'juice' of the pandanus nuts, . . . it's the same as the 'water' of a man, the same as a man's 'juice' [semen]. And I like to eat a lot of it [because it can give me more water], . . . for the milk of women is also the same as the milk of men. Milk [breast milk] is for when she carries a child—it belongs to the infant who drinks it." The association between semen and the infant's breast food is also explicit in this observation by Gaimbako, a second-stage initiate: "Semen is the same kind as that [breast milk] of women. . . . It's the very same kind as theirs, . . . the same as pandanus nuts too. . . . But when milk [semen] falls into my mouth [during fellatio], I think it's the milk of women." So the boys are taught beliefs that are highly motivating in support of same-gender sexual relations.

But the ritual also creates in boys a new awareness about their subordination to the older men. Kambo related this thought as his immediate response to the penis teaching of the flute ceremony: "I was afraid of penis. It's the same as mine—why should I eat it? It's the same kind; [our penises are] only one kind. We're men, not *different* kinds." This supposition is fundamental and implied in many boys' understandings. Kambo felt that males are of one kind, that is, "one sex," as distinct from females. This implies tacit recognition of the sameness of men, which ironically suggests that they should be not sexually involved but in competition for the other gender. Remember, too, the coercive character of the setting: The men's attempt to have boys suck the flutes is laden with overt hostility, much stronger than the latent hostility expressed in lewd homosexual jokes made during the preceding body decoration. The boys are placed in a sexually subordinate position, a fact that is symbolically communicated in the idiom that the novices are "married" to the flutes. (Novices suck the small flute, which resembles the mature glans penis, the men say.) The men thus place the boys in an invidious state of subordination during which the boys may sense that they are being treated too much like women. Sometimes this makes them panic and creates fear and shame. In time, however, a different feeling about the practice sets in.

Nearly all the novices perform their first act of fellatio during the days of initiation, and their story helps us to understand what happens later in their masculine development. Let me cite several responses of Moondi to this highly emotional act:

I was wondering what they [elders] were going to do to us. And . . . I felt afraid. What will they do to us next? But they put the bamboo in and out of the mouth; and I wondered, what are they doing? Then, when they tried out our mouths, I began to understand . . . that they were talking about the penis. Oh, that little bamboo is the penis of the men. . . . My whole body was afraid, completely afraid, . . . and I was heavy, I wanted to cry.

At that point my thoughts went back to how I used to think it was the *aatmwogwambu* [flute spirit], but then I knew that the men did it [made the sounds]. And . . . I felt a little better, for before [I thought that] the aatmwogwambu would get me. But now I saw that they [the men] did it.

They told us the penis story. . . . Then I thought a lot, as my thoughts raced quickly. I was afraid—not good that the men "shoot" me [penetrate my mouth] and break my neck. Aye! Why should they put that [penis] inside our mouths! It's not a good thing. They all hide it [the penis] inside their grass skirts, and it's got lots of hair too!

"You must listen well," the elders said. "You all won't grow by yourselves; if you sleep with the men you'll become a *strong* man." They said that; I was afraid. . . . And then they told us clearly: semen is inside—and when you hold a man's penis, you must put it inside your mouth—he can give you semen. . . . It's the same as your mother's breast milk.

"This is no lie!" the men said. "You can't go tell the children, your sisters." . . . And then later I tried it [fellatio], and I thought: Oh, they told us about *aamoonaalyi* [breast milk; Moondi means semen]—it [semen] is in there.

Despite great social pressures, some boys evince a low interest in the practice from the start, and they seldom participate in fellatio. Some novices feverishly join in. Those are the extremes. The great majority of Sambia boys regularly engage in fellatio for years as constrained by taboo. Homoerotic activities are a touchy subject among males for many reasons. These activities begin with ceremony, it is true, but their occurrence and meaning fan out to embrace a whole secret way of life. What matters is that the boys become sharers of this hidden tradition; and we should expect them to acquire powerful feelings about bachelors, fellatio, semen, and the whole male sexual culture.

One story must stand for many in the way that the Sambia boys grow into this sexual lifeway. One day, while I was talking idly with Kambo, he mentioned singing to himself as he walked in the forest. I asked him what he sang about; and from this innocuous departure point, he said this: "When I think of men's name songs then I sing them: that of a bachelor who is sweet on me; a man of another line or my own line. When I sing the song of a creek in the forest I am happy about that place. . . . Or some man who sleeps with me—when he goes elsewhere, I sing his song. I think of that man who gave me a lot of semen; later, I must sleep with him. I feel like this: he gave me a lot of water [semen]. . . . Later, I will have a lot of water like him."

Here we see established in Kambo's thought the male emphasis on "accumulating semen" and the powerful homoerotic relationships that accompany it. Even a simple activity like singing can create a mood of subjective association with past fellatio and same-gender relationships with the older males. Kambo's last sentence contains a wish: that he will acquire abundant manliness, like that of the friend of whom he sings.

No issue in recent reviews has inspired more debate than the basic question of whether—or to what extent—sexual feelings and erotic desires are motives or consequences of these cultural practices. Does the Sambia boy desire sexual intercourse with the older male? Is the older male sexually attracted to the boy? Indeed, what does "erotic" or "sexual" mean in this context, and is "desire" the proper concept with which to gauge the ontology? Or do other factors, such as power or kinship, produce the sexual attraction and excitement (conscious or unconscious) necessary to produce arousal and uphold the tradition (Herdt 1991)?

Although Sambia culture requires that men eventually change their focus to marriage and give up boy-inseminating, some of the men continue to practice age-structured relations because they find them so pleasurable. A small number of individual men enjoy inseminating boys too much to give up the practice. They develop favorites among the boys and even resort to payment of meat when they find it difficult to obtain a boy who will service them. In our culture these men would probably be called homosexuals because of their preference for the boys, their desires, and their need to mask their activities within the secret domain of ritual. But such an identity of homosexual or gay does not exist for the Sambia, and we must be careful not to project these meanings onto them, for that would be ethnocentric. We can, however, see how they live and what it means to have such an experience—in the absence of the sexual identity system of western culture.

One of these men, Kalutwo, has been interviewed by me over a long period of time, and his sexual and social history reveals a pattern of broken, childless marriages and an exclusive attraction to boys. As he got older, he would have to "pay" the boys with gifts to engage in sex, but when he was younger, some of the boys were known to be fond of him as well (Herdt and Stoller 1990). Several other males are different from Kalutwo in liking boys but also liking women and being successfully married with children. They would be called bisexual in our society. They seem to enjoy sexual pleasure with women and take pride in making babies through their wives, yet they continue illicitly to enjoy oral sex with boys. But Kalutwo disliked women sexually and generally preferred the closeness, sexual intimacy, and emotional security of young men and boys. As he got older, it was increasingly difficult for him to obtain boys as sexual partners, and this seemed to make him feel depressed. Moreover, as he got older, he was increasingly at odds with his male peers socially and stood out from the crowd, having no wife or children, as expected of customary adult manhood. Some people made fun of him behind his back; so did some of the boys. In a society that had a homosexual role, Kalutwo might have found more social support or comfort and perhaps might have been able to make a different transition into middle age. But his village still accepts him, and he has not been turned away or destroyed—as might have occurred in another time had he lived in a western country.

Perhaps in these cases we begin to understand the culture of male camaraderie and emotional intimacy that created such deeply felt desire for same-gender relations in ancient Greece and Japan, in which sexual pleasures and social intimacies with the same gender were as prized as those of intercourse and family life with women. No difficulty was posed to society or to self-esteem so long as these men met their social and sexual obligations and were honorable in their relations with younger males. We know from the anthropological reports from New Guinea that such individuals existed elsewhere as well, and among the Malekula and Marind-anim tribes, for example, adult married men would continue such relations with boys even after reaching the age of being grandfathers in the group, for this was expected.

Mojave Two-Spirit Initiation

My reading of the gender-transformed role among American Indians has shown the importance of two spirits in Native American society for the broader understanding of alternative sexualities. What I have not established thus far is the development of the role in the life of the individual. Among the Mojave Indians, a special ceremony in late childhood marked a transition into the third-gender role that allowed for homoerotic relations so long as they were between people in different gender roles. The two spirit was the product of a

long cultural history that involved myth and ceremonial initiation. The ceremonies were sacred and of such importance that their official charter was established in the origin myths of the tribe, known from time immemorial. The meanings of this transition deserve to be highlighted as another variation on coming of age ceremonies in nonwestern cultures.

The Mojave child was only about ten years old when he participated in the ceremony for determining whether a change to two spirit would occur. Perhaps this seems young for a coming of age ceremony; but it might be that the very degree of change and the special nature of the desires to become a man-woman required a childhood transition. In the Mojave case, it was said that a Mojave boy could act "strangely" at the time, turning away from male tasks and refusing the toys of his own sex. The parents would view this as a sign of personal and gender change. Recall that mothers had dreams that their sons would grow up to become two spirits. No doubt this spiritual sign helped to lend religious support for the ceremony. At any rate these signs of gender change were said by the Mojave to express the "true" intentions of the child to change into a man-woman. Nahwera, a Mojave elder, stated: "When there is a desire in a child's heart to become a transvestite that child will act different. It will let people become aware of that desire" (Devereux 1937, 503). Clearly, the child was beginning to act on desires that transgressed his role and required an adjustment, through ritual, to a new kind of being and social status in the culture.

Arrangements for the ceremony were made by the parents. The boy was reported to have been "surprised" by being offered "female apparel," whereon the relatives waited nervously to see his response. Devereux reported that this was considered both an initiation and an ultimate test of the child's true desires. "If he submitted to it, he was considered a genuine homosexual. . . . If the boy acted in the expected fashion during the ceremony he was considered an initiated homosexual, if not, the gathering scattered, much to the relief of the boy's family" (Devereux 1937, 508). The story suggests that the parents in general may have been ambivalent about this change and may not have wanted it. Nevertheless, true to Mojave culture, they accepted the actions of the boy and supported his decision to become a two-spirit person. The Mojave thus allowed a special combination of a child's ontological being and the support of the family to find its symbolic expression in a ready-made institutionalized cultural practice. It only awaited the right individual and circumstances for the two-spirit person to emerge in each community in each generation.

Both the Sambia example of age-structured relations and the Mojave illustration of gender-transformed homosexuality reveal transitions in late childhood up to age ten. What is magical about age ten? It may be that certain critical developmental changes begin to occur around this time—desires and attractions that indicate the first real sexuality and growing sense of becoming a sexual person. In fact, our study in Chicago revealed that nine and one-half years for boys and ten years for girls were the average age when they were first attracted to the same gender (Herdt and Boxer 1996).

Coming Out—Gay and Lesbian Teens in America

Ours is a culture that defines male and female as absolutely different and then goes to great lengths to deny having done so; American culture reckons "heterosexual" and "homosexual" as fundamentally distinctive kinds of "human nature" but then struggles to find a place for both. Although such gender dimorphism is common in the thinking of nonwestern peoples, the latter idea is rare in, even absent from, many cultures—including our own cultural ancestors, the ancient Greeks. The Greeks described people's sexual behaviors but not their being as homosexual or heterosexual. As we have seen, the Greeks did not place people in categories of sexuality or create sexual classifications that erased all other cultural and personality traits. In our society today this kind of thinking is common and permeates the great symbolic types that define personal being and social action in most spheres of our lives. For many heterosexuals, their worldview and life course goals remain focused on the greatest ritual of reproduction: the church-ordained marriage. And this leads to parenting and family formation. Many think of this ritual process as "good" in all of its aspects. Others see same-gender desire as an attack on that reproductive and moral order, a kind of crisis of gender and sexuality that requires the assertion of a mythical "family values," descended from nineteenth-century ideals, that are seldom relevant to heterosexuals today, let alone to gays and lesbians.

Coming out is another form of ritual that intensifies change in a young person's sexual identity development and social being. It gives public expression to desires long felt to be basic to the person's sexual nature but formerly hidden because of social taboos and homophobia. The process leads to many events that reach a peak in the person's young adult years, especially in the development of gay or lesbian selves, roles, and social relations. Coming out continues to unfold across the entire course of life: There is never really an end to the process for the simple reason that as gay or lesbian people age and their social situations change, they continue to express in new, relevant ways what it means to be gay or lesbian. Such a social and existential crisis of identity—acted out on the stage of the lesbian and gay community—links the social drama of American youths' experiences with those of tribal initiations, such as those of the Sambia and Mojave, played out in the traditional communities. Of course, these two kinds of drama are different and should not be confused, but they share the issues of handling same-gender desires in cultural context.

Two different processes are involved. First is the secretive act of "passing" as heterosexual, involving the lone individual in largely hidden social networks and secret social spaces. . . . In many towns and cities, especially unsophisticated and traditionally conservative areas of the country, the possibilities are only now emerging for gay/lesbian identification and social action. Second is the coming out in adolescence or young adulthood.

Initially the gay or lesbian grows up with the assumption of being heterosexual. As an awareness of same-gender desires emerges, a feeling of having to hide these desires and pretend otherwise, of acting straight, leads to many moments of secrecy. Later, however, sexual and social experiences may yield a divergent awareness and a desire to be open. What follows is a process of coming out—typically begun in urban centers, sometimes in high school, sometimes later, after the young person has left home for college, work, or the service—that leads to self-identification as gay or lesbian. Through these ritual steps of disclosure all kinds of new socialization and opportunities emerge, including entrance into the gay and lesbian community.

Being and doing gay life are provisioned by the rituals of coming out, and they open significant questions for thinking about youths in search of positive same-gender roles. American teenagers may seem less exotic to the gay or lesbian reader; but they are more of an oddity to the heterosexual adult community as they come out. To many in our own society, these youths look "queer" and "strange" and "diseased," attitudes that reflect historical stereotypes and cultural homophobia.

The growing visibility of the lesbian and gay movement in the United States has made it increasingly possible for people to disclose their desires and "come out" at younger ages. Over the past quarter century, the evidence suggests that the average age of the declaration of same-gender desires has gotten earlier—a lot earlier, as much as ten years earlier than it was in the 1970s—and is for the first time in history a matter of adolescent development. It is not a matter for everyone, of course, but increasingly for those who become aware and are lucky to have the opportunities to begin a new life. In our study of gay and lesbian self-identified youths in Chicago, we found that the average age for boys and girls' "coming out" was sixteen. But we also found that the earliest awareness of same-gender attraction begins at about age ten, which suggests that the desires are a part of the deeper being of the gay or lesbian person.

Gay and lesbian teenagers are growing up with all of the usual problems of our society, including the political, economic, and social troubles of our country, as well as the sexual and social awakening that typifies the adolescent experience. I have already noted how American society and western cultures in general have changed in the direction of more positive regard for gays. This does not mean, however, that the hatred and homophobia of the past are gone or that the secrecy and fear of passing have faded away. People still fear, and rightly so, the effects of coming out on their lives and safety, their well-being and jobs, their social standing and community prestige. These youths are opting to come out as openly lesbian or gay earlier in the life course than ever before in our society. Yet they experience the troubles of feeling themselves attracted to the same gender, with its taboos and sorrows of stigma and shame, not knowing what to do about it. Fortunately, the gay and lesbian culture provides new contexts of support; these youths have institutions and media that talk about it; they learn from adult role models that they can live relatively happy and rewarding lives with their desires.

We can study how one group of adolescents in Chicago has struggled with these issues while preparing for socialization and coming out in the context of the lesbian and gay community. The study of gay, lesbian, and bisexual youths in Chicago was located in the largest gay social services agency of the city, Horizons Community Services. Horizons was created in the early 1970s out of the gay liberation movement, and by 1979 it had founded a gay and lesbian youth group, one of the first in the United States. The agency is based in the gay neighborhood of the city, and it depends on volunteers and the goodwill and interest of friends of the agency. In recent years the youths have led the Gay and Lesbian Pride Day Parade in Chicago and have become a symbol of social and political progress in gay culture in the city.

The Horizons study was organized around the youth group, for ages thirteen to twenty, but the average age of the youths interviewed in depth was about eighteen. We interviewed a total of 202 male and female youths of all backgrounds from the suburbs and inner city, white and black and brown. Many people of color and of diverse ethnic subcultures in Chicago have experienced racism and many forms of homophobia, and these have effectively barred their coming out. The group tries to find a place for all of these diverse adolescents; no one is turned away. Group meetings are coordinated by lesbian and gay adults, esteemed role models of the teens. They facilitate a discussion of a variety of topics, particularly in matters of the coming out process, such as fears and homophobic problems at school or home, and issues of special interest to the teens. The youth group has an active social life as well, hosting parties and organizing social events, such as the annual alternative gay and lesbian prom, held on the weekend of high school proms in Chicago, for the youth members.

Protecting teens from the risk of infection from AIDS is another key goal of Horizons' sponsorship of the youth group. AIDS has become an increasingly important element of the youth group discussions. "Safe sex" is promoted through educational material and special public speakers. In general, the socialization rituals of the group prepare the youths for their new status in the gay and lesbian community, and the rituals culminate in marching in the Gay and Lesbian Pride Day Parade every June.

The lesbian or gay youth is in the throes of moving through the symbolic "death" of the heterosexual identity and role and into the "rebirth" of their social being as gay. As a life crisis and a passage between the past and future, the person is betwixt and between normal social states, that is, between the heterosexual worlds of parents and the cultural system of gay and lesbian adults. To the anthropologist, the youths are symbolically exiting what was once called "homosexuality" and entering what is now called "gay and lesbian." To the psychologist, their transition is from dependence and internalized homophobia to a more open and mature competence and pride in the sexual/gender domains of their lives. The transformative power contained in the rituals of coming out as facilitated by Horizons helps in the newfound development of the person. But it also helps in the lives of everyone touched by a youth who is coming out. As long as this process is blocked or resisted, the pull back into passing as heterosexual is very tempting.

Back in the 1960s, . . . coming out was a secret incorporation into the closet "homosexual" community. Studies at the time showed that the more visible contexts of engaging in same-sex contacts might lead to de facto coming out, but these were generally marginal and dangerous places, such as public toilets, where victimization and violence could occur. To come out in secret bars, the military, toilets, or bus depots did not create a positive identification with the category of gay/lesbian. There was generally no identity that positively accorded with gay or lesbian self-esteem as we think of it today. Thus, we can understand how many people found it revolutionary to fight back against homophobia and begin to march openly in parades in the 1970s. Nevertheless, the change was uneven and difficult.

People who continue to pass as straight when they desire people of the same gender and may in fact have sexual relations with them present a perplexing issue—not only for lesbians and gay men but also for society as a whole. This kind of person, through secrecy and passing, serves as a negative role model of what not to be. Alas, there are many movie stars, celebrities, and sports heroes who live closeted lives of this kind—until they are discovered or "outed" by someone. Many youths are frightened or intimidated when they discover adults they know and love, such as teachers, uncles, family friends, or pastors, who pass as heterosexual but have been discovered to desire the same gender. Adolescents can be angered to discover that a media person they admire has two lives, one publicly heterosexual and one privately homosexual. This is a cultural survival of the nineteenth-century system of closet homosexuality, with its hide-and-seek games to escape the very real dangers of homophobia. In contrast, positive role models provided by the largely white middle-class adult advisers at Horizons are the crucial source for learning how to enter the gay and lesbian community.

Cultural homophobia in high school is a powerful force against coming out. Learning to hide one's desires is crucial for the survival of some youths, especially at home and at school, the two greatest institutions that perpetuate homophobia in the United States. Our informants tell us that standard slurs to put people down in the schools remain intact. To be slurred as a "dyke" or a "faggot" is a real blow to social esteem. But "queer" is the most troubling epithet of all. To be targeted as a "queer" in high school is enormously troubling for the youths, somehow more alienating and isolating, an accusation not just of doing something "different" but of being something "unnatural." One seventeen-year-old eleventh grade boy remarked to us that he was secretive at school. "I'm hidden mostly—cause of the ways they'll treat you. Okay, there are lots of gangs. . . . They find out you're [what they call] a faggot and they beat on you and stuff. If they ask me I say it's none of their business." The role of secrecy, passing, and hiding continues the homophobia. Ironically, as Michelle Fine (1988, 36) notes in her study of black adolescent girls in New York City high schools, it was the gay and lesbian organization in the school that was the most open and safe environment in which young African-American girls could access their own feelings. They could, with the support of the lesbian and gay teenage group, start to become the agents of their *own* desires. Our study has shown that in Chicago most lesbian or gay youths have experienced harassment in school; and when this is combined with harassment and problems at home, it signals a serious mental health risk, especially for suicide. And the risk of suicide before lesbian or gay youths come to find the support of the Horizons group is very great.

The ritual of coming out means giving up the secrecy of the closet. This is a positive step toward mental health, for life in the closet involves not only a lot of hiding but also a good deal of magical thinking, which may be detrimental to the person's well-being. By magical thinking, I mean mainly contagious beliefs about homosexuality such as the common folk ideas of our culture that stereotype homosexuality as a disease that spreads, as well as the historical images of homosexuality as a mental illness or a crime against nature. These magical beliefs support homophobia and warn about the dangers of going to a gay community organization, whispering how the adolescent might turn into a monster or sex fiend or be raped or murdered or sold into slavery.

Another common contagious fear is the belief that by merely contacting other gays, the adolescent's "sin or disease" will spread to the self and will then unwittingly spread to others, such as friends and siblings. One of the common magical beliefs of many adults and parents is that the youth has merely to avoid other gays and lesbians in order to "go straight." This is surely another cultural "leftover" from the dark myth of homosexuality as evil. . . . If the adolescent will only associate with straights, the parent feels, this strange period of "confusion" will pass, and he or she will become heterosexual like everyone else. Such silly stereotypes are strongly associated with the false notion that all gay or lesbian teens are simply "confused," which was promoted by psychologists in the prior generation. This belief is based on the cultural myth that same-sex desires are "adolescent" desires of a transient nature that may be acquired or learned but can go away; and if the self ignores them, the desire for the opposite sex will grow in their place. Magical fears of contracting AIDS is a new and most powerful deterrent to coming out among some youths. Many youths fear their initial social contact with anyone gay because they think they might contagiously contract AIDS by being gay or lesbian or by interacting socially with gays.

The gender difference in the experience of coming out as a male or a female highlights the cultural pressures that are still exerted on teens to conform to the norm of heterosexuality in our society. Girls typically have more heterosexual experience in their histories, with two-thirds of the girls having had significant heterosexual contact before they came to Horizons. Since the age of our sample was about eighteen, it is easy to see that relatively early on, between the ages of thirteen and seventeen, girls were being inducted into sexual relations with boys. We face here the problem of what is socially necessary and what is preferred. Only one-third of the boys had had heterosexual experience, and fully two-fifths of them had had no sexual experience with girls. Note also that for many of the boys, their sexual contacts with girls were their lesbian-identified friends at the Horizons youth group. The boys tended to achieve sexual experiences earlier than the girls, by age sixteen, at which point the differences in development had evened out. Both genders were beginning to live openly lesbian or gay lives.

Clearly, powerful gender role pressures are exerted on girls to conform to the wishes of parents, siblings, peers, and boyfriends. Some of this, to use a phrase by Nancy Chodorow (1992) about heterosexuality as a compromise formation, results in a compromise of their desires, even of their personal integrity, in the development of their sexual and self-concept. But as we know from the work of Michele Fine (1988), who studied adolescent sexuality among African-American girls in the New York City schools, females were not able to explore and express their desires until they located a safe space that enabled them to think out loud. In fact, they could not become the agents of their own desires until they had located the gay and lesbian youth group in the high school! There, some of them had to admit, contrary to their stereotypes, they found the gay youths more accepting and open of variations than any of their peers or the adults. The lesson here is that when a cultural space is created, people can explore their own desires and better achieve their own identities and sociosexual goals in life.

We have found that four powerful magical beliefs exist in the implicit learning of homophobia and self-hatred among gay and lesbian youths. First is the idea that homosexuals are crazy and heterosexuals are sane. Unlearning this idea involves giving up the assumption of heterosexual normalcy in favor of positive attitudes and role models. Second is the idea that the problem with same-gender desires is in the self, not in society. Unlearning this belief means recognizing cultural homophobia and discovering that the problem with hatred lies not in the self but in society. Third is the magical belief that to have same-gender desires means giving up gendered roles as they were previously known and acting as a gender-transformed person, a boy acting or dressing as a girl, a girl living as a boy, or either living as an androgyne. There is nothing wrong with these transformations. What we have seen in the cross-cultural study, however, is that there are a variety of ways to organize same-gender desires. The old ways of gender inversion from the nineteenth century are only one of these. Unlearning gender reversal means accepting one's own gendered desires and enactments of roles, whatever these are, rather than living up to social standards—either in the gay or straight community.

Fourth is the belief that if one is going to be gay, there are necessary goals, rules, roles, and political and social beliefs that must be performed or expressed. This idea goes against the grain of American expressive individualism, in which we feel that each one of us is unique and entitled to "know thyself" as the means of social fulfillment. The key is that there is not one perfect way to be gay; there are many divergent ways. Nor is there any single event, or magic pill, that will enable the process of coming out. It is a lifelong process, as long as it takes to live and find a fulfilling social and spiritual lifeway in our culture.

Lesbian and gay youths have shown that coming out is a powerful means of confronting the unjust, false, wrongful social faces and values of prejudice in our culture. Before being out, youths are asking, "What can we be?" or "How can we fit into this society?" Emerging from the secrecy, these youths are making new claims on society to live up to its own standards of justice. The rituals of coming out are a way of unlearning and creating new learning about living with same-gender desires and creating a positive set of relationships around them. Surely the lesson of the gay movement is that hiding desires and passing as something other than what one is are no less injurious to the normal heart and the healthy mind of gay youths than was, say, passing as a Christian if one was a Jew in Nazi Germany or passing as white in the old South or in South Africa under apartheid.

Lesbian and gay youths are challenging society in ways that are no less revolutionary than discriminations based on skin color, gender, or religion. A new of kind of social and political activism has arisen; it goes beyond AIDS/HIV, but builds on the grief and anger that the entire generation feels about the impact of the pandemic on gay and lesbian culture. Some call this new generation queer. But others prefer lesbian or gay or bisexual or transgendered. Perhaps the word is less important than the commitment to building a rich and meaningful social world in which all people, including lesbians and gays, have a place to live and plan for the future.

We have seen in this chapter how a new generation of lesbian- and gay-identified youths has utilized transition rituals to find a place in the gay and lesbian community. It was the activism and social progress of the lesbian and gay culture that made this huge transformation possible. The emergence of a community enabled the support of youth groups and other institutions for the creation of a new positive role model and self-concept. Youths are beginning to take up new status rights and duties, having a new set of cultural ideas to create the moral voice of being gay, bisexual, lesbian, or queer. The rituals, such as the annual Gay and Lesbian Pride Day Parade, make these newly created traditions a lived reality; they codify and socialize gay and lesbian ideals, knowledge, and social roles, bonding past and future in a timeless present that will enable these youths to find a place in a better society.

References

Benedict, Ruth. 1938. "Continuities and discontinuities in cultural conditioning." *Psychiatry* 1:161–167.

Chodorow, Nancy J. 1992. "Heterosexuality as a Compromise Formation: Reflections on the Psychoanalytic Theory of Sexual Development." *Psychoanalysis and Contemporary Thought* 15:267–304.

Devereux, George. 1937. "Institutionalized Homosexuality Among the Mohave Indians." *Human Biology* 9:498–527.

Fine, Michelle. 1988. "Sexuality, Schooling, and Adolescent Females: The Missing Discourse of Desire." *Harvard Education Review* 58:29–53.

Hart, C. W. M. 1963. "Contrasts Between Prepubertal and Postpubertal Education." In *Education and Culture,* ed. G. Spindler, pp. 400–425. New York: Holt, Rinehart and Winston.

Herdt, Gilbert. 1981. *Guardians of the Flutes: Idioms of Masculinity.* New York: McGraw-Hill.

———. 1982. "Fetish and Fantasy in Sambia Initiation." In *Rituals of Manhood,* ed. G. Herdt., pp. 44–98. Berkeley and Los Angeles: University of California Press.

———. 1984b. "Semen Transactions in Sambia Culture." In *Ritualized Homosexuality in Melanesia,* ed. G. Herdt, pp. 167–210. Berkeley and Los Angeles: University of California Press.

———. 1991. "Representations of Homosexuality in Traditional Societies: An Essay on Cultural Ontology and Historical Comparison, Part II." *Journal of the History of Sexuality* 2:603–632.

———. 1993. "Introduction." In *Ritualized Homosexuality in Melanesia,* ed. G. Herdt, pp. vii–xliv. Berkeley and Los Angeles: University of California Press.

———, and Andrew Boxer. 1996. *Children of Horizons: How Gay and Lesbian Youth Are Forging a New Way Out of the Closet.* Boston: Beacon Press.

———, and Robert J. Stoller. 1990. *Intimate Communications: Erotics and the Study of Culture.* New York: Columbia University Press.

Is Female Genital Mutilation an Islamic Problem?

THOMAS VON DER OSTEN-SACKEN AND THOMAS UWER

Among social activists and feminists, combating female genital mutilation (FGM) is an important policy goal. Sometimes called female circumcision or female genital cutting, FGM is the cutting of the clitoris of girls in order to curb their sexual desire and preserve their sexual honor before marriage. The practice, prevalent in some majority Muslim countries, has a tremendous cost: many girls bleed to death or die of infection. Most are traumatized. Those who survive can suffer adverse health effects during marriage and pregnancy. New information from Iraqi Kurdistan raises the possibility that the problem is more prevalent in the Middle East than previously believed and that FGM is far more tied to religion than many Western academics and activists admit.

Many Muslims and academics in the West take pains to insist that the practice is not rooted in religion[1] but rather in culture. "When one considers that the practice does not prevail and is much condemned in countries like Saudi Arabia, the center of the Islamic world, it becomes clear that the notion that it is an Islamic practice is a false one," Haseena Lockhat, a child clinical psychologist at North Warwickshire Primary Care Trust, wrote.[2] True, FGM occurs in non-Muslim societies in Africa. And in Arab states such as Egypt, where perhaps 97 percent of girls suffer genital mutilation,[3] both Christian Copts and Muslims are complicit.

But at the village level, those who commit the practice believe it to be religiously mandated. Religion is not only theology but also practice.

And the practice is widespread throughout the Middle East. Many diplomats, international organization workers, and Arabists argue that the problem is localized to North Africa or sub-Saharan Africa,[4] but they are wrong. The problem is pervasive throughout the Levant, the Fertile Crescent, and the Arabian Peninsula, and among many immigrants to the West from these countries. Silence on the issue is less reflective of the absence of the problem than insufficient freedom for feminists and independent civil society to raise the issue.

Detecting Female Genital Mutilation

It is perhaps understandable that many diplomats and academics do not recognize the scope of the problem. Should someone wish to understand the sexual habits of Westerners, he would not face a difficult task. He could survey personal advertisements, watch talk shows, and read magazine articles explaining the best ways to enhance sexual experience, not to mention numerous scientific publications on sex and gender relations. Public knowledge of trivial and even painful matters is incumbent in Western culture. The multitude of sexual habits and gender relations represents a vital element of life in the West, much the same as the economy, politics, sports, and culture.

If, however, someone wants to study sexual relations and habits in Middle Eastern societies, it would be difficult to find comparable traces in public. Almost everything connected with sexuality and personal relations is hidden in a private

Thomas von der Osten-Sacken and Thomas Uwer, "Is Female Genital Mutilation an Islamic Problem?" *Middle East Quarterly*, Winter 2007, pp. 29–36. Reprinted by permission of *Middle East Quarterly*.

sphere. Advisory books and research on sexual habits are almost nonexistent beyond comprehensive rules and prohibitions outlined by Islamic law or, in Shi'ite societies, beyond the questions and responses submitted to senior ayatollahs. Sex education is not taught at the university, let alone in any high school. Psychology remains a shadow discipline, almost absent in the eastern Middle East and only slightly more present in North Africa where more than a century of French rule offered more opportunity for it to take root. The Library of the British Psychoanalytical Society, for example, holds only one journal on psychotherapy or psychoanalysis in Arabic. Arab psychoanalyst Jihad Mazarweh gave an interview in the German weekly *Die Zeit* in which he said, "For most people, speaking about sexuality, as it happens in psychoanalysis, is almost unthinkable."[5] It would be a mistake to interpret lack of public discussion of many sexual issues in the Middle East as indicative of a lack of problems. Rather, the silence only reflects the strength of taboo.

Female genital mutilation has been a top priority for United Nations agencies and nongovernmental organizations (NGOs) for almost three decades. As early as 1952, the U.N. Commission on Human Rights adopted a resolution condemning the practice.[6] International momentum against the practice built when, in 1958, the Economic and Social Council invited the World Health Organization to study the persistence of customs subjecting girls to ritual operations.[7] They repeated their call three years later.[8] The 1979 Convention on the Elimination of All Forms of Discrimination against Women denounced the practice,[9] and the 1989 Convention on the Rights of the Child identified female genital mutilation as a harmful traditional practice.[10] According to the Demographic and Health Surveys Program, a project funded by the United States Agency for International Development to assist in undertaking medical and reproductive health surveys, FGM affects 130 million women in twenty-eight African countries.[11] Rather than diminishing as countries modernize, FGM is expanding.[12]

Anthropologists and activists identify three main types of FGM. Pharaonic circumcision refers to the removal of the entire clitoris; the labia minora and medial part of the labia majora are cut with both sides of the organ stitched together to leave only a small opening. Clitorectomy requires the removal of the entire clitoris along with part of the labia minora. Sunna circumcision, the most common form in the Islamic world, requires removal of the prepuce of the clitoris.

Genital Mutilation: An African Phenomenon?

Many experts hold that FGM is an African practice. Nearly half of the FGM cases represented in official statistics occur in Egypt and Ethiopia; Sudan also records high prevalence of the practice.[13] True, Egypt is part of the African continent but, from a cultural, historical, and political perspective, Egypt has closer ties to the Arab Middle East than to sub-Saharan Africa. Egypt was a founding member of the Arab League, and Egyptian president Gamal Abdel Nasser came to personify Arab nationalism between 1952 until his death in 1970. That FGM is so prevalent in Egypt should arouse suspicion about the practice elsewhere in the Arab world, especially given the low appreciation for women's rights in Arab societies. But most experts dismiss the connection of the practice with Islam. Instead, they explain the practice as rooted in poverty, lack of education, and superstition.

Few reports mention the existence of FGM elsewhere in the Middle East, except in passing. A UNICEF report on the issue, for example, focuses on Africa and makes only passing mention of "some communities on the Red Sea coast of Yemen." UNICEF then cites reports, but no evidence, that the practice also occurs to a limited degree in Jordan, Gaza, Oman, and Iraqi Kurdistan.[14] The German semigovernmental aid agency, the Gesellschaft fur Technische Zusammenarbeit, reports that FGM is prevalent in twenty-eight African countries but only among small communities "in a few Arab and Asian countries" (e.g., Yemen, a few ethnic groups in Oman, Indonesia, and Malaysia).[15] Some scholars have asserted that the practice does not exist at all in those countries east of the Suez Canal.[16] Such assertions are wrong. FGM is a widespread practice in at least parts of these countries.[17]

Latest findings from northern Iraq suggest that FGM is practiced widely in regions outside Africa. Iraqi Kurdistan is an instructive case. Traditionally, Kurdish society is agrarian. A significant part of the population lives outside cities. Women face a double-burden: they are sometimes cut off from even the most basic public services and are subject to a complex of patriarchal rules. As a result, living conditions for women are poor. Many of the freedoms and rights introduced by political leaders in Iraqi Kurdistan after the establishment of the safe-haven in 1991 are, for many women, more theoretical than actual.

In early 2003, WADI, a German-Austrian NGO focusing on women's issues,[18] started to work with mobile teams to take medical aid and social support to women in peripheral Kurdish areas such as in the Garmian region of Iraqi Kurdistan. These all-female teams consisting of a physician, a nurse, and a social worker built trust and opened doors in local communities otherwise sealed against outsiders. After more than a year of working in the area, women began to speak about FGM. Kurds in the area practice Sunna circumcision. Midwives often perform the operation with unsterilized instruments or even broken glass and without anesthesia on girls four to twelve years old. The extent of mutilation depends on the experience of the midwife and the luck of the girl. The wound is then treated with ash or mud with the girls then forced to sit in a bucket of iced water. Many Kurdish girls die, and others suffer chronic pain, infection, and infertility. Many say they suffer symptoms consistent with posttraumatic stress disorder syndrome.[19]

Subsequent research found that 907 out of 1,544 women questioned had undergone genital circumcision, a cutting rate of nearly 60 percent.[20] Follow-up research in the Irbil and Kirkuk governorates suggests rates of FGM consistent with those in Garmian. Nearly every woman questioned declared FGM to be a "normal" practice. Most women referred to the practice as both a tradition and a religious obligation. When asked why they subject their daughters to the operation, many women respond "it has always been like that." Because the clitoris is considered to be "dirty" (haram, the connotation is forbidden by religion), women fear that they cannot find husbands for their daughters if they have not been mutilated; many believe men prefer sex with a mutilated wife. Others stress the religious necessity of FGM even though Islamic law is unclear with regard to FGM. While Western scholars may dismiss the religious roots of the practice, what counts is that many Islamic clerics in northern Iraq advise women to practice FGM. Should a woman consider abandoning the practice, she must be aware that she could appear as disreputable in the public eye.[21] Men usually avoid offering a clear statement about whether FGM is a good practice; rather, they refer to FGM as a female practice in which men should not interfere. None of the men said he had ever discussed the question with his wife.[22]

The reaction of locals to the findings has been instructive. When confronted with the study results, only a few women's activists in the Iraqi Kurdish city of Sulaimaniya expressed surprise although most said they did not realize just how high a proportion of women was affected.[23] While local researcher and women's rights activist Ronak Faraj had published a study on female circumcision in Sulaimaniya in 2004,[24] the fact that an international NGO had become aware of the problem bolstered public attention. While many Kurdish authorities were at first reluctant to address the issue for fear that the Kurdish region might appear backward, they now acknowledge the problem and are working to confront it with both an awareness campaign and with legislation.[25] But some members of influential Islamic and Arabic organizations in the diaspora scandalized the findings, accusing WADI of trying to insult Islam and spread anti-Islamic propaganda. Tarafa Baghajati and Omar al-Rawi, both members of the Initiative of Muslim Austrians, called the data part of an "Islamophobic campaign" and declared no FGM exists in Iraq.[26] That Islamic and Arabic organizations in Austria, for example, make such arguments is indicative of the problem affecting FGM data: these groups believe that if there are no such anti-FGM campaigns or studies, then they can bypass an embarrassing problem.

Such campaigns take time. In Egypt, anti-FGM education campaigns inaugurated in the mid-1990s are only now bearing fruit.[27] The idea that rooted practices cannot be changed is false. For centuries, foot-binding crippled Chinese women. An anti-foot-binding society formed only in 1874, but the activists were successful in scaling back and, eventually, eliminating the practice.[28] In Western societies, too, open public discourse on sexuality became possible only by persistent struggle in the face of stark opposition. The heated reactions to the 1948 *Kinsey Report*—and the portion concerning female sexuality published in 1953—are a case in point.[29]

How Widespread Is Female Genital Mutilation?

The discovery of widespread FGM in Iraqi Kurdistan suggests the assumption to be incorrect that FGM is primarily an African phenomenon with only marginal occurrence in the eastern Islamic world. If FGM is practiced at a rate of nearly 60 percent by Iraqi Kurds, then how prevalent is the practice in neighboring Syria where living conditions and cultural and religious practices are comparable? According to Fran Hosken, late founder of the Women's International Network News and author of groundbreaking research on FGM in 1975, "There is little doubt that similar practices—excision, child marriage, and putting rock salt into the vagina of women after childbirth—exist in other parts of the Arabian Peninsula and around the Persian Gulf."[30] That no firsthand medical records are available for Saudi Arabia or from any other countries in that region does not mean that these areas are free of FGM, only that the societies are not free enough to permit formal study of societal problems. That diplomats and international aid workers do not detect FGM in other societies also should not suggest that the problem does not exist. After all, FGM was prevalent in Iraqi Kurdistan for years but went undetected by the World Health Organization, UNICEF, and many other international NGOs in the region. Perhaps the most important factor enabling an NGO to

uncover FGM in Iraqi Kurdistan was the existence of civil society structures and popular demand for individual rights. Such conditions simply do not exist in Syria, Saudi Arabia, or even the West Bank and Gaza where local authorities fight to constrain individual freedoms rather than promote them.

But the problem is not only that autocratic regimes tend to suppress the truth. There also must be someone in place to conduct surveys. Prior to Iraq's liberation, it was impossible to undertake independent surveys on issues such as malnutrition and infant mortality. Saddam Hussein's regime preferred to supply data to the U.N. rather than to enable others to collect their own data which might not support the conclusions the Baathist regime desired to show. The oft-cited 1999 UNICEF study claiming that U.N. sanctions had led to the deaths of 500,000 children was based on figures supplied by Saddam's regime, not an independent survey.[31] The U.N. undertook its first reliable statistical research on the living conditions in Iraq only after liberation.[32] Syrian, Saudi, and Iranian authorities simply do not let NGOs operate without restriction, especially when they deal with sensitive social issues.

Taboo—not social but political—is another factor undercutting research on FGM in Arab countries. Many academics and NGO workers in the region find it objectionable to criticize the predominant Muslim or Arab cultures. They will bend over backwards to avoid the argument that FGM is rooted in Arab or Muslim cultures even though no one argues that FGM is exclusively an Arab or Muslim problem. Statistical data from African countries indicate no clear relationship between FGM and a specific religion.[33] Still, this does not mean that the causes of FGM do not vary across regions and that religion has no influence. As California State University anthropologist Ellen Gruenbaum has explained, "People have different and multiple reasons [for FGM] . . . For some it is a rite of passage. For others it is not. Some consider it aesthetically pleasing. For others, it is mostly related to morality or sexuality."[34] Hanny Lightfoot-Klein, an internationally known expert on FGM who spent years in Kenya, Egypt, and Sudan, explains that "it is believed in the Sudan that the clitoris will grow to the length of a goose's neck until it dangles between the legs, in rivalry with the male's penis, if it is not cut."[35]

Most studies speak of "justifications"[36] and "rationalizations"[37] for FGM but do not speak of causes since this could implicate Islamic rules relating to women and sexual morality. Islam is regarded as a wrong "justification," often with a citation that the Qur'an does not require FGM. That many women in northern Iraq—and presumably many women in Egypt—believe that the practice is rooted in religion is a factor ignored by Western universities and international organizations.

Islamic Scholars on Female Genital Mutilation

Islamic scholars disagree on FGM: some say no obligatory rules exist while others refer to the mention of female circumcision in the Hadith. According to Sami A. Aldeeb Abu Sahlieh, a Palestinian-Swiss specialist in Islamic law:

> The most often mentioned narration reports a debate between Muhammed and Um Habibah (or Um 'Atiyyah). This woman, known as an exciser of female slaves, was one of a group of women who had immigrated with Muhammed. Having seen her, Muhammad asked her if she kept practicing her profession. She answered affirmatively, adding: "unless it is forbidden, and you order me to stop doing it." Muhammed replied: "Yes, it is allowed. Come closer so I can teach you: if you cut, do not overdo it, because it brings more radiance to the face, and it is more pleasant for the husband."[38]

Abu Sahlieh further cited Muhammad as saying, "Circumcision is a *sunna* (tradition) for the men and *makruma* (honorable deed) for the women."[39]

While some clerics say circumcision is not obligatory for women, others say it is. "Islam condones the sunna circumcision . . . What is forbidden in Islam is the pharaonic circumcision,"[40] one religious leader explained. Others, such as the late rector of Al-Azhar University, Sheikh Gad al-Haq, said that since the Prophet did not ban female circumcision, it was permissible and, at the very least, could not be banned.[41]

In short, some clerics condemn FGM as an archaic practice, some accept it, and still others believe it to be obligatory. It is the job of clerics to interpret religious literature; it is not the job of FGM researchers and activists. There is a certain tendency to confuse a liberal interpretation of Islam with the reality women face in many predominately Islamic regions. To counter FGM as a practice, it is necessary to accept that Islam is more than just a written text. It is not the book that cuts the clitoris, but its interpretations aid and abet the mutilation.

Conclusions

There are indications that FGM might be a phenomenon of epidemic proportions in the Arab Middle East. Hosken, for instance, notes that traditionally all women in the Persian Gulf region were mutilated.[42] Arab governments refuse to address the problem. They prefer to believe that lack of statistics will enable international organizations to conclude that the problem does not exist in their jurisdictions. It is not enough to consult Islamic clerics to learn about the mutilation of girls in Islamic societies—that is like asking the cook if the guests like the meal. U.N. agencies operating in the region ignore FGM statistics saying they have no applicable mandate to gather such data. Hosken describes it as a cartel of silence: men from countries where FGM is practiced "enjoy much influence at the U.N."[43] and show no interest in tackling pressing social problems.

To tackle the problem, Western countries and human rights organizations need to continue to break down the wall of silence and autocracy that blights the Arab Middle East and better promote the notion of individual rights. They should withhold conclusions about the breadth of FGM and, for that matter, other social problems or political attitudes until they can conduct independent field research.

Notes

1. See, for example, Marie José Simonet, "FMG: Sunna oder Verbrechen aus Tradition," stopFMG.net, Vienna, June 24, 2005.
2. Haseena Lockhat, *Female Genital Mutilation: Treating the Tears* (London: Middlesex University Press, 2004), p. 16.

3. *Weibliche Genitalverstümmelung: Geschichte, Ausmaß, Formen und Folgen* (Vienna: Renner Institut, 2004), p. 6.

4. See, for example, *Innocenti Digest: Changing a Harmful Social Convention: Female Genital Mutilation/Cutting* (Florence: UNICEF, 2005).

5. *Die Zeit* (Hamburg), May 11, 2006.

6. See, for example, *Changing a Harmful Social Convention*, p. VII.

7. "Fact Sheet no. 23, Harmful Traditional Practices Affecting the Health of Women and Children," U.N. Office of the High Commissioner for Human Rights, Geneva, accessed Aug. 11, 2006.

8. ECOSOC resolution 821 II (XXXII); ibid.

9. "Convention on the Elimination of All Forms of Discrimination against Women," U.N. General Assembly resolution 34/180, Dec. 18, 1979.

10. "Convention on the Rights of the Child," U.N. General Assembly resolution 44/25, Nov. 20, 1989, art. 24, 3.

11. Dara Carr, *Female Genital Cutting: Findings from the Demographic and Health Surveys Program* (Calverton, Md.: Macro International, 1997), p. 1.

12. Gerry Mackie, "A Way to End Female Genital Cutting," Female Genital Cutting Education and Networking Project, Tallahassee, Fla., accessed Aug. 4, 2006.

13. Eiman Okro, "Weibliche Genitalverstümmelung im Sudan," PhD dissertation, Humboldt University, Berlin (Hamburg: Akademos Science Publishing House, 2001); "Female Genital Mutilation in Africa: Information by Country," Amnesty International, accessed Sept. 1, 2006.

14. *Changing a Harmful Social Convention*, p. 3.

15. "What Is Female Genital Mutilation?" Gesellschaft fuer Technische Zusammenarbeit, Frankfurt, Ger., 2005, accessed Aug. 4, 2006.

16. See, for example, "Female Genital Mutilation (FGM) in Africa, the Middle East and Far East: Where, Why and How It Is Done," Ontario Consultants on Religious Tolerance, updated Mar. 2005.

17. Fran P. Hosken, *The Hosken Report: Genital and Sexual Mutilation of Females* (Lexington: The Women's International Network News, 1993), pp. 275–8.

18. WADI, offices in Frankfurt and Sulaimaniya.

19. Janet Menage, "Post-Traumatic Stress Disorder in Women Who Have Undergone Obstetric and/or Gynecological Procedures. A Consecutive Series of 30 Cases of PTSD," *Journal of Reproductive and Infant Psychology*, 11(1993): 221–8.

20. Data derived from WADI field research in the Garmian region of Iraqi Kurdistan, 2005; *Christian Science Monitor*, Aug. 10, 2005; Radio Free Europe/Radio Liberty, Jan. 21, 2005; "Widespread FGM in Northern Iraq," Global Health Council, Jan. 6, 2005; "Iraq: Decades of Suffering, Now Women Deserve Better," Amnesty International, London, Feb. 22, 2005.

21. Mackie, "A Way to End Female Genital Cutting."

22. WADI field research, 2005.

23. U.N. Integrated Regional Information Networks (IRIN), Mar. 16, 2005.

24. Ronak Faraj, "Female Circumcision," Women Information and Culture Center, Sulaimaniya, Iraq, 2004.

25. *The Irish Times* (Dublin), Oct. 25, 2005.

26. Judith Götz, "Anmerkungen zu einer Veranstaltung Die politische Lage im Irak," Jan. 28, 2005, accessed Oct. 11, 2006.

27. *NBC News*, Oct. 21, 2004.

28. Mackie, "A Way to End Female Genital Cutting"; Marie Vento, "One Thousand Years of Chinese Footbinding: Its Origins, Popularity and Demise," paper, City University of New York, Mar. 7, 1998.

29. "American Experience: Kinsey in the News," Public Broadcasting Service, Jan. 27, 2005.

30. Hosken, *The Hosken Report*, p. 278.

31. Michael Rubin, "Sanctions on Iraq: A Valid Anti-American Grievance?" *Middle East Review of International Affairs*, June, 2002.

32. "Iraq Living Conditions Survey 2004," United Nations Development Program, Baghdad, 2005.

33. *Female Genital Mutilation/Cutting. A Statistical Exploration* (New York: UNICEF, 2005), p. 10.

34. Ellen Gruenbaum, *The Female Circumcision Controversy: An Anthropological Perspective* (Philadelphia: University of Pennsylvania Press, 2000), p. 33.

35. Hanny Lightfoot-Klein. "Prisoners of Ritual: Some Contemporary Developments in the History of Female Genital Mutilation," presented at the Second International Symposium on Circumcision in San Francisco, Apr. 30-May 3, 1991.

36. Julia M. Masterson and Julie Hanson Swanson, *Female Genital Cutting: Breaking the Silence, Enabling Change* (Washington, D.C.: International Center for Research on Women and the Center for Development and Population Activities, 2000), p. 5.

37. "Female Genital Mutilation: A Joint WHO/UNICEF/UNFPA Statement," Geneva, 1997.

38. Sami A. Aldeeb Abu Sahlieh, "To Mutilate in the Name of Jehovah or Allah: Legitimization of Male and Female Circumcision," *Medicine and Law*, July 1994, pp. 575–622.

39. Ibid.

40. *Razor's Edge: The Controversy of Female Genital Mutilation*, IRIN, Mar. 2005; Sheikh Omer, interview, IRINnews.org, U.N. Office for the Coordination of Humanitarian Affairs, Mar. 8, 2005.

41. "Appendix: Is Female Circumcision Required?" Jannah.org, accessed Aug. 11, 2005.

42. Hosken, *The Hosken Report*, p. 277.

43. Ibid., p. 375.

The Psychology of Sex Roles

Even if biology were destiny, the founder of psychoanalysis Sigmund Freud argued, the process by which biological males and females become gendered men and women does not happen naturally nor inevitably. Gender identity, he argued, is an achievement—the outcome of a struggle for boys to separate from their mothers and identify with their fathers, and of a parallel and complementary struggle for girls to reconcile themselves to their sexual inadequacy and therefore maintain their identification with their mothers.

Subsequent generations of psychologists have attempted to specify the content of that achievement of gender identity and how it might be measured. In the early 1930s, Lewis Terman, one of the country's most eminent social psychologists, codified gender identity into a set of attitudes, traits, and behaviors that enabled researchers to pinpoint exactly where any young person was on a continuum between masculinity and femininity. If one had successfully acquired the "appropriate" collection of traits and attitudes, one (and one's parents) could rest assured that one would continue to develop "normally." Gender nonconformity—boys who scored high on the femininity side of the continuum or girls who scored high on the masculine side—was a predictor, Terman argued, for sexual nonconformity. Homosexuality was the sexual behavioral outcome of a gender problem, of men

who had not successfully mastered masculinity or women who had not successfully mastered femininity.

In this section Janet Shibley Hyde reviews all the studies of gender difference
in psychology—traits, attitudes, and behaviors—and finds few, if any, really big
differences. It turns out that the empirical research reveals that we're all from
planet Earth.

Despite these similarities, an enormous cultural and psychological edifice is
concerned with creating, sustaining, and reproducing gender difference, and then
convincing us that it's natural, inevitable, and biologically based. C. J. Pascoe as
well as May Ling Halim and her colleagues show how homophobic teasing and
bullying serve as a sort of policing device to make sure that boys (and to a lesser
extent girls) remain conformists to gender norms. And Robb Willer and his colleagues show how guys often overcompensate when they feel their masculinity is
threatened.

The Gender Similarities Hypothesis

JANET SHIBLEY HYDE

The mass media and the general public are captivated by findings of gender differences. John Gray's (1992) *Men Are from Mars, Women Are from Venus*, which argued for enormous psychological differences between women and men, has sold over 30 million copies and been translated into forty languages (Gray, 2005). Deborah Tannen's (1991) *You Just Don't Understand: Women and Men in Conversation* argued for the *different cultures hypothesis:* that men's and women's patterns of speaking are so fundamentally different that men and women essentially belong to different linguistic communities or cultures. That book was on the *New York Times* bestseller list for nearly four years and has been translated into twenty-four languages (AnnOnline, 2005). Both of these works, and dozens of others like them, have argued for the *differences hypothesis:* that males and females are, psychologically, vastly different. Here, I advance a very different view—the *gender similarities hypothesis* (for related statements, see Epstein, 1988; Hyde, 1985; Hyde & Plant, 1995; Kimball, 1995).

The Hypothesis

The gender similarities hypothesis holds that males and females are similar on most, but not all, psychological variables. That is, men and women, as well as boys and girls, are more alike than they are different. In terms of effect sizes, the gender similarities hypothesis states that most psychological gender differences are in the close-to-zero ($d \leq 0.10$) or small ($0.11 < d < 0.35$) range, a few are in the moderate range ($0.36 < d < 0.65$), and

very few are large ($d = 0.66$–1.00) or very large ($d > 1.00$).

Although the fascination with psychological gender differences has been present from the dawn of formalized psychology around 1879 (Shields, 1975), a few early researchers highlighted gender similarities. Thorndike (1914), for example, believed that psychological gender differences were too small, compared with within-gender variation, to be important. Leta Stetter Hollingworth (1918) reviewed available research on gender differences in mental traits and found little evidence of gender differences. Another important reviewer of gender research in the early 1900s, Helen Thompson Woolley (1914), lamented the gap between the data and scientists' views on the question:

> The general discussions of the psychology of sex, whether by psychologists or by sociologists show such a wide diversity of points of view that one feels that the truest thing to be said at present is that scientific evidence plays very little part in producing convictions. (p. 372)

The Role of Meta-Analysis in Assessing Psychological Gender Differences

Reviews of research on psychological gender differences began with Woolley's (1914) and Hollingworth's (1918) and extended through Maccoby and Jacklin's (1974) watershed book *The Psychology of Sex Differences*, in which they reviewed more than 2,000 studies of gender differences in a wide variety of domains, including abilities, personality, social behavior, and memory. Maccoby and Jacklin dismissed as unfounded many popular beliefs in psychological gender differences, including beliefs that girls are more "social" than boys; that girls are more suggestible; that girls have lower self-esteem; that girls are better at rote learning and simple tasks, whereas boys are better at higher level cognitive processing; and that girls lack achievement motivation. Maccoby and Jacklin concluded that gender differences were well established in only four areas: verbal ability, visual-spatial ability, mathematical ability, and aggression. Overall, then, they found much evidence for gender similarities. Secondary reports of their findings in textbooks and other sources, however, focused almost exclusively on their conclusions about gender differences (e.g., Gleitman, 1981; Lefrançois, 1990).

Shortly after this important work appeared, the statistical method of meta-analysis was developed (e.g., Glass, McGaw, & Smith, 1981; Hedges & Olkin, 1985; Rosenthal, 1991). This method revolutionized the study of psychological gender differences. Meta-analyses quickly appeared on issues such as gender differences in influenceability (Eagly & Carli, 1981), abilities (Hyde, 1981; Hyde & Linn, 1988; Linn & Petersen, 1985), and aggression (Eagly & Steffen, 1986; Hyde, 1984, 1986).

Meta-analysis is a statistical method for aggregating research findings across many studies of the same question (Hedges & Becker, 1986). It is ideal for synthesizing research on gender differences, an area in which often dozens or even hundreds of studies of a particular question have been conducted.

Crucial to meta-analysis is the concept of effect size, which measures the magnitude of an effect—in this case, the magnitude of gender difference....

The Evidence

To evaluate the gender similarities hypothesis, I collected the major meta-analyses that have been conducted on psychological gender differences. They are listed in Table 1, grouped roughly into six categories: those that assessed cognitive variables, such as abilities; those that assessed verbal or nonverbal communication; those that assessed social or personality variables, such as aggression or leadership; those that assessed measures of psychological well-being, such as self-esteem; those that assessed motor behaviors, such as throwing distance; and those that assessed miscellaneous constructs, such as moral reasoning. . . .

Inspection of the effect sizes shown in the rightmost column of Table 1 reveals strong evidence for the gender similarities hypothesis. These effect sizes are summarized in Table 2. Of the 128 effect sizes shown in Table 1, 4 were unclassifiable because the meta-analysis provided such a wide range for the estimate. The remaining 124 effect sizes were classified into the categories noted earlier: close-to-zero ($d \leq 0.10$), small ($0.11 < d < 0.35$), moderate ($0.36 < d < 0.65$), large ($d = 0.66-1.00$), or very large (> 1.00). The striking result is that 30% of the effect sizes are in the close-to-zero range, and an additional 48% are in the small range. That is, 78% of gender differences are small or close to zero. This result is similar to that of Hyde and Plant (1995), who found that 60% of effect sizes for gender differences were in the small or close-to-zero range.

The small magnitude of these effects is even more striking given that most of the meta-analyses addressed the classic gender differences questions—that is, areas in which gender differences were reputed to be reliable, such as mathematics performance, verbal ability, and aggressive behavior. For example, despite Tannen's (1991) assertions, gender differences in most aspects of communication are small. Gilligan (1982) has argued that males and females speak in a different moral "voice," yet meta-analyses show that gender differences in moral reasoning and moral orientation are small (Jaffee & Hyde, 2000).

The Exceptions

As noted earlier, the gender similarities hypothesis does not assert that males and females are similar in absolutely every domain. The exceptions—areas in which gender differences are moderate or large in magnitude—should be recognized.

The largest gender differences in Table 1 are in the domain of motor performance, particularly

TABLE I. Major Meta-Analyses of Research on Psychological Gender Differences

Study and Variable	Age	No. of Reports	d
Cognitive Variables			
Hyde, Fennema, & Lamon (1990)			
Mathematics computation	All	45	−0.14
Mathematics concepts	All	41	−0.03
Mathematics problem solving	All	48	+0.08
Hedges & Nowell (1995)			
Reading comprehension	Adolescents	5*	−0.09
Vocabulary	Adolescents	4*	+0.06
Mathematics	Adolescents	6*	+0.16
Perceptual speed	Adolescents	4*	−0.28
Science	Adolescents	4*	+0.32
Spatial ability	Adolescents	2*	+0.19
Hyde, Fennema, Ryan, et al. (1990)			
Mathematics self-confidence	All	56	+0.16
Mathematics anxiety	All	53	−0.15
Feingold (1988)			
DAT spelling	Adolescents	5*	−0.45
DAT language	Adolescents	5*	−0.40
DAT verbal reasoning	Adolescents	5*	−0.02
DAT abstract reasoning	Adolescents	5*	−0.04
DAT numerical ability	Adolescents	5*	−0.10
DAT perceptual speed	Adolescents	5*	−0.34
DAT mechanical reasoning	Adolescents	5*	+0.76
DAT space relations	Adolescents	5*	+0.15
Hyde & Linn (1988)			
Vocabulary	All	40	−0.02
Reading comprehension	All	18	−0.03
Speech production	All	12	−0.33
Linn & Petersen (1985)			
Spatial perception	All	62	+0.44
Mental rotation	All	29	+0.73
Spatial visualization	All	81	+0.13
Voyer et al. (1995)			
Spatial perception	All	92	+0.44
Mental rotation	All	78	+0.56
Spatial visualization	All	116	+0.19
Lynn & Irwing (2004)			
Progressive matrices	6–14 years	15	+0.02
Progressive matrices	15–19 years	23	+0.16
Progressive matrices	Adults	10	+0.30

(continued)

TABLE I. *(continued)*

Study and Variable	Age	No. of Reports	d
Cognitive Variables			
Whitley et al. (1986)			
Attribution of success to ability	All	29	+0.13
Attribution of success to effort	All	29	−0.04
Attribution of success to task	All	29	−0.01
Attribution of success to luck	All	29	−0.07
Attribution of failure to ability	All	29	+0.16
Attribution of failure to effort	All	29	+0.15
Attribution of failure to task	All	29	−0.08
Attribution of failure to luck	All	29	−0.15
Communication			
Anderson & Leaper (1998)			
Interruptions in conversation	Adults	53	+0.15
Intrusive interruptions	Adults	17	+0.33
Leaper & Smith (2004)			
Talkativeness	Children	73	−0.11
Affiliative speech	Children	46	−0.26
Assertive speech	Children	75	+0.11
Dindia & Allen (1992)			
Self-disclosure (all studies)	—	205	−0.18
Self-disclosure to stranger	—	99	−0.07
Self-disclosure to friend	—	50	−0.28
LaFrance et al. (2003)			
Smiling	Adolescents and adults	418	−0.40
Smiling: Aware of being observed	Adolescents and adults	295	−0.46
Smiling: Not aware of being observed	Adolescents and adults	31	−0.19
McClure (2000)			
Facial expression processing	Infants	29	−0.18 to −0.92
Facial expression processing	Children and adolescents	89	−0.13 to −0.18
Social and Personality Variables			
Hyde (1984, 1986)			
Aggression (all types)	All	69	+0.50
Physical aggression	All	26	+0.60
Verbal aggression	All	6	+0.43
Eagly & Steffen (1986)			
Aggression	Adults	50	+0.29

TABLE I. *(continued)*

Study and Variable	Age	No. of Reports	d
Social and Personality Variables *(continued)*			
Eagly & Steffen (1986)			
Physical aggression	Adults	30	+0.40
Psychological aggression	Adults	20	+0.18
Knight et al. (2002)			
Physical aggression	All	41	+0.59
Verbal aggression	All	22	+0.28
Aggression in low emotional arousal context	All	40	+0.30
Aggression in emotional arousal context	All	83	+0.56
Bettencourt & Miller (1996)			
Aggression under provocation	Adults	57	+0.17
Aggression under neutral conditions	Adults	50	+0.33
Archer (2004)			
Aggression in real-world settings	All	75	+0.30 to +0.63
Physical aggression	All	111	+0.33 to +0.84
Verbal aggression	All	68	+0.09 to +0.55
Indirect aggression	All	40	−0.74 to +0.05
Stuhlmacher & Walters (1999)			
Negotiation outcomes	Adults	53	+0.09
Walters et al. (1998)			
Negotiator competitiveness	Adults	79	10.07
Eagly & Crowley (1986)			
Helping behavior	Adults	99	+0.13
Helping: Surveillance context	Adults	16	+0.74
Helping: No surveillance	Adults	41	−0.02
Oliver & Hyde (1993)			
Sexuality: Masturbation	All	26	+0.96
Sexuality: Attitudes about casual sex	All	10	+0.81
Sexual satisfaction	All	15	−0.06
Attitudes about extramarital sex	All	17	+0.29
Murnen & Stockton (1997)			
Arousal to sexual stimuli	Adults	62	+0.31
Eagly & Johnson (1990)			
Leadership: Interpersonal style	Adults	153	−0.04 to −0.07
Leadership: Task style	Adults	154	0.00 to −0.09
Leadership: Democratic vs. autocratic	Adults	28	+0.22 to +0.34
Eagly et al. (1992)			
Leadership: Evaluation	Adults	114	+0.05
Eagly et al. (1995)			
Leadership: Effectiveness	Adults	76	−0.02

(continued)

TABLE I. *(continued)*

Study and Variable	Age	No. of Reports	d
Social and Personality Variables *(continued)*			
Eagly et al. (2003)			
Leadership: Transformational	Adults	44	−0.10
Leadership: Transactional	Adults	51	−0.13 to +0.27
Leadership: Laissez-faire	Adults	16	+0.16
Feingold (1994)			
Neuroticism: Anxiety	Adolescents and adults	13*	−0.32
Neuroticism: Impulsiveness	Adolescents and adults	6*	−0.01
Extraversion: Gregariousness	Adolescents and adults	10*	−0.07
Extraversion: Assertiveness	Adolescents and adults	10*	+0.51
Extraversion: Activity	Adolescents and adults	5	+0.08
Openness	Adolescents and adults	4*	+0.19
Agreeableness: Trust	Adolescents and adults	4*	−0.35
Agreeableness: Tendermindedness	Adolescents and adults	10*	−0.91
Conscientiousness	Adolescents and adults	4	−0.18
Psychological Well-Being			
Kling et al. (1999, Analysis I)			
Self-esteem	All	216	+0.21
Kling et al. (1999, Analysis II)			
Self-esteem	Adolescents	15*	+0.04 to +0.16
Major et al. (1999)			
Self-esteem	All	226	+0.14
Feingold & Mazzella (1998)			
Body esteem	All	—	+0.58
Twenge & Nolen-Hoeksema (2002)			
Depression symptoms	8–16 years	310	+0.02
Wood et al. (1989)			
Life satisfaction	Adults	17	−0.03
Happiness	Adults	22	−0.07
Pinquart & Sörensen (2001)			
Life satisfaction	Elderly	176	+0.08
Self-esteem	Elderly	59	+0.08
Happiness	Elderly	56	−0.06

TABLE 1. *(continued)*

Study and Variable	Age	No. of Reports	*d*
Psychological Well-Being *(continued)*			
Tamres et al. (2002)			
Coping: Problem-focused	All	22	−0.13
Coping: Rumination	All	10	−0.19
Motor Behaviors			
Thomas & French (1985)			
Balance	3–20 years	67	+0.09
Grip strength	3–20 years	37	+0.66
Throw velocity	3–20 years	12	+2.18
Throw distance	3–20 years	47	+1.98
Vertical jump	3–20 years	20	+0.18
Sprinting	3–20 years	66	+0.63
Flexibility	5–10 years	13	−0.29
Eaton & Enns (1986)			
Activity level	All	127	+0.49
Miscellaneous			
Thoma (1986)			
Moral reasoning: Stage	Adolescents and adults	56	−0.21
Jaffee & Hyde (2000)			
Moral reasoning: Justice orientation	All	95	+0.19
Moral reasoning: Care orientation	All	160	−0.28
Silverman (2003)			
Delay of gratification	All	38	−0.12
Whitley et al. (1999)			
Cheating behavior	All	36	+0.17
Cheating attitudes	All	14	+0.35
Whitley (1997)			
Computer use: Current	All	18	+0.33
Computer self-efficacy	All	29	+0.41
Konrad et al. (2000)			
Job attribute preference: Earnings	Adults	207	+0.12
Job attribute preference: Security	Adults	182	−0.02
Job attribute preference: Challenge		63	+0.05
Job attribute preference: Physical work environment	Adults	96	−0.13
Job attribute preference: Power	Adults	68	+0.04

Note: Positive values of *d* represent higher scores for men and/or boys; negative values of *d* represent higher scores for women and/or girls. Asterisks indicate that data were from major, large national samples. Dashes indicate that data were not available (i.e., the study in question did not provide this information clearly). No. = number; DAT = Differential Aptitude Test.

TABLE 2. Effect Sizes (n = 124) for Psychological Gender Differences, Based on Meta-Analyses, Categorized by Range of Magnitude

	Effect Size Range				
Effect Sizes	0–0.10	0.11–0.35	0.36–0.65	0.66–1.00	>1.00
Number	37	59	19	7	2
% of total	30	48	15	6	2

for measures such as throwing velocity (*d* = 2.18) and throwing distance (*d* = 1.98) (Thomas & French, 1985). These differences are particularly large after puberty, when the gender gap in muscle mass and bone size widens.

A second area in which large gender differences are found is some—but not all—measures of sexuality (Oliver & Hyde, 1993). Gender differences are strikingly large for incidences of masturbation and for attitudes about sex in a casual, uncommitted relationship. In contrast, the gender difference in reported sexual satisfaction is close to zero.

Across several meta-analyses, aggression has repeatedly shown gender differences that are moderate in magnitude (Archer, 2004; Eagly & Steffen, 1986; Hyde, 1984, 1986). The gender difference in physical aggression is particularly reliable and is larger than the gender difference in verbal aggression. Much publicity has been given to gender differences in relational aggression, with girls scoring higher (e.g., Crick & Grotpeter, 1995). According to the Archer (2004) meta-analysis, indirect or relational aggression showed an effect size for gender differences of −0.45 when measured by direct observation, but it was only −0.19 for peer ratings, −0.02 for self-reports, and −0.13 for teacher reports. Therefore, the evidence is ambiguous regarding the magnitude of the gender difference in relational aggression. . . .

Developmental Trends

Not all meta-analyses have examined developmental trends and, given the preponderance of psychological research on college students, developmental analysis is not always possible. However, meta-analysis can be powerful for identifying age trends in the magnitude of gender differences.

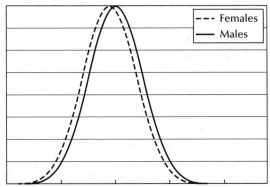

Figure 1. Graphic Representation of a 0.21 Effect Size. Source: From "Gender Differences in Self-Esteem: A Meta-Analysis," by K. C. Kling, J. S. Hyde, C. J. Showers, and B. N. Buswell, 1999, *Psychological Bulletin*, 125, p. 484. Copyright © 1999 by the American Psychological Association. Note: Two normal distributions that are 0.21 standard deviations apart (i.e., *d* = 0.21). This is the approximate magnitude of the gender difference in self-esteem, averaged over all samples, found by Kling et al. (1999).

Here, I consider a few key examples of meta-analyses that have taken this developmental approach (see Table 3).

At the time of the meta-analysis by Hyde, Fennema, and Lamon (1990), it was believed that gender differences in mathematics performance were small or nonexistent in childhood and that the male advantage appeared beginning around the time of puberty (Maccoby & Jacklin, 1974). It was also believed that males were better at high-level mathematical problems that required complex processing, whereas females were better at low-level mathematics that required only simple computation. Hyde and colleagues addressed both hypotheses in their meta-analysis. They found a small gender difference favoring girls in computation in elementary school and middle school and no

TABLE 3. Selected Meta-Analyses Showing Developmental Trends in the Magnitude of Gender Differences

Study and Variable	Age (years)	No. of Reports	*d*
Hyde, Fennema, & Lamon (1990)			
Mathematics: Complex problem solving	5–10	11	0.00
	11–14	21	−0.02
	15–18	10	+0.29
	19–25	15	+0.32
Kling et al. (1999)			
Self-esteem	7–10	22	+0.16
	11–14	53	+0.23
	15–18	44	+0.33
	19–22	72	+0.18
	23–59	16	+0.10
	>60	6	−0.03
Major et al. (1999)			
Self-esteem	5–10	24	+0.01
	11–13	34	+0.12
	14–18	65	+0.16
	19 or older	97	+0.13
Twenge & Nolen-Hoeksema (2002)			
Depressive symptoms	8–12	86	−0.04
	13–16	49	+0.16
Thomas & French (1985)			
Throwing distance	3–8	—	+1.50 to +2.00
	16–18	—	+3.50

Note: Positive values of *d* represent higher scores for men and/or boys; negative values of *d* represent higher scores for women and/or girls. Dashes indicate that data were not available (i.e., the study in question did not provide this information clearly). No. = number.

gender difference in computation in the high school years. There was no gender difference in complex problem solving in elementary school or middle school, but a small gender difference favoring males emerged in the high school years ($d = 0.29$). Age differences in the magnitude of the gender effect were significant for both computation and problem solving.

Kling et al. (1999) used a developmental approach in their meta-analysis of studies of gender differences in self-esteem, on the basis of the assertion of prominent authors such as Mary Pipher (1994) that girls' self-esteem takes a nosedive at the beginning of adolescence. They found that the magnitude of the gender difference did grow larger from childhood to adolescence: In childhood (ages 7–10), $d = 0.16$; for early adolescence (ages 11–14), $d = 0.23$; and for the high school years (ages 15–18), $d = 0.33$. However, the gender difference did not suddenly become large in early adolescence, and even in high school the difference was still not large. Moreover, the gender difference was smaller in older samples; for example, for ages 23–59, $d = 0.10$.

Whitley's (1997) analysis of age trends in computer self-efficacy is revealing. In grammar school samples, $d = 0.09$, whereas in high school samples, $d = 0.66$. This dramatic trend leads to questions about what forces are at work transforming girls from feeling as effective with computers as boys do to showing a large difference in self-efficacy by high school.

These examples illustrate the extent to which the magnitude of gender differences can fluctuate with age. Gender differences grow larger or smaller at different times in the life span, and meta-analysis is a powerful tool for detecting these trends. Moreover, the fluctuating magnitude of gender differences at different ages argues against the differences model and notions that gender differences are large and stable.

The Importance of Context

Gender researchers have emphasized the importance of context in creating, erasing, or even reversing psychological gender differences (Bussey & Bandura, 1999; Deaux & Major, 1987; Eagly & Wood, 1999). Context may exert influence at numerous levels, including the written instructions given for an exam, dyadic interactions between participants or between a participant and an experimenter, or the sociocultural level.

In an important experiment, Lightdale and Prentice (1994) demonstrated the importance of gender roles and social context in creating or erasing the purportedly robust gender difference in aggression. Lightdale and Prentice used the technique of deindividuation to produce a situation that removed the influence of gender roles. *Deindividuation* refers to a state in which the person has lost his or her individual identity; that is, the person has become anonymous. Under such conditions, people should feel no obligation to conform to social norms such as gender roles. Half of the participants, who were college students, were assigned to an individuated condition by having them sit close to the experimenter, identify themselves by name, wear large name tags, and answer personal questions. Participants in the deindividuation condition sat far from the experimenter, wore no name tags, and were simply told to wait. All participants were also told that the experiment required information from only half of the participants, whose behavior would be monitored, and that the other half would remain anonymous. Participants then played an interactive video game in which they first defended and then attacked by dropping bombs. The number of bombs dropped was the measure of aggressive behavior.

The results indicated that in the individuated condition, men dropped significantly more bombs ($M = 31.1$) than women did ($M = 26.8$). In the deindividuated condition, however, there were no significant gender differences and, in fact, women dropped somewhat more bombs ($M = 41.1$) than men ($M = 36.8$). In short, the significant gender difference in aggression disappeared when gender norms were removed.

Steele's (1997; Steele & Aronson, 1995) work on stereotype threat has produced similar evidence in the cognitive domain. Although the original experiments concerned African Americans and the stereotype that they are intellectually inferior, the theory was quickly applied to gender and stereotypes that girls and women are bad at math (Brown & Josephs, 1999; Quinn & Spencer, 2001; Spencer, Steele, & Quinn, 1999; Walsh, Hickey, & Duffy, 1999). In one experiment, male and female college students with equivalent math backgrounds were tested (Spencer et al., 1999). In one condition, participants were told that the math test had shown gender difference in the past, and in the other condition, they were told that the test had been shown to be gender fair—that men and women had performed equally on it. In the condition in which participants had been told that the math test was gender fair, there were no gender differences in performance on the test. In the condition in which participants expected gender differences, women underperformed compared with men. This simple manipulation of context was capable of creating or erasing gender differences in math performance.

Meta-analysts have addressed the importance of context for gender differences. In one of the earliest demonstrations of context effects, Eagly and Crowley (1986) meta-analyzed studies of gender differences in helping behavior, basing the analysis in social-role theory. They argued that certain kinds of helping are part of the male role: helping that is heroic or chivalrous. Other kinds of helping are part of the female role: helping that is nurturant and caring, such as caring for children. Heroic helping involves danger to the self, and both heroic and chivalrous helping are facilitated when onlookers are present. Women's nurturant helping more often occurs in private, with no onlookers. Averaged over all studies, men helped more ($d = 0.34$). However, when studies were separated into those in which onlookers were present and participants were aware of it, $d = 0.74$. When no onlookers were present, $d = 20.02$. Moreover, the magnitude of the gender difference was highly correlated with the degree of danger in the helping situation; gender differences were largest favoring males in situations with the most danger. In short, the gender difference in helping behavior can be large, favoring males, or close to zero, depending on the social context in which the behavior is measured. Moreover, the pattern of gender differences is consistent with social-role theory.

Anderson and Leaper (1998) obtained similar context effects in their meta-analysis of gender differences in conversational interruption. At the time of their meta-analysis, it was widely believed that men interrupted women considerably more than the reverse. Averaged over all studies, however, Anderson and Leaper found a d of 0.15, a small effect. The effect size for intrusive interruptions (excluding back-channel interruptions) was larger: 0.33. It is important to note that the magnitude of the gender difference varied greatly depending on the social context in which interruptions were studied. When dyads were observed, $d = 0.06$, but with larger groups of three or more, $d = 0.26$. When participants were strangers, $d = 0.17$, but when they were friends, $d = -0.14$. Here, again, it is clear that gender differences can be created, erased, or reversed, depending on the context.

In their meta-analysis, LaFrance, Hecht, and Paluck (2003) found a moderate gender difference in smiling ($d = -0.41$), with girls and women smiling more. Again, the magnitude of the gender difference was highly dependent on the context. If participants had a clear awareness that they were being observed, the gender difference was larger ($d = -0.46$) than it was if they were not aware of

being observed ($d = -0.19$). The magnitude of the gender difference also depended on culture and age.

Dindia and Allen (1992) and Bettencourt and Miller (1996) also found marked context effects in their gender meta-analyses. The conclusion is clear: The magnitude and even the direction of gender differences depend on the context. These findings provide strong evidence against the differences model and its notions that psychological gender differences are large and stable.

Costs of Inflated Claims of Gender Differences

The question of the magnitude of psychological gender differences is more than just an academic concern. There are serious costs of overinflated claims of gender differences (for an extended discussion of this point, see Barnett & Rivers, 2004; see also White & Kowalski, 1994). These costs occur in many areas, including work, parenting, and relationships.

Gilligan's (1982) argument that women speak in a different moral "voice" than men is a well-known example of the differences model. Women, according to Gilligan, speak in a moral voice of caring, whereas men speak in a voice of justice. Despite the fact that meta-analyses disconfirm her arguments for large gender differences (Jaffee & Hyde, 2000; Thoma, 1986; Walker, 1984), Gilligan's ideas have permeated American culture. One consequence of this overinflated claim of gender differences is that it reifies the stereotype of women as caring and nurturant and men as lacking in nurturance. One cost to men is that they may believe that they cannot be nurturant, even in their role as father. For women, the cost in the workplace can be enormous. Women who violate the stereotype of being nurturant and nice can be penalized in hiring and evaluations. Rudman and Glick (1999), for example, found that female job applicants who displayed agentic qualities received considerably lower hireability ratings than agentic male applicants ($d = 0.92$) for a managerial job that had been "feminized" to require not only technical skills and the ability to work under pressure but also the ability to be helpful and sensitive to the needs of others. The researchers concluded that women must present themselves as competent and agentic to be hired, but they may then be viewed as interpersonally deficient and uncaring and receive biased work evaluations because of their violation of the female nurturance stereotype.

A second example of the costs of unwarranted validation of the stereotype of women as caring nurturers comes from Eagly, Makhijani, and Klonsky's (1992) meta-analysis of studies of gender and the evaluation of leaders. Overall, women leaders were evaluated as positively as men leaders ($d = 0.05$). However, women leaders portrayed as uncaring autocrats were at a more substantial disadvantage than were men leaders portrayed similarly ($d = 0.30$). Women who violated the caring stereotype paid for it in their evaluations. The persistence of the stereotype of women as nurturers leads to serious costs for women who violate this stereotype in the workplace.

The costs of overinflated claims of gender differences hit children as well. According to stereotypes, boys are better at math than girls are (Hyde, Fennema, Ryan, Frost, & Hopp, 1990). This stereotype is proclaimed in mass media headlines (Barnett & Rivers, 2004). Meta-analyses, however, indicate a pattern of gender similarities for math performance. Hedges and Nowell (1995) found a d of 0.16 for large national samples of adolescents, and Hyde, Fennema, and Lamon (1990) found a d of -0.05 for samples of the general population (see also Leahey & Guo, 2000). One cost to children is that mathematically talented girls may be overlooked by parents and teachers because these adults do not expect to find mathematical talent among girls. Parents have lower expectations for their daughters' math success than for their sons' (Lummis & Stevenson, 1990), despite the fact that girls earn better grades in math than boys do (Kimball, 1989). Research has shown repeatedly that parents' expectations for their children's mathematics success relate strongly to outcomes such as the child's mathematics self-confidence and performance, with support for a model in which parents' expectations influence children (e.g., Frome & Eccles, 1998). In short, girls may find their confidence in their ability to succeed in challenging math courses or in a mathematically oriented career undermined by parents' and teachers' beliefs that girls are weak in math ability.

In the realm of intimate heterosexual relationships, women and men are told that they are as different as if they came from different planets and that they communicate in dramatically different ways (Gray, 1992; Tannen, 1991). When relationship conflicts occur, good communication is essential to resolving the conflict (Gottman, 1994). If, however, women and men believe what they have been told—that it is almost impossible for them to communicate with each other—they may simply give up on trying to resolve the conflict through better communication. Therapists will need to dispel erroneous beliefs in massive, unbridgeable gender differences.

Inflated claims about psychological gender differences can hurt boys as well. A large gender gap in self-esteem beginning in adolescence has been touted in popular sources (American Association of University Women, 1991; Orenstein, 1994; Pipher, 1994). Girls' self-esteem is purported to take a nosedive at the beginning of adolescence, with the implication that boys' self-esteem does not. Yet meta-analytic estimates of the magnitude of the gender difference have all been small or close to zero: $d = 0.21$ (Kling et al., 1999, Analysis I), $d = 0.04–0.16$ (Kling et al., 1999, Analysis II), and $d = 0.14$ (Major, Barr, Zubek, & Babey, 1999). In short, self-esteem is roughly as much a problem for adolescent boys as it is for adolescent girls. The popular media's focus on girls as the ones with self-esteem problems may carry a huge cost in leading parents, teachers, and other professionals to overlook boys' self-esteem problems, so that boys do not receive the interventions they need.

As several of these examples indicate, the gender similarities hypothesis carries strong implications for practitioners. The scientific evidence does not support the belief that men and women have inherent difficulties in communicating across gender. Neither does the evidence support the belief that adolescent girls are the only ones with self-esteem problems. Therapists who base their practice in the differences model should reconsider their approach on the basis of the best scientific evidence.

Conclusion

The gender similarities hypothesis stands in stark contrast to the differences model, which holds that men and women, and boys and girls, are vastly different psychologically. The gender similarities hypothesis states, instead, that males and females are alike on most—but not all—psychological variables. Extensive evidence from meta-analyses of research on gender differences supports the gender similarities hypothesis. A few notable exceptions are some motor behaviors (e.g., throwing distance) and some aspects of sexuality, which show large gender differences. Aggression shows a gender difference that is moderate in magnitude.

It is time to consider the costs of overinflated claims of gender differences. Arguably, they cause harm in numerous realms, including women's opportunities in the workplace, couple conflict and communication, and analyses of self-esteem problems among adolescents. Most important, these claims are not consistent with the scientific data.

References

American Association of University Women. (1991). *Shortchanging girls, shortchanging America: Full data report*. Washington, DC: Author.

Anderson, K. J., & Leaper, C. (1998). Meta-analyses of gender effects on conversational interruption: Who, what, when, where, and how. *Sex Roles, 39*, 225–252.

AnnOnline. (2005). *Biography: Deborah Tannen*. Retrieved January 10, 2005, from http://www.annonline.com.

Archer, J. (2004). Sex differences in aggression in real-world setting: A meta-analytic review. *Review of General Psychology, 8*, 291–322.

Barnett, R., & Rivers, C. (2004). *Same difference: How gender myths are hurting our relationships, our children, and our jobs*. New York: Basic Books.

Bettencourt, B. A., & Miller, N. (1996). Gender differences in aggression as a function of provocation: A meta-analysis. *Psychological Bulletin, 119*, 422–447.

Brown, R. P., & Josephs, R. A. (1999). A burden of proof: Stereotype relevance and gender differences in math performance. *Journal of Personality and Social Psychology, 76*, 246–257.

Bussey, K., & Bandura, A. (1999). Social cognitive theory of gender development and differentiation. *Psychological Review, 106*, 676–713.

Crick, N. R., & Grotpeter, J. K. (1995). Relational aggression, gender, and social–psychological adjustment. *Child Development, 66*, 710–722.

Deaux, K., & Major, B. (1987). Putting gender into context: An interactive model of gender-related behavior. *Psychological Review, 94*, 369–389.

Dindia, K., & Allen, M. (1992). Sex differences in self-disclosure: A meta-analysis. *Psychological Bulletin, 112*, 106–124.

Eagly, A. H., & Carli, L. L. (1981). Sex of researchers and sex-typed communications as determinants of sex differences in influenceability: A meta-analysis of social influence studies. *Psychological Bulletin, 90*, 1–20.

Eagly, A. H., & Crowley, M. (1986). Gender and helping behavior: A meta-analytic review of the social psychological literature. *Psychological Bulletin, 100*, 283–308.

Eagly, A. H., Johannesen-Schmidt, M. C., & van Engen, M. L. (2003). Transformational, transactional, and laissez-faire leadership styles: A meta-analysis comparing women and men. *Psychological Bulletin, 129*, 569–591.

Eagly, A. H., & Johnson, B. T. (1990). Gender and leadership style: A meta-analysis. *Psychological Bulletin, 108*, 233–256.

Eagly, A. H., Karau, S. J., & Makhijani, M. G. (1995). Gender and the effectiveness of leaders: A meta-analysis. *Psychological Bulletin, 117*, 125–145.

Eagly, A. H., Makhijani, M. G., & Klonsky, B. G. (1992). Gender and the evaluation of leaders: A meta-analysis. *Psychological Bulletin, 111*, 3–22.

Eagly, A. H., & Steffen, V. (1986). Gender and aggressive behavior: A meta-analytic review of the social psychological literature. *Psychological Bulletin, 100*, 309–330.

Eagly, A. H., & Wood, W. (1999). The origins of sex differences in human behavior: Evolved dispositions versus social roles. *American Psychologist, 54*, 408–423.

Eaton, W. O., & Enns, L. R. (1986). Sex differences in human motor activity level. *Psychological Bulletin, 100*, 19–28.

Epstein, C. F. (1988). *Deceptive distinctions: Sex, gender, and the social order*. New Haven, CT: Yale University Press.

Feingold, A. (1988). Cognitive gender differences are disappearing. *American Psychologist, 43,* 95–103.

———. (1994). Gender differences in personality: A meta-analysis. *Psychological Bulletin, 116,* 429–456.

Feingold, A., & Mazzella, R. (1998). Gender differences in body image are increasing. *Psychological Science, 9,* 190–195.

Frome, P. M., & Eccles, J. S. (1998). Parents' influence on children's achievement-related perceptions. *Journal of Personality and Social Psychology, 74,* 435–452.

Gilligan, C. (1982). *In a different voice: Psychological theory and women's development.* Cambridge, MA: Harvard University Press.

Glass, G. V., McGaw, B., & Smith, M. L. (1981). *Meta-analysis in social research.* Beverly Hills, CA: Sage.

Gleitman, H. (1981). *Psychology.* New York: Norton.

Gottman, J. (1994). *Why marriages succeed or fail.* New York: Simon & Schuster.

Gray, J. (1992). *Men are from Mars, women are from Venus: A practical guide for improving communication and getting what you want in your relationships.* New York: HarperCollins.

———. (2005). *John Gray, Ph.D. is the best-selling relationship author of all time.* Retrieved January 10, 2005, from http://www.marsvenus.com.

Hedges, L. V., & Becker, B. J. (1986). Statistical methods in the meta-analysis of research on gender differences. In J. S. Hyde & M. C. Linn (Eds.), *The psychology of gender: Advances through meta-analysis* (pp. 14–50). Baltimore: Johns Hopkins University Press.

Hedges, L. V., & Nowell, A. (1995, July 7). Sex differences in mental test scores, variability, and numbers of high-scoring individuals. *Science, 269,* 41–45.

Hedges, L. V., & Olkin, I. (1985). *Statistical methods for meta-analysis.* San Diego, CA: Academic Press.

Hollingworth, L. S. (1918). Comparison of the sexes in mental traits. *Psychological Bulletin, 15,* 427–432.

Hyde, J. S. (1981). How large are cognitive gender differences? A meta-analysis using w^2 and d. *American Psychologist, 36,* 892–901.

———. (1984). How large are gender differences in aggression? A developmental meta-analysis. *Developmental Psychology, 20,* 722–736.

———. (1985). *Half the human experience: The psychology of women* (3rd ed.). Lexington, MA: Heath.

———. (1986). Gender differences in aggression. In J. S. Hyde & M. C. Linn (Eds.), *The psychology of gender: Advances through meta-analysis* (pp. 51–66). Baltimore: Johns Hopkins University Press.

Hyde, J. S., Fennema, E., & Lamon, S. (1990). Gender differences in mathematics performance: A meta-analysis. *Psychological Bulletin, 107,* 139–155.

Hyde, J. S., Fennema, E., Ryan, M., Frost, L. A., & Hopp, C. (1990). Gender comparisons of mathematics attitudes and affect: A meta-analysis. *Psychology of Women Quarterly, 14,* 299–324.

Hyde, J. S., & Linn, M. C. (1988). Gender differences in verbal ability: A meta-analysis. *Psychological Bulletin, 104,* 53–69.

Hyde, J. S., & Plant, E. A. (1995). Magnitude of psychological gender differences: Another side to the story. *American Psychologist, 50,* 159–161.

Jaffee, S., & Hyde, J. S. (2000). Gender differences in moral orientation: A meta-analysis. *Psychological Bulletin, 126,* 703–726.

Kimball, M. M. (1989). A new perspective on women's math achievement. *Psychological Bulletin, 105,* 198–214.

———. (1995). *Feminist visions of gender similarities and differences.* Binghamton, NY: Haworth Press.

Kling, K. C., Hyde, J. S., Showers, C. J., & Buswell, B. N. (1999). Gender differences in self-esteem: A meta-analysis. *Psychological Bulletin, 125,* 470–500.

Knight, G. P., Guthrie, I. K., Page, M. C., & Fabes, R. A. (2002). Emotional arousal and gender differences in aggression: A meta-analysis. *Aggressive Behavior, 28,* 366–393.

Konrad, A. M., Ritchie, J. E., Lieb, P., & Corrigall, E. (2000). Sex differences and similarities in job attribute preferences: A meta-analysis. *Psychological Bulletin, 126,* 593–641.

LaFrance, M., Hecht, M. A., & Paluck, E. L. (2003). The contingent smile: A meta-analysis of sex differences in smiling. *Psychological Bulletin, 129,* 305–334.

Leahey, E., & Guo, G. (2000). Gender differences in mathematical trajectories. *Social Forces, 80,* 713–732.

Leaper, C., & Smith, T. E. (2004). A meta-analytic review of gender variations in children's language use: Talkativeness, affiliative speech, and assertive speech. *Developmental Psychology, 40,* 993–1027.

Lefrançois, G. R. (1990). *The lifespan* (3rd ed.). Belmont, CA: Wadsworth.

Lightdale, J. R., & Prentice, D. A. (1994). Rethinking sex differences in aggression: Aggressive behavior in the absence of social roles. *Personality and Social Psychology Bulletin, 20,* 34–44.

Linn, M. C., & Petersen, A. C. (1985). Emergence and characterization of sex differences in spatial ability: A meta-analysis. *Child Development, 56,* 1479–1498.

Lummis, M., & Stevenson, H. W. (1990). Gender differences in beliefs and achievement: A cross-cultural study. *Developmental Psychology, 26,* 254–263.

Lynn, R., & Irwing, P. (2004). Sex differences on the progressive matrices: A meta-analysis. *Intelligence, 32,* 481–498.

Maccoby, E. E., & Jacklin, C. N. (1974). *The psychology of sex differences.* Stanford, CA: Stanford University Press.

Major, B., Barr, L., Zubek, J., & Babey, S. H. (1999). Gender and self-esteem: A meta-analysis. In W.B. Swann, J. H. Langlois, & L. A. Gilbert (Eds.), *Sexism and stereotypes in modern society: The gender science of Janet Taylor Spence* (pp. 223–253). Washington, DC: American Psychological Association.

McClure, E. B. (2000). A meta-analytic review of sex differences in facial expression processing and their development in infants, children, and adolescents. *Psychological Bulletin, 126,* 424–453.

Murnen, S. K., & Stockton, M. (1997). Gender and self-reported sexual arousal in response to sexual stimuli: A meta-analytic review. *Sex Roles, 37,* 135–154.

Oliver, M. B., & Hyde, J. S. (1993). Gender differences in sexuality: A meta-analysis. *Psychological Bulletin, 114,* 29–51.

Orenstein, P. (1994). *Schoolgirls: Young women, self-esteem, and the confidence gap.* New York: Anchor Books.

Pinquart, M., & Sörensen (2001). Gender differences in self-concept and psychological well-being in old age: A meta-analysis. *Journal of Gerontology: Psychological Sciences, 56B,* P195–P213.

Pipher, M. (1994). *Reviving Ophelia: Saving the selves of adolescent girls.* New York: Ballantine Books.

Quinn, D. M., & Spencer, S. J. (2001). The interference of stereotype threat with women's generation of mathematical problem-solving strategies. *Journal of Social Issues, 57,* 55–72.

Rosenthal, R. (1991). *Meta-analytic procedures for social research* (Rev. ed.). Newbury Park, CA: Sage.

Rudman, L. A., & Glick, P. (1999). Feminized management and backlash toward agentic women: The hidden costs to women of a kinder, gentler image of middle managers. *Journal of Personality and Social Psychology, 77,* 1004–1010.

Shields, S. A. (1975). Functionalism, Darwinism, and the psychology of women: A study in social myth. *American Psychologist, 30,* 739–754.

Silverman, I. W. (2003). Gender differences in delay of gratification: A meta-analysis. *Sex Roles, 49,* 451–463.

Spencer, S. J., Steele, C. M., & Quinn, D. M. (1999). Stereotype threat and women's math performance. *Journal of Experimental Social Psychology, 35,* 4–28.

Steele, C. M. (1997). A threat in the air: How stereotypes shape intellectual identity and performance. *American Psychologist, 52,* 613–629.

Steele, C. M., & Aronson, J. (1995). Stereotype threat and the intellectual test performance of African Americans. *Journal of Personality and Social Psychology, 69,* 797–811.

Stuhlmacher, A. C., & Walters, A. E. (1999). Gender differences in negotiation outcome: A meta-analysis. *Personnel Psychology, 52,* 653–677.

Tamres, L. K., Janicki, D., & Helgeson, V. S. (2002). Sex differences in coping behavior: A meta-analytic review and an examination of relative coping. *Personality and Social Psychology Review, 6,* 2–30.

Tannen, D. (1991). *You just don't understand: Women and men in conversation.* New York: Ballantine Books.

Thoma, S. J. (1986). Estimating gender differences in the comprehension and preference of moral issues. *Developmental Review, 6,* 165–180.

Thomas, J. R., & French, K. E. (1985). Gender differences across age in motor performance: A meta-analysis. *Psychological Bulletin, 98,* 260–282.

Thorndike, E. L. (1914). *Educational psychology* (Vol. 3). New York: Teachers College, Columbia University.

Twenge, J. M., & Nolen-Hoeksema. S. (2002). Age, gender, race, socioeconomic status, and birth cohort differences on the Children's Depression Inventory: A meta-analysis. *Journal of Abnormal Psychology, 111,* 578–588.

Voyer, D., Voyer, S., & Bryden, M. P. (1995). Magnitude of sex differences in spatial abilities: A meta-analysis and consideration of critical variables. *Psychological Bulletin, 117,* 250–270.

Walker, L. J. (1984). Sex differences in the development of moral reasoning: A critical review. *Child Development, 55,* 677–691.

Walsh, M., Hickey, C., & Duffy, J. (1999). Influence of item content and stereotype situation on gender differences in mathematical problem solving. *Sex Roles, 41,* 219–240.

Walters, A. E., Stuhlmacher, A. F., & Meyer, L. L. (1998). Gender and negotiator competitiveness: A meta-analysis. *Organizational Behavior and Human Decision Processes, 76,* 1–29.

White, J. W., & Kowalski, R. M. (1994). Deconstructing the myth of the nonaggressive woman: A feminist analysis. *Psychology of Women Quarterly, 18,* 487–508.

Whitley, B. E. (1997). Gender differences in computer-related attitudes and behavior: A meta-analysis. *Computers in Human Behavior, 13,* 1–22.

Whitley, B. E., McHugh, M. C., & Frieze, I. H. (1986). Assessing the theoretical models for sex differences in causal attributions of success and failure. In J. S. Hyde & M. C. Linn (Eds.), *The psychology of gender: Advances through meta-analysis* (pp. 102–135). Baltimore: Johns Hopkins University Press.

Whitley, B. E., Nelson, A. B., & Jones, C. J. (1999). Gender differences in cheating attitudes and classroom cheating behavior: A meta-analysis. *Sex Roles, 41,* 657–677.

Wood, W., Rhodes, N., & Whelan, M. (1989). Sex differences in positive well-being: A consideration of emotional style and marital status. *Psychological Bulletin, 106,* 249–264.

Woolley, H. T. (1914). The psychology of sex. *Psychological Bulletin, 11,* 353–379.

"Dude, You're a Fag": Adolescent Masculinity and the Fag Discourse

C. J. PASCOE

"There's a faggot over there! There's a faggot over there! Come look!" yelled Brian, a senior at River High School, to a group of 10-year-old boys. Following Brian, the 10-year-olds dashed down a hallway. At the end of the hallway Brian's friend, Dan, pursed his lips and began sashaying towards the 10-year-olds. He minced towards them, swinging his hips exaggeratedly and wildly waving his arms. To the boys Brian yelled, "Look at the faggot! Watch out! He'll get you!" In response the 10-year-olds raced back down the hallway screaming in terror.

(From author's fieldnotes)

The relationship between adolescent masculinity and sexuality is embedded in the specter of the faggot. Faggots represent a penetrated masculinity in which "to be penetrated is to abdicate power" (Bersani, 1987: 212). Penetrated men symbolize a masculinity devoid of power, which, in its contradiction, threatens both psychic and social chaos. It is precisely this specter of penetrated masculinity that functions as a regulatory mechanism of gender for contemporary American adolescent boys.

Feminist scholars of masculinity have documented the centrality of homophobic insults to

C. J. Pascoe, "'Dude, You're a Fag': Adolescent Masculinity and the Fag Discourse," *Sexualities,* Vol. 8, No. 3 (2005), pp. 329–346. Copyright © 2005 by SAGE Publications. Reprinted by permission of SAGE Publications.

masculinity (Lehne, 1998; Kimmel, 2001) especially in school settings (Wood, 1984; Smith, 1998; Burn, 2000; Plummer, 2001; Kimmel, 2003). They argue that homophobic teasing often characterizes masculinity in adolescence and early adulthood, and that anti-gay slurs tend to primarily be directed at other gay boys.

This article both expands on and challenges these accounts of relationships between homophobia and masculinity. Homophobia is indeed a central mechanism in the making of contemporary American adolescent masculinity. This article both critiques and builds on this finding by (1) pointing to the limits of an argument that focuses centrally on homophobia, (2) demonstrating that the fag is not only an identity linked to homosexual boys[1] but an identity that can temporarily adhere to heterosexual boys as well and (3) highlighting the racialized nature of the fag as a disciplinary mechanism.

"Homophobia" is too facile a term with which to describe the deployment of "fag" as an epithet. By calling the use of the word "fag" homophobia—and letting the argument stop with that point—previous research obscures the gendered nature of sexualized insults (Plummer, 2001). Invoking homophobia to describe the ways in which boys aggressively tease each other overlooks the powerful relationship between masculinity and this sort of insult. Instead, it seems incidental in this conventional line of argument that girls do not harass each other and are not harassed in this same manner.[2] This framing naturalizes the relationship between masculinity and homophobia, thus obscuring the centrality of such harassment in the formation of a gendered identity for boys in a way that it is not for girls.

"Fag" is not necessarily a static identity attached to a particular (homosexual) boy. Fag talk and fag imitations serve as a discourse with which boys discipline themselves and each other through joking relationships.[3] Any boy can temporarily become a fag in a given social space or interaction. This does not mean that those boys who identify as or are perceived to be homosexual are not subject to intense harassment. But becoming a fag has as much to do with failing at the masculine tasks

of competence, heterosexual prowess and strength or in any way revealing weakness or femininity, as it does with a sexual identity. This fluidity of the fag identity is what makes the specter of the fag such a powerful disciplinary mechanism. It is fluid enough that boys police most of their behaviors out of fear of having the fag identity permanently adhere and definitive enough so that boys recognize a fag behavior and strive to avoid it.

The fag discourse is racialized. It is invoked differently by and in relation to white boys' bodies than it is by and in relation to African-American boys' bodies. While certain behaviors put all boys at risk for becoming temporarily a fag, some behaviors can be enacted by African-American boys without putting them at risk of receiving the label. The racialized meanings of the fag discourse suggest that something more than simple homophobia is involved in these sorts of interactions. An analysis of boys' deployments of the specter of the fag should also extend to the ways in which gendered power works through racialized selves. It is not that this gendered homophobia does not exist in African-American communities. Indeed, making fun of "Negro faggotry seems to be a rite of passage among contemporary black male rappers and filmmakers" (Riggs, 1991: 253). However, the fact that "white women and men, gay and straight, have more or less colonized cultural debates about sexual representation" (Julien and Mercer, 1991: 167) obscures varied systems of sexualized meanings among different racialized ethnic groups (Almaguer, 1991; King, 2004).

Theoretical Framing

The sociology of masculinity entails a "critical study of men, their behaviors, practices, values and perspectives" (Whitehead and Barrett, 2001: 14). Recent studies of men emphasize the multiplicity of masculinity (Connell, 1995) detailing the ways in which different configurations of gender practice are promoted, challenged or reinforced in given social situations. This research on how men do masculinities has explored gendered practices in a wide range of social institutions, such as families (Coltrane, 2001), schools (Skelton, 1996; Parker, 1996;

Mac and Ghaill, 1996; Francis and Skelton, 2001), workplaces (Cooper, 2000), media (Craig, 1992), and sports (Messner, 1989; Edly and Wetherel, 1997; Curry, 2004). Many of these studies have developed specific typologies of masculinities: gay, Black, Chicano, working class, middle class, Asian, gay Black, gay Chicano, white working class, militarized, transnational business, New Man, negotiated, versatile, healthy, toxic, counter, and cool masculinities, to name a few (Messner, 2004). In this sort of model the fag could be (and often has been) framed as a type of subordinated masculinity attached to homosexual adolescent boys' bodies.

Heeding Timothy Carrigan's admonition that an "analysis of masculinity needs to be related as well to other currents in feminism" (Carrigan et al., 1987: 552), in this article I integrate queer theory's insights about the relationships between gender, sexuality, identities and power with the attention to men found in the literature on masculinities. Like the sociology of gender, queer theory destabilizes the assumed naturalness of the social order (Lemert, 1996). Queer theory is a "conceptualization which sees sexual power as embedded in different levels of social life" and interrogates areas of the social world not usually seen as sexuality (Stein and Plummer, 1994). In this sense queer theory calls for sexuality to be looked at not only as a discrete arena of sexual practices and identities, but also as a constitutive element of social life (Warner, 1993; Epstein, 1996).

While the masculinities' literature rightly highlights very real inequalities between gay and straight men (see for instance Connell, 1995), this emphasis on sexuality as inhered in static identities attached to male bodies, rather than major organizing principles of social life (Sedgwick, 1990), limits scholars' ability to analyze the myriad ways in which sexuality, in part, constitutes gender. This article does not seek to establish that there are homosexual boys and heterosexual boys and the homosexual ones are marginalized. Rather this article explores what happens to theories of gender if we look at a *discourse* of sexualized identities in addition to focusing on seemingly static identity categories inhabited by men. This is not

to say that gender is reduced only to sexuality, indeed feminist scholars have demonstrated that gender is embedded in and constitutive of a multitude of social structures—the economy, places of work, families and schools. In the tradition of post-structural feminist theorists of race and gender who look at "border cases" that explode taken-for-granted binaries of race and gender (Smith, 1994), queer theory is another tool which enables an integrated analysis of sexuality, gender and race.

As scholars of gender have demonstrated, gender is accomplished through day-to-day interactions (Fine, 1987; Hochschild, 1989; West and Zimmerman, 1991; Thorne, 1993). In this sense, gender is the "activity of managing situated conduct in light of normative conceptions of attitudes and activities appropriate for one's sex category" (West and Zimmerman, 1991: 127). Similarly, queer theorist Judith Butler argues that gender is accomplished interactionally through "a set of repeated acts within a highly rigid regulatory frame that congeal over time to produce the appearance of substance, of a natural sort of being" (Butler, 1999: 43). Specifically she argues that gendered beings are created through processes of citation and repudiation of a "constitutive outside" (Butler, 1993: 3) in which is contained all that is cast out of a socially recognizable gender category. The "constitutive outside" is inhabited by abject identities, unrecognizably and unacceptably gendered selves. The interactional accomplishment of gender in a Butlerian model consists, in part, of the continual iteration and repudiation of this abject identity. Gender, in this sense, is "constituted through the force of exclusion and abjection, on which produces a constitutive outside to the subject, an abjected outside, which is, after all, 'inside' the subject as its own founding repudiation" (Butler, 1993: 3). This repudiation creates and reaffirms a "threatening specter" (Butler, 1993: 3) of failed, unrecognizable gender, the existence of which must be continually repudiated through interactional processes.

I argue that the "fag" position is an "abject" position and, as such, is a "threatening specter" constituting contemporary American adolescent masculinity. The fag discourse is the interactional process through which boys name and repudiate this abjected identity. Rather than analyzing the fag as an identity for homosexual boys, I examine uses of the discourse that imply that any boy can become a fag, regardless of his actual desire or self-perceived sexual orientation. The threat of the abject position infuses the faggot with regulatory power. This article provides empirical data to illustrate Butler's approach to gender and indicates that it might be a useful addition to the sociological literature on masculinities through highlighting one of the ways in which a masculine gender identity is accomplished through interaction.

Method
Research Site

I conducted fieldwork at a suburban high school in north-central California which I call River High.[4] River High is a working class, suburban 50-year-old high school located in a town called Riverton. With the exception of the median household income and racial diversity (both of which are elevated due to Riverton's location in California), the town mirrors national averages in the percentages of white-collar workers, rates of college attendance and marriages, and age composition (according to the 2000 census). It is a politically moderate to conservative, religious community. Most of the students' parents commute to surrounding cities for work.

On average, Riverton is a middle-class community. However, students at River are likely to refer to the town as two communities: "Old Riverton" and "New Riverton." A busy highway and railroad tracks bisect the town into these two sections. River High is literally on the "wrong side of the tracks," in Old Riverton. Exiting the freeway, heading north to Old Riverton, one sees a mix of 1950s-era ranch-style homes, some with neatly trimmed lawns and tidy gardens, others with yards strewn with various car parts, lawn chairs and appliances. Old Riverton is visually bounded by smoke-puffing factories. On the other side of the freeway New Riverton is characterized by wide sidewalk-lined streets and new walled-in home developments. Instead of smokestacks, a forested mountain, home to a state park, rises

majestically in the background. The teens from these homes attend Hillside High, River's rival.

River High is attended by 2,000 students. River High's racial/ethnic breakdown roughly represents California at large: 50 percent white, 9 percent African-American, 28 percent Latino and 6 percent Asian (as compared to California's 46, 6, 32, and 11 percent, respectively, according to census data and school records). The students at River High are primarily working class.

Research

I gathered data using the qualitative method of ethnographic research. I spent a year and a half conducting observations, formally interviewing 49 students at River High (36 boys and 13 girls), one male student from Hillside High, and conducting countless informal interviews with students, faculty and administrators. I concentrated on one school because I explore the richness rather than the breadth of data (for other examples of this method see Willis, 1981; MacLeod, 1987; Eder et al., 1995; Ferguson, 2000).

I recruited students for interviews by conducting presentations in a range of classes and hanging around at lunch, before school, after school and at various events talking to different groups of students about my research, which I presented as "writing a book about guys." The interviews usually took place at school, unless the student had a car, in which case he or she met me at one of the local fast food restaurants where I treated them to a meal. Interviews lasted anywhere from half an hour to two hours.

The initial interviews I conducted helped me to map a gendered and sexualized geography of the school, from which I chose my observation sites. I observed a "neutral" site—a senior government classroom, where sexualized meanings were subdued. I observed three sites that students marked as "fag" sites—two drama classes and the Gay/Straight Alliance. I also observed two normatively "masculine" sites—auto-shop and weightlifting.[5] I took daily fieldnotes focusing on how students, faculty and administrators negotiated, regulated and resisted particular meanings of gender and sexuality. I attended major school rituals such as

Winter Ball, school rallies, plays, dances and lunches. I would also occasionally "ride along" with Mr. Johnson (Mr. J.), the school's security guard, on his battery-powered golf cart to watch which, how and when students were disciplined. Observational data provided me with more insight to the interactional processes of masculinity than simple interviews yielded. If I had relied only on interview data, I would have missed the interactional processes of masculinity which are central to the fag discourse.

Given the importance of appearance in high school, I gave some thought as to how I would present myself, deciding to both blend in and set myself apart from the students. In order to blend in I wore my standard graduate student gear— comfortable, baggy cargo pants, a black t-shirt or sweater and tennis shoes. To set myself apart I carried a messenger bag instead of a back-pack, didn't wear makeup, and spoke slightly differently than the students by using some slang, but refraining from uttering the ubiquitous "hecka" and "hella."

The boys were fascinated by the fact that a 30-something white "girl" (their words) was interested in studying them. While at first many would make sexualized comments asking me about my dating life or saying that they were going to "hit on" me, it seemed eventually they began to forget about me as a potential sexual/romantic partner. Part of this, I think, was related to my knowledge about "guy" things. For instance, I lift weights on a regular basis and as a result the weightlifting coach introduced me as a "weight-lifter from U.C. Berkeley" telling the students they should ask me for weightlifting advice. Additionally, my taste in movies and television shows often coincided with theirs. I am an avid fan of the movies "Jackass" and "Fight Club," both of which contain high levels of violence and "bathroom" humor. Finally, I garnered a lot of points among boys because I live off a dangerous street in a nearby city famous for drug deals, gang fights, and frequent gun shots.

What Is a Fag?

"Since you were little boys you've been told, 'hey, don't be a little faggot,'" explained Darnell, an African-American football player, as we sat on a bench next to the athletic field. Indeed, both the boys and girls I interviewed told me that "fag" was the worst epithet one guy could direct at another. Jeff, a slight white sophomore, explained to me that boys call each other fag because "gay people aren't really liked over here and stuff." Jeremy, a Latino junior, told me that this insult literally reduced a boy to nothing: "To call someone gay or fag is like the lowest thing you can call someone. Because that's like saying that you're nothing."

Most guys explained their or others' dislike of fags by claiming that homophobia is just part of what it means to be a guy. For instance Keith, a white soccer-playing senior, explained, "I think guys are just homophobic." However, it is not just homophobia, it is a *gendered* homophobia. Several students told me that these homophobic insults only applied to boys and not girls. For example, while Jake, a handsome white senior, told me that he didn't like gay people, he quickly added, "Lesbians, okay that's *good*." Similarly Cathy, a popular white cheerleader, told me "Being a lesbian is accepted because guys think 'oh that's cool.'" Darnell, after telling me that boys were told not to be faggots, said of lesbians, "They're [guys are] fine with girls. I think it's the guy part that they're like ewwww!" In this sense it is not strictly homophobia, but a gendered homophobia that constitutes adolescent masculinity in the culture of this school. However, it is clear, according to these comments, that lesbians are "good" because of their place in heterosexual male fantasy, not necessarily because of some enlightened approach to same-sex relationships. It does, however, indicate that using only the term homophobia to describe boys' repeated use of the word "fag" might be a bit simplistic and misleading.

Additionally, girls at River High rarely deployed the word "fag" and were never called "fags." I recorded girls uttering "fag" only three times during my research. In one instance, Angela, a Latina cheerleader, teased Jeremy, a well-liked white senior involved in student government, for not ditching school with her, "You wouldn't 'cause you're a faggot." However, girls did not use this word as part of their regular lexicon. The sort of gendered homophobia that constitutes adolescent masculinity does not constitute adolescent femininity. Girls were not called dykes or lesbians in any sort of regular or systematic way. Students did tell me that "slut" was the worst thing a girl could be called. However, my fieldnotes indicate that the word "slut" (or its synonym "ho") appears one time for every eight times the word "fag" appears. Even when it does occur, "slut" is rarely deployed as a direct insult against another girl.

Highlighting the difference between the deployment of "gay" and "fag" as insults brings the gendered nature of this homophobia into focus. For boys and girls at River High "gay" is a fairly common synonym for "stupid." While this word shares the sexual origins of "fag," it does not *consistently* have the skew of gender-loaded meaning. Girls and boys often used "gay" as an adjective referring to inanimate objects and male or female people, whereas they used "fag" as a noun that denotes only un-masculine males. Students used "gay" to describe anything from someone's clothes to a new school rule that the students did not like, as in the following encounter:

> In auto-shop Arnie pulled out a large older version black laptop computer and placed it on his desk. Behind him Nick said "That's a gay laptop! It's five inches thick!"

A laptop can be gay, a movie can be gay or a group of people can be gay. Boys used "gay" and "fag" interchangeably when they refer to other boys, but "fag" does not have the non-gendered attributes that "gay" sometimes invokes.

While its meanings are not the same as "gay," "fag" does have multiple meanings which do not necessarily replace its connotations as a homophobic slur, but rather exist alongside. Some boys took pains to say that "fag" is not about sexuality. Darnell told me "It doesn't even have anything to do with being gay." J. L., a white sophomore at Hillside High (River High's cross-town rival), asserted "Fag, seriously, it has nothing to do with sexual preference at all. You could just be calling somebody an idiot you know?" I asked Ben, a quiet, white sophomore who wore heavy metal t-shirts to auto-shop each day, "What kind of things do guys get called a fag for?" Ben answered

"Anything . . . literally, anything. Like you were trying to turn a wrench the wrong way, 'dude, you're a fag.' Even if a piece of meat drops out of your sandwich, 'you fag!'" Each time Ben said "you fag" his voice deepened as if he were imitating a more masculine boy. While Ben might rightly *feel* like a guy could be called a fag for "anything . . . literally, anything," there are actually specific behaviors which, when enacted by most boys, can render him more vulnerable to a fag epithet. In this instance Ben's comment highlights the use of "fag" as a generic insult for incompetence, which in the world of River High, is central to a masculine identity. A boy could get called a fag for exhibiting any sort of behavior defined as non-masculine (although not necessarily behaviors aligned with femininity) in the world of River High: being stupid, incompetent, dancing, caring too much about clothing, being too emotional or expressing interest (sexual or platonic) in other guys. However, given the extent of its deployment and the laundry list of behaviors that could get a boy in trouble it is no wonder that Ben felt like a boy could be called "fag" for "anything."

One-third (13) of the boys I interviewed told me that, while they may liberally insult each other with the term, they would not actually direct it at a homosexual peer. Jabes, a Filipino senior, told me

> I actually say it [fag] quite a lot, except for when I'm in the company of an actual homosexual person. Then I try not to say it at all. But when I'm just hanging out with my friends I'll be like, "shut up, I don't want to hear you any more, you stupid fag."

Similarly J. L. compared homosexuality to a disability, saying there is "no way" he'd call an actually gay guy a fag because

> There's people who are the retarded people who nobody wants to associate with. I'll be so nice to those guys and I hate it when people make fun of them. It's like, "bro do you realize that they can't help that?" And then there's gay people. They were born that way.

According to this group of boys, gay is a legitimate, if marginalized, social identity. If a man is gay, there may be a chance he could be considered masculine by other men (Connell, 1995). David, a handsome white senior dressed smartly in khaki pants and a white button-down shirt, said, "Being gay is just a lifestyle. It's someone you choose to sleep with. You can still throw around a football and be gay." In other words there is a possibility, however slight, that a boy can be gay and masculine. To be a fag is, by definition, the opposite of masculine, whether or not the word is deployed with sexualized or non-sexualized meanings. In explaining this to me, Jamaal, an African-American junior, cited the explanation of popular rap artist, Eminem:

> Although I don't like Eminem, he had a good definition of it. It's like taking away your title. In an interview they were like, "you're always capping on gays, but then you sing with Elton John." He was like "I don't mean gay as in gay."

This is what Riki Wilchins calls the "Eminem Exception." Eminem explains that he doesn't call people 'faggot' because of their sexual orientation but because they're weak and unmanly" (Wilchins, 2003). This is precisely the way in which this group of boys at River High uses the term "faggot." While it is not necessarily acceptable to be gay, at least a man who is gay can do other things that render him acceptably masculine. A fag, by the very definition of the word, indicated by students' usages at River High, cannot be masculine. This distinction between "fag" as an unmasculine and problematic identity and "gay" as a possibly masculine, although marginalized, sexual identity is not limited to a teenage lexicon, but is reflected in both psychological discourses (Sedgwick, 1995) and gay and lesbian activism.

Becoming a Fag

"The ubiquity of the word faggot speaks to the reach of its discrediting capacity" (Corbett, 2001: 4). It is almost as if boys cannot help but shout it out on a regular basis—in the hallway, in class, across campus as a greeting, or as a joke. In my fieldwork I was amazed by the way in which the word seemed to pop uncontrollably out of boys' mouths in all kinds of situations. To quote just one of many instances from my fieldnotes:

> Two boys walked out of the P.E. locker room and one yelled "fucking faggot!" at no one in particular.

This spontaneous yelling out of a variation of fag seemingly apropos of nothing happened repeatedly among boys throughout the school.

The fag discourse is central to boys' joking relationships. Joking cements relationships between boys (Kehily and Nayak, 1997; Lyman, 1998) and helps to manage anxiety and discomfort (Freud, 1905). Boys invoked the specter of the fag in two ways: through humorous imitation and through lobbing the epithet at one another. Boys at River High imitated the fag by acting out an exaggerated "femininity," and/or by pretending to sexually desire other boys. As indicated by the introductory vignette in which a predatory "fag" threatens the little boys, boys at River High link these performative scenarios with a fag identity. They lobbed the fag epithet at each other in a verbal game of hot potato, each careful to deflect the insult quickly by hurling it toward someone else. These games and imitations make up a fag discourse which highlights the fag not as a static but rather as a fluid identity which boys constantly struggle to avoid.

In imitative performances the fag discourse functions as a constant reiteration of the fag's existence, affirming that the fag is out there; at any moment a boy can become a fag. At the same time these performances demonstrate that the boy who is invoking the fag is *not* a fag. By invoking it so often, boys remind themselves and each other that at any point they can become fags if they are not sufficiently masculine.

> Mr. McNally, disturbed by the noise outside of the classroom, turned to the open door saying "We'll shut this unless anyone really wants to watch sweaty boys playing basketball." Emir, a tall skinny boy, lisped "I wanna watch the boys play!" The rest of the class cracked up at his imitation.

Through imitating a fag, boys assure others that they are not a fag by immediately becoming masculine again after the performance. They mock their own performed femininity and/or same-sex desire, assuring themselves and others that such an identity is one deserving of derisive laughter. The fag identity in this instance is fluid, detached from Emir's body. He can move in and out of this "abject domain" while simultaneously affirming his position as a subject.

Boys also consistently tried to put another in the fag position by lobbing the fag epithet at one another.

> Going through the junk-filled car in the auto-shop parking lot, Jay poked his head out and asked "Where are Craig and Brian?" Neil, responded with "I think they're over there," pointing, then thrusting his hips and pulling his arms back and forth to indicate that Craig and Brian might be having sex. The boys in auto-shop laughed.

This sort of joke temporarily labels both Craig and Brian as faggots. Because the fag discourse is so familiar, the other boys immediately understand that Neil is indicating that Craig and Brian are having sex. However these are not necessarily identities that stick. Nobody actually thinks Craig and Brian are homosexuals. Rather the fag identity is a fluid one, certainly an identity that no boy wants, but one that a boy can escape, usually by engaging in some sort of discursive contest to turn another boy into a fag. However, fag becomes a hot potato that no boy wants to be left holding. In the following example, which occurred soon after the "sex" joke, Brian lobs the fag epithet at someone else, deflecting it from himself:

> Brian initiated a round of a favorite game in auto-shop, the "cock game." Brian quietly, looking at Josh, said, "Josh loves the cock," then slightly louder, "Josh loves the cock." He continued saying this until he was yelling "JOSH LOVES THE COCK!" The rest of the boys laughed hysterically as Josh slinked away saying "I have a bigger dick than all you mother fuckers!"

These two instances show how the fag can be mapped, momentarily, on to one boy's body and how he, in turn, can attach it to another boy, thus deflecting it from himself. In the first instance Neil makes fun of Craig and Brian for simply hanging out together. In the second instance Brian goes from being a fag to making Josh into a fag, through the "cock game." The "fag" is transferable. Boys move in and out of it by discursively creating another as a fag through joking interactions. They, somewhat ironically, can move in and out of the fag position by transforming themselves, temporarily, into a fag, but this has the effect of reaffirming their masculinity when they return to a heterosexual position after imitating the fag.

These examples demonstrate boys invoking the trope of the fag in a discursive struggle in which the boys indicate that they know what a fag is—and that they are not fags. This joking cements bonds between boys as they assure themselves and each other of their masculinity through repeated repudiations of a non-masculine position of the abject.

Racing the Fag

The fag trope is not deployed consistently or identically across social groups at River High. Differences between white boys' and African-American boys' meaning making around clothes and dancing reveal ways in which the fag as the abject position is racialized.

Clean, oversized, carefully put together clothing is central to a hip-hop identity for African-American boys who identify with hip-hop culture.[6] Richard Majors calls this presentation of self a "cool pose" consisting of "unique, expressive and conspicuous styles of demeanor, speech, gesture, clothing, hairstyle, walk, stance and handshake," developed by African-American men as a symbolic response to institutionalized racism (Majors, 2001: 211). Pants are usually several sizes too big, hanging low on a boy's waist, usually revealing a pair of boxers beneath. Shirts and sweaters are similarly oversized, often hanging down to a boy's knees. Tags are frequently left on baseball hats worn slightly askew and sit perched high on the head. Meticulously clean, unlaced athletic shoes with rolled up socks under the tongue complete a typical hip-hop outfit.

This amount of attention and care given to clothing for white boys not identified with hip-hop culture (that is, most of the white boys at River High) would certainly cast them into an abject, fag position. White boys are not supposed to appear to care about their clothes or appearance, because only fags care about how they look. Ben illustrates this:

> Ben walked in to the auto-shop classroom from the parking lot where he had been working on a particularly oily engine. Grease stains covered his jeans. He looked down at them, made a face and walked toward me with limp wrists, laughing and lisping in a high pitch sing-song voice "I got my good panths all dirty!"

Ben draws on indicators of a fag identity, such as limp wrists, as do the boys in the introductory vignette to illustrate that a masculine person certainly would not care about having dirty clothes. In this sense, masculinity, for white boys, becomes the carefully crafted appearance of not caring about appearance, especially in terms of cleanliness.

However, African-American boys involved in hip-hop culture talk frequently about whether or not their clothes, specifically their shoes, are dirty:

> In drama class both Darnell and Marc compared their white Adidas basketball shoes. Darnell mocked Marc because black scuff marks covered his shoes, asking incredulously "Yours are a week old and they're dirty—I've had mine for a month and they're not dirty!" Both laughed.

Monte, River High's star football player, echoed this concern about dirty shoes when looking at the fancy red shoes he had lent to his cousin the week before, told me he was frustrated because after his cousin used them, the "shoes are hella scuffed up." Clothing, for these boys, does not indicate a fag position, but rather defines membership in a certain cultural and racial group (Perry, 2002).

Dancing is another arena that carries distinctly fag associated meanings for white boys and masculine meanings for African-American boys who participate in hip-hop culture. White boys often associate dancing with "fag." J. L. told me that guys think "'nSync's gay" because they can dance. 'nSync is an all white male singing group known for their dance moves. At dances white boys frequently held their female dates tightly, locking their hips together. The boys never danced with one another,

unless engaged in a round of "hot potato." White boys often jokingly danced together in order to embarrass each other by making someone else into a fag:

> Lindy danced behind her date, Chris. Chris's friend, Matt, walked up and nudged Lindy aside, imitating her dance moves behind Chris. As Matt rubbed his hands up and down Chris's back, Chris turned around and jumped back startled to see Matt there instead of Lindy. Matt cracked up as Chris turned red.

However dancing does not carry this sort of sexualized gender meaning for all boys at River High. For African-American boys dancing demonstrates membership in a cultural community (Best, 2000). African-American boys frequently danced together in single sex groups, teaching each other the latest dance moves, showing off a particularly difficult move or making each other laugh with humorous dance moves. Students recognized K. J. as the most talented dancer at the school. K. J. is a sophomore of African-American and Filipino descent who participated in the hip-hop culture of River High. He continually wore the latest hip-hop fashions. K. J. was extremely popular. Girls hollered his name as they walked down the hall and thrust urgently written love notes folded in complicated designs into his hands as he sauntered to class. For the past two years K. J. won first place in the talent show for dancing. When he danced at assemblies the room reverberated with screamed chants of "Go K. J.! Go K. J.! Go K. J.!" Because dancing for African-American boys places them within a tradition of masculinity, they are not at risk of becoming a fag for this particular gendered practice. Nobody called K. J. a fag. In fact in several of my interviews boys of multiple racial/ethnic backgrounds spoke admiringly of K. J.'s dancing abilities.

Implications

These findings confirm previous studies of masculinity and sexuality that position homophobia as central to contemporary definitions of adolescent masculinity. These data extend previous research by unpacking multilayered meanings that boys deploy through their uses of homophobic language and joking rituals. By attending to these meanings I reframe the discussion as one of a fag discourse, rather than simply labeling this sort of behavior as homophobia. The fag is an "abject" position, a position outside of masculinity that actually constitutes masculinity. Thus, masculinity, in part becomes the daily interactional work of repudiating the "threatening specter" of the fag.

The fag extends beyond a static sexual identity attached to a gay boy. Few boys are permanently identified as fags; most move in and out of fag positions. Looking at "fag" as a discourse rather than a static identity reveals that the term can be invested with different meanings in different social spaces. "Fag" may be used as a weapon with which to temporarily assert one's masculinity by denying it to others. Thus "fag" becomes a symbol around which contests of masculinity take place.

The fag epithet, when hurled at other boys, may or may not have explicit sexual meanings, but it always has gendered meanings. When a boy calls another boy a fag, it means he is not a man, not necessarily that he is a homosexual. The boys in this study know that they are not supposed to call homosexual boys "fags" because that is mean. This, then, has been the limited success of the mainstream gay rights movement. The message absorbed by some of these teenage boys is that "gay men can be masculine, just like you." Instead of challenging gender inequality, this particular discourse of gay rights has reinscribed it. Thus we need to begin to think about how gay men may be in a unique position to challenge gendered as well as sexual norms.

This study indicates that researchers who look at the intersection of sexuality and masculinity need to attend to the ways in which racialized identities may affect how "fag" is deployed and what it means in various social situations. While researchers have addressed the ways in which masculine identities are racialized (Connell, 1995; Ross, 1998; Bucholtz, 1999; Davis, 1999; Price, 1999; Ferguson, 2000; Majors, 2001) they have not paid equal attention to the ways in which "fag" might be a racialized epithet. It is important to look at

when, where and with what meaning "the fag" is deployed in order to get at how masculinity is defined, contested, and invested in among adolescent boys.

Research shows that sexualized teasing often leads to deadly results, as evidenced by the spate of school shootings in the 1990s (Kimmel, 2003). Clearly the fag discourse affects not just homosexual teens, but all boys, gay and straight. Further research could investigate these processes in a variety of contexts: varied geographic locations, sexualized groups, classed groups, religious groups and age groups.

Notes

1. While the term "homosexual" is laden with medicalized and normalizing meanings, I use it instead of "gay" because "gay" in the world of River High has multiple meanings apart from sexual practices or identities.
2. Girls do insult one another based on sexualized meanings. But in my own research I found that girls and boys did not harass girls in this manner with the same frequency that boys harassed each other through engaging in joking about the fag.
3. I use discourse in the Foucauldian sense, to describe truth producing practices, not just text or speech (Foucault, 1978).
4. The names of places and respondents have been changed.
5. Auto-shop was a class in which students learned how to build and repair cars. Many of the students in this course were looking into careers as mechanics.
6. While there are several white and Latino boys at River High who identify with hip-hop culture, hip-hop is identified by the majority of students as an African-American cultural style.

References

Almaguer, Tomas (1991) "Chicano Men: A Cartography of Homosexual Identity and Behavior," *Differences* 3: 75–100.

Bersani, Leo (1987) "Is the Rectum a Grave?" *October* 43: 197–222.

Best, Amy (2000) *Prom Night: Youth, Schools and Popular Culture.* New York: Routledge.

Bucholtz, Mary (1999) "'You Da Man': Narrating the Racial Other in the Production of White Masculinity," *Journal of Sociolinguistics* 3/4: 443–60.

Burn, Shawn M. (2000) "Heterosexuals' Use of 'Fag' and 'Queer' to Deride One Another: A Contributor to Heterosexism and Stigma," *Journal of Homosexuality* 40: 1–11.

Butler, Judith (1993) *Bodies that Matter*. New York: Routledge.

———. (1999) *Gender Trouble*. New York: Routledge.

Carrigan, Tim, Connell, Bob and Lee, John (1985) "Toward a New Sociology of Masculinity," *Theory and Society*, 14(5), 551–604.

Coltrane, Scott (2001) "Selling the Indispensable Father," paper presented at *Pushing the Boundaries Conference: New Conceptualizations of Childhood and Motherhood*, Philadelphia.

Connell, R. W. (1995) *Masculinities*. Berkeley: University of California Press.

Cooper, Marianne (2000) "Being the 'Go-To Guy': Fatherhood, Masculinity and the Organization of Work in Silicon Valley," *Qualitative Sociology* 23: 379–405.

Corbett, Ken (2001) "Faggot = Loser," *Studies in Gender and Sexuality* 2: 3–28.

Craig, Steve (1992) *Men, Masculinity and the Media*. Newbury Park: Sage.

Curry, Timothy J. (2004) "Fraternal Bonding in the Locker Room: A Profeminist Analysis of Talk About Competition and Women," in Michael Messner and Michael Kimmel (eds.) *Men's Lives*. Boston, MA: Pearson.

Davis, James E. (1999) "Forbidden Fruit, Black Males' Constructions of Transgressive Sexualities in Middle School," in William J. Letts IV and James T. Sears (eds.) *Queering Elementary Education: Advancing the Dialogue About Sexualities and Schooling*, pp. 49 ff. Lanham, MD: Rowan & Littlefield.

Eder, Donna, Evans, Catherine and Parker, Stephen (1995) *School Talk: Gender and Adolescent Culture*. New Brunswick, NJ: Rutgers University Press.

Edly, Nigel and Wetherell, Margaret (1997) "Jockeying for Position: The Construction of Masculine Identities," *Discourse and Society* 8: 203–17.

Epstein, Steven (1996) "A Queer Encounter," in Steven Seidman (ed.) *Queer Theory/Sociology*, pp. 188–202. Cambridge, MA: Blackwell.

Ferguson, Ann (2000) *Bad Boys: Public Schools in the Making of Black Masculinity*. Ann Arbor: University of Michigan Press.

Fine, Gary (1987) *With the Boys: Little League Baseball and Preadolescent Culture*. Chicago, IL: University of Chicago Press.

Foucault, Michel (1978) *The History of Sexuality, Volume I*. New York: Vintage Books.

Francis, Becky and Skelton, Christine (2001) "Men Teachers and the Construction of Heterosexual Masculinity in the Classroom," *Sex Education* 1: 9–21.

Freud, Sigmund (1905) *The Basic Writings of Sigmund Freud* (translated and edited by A. A. Brill). New York: The Modern Library.

Hochschild, Arlie (1989) *The Second Shift*. New York: Avon.

Julien, Isaac and Mercer, Kobena (1991) "True Confessions: A Discourse on Images of Black Male Sexuality," in Essex Hemphill (ed.) *Brother to Brother: New Writings by Black Gay Men*, pp. 167–73. Boston, MA: Alyson Publications.

Kehily, Mary Jane and Nayak, Anoop (1997) "Lads and Laughter: Humour and the Production of Heterosexual Masculinities," *Gender and Education* 9: 69–87.

Kimmel, Michael (2001) "Masculinity as Homophobia: Fear, Shame, and Silence in the Construction of Gender Identity," in Stephen Whitehead and Frank Barrett (eds.) *The Masculinities Reader*, pp. 266–87. Cambridge: Polity.

———. (2003) "Adolescent Masculinity, Homophobia, and Violence: Random School Shootings, 1982–2001," *American Behavioral Scientist* 46: 1439–58.

King, D. L. (2004) *Double Lives on the Down Low*. New York: Broadway Books.

Lehne, Gregory (1998) "Homophobia Among Men: Supporting and Defining the Male Role," in Michael Kimmel and Michael Messner (eds.) *Men's Lives*, pp. 237–49. Boston, MA: Allyn and Bacon.

Lemert, Charles (1996) "Series Editor's Preface," in Steven Seidman (ed.) *Queer Theory/Sociology*. Cambridge, MA: Blackwell.

Lyman, Peter (1998) "The Fraternal Bond as a Joking Relationship: A Case Study of the Role of Sexist Jokes in Male Group Bonding," in Michael Kimmel and Michael Messner (eds.) *Men's Lives*, pp. 171–93. Boston, MA: Allyn and Bacon.

Mac and Ghaill, Martain (1996) "What about the Boys—School, Class and Crisis Masculinity," *Sociological Review* 44: 381–97.

MacLeod, Jay (1987) *Ain't No Makin It: Aspirations and Attainment in a Low Income Neighborhood.* Boulder, CO: Westview Press.

Majors, Richard (2001) "Cool Pose: Black Masculinity and Sports," in Stephen Whitehead and Frank Barrett (eds.) *The Masculinities Reader*, pp. 208–17. Cambridge: Polity.

Messner, Michael (1989) "Sports and the Politics of Inequality," in Michael Kimmel and Michael Messner (eds.) *Men's Lives.* Boston, MA: Allyn and Bacon.

———. (2004) "On Patriarchs and Losers: Rethinking Men's Interests," paper presented at Berkeley *Journal of Sociology* Conference, Berkeley.

Parker, Andrew (1996) "The Construction of Masculinity Within Boys' Physical Education," *Gender and Education* 8: 141–57.

Perry, Pamela (2002) *Shades of White: White Kids and Racial Identities in High School.* Durham, NC: Duke University Press.

Plummer, David C. (2001) "The Quest for Modern Manhood: Masculine Stereotypes, Peer Culture and the Social Significance of Homophobia," *Journal of Adolescence* 24: 15–23.

Price, Jeremy (1999) "Schooling and Racialized Masculinities: The Diploma, Teachers and Peers in the Lives of Young, African-American Men," *Youth and Society* 31: 224–63.

Riggs, Marlon (1991) "Black Macho Revisited: Reflections of a SNAP! Queen," in Essex Hemphill (ed.) *Brother to Brother: New Writings by Black Gay Men*, pp. 153–260. Boston, MA: Alyson Publications.

Ross, Marlon B. (1998) "In Search of Black Men's Masculinities," *Feminist Studies* 24: 599–626.

Sedgwick, Eve K. (1990) *Epistemology of the Closet.* Berkeley: University of California Press.

———. (1995) "Gosh, Boy George, You Must Be Awfully Secure in Your Masculinity!" in Maurice Berger, Brian Wallis and Simon Watson (eds.) *Constructing Masculinity*, pp. 11–20. New York: Routledge.

Skelton, Christine (1996) "Learning to Be Tough: The Fostering of Maleness in One Primary School," *Gender and Education* 8: 185–97.

Smith, George W. (1998) "The Ideology of 'Fag': The School Experience of Gay Students," *The Sociological Quarterly* 39: 309–35.

Smith, Valerie (1994) "Split Affinities: The Case of Interracial Rape," in Anne Herrmann and Abigail Stewart (eds.) *Theorizing Feminism*, pp. 155–70. Boulder, CO: Westview Press.

Stein, Arlene and Plummer, Ken (1994) "'I Can't Even Think Straight': 'Queer' Theory and the Missing Sexual Revolution in Sociology," *Sociological Theory* 12: 178 ff.

Thorne, Barrie (1993) *Gender Play: Boys and Girls in School.* New Brunswick, NJ: Rutgers University Press.

Warner, Michael (1993) "Introduction," in Michael Warner (ed.) *Fear of a Queer Planet: Queer Politics and Social Theory*, pp. vii–xxxi. Minneapolis: University of Minnesota Press.

West, Candace and Zimmerman, Don (1987) "Doing Gender." *Gender and Society*, 1(2), 125–151.

Whitehead, Stephen and Barrett, Frank (2001) "The Sociology of Masculinity," in Stephen Whitehead and Frank Barrett (eds.) *The Masculinities Reader*, pp. 1–29. Cambridge: Polity.

Wilchins, Riki (2003) "Do You Believe in Fairies?" *The Advocate*, 4 February.

Willis, Paul (1981) *Learning to Labor: How Working Class Kids Get Working Class Jobs.* New York: Columbia University Press.

Wood, Julian (1984) "Groping Toward Sexism: Boy's Sex Talk," in Angela McRobbie and Mica Nava (eds.) *Gender and Generation.* London: Macmillan Publishers.

Pink Frilly Dresses and the Avoidance of All Things "Girly": Children's Appearance Rigidity and Cognitive Theories of Gender Development

MAY LING HALIM, DIANE N. RUBLE, CATHERINE S. TAMIS-LEMONDA, KRISTINA M. ZOSULS,

LEAH E. LURYE, AND FAITH K. GREULICH

Our appearances are a symbolic representation of our self-concepts and convey messages to others about how we would like to be perceived. Clothing is a critical way we communicate our identity to others (e.g., Feinberg, Mataro, & Burroughs, 1992) and can signal membership in or separation from social groups (e.g., Freitas, Kaiser, & Hammidi, 1996). It is surprising, then, that the topic of children's gender-typed appearances has been virtually ignored in the gender identity development literature. The study of gender development has been dominated by a focus on gender stereotyping or activity preferences and behaviors (Zosuls, Miller, Ruble, Martin, & Fabes, 2011), despite numerous calls to focus on multiple domains (Huston, 1983; Ruble, Martin, & Berenbaum, 2006). Children's gender-typed appearance is also unique from other aspects of gender-typing. During the course of a day, playing with toys or with same- or other-gender peers is a transitory behavior, yet appearances are comparatively stable. Clothing thus allows a child to announce to the world, "This is who I am" as a girl or boy.

Appearance rigidity, adherence to conforming to gender norms in one's appearance through gender-stereotypical dress, is one particular phenomenon that might elucidate this appearance–identity link in young children. Some young girls, it seems, according to parent anecdotes and informal observations, go through a phase in which they refuse to wear anything but pink, frilly dresses (Ruble, Lurye, & Zosuls, 2007). Parents have reported that this "rigidity" can be seen in the level of gender stereotypicality (e.g., wearing pink from head to toe) and in the frequency of its occurrence (e.g., insisting on wearing a dress every single day, rain or shine).

We might speculate that this kind of behavior is linked to socialization processes, especially pressures from advertising. Girls might copy Disney princesses (England, Descartes, & Collier-Meek, 2011), and others might reinforce their behavior with praise. However, such an interpretation seems incomplete. For example, in line with theories about the benefits of androgyny (Bem, 1981), the insistence on wearing ultra-feminine clothing might upset some parents, causing them to feel that they have failed to raise their daughters in a gender-neutral fashion, as the popular media has noted (Fine, 2010; Orenstein, 2010; Padawar, 2012). In addition, about a third of young children exhibit other forms of rigidity or "extremely intense interests" beyond those that involve gender identity (DeLoache, Simcock, & Macari, 2007). Moreover parents reported that these preoccupations originated from the child rather than being encouraged

May Ling Halim, Diane N. Ruble, Catherine S. Tamis-LeMonda, Kristina M. Zosuls, Leah E. Lurye, and Faith K. Gruelich, "Pink Frilly Dresses and the Avoidance of All Things 'Girly': Children's Appearance Rigidity and Cognitive Theories of Gender Development," *Developmental Psychology,* Vol. 50, No. 4 (April 2014), pp. 1091–1101. Copyright © 2014 by the American Psychological Association. Reproduced with permission. The use of this information does not imply endorsement by the publisher.

by others. These counterefforts by some parents and children's intense interests across domains suggest that appearance rigidity might emanate, at least in part, from factors other than external socialization, such as cognitive–developmental and motivational processes, referred to here as *self-socialization*.

Cognitive Theories of Gender Development

Cognitive theories of gender development emphasize three key features (Martin, Ruble, & Szkrybalo, 2002). First, children are viewed as active, internally motivated agents who construct the meaning of gender categories (Tobin et al., 2010). Once children understand that they belong to a gender category, they embark on an investigation as "gender detectives," attending to information about their own gender and about differences between girls and boys (Martin & Ruble, 2004). Second, children's emerging understanding of gender concepts motivates them to master gender categories by behaving in gender-appropriate ways (Stangor & Ruble, 1987). Third, there exists a developmental trajectory of gender typing. Once children recognize an important categorical distinction such as gender, they might exhibit phase-like shifts in the rigidity of category-relevant beliefs and behaviors, moving from a beginning awareness, to rigidity, to flexibility (Ruble, 1994), a trajectory supported by research on children's endorsement of gender stereotypes (Miller, Trautner, & Ruble, 2006; Trautner et al., 2005).

Children's gender appearance is an ideal behavior to test cognitive theories of gender development, as it is a clear marker of gender typing that is relatively permanent across situations. Moreover, appearances are both highly salient and important to young children as their person perception relies on peripheral characteristics such as physical appearance (Ruble & Dweck, 1995). We propose that increases in children's adherence to wearing feminine or masculine clothing might be viewed as a manifestation of their passage through the rigidity phase in the trajectory of gender development (Halim, Ruble, & Amodio, 2011), reflecting cognitions about basic gender identity as a girl or boy,

along with early-acquired and highly visible gender-stereotype knowledge (Miller, Lurye, Zosuls, & Ruble, 2009).

Goals and Predictions for the Present Studies

Appearance rigidity among girls has been described previously (i.e., the "pink, frilly dress" phenomenon, or PFD; Ruble, Lurye, et al., 2007), but there has been no direct empirical inquiry to date regarding the phenomenon. In our present research, we aimed to (a) describe children's appearance rigidity, (b) examine whether gender identity predicts children's gender appearance rigidity, and (c) explore whether appearance rigidity generalizes to diverse populations.

Appearance Rigidity

We examined the alternative hypotheses that appearance rigidity might be seen in only a few, select young girls or that appearance rigidity might be relatively common in young girls. We were also interested to see whether boys would exhibit their own version of appearance rigidity. Because appearance rigidity is an appearance-based phenomenon, we expected a lower prevalence among boys, given past research suggesting that stereotypes of girls revolve around appearances and stereotypes of boys might revolve more around activities (Miller et al., 2009; Cristofaro & Tamis-LeMonda, 2008). Nevertheless, if appearance rigidity is found in boys, we expected it to include the embracing of superhero outfits (Neppl & Murray, 1997; Paley, 1986) or the donning of other masculine items such as suits and ties. We further anticipated that boys might exhibit appearance rigidity by *avoiding* feminine clothing as gender-role behavior is sometimes more often defined and exhibited as something boys should *not* do, rather than what they should do (Chiu et al., 2006; Hartley, 1959; Pickering & Repacholi, 2001).

We also hypothesized that the prevalence of gender-related appearance would show a trajectory of rigidity followed by flexibility across age as predicted by cognitive theories of gender development. Namely, because gender labeling and identity are evident in many children by age 2 (Zosuls et al.,

2009) and gender stability usually emerges by age 3 or 4 (Ruble et al., 2006), we expected 3- and 4-year-old children to show more appearance rigidity than 5- and 6-year-old children. In addition, we anticipated that boys would show appearance rigidity later than girls because girls' gender development sometimes precedes boys' (Ruble et al., 2006; Zosuls et al., 2009).

Gender Identity and Gender-Typed Appearance

Our second aim was to examine the link between appearance rigidity and two aspects of gender identity development that capture the motivational (gender centrality and evaluation) and knowledge (gender constancy) components of cognitive theories of gender development. Gender centrality refers to the importance of gender to the self-concept and evaluation refers to personal regard for one's own gender (see Egan & Perry, 2001).

There has been little research directly examining connections between gender centrality/evaluation and gender-typed behaviors in young children. We hypothesized that higher levels of identification with one's own gender would be associated with higher levels of gender-typed appearances. Children who feel that their gender identities are important and positive might desire for others to recognize their gender identities and go to great lengths to convey the right message with their clothing.

Full gender constancy involves learning three increasingly sophisticated gender category concepts by approximately the age of 6 or 7 years: (a) identity—that they and others are either boys or girls; (b) stability—that one's sex remains stable over time (e.g., knowing that a baby girl will become a woman); and (c) consistency—that despite superficial changes (e.g., if a boy wears a dress), sex does not change (Slaby & Frey, 1975). Researchers examining the connection between gender constancy and gender-typed behaviors have reached mixed conclusions (Halim & Ruble, 2010). Some find positive associations, whereas others find no associations (see Martin et al., 2002). Recent analyses parsing the stages of constancy have suggested that stability might be a better predictor of gender rigidity compared with gender consistency (Smetana &

Letourneau, 1984), which has been related to decreased rather than increased gender rigidity (Ruble, Taylor, et al., 2007; Zucker et al., 1999). Thus, we hypothesized that gender stability would predict gender-typed appearance. We reasoned that if children have attained gender stability, they might feel more committed to their gender and thus dress in more gender-stereotypical ways.

Appearance Rigidity in Multiple Cultures

A third goal was to explore whether appearance rigidity would be seen in children from diverse ethnic backgrounds. There might be large variation in the gender attitudes, gender roles, and gender stereotyping of different cultural communities due to historical and philosophical influences (Kane, 2000). For example, *machismo* and *marianismo*, or, broadly, male dominance and female submissiveness, might characterize Latino culture (Julian, McKenry. & McKenry, 1994). Chinese Confucian teachings emphasize male dominance in a patriarchal clan system (Hofstede, 1980), while dictating that the female role is to serve (Tu, 1985). In contrast, some have argued that workforce participation by African American women and the value of equality in American culture more broadly have created greater gender equality in African American families (Gutman, 1976; Tamis-LeMonda & McFadden, 2009). In light of the gendered contexts of different communities, examining gender appearance rigidity across ethnically diverse children from different social classes provides a stringent test of the prevalence and generality of the phenomenon.

Overview

We conducted two studies. Study 1a investigated whether gender appearance rigidity is apparent in early childhood in a middle-class, mostly White sample. We also investigated whether parents' preferences are associated with children's gender appearance rigidity. In Study 1b, we tested cognitive theories of gender development by examining whether appearance rigidity was connected to children's gender identification and understanding of gender stability. In Study 2, we tested whether appearance rigidity was generalizable to populations of children from different ethnicities and from a different socioeconomic class.

Study Ia

Plan of analyses

We first describe the distributions of children who have ever exhibited ("lifetime") appearance rigidity, then provide details about how many children displayed current appearance rigidity. Next, to explore trajectories of gender-typed appearance, we examine gender by cohort interactions for lifetime and current gender-typed appearance using chi-squares and analyses of variance (ANOVAs). Finally, we investigate whether parent preferences conceding clothing were associated with children's current gender-typed appearance using multiple regressions.

Prevalence and extremity

Analyses of the lifetime appearance rigidity measure indicated that 54% of the girls (68% in the younger cohort and 40% in the older cohort) were reported as having ever exhibited appearance rigidity (this finding also means that 46% either had never exhibited appearance rigidity or had shown a little bit or some interest: see Table 1). In contrast, 27% of the boys (11% in the younger cohort and 44% in the older cohort) were reported to have been insistent on wearing gender-typed clothing at some point in their early childhood. This result

also means that 73% of boys either had never exhibited appearance rigidity or had shown a little bit or some interest.

Parents' comments indicated that this lifetime appearance rigidity was quite extreme for some of the girls. About a quarter of the parents of girls who had exhibited appearance rigidity (24%) used expressions such as "has to," "no option," "won't wear anything else," "not a choice," or "that's it." Parents also pointed to children's refusals or rejections of certain items of clothing (80% of boys and 19% of girls who exhibited appearance rigidity).

Ways in which children express lifetime appearance rigidity

For girls, parent responses clustered around the adherence to dresses and skirts and the avoidance of pants (see Table 2 and Figure 1). For boys, parent responses converged on the avoidance of feminine clothing and in some cases the donning of superhero costumes and formal menswear. Children insisted on wearing gender-typed clothing on a daily basis and often refused other, less gender-typed, suggested options. About 17% of children showed lifetime appearance rigidity in only one category (i.e., dresses); 32% showed rigidity in two or three ways (i.e., dresses and pink); and 12% showed rigidity in between four and six ways. About 40% of parents did not mention specific clothing elements, usually answering with unequivocal yes's or no's.

TABLE 1.　**Percentage of Children Who Have Shown Appearance Rigidity (Lifetime Appearance Rigidity)**

Gender/age groups	No interest	Little interest	Pretty interested	Insistent
Girls				
3- & 4-year-olds	16	11	5	68
5- & 6-year-olds	35	15	10	40
All girls	26	13	8	54
Boys				
3- & 4-year-olds	68	21	0	11
5- & 6-year-olds	33	6	17	44
All boys	51	14	8	27
All 3- & 4-year-olds	16	11	5	68
All 5- & 6-year-olds	35	15	10	40
All children	38	13	8	41

Note: Percentages are calculated for each row.

TABLE 2. Study 1a: Characteristic Examples of Lifetime Appearance Rigidity

Gender/clothing item	Parent quotes
Girls	
Dresses and skirts	"No option, she wears dresses and won't wear anything else, always stockings even when it is cold out."
	"All the time, skirts pastel colors, [she] has to wear skirts, [she's] always done this since [she] turned 3."
	"[She] always prefers a dress. I have to convince her if it's cold to wear leggings."
	"[Her typical outfit is] a dress or a skirt. We do negotiate if [we're] going to the park, but [she] doesn't like jeans unless [they] have embroidered flowers [on them]."
	"Pretty dress—pink and frilly."
	"Dress, tights, Mary Jane shoes; pink is [her] favorite color now."
Avoidance of pants	"Pants are not a choice. [She says,] 'I want to wear a dress, and that's it.'
	"Dress over skort."
	"I bought two pairs of corduroy pants [for her]. She won't wear them because [they're] too masculine."
	"[She] refuses to wear pants—I have to persuade her. [My daughter says,] 'I want to wear a dress—I don't like pants.'"
Other	"She'd wear [her pink ballet slippers] all the time if she could."
Boys	
Avoidance of feminine clothing	"He wouldn't be caught dead in girls' clothing."
	"Negated burgundy pants because 'red is for girls.'"
	"He wouldn't wear a sweater that is feminine—he won't wear hand-me-downs from his big sister."
	"At [his] grandmother's, he had no underwear. She put hers on him. He got upset."
	"Won't wear his sister's pink hand-me-downs."
	"Won't wear pink or purple. Says boys' stuff is better in general."
	"He refuses colors 'for girls.'"
	"Wouldn't wear sandals because they looked like girls' [sandals]."
Superhero	"Superhero costumes—Superman, Spiderman."
	"Batman outfits."
Formal menswear	"Suit and tie and shoes and briefcase! [He says to me,] 'Don't I look handsome!'"
	"Loves to wear shirts and ties."
Other	"[He] loves to wear baggy cargo pants."

Note: Reponses to the question, "Has your daughter/son ever insisted on wearing traditional feminine/masculine clothes whenever she/he went out? Please describe."

Differences by gender and cohort

We examined gender and cohort differences in both lifetime and current appearance rigidity. Because the distribution of lifetime appearance rigidity was non-parametric (79% of children at the ends of the distribution), we contrasted the most rigid children . . . with everyone else. Results revealed that, across cohorts, more girls than boys showed lifetime appearance rigidity. . . . In addition, there was a gender by cohort interaction. . . . Among girls, lifetime appearance rigidity was marginally more prevalent in the younger

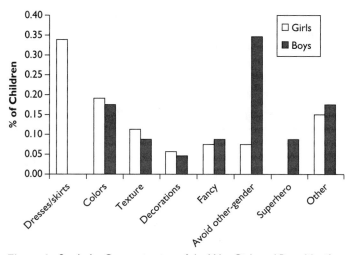

Figure 1. Study 1a: Categorization of the Way Girls and Boys Manifest Appearance Rigidity Based on Parents' Reports.

than in the older cohort . . . (see Figure 2). It seems possible that given the high frequency of lifetime appearance rigidity among 3- to 4-year-olds, some parents of 5- to 6-year-old girls might have under-reported past gender-rigid behavior among their daughters. In contrast, lifetime appearance rigidity was more prevalent in boys in the older (44%) than in the younger (11%) cohort. . . .

For current gender-typed appearance, . . . [a]s expected, girls in the younger . . . compared with the older . . . cohort were rated as exhibiting a higher level of current gender-typed appearance. . . . In contrast, boys in the older . . . compared with the younger . . . cohort did not significantly differ. Overall, children currently dressed in rather gender-typed ways . . . especially girls in the younger cohort. . . .

The role of parents

Finally, we examined the possible association between parents' preferences and children's appearance rigidity. We did this in several ways. First, we examined the parents' open-ended responses for spontaneous reactions to this behavior. In their open-ended responses concerning lifetime appearance rigidity, none of the parents of children who insisted on wearing gender-typed clothing reported actively encouraging or supporting their children to wear gender-typed clothing. Indeed, some

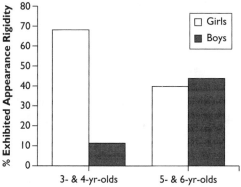

Figure 2. Study 1a: Prevalence of Lifetime Appearance Rigidity by Gender and Cohort.

parents reported having to resort to some sort of negotiation or persuasion to dress their daughters in a manner that deviated from their daughters' wishes (e.g., "[She] always prefers a dress. I have to convince her if it's cold to wear leggings"). Second, we asked parents, "During an average week, how frequently do you attempt to influence your child's clothing?" (0 = *never*, 1 = *rarely*, 2 = *a couple times*, 3 = *often*, 4 = *a lot*). The average response indicated low parental attempts to influence children's outfits. . . .

Third, we examined whether parents' preferences for their children's clothing in terms of femininity/masculinity were associated with their child's current appearance rigidity. We conducted a hierarchical multiple regression, in which children's current expression of appearance rigidity served as the dependent variable with age and gender entered on the first step, parent preferences entered on the second step, the 3 two-way interactions entered on the third step, and the three-way interaction entered on the fourth step. No significant effects were found. The largest coefficient for parents' preferences predicting children's current appearance rigidity was found on the second step but was not significant. . . .

Discussion

These data are the first to document the prevalence of gender appearance rigidity in young children. We used strict criteria for calculating the prevalence of lifetime appearance rigidity, and using these criteria, we found that more than half of girls and a little more than a quarter of boys had at some point strongly insisted on wearing gender-typed clothing (Table 2). On the other end of the spectrum, about a quarter of girls and about half of boys had never shown any appearance rigidity over their lifetimes. These data point to the variability in children's appearance rigidity.

As expected, lifetime gender appearance rigidity was reported to be more prevalent in girls than in boys. In addition, we found that lifetime appearance rigidity was marginally reported more often for 3- and 4-year-old girls (68%) compared with 5- and 6-year-old girls (40%), whereas lifetime appearance rigidity was reported more often for 5- and 6-year-old boys (40%) compared with 3- and 4-year-old boys (11%). Current appearance rigidity showed similar, and significant, patterns for girls, but no differences by cohort for boys. Together these results tentatively suggest a later onset of appearance rigidity for boys. This delay would mirror research showing that girls are often a little ahead of boys in gender development (Zosuls et al., 2009). Alternatively, because boys most frequently expressed appearance rigidity by avoiding anything feminine, it might be that it takes longer to learn what to avoid about the other gender (e.g., Chiu et al., 2006), than to learn what to embrace about one's own gender.

The qualitative data on lifetime appearance rigidity suggested that some children were quite insistent on wearing or avoiding feminine clothing. Qualitatively, parent-reported reactions ranged from tolerance to reasoning with or making compromises with their children. Interestingly, only parents of daughters explicitly mentioned conflict. Perhaps parents of sons were very comfortable with their boys wearing 'boyish' clothing. Somewhat surprisingly, parents' preferences did not predict children's current gender appearance rigidity.

Study 1b

In Study 1b, we used child interviews to test whether two aspects of self-socialization in gender identity development—(a) feelings of importance and positive evaluation of one's gender and (b) understanding of the permanence of gender categories—could help explain why young children want to dress like girly girls and masculine boys. We tested these hypotheses by examining the association between these aspects of gender identity development with their current gender appearance rigidity as reported by their parents in Study 1a. . . .

Results

Gender centrality and evaluation

Consistent with our hypothesis, gender centrality/evaluation positively predicted children's current appearance rigidity adjusting for age and gender. . . . We found no other significant effects.

Gender stability

Confirming our hypothesis, an understanding of gender stability was associated with children's current appearance rigidity. . . . We found no other significant effects. . . .

Discussion

The data lend support to cognitive theories of gender development regarding children's appearance rigidity. First, we found that gender centrality and evaluation positively predicted children's current appearance rigidity across age and gender. These findings suggest that children exhibiting appearance rigidity might be doing so, in part, because they consider their gender identity to be an important and positive aspect of themselves. In addition, we found that a greater understanding of gender stability predicted children's current appearance rigidity across gender. These data indicate that children's current appearance rigidity might mark a solidified commitment to their gender identities, once children know that gender is relatively permanent over time. These associations are consistent with predictions from the phase model of transitions (Ruble. 1994) with children's cognitive development predicting their identity-displaying behavior.

A limitation of Study 1 was the homogeneity of our sample. We suggest that appearance rigidity could be found in any culture in which gender is an important and salient categorical distinction and in which certain appearance characteristics are closely connected with gender. Hence, to examine the generalizability of gender appearance rigidity during early childhood to other cultural communities, we conducted a second study on a different, diverse population.

Study 2

Study 2 examined whether the identified patterns of gender appearance found in Study 1 would generalize to 4-year-old children from ethnically diverse backgrounds (Mexican, Chinese, Dominican, and African American) and from low-income neighborhoods. Based on the responses of parents in Study 1, we constructed closed-ended questions to assess children's appearance rigidity. We examined mothers of 4-year-olds, in particular, because Study 1 showed that appearance rigidity was prevalent at age 4 and cognitive theories of gender development would also predict a peak in gender-typed appearance at this time. We chose these four particular cultural backgrounds based on their increasing presence in the United States and because they each have unique histories and traditions that might affect children's gender typing. In terms of ethnic group differences, African American children might be expected to display less appearance rigidity than the three immigrant groups because gender distinctions might be less salient among African American families in light of high employment and economic responsibilities of mothers (Hill, 2002; Jarrett, Roy, & Burton, 2002). . . .

Results

Prevalence of gender appearance rigidity by gender

We analyzed girls' and boys' appearance rigidity separately. Among girls, gender appearance rigidity was very high. . . . In fact, 69% of girls were reported to exhibit appearance rigidity, scoring 4 (*very true*) or 5 (*extremely true*) on the response scale. This also means that 31% of girls exhibited some (23%), little (5%), or no (3%) appearance rigidity, indicated by scores of 1 (*not at all true*), 2 (*a little bit true*), or 3 (*somewhat true*). Among boys, gender appearance rigidity was also high. . . . A little more than half (56%) of boys were reported to exhibit appearance rigidity (scoring 4's or 5's). Thus, 44% of boys exhibited some (20%), little (17%), or no (7%) gender appearance rigidity.

Ethnic group differences in prevalence of gender appearance rigidity

Among girls, there were significant differences by ethnicity. . . . Fewer Mexican American girls (50%) showed appearance rigidity compared with Dominican (82%; $p = .012$), Chinese (73%; $p = .036$), and African American (72%; $p = .093$) girls, who did not significantly differ from each other. . . . Hence, appearance rigidity was generally prevalent in these 4-year-old girls from low-income, ethnically diverse backgrounds.

Among boys, there was a marginally significant effect for ethnicity. . . . More Dominican American boys (77%) were reported to express appearance rigidity than did boys from the other ethnic groups—Mexican (48%), Chinese (51%), African American (50% . . .)—who did not significantly differ from each other. Thus, appearance rigidity was found among more than half of these 4-year-old boys across a diverse number of cultural groups and was even more prevalent among Dominican American boys.

Discussion

Study 2 showed that appearance rigidity is not limited to White, middle-class samples. Two thirds of 4-year-old girls and more than half of 4-year-old boys from diverse ethnic backgrounds, including Chinese, Dominican, and Mexican immigrant children, as well as African American children, on average showed a moderately high to very high degree of gender appearance rigidity. As in Study 1, the data also point to variability in children's appearance rigidity. One third of ethnic minority 4-year-old girls and 44% of ethnic minority 4-year-old boys showed a more tempered interest or no interest in gender-typed clothing. Perhaps these children might be low on gender typing generally; perhaps their gender identities are not as central to their general self-identities; or perhaps gender is made less salient in their peer environments.

We found a few ethnic differences. Unexpectedly, Mexican girls showed the least amount of gender appearance rigidity, which contrasts with assumptions that Latino culture might endorse more gender typing. Moreover, African American girls showed as much gender appearance rigidity as girls in the other ethnic groups, contrary to the idea that African American girls might endorse gender roles less because of African American family structures (e.g., Hill, 2002). Gender is multidimensional (Ruble et al., 2006); thus, gender rigidity might be expressed in different ways depending on what is emphasized in one's culture. Perhaps as an alternative to appearance, Mexican girls express their gender in their play or peer preferences (Halim, Ruble, Tamis-LeMonda, & Shrout, 2013). And perhaps African American girls learn that appearance is particularly important in order to ensure a sense of respectability and social status (Wolcott, 2001). In the case of the ethnic group difference among boys, Dominican boys showed marginally more appearance rigidity than the boys in all the other ethnic groups. Scholars have noted that gender roles are often clearly defined in Dominican culture (Lopez. 2002; Cristofaro & Tamis-LeMonda, 2008). Perhaps gender is particularly salient to Dominican boys, and they are choosing appearance as the choice avenue of gender identity expression.

General Discussion

Across multiple studies, mixed methods, and diverse samples, we found that most girls were reported to show a keen interest in dressing in gender-typed ways at some point in early childhood (68% of 3- and 4-year-olds in Study 1; 69% of

4-year-olds in Study 2). Similarly, but to a lesser degree, a number of boys (more than half of ethnic minority boys, about a quarter of White middle-class boys) also were reported to show an affinity for especially masculine clothing. We consider this prevalence among boys to be remarkable given our expectations that appearance rigidity would be a phenomenon found primarily among girls. Although gender might be more or less salient in different cultural communities, children from multiple ethnic backgrounds—particularly girls—on average exhibited a penchant for gendered clothing, thereby demonstrating the robustness of gender appearance rigidity in early childhood.

Gender Differences

Girls generally were reported to exhibit more gender appearance rigidity than were boys across both studies. This contrast might be due to gender differences in the construction of the meaning of gender identity. For girls, being a girl might mean *looking* like a girl. For boys, we speculate that being a boy might largely mean something else, such as *acting* like a boy. Children's stereotypes about girls are largely defined by appearance, whereas children's stereotypes about boys are more often defined by behavior and activities (Miller et al., 2009). It is also possible that boys do not have to be obsessed with appearances because their wardrobe choices are more constrained, as boys' clothing already usually excludes feminine options. Boys might have less choice in what they wear and thus find other avenues for the expression of their gender identities.

Although appearance rigidity was less prevalent among boys, when boys did show appearance rigidity, it often revolved around avoiding other-gender-typed clothing, as in Study 1. We speculate that knowledge of status differences could be emerging; thus, boys might desire to avoid looking feminine because females have lower status than males (Rudman & Glick, 2012). It is also possible that boys might be punished more for looking feminine than vice versa (Smetana, 1986). Perhaps also, at an early age, boys' avoidance of femininity can be seen in their avoidance of feminine clothing, and later on in development this type of avoidance is extended to other domains such as boys' self-censorship in expressing certain emotions (Adler, Kless, & Adler, 1992). Because the avoidance of femininity was a noticeable theme among boys, it would be beneficial in future research to directly and systematically assess the avoidance of cross-gender-typed clothing.

Ethnic Similarities and Differences

Studies 1 and 2 showed that appearance rigidity was comparably prevalent in both White (68% of 3- and 4-year-olds) and ethnic minority (69% of 4-year-olds) young girls. Thus across five different ethnic groups, appearance rigidity was the norm among young girls, although in each sample there were girls who did not express the highest levels of appearance rigidity as well (31%–32% in 3- or 4-year-olds). In contrast, cross-cultural comparisons among boys revealed an interesting finding. In Study 1, only 11% of 3- and 4-year-old White boys showed appearance rigidity. Based on these results, it was unexpected to find that more than half (56%) of 4-year-old ethnic minority boys expressed appearance rigidity (and among Dominican 4-year-old boys, the prevalence rate was 77%). This finding suggests that appearances might be more integral to the gender identities of ethnic minority boys (see Archer & Yamshita, 2003). Alternatively, as 44% of 5- and 6-year-old White boys in Study 1 showed appearance rigidity, nearing the 56% of the 4-year-old ethnic minority boys, it is possible that appearance rigidity has an earlier developmental course for ethnic minority boys than White boys. A future, direct cross-cultural comparison and a longitudinal study on the developmental trajectories of appearance rigidity could elucidate this finding. If other dimensions of gender typing (sex segregation, play) also showed earlier developmental courses for ethnic minority boys than for White boys, this might suggest that general gender identity development might begin earlier for them than for White boys. We speculate that perhaps gender is more salient in the environments of ethnic minority boys compared with the environments of White boys.

Another interesting cultural difference was that in the White, Chinese, and African American groups, appearance rigidity was more prevalent in girls than in boys. However, both Latino groups showed parity in appearance rigidity between girls and boys (82% and 77% of Dominican girls and boys, respectively; 50% and 48% of Mexican girls and boys, respectively). We speculate that the importance of looking feminine or masculine might be stressed equally for girls and boys in Latino groups. . . .

Limitations and Future Directions

In the current study, parent preferences were not associated with children's gender-typed appearances. However, because our primary focus concerned testing cognitive theories of gender development, our measures of parent preferences were limited in the number of items used. Also, it is possible that some parents might have been biased in their reports, either being unaware of or downplaying how much they actually encourage their children to dress in stereotypical ways. In addition, it is possible that parent preferences interact with some other factors, such as children's cognitive development, in affecting their gender-typed dress, but we lacked the statistical power to adequately examine this kind of interaction. Nevertheless, our parent measures had the benefit of being very specific (Zosuls, Ruble, Tamis-LeMonda, & Martin, 2013). More research is needed to understand the intersection between parent preferences and children's gender-typed dress. Perhaps a more nuanced measure would capture a bidirectional influence between children and parents in determining children's gendered appearances. Alternatively, parent preferences might not be as strongly connected to appearance rigidity at this age, but at earlier ages, when children are not as attuned to gender categories and are not as invested in their gender identities.

Another limitation was that our measure of appearance rigidity in Study 2 showed low correlations for some of the ethnic by gender groups. However, sample sizes were relatively small when split by ethnic and gender group. Thus, we lacked the power to draw firm conclusions about the cross-cultural equivalence of the measure (Cohen, 1992). In addition, because the items in the measure were very concrete ("skirts," "baseball caps") and did not ask about abstract concepts (like "appearance rigidity"), we are confident that mothers from all ethnic groups understood the questions. Nevertheless, it would be interesting for investigators in a future study to directly examine the particular ways gender manifests itself in the adornments and dress of different cultural groups.

The present findings suggest a number of other important directions for future research. One issue concerns the social identity implications of gender-related appearance rigidity. For example, if appearance rigidity represents strong gender identification, as our research suggests, then children who are rigid might show more ingroup favoritism than those who are more flexible. Our finding that girls showed more gender appearance rigidity than boys is consistent with literature sometimes reporting that girls show more intergroup bias than do boys (Leroux, 2008; Powlishta, 1995; Susskind & Hodges, 2007; Zosuls et al., 2011).

Another important direction concerns the causes and consequences of individual differences in appearance rigidity. Although we have emphasized how prevalent appearance rigidity is for girls, it is important to remember that there was also a subset of girls who exhibited no appearance rigidity. And although, depending on the sample, about a quarter to almost half of boys exhibited appearance rigidity, many boys never did. What makes these individuals different from one another? Some children could be generally more gender-typed than others due to experiencing different hormonal environments in utero (e.g., girls exposed to high levels of androgens could prefer more masculine dress, activities, and peers; Berenbaum & Snyder, 1995) or experiencing different amounts of felt pressure to conform to gender norms from family, peers, or the media (Egan & Perry, 2001). Alternatively, perhaps some children are defining their gender through other avenues besides their appearance.

Whatever the explanation for these individual differences, it would be interesting to track these differences over time and understand the developmental trajectory of appearance rigidity.

Journalists have increasingly discussed the negative impact of the princess culture on girls' development (e.g., Fine, 2010; Orenstein, 2010). On the one hand, in light of the lower levels of appearance rigidity among older girls in Study 1, which suggests a dearth of elementary-school-aged girls who wear pink, frilly dresses (Halim et al., 2011), we posit that appearance rigidity might he a short-lived phase. If so, then perhaps appearance rigidity need not elicit stress around parent–child interactions, potentially damaging parent–child relationships and making children perceive that expressing one's gender identity is bad. On the other hand, if appearance rigidity is more long-term and stable, then it might lead children, and especially girls, to focus too much on their physical appearance, especially if they are continually praised by others for looking pretty. Appearance rigidity might then feed into defining one's self and one's self-worth in terms of how one looks. In turn, one's self-esteem might become contingent on self-perceived attractiveness, which can contribute to psychological distress (Crocker & Wolfe, 2001; Eccles, Barber, Jozefowicz, Malenchuk, & Vida, 1999). A hyper-focus on one's physical appearance might also feed into girls' self-objectification, which has also been associated with poor psychological adjustment and math performance (e.g., Fredrickson, Roberts, Noll, Quinn, & Twenge, 1998).

Conclusion

In conclusion, through multiple methods and across studies in a large and diverse sample, our study emphasizes that the clothing that children put on each day has significance and is a central, but previously missing, piece in the study of gender and identity development. Whether a girl dons a pink, frilly dress or a boy wears a red and blue Spiderman T-shirt might reflect changing understandings of gender categories and developing motivations to master these categories. Thus, the present findings support the view of young children as active self-socializing agents, picking up clues on what gender looks like and doggedly following their deductions.

References

Adler, P. A., Kless, S. J., & Adler, P. (1992). Socialization to gender roles: Popularity among elementary school boys and girls. *Sociology of Education, 65,* 169–187. doi:10.2307/2112807

Archer, L., & Yamashita, H. (2003). Theorising inner-city masculinities: "Race," class, gender and education. *Gender and Education, 15,* 115–132. doi:10.1080/09540250303856

Bem, S. L. (1981). Gender schema theory: A cognitive account of sex typing. *Psychological Review, 88,* 354–364. doi:10.1037/0033-295X.88.4.354

Berenbaum, S. A., & Snyder, E. (1995). Early hormonal influences on childhood sex-typed activity and playmate preferences: Implications for the development of sexual orientation. *Developmental Psychology, 31,* 31–42. doi:10.1037/0012-1649.31.1.31

Chiu, S. W., Gervan, S., Fairbrother, C., Johnson, L. L., Owen-Anderson, A. F. H., Bradley, S. J., & Zucker, K. J. (2006). Sex-dimorphic color preference in children with gender identity disorder: A comparison to clinical and community controls. *Sex Roles, 55,* 385–395. doi:10.1007/s11199-006-9089-9

Cohen, J. (1992). A power primer, *Psychological Bulletin, 112,* 155–159. doi:10.1037/0033-2909.112.1.155

Cristofaro, T. N., & Tamis-LeMonda, C. S. (2008). Lessons in mother–child and father–child personal narratives in Latino families. In A. McCabe, A. Balley, & G. Melzi (Eds.), *Spanish-language narration and literacy: Culture, cognition, and emotion* (pp. 54–91). Cambridge, MA: Cambridge University Press. doi:10.1017/CBO9780511815669.006

Crocker, J., & Wolfe, C. T. (2001). Contingencies of self-worth. *Psychological Review, 108,* 593–623. doi:10.1037/0033-295X,108.3.593

DeLoache, J. S., Simcock, G., & Macari, S. (2007). Planes, trains, automobiles—and tea sets: Extremely intense interests in very young children. *Developmental Psychology, 43,* 1579–1586. doi:10.1037/0012-1649.43.6.1579

Eccles, J., Barber, B., Jozefowicz, D., Malenchuk, O., & Vida, M. (1999). Self-evaluations of competence, task values, and self-esteem. In N. G. Johnson, M. C. Roberts, & J, Worell (Eds.), *Beyond appearance: A new look at adolescent girls* (pp. 53–83). Washington, DC: American Psychological Association. doi:10.1037/10325-002

Egan, S. K., & Perry, D. G. (2001). Gender identity: A multidimensional analysis with implications for psychosocial adjustment. *Developmental Psychology, 37,* 451–463. doi:10.1037/0012-1649.37.4.451

England, D. E., Descartes, L., & Collier-Meek, M. A. (2011). Gender role portrayal and the Disney princesses. *Sex Roles, 64,* 555–567. doi:10.1007/s11199-011-9930-7

Feinberg, R. A., Mataro, L., & Burroughs, W. J. (1992). Clothing and social identity. *Clothing & Textiles Research Journal, 11,* 18–23. doi:10.1177/0887302X9201100103

Fine, C. (2010). *Delusions of gender.* New York, NY: Norton.

Fredrickson, B. L., Roberts, T., Noll, S. M., Quinn, D. M., & Twenge, J. M. (1998). That swimsuit becomes you: Sex differences in self-objectification, restrained eating, and math performance. *Journal of Personality and Social Psychology, 75,* 269–284. doi:10.1037/0022-3514.75.1.269

Freitas, A., Kaiser, S., & Hammidi, T. (1996). Communities, commodities, cultural space, and style. *Journal of Homosexuality, 31,* 83–107.

Gutman, H. G. (1976). *The Black family in slavery and freedom.* New York, NY: Vintage.

Halim, M. L., & Ruble, D. N. (2010). Gender identity and stereotyping in early and middle childhood. In J. Chrisler & D. McCreary (Eds.), *Handbook of gender research in psychology* (pp. 495–525). New York, NY: Springer. doi:10.1007/978-1-4419-1465-1_24

Halim, M. L., Ruble, D. N., & Amodio, D. M. (2011). From pink frilly dresses to "one of the boys": A social–cognitive analysis of gender identity development and gender bias. *Social and Personality Psychology Compass, 5,* 933–949. doi:10.1111/j.1751-9004.2011.00399.x

Halim, M. L., Ruble, D. N., Tamis-LeMonda, C. S., & Shrout, P. E. (2013). Rigidity in gender-typed behaviors in early childhood: A longitudinal study of ethnic minority children. *Child Development, 84,* 1269–1284.

Harter, S. (1982). The Perceived Competence Scale for Children. *Child Development, 53,* 87–97. doi:10.2307/1129640

Hartley, R. E. (1959). Sex-role pressures and socialization of the male child. *Psychological Reports, 5,* 457–468. doi:10.2466/PR0.5.457-468

Hill, S. A. (2002). Teaching and doing gender in African American families. *Sex Roles, 47*, 493–506. doi:10.1023/A:1022026303937

Hofstede, F. (1980). *Culture's consequences.* London, United Kingdom: Sage.

Huston, A. C. (1983). Sex-typing. In E. M. Hetherington (Ed.) & P. H. Mussen (Series Ed.), *Handbook of child psychology: Vol. 4. Socialization, personality, and social development* (pp. 387–467), New York, NY: Wiley.

Jarrett, R., Roy, K., & Burton, L. (2002). Fathers in the 'hood: Qualitative research on African American men. In C. Tamis-LeMonda & N. Cabrera (Eds.), *Handbook of father involvement: Multidisciplinary perspectives* (pp. 211–248). Hillsdale, NJ: Erlbaum.

Julian, T. W., McKenry, P. C., & McKelvey, M. W. (1994). Cultural variations in parenting: Perceptions of Caucasian, African-American, Hispanic, and Asian-American parents. *Family Relations, 43*, 30–37. doi:10.2307/585139

Kane, E. W. (2000), Racial and ethnic variations in gender-related attitudes. *Annual Review of Sociology, 26*, 419–439. doi:10.1146/annurev.soc.26.1.419

Leroux, A. (2008). *Do children with gender identity disorder have an in-group or an out-group gender-based bias?* (Unpublished master's thesis). Ontario Institute for the Study in Education of the University of Toronto, Toronto, Ontario, Canada.

Lopez, N. (2002). *Hopeful girls, troubled boys: Race and gender disparity in urban education.* New York, NY: Routledge.

Martin, C. L., & Ruble, D. N. (2004). Children's search for gender cues: Cognitive perspectives on gender development. *Current Directions in Psychological Science, 13*, 67–70. doi:10.1111/j.0963-7214.2004.00276.x

Martin, C. L., Ruble, D. N., & Szkrybalo, J. (2002). Cognitive theories of early gender development. *Psychological Bulletin, 128*, 903–933. doi:10.1037/0033-2909,128.6.903

Miller, C. F., Lurye, L. E., Zosuls, K. M., & Ruble, D. N. (2009). Accessibility of gender stereotypes domains: Developmental and gender differences in children. *Sex Roles, 60*, 870–881. doi:10.1007/s11199-009-9584-x

Miller, C. F., Trautner, H., & Ruble, D. N. (2006). The role of gender stereotypes in children's preferences and behavior. In L. Balter & C. S. Tamis-LeMonda (Eds.), *Child psychology: A handbook of contemporary issues* (pp. 293–323). New York, NY: Psychology Press.

Neppl, T. K., & Murray, A. D. (1997). Social dominance and play patterns among preschoolers: Gender comparisons. *Sex Roles, 36*, 381–393. doi:10.1007/BF02766654

Orenstein, P. (2010). *Cinderella ate my daughter.* New York, NY: Harper.

Padawar, R. (2012, August 12). Boygirl. *New York Times Magazine*, pp. 18–23, 36, 46.

Paley, V. G. (1986). *Boys and girls: Superheroes in the doll corner.* Chicago, IL: University of Chicago Press.

Pickering, S., & Repacholi, B. (2001). Modifying children's gender-typed musical instrument preferences: The effects of gender and age. *Sex Roles, 45*, 623–643. doi:10.1023/A:1014863609014

Powlishta, K. K. (1995). Intergroup processes in childhood: Social categorization and sex role development. *Developmental Psychology, 31*, 781–788. doi:10.1037/0012-1649.31.5.781

Ruble, D. N. (1994). A phase model of transitions: Cognitive and motivational consequences. In M. Zanna (Ed.), *Advances in experimental social psychology* (pp. 163–214). New York, NY: Academic Press. doi:10.1016/S0065-2601(08)60154-9

Ruble, D. N., & Dweck, C. S. (1995). Self-perceptions, person conceptions, and their development. In N. Eisenberg (Ed.), *Social development* (pp. 109–139). Thousand Oaks, CA: Sage.

Ruble, D. N., Lurye, L. E., & Zosuls, K. M. (2007). Pink frilly dresses (PFD) and early gender identity. *Princeton Report on Knowledge (P-ROK), 2*(2). Retrieved from http://www.princeton.edu/prok/issues/2-2/pink_frilly-xml

Ruble, D. N., Martin, C., & Berenbaum, S. (2006). Gender development. In N. Eisenberg (Vol. Ed.), W. Damon, & R. M. Lerner (Series Eds.), *Handbook of child psychology: Vol. 3. Personality and social development* (6th ed., pp. 858–932). New York, NY: Wiley.

Ruble, D. N., Taylor, L. J., Cyphers, L., Greulich, F. K., Lurye, L. E., & Shrout, P. E. (2007). The role of gender constancy in early gender development. *Child Development, 78*, 1121–1136. doi:10.1111/j.1467-8624.2007.01056.x

Rudman, L. A., & Glick, P. (2012). *Social psychology of gender: How power and intimacy shape gender relations.* New York, NY: Guilford Press.

Slaby, R. G., & Frey, K. S. (1975). Development of gender constancy and selective attention to same-sex models. *Child Development, 46,* 849–856. doi:10.2307/1128389

Smetana, J. G. (1986). Preschool children's conceptions of sex-role transgressions. *Child Development, 57,* 862–871. doi:10.2307/1130363

Smetana, J. G., & Letourneau, K. J. (1984). Development of gender constancy and children's sex-typed free play behavior. *Developmental Psychology, 20,* 691–696. doi:10.1037/0012-1649.20.4.691

Stangor, C., & Ruble, D. N. (1987). Development of gender role knowledge and gender constancy. In L. S. Liben & M. L. Signorella (Eds.), *New directions for child development: Vol. 39. Children's gender schemata* (pp. 5–22). San Francisco, CA: Jossey–Bass.

Susskind, J. E., & Hodges, C. (2007). Decoupling children's gender-based in-group positivity from out-group negativity. *Sex Roles, 56,* 707–716. doi:10.1007/s11199-007-9235-z

Tamis-LeMonda, C. S., & McFadden, K. E. (2009). The United States of America. In M. H. Bornstein (Ed.), *Handbook of cultural developmental science* (pp. 299–322). New York, NY: Psychology Press.

Tobin, D. D., Menon, M., Menon, M., Spatta, B. C., Hodges, E. V. E., & Perry, D. G. (2010). The intrapsychics of gender: A model of self-socialization. *Psychological Review, 117,* 601–622. doi:10.1037/a0018936

Trautner, H. M., Ruble, D. N., Cyphers, L. Kirsten, B., Behrendt, R., & Hartmann, P. (2005). Rigidity and flexibility of gender stereotypes in children:

Developmental or differential? *Infant and Child Development, 14,* 365–381. doi:10.1002/icd.399

Tu, W. M. (1985). Selfhood and otherness in Confucian thought. In A. J. Marsella, G. De Vos, & F. L. K. Hsu (Eds.), *Culture and the self* (pp. 231–251). New York, NY: Tavistock.

Wolcott, V. W. (2001). *Remaking respectability: African American women in interwar Detroit.* Chapel Hill, NC: University of North Carolina Press.

Zosuls, K. M., Miller, C. F., Ruble, D. N., Martin, C. L., & Fabes, R. A. (2011). Gender development research in sex roles: Historical trends and future directions. *Sex Roles, 64,* 826–842. doi:10.1007/s11199-010-9902-3

Zosuls, K. M., Ruble, D. N., Tamis-LeMonda, C. S., & Martin, C. L. (2013). Does your infant say the words "girl" and "boy"? How gender labels matter in early gender development. In M. R. Banaji & S. A. Gelman (Eds.), *Navigating the social world: What infants, children, and other species can teach us* (pp. 301–305). Oxford, United Kingdom: Oxford University Press.

Zosuls, K. M., Ruble, D. N., Tamis-LeMonda, C. S., Shrout, P. E., Bornstein, M. H., & Greulich, F. K. (2009). The acquisition of gender labels in infancy: Implications for sex-typed play. *Developmental Psychology, 45,* 688–701. doi:10.1037/a0014053

Zucker, K. J., Bradley, M. D., Kuksis, M., Pecore, K., Birkenfeld-Adams, A., & Doering, R. W. (1999). Gender constancy judgments in children with a gender identity disorder: Evidence for a developmental lag. *Archives of Sexual Behavior, 28,* 475–502. doi:10.1023/A:1018713115866

Overdoing Gender: A Test of the Masculine Overcompensation Thesis

ROBB WILLER, BRIDGET CONLON, CHRISTABEL L. ROGALIN, AND MICHAEL T. WOJNOWICZ

Introduction

The 1964 film *Dr. Strangelove, or How I Learned to Stop Worrying and Love the Bomb* depicts the initiation of World War III as a great act of overcompensation by a sexually impotent general. This line of reasoning is not unusual, appearing not only in popular but also academic (e.g., Adler [1910] 1956) discourse. Masculine overcompensation is invoked as an explanation for a variety of behaviors from the everyday—men purportedly purchasing sports cars at the onset of "midlife crises"—to the world-changing—as in analyses of Lyndon Johnson's escalation of the Vietnam War (Fasteau 1974; Kimmel 1996).

The masculine overcompensation thesis asserts that men react to masculine insecurity by enacting extreme demonstrations of their masculinity. Men's pursuit of masculinity in the face of threats is driven by desires to recover masculine status both in their own and others' eyes. The overcompensation dynamic is different from mere compensation. Where compensation would lead men to behave roughly as they would normally, their behavior apparently unaffected by the threat, overcompensation suggests a dynamic of relatively extreme reaction, over and above men's behavior in the absence of threats. In this way, men may inadvertently reveal feelings of threat by behaving in a more extremely masculine way than they otherwise would. If true, the thesis implies that extreme,

caricatured demonstrations of masculinity among men may in fact serve as tell-tale signs of underlying insecurity, not self-assured confidence. Those men who exhibit the most masculine traits may actually be seeking cover for lurking insecurities, their outsized masculine displays in fact strategic claims at masculine status, efforts to pass as something they fear they are not.

But while the logic is familiar—the notion that people would act to cover up their self-perceived deficits is often cited in settings beyond gender identity (e.g., Willer, Kuwabara, and Macy 2009)—it is not known whether the claim is valid. Do men overcompensate in response to gender identity threats? In this article we review the theoretical bases for the masculine overcompensation thesis, establishing the theoretical claims underlying the dynamic. We then test the idea of masculine overcompensation in a series of laboratory experiments and a large-scale survey. Finally, we conclude by discussing implications of our research.

Theory

The theoretical roots of the masculine overcompensation thesis lie in psychoanalytic theory, specifically Adler's notion that men engage in "masculine protest" as a response to feelings of inferiority ([1910] 1956). Masculine overcompensation also derives from Freud's notion of "reaction formation" ([1898] 1962), which describes the tendency of

Robb Willer, Bridget Conlon, Christabel L. Rogalin, and Michael T. Wojnowicz, "Overdoing Gender: A Test of the Masculine Overcompensation Thesis," *American Journal of Sociology*, Vol. 118, No. 4 (January 2013), pp. 980–1022. Copyright © 2013 by The University of Chicago.

individuals to respond to the suggestion that they possess a socially unacceptable trait by enacting its opposite, often in the extreme. While empirical support for psychoanalytic theory in general—and Freud's defense mechanisms in particular—is decidedly spotty, research is generally supportive of reaction formation (Baumeister, Dale, and Sommer 1998).

In perhaps the best-known empirical demonstration of reaction formation, one study found that more homophobic men actually showed greater sexual arousal (as indicated by penile circumference measured via a penile plethysmograph) than less homophobic men when watching videos of homosexual intercourse, though they reported lower levels of arousal (Adams, Wright, and Lohr 1996). This finding suggests that homophobia may be a case of reaction formation for men with same-sex attraction and strong concerns about the social implications of being seen as gay (see also Weinstein et al. 2012). The masculine overcompensation thesis follows a similar line of reasoning: men who fear they have insufficient masculinity overcompensate by enacting extreme masculine behaviors and attitudes designed to create the impression that they are quite masculine.

Here we review two additional lines of theory that together provide a theoretical basis for the masculine overcompensation thesis. First, masculinity theory, which argues that masculinity is both more narrowly defined (making masculinity more easily threatened) and socially valued (making men more motivated to recover it) than femininity. Second, theories of identity, which argue that individuals tend to react to feedback that threatens valued identities with overcompensation, enacting attitudes and behaviors associated with the identity to a more extreme extent than they would have in the absence of threats.

Masculinity Theory

Masculinity theorists have traditionally argued that, while definitions of masculinity vary across contexts, within a given culture men are typically measured against a monolithic standard of "hegemonic masculinity" (Connell 1983). Hegemonic masculinity describes the most legitimate and respected conception of masculinity in a given culture, prescribing a particular set of behaviors and traits that are viewed as most socially desirable in men (Carrigan, Connell, and Lee 1985; Connell 1987). Because femininity and other masculinities are less valued and respected than hegemonic masculinity, the stakes associated with maintaining a masculine identity that hews closely to this ideal are relatively high for men. While the specific characteristics of hegemonic masculinity vary across groups and contexts (Connell and Messerschmidt 2005), several aspects are common (Schrock and Schwalbe 2009), including competitiveness, assertiveness, physical strength, aggression, risk-taking, courage, heterosexuality, and lack of feminine traits. Researchers have emphasized that dominance and control are central to hegemonic masculinity in the American context (Johnson 2005).

In recent years, some masculinity researchers have turned their attention to the changing definition of masculinity in American culture and to an expansion of what are viewed as acceptable masculine attitudes and behaviors (e.g., Anderson 2009). But despite this work most agree that the cultural definition of what are acceptable and respected traits is narrower for masculinity than for femininity (e.g., Schrock and Schwalbe 2009). For example, within the literature on children and adolescents, it is clear that while cultural expectations for girls have shown a remarkable transformation in recent years, moving toward acceptance of expressions of self typically associated with masculinity (Adams and Bettis 2003), there is a much more halting cultural acceptance of behaviors associated with femininity in boys (Kimmel and Mahler 2003; Pascoe 2005).

Masculinity theorists emphasize that sensitivity and responsiveness to masculinity threats are common in men (e.g., Kimmel 1994). The social pressure to maintain an esteemed masculine gender identity is strong, though it is different from other forms of normative pressure in that total conformity is likely impossible. Indeed, the standards of true masculinity are so exacting as to be virtually unattainable, leading men to continually strive to satisfy them (Connell 1987, 1995). As a result, though certain circumstances may be more emasculating than others, the feeling that one is insufficiently masculine is far from an occasional event. Instead, insecurity, feelings of emasculation, and the suspicion of inadequate masculinity are ubiquitous for men. These concerns and feelings of deficiency instigate the enactment of masculinity in everyday life. Because true masculinity is narrowly defined, esteemed, and unattainable, a strain always exists, and the result of that strain is overcompensation and the continual striving for ever greater masculinity.

Kimmel emphasizes the role of men as a sort of "gender police," describing homophobia as the fear among men that other men will detect their insufficient masculinity (1994). This fear, however, is itself a source of shame and must be covered up, along with any possible feminine or inadequately masculine characteristics, ideally with bold demonstrations of strength and masculinity: "What we call masculinity is often a hedge against being revealed as a fraud, an exaggerated set of activities that keep others from seeing through us, and a frenzied effort to keep at bay those fears within ourselves . . . the reigning definition of masculinity is a defensive effort to prevent being emasculated" (Kimmel 1994, p. 103).

Empirical research across a variety of cultures supports the view that masculinity is not easily attained but rather must be continually pursued in the face of threats and challenges (Gilmore 1990). Social psychology research on "precarious manhood" supports this view of men as plagued by chronic doubts (Bosson et al. 2009). In one study researchers found that student participants were able to spontaneously report numerous ways that a man could lose his masculinity (e.g., losing his job) but relatively fewer ways that women could lose femininity (Vandello et al. 2008). Thus, people find it intuitive that men's masculine status is tenuous and easily undermined but do not view femininity in the same way.

One reason that masculinity is easily threatened is that masculine status is relative and hierarchical (Kimmel 1994). Thus, as one man establishes his masculine standing, he necessarily diminishes the standing of other men. Indeed, one way to establish one's own masculinity is by insulting that of another man, creating a self-reinforcing dynamic

in which men feed the social pressure that compelled their own masculinity striving in the first place. Thus, masculine insecurity may be in a sense contagious, as it creates in men the seeds of its own perpetuation.

Past research on gender and masculinity in the field and laboratory highlights men's sensitivity to threats. For example, Macmillan and Gartner found that employed wives of unemployed husbands face a greater risk of domestic abuse, perhaps because their employment constitutes a threat to the masculinity of their spouse (1999), a finding also shown for relative spousal income levels (McCloskey 1996). Further, men who are more economically dependent on their wives tend to do less housework (Brines 1994; but see also Bittman et al. 2003), perhaps acting to distance themselves from behaviors seen as feminine. In one experimental study, social psychologists found that men whose masculinity was threatened via bogus feedback on a gender identity survey were more likely to subsequently sexually harass a female participant in the study (Maass et al. 2003). This body of research supports masculinity theorists' contention that men are highly attentive to their masculine status, responding to threats by enacting behaviors associated with masculinity, including aggression and violence.

From this literature we cull two main theoretical claims: (1) a narrower definition exists for what are acceptable and respected masculine traits, as opposed to feminine traits, and (2) masculinity tends to be more respected than femininity (e.g., Ridgeway 2011). Together, these dynamics lead men to be both vulnerable to masculinity threats, due to the narrow definition of masculinity, and motivated to reclaim a masculine gender identity, due to the prestige attached to it. This is not to say that social expectations do not also compel women to "do gender" (West and Zimmerman 1987; Butler 1990; Bordo 1993), and indeed researchers have argued that a corresponding ideal of "hegemonic femininity" exists (e.g., Ussher 1997; Krane et al. 2004) and that women sometimes strive to reestablish their femininity in the face of threats (Griffin 1998; Munsch and Wilier 2012). But we argue here that women should be less readily threatened by feedback suggesting they lack femininity and less motivated to reclaim a feminine identity. Thus, in the current investigation we expect stronger reactions to gender identity threats among men than among women. We return in the General Discussion section to the issue of feminine overcompensation and under what conditions we expect that it would be most likely.

Theories of Identity

The above theoretical reasoning clarifies why we expect greater responsiveness to gender identity threats in men than in women, but it does not explain why we predict that men will overcompensate in the face of such threats. We draw upon theories of identity for a characterization of how individuals recover valued identities in the face of disconfirming feedback. Identity theorists argue that people strive to maintain identities that are deeply held (Burke and Tully 1977; McCall and Simmons 1978; Stets and Burke 2000b) and socially esteemed (Cialdini et al. 1976). Identity theorists often posit a hierarchy of identities of varying strength (e.g., Stryker 1980), asserting that people are more motivated to act in ways that maintain strongly held and fundamental identities.

Identity theories offer insight on how individuals enact and maintain valued identities in the course of interaction. For example, identity control theory (Burke 2004) proposes a cybernetic model of the relationships between self-concept, behavior, and situational feedback. In the model, individuals receive information that is relevant to a given, salient identity and assess whether this feedback is consistent with the identity. When discrepancies are detected, they behave in ways designed to bring situational feedback in line with their identity standard. Importantly, many theories of identity would predict that when people receive social feedback that is not consistent with a given identity standard, they will enact more extreme versions of behaviors associated with that identity (Burke 1991; Heise 2007; Burke and Stets 2009). Importantly, under such conditions individuals are expected not merely to compensate but to overcompensate in an effort to recover the identity.

For example, if a person assuming a role (e.g., mother, athlete) strongly associated with some characteristic (e.g., warmth, competitiveness) received feedback that she or he failed to convey this trait in interaction (e.g., behaving coldly or passively), that person would be likely to enact an extreme form of the characteristic in an effort to restore an average presentation of self closer to the desired level. This view of identity maintenance is akin to the workings of a thermostat, which does not maintain a steady temperature but instead starts heating cycles that lift a room's temperature beyond the desired level upon receiving feedback that the temperature has fallen too far below its target. Thus, individuals responding to feedback that they have fallen short of expectations associated with a valued self-concept are expected to go beyond prototypical behaviors associated with the identity, acting in ways that are extreme versions of the identity in order to reclaim it. Nonetheless, such a response can be self-defeating as the feelings of inadequacy motivating the response are detectable in the extremity of the individual's reaction.

In research on identity processes, gender identification as masculine or feminine drives gender-relevant behaviors, such as men who identify as highly masculine behaving in a more dominant or competitive fashion (Burke 1989; Stets and Burke 2000a). Gender identities are thought to typically be strongly held (Burke and Tully 1977). Further, other research on identity maintenance finds that individuals are more motivated to maintain identities that are highly socially valued (Cialdini et al. 1976). As a result, we would expect men to be strongly driven to recover a masculine gender identity when faced with situational feedback suggesting they lack masculinity, more than we would expect women to strive to recover femininity. Further, men's behavior in the face of threat should not simply be compensatory, but rather overcompensatory. In an effort to project an overall impression of sufficient masculinity for themselves and others, men should enact extreme masculine behaviors when they receive feedback suggesting a lack of masculinity.

Testosterone and Masculinity

A mounting body of physiological research has explored relationships between levels of the steroid hormone testosterone and a variety of social behaviors in humans. Most notably for the present investigation, several studies have linked testosterone levels with masculine behaviors and attitudes related to dominance, aggression, power, risk-taking, and competitiveness (e.g., Mazur and Booth 1998; Booth et al. 2006; Carney, Cuddy, and Yap 2010). Most relevant to the present investigation, past research finds that testosterone levels are associated with (1) sensitivity to threats and status standing (van Honk et al. 1999; Josephs et al. 2006; Terburg, Aarts, and van Honk 2012) and (2) the enactment of dominance behaviors (Mazur and Booth 1998; Mehta, Jones, and Josephs 2008). This body of work and the fact that testosterone levels are typically found at significantly higher levels in men than women suggest the possibility that testosterone levels might play a role in masculine overcompensation.

But how exactly might testosterone levels and overcompensation be linked? Research on testosterone and masculine-typed behaviors like aggression and dominance has typically failed to find consistent main effects of testosterone levels on behavior (Rowe et al. 2004; Archer 2006), suggesting that the link between testosterone and behavior is more nuanced than often assumed (Booth et al. 2006). Most research supports the view that testosterone plays a complex role in influencing traits and behaviors associated with masculinity, both in general and in the specific domain of men's responses to threats and challenges (Kemper 1990; Josephs et al. 2006).

One possibility is that men's testosterone levels might mediate the overcompensation effect. It could be that testosterone increases when men are faced with a masculinity threat and these higher levels in turn lead to more masculine behaviors. This possibility is consistent with research on the "challenge hypothesis." Originally developed to explain the role of testosterone in nonhuman animals (Wingfield et al. 1990), applied to humans the hypothesis argues that threatened men will exhibit increased testosterone levels, which in turn leads to higher levels of aggression and dominance (Archer 2006; Trumble et al. 2012). Consistent with this, Cohen et al. (1996) found that men who were bumped and insulted in a laboratory experiment showed significant testosterone increases and

more aggressive behavior, especially if they were from the American South, where the researchers argue such actions are culturally understood to be more threatening to a man's standing.

A more likely alternative is that testosterone levels could moderate the masculine overcompensation effect. It could be the case, for example, that men with higher basal testosterone levels are more responsive to masculinity threats. This is suggested by research on "the mismatch effect," which shows that higher-testosterone men are more concerned with their status and dominance and more sensitive to threats to their standing (Newman, Sellers, and Josephs 2005; Josephs et al. 2006). For example, research has found that higher-testosterone individuals look longer at pictures of threatening faces than those with lower testosterone (van Honk et al. 1999). Further, studies show that when the status of higher-testosterone individuals is challenged, they react with emotional arousal, increased heart rate, and greater focus on status and power concerns (Josephs et al. 2003; Josephs et al. 2006). Taken together, these findings suggest the possibility that masculine overcompensation is more pronounced among higher-testosterone men.

Present Research

The above-reviewed theory and research suggests the plausibility of our central claim. On the one hand, masculinity theorists argue that masculinity is both narrowly defined and highly socially valued, making men relatively more likely to perceive threats to their masculinity and more motivated to respond to them. Theories of identity explain how individuals strive to maintain deeply held and socially valued identities like masculinity, positing that such identities are maintained via an overcompensation dynamic in which individuals respond to threats with extreme forms of identity-consistent attitudes and behavior. Finally, research has linked testosterone levels with responsiveness to threats and the enactment of masculine traits like dominance, though it remains an open question whether testosterone levels might mediate or moderate the masculine overcompensation dynamic.

Based on the above, we hypothesize that men will react to masculinity threats with extreme demonstrations of masculinity but that women will be far less affected by corresponding threats to their femininity. We test this claim across a series of studies. Study 1 is a laboratory experiment in which we tested whether men whose masculinity was threatened would adopt more masculine attitudes. In study 2 we conducted another laboratory experiment in an effort to identify what aspect of masculinity men enact through overcompensation. Study 3 tests the masculine overcompensation thesis in a more diverse sample, using a national survey to examine whether men who report greater feelings that social changes threaten the status of men also tend to espouse more masculine attitudes. In each of these studies, we also test for possible effects for women. Finally, in study 4 we returned to a laboratory setting to explore the possible mediating or moderating role that men's testosterone levels might play in the overcompensation process.

Study 1: An Experimental Test

We conducted a laboratory experiment as an initial test of the masculine overcompensation thesis. In the study we administered a gender identity survey to men and women and then gave them randomly determined feedback indicating that they had scored in either the "masculine" or "feminine" range relative to past study participants. We then looked at how this feedback might affect their responses on subsequent surveys. Specifically we measured participants' support for the Iraq War, views of homosexuality, and interest in purchasing a sport utility vehicle (SUV), all views that were considered masculine in the study population.[1] Based on the above theoretical reasoning, we expect men whose masculinity is threatened to express more support for the Iraq War, more negative views of homosexuality, and more interest in buying an SUV. While we predict effects of masculinity threats but weak or no effects for femininity threats among women, we include women in our study to establish that our predicted effects are in fact unique to men. That said, because the dependent measures we employ are selected to capture masculine attitudes, this study offers limited insight on whether and when women would exhibit overcompensation. . . .

Results

Table 1 gives means for men's and women's attitudes toward the Iraq War and homosexuality. Ratings are mostly low relative to each composite scale's midpoint of "4," suggesting that

TABLE 1. The Effects of Gender Identity Feedback on Men's and Women's Support for the Iraq War, Views of Homosexuality, and Desire to Purchase an SUV

	Gender Identity Threatened (Mean)	Gender Identity Not Threatened (Mean)	t
Men (N = 51):			
Support for Iraq War	3.64 (1.85)	2.65 (1.52)	2.06*
Negative views of homosexuality	4.03 (1.68)	2.77 (1.60)	2.70**
SUV desirability	6.56 (2.63)	4.84 (3.16)	2.09*
SUV pay (in thousands of dollars)	28.00 (13.76)	20.68 (10.63)	2.10*
Women (N = 60):			
Support for Iraq War	2.52 (1.59)	2.40 (1.39)	.30
Negative views of homosexuality	2.54 (1.81)	2.20 (1.52)	.80
SUV desirability	5.20 (3.03)	5.17 (2.74)	.05
SUV pay (in thousands of dollars)	22.52 (14.6)	25.38 (19.52)	.63

Note: SDs are in parentheses.
*P < .05.
**P < .01.

participants reported generally positive views of homosexuality and low support for war. Turning to our predictions, we find that men whose masculinity was threatened reported significantly greater support for the Iraq War and more negative views of homosexuality than did men in the study whose masculinity was not threatened (P's < .05). Women, however, showed no significant differences across conditions in their reported attitudes.

Turning to our predictions regarding vehicle preferences, men whose masculinity was threatened reported viewing the SUV as more desirable and reported being willing to spend more money to purchase it than did unthreatened men. On average, men whose masculinity was threatened reported a willingness to pay $7,320 more for the SUV than did men whose masculinity was not. . . . Women showed no significant differences across conditions in how desirable they felt any of the vehicles were, nor in how much they were willing to pay for them. Finally, a higher proportion of threatened men (40%) than unthreatened men (16%) reported being most likely to buy the SUV from among the four vehicles ($\chi^2(1) =$. 3.57, $P = .059$); however, we found no difference between threatened (17%) and unthreatened women (17%).

We also explored participants' reported emotions. These analyses were largely exploratory. One could imagine that men whose masculinity was threatened might report greater negative affect. Alternatively, threatened men might express lower levels of emotions in general in effort to appear more masculine. Results supported the former prediction as threatened men reported feeling more guilty, ashamed, upset, and hostile than unthreatened men (P's < .05). Women showed no differences across conditions with one exception; women given feedback that they were masculine reported feeling higher levels of nervousness than women who were told they were feminine ($P < .03$).[2]

Discussion

Results of study 1 support the masculine overcompensation thesis. As predicted, men whose masculinity was threatened expressed more masculine attitudes than did men whose masculinity was not. Threatened men reported greater support for war, more negative views of homosexuality, and greater interest in purchasing an SUV, all attitudes that a pretest confirmed were viewed as masculine in the study population. Threatened men also reported significantly greater negative affect on multiple emotion survey items. In contrast, women showed no significant effects of the gender identity feedback.

One possible concern regarding the results of this study is that random assignment might have failed to equalize important characteristics across conditions of the study. As one way to test for this concern, we looked at participants' self-reported liberalism as reported on the demographic questionnaire administered before the experimental manipulation. Men reported effectively the same levels of liberalism in the threatened and unthreatened conditions ($t = .87$, $P = .39$). If anything, more liberal men were more often assigned to the threat condition, an initial difference that would make the predicted effects for support for war and expressed homophobia less likely. Indeed, in a multivariate analysis of these effects controlling for self-reported liberalism, the effects of threat for men become slightly more statistically significant. Women's reported liberalism also did not differ significantly across conditions ($t = -.26$, $P = .80$). We also analyzed participant's scores on the Bem Sex Role Inventory. Masculinity and femininity scores for men and women did not vary across conditions (P's > .29); nor did they interact with any of the main effects reported here.

Thus, we have evaluated several alternative accounts for the data beside the masculine overcompensation thesis, including the possibilities that (1) men and women react to gender identity threat with extreme gender-typed behaviors, (2) men assigned to the masculinity-threat condition were simply more politically conservative, and (3) men assigned to the masculinity-threat condition were more (or less) masculine (or feminine). In each case we found no support for these alternative explanations.

Study 2: Masculinity Threats and Dominance

The purpose of study 2 is to develop a more general understanding of what aspect of masculinity men seek to bolster in response to masculinity threats. One possibility suggested by the results of study 1 is that men respond to masculinity threats by seeking to reacquire feelings of dominance and power, core characteristics of masculinity (Kimmel 1994). If so, it is possible that threatened men in study 1 sought to reassert their desire and support for dominance in advocating aggressive military action, subordination of a population perceived as violating traditional gender roles, and expressing a desire to purchase a large, powerful vehicle.

To test this reasoning more directly, we replicated the methodology of study 1, employing new dependent measures, including a standard measure of desire for dominance and support for dominance hierarchies, "social dominance orientation" (Pratto et al. 1994). Past research suggests that social dominance orientation could be implicated in masculine overcompensation. Dominance attitudes tend to be higher in men than women (Sidanius, Pratto, and Bobo 1996). Men who identify more strongly as men hold stronger dominance

attitudes, while the opposite pattern is observed among women (Wilson 2005). Men higher in dominance attitudes are more responsive to masculinity threats (Maass et al. 2003). In turn, dominance attitudes predict support for war and nonegalitarian political attitudes (Sidanius and Pratto 1999).

A secondary purpose of this study is to address a potential alternative explanation for study 1. One commonality among two of the dependent measures used in our first study—support for the Iraq War and opposition to homosexuality—is that each is related to conservatism in the contemporary United States. Thus, it could be that men whose masculinity was threatened in that study adopted more conservative political attitudes, perhaps because of cultural associations between masculinity and political conservatism (e.g., Ducat 2004). To test this possibility we added multiple surveys tapping aspects of political conservatism as dependent measures. . . .

Results and Discussion

First, we find support for our central prediction (see table 2). Men whose masculinity was threatened did express stronger dominance attitudes than unthreatened men ($P < .04$). However, there

TABLE 2. The Effects of Gender Identity Feedback on Men's and Women's Dominance Attitudes, Political Conservatism, System Justification, and Traditionalism

	Gender Identity Threatened (Mean)	Gender Identity Not Threatened (Mean)	t
Men ($N = 40$):			
Dominance attitudes	4.36 (1.53)	3.26 (1.61)	2.22*
Political conservatism	3.77 (1.07)	3.41 (.96)	1.12
System justification	5.06 (1.43)	5.04 (1.08)	.05
Traditionalism	2.23 (.95)	2.96 (1.23)	2.11*
Women ($N = 60$):			
Dominance attitudes	2.91 (1.43)	2.57 (1.78)	.80
Political conservatism	3.07 (.73)	3.27 (.61)	1.15
System justification	4.45 (1.00)	4.55 (.91)	.41
Traditionalism	2.72 (.93)	2.65 (.95)	.31

Note: SDs are in parentheses.
* $P < .05$.
** $P < .01$.

was no effect of gender identity feedback on the reported dominance attitudes of women ($P > .40$). This finding supports our reasoning that men react to masculinity threats with stronger dominance-related attitudes, in this case reflected in their greater desire for dominance and support for dominance hierarchies in society. This finding suggests that increased desire and support for dominance among threatened men may have driven the results of study 1.

We found no support, however, for the notion that masculinity threats simply made men more conservative in general. Threatened men did not report more conservative views on a battery measuring attitudes on several political issues, nor greater system justification (P's $> .25$). In fact, threatened men reported significantly less traditionalism ($P < .05$), a result we did not expect. Revisiting the items used to assess this construct, it may have been that men whose masculinity was threatened were disinclined to show deference to the ideas of those who came before them, preferring to go with newer, riskier ideas of their own. If so, this finding could be consistent with the notion that men sought to reclaim masculinity by expressing masculine-typed views associated with strength, power, and dominance. We found no effects of gender identity feedback on women's reported levels of political conservatism, system justification, or traditionalism (P's $> .25$).

Study 3: Correlational Analyses in a Diverse Sample

Studies 1 and 2 demonstrated in laboratory settings that men whose masculinity was threatened reacted with more extreme masculine attitudes, in particular views associated with dominance. These studies were, however, conducted within a relatively small, homogeneous population, creating external validity concerns (e.g., Lieberson 1987; but see also Lucas 2003). While laboratory experiments have several unique advantages, for example, random assignment to controlled conditions sharply reduces spuriousness concerns, constraining the scope of alternative explanations—the use of demographically homogeneous convenience samples limits confidence in the generality of findings.

There may have been something unique to the population studied that partially drove the observed effects; for example, it could be that young men are uniquely sensitive to threats to their masculinity where older men might not be. Indeed, ample masculinity research suggests that the dynamics of masculinity can vary substantially by race, class, and age (Schrock and Schwalbe 2009).

One way to address these concerns would be to look at the correlation between masculinity threat and extreme masculine attitudes in a large-scale survey that provides greater demographic heterogeneity. Such a study would offer less certainty that the relationship between the variables was causal, given the threat of spurious and/or reverse causation in correlational research, but it would offer much greater confidence that the findings of studies 1 and 2 are externally valid. Specifically, it would reduce concerns that the results of studies 1 and 2 were driven by the use of a sample that was somehow uniquely vulnerable to masculinity threat. In this way, laboratory experiments and correlational analysis of large-scale surveys involving diverse samples are uniquely complementary methods, as experiments offer leverage on causal inference lacking in correlational research and large-scale surveys on diverse samples offer the external validity lacking in laboratory experiments.

Ideally we would have tested our claims in a large, representative data set, but we were unable to find one with an adequate measure of our central, independent variable: masculinity threat. We were, however, able to partner with a private research firm on the construction of a large-scale survey featuring a diverse sample of Americans, adding to the survey an item gauging perceptions of threat to gender status as well as measures of several of the dependent variables from studies 1 and 2. While the survey was not nationally representative and is essentially a convenience sample, it does provide substantial sample diversity. If our results are robust in analyses on this data set, it would provide evidence that the results of studies 1 and 2 were not driven by some unique characteristic of the samples used in those studies.

In study 3 we test for relationships between men's reported feelings that social changes threaten the status of men and a variety of masculine-typed attitudes. We anticipate that men's feelings of threat will be related to these attitudes but that there will be no association between feelings of gender threat and the same attitudes among women. In addition to addressing external validity concerns, study 3 is intended to substantively extend the findings of studies 1 and 2. While studies 1 and 2 conceptualized masculinity threat as a situational variable, study 3 posits that perceptions that the status of men in the larger society is declining may also threaten men's masculinity. Theorists have argued that men may be highly responsive to their perception of the macrolevel status of their gender, being threatened by the rise of feminism, the gay rights movement, and other social trends that could challenge men's traditional status advantage (e.g., Kimmel 1996; Schrock and Shwalbe 2009). In addition, laboratory research suggests that men's perception that the status difference between men and women has declined are linked to overcompensatory behaviors, like sexual harassment (e.g., Dall'Ara and Maass 2000; Maass et al. 2003).

Study 3 also extends our study of what masculine-typed attitudes and behaviors can be shaped by feelings of threat. In study 3 we again look at the relationship between gender identity threat and support for the Iraq War, views of homosexuality, and dominance attitudes. We also now look at another attitude—belief in male superiority—that theorists have argued is closely tied to men's maintenance of a masculine gender identity (e.g., Kimmel 1994; Beneke 1997). . . .

Results

. . . We predicted that threat to gender status would be associated with more extreme masculine attitudes among men, but not women. . . . Among the control variables, only political conservatism had consistent effects on the dependent variables, being significantly related to the dependent variable in all models presented here. In addition, college-educated respondents tended to show less endorsement of the attitudes we studied.

Looking at our predicted effects, across all four models the effect of gender status threat was significant and in the expected direction for men

(P's $<$ 05). These effects indicate that the more men felt that the status of their gender was threatened by social changes the more they tended to support the Iraq War, hold negative views of homosexuality, believe in male superiority, and hold strong dominance attitudes. . . . [A]s predicted, we see that women's reported feelings . . . show that there was no relationship between women's feelings that the status of their gender was under threat and the attitudes we studied (P's $>$ .55).

We also conducted a variety of analyses investigating whether the relationship between gender status threat and men's attitudes might vary significantly by race, age, income, or education. Analyses showed no consistent interaction effects of threat with these demographic variables. Nonetheless, it is likely that these and other factors can influence the magnitude and character of masculine overcompensation, a potentially fruitful area for future research.

Discussion

Study 3 offers further support for the masculine overcompensation thesis, this time in a more diverse sample than those used in studies 1 and 2. Men who reported that social changes threatened the status of men reported greater support for war, more negative views of homosexuality, stronger belief in male superiority, and stronger dominance attitudes. Women, on the other hand, showed no such relationships.

Perhaps the most significant concern with the study involves inference of causation from the correlations we found. These correlations could, for example, be driven by a reverse causal process: a tendency for individuals adopting more traditional masculine attitudes to more readily perceive that the status of masculinity is under threat, perhaps because they endorse a narrower conception of masculinity. Alternatively, some third variable that we failed to control for in our models could drive the observed associations. For example, though we controlled for political conservatism, it could be that individuals with a more traditional cultural worldview are more inclined to see cultural change as threatening and to adopt traditionally masculine attitudes. We believe these are credible concerns and that the relationships we found could be driven in part by these processes. The results of the controlled experiments of studies 1 and 2, however, offer strong evidence for a causal effect of perceived masculinity threat on men's masculine attitudes. This experimental evidence helps to address the limited capacity for correlational research to support causal conclusions, providing credibility to our causal claims.

Another concern with this study is that the nonrepresentativeness of the sample and the very low response rate might threaten the validity of the data. These aspects of the data set pose serious concerns for matching the magnitude of the coefficients and intercepts from our regression models with the "true" effects that exist in the population. However, our purpose here was to test whether the relationship between threat and masculine attitudes would be significant and positive for men (but not women) in a more diverse sample than those used in studies 1 and 2. The biggest threat posed by the non-representativeness and the low response rate of the survey we used is the possibility that selection into our sample might somehow be correlated with our predicted effects. Although this is possible, we see little reason why a group that is overrepresented in our sample would be uniquely sensitive to masculinity (but not femininity) threats, thus driving the associations (and nonassociations) we observe. Further, many of the effects for control variables . . . are consistent with past research, that is, the link between conservatism and support for war (Zaller 1991)—suggesting that the data set's validity is not fundamentally compromised by the response rate.

One possible alternative explanation for our findings in study 3 is that the rising status of women in educational and professional domains may have led women to report low levels of perceived status threat, impairing our ability to detect any possible effects on gendered attitudes. However, while men did report significantly higher levels of threat ($M = 2.41$) than women ($M = 2.32$; $t = 2.36$; $P = .02$), the magnitude of the difference was likely too small to support this alternative explanation.

These results extend the findings of our prior studies in several ways. First, they offer external validity for the findings of studies 1 and 2, demonstrating a relationship between men's feelings of masculinity threat and more extreme masculine attitudes in a diverse sample of Americans studied outside of a laboratory setting. They further suggest that perception that social changes have diminished the status of men may affect men in ways similar to the individual-level gender identity threats of studies 1 and 2.

Study 4: Testosterone and Overcompensation

The results of studies 1–3 show a close tie between threats to men's masculinity and men's enactment of more extreme masculine attitudes, especially dominance-related attitudes. As noted above, past research has linked men's testosterone levels with sensitivity to status threats and dominance behaviors, suggesting the possibility that testosterone might be implicated in the masculine overcompensation process.

Here we explore two rival hypotheses suggested by past work regarding the role of testosterone in masculine overcompensation. First, it is possible that testosterone levels mediate the relationship between threats and extreme masculine attitudes, with threats leading to increased testosterone levels and, thereafter, masculine attitudes. Alternatively, basal testosterone levels could moderate the strength of the effect of threats on masculine attitudes, with men higher in basal testosterone being more prone to overcompensation.

To test these possibilities, we returned to a laboratory context. Our study was largely identical to study 1 except that it was conducted only among men and at several points participants were asked to provide saliva samples. These samples were subsequently used to measure testosterone levels, allowing us to test whether testosterone mediates or moderates the masculine overcompensation effect. . . .

Results

Mediation

The mediation hypothesis predicts that men whose masculinity is threatened will exhibit increased testosterone, and this higher testosterone will in turn lead to more masculine attitudes. As a first step in evaluating the mediation claim, we tested to see if the masculinity threat had a significant effect on testosterone levels. We found no significant difference between the postmanipulation testosterone levels of threatened participants ($M = 109.54$ pg/ml) and those of unthreatened participants ($M = 119.28$ pg/ml; $t(54) = 1.35$, $P > .15$).[3] We also tested the effect of masculinity threat on postmanipulation testosterone levels while controlling for premanipulation testosterone levels in a multiple regression analysis. Again, we found no significant effect of threat on subsequent testosterone levels ($P > .65$).

Moderation

Finding no evidence for mediation, we turn next to the possibility that basal testosterone levels might moderate the masculine overcompensation effect. To test for moderation, we first centered our measure of participant's basal testosterone (Aiken and West 1991). To test whether participants of different testosterone levels responded differently to masculinity threats, we conducted a series of multiple regression analyses entering basal testosterone level, masculinity threat, and the interaction of the two as predictors of support for the Iraq War, negative views of homosexuality, and support for President Bush.[4]

Looking first at participants' support for the Iraq War, we found a nonsignificant main effect of basal testosterone level. We also found a marginally significant, positive effect of masculinity threat, indicating that at the mean level of basal testosterone, threatened men reported greater support for the Iraq War. Most relevant to the moderation hypothesis, the interaction of masculinity threat and testosterone level is positive and significant. These relationships are depicted in figure 1, which shows that responses to masculinity threats were more pronounced among higher-testosterone men. While higher-testosterone men responded to masculinity threats with greater support for the Iraq War, lower-testosterone men whose masculinity was threatened actually tended to report lower levels of support for the war.

Turning to participants' views of homosexuality, here we find nonsignificant effects of both basal testosterone level and masculinity threat. The interaction of these terms, however, was again positive and significant. Figure 2 illustrates this interaction effect showing that the effect of masculinity threats on men's views of homosexuality varied greatly depending on premanipulation testosterone levels. The higher were men's testosterone levels, the more they responded to masculinity threats with negative views of homosexuality.

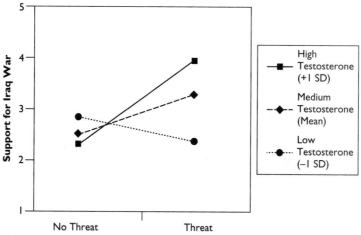

Figure 1. Effects of Testosterone and Masculinity Threat on Support for the Iraq War.

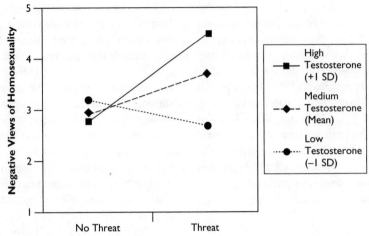

Figure 2. Effects of Testosterone and Masculinity Threat on Negative Views of Homosexuality.

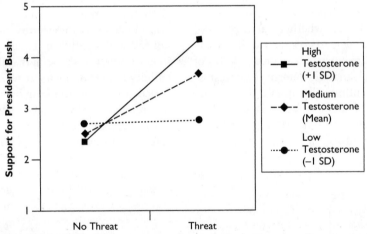

Figure 3. Effects of Testosterone and Masculinity Threat on Support for President Bush.

Low-testosterone men, however, showed the opposite pattern, with threat leading to less negative views of homosexuality.

Finally, analyzing participants' support for [President George W.] Bush, we found a nonsignificant effect of basal testosterone level and a positive, significant effect of masculinity threat. The latter effect indicates that, at the mean level of testosterone level, masculinity threats led participants to report greater support for Bush.

The moderation hypothesis was again supported, as the interaction of testosterone and threat was significant and positive. As shown in figure 3, at higher levels of basal testosterone, participants were more likely to react to masculinity threats with support for Bush. Higher-testosterone men reported greater support for Bush than their unthreatened counterparts, but lower testosterone men showed no change in support for Bush as a result of threats.

Discussion

While we found no evidence that testosterone mediated the masculine overcompensation effect, in study 4 we found consistent support for a moderation effect. The interaction of basal testosterone and masculinity threat was significant for all three dependent measures we investigated: support for the Iraq War, negative views of homosexuality, and support for President Bush. In all cases higher-testosterone men were more likely to react to masculinity threats by adopting more masculine attitudes.

We found that the effects of testosterone were highly contingent. For example, among men whose masculinity was not threatened, we found no main effects of testosterone as higher- and lower-testosterone men indicated roughly equivalent support for the Iraq War, negative views of homosexuality, and support for President Bush. By contrast, the significant effects we found for the interaction of masculinity threats and basal testosterone levels indicate that, when masculinity was threatened, basal testosterone levels were positively associated with masculine attitudes. These results fit well with a growing body of research showing that levels of testosterone do not typically have significant main effects but that in combination with social stimuli like masculinity or status threats, they can have quite strong interaction effects (e.g., Kemper 1990; Josephs et al. 2006). In a sense, the effects of testosterone levels must be "activated" by situational factors if they are to affect behavior or attitudes. Taken together with past research, our findings suggest that higher-testosterone men are more attentive and responsive to threats to their status, reacting to them with dominance-related behaviors and attitudes. More generally, these findings are promising for future research on the interaction of hormones and social context.[5]

General Discussion

Results of four studies offer consistent support for the masculine overcompensation thesis. In study 1, men whose masculinity was threatened expressed more masculine attitudes than men whose masculinity was not. Women, however, were apparently unaffected by equivalent feedback. Results of study 2 showed that men whose masculinity was threatened adopted stronger dominance attitudes, suggesting that these threats motivate men to reassert their support for such hierarchies and their position in them. Study 3 replicated these findings in the context of a large-scale survey study, showing that results were robust in a more diverse sample. Results of study 3 further suggested that perceptions that cultural changes threaten men's standing may serve as masculinity threats in a way similar to the individual-level threats of studies 1 and 2.

Finally, because past research has linked masculinity and dominance with testosterone levels, study 4 investigated what role testosterone might play in masculine overcompensation. While we found no evidence that testosterone levels mediated the effect, we did find evidence for moderation. Men who were higher in basal testosterone were more responsive to masculinity threats, expressing more masculine attitudes following these threats. Low-testosterone men, on the other hand, did not overcompensate.

Taken together these findings help establish the validity of masculine overcompensation. Multiple studies using both laboratory experimental and correlational field methods supported the claim. These findings offer more convincing support together as experiments are uniquely able to answer the weaknesses of correlational field research, establishing causality by controlling for possible confounding variables, thus reducing concerns that observed correlations could be spurious. Conversely, large-scale, correlational field research addresses weaknesses of laboratory experiments by testing hypothesized relationships outside the potentially artificial laboratory context and investigating whether results are robust in more diverse populations than the convenience samples typical of laboratory studies. In addition, the present research also looked at masculine overcompensation at three different levels of analysis, showing how this interactional process may be implicated in macrolevel patterns of political and cultural attitudes, while itself being shaped by endocrinological factors.

More generally, the present research is consistent with theoretical work on both masculinity and identity. In accordance with identity theories, we found that men did not simply strive to compensate when their masculinity was threatened. Rather, they overcompensated, as if striving to pull their average level of masculinity up to more acceptable levels.

Masculinity theorists have typically argued that masculinity is both narrowly defined and more socially valued than femininity, at least in contemporary American culture. Our results are also consistent with these arguments, as men but not women showed consistent responsiveness to threats in our studies. Men not only responded by adjusting their attitudes to be more masculine upon receiving feedback that they lacked masculinity, they also reported greater negative affect (study 1), suggesting greater sensitivity to threat. We found no corresponding tendency for gender identity threats to foster negative emotions in women.

Our application of masculinity theory here also suggests that the extent to which men will overcompensate in the face of masculinity threats is likely to vary across cultures. We expect masculine overcompensation to be most likely and most pronounced in cultural contexts that (1) conceptualize acceptable masculinity in a very narrow way and (2) value masculinity at a relatively high level. Where these factors are both low, where masculinity is more broadly defined and valued similarly to femininity, it should be harder to threaten men's masculinity and they should be less motivated to reclaim it. Future cross-cultural research should explore whether these macrocultural factors do in fact moderate the performance of masculinity in everyday life in the way we theorize. In addition, future research could explore causal links between the definition and valuation of gender identities across social contexts. For example, it may be that the high valuation of masculinity tends to lead to it being narrowly defined as people struggle to understand why someone would violate the standards of a highly valued identity.

Theorists further argue that striving for masculinity in the face of threats is a near ubiquitous aspect of men's lives because of the hierarchical nature of masculinity, the esteem accorded to it, and the presence of a narrowly defined set of ideal masculine traits. Our results are consistent with the prominent role of threat in the maintenance of masculinity. We found evidence linking masculinity threats to diverse outcomes, including domestic and foreign policy views, cultural attitudes, consumption practices, and more general views of hierarchy and inequality between groups. We also found that both situationally induced threats (studies 1, 2, and 4) and perceptions of the declining status of men in the larger society (study 3) were related to the expression of relatively extreme masculine attitudes.

We found evidence that the core aspect of masculinity that men enacted in the face of threats was dominance, a fundamental basis of hierarchy and status differentiation among men and boys (e.g., Johnson 2005; Martin 2009). Experimental and field data showed that threatened men expressed both greater desire for standing within, and support for the existence of, dominance hierarchies. Further, the effects we found for belief in the superiority of men, derogation of homosexuals, support for war, and desire for a large, powerful vehicle may also reflect such dominance striving. These results fit well with past arguments that masculinity is arrayed hierarchically, with men competing to pursue greater masculine status according to reigning cultural definitions of what are valued masculine traits. On such a playing field men must respond to threats and provocations with demonstrations of aggression, power, and dominance if they hope to achieve masculine status relative to other men.

Limitations and Future Directions

Still, the present research leaves open important questions that present fruitful opportunities for future research. A critical point in our argument is that women will typically react less to femininity threats than men do to masculinity threats. But there are other, alternative explanations for the gender asymmetry we observed in our studies. For example, it could be that women are equally responsive to gender identity threats but that our focus on masculine attitudes did not allow us to detect women's efforts to restore a feminine gender identity. While plausible, this interpretation cannot account for the fact that threats led men but not women in study 1 to report greater negative affect, consistent with our reasoning that gender identity threats affect men more than women.

But this is not to say that feminine overcompensation is impossible. On the contrary, past theory and research argue that a hegemonic feminine ideal exists for women (e.g., Ussher 1997; Krane et al. 2004) and find that, accordingly, women sometimes overcompensate in the face of threats to their femininity (e.g., Griffin 1998). We argue here that, in the American context, feminine overcompensation will typically require larger threats than those studied here and will be more likely in cultural contexts where femininity is defined in narrow, traditional ways.

Further, our application of masculinity theory suggests that the more narrowly defined and highly socially valued femininity is in a given cultural context, the more likely feminine overcompensation will be. Future cross-cultural research could explore if feminine overcompensation is more common in cultures that construct acceptable femininity in very specific terms and value it more highly, relative to cultures lower on these two criteria.

Another very fundamental issue that this research leaves unresolved is whether masculine overcompensation is driven more by identity or reputational concerns. When men respond to threats with masculinity striving, are they seeking to restore a fundamental aspect of their self-concept that they deeply value or to restore reputational standing in the eyes of others? The relatively high social esteem associated with masculinity could affect either process, increasing the reputational rewards for men who behave in a masculine way and also increasing men's private valuation of a masculine gender identity. The dependent measures used in the present research involved anonymous surveys of masculine-typed attitudes, suggesting it is unlikely that greater masculinity was motivated by a desire to impress others. But despite this we think it is most likely that masculine overcompensation is motivated by both identity and status concerns. It could be that responses on our anonymous surveys reflect heuristics developed in public settings where masculine status is at stake. This interpretation was not directly tested here, however, and should be evaluated. For example, as a way to get at the roles of identity versus status concerns, future research could experimentally manipulate whether participants' gender

identity feedback was kept private or made public to several other study participants (see Lightdale and Prentice 1994).

A possible concern with the present research is that participants in studies 1, 2, and 4 might have construed the feedback they received about their masculinity as referring more to their sexual orientation than masculinity per se. This alternative interpretation of our results is suggested by past research noting that, for young American men, being masculine is deeply intertwined with maintaining a heterosexual identity (Pascoe 2005). While possible, we believe that the feedback we gave in our studies was primarily interpreted as referring to participants' masculinity and femininity. The gender identity test that participants completed (see app. A) made no reference to sexuality nor did the feedback participants received. In addition, we found convergent results in study 3, which employed a self-report measure of perceived gender identity threat. Nonetheless, it would be a worthwhile line of future research to explore how much masculinity feedback is subjectively construed as sexuality feedback. It could also be interesting to investigate the opposite mediating process, that the effect of sexual orientation feedback on men's subsequent behavior might be mediated by feelings of masculinity threat.

The Role of Testosterone

While we have consistently found no results of gender identity threat for women in the studies reported here, the results of study 4 might lead one to wonder if women high in basal testosterone could also be responsive to gender identity feedback, perhaps even being sensitive to the suggestion that they possess feminine traits. A variety of research suggests that links between testosterone and behavior operate in similar ways for men and women (Mazur and Booth 1998; Josephs et al. 2003; Newman et al. 2005), and some past studies have shown that basal testosterone moderates responses to status-relevant feedback in both men and women (e.g., Mehta et al. 2008). The distributions of basal testosterone among men and women are such that basal testosterone levels at the top end of typical distributions for women are similar to the lowest levels seen among men (Salimetrics 2010), meaning that only women with extremely high basal testosterone (roughly, the top 5% of the distribution) would possess levels akin to the men in study 4 who showed responses to masculinity threats. Thus, a worthwhile avenue for future research could be to explore whether women with very high testosterone might be responsive to threatening gender identity feedback in a way analogous to men.

This reasoning also suggests an intriguing, alternate theory to the one presented here. It might be that who engages in overcompensation is a matter of basal testosterone level more than gender, with moderate- and high-testosterone men (and perhaps extremely high-testosterone women) exhibiting strong responses to gender identity-threatening feedback and low-testosterone men and most women being largely unaffected. Additionally, past research indicates that those high in basal testosterone may be sensitive to feedback threatening their status in general (Josephs et al. 2006; Mehta et al. 2008), not just gender identity feedback. Taken together with the present research, this suggests the possibility that people with relatively higher basal testosterone levels react to low status feedback by enacting attitudes and behaviors intended to assert or reclaim dominance. This alternate theory fits well with contemporary testosterone research, but it diverges in important ways from the theoretical reasoning presented here and merits further empirical examination.

Is Overcompensation a Biological Process?

One interpretation of the results of study 4 is that masculine overcompensation should be viewed as a biological process, but we would caution against this interpretation. First, the study fits well with other research showing that testosterone levels rarely have main effects on human behavior; more common are findings that testosterone levels interact with social stimuli to affect behavior (e.g., Newman et al. 2005; Josephs et al. 2006). Further, in our research we found main effects of situational threats on masculine behaviors across three studies where testosterone levels were not considered. But, as shown in figures 1–3, we found no differences in masculine attitudes by basal testosterone

level among unthreatened men. Testosterone effects were only observed when a situational threat, in a sense, "activated" them.

But, more generally, viewing biological and social factors as necessarily separate and competing to explain zero-sum variance in human behavior reinforces a false and antiquated dichotomy. Social and biological processes are deeply intertwined. Just as we have documented here a physiological factor that influences human behavior, social factors shape biological processes in important ways. For example, life course events (Archer 2006) and situational stimuli (Schultheiss et al. 1999; Schultheiss and Rohde 2002) shape individuals' testosterone levels and, as documented here and elsewhere, these levels in turn interact with social factors in affecting behavior (Josephs et al. 2006). We hope these results suggest the usefulness of incorporating hormonal and other physiological measurement in sociological research, though the vast majority of sociological research questions can be productively studied without regard for this level of analysis.

Conclusion

Because the notion of overcompensation is so common in popular discourse, it may be hard to see that these study results could once have been viewed as counterintuitive. It is not so intuitive, however, for individuals to enact extreme behaviors as a cover for their insecurity. Perhaps the most successful way for men to disguise their masculine insecurity would be to behave in the same way as unthreatened men do. In the present research, this would have resulted in no observed differences between threatened and unthreatened men. Instead, men tend to overcompensate, in a sense overdoing gender, and in so doing inadvertently reveal themselves to be sensitive to threats. One implication of this finding is that extreme masculine behaviors may in fact serve as telltale signs of threats and insecurity. Perhaps those men who appear most assuredly masculine, who in their actions communicate strength, power, and dominance at great levels, may actually be acting to conceal underlying concerns that they lack exactly those qualities they strive to project.

Appendix 1
Gender Identity Survey

The gender identity survey given to participants in studies 1, 2, and 4 is printed below (see Bem 1974).

Please answer the questions that follow as well as you can. Do not skip questions. If you are unsure of an answer, please give the answer that seems best to you.

For each of the following words, please pick a number from the following scale that best indicates how well you think the word describes yourself:

Never or Almost Never True 1-2-3-4-5-6-7 Always or Almost Always True

Once you have picked the number that best describes yourself, enter it into the blank next to the word and move on.

1. Self-reliant _____

2. Yielding _____

3. Helpful _____

4. Defends own beliefs _____

5. Cheerful _____

6. Moody _____

7. Independent _____

8. Shy _____

9. Conscientious _____

10. Athletic _____

11. Affectionate _____

12. Theatrical _____

13. Assertive _____

14. Flatterable _____

15. Happy _____

16. Strong personality _____

17. Loyal _____

18. Unpredictable _____

19. Forceful _____

20. Feminine _____

21. Reliable _____

22. Analytical _____

23. Sympathetic _____

24. Jealous _____

25. Has leadership abilities _____

26. Truthful _____

27. Sensitive to the needs of others _____

28. Willing to take risks _____

29. Understanding _____

30. Secretive _____

31. Makes decisions easily _____

32. Compassionate _____

33. Sincere _____

34. Self-sufficient _____

35. Eager to soothe hurt feelings _____

36. Conceited _____

37. Dominant _____

38. Soft spoken _____

39. Likable _____

40. Masculine _____

41. Warm _____

42. Solemn _____

43. Willing to take a stand _____

44. Tender _____

45. Friendly _____

46. Aggressive _____

47. Gullible _____

48. Inefficient _____

49. Acts as a leader _____

50. Childlike _____

51. Adaptable _____

52. Individualistic _____

53. Does not use harsh language _____

54. Unsystematic _____

55. Competitive _____

56. Loves children _____

57. Tactful _____

58. Ambitious _____

59. Gentle _____

60. Conventional _____

Notes

1. Past theory and research have linked masculinity with support for war (Connell 1985; Christensen and Ferree 2008; Messerschmidt 2010), homophobia (Kimmel 1994), and SUV ownership (Bradsher 2002). Conceptions of masculinity, however, vary across groups (Connell and Messerschmidt. 2005), thus we conducted a pretest ($N = 60$) in a separate sample to assess whether these dependent variables were viewed as masculine among members of the population. Participants rated Iraq War support, negative views of homosexuality, and SUV ownership to be more masculine than they were feminine (P's $< .001$) and more masculine than opposing war, having positive views of homosexuality, or owning one of the other three vehicles tested (P's $< .05$).

2. One would expect one of the 20 items to be significant by chance using a .05 significance standard.

3. Because changes in levels of testosterone might not be detectable for longer than we anticipated, or might attenuate, we also tested for effects of the masculinity threat in the third and fourth samples individually and found none (P's $= .20$, .21, respectively).

4. Past research on the moderating role of testosterone has treated it as either a continuous (Mehta et al. 2008) or dichotomous (e.g., Newman et al. 2005; Josephs et al. 2006) variable. Accordingly, we explored alternate versions of the regression models given here in which testosterone was either trichotomized or dichotomized in various ways (e.g., median split, highest third of distribution vs. lowest two-thirds). Bayesian information criterion (BIC) statistics for these models indicated that the continuous analyses reported here fit the data as well as, or better than, any of these alternatives.

5. These results are the first showing a causal effect of hormone levels on political attitudes. Note that one past study showed an effect of election outcomes on partisans' testosterone levels (Stanton et al. 2009).

References

Adams, Henry E., Lester W. Wright Jr., and Bethany Lohr. 1996. "Is Homophobia Associated with Homosexual Arousal?" *Journal of Abnormal Psychology* 105:440–45.

Adams, Natalie, and Pamela Bettis. 2003. "Commanding the Room in Short Skirts: Cheering as the Embodiment of Ideal Girlhood." *Gender and Society* 17:73–91.

Adler, Alfred. (1910) 1956. "Inferiority Feeling and Masculine Protest." Pp. 45–52 in *The Individual Psychology of Alfred Adler: A Systematic Presentation in Selections from His Writings*, edited by Heinz L. Ansbacher and Rowena R. Ansbacher. New York: Basic Books.

Aiken, Leona S., and Stephen G. West. 1991. *Multiple Regression: Testing and Interpreting Interactions.* Thousand Oaks, Calif.: Sage.

Anderson, Eric. 2009. *Inclusive Masculinity: The Changing Nature of Masculinities.* New York: Routledge.

Archer, John. 2006. "Testosterone and Human Aggression: An Evaluation of the Challenge Hypothesis." *Neuroscience and Biobehavioral Reviews* 30:319–45.

Baumeister, Roy F., Karen Dale, and Kristin L. Sommer. 1998. "Freudian Defense Mechanisms and Empirical Findings in Modern Social Psychology: Reaction Formation, Projection, Displacement,

Undoing, Isolation, Sublimation, and Denial." *Journal of Personality* 66:1081–1124.

Bem, Sandra L. 1974. "The Measurement of Psychological Androgyny." *Journal of Consulting and Clinical Psychology* 42 (2): 155–62.

Beneke, Timothy. 1997. *Proving Manhood: Reflections on Men and Sexism.* Berkeley and Los Angeles: University of California.

Bittman, Michael, Paula England, Liana Sayer, Nancy Folbre, and George Matheson. 2003. "When Does Gender Trump Money? Bargaining and Time in Household Work." *American Journal of Sociology* 109:186–214.

Booth, Allan, Douglas A. Granger, Allan Mazur, and Katie T. Kivlighan. 2006. "Testosterone and Social Behavior." *Social Forces* 85:167–91.

Bordo, Susan. 1993. *Unbearable Weight: Feminism, Western Culture, and the Body.* Berkeley and Los Angeles: University of California Press.

Bosson, Jennifer K., Joseph A. Vandello, Rochelle M. Burnaford, Jonathan R. Weaver, and S. Arzu Wasti. 2009. "Precarious Manhood and Displays of Physical Aggression." *Personality and Social Psychology Bulletin* 35:623–34.

Bradsher, Keith. 2002. *High and Mighty: SUVS—The World's Most Dangerous Vehicles and How They Got That Way.* New York: Public Affairs.

Brines, Julie. 1994. "Economic Dependency, Gender, and the Division of Labor at Home." *American Journal of Sociology* 100:652–88.

Burke, Peter J. 1989. "Gender Identity, Sex, and School Performance." *Social Psychology Quarterly* 52:159–69.

———. 1991. "Identity Processes and Social Stress." *American Sociological Review* 56:836–49.

———. 2004. "Identities and Social Structure: The 2003 Cooley-Mead Award Address." *Social Psychology Quarterly* 67:5–15.

Burke, Peter J., and Jan E. Stets. 2009. *Identity Theory.* New York: Oxford University Press.

Burke, Peter J., and Judy Tully. 1977. "The Measurement of Role/Identity." *Social Forces* 55:880–97.

Butler, Judith. 1990. *Gender Trouble: Feminism and the Subversion of Identity.* New York: Routledge.

Carney, Dana R., Amy J. C. Cuddy, and Andy J. Yap. 2010. "Power Posing: Brief Nonverbal Displays Affect Neuroendocrine Levels and Risk Tolerance." *Psychological Science* 21:1363–38.

Carrigan, Tim, Bob Connell, and John Lee. 1985. "Toward a New Sociology of Masculinity." *Theory and Society* 14:551–604.

Christensen, Wendy M., and Myra Marx Ferree. 2008. "Cowboy of the World? Gender Discourse and the Iraq War Debate." *Qualitative Sociology* 31:287–306.

Cialdini, Robert B., Richard J. Borden, Avril Thorne, Marcus R. Walker, Stephen Freeman, and Lloyd Reynolds Sloan. 1976. "Basking in Reflected Glory: Three (Football) Field Studies." *Journal of Personality and Social Psychology* 34:366–75.

Cohen, Dov, Richard E. Nisbett, Brian F. Bowdle, and Norbert Schwartz. 1996. "Insult, Aggression, and the Southern Culture of Honor: An 'Experimental Ethnography.'" *Journal of Personality and Social Psychology* 70:945–60.

Connell, Robert W. 1983. *Which Way Is Up? Essays on Sex, Class, and Culture,* Sydney: Allen & Unwin.

———. 1985. "Masculinity, Violence, and War." Pp. 4–10 in *War/Masculinity,* edited by Paul Patton and Ross Poole. Melbourne: Intervention.

———. 1987. *Gender and Power.* Stanford, Calif.: Stanford University Press.

———. 1995. *Masculinities.* Berkeley and Los Angeles: University of California Press.

Connell, Robert W. and James W. Messerschmidt. 2005. "Hegemonic Masculinity: Rethinking the Concept." *Gender and Society* 19:829–59.

Dall'Ara, Elena, and Anne Maass. 2000. "Studying Sexual Harassment in the Laboratory: Are Egalitarian Women at Higher Risk?" *Sex Roles* 41:681–704.

Ducat, Stephen. 2004. *The Wimp Factor: Gender Gaps, Holy Wars, and the Politics of Anxious Masculinity.* Boston: Beacon.

Fasteau, Marc F. 1974. *The Male Machine.* New York: McGraw-Hill.

Freud, Sigmund. (1898) 1962. "The Neuro-Psychoses of Defense." Pp. 43–70 in *The Standard Edition of the Complete Psychological Works of Sigmund Freud,* vol. 3. London: Hogarth.

Gilmore, David D. 1990. *Manhood in the Making.* New Haven, Conn.: Yale University Press.

Griffin, Pat. 1998. *Strong Women, Deep Closets: Lesbians and Homophobia in Sport.* Champaign, Ill.: Human Kinetics.

Heise, David R. 2007. *Expressive Order: Confirming Sentiments in Social Actions.* New York: Springer.

Johnson, Allan G. 2005. *The Gender Knot: Unraveling our Patriarchal Legacy*. Philadelphia: Temple University Press.

Josephs, Robert A., Matthew L. Newman, Ryan P. Brown, and Jeremy M. Beer. 2003. "Status, Testosterone, and Human Intellectual Performance: Stereotype Threat as Status Concern." *Psychological Science* 14:158–63.

Josephs, Robert A., Jennifer G. Sellers, Matthew L. Newman, and Pranjal H. Mehta. 2006. "The Mismatch Effect: When Testosterone and Status Are at Odds." *Journal of Personality and Social Psychology* 90:999–1013.

Kemper, Theodore D. 1990. *Social Structure and Testosterone*. New Brunswick, N.J.: Rutgers University Press.

Kimmel, Michael S. 1994. "Masculinity as Homophobia: Fear, Shame, and Silence in the Construction of Gender Identity." Pp. 119–41 in *Theorizing Masculinities*, edited by Harry Brod and Michael Kaufman. Newbury Park, Calif.: Sage.

———. 1996. *Manhood in America: A Cultural History*. New York: Free Press.

Kimmel, Michael S., and Matthew Mahler. 2003. "Adolescent Masculinity, Homophobia, and Violence: Random School Shootings, 1982–2001." *American Behavioral Scientist* 46:1439–58.

Krane, Vikki, Precilla Y. L. Choi, Shannon M. Baird, Christine M. Aimar, and Kerri J. Kauer. 2004. "Living the Paradox: Female Athletes Negotiate Femininity and Muscularity." *Sex Roles* 50:315–29.

Lieberson, Stanley. 1987. *Making It Count: The Improvement of Social Research and Theory*. Berkeley and Los Angeles: University of California Press.

Lightdale, Jennifer R., and Deborah A. Prentice. 1994. "Rethinking Sex Differences in Aggression: Aggressive Behavior in the Absence of Social Roles." *Personality and Social Psychology Bulletin* 20:34–44.

Lucas, Jeffrey W. 2003. "Theory Testing, Generalization, and the Problem of External Validity." *Sociological Theory* 21:236–53.

Maass, Anne, Mara Cadinu, Gaia Guarnieri, and Annalisa Grasselli. 2003. "Sexual Harassment under Social Identity Threat: The Computer Harassment Paradigm." *Journal of Personality and Social Psychology* 85 (5): 853–70.

Macmillan, Ross, and Rosemary Gartner. 1999. "When She Brings Home the Bacon: Labor-Force Participation and the Risk of Spousal Violence against Women." *Journal of Marriage and the Family* 61:947–58.

Martin, John Levi. 2009. "Formation and Stabilization of Vertical Hierarchies among Adolescents: Towards a Quantitative Ethology of Dominance among Humans." *Social Psychology Quarterly* 72:241–64.

Mazur, Allan, and Allan Booth. 1998. "Testosterone and Dominance." *Behavioral and Brain Sciences* 21:353–63.

McCall, George J., and J. L. Simmons. 1978. *Identities and Interactions*. New York: Free Press.

McCloskey, Lann A. 1996. "Socioeconomic and Coercive Power within the Family." *Gender and Society* 10:449–63.

Mehta, Pranjal H., Amanda C. Jones, and Robert A. Josephs. 2008. "The Social Endocrinology of Dominance: Basal Testosterone Predicts Cortisol Changes and Behavior following Victory and Defeat." *Journal of Personality and Social Psychology* 94:1078–93.

Messerschmidt, James W. 2010. *Hegemonic Masculinities and Camouflaged Politics: Unmasking the Bush Dynasty and Its War against Iraq*. Boulder, Colo.: Paradigm.

Munsch, Christin, and Robb Willer. 2012. "The Role of Gender Identity Threat in Perceptions of Date Rape and Sexual Coercion." *Violence against Women* 18(10): 1125–46.

Newman, Matthew L., Jennifer G. Sellers, and Robert A. Josephs. 2005. "Testosterone, Cognition, and Social Status." *Hormones and Behavior* 47:205–11.

Pascoe, C. J. 2005. "'Dude, You're a Fag': Adolescent Masculinity and the Fag Discourse." *Sexualities* 8:329–46.

Pratto, Felicia, James Sidanius, Lisa M. Stallworth, and Bertram F. Malle. 1994. "Social Dominance Orientation: A Personality Variable Predicting Social and Political Attitudes." *Journal of Personality and Social Psychology* 67:741–63.

Ridgeway, Cecilia L. 2011. *Framed by Gender: How Gender Inequality Persists in the Modern World*. New York: Oxford University Press.

Rowe, Richard, Barbara Maughan, Carol M. Worthman, E. Jane Costello, and Adrian Angold.

2004. "Testosterone, Antisocial Behavior, and Social Dominance in Boys: Pubertal Development and Biosocial Interaction." *Biological Psychiatry* 55:546–52.

Salimetrics, LLC. 2010. *Expanded Range Salivary Testosterone Enzyme Immunoassay Kit.* State College, Pa.: Salimetrics, LLC.

Schrock, Douglas, and Michael Schwalbe. 2009. "Men, Masculinity, and Manhood Acts." *Annual Review of Sociology* 35:277–95.

Schultheiss, Oliver C., Kenneth L. Campbell, and David C. McClelland. 1999. "Implicit Power Motivation Moderates Men's Testosterone Response to Imagined and Real Dominance Success." *Hormones and Behavior* 36:234–41.

Schultheiss, Oliver C., and Wolfgang Rohde. 2002. "Implicit Power Motivation Predicts Men's Testosterone Changes and Implicit Learning in a Contest Situation." *Hormones and Behavior* 41:195–202.

Sidanius, Jim, and Felicia Pratto. 1999. *Social Dominance: An Intergroup Theory of Social Hierarchy and Oppression.* New York: Cambridge University Press.

Sidanius, Jim, Felicia Pratto, and Lawrence Bobo. 1996. "Racism, Conservatism, Affirmative Action, and Intellectual Sophistication: A Matter of Principled Conservatism or Group Dominance?" *Journal of Personality and Social Psychology* 70:476–90.

Stanton, Steven J., Jacinta C. Beehner, Ekjyhot K. Saini, Cynthia M. Kuhn, and Kevin S. LaBar. 2009. "Dominance, Politics, and Physiology: Voters' Testosterone Changes on the Night of the 2008 United States Presidential Election." *PLoS One* 4 (10): e7543.

Stets, Jan E. and Peter J. Burke. 2000a. "Femininity/Masculinity." Pp. 997–1005 in *Encyclopedia of Sociology,* rev. ed. Edited by Edgar F. Borgatta and Rhonda J. V. Montgomery. New York: Macmillan.

———. 2000b. "Identity Theory and Social Identity Theory." *Social Psychology Quarterly* 63:224–37.

Stryker, Sheldon. 1980. *Symbolic Interactionism: A Social Structural Version.* Menlo Park, Calif.: Cummings.

Terburg, David, Henk Aarts, and Jack van Honk. 2012. "Testosterone Affects Gaze Aversion from Angry Faces outside of Conscious Awareness." *Psychological Science* 23:459–63.

Trumble, Benjamin C., Daniel Cummings, Christopher von Rueden, Kathleen A. O'Connor, Eric A. Smith, Michael Gurven, and Hillard Kaplan. 2012. "Physical Competition Increases Testosterone among Amazonian Forager-Horticulturalists: A Test of the 'Challenge Hypothesis.'" *Proceedings of the Royal Society of London B: Biological Sciences* 279:2907–12.

Ussher, Jane M. 1997. *Fantasies of Femininity: Reframing the Boundaries of Sex.* New Brunswick, N.J.: Rutgers University Press.

Vandello, Joseph, Jennifer K. Bosson, Dov Cohen, Rochelle M. Burnaford, and Jonathan R. Weaver. 2008. "Precarious Manhood." *Journal of Personality and Social Psychology* 95:1325–39.

van Honk, Jack, Adriaan Tuiten, Rien Verbaten, Marcel van den Hout, Hans Koppescaar, Jos Thijssen, and Edward de Haan. 1999. "Correlations among Salivary Testosterone, Mood, and Selective Attention to Threat in Humans." *Hormones and Behavior* 36:17–24.

Weinstein, Netta, William S. Ryan, Cody R. DeHaan, Andrew K. Przybylski, Nicole Legate, and Richard M. Ryan. 2012. "Parental Autonomy Support and Discrepancies between Implicit and Explicit Sexual Identities: Dynamics of Self-Acceptance and Defense." *Journal of Personality and Social Psychology* 102:815–32.

West, Candace, and Don H. Zimmerman. 1987. "Doing Gender." *Gender and Society* 1:125–51.

Willer, Robb, Ko Kuwabara, and Michael W. Macy. 2009. "The False Enforcement of Unpopular Norms." *American Journal of Sociology* 115:451–90.

Wilson, Marc S. 2005. "Gender Group Identity as a Moderator of Sex Differences in Interpersonal and Intergroup Dominance." Pp. 145–67 in *Psychology of Gender Identity,* edited by Janice W. Lee. New York: Nova.

Wingfield, John C., Robert E. Hegner, Alfred M. Dufty Jr., and Gregory F. Ball. 1990. "The 'Challenge Hypothesis': Theoretical Implications for Patterns of Testosterone Secretion, Mating Systems, and Breeding Strategies." *American Naturalist* 136:829–46.

Zaller, John. 1991. "Information, Values, and Opinions." *American Political Science Review* 85:1215–37.

The Social Construction of Gender Relations

To sociologists, the psychological discussion of sex roles—that collection of attitudes, traits, and behaviors that are normative for either boys or girls— exposes the biological sleight of hand that suggests that what is normative— enforced, socially prescribed—is actually normal. But psychological models themselves do not go far enough, unable to fully explain the variations *among* men or women based on class, race, ethnicity, sexuality, and age, or to explain the ways in which one gender consistently enjoys power over the other. And, most importantly to sociologists, psychological models describe how individuals acquire sex role identity, but then assume that these gendered individuals enact their gendered identities in institutions that are gender-neutral.

Sociologists have taken up each of these themes in exploring (1) how the institutions in which we find ourselves are also gendered, (2) the ways in which those psychological prescriptions for gender identity reproduce *both* gender difference and male domination, and (3) the ways in which gender is accomplished and expressed in everyday interaction.

In this section, Rosalind Barnett and Caryl Rivers reveal the problems with the "interplanetary theory" of gendered communication. Then, Candace West and Don Zimmerman make clear that gender is not a property of the individual, something that one *has*, but rather is a process that one *does* in everyday interaction with others. And that what one is doing is not simply doing gender, but also doing difference, which in our society also means doing inequality. Finally, Laurel Westbrook and Kristin Schilt expand on that link between doing gender and inequality in their essay about how the transgender community reproduces, challenges, and reverses gender assumptions.

Men and Women Are from Earth

ROSALIND BARNETT AND CARYL RIVERS

Do men and women come from two separate "communication cultures" that make it difficult for them to hear one another? Are they doomed to moan, eternally, "You just don't understand?" Are women the caring, sharing, open sex, while men are hardwired to be strong, silent, self-absorbed, and uncomfortable with emotions? This portrait of the sexes has become conventional wisdom, promoted in best sellers like John Gray's *Men Are from Mars, Women Are from Venus* and Deborah Tannen's *You Just Don't Understand.* The idea has also leached into the academic and therapy arenas.

The textbook *Language and Social Identity,* by Daniel N. Maltz and Ruth A. Borker, states flatly, "American men and women come from different sociolinguistic subcultures, having learned to do different things with words in a conversation."

In this scenario, women are the relationship experts, holding marriages and friendships together by putting others first, avoiding conflict at the cost of their own wishes, and not putting burdens on men by demanding intimacy or understanding. Women speak "in a different voice," as feminist psychologist Carol Gilligan put it, because they are so tuned in to others. Men, in contrast, lack empathy with others. If a friend or coworker approaches them to talk about problems, they change the subject or make a joke. In personal relationships men don't have a clue, and as parents, they are the inferior sex. They lack the inherent communication abilities necessary for parenting that nature confers on women.

Is this dismal picture accurate? Do the best sellers, some textbooks, and the media's pop psychologists have it right? Are men and women so hamstrung by their communication styles that they are perpetually destined to misunderstand each other—ships eternally passing in the night?

As poetic and familiar as this idea seems, it is more fantasy than fact. New research tears this conventional wisdom to shreds. Women and men are far more alike than different in how they listen to people, the ways they react to others who are in trouble, and their ability to be open and honest in communication. As University of Wisconsin psychologists Kathryn Dindia and Mike Allen say, "It is time to stop perpetuating the myth that there are large sex differences in men's and women's self disclosure."

Women, Deborah Tannen says, use their unique conversational style to show involvement, connection, and participation, while men use speech to indicate independence and position in a hierarchy. Women seek connection and want to be liked, while men just want to press their own agenda. Tannen also states as fact that men always interrupt women. Is this really how men and women behave? Sometimes yes, sometimes no. Tannen's problem is that she often sees gender as the main driver of communication, ignoring a whole host of other important factors—such as power, individual personalities, and the situation you're in when you are about to speak. Do men always interrupt women? In fact, the sex differences here are trivial, conclude researchers Kristen Anderson and Campbell Leaper of the University of California at Santa Cruz, based on their meta-analyses of 43 studies. (A meta-analysis summarizes the findings of many studies.) The key to understanding interruptions is the situation—or, as the researchers put it, "The What, When, Where and How." Power is often the key.

Psychologist Elizabeth Aries of Amherst College found that men often interrupt women in conversation. But, when traditional power relationships are reversed—such as in many contemporary couples where the woman is the higher earner, or when male subordinates interact with female superiors—speech patterns also undergo a reversal. The person with less power interrupts less and works harder to keep the conversation going, whether that person is female or male. Those with more power, male or female, are likely to take control of the conversation. Do we really believe that Secretary of State Condoleezza Rice is often interrupted by her male aides? Or that a male law clerk would break into the sentences of Justice Ruth Bader Ginsberg? It's impossible to see the true communication dynamic if we are blinded by the notion that something buried deep in women's psyches chains them to the speech styles of the powerless.

As for men, are they in fact handcuffed by deep-seated inabilities to engage in conversations about emotion? According to essentialist theorists, who believe differences between men and women are innate rather than socially constructed, men are uncomfortable with any kind of communication that has to do with personal conflicts. They avoid talking about their problems. They avoid responding too deeply to other people's problems, instead giving advice, changing the subject, making a joke, or giving no response. Unlike women, they don't react to "troubles talk" by empathizing with others and expressing sympathy. These ideas are often cited in textbooks and in popular manuals, like those written by John Gray, of Mars and Venus fame.

After Gray nabs us with his attention-grabbing titles, he tells us that men are naturally programmed to go into their "caves" and not communicate with other people. Women must never try to talk to men when they withdraw, but must honor their behavior. A woman must not offer help to a man, because it makes him feel weak and incompetent. A woman must never criticize a man or try to change his behavior. She should never show anger. If she feels angry, she must wait until she is "more loving and centered" to talk to him. Only when she is loving and forgiving can she share her feelings. If a man pulls away from her, "he is just fulfilling a valid need to take care of himself for a while."

Gray cites the case of "Bill," who asks his wife, "Mary," to make a phone call for him while he is sitting on the couch watching TV. Mary reacts with a frustrated and helpless tone of voice. She says, "I can't right now, I already have too much to do, I have to change the baby's diaper, I have to clean up this mess, balance the checkbook, finish the wash, and tonight we are going out to a movie. I have too much to do. I just can't do it all!"

Bill goes back to watching TV and disconnects from her feelings. Bill, says Gray, is angry at Mary for making him feel like a failure. He retreats to his cave, "just taking care of himself." If Mary realized this, Gray suggests, she would smile at his request to do still one more chore and say sweetly that she's running behind. As for Bill, all he has to do, Gray suggests, is to say admiringly to Mary, "I just don't know how you do it!" That line might just get Bill a damp diaper in the face. Gray does not suggest that Bill might A) change the baby's diaper, B) help clean up the house, C) balance the checkbook, or D) help with the wash. Who has the power in this marriage—and isn't this really the issue? Gray's scenario puts women in a tight bind, while requiring little from men. Gray's prescription for heterosexual relationships is for the woman to leave the man alone while she supervises the kids' homework, cooks dinner, and cleans up. That's advice that gets couples into trouble, not out of it. A woman who takes Gray's advice at face value may be at serious risk for high stress. Unable to express her anger openly and to ask for what she really needs, always on edge because she must sense a man's every whim and need, she is likely to turn her anger inward. This situation makes her communication inauthentic.

She feels anger, but can't communicate it, and as a result she feels worse and worse about herself and her marriage. She is living a lie—and how good can anyone feel about that? On top of that, her husband has no idea of what she's feeling. There's no way he could be the helpful person he may actually want to be.

In fact, if women expected men to be unable to relate to other people's problems, they would never bother talking to men about such things.

Systematic research does not support those ideas. Erina L. MacGeorge, of Purdue University, and her colleagues at the University of Pennsylvania find no support for the idea that women and men constitute different "communication cultures." Based on three studies that used questionnaires and interviews to sample 738 people—417 women and 321 men—they conclude that: Both men and women view the provision of support as a central element of close personal relationships; both value the supportive communication skills of their friends, lovers, and family members; both make similar judgments about what counts as sensitive, helpful support; and both respond quite similarly to various support efforts.

When someone comes to men with a problem, they don't joke, tell the person to cheer up, change the topic, or run away as Gray and Tannen suggest they do. Both sexes are instead likely to offer sympathy and advice. If men are having a problem, and someone offers a sympathetic response, they don't get angry, minimize, or push the other person away. Like women, they are comforted when people are concerned about them. There are no differences in how men and women handle emotional issues—theirs or others'.

Kristen Neff of the University of Texas at Austin and Susan Harter of the University of Denver uncovered a similar lack of difference in men's and women's styles of conflict resolution. They found that 62 percent of men and 61 percent of women reported that they typically resolved conflicts in their relationships by compromising with their partners. This is a far cry from the idea that women always retreat, and men always insist on getting their way.

Similar doubts have also been raised about the "fact" that men can't share their feelings, and that they always retreat to their caves or take refuge in silence. A huge meta-analysis of 24,000 subjects in 205 peer-reviewed studies found that women disclose slightly more than men—but the effect was trivial. Practically speaking, there were no differences between the sexes. Because therapists (and others) contend that the ability to self-disclose is crucial to success in therapy, they believe that men's chances of being helped are relatively poor. But this is not so, according to these research findings. Even more importantly, the idea that women can't expect men to share, to lend a sympathetic ear, to compromise in settling issues, or to be good listeners can have disastrous consequences. Women who cling to such stereotypes will miss out on close relationships with their male partners and of course men will be further pigeonholed as distant, remote, and unavailable creatures. If that's how they are treated, maybe that's what they will turn into. And if men assume that women are too emotional to discuss problems rationally, they will simply clam up and miss the help and support they really need. Either way, rigid sex stereotypes promote self-fulfilling prophecies.

Unfortunately, the essentialist perspective has so colored the dialogue about the sexes that there is scant room for any narrative other than difference. As we've seen, the difference rhetoric can harm both men and women. Given how little empirical support exists for essentialist ideas, it's high time to broaden the dialogue. We believe that men and women are far more similar than different, a provocative idea that is backed by considerable research. We challenge the conventional wisdom, and we encourage others to do the same.

Doing Gender

CANDACE WEST AND DON H. ZIMMERMAN

In the beginning, there was sex and there was gender. Those of us who taught courses in the area in the late 1960s and early 1970s were careful to distinguish one from the other. Sex, we told students, was what was ascribed by biology: anatomy, hormones, and physiology. Gender, we said, was an achieved status: that which is constructed through psychological, cultural, and social means. To introduce the difference between the two, we drew on singular case studies of hermaphrodites and anthropological investigations of "strange and exotic tribes."

Inevitably (and understandably), in the ensuing weeks of each term, our students became confused. Sex hardly seemed a "given" in the context of research that illustrated the sometimes ambiguous and often conflicting criteria for its ascription. And gender seemed much less an "achievement" in the context of the anthropological, psychological, and social imperatives we studied—the division of labor, the formation of gender identities, and the social subordination of women by men. Moreover, the received doctrine of gender socialization theories conveyed the strong message that while gender may be "achieved," by about age five it was certainly fixed, unvarying, and static—much like sex.

Since about 1975, the confusion has intensified and spread far beyond our individual classrooms. For one thing, we learned that the relationship between biological and cultural processes was far more complex—and reflexive—than we previously had supposed. For another, we discovered that certain structural arrangements, for example, between work and family, actually produce or enable some capacities, such as to mother, that we formerly associated with biology. In the midst of all this, the notion of gender as a recurring achievement somehow fell by the wayside.

Our purpose in this article is to propose an ethnomethodologically informed, and therefore distinctively sociological, understanding of gender as a routine, methodical, and recurring accomplishment. We contend that the "doing" of gender is undertaken by women and men whose competence as members of society is hostage to its production. Doing gender involves a complex of socially guided perceptual, interactional, and micropolitical activities that cast particular pursuits as expressions of masculine and feminine "natures."

When we view gender as an accomplishment, an achieved property of situated conduct, our attention shifts from matters internal to the individual and focuses on interactional and, ultimately, institutional arenas. In one sense, of course, it is individuals who "do" gender. But it is a situated doing, carried out in the virtual or real presence of others who are presumed to be oriented to its production. Rather than as a property of individuals, we conceive of gender as an emergent feature of social situations: both as an outcome of and a rationale for various social arrangements and as a means of legitimating one of the most fundamental divisions of society.

To advance our argument, we undertake a critical examination of what sociologists have meant

Candace West and Don H. Zimmerman, "Doing Gender," *Gender & Society*, Vol. 1, No. 2 (June 1987), pp. 125–151. Copyright © 1987 by Sociologists for Women in Society. Reprinted by permission of SAGE Publications.

by *gender,* including its treatment as a role enactment in the conventional sense and as a "display" in Goffman's (1976) terminology. Both *gender role* and *gender display* focus on behavioral aspects of being a woman or a man (as opposed, for example, to biological differences between the two). However, we contend that the notion of gender as a role obscures the work that is involved in producing gender in everyday activities, while the notion of gender as a display relegates it to the periphery of interaction. We argue instead that participants in interaction organize their various and manifold activities to reflect or express gender, and they are disposed to perceive the behavior of others in a similar light.

To elaborate our proposal, we suggest at the outset that important but often overlooked distinctions be observed among *sex, sex category,* and *gender. Sex* is a determination made through the application of socially agreed upon biological criteria for classifying persons as females or males. The criteria for classification can be genitalia at birth or chromosomal typing before birth, and they do not necessarily agree with one another. Placement in a *sex category* is achieved through application of the sex criteria, but in everyday life, categorization is established and sustained by the socially required identificatory displays that proclaim one's membership in one or the other category. In this sense, one's sex category presumes one's sex and stands as proxy for it in many situations, but sex and sex category can vary independently; that is, it is possible to claim membership in a sex category even when the sex criteria are lacking. *Gender,* in contrast, is the activity of managing situated conduct in light of normative conceptions of attitudes and activities appropriate for one's sex category. Gender activities emerge from and bolster claims to membership in a sex category.

We contend that recognition of the analytical independence of sex, sex category, and gender is essential for understanding the relationships among these elements and the interactional work involved in "being" a gendered person in society. While our primary aim is theoretical, there will be occasion to discuss fruitful directions for empirical research following from the formulation of gender that we propose.

We begin with an assessment of the received meaning of gender, particularly in relation to the roots of this notion in presumed biological differences between women and men.

Perspectives on Sex and Gender

In Western societies, the accepted cultural perspective on gender views women and men as naturally and unequivocally defined categories of being with distinctive psychological and behavioral propensities that can be predicted from their reproductive functions. Competent adult members of these societies see differences between the two as fundamental and enduring—differences seemingly supported by the division of labor into women's and men's work and an often elaborate differentiation of feminine and masculine attitudes and behaviors that are prominent features of social organization. Things are the way they are by virtue of the fact that men are men and women are women—a division perceived to be natural and rooted in biology, producing in turn profound psychological, behavioral, and social consequences. The structural arrangements of a society are presumed to be responsive to these differences.

Analyses of sex and gender in the social sciences, though less likely to accept uncritically the naive biological determinism of the view just presented, often retain a conception of sex-linked behaviors and traits as essential properties of individuals. The "sex differences approach" is more commonly attributed to psychologists than to sociologists, but the survey researcher who determines the "gender" of respondents on the basis of the sound of their voices over the telephone is also making trait-oriented assumptions. Reducing gender to a fixed set of psychological traits or to a unitary "variable" precludes serious consideration of the ways it is used to structure distinct domains of social experience.

Taking a different tack, role theory has attended to the social construction of gender categories, called "sex roles" or, more recently, "gender roles" and has analyzed how these are learned and enacted. Beginning with Linton (1936) and continuing through the works of Parsons (Parsons 1951; Parsons and Bales 1955) and Komarovsky (1946, 1950), role theory has emphasized the social and dynamic aspect of role construction and enactment. But at the level of face-to-face interaction, the application of role theory to gender poses problems of its own. Roles are *situated* identities—assumed and relinquished as the situation demands—rather than *master identities*, such as sex category, that cut across situations. Unlike most roles, such as "nurse," "doctor," and "patient" or "professor" and "student," gender has no specific site or organizational context.

Moreover, many roles are already gender marked, so that special qualifiers—such as "female doctor" or "male nurse"—must be added to exceptions to the rule. Thorne (1980) observes that conceptualizing gender as a role makes it difficult to assess its influence on other roles and reduces its explanatory usefulness in discussions of power and inequality. Drawing on Rubin (1975), Thorne calls for a reconceptualization of women and men as distinct social groups, constituted in "concrete, historically changing—and generally unequal— social relationships" (Thorne 1980, p. 11).

We argue that gender is not a set of traits, nor a variable, nor a role, but the product of social doings of some sort. What then is the social doing of gender? It is more than the continuous creation of the meaning of gender through human actions. We claim that gender itself is constituted through interaction. To develop the implications of our claim, we turn to Goffman's (1976) account of "gender display." Our object here is to explore how gender might be exhibited or portrayed through interaction, and thus be seen as "natural," while it is being produced as a socially organized achievement.

Gender Display

Goffman contends that when human beings interact with others in their environment, they assume that each possesses an "essential nature"—a nature that can be discerned through the "natural signs given off or expressed by them" (1976, p. 75). Femininity and masculinity are regarded as

"prototypes of essential expression—something that can be conveyed fleetingly in any social situation and yet something that strikes at the most basic characterization of the individual" (1976, p. 75). The means through which we provide such expressions are "perfunctory, conventionalized acts" (1976, p. 69), which convey to others our regard for them, indicate our alignment in an encounter, and tentatively establish the terms of contact for that social situation. But they are also regarded as expressive behavior, testimony to our "essential natures."

Goffman (1976, pp. 69–70) sees *displays* as highly conventionalized behaviors structured as two-part exchanges of the statement-reply type, in which the presence or absence of symmetry can establish deference or dominance. These rituals are viewed as distinct from but articulated with more consequential activities, such as performing tasks or engaging in discourse. Hence, we have what he terms the "scheduling" of displays at junctures in activities, such as the beginning or end, to avoid interfering with the activities themselves. Goffman (1976, p. 69) formulates *gender display* as follows:

> If gender be defined as the culturally established correlates of sex (whether in consequence of biology or learning), then gender display refers to conventionalized portrayals of these correlates.

These gendered expressions might reveal clues to the underlying, fundamental dimensions of the female and male, but they are, in Goffman's view, optional performances. Masculine courtesies may or may not be offered and, if offered, may or may not be declined (1976, p. 71). Moreover, human beings "themselves employ the term 'expression,' and conduct themselves to fit their own notions of expressivity" (1976, p. 75). Gender depictions are less a consequence of our "essential sexual natures" than interactional portrayals of what we would like to convey about sexual natures, using conventionalized gestures. Our human nature gives us the ability to learn to produce and recognize masculine and feminine gender displays—"a capacity [we] have by virtue of being persons, not males and females" (1976, p. 76).

Upon first inspection, it would appear that Goffman's formulation offers an engaging sociological corrective to existing formulations of gender. In his view, gender is a socially scripted dramatization of the culture's *idealization* of feminine and masculine natures, played for an audience that is well schooled in the presentational idiom. To continue the metaphor, there are scheduled performances presented in special locations, and like plays, they constitute introductions to or time out from more serious activities.

There are fundamental equivocations in this perspective. By segregating gender display from the serious business of interaction, Goffman obscures the effects of gender on a wide range of human activities. Gender is not merely something that happens in the nooks and crannies of interaction, fitted in here and there and not interfering with the serious business of life. While it is plausible to contend that gender displays—construed as conventionalized expressions—are optional, it does not seem plausible to say that we have the option of being seen by others as female or male.

It is necessary to move beyond the notion of gender display to consider what is involved in doing gender as an ongoing activity embedded in everyday interaction. Toward this end, we return to the distinctions among sex, sex category, and gender introduced earlier.

Sex, Sex Category, and Gender

Garfinkel's (1967, pp. 118–40) case study of Agnes, a transsexual raised as a boy who adopted a female identity at age 17 and underwent a sex reassignment operation several years later, demonstrates how gender is created through interaction and at the same time structures interaction. Agnes, whom Garfinkel characterized as a "practical methodologist," developed a number of procedures for passing as a "normal, natural female" both prior to and after her surgery. She had the practical task of managing the fact that she possessed male genitalia and that she lacked the social resources a girl's biography would presumably provide in everyday interaction. In short, she needed to display herself as a woman, simultaneously learning what it was to be a woman. Of necessity, this full-time pursuit took place at a time when most people's gender would be well-accredited and routinized. Agnes had to consciously contrive what the vast majority of women do without thinking. She was not "faking" what "real" women do naturally. She was obliged to analyze and figure out how to act within socially structured circumstances and conceptions of femininity that women born with appropriate biological credentials come to take for granted early on. As in the case of others who must "pass," such as transvestites, Kabuki actors, or Dustin Hoffman's "Tootsie," Agnes's case makes visible what culture has made invisible—the accomplishment of gender.

Garfinkel's (1967) discussion of Agnes does not explicitly separate three analytically distinct, although empirically overlapping, concepts—sex, sex category, and gender.

Sex

Agnes did not possess the socially agreed upon biological criteria for classification as a member of the female sex. Still, Agnes regarded herself as a female, albeit a female with a penis, which a woman ought not to possess. The penis, she insisted, was a "mistake" in need of remedy (Garfinkel 1967, pp. 126–27, 131–32). Like other competent members of our culture, Agnes honored the notion that there are "essential" biological criteria that unequivocally distinguish females from males. However, if we move away from the commonsense viewpoint, we discover that the reliability of these criteria is not beyond question. Moreover, other cultures have acknowledged the existence of "cross-genders" and the possibility of more than two sexes.

More central to our argument is Kessler and McKenna's (1978, pp. 1–6) point that genitalia are conventionally hidden from public inspection in everyday life; yet we continue through our social rounds to "observe" a world of two naturally, normally sexed persons. It is the *presumption* that essential criteria exist and would or should be there if looked for that provides the basis for sex categorization. Drawing on Garfinkel, Kessler and McKenna argue that "female" and "male" are cultural events—products of what they term the "gender attribution process"—rather than some collection of traits, behaviors, or even physical attributes. Illustratively they cite the child who, viewing a picture of someone clad in a suit and a tie, contends, "It's a man, because he has a pee-pee" (Kessler and McKenna 1978, p. 154). Translation: "He must have a pee-pee [an essential characteristic] because I see the *insignia* of a suit and tie." Neither initial sex assignment (pronouncement at birth as a female or male) nor the actual existence of essential criteria for that assignment (possession of a clitoris and vagina or penis and testicles) has much—if anything—to do with the identification of sex category in everyday life. There, Kessler and McKenna note, we operate with a moral certainty of a world of two sexes. We do not think, "Most persons with penises are men, but some may not be" or "Most persons who dress as men have penises." Rather, we take it for granted that sex and sex category are congruent—that knowing the latter, we can deduce the rest.

Sex Categorization

Agnes's claim to the categorical status of female, which she sustained by appropriate identificatory displays and other characteristics, could be *discredited* before her transsexual operation if her possession of a penis became known and after by her surgically constructed genitalia. In this regard, Agnes had to be continually alert to actual or potential threats to the security of her sex category. Her problem was not so much living up to some prototype of essential femininity but preserving her categorization as female. This task was made easy for her by a very powerful resource, namely, the process of commonsense categorization in everyday life.

The categorization of members of society into indigenous categories such as "girl" or "boy," or "woman" or "man," operates in a distinctively social way. The act of categorization does not involve a positive test, in the sense of a well-defined set of criteria that must be explicitly satisfied prior to making an identification. Rather, the application of membership categories relies on an "if-can" test in everyday interaction. This test stipulates that if people *can be seen* as members of relevant categories, *then categorize them that way*. That is, use the category that seems appropriate, except in the presence of discrepant information or obvious features that would rule out its use. This procedure is quite in keeping with the attitude of everyday life, which has us take appearances at face value unless we have special reason to doubt. It should be added that it is precisely when we have special reason to doubt that the issue of applying rigorous criteria arises, but it is rare, outside legal or bureaucratic contexts, to encounter insistence on positive tests.

Agnes's initial resource was the predisposition of those she encountered to take her appearance (her figure, clothing, hair style, and so on) as the undoubted appearance of a normal female. Her further resource was our cultural perspective on the properties of "natural, normally sexed persons." Garfinkel (1967, pp. 122–28) notes that in everyday life, we live in a world of two—and only two—sexes. This arrangement has a moral status, in that we include ourselves and others in it as "essentially, originally, in the first place, always have been, always will be, once and for all, in the final analysis, either 'male' or 'female'" (Garfinkel 1967, p. 122).

Consider the following case:

This issue reminds me of a visit I made to a computer store a couple of years ago. The person who answered my questions was truly a *salesperson*. I could not categorize him/her as a woman or a man. What did I look for? (1) Facial hair: She/he was smooth skinned, but some men have little or no facial hair. (This varies by race, Native Americans and Blacks often have none.) (2) Breasts: She/he was wearing a loose shirt that hung from his/her shoulders. And, as many women who suffered through a 1950s' adolescence know to their shame, women are often flat-chested. (3) Shoulders: His/hers were small and round for a man, broad for a woman. (4) Hands: Long and slender fingers, knuckles a bit large for a woman, small for a man. (5) Voice: Middle range, unexpressive for a woman, not at all the exaggerated tones some gay males affect. (6) His/her treatment of me: Gave off no signs that would let me know if I were of the same or different sex as this person. There were not even any signs that he/she knew his/her sex would be difficult to categorize and I wondered about that even as I did my best to hide these questions so I would not embarrass him/her while we talked of computer paper. I left still not knowing the sex of my salesperson, and was disturbed by that unanswered question (child of my culture that I am). (Diane Margolis, personal communication)

What can this case tell us about situations such as Agnes's or the process of sex categorization in general? First, we infer from this description that the computer salesclerk's identificatory display was ambiguous, since she or he was not dressed or adorned in an unequivocally female or male fashion. It is when such a display *fails* to provide grounds for categorization that factors such as facial hair or tone of voice are assessed to determine membership in a sex category. Second, beyond the fact that this incident could be recalled after "a couple of years," the customer was not only "disturbed" by the ambiguity of the salesclerk's category but also assumed that to acknowledge this ambiguity would be embarrassing to the salesclerk. Not only do we want to know the sex category of those around us (to see it at a glance, perhaps), but we presume that others are displaying it for us, in as decisive a fashion as they can.

Gender

Agnes attempted to be "120 percent female" (Garfinkel 1967, p. 129), that is, unquestionably in all ways and at all times feminine. She thought she could protect herself from disclosure before and after surgical intervention by comporting herself in a feminine manner, but she also could have given herself away by overdoing her performance. Sex categorization and the accomplishment of gender are not the same. Agnes's categorization could be secure or suspect, but did not depend on whether or not she lived up to some ideal conception of femininity. Women can be seen as unfeminine, but that does not make them "unfemale." Agnes faced an ongoing task of being a woman—something beyond style of dress (an identificatory

display) or allowing men to light her cigarette (a gender display). Her problem was to produce configurations of behavior that would be seen by others as normative gender behavior.

Agnes's strategy of "secret apprenticeship," through which she learned expected feminine decorum by carefully attending to her fiancé's criticisms of other women, was one means of masking incompetencies and simultaneously acquiring the needed skills (Garfinkel 1967, pp. 146–47). It was through her fiancé that Agnes learned that sunbathing on the lawn in front of her apartment was "offensive" (because it put her on display to other men). She also learned from his critiques of other women that she should not insist on having things her way and that she should not offer her opinions or claim equality with men (Garfinkel 1967, pp. 147–48). (Like other women in our society, Agnes learned something about power in the course of her "education.")

Popular culture abounds with books and magazines that compile idealized depictions of relations between women and men. Those focused on the etiquette of dating or prevailing standards of feminine comportment are meant to be of practical help in these matters. However, the use of any such source *as a manual of procedure* requires the assumption that doing gender merely involves making use of discrete, well-defined bundles of behavior that can simply be plugged into interactional situations to produce recognizable enactments of masculinity and femininity. The man "does" being masculine by, for example, taking the woman's arm to guide her across a street, and she "does" being feminine by consenting to be guided and not initiating such behavior with a man.

Agnes could perhaps have used such sources as manuals, but, we contend, doing gender is not so easily regimented. Such sources may list and describe the sorts of behaviors that mark or display gender, but they are necessarily incomplete. And to be successful, marking or displaying gender must be finely fitted to situations and modified or transformed as the occasion demands. Doing gender consists of managing such occasions so that, whatever the particulars, the outcome is seen and seeable in context as gender-appropriate or, as the case may be, gender-*in*appropriate, that is, *accountable.*

Gender and Accountability

As Heritage (1984, pp. 136–37) notes, members of society regularly engage in "descriptive account-ings of states of affairs to one another," and such accounts are both serious and consequential. These descriptions name, characterize, formulate, explain, excuse, excoriate, or merely take notice of some circumstance or activity and thus place it within some social framework (locating it relative to other activities, like and unlike).

Such descriptions are themselves accountable, and societal members orient to the fact that their activities are subject to comment. Actions are often designed with an eye to their accountability, that is, how they might look and how they might be characterized. The notion of accountability also encompasses those actions undertaken so that they are specifically unremarkable and thus not worthy of more than a passing remark, be-cause they are seen to be in accord with culturally approved standards.

Heritage (1984, p. 179) observes that the process of rendering something accountable is interac-tional in character:

> [This] permits actors to design their actions in re-lation to their circumstances so as to permit others, by methodically taking account of cir-cumstances, to recognize the action for what it is.

The key word here is *circumstances.* One circum-stance that attends virtually all actions is the sex category of the actor. As Garfinkel (1967, p. 118) comments:

> [T]he work and socially structured occasions of sexual passing were obstinately unyielding to [Agnes's] attempts to routinize the grounds of daily activities. This obstinacy points to the *om-nirelevance* of sexual status to affairs of daily life as an invariant but unnoticed background in the texture of relevances that compose the changing actual scenes of everyday life. (italics added)

If sex category is omnirelevant (or even approaches being so), then a person engaged in virtually any activity may be held accountable for performance of that activity as a *woman* or a *man,* and their incumbency in one or the other sex category can be used to legitimate or discredit their other ac-tivities. Accordingly, virtually any activity can be assessed as to its womanly or manly nature. And note, to "do" gender is not always to live up to nor-mative conceptions of femininity or masculinity; it is to engage in behavior *at the risk of gender as-sessment.* While it is individuals who do gender, the enterprise is fundamentally interactional and institutional in character, for accountability is a feature of social relationships and its idiom is drawn from the institutional arena in which those relationships are enacted. If this be the case, can we ever *not* do gender? Insofar as a society is partitioned by "essential" differences between women and men and placement in a sex category is both relevant and enforced, doing gender is unavoidable.

Resources for Doing Gender

Doing gender means creating differences be-tween girls and boys and women and men, differences that are not natural, essential, or biological. Once the differences have been con-structed, they are used to reinforce the "essen-tialness" of gender. In a delightful account of the "arrangement between the sexes," Goffman (1977) observes the creation of a variety of in-stitutionalized frameworks through which our "natural, normal sexedness" can be enacted. The physical features of social setting provide one obvious resource for the expression of our "essential" differences. For example, the sex seg-regation of North American public bathrooms distinguishes "ladies" from "gentlemen" in mat-ters held to be fundamentally biological, even though both "are somewhat similar in the ques-tion of waste products and their elimination" (Goffman 1977, p. 315). These settings are fur-nished with dimorphic equipment (such as uri-nals for men or elaborate grooming facilities for women), even though both sexes may achieve the same ends through the same means (and appar-ently do so in the privacy of their own homes). To be stressed here is the fact that:

The *functioning* of sex-differentiated organs is involved, but there is nothing in this functioning that biologically recommends segregation; that arrangement is a totally cultural matter . . . toilet segregation is presented as a natural consequence of the difference between the sex-classes when in fact it is a means of honoring, if not producing, this difference. (Goffman 1977, p. 316)

Standardized social occasions also provide stages for evocations of the "essential female and male natures." Goffman cites organized sports as one such institutionalized framework for the expression of manliness. There, those qualities that ought "properly" to be associated with masculinity, such as endurance, strength, and competitive spirit, are celebrated by all parties concerned—participants, who may be seen to demonstrate such traits, and spectators, who applaud their demonstrations from the safety of the sidelines (1977, p. 322).

Assortative mating practices among heterosexual couples afford still further means to create and maintain differences between women and men. For example, even though size, strength, and age tend to be normally distributed among females and males (with considerable overlap between them), selective pairing ensures couples in which boys and men are visibly bigger, stronger, and older (if not "wiser") than the girls and women with whom they are paired. So, should situations emerge in which greater size, strength, or experience is called for, boys and men will be ever ready to display it and girls and women, to appreciate its display.

Gender may be routinely fashioned in a variety of situations that seem conventionally expressive to begin with, such as those that present "helpless" women next to heavy objects or flat tires. But, as Goffman notes, heavy, messy, and precarious concerns can be constructed from *any* social situation, "even though by standards set in other settings, this may involve something that is light, clean, and safe" (Goffman 1977, p. 324). Given these resources, it is clear that any interactional situation sets the stage for depictions of "essential" sexual natures. In sum, these situations "do not so much allow for the expression of natural differences as for the production of that difference itself" (Goffman 1977, p. 324).

Many situations are not clearly sex categorized to begin with, nor is what transpires within them obviously gender relevant. Yet any social encounter can be pressed into service in the interests of doing gender. Thus, Fishman's (1978) research on casual conversations found an asymmetrical "division of labor" in talk between heterosexual intimates. Women had to ask more questions, fill more silences, and use more attention-getting beginnings in order to be heard. Her conclusions are particularly pertinent here:

> Since interactional work is related to what constitutes being a woman, with what a woman is, the idea that it is work is obscured. The work is not seen as what women do, but as part of what they are. (Fishman 1978, p. 405)

We would argue that it is precisely such labor that helps to constitute the essential nature of women as women in interactional contexts.

Individuals have many social identities that may be donned or shed, muted or made more salient, depending on the situation. One may be a friend, spouse, professional, citizen, and many other things to many different people—or, to the same person at different times. But we are always women or men—unless we shift into another sex category. What this means is that our identificatory displays will provide an ever-available resource for doing gender under an infinitely diverse set of circumstances.

Some occasions are organized to routinely display and celebrate behaviors that are conventionally linked to one or the other sex category. On such occasions, everyone knows his or her place in the interactional scheme of things. If an individual identified as a member of one sex category engages in behavior usually associated with the other category, this routinization is challenged. Hughes (1945, p. 356) provides an illustration of such a dilemma:

> [A] young woman . . . became part of that virile profession, engineering. The designer of an airplane is expected to go up on the maiden flight of the first plane built according to the design.

He [sic] then gives a dinner to the engineers and workmen who worked on the new plane. The dinner is naturally a stag party. The young woman in question designed a plane. Her co-workers urged her not to take the risk—for which, presumably, men only are fit—of the maiden voyage. They were, in effect, asking her to be a lady instead of an engineer. She chose to be an engineer. She then gave the party and paid for it like a man. After food and the first round of toasts, she left like a lady.

On this occasion, parties reached an accommodation that allowed a woman to engage in presumptively masculine behaviors. However, we note that in the end, this compromise permitted demonstration of her "essential" femininity, through accountably "ladylike" behavior.

Hughes (1945, p. 357) suggests that such contradictions may be countered by managing interactions on a very narrow basis, for example, "keeping the relationship formal and specific." But the heart of the matter is that even—perhaps, especially—if the relationship is a formal one, gender is still something one is accountable for. Thus a woman physician (notice the special qualifier in her case) may be accorded respect for her skill and even addressed by an appropriate title. Nonetheless, she is subject to evaluation in terms of normative conceptions of appropriate attitudes and activities for her sex category and under pressure to prove that she is an "essentially" feminine being, despite appearances to the contrary. Her sex category is used to discredit her participation in important clinical activities, while her involvement in medicine is used to discredit her commitment to her responsibilities as a wife and mother. Simultaneously, her exclusion from the physician colleague community is maintained and her accountability *as a woman* is ensured.

In this context, "role conflict" can be viewed as a dynamic aspect of our current "arrangement between the sexes" (Goffman 1977), an arrangement that provides for occasions on which persons of a particular sex category can "see" quite clearly that they are out of place and that if they were not there, their current troubles would not exist. What is at stake is, from the standpoint of interaction, the management of our "essential" natures, and from the standpoint of the individual, the continuing accomplishment of gender. If, as we have argued, sex category is omnirelevant, then any occasion, conflicted or not, offers the resources for doing gender.

We have sought to show that sex category and gender are managed properties of conduct that are contrived with respect to the fact that others will judge and respond to us in particular ways. We have claimed that a person's gender is not simply an aspect of what one is, but, more fundamentally, it is something that one does, and *does* recurrently, in interaction with others.

What are the consequences of this theoretical formulation? If, for example, individuals strive to achieve gender in encounters with others, how does a culture instill the need to achieve it? What is the relationship between the production of gender at the level of interaction and such institutional arrangements as the division of labor in society? And, perhaps most important, how does doing gender contribute to the subordination of women by men?

Research Agendas

To bring the social production of gender under empirical scrutiny, we might begin at the beginning, with a reconsideration of the process through which societal members acquire the requisite categorical apparatus and other skills to become gendered human beings.

Recruitment to Gender Identities

The conventional approach to the process of becoming girls and boys has been sex-role socialization. In recent years, recurring problems arising from this approach have been linked to inadequacies inherent in role theory *per se*—its emphasis on "consensus, stability and continuity" (Stacey and Thorne 1985, p. 307), its historical and depoliticizing focus (Thorne 1980, p. 9; Stacey and Thorne 1985, p. 307), and the fact that its "social" dimension relies on "a general assumption that people choose to maintain existing customs" (Connell 1985, p. 263).

In contrast, Cahill (1982, 1986a, 1986b) analyzes the experiences of preschool children using a social model of recruitment into normally gendered identities. Cahill argues that categorization practices are fundamental to learning and displaying feminine and masculine behavior. Initially, he observes, children are primarily concerned with distinguishing between themselves and others on the basis of social competence. Categorically, their concern resolves itself into the opposition of "girl/boy" classification versus "baby" classification (the latter designating children whose social behavior is problematic and who must be closely supervised). It is children's concern with being seen as socially competent that evokes their initial claims to gender identities:

> During the exploratory stage of children's socialization . . . they learn that only two social identities are routinely available to them, the identity of "baby," or, depending on the configuration of their external genitalia, either "big boy" or "big girl." Moreover, others subtly inform them that the identity of "baby" is a discrediting one. When, for example, children engage in disapproved behavior, they are often told "You're a baby" or "Be a big boy." In effect, these typical verbal responses to young children's behavior convey to them that they must behaviorally choose between the discrediting identity of "baby" and their anatomically determined sex identity. (Cahill 1986a, p. 175)

Subsequently, little boys appropriate the gender ideal of "efficaciousness," that is, being able to affect the physical and social environment through the exercise of physical strength or appropriate skills. In contrast, little girls learn to value "appearance," that is, managing themselves as ornamental objects. Both classes of children learn that the recognition and use of sex categorization in interaction are not optional, but mandatory.

Being a "girl" or a "boy" then, is not only being more competent than a "baby," but also being competently female or male, that is, learning to produce behavioral displays of one's "essential" female or male identity. In this respect, the task of four- to five-year-old children is very similar to Agnes's:

> For example, the following interaction occurred on a preschool playground. A 55-month-old boy (D) was attempting to unfasten the clasp of a necklace when a preschool aide walked over to him.
> A: Do you want to put that on?
> D: No. It's for girls.
> A: You don't have to be a girl to wear things around your neck. Kings wear things around their necks. You could pretend you're a king.
> D: I'm not a king. I'm a boy. (Cahill 1986a, p. 176)

As Cahill notes of this example, although D may have been unclear as to the sex status of a king's identity, he was obviously aware that necklaces are used to announce the identity "girl." Having claimed the identity "boy" and having developed a behavioral commitment to it, he was leery of any display that might furnish grounds for questioning his claim.

In this way, new members of society come to be involved in a *self-regulating process* as they begin to monitor their own and others' conduct with regard to its gender implications. The "recruitment" process involves not only the appropriation of gender ideals (by the valuation of those ideals as proper ways of being and behaving) but also *gender identities* that are important to individuals and that they strive to maintain. Thus gender differences, or the sociocultural shaping of "essential female and male natures," achieve the status of objective facts. They are rendered normal, natural features of persons and provide the tacit rationale for differing fates of women and men within the social order.

Additional studies of children's play activities as routine occasions for the expression of gender-appropriate behavior can yield new insights into how our "essential natures" are constructed. In particular, the transition from what Cahill (1986a) terms "apprentice participation" in the sex-segregated worlds that are common among elementary school children to "bona fide participation" in the heterosocial world so frightening to adolescents is likely to be a keystone in our understanding of the recruitment process.

Gender and the Division of Labor

Whenever people face issues of *allocation*—who is to do what, get what, plan or execute action, direct or be directed, incumbency in significant social categories such as "female" and "male" seems to become pointedly relevant. How such issues are resolved conditions the exhibition, dramatization, or celebration of one's "essential nature" as a woman or man.

Berk (1985) offers elegant demonstration of this point in her investigation of the allocation of household labor and the attitudes of married couples toward the division of household tasks. Berk found little variation in either the actual distribution of tasks or perceptions of equity in regard to that distribution. Wives, even when employed outside the home, do the vast majority of household and child-care tasks. Moreover, both wives and husbands tend to perceive this as a "fair" arrangement. Noting the failure of conventional sociological and economic theories to explain this seeming contradiction, Berk contends that something more complex is involved than rational arrangements for the production of household goods and services:

> Hardly a question simply of who has more time, or whose time is worth more, who has more skill or more power, it is clear that a complicated relationship between the structure of work imperatives and the structure of normative expectations attached to work as *gendered* determines the ultimate allocation of members' time to work and home. (Berk 1985, pp. 195–96)

She notes, for example, that the most important factor influencing wives' contribution of labor is the total amount of work demanded or expected by the household; such demands had no bearing on husbands' contributions. Wives reported various rationales (their own and their husbands') that justified their level of contribution and, as a general matter, underscored the presumption that wives are essentially responsible for household production.

Berk (1985, p. 201) contends that it is difficult to see how people "could rationally establish the arrangements that they do solely for the production of household goods and services"—much less, how people could consider them "fair." She argues that our current arrangements for the domestic division of labor support *two* production processes: household goods and services (meals, clean children, and so on) and, at the same time, gender. As she puts it:

> Simultaneously, members "do" gender, as they "do" housework and child care, and what [has] been called the division of labor provides for the joint production of household labor and gender; it is the mechanism by which both the material and symbolic products of the household are realized. (1985, p. 201)

It is not simply that household labor is designated as "women's work," but that for a woman to engage in it and a man not to engage in it is to draw on and exhibit the "essential nature" of each. What is produced and reproduced is not merely the activity and artifact of domestic life, but the material embodiment of wifely and husbandly roles, and derivatively, of womanly and manly conduct. What are also frequently produced and reproduced are the dominant and subordinate statuses of the sex categories.

How does gender get done in work settings outside the home, where dominance and subordination are themes of overarching importance? Hochschild's (1983) analysis of the work of flight attendants offers some promising insights. She found that the occupation of flight attendant consisted of something altogether different for women than for men:

> As the company's main shock absorbers against "mishandled" passengers, their own feelings are more frequently subjected to rough treatment. In addition, a day's exposure to people who resist authority in a woman is a different experience than it is for a man. . . . In this respect, it is a disadvantage to be a woman. And in this case, they are not simply women in the biological sense. They are also a highly visible distillation of middle-class American notions of femininity. They symbolize

Woman. Insofar as the category "female" is mentally associated with having less status and authority, female flight attendants are more readily classified as "really" females than other females are. (Hochschild 1983, p. 175)

In performing what Hochschild terms the "emotional labor" necessary to maintain airline profits, women flight attendants simultaneously produce enactments of their "essential" femininity.

Sex and Sexuality

What is the relationship between doing gender and a culture's prescription of "obligatory heterosexuality"? As Frye (1983, p. 22) observes, the monitoring of sexual feelings in relation to other appropriately sexed persons requires the ready recognition of such persons "before one can allow one's heart to beat or one's blood to flow in erotic enjoyment of that person." The appearance of heterosexuality is produced through emphatic and unambiguous indicators of one's sex, layered on in ever more conclusive fashion (Frye 1983, p. 24). Thus, lesbians and gay men concerned with passing as heterosexuals can rely on these indicators for camouflage; in contrast, those who would avoid the assumption of heterosexuality may foster ambiguous indicators of their categorical status through their dress, behaviors, and style. But "ambiguous" sex indicators are sex indicators nonetheless. If one wishes to be recognized as a lesbian (or heterosexual woman), one must first establish a categorical status as female. Even as popular images portray lesbians as "females who are not feminine" (Frye 1983, p. 129), the accountability of persons for their "normal, natural sexedness" is preserved.

Nor is accountability threatened by the existence of "sex-change operations"—presumably, the most radical challenge to our cultural perspective on sex and gender. Although no one coerces transsexuals into hormone therapy, electrolysis, or surgery, the alternatives available to them are undeniably constrained:

When the transsexual experts maintain that they use transsexual procedures only with people who ask for them, and who prove that they can "pass," they obscure the social reality. Given patriarchy's

prescription that one must be *either* masculine or feminine, free choice is conditioned. (Raymond 1979, p. 135, italics added)

The physical reconstruction of sex criteria pays ultimate tribute to the "essentialness" of our sexual natures—as women *or* as men.

Gender, Power, and Social Change

Let us return to the question: Can we avoid doing gender? Earlier, we proposed that insofar as sex category is used as a fundamental criterion for differentiation, doing gender is unavoidable. It is unavoidable because of the social consequences of sex-category membership: the allocation of power and resources not only in the domestic, economic, and political domains but also in the broad arena of interpersonal relations. In virtually any situation, one's sex category can be relevant, and one's performance as an incumbent of that category (i.e., gender) can be subjected to evaluation. Maintaining such pervasive and faithful assignment of lifetime status requires legitimation.

But doing gender also renders the social arrangements based on sex category accountable as normal and natural, that is, legitimate ways of organizing social life. Differences between women and men that are created by this process can then be portrayed as fundamental and enduring dispositions. In this light, the institutional arrangements of a society can be seen as responsive to the differences—the social order being merely an accommodation to the natural order. Thus if, in doing gender, men are also doing dominance and women are doing deference, the resultant social order, which supposedly reflects "natural differences," is a powerful reinforcer and legitimator of hierarchical arrangements. Frye observes:

For efficient subordination, what's wanted is that the structure not appear to be a cultural artifact kept in place by human decision or custom, but that it appear *natural*—that it appear to be quite a direct consequence of facts about the beast which are beyond the scope of human manipulation.... That we are trained to behave so differently as women and men, and to behave so differently toward women and men, itself contributes mightily to the appearance of extreme dimorphism, but also, the *ways* we act as women and men, and the *ways* we act toward women and men, mold our bodies and our minds to the shape of subordination and dominance. We do become what we practice being. (Frye 1983, p. 34)

If we do gender appropriately, we simultaneously sustain, reproduce, and render legitimate the institutional arrangements that are based on sex category. If we fail to do gender appropriately, we as individuals—not the institutional arrangements—may be called to account (for our character, motives, and predispositions).

Social movements such as feminism can provide the ideology and impetus to question existing arrangements, and the social support for individuals to explore alternatives to them. Legislative changes, such as that proposed by the Equal Rights Amendment, can also weaken the accountability of conduct to sex category, thereby affording the possibility of more widespread loosening of accountability in general. To be sure, equality under the law does not guarantee equality in other arenas. As Lorber (1986, p. 577) points out, assurance of "scrupulous equality of categories of people considered essentially different needs constant monitoring." What such proposed changes can do is provide the warrant for asking why, if we wish to treat women and men as equals, there needs to be two sex categories at all.

The sex category/gender relationship links the institutional and interactional levels, a coupling that legitimates social arrangements based on sex category and reproduces their asymmetry in face-to-face interaction. Doing gender furnishes the interactional scaffolding of social structure, along with a built-in mechanism of social control. In appreciating the institutional forces that maintain distinctions between women and men, we must not lose sight of the interactional validation of those distinctions that confers upon them their sense of "naturalness" and "rightness."

Social change, then, must be pursued both at the institutional and cultural level of sex category and at the interactional level of gender. Such a conclusion is hardly novel. Nevertheless, we suggest that it is important to recognize that the

analytical distinction between institutional and interactional spheres does not pose an either/or choice when it comes to the question of effecting social change. Reconceptualizing gender not as a simple property of individuals but as an integral dynamic of social orders implies a new perspective on the entire network of gender relations:

> [T]he social subordination of women, and the cultural practices which help sustain it; the politics of sexual object-choice, and particularly the oppression of homosexual people; the sexual division of labor, the formation of character and motive, so far as they are organized as femininity and masculinity; the role of the body in social relations, especially the politics of childbirth; and the nature of strategies of sexual liberation movements. (Connell 1985, p. 261)

Gender is a powerful ideological device, which produces, reproduces, and legitimates the choices and limits that are predicated on sex category. An understanding of how gender is produced in social situations will afford clarification of the interactional scaffolding of social structure and the social control processes that sustain it.

References

Berk, Sarah F. 1985. *The Gender Factory: The Apportionment of Work in American Households.* New York: Plenum.

Cahill, Spencer E. 1982. "Becoming Boys and Girls." Ph.D. dissertation, Department of Sociology, University of California, Santa Barbara.

———. 1986a. "Childhood Socialization as Recruitment Process: Some Lessons from the Study of Gender Development." Pp. 163–86 in *Sociological Studies of Child Development,* edited by P. Adler and P. Adler. Greenwich, CT: JAI Press.

———. 1986b. "Language Practices and Self-Definition: The Case of Gender Identity Acquisition." *The Sociological Quarterly* 27:295–311.

Connell, R.W. 1985. "Theorizing Gender." *Sociology* 19:260–72.

Fishman, Pamela. 1978. "Interaction: The Work Women Do." *Social Problems* 25:397–406.

Frye, Marilyn. 1983. *The Politics of Reality: Essays in Feminist Theory.* Trumansburg, NY: The Crossing Press.

Garfinkel, Harold. 1967. *Studies in Ethnomethodology.* Englewood Cliffs, NJ: Prentice-Hall.

Goffman, Erving. 1976. "Gender Display." *Studies in the Anthropology of Visual Communication* 3:69–77.

———. 1977. "The Arrangement Between the Sexes." *Theory and Society* 4:301–31.

Heritage, John. 1984. *Garfinkel and Ethnomethodology.* Cambridge, England: Polity Press.

Hochschild, Arlie R. 1983. *The Managed Heart. Commercialization of Human Feeling.* Berkeley: University of California Press.

Hughes, Everett C. 1945. "Dilemmas and Contradictions of Status." *American Journal of Sociology* 50:353–59.

Kessler, Suzanne J., and Wendy McKenna. 1978. *Gender: An Ethnomethodological Approach.* New York: Wiley.

Komarovsky, Mirra. 1946. "Cultural Contradictions and Sex Roles." *American Journal of Sociology* 52:184–89.

———. 1950. "Functional Analysis of Sex Roles." *American Sociological Review* 15:508–16.

Linton, Ralph. 1936. *The Study of Man.* New York: Appleton-Century.

Lorber, Judith. 1986. "Dismantling Noah's Ark." *Sex Roles* 14:567–80.

Parsons, Talcott. 1951. *The Social System.* New York: Free Press.

———, and Robert F. Bales. 1955. *Family, Socialization and Interaction Process.* New York: Free Press.

Raymond, Janice G. 1979. *The Transsexual Empire.* Boston: Beacon.

Rubin, Gayle. 1975. "The Traffic in Women: Notes on the 'Political Economy' of Sex." Pp. 157–210 in *Toward an Anthropology of Women*, edited by R. Reiter. New York: Monthly Review Press.

Stacey, Judith, and Barrie Thorne. 1985. "The Missing Feminist Revolution in Sociology." *Social Problems* 32:301–16.

Thorne, Barrie. 1980. "Gender . . . How Is It Best Conceptualized?" Unpublished manuscript.

Doing Gender, Determining Gender: Transgender People, Gender Panics, and the Maintenance of the Sex/Gender/Sexuality System

LAUREL WESTBROOK AND KRISTEN SCHILT

In 1989, Christie Lee Cavazos married Jonathon Littleton, a marriage that lasted until Jonathon's untimely death in 1996. Christie filed a medical malpractice suit against the Texas doctor she alleged had misdiagnosed her husband. What might have been an open-and-shut case, however, was complicated by her biography: In the 1970s she had undergone what was then termed a

Laurel Westbrook and Kristen Schilt, "Doing Gender, Determining Gender: Transgender People, Gender Panics, and the Maintenance of the Sex/Gender/Sexuality System," *Gender & Society*, Vol. 28, No. 1 (2013), pp. 32–57. Copyright © 2013 by Laurel Westbrook and Kristen Schilt. Reprinted by permission of SAGE Publications.

surgical "sex change" operation. Before considering her case, the court first examined the validity of her marriage as a transgender woman to a cis-gender man. At the center of this case was the determination of her gender. Christie had undergone genital surgery, legally amended all of her government documents to categorize her as "female," had a legal marriage, lived as a woman for 20 years, and had medical experts who testified that she was, physically and psychologically, a woman. Yet, the court ruled that she was, and would always be, chromosomally male and, therefore, could not file a malpractice suit as a spouse. Musing about the nature of gender in his ruling, Chief Justice Hardberger wrote, "There are some things you cannot will into being. They just are" (*Littleton v. Prange* 1999).

The Littleton case illustrates two competing cultural ideologies about how a person's gender[1] is to be authenticated by other people. The judge's ruling that gender is an unchangeable, innate fact illustrates what we term a "biology-based determination of gender." In contrast, the validation of Littleton's identity as a woman by others highlights what we term an "identity-based determination of gender." Such a premise does not mean seeing gender identity as fluid, or as an "anything goes" proposition. Rather, under an identity-based gender ideology, people can be recognized as a member of the gender category with which they identify if their identity claim is accepted as legitimate by other people determining their gender—in the Littleton case, her husband, friends, and medical experts.

We term this social process of authenticating another person's gender identity "determining gender." In face-to-face interactions, determining gender is the response to doing gender. When people do gender in interactions, they present information about their gender. Others then interpret this information, placing them in gender categories and determining their gender. Yet, the process of gender determination does not always rely on visual and behavioral cues. Expanding upon interactional theories of gender attribution (Kessler and McKenna 1978; West and Zimmerman 1987), we examine gender determination criteria in policy and court cases, where a great deal of biographical and bodily knowledge is known about the person whose gender is in question, as well as how gender is determined in imagined interactions—namely, cis-people's imagined interactions with trans-people, where the knowledge about the person's body and identity are hypothetical. We use "determining gender" as an umbrella term for these diverse practices of placing a person in a gender category. Additionally, we explore the consequences of gender determination, an exploration that goes beyond "How is gender socially attributed?" to an analysis of "How does gender attribution challenge or maintain the sex/gender/sexuality system?"

We examine the criteria for gender determination in moments of ideological collision. As we have previously argued (Schilt and Westbrook 2009; Westbrook 2009), many people use genitalia (biological criteria) to determine another person's gender in (hetero)sexual[2] and sexualized interactions. Yet, since the advent of the "liberal moment" (Meyerowitz 2002), a cultural turn in the 1960s toward values of autonomy and equality, there has been more acceptance of a person's gender self-identity in spaces defined as nonsexual,[3] such as many workplaces (Schilt 2010). When questions of access to gender-segregated locations arise, however, identity-based and biology-based determinations clash. We center our analysis on three such moments: (1) federal and state proposals made between 2009 and 2011 to prohibit discrimination based on gender identity and expression in the arena of employment, housing, and public accommodations (often called "transgender rights bills"); (2) a 2006 proposed policy in New York City to remove the genital surgery requirement for a change of sex marker on birth certificates; and (3) controversies over trans-people participating in competitive sports.

Our cases address different social milieu: sports, employment, and government documents. Yet, each case is, at its core, about upholding the logic of gender segregation. In these ideological collisions, social actors struggle with where actual and imagined trans-people fit in gender-segregated spaces, such as public restrooms. These struggles provoke what we term "gender panics," situations where people react to disruptions to biology-based gender ideology by frantically reasserting the naturalness of a male–female binary. When successful, this labor, which we term "gender naturalization work," quells the panics. In our cases, enacting policies requiring surgical and hormonal criteria for admission into gender-segregated spaces ends the panic. As in sexual and sexualized interactions, genitals determine gender in gender-segregated spaces, as it is often fears of unwanted (hetero)sexuality that motivates gender identity policing.

These cases demonstrate that criteria for determining gender vary across social situations. In gender-integrated public settings, such as the workplace, identity-based criteria can suffice to determine a person's gender. However, in interactional situations that derive their form and logic from gender oppositeness, such as heterosexual acts and gender-segregated sports competitions, social actors tend to enforce more rigid, biology-based criteria. Yet, gender-segregated spaces are not evenly policed, as the criteria for access are heavily interrogated only for women's spaces. Exploring the implications of this difference, we posit that bodies (mainly the presence or absence of the penis) matter for determining gender in women's spaces because of cultural ideologies of women as inherently vulnerable and in need of protection (Hollander 2001) that reproduce gender inequality under the guise of protecting women. We argue that, in the liberal moment of gender, access to gender-segregated spaces is not determined by unchangeable measures such as chromosomes but, instead, by genitals—a move that suggests a greater acceptance of an identity-based determination of gender. However, as we show, by using changeable bodily aspects to determine gender, the basic premises of the "sex/gender/sexuality system" (Seidman 1995) are maintained, as the system repatriates those whose existence potentially calls it into question, thereby naturalizing gender difference and gender inequality.

Conceptual Framework

Sociologists of gender emphasize the social, rather than biological, processes that produce a person's gender. Focused on the interactional level, such theories illustrate how people sort each other into the category of "male" or "female" in social situations on the basis of visual information cues (such as facial hair) and implicit rules for assigning characteristics to particular genders (women wear skirts; men do not). Such visual cues act as proxies for biological criteria invisible in many interactions. This categorization process, termed "gender attribution" (Kessler and McKenna 1978, 2) or "sex categorization" (West and Zimmerman 1987, 127), is theorized as an inescapable but typically unremarkable hallmark of everyday social interactions—except in instances of ambiguity, which can create an interactional breakdown, generating anxiety, concern, and even anger (Schilt 2010; West and Zimmerman 1987).

This theory is a useful counterpoint to essentialism. Yet, the focus on face-to-face interactions can be analytically limiting. Kessler and McKenna note, "The only physical characteristics that can play a role in gender attribution in everyday life are those that are visible" (Kessler and McKenna 1978, 76). West and Zimmerman, too, see characteristics that are visible in interaction as paramount to sex categorization, arguing, "Neither initial sex assignment (pronouncement at birth as female or male) nor the actual existence of essential criteria for that assignment (possession of a clitoris and vagina or penis and testicles) has much—if anything—to do with the identification of sex category in everyday life" (West and Zimmerman 1987, 132). While such propositions may hold in many nonsexual interactions, genitals play a much more key role in gender determination in sexual and sexualized interactions (Schilt and Westbrook 2009). In addition, as the Littleton case demonstrates, invisible characteristics, such as chromosomes, can override visual cues as the appropriate criteria for determining gender when legal rights are at stake.

We seek to expand these theories beyond face-to-face interactions by proposing a broader conceptualization, offering "determining gender" as an umbrella term for the different subprocesses of attributing or, in some cases, officially deciding another person's gender. Gender determination does occur at the level of *everyday interaction*, a process already well documented in the literature. Both cis- and transwomen, for instance, may find their biological claim to use a public women's restroom challenged by other women if they do not present the expected visual cues warranted for access (Cavanagh 2010), while both groups may have their gender self-identity affirmed in gender-integrated interactions. Gender determination also occurs at the level of *legal cases* and *policy decisions,* where social actors with organizational power devise criteria for who counts as a man or a woman (and therefore who gains or is denied access to gender-specific rights and social settings) (Meadow 2010). In addition, gender determinations occur at the level of the *imaginary.* Illustrating this point, as trans-inclusive policies and laws are discussed in the media, opponents and supporters often draw on hypothetical interactions with trans-people in gender-segregated spaces, such as bathrooms. In these imagined interactions, hypothetical knowledge of the person's genitals or their self-identity, rather than visible gender cues, is used to determine their gender.

When social actors officially or unofficially determine another person's gender, accepted criteria differ across contexts. Face-to-face interactions rely mostly on implicit, culturally agreed on criteria. Imagined interactions and legal or policy decisions, in contrast, often demand more explicit, officially defined criteria. Such a focus on developing explicit criteria for determining gender has grown alongside new surgical possibilities for gender transitions (Meyerowitz 2002). To receive legal and medical gender validation, trans-people have had to follow particular protocols, such as genital reconstructive surgery, that symbolically repatriate them from one side of the gender binary to the other. These criteria, which reflect dominant understandings of sex/gender/sexuality, allowed liberal values of self-determination to co-exist with beliefs about the innateness of the gender binary (Meyerowitz 2002).

This co-existence faced greater challenges in the 1990s when the hegemony of the "stealth model" of transitioning (Schilt 2010) began to dissipate, and transsexual, intersex, and transgender groups organized in an effort to gain greater cultural

recognition and civil rights (Stryker 2008). With this push came wider coverage of trans-people in the media, including debates about where transmen and transwomen fit in institutions, such as legal marriage, and in public gender-segregated spaces, such as bathrooms, prisons, and sports competitions. Policy and lawmakers began to grapple with how to balance trans-inclusivity in a social system predicated on clear, fixed distinctions between men and women, and how to address some cis-gender concerns that the cultural validation of trans-people was a direct challenge to a biologically-determined and/or God-given gender binary.

Cultural beliefs about the sanctity of gender binarism naturalize a sex/gender/sexuality system in which heterosexuality is positioned as the only natural and desirable sexual form. Showing the interrelatedness of ideas about (hetero)sexuality and gender difference, men and women's assumed psychological and embodied distinctions are widely held to be complementary and to require particular relationships with one another (Connell 1995). In nonsexual interactions, in contrast, men and women sometimes are physically segregated on the basis of those same assumed differences in their bodies, capabilities, and interests (Fausto-Sterling 2000; Goffman 1977; Lorber 1993), as well as widely shared beliefs about what activities are normal and appropriate for each gender. While men and women freely interact in many social settings, such as the workplace, the creation of "men's space" and "women's space" "ensure[s] that subcultural differences can be reaffirmed and reestablished in the face of contact between the sexes" (Goffman 1977, 314). In these spaces, gender differences are highlighted, though the same differences are minimized in other settings.

Media coverage of transgender people in the late 2000s provides a useful case study for how gender is determined in various social spaces, what larger cultural beliefs motivate deployment of biology-based and identity-based criteria, and how such criteria are forged in moments of gender ideology collision. We develop the concept of gender determination beyond face-to-face interactions through an analysis of policy and law debates and imagined interactions, situations that often display a call for explicit criteria for deciding who counts as a man or as a woman. At stake in such determinations are the criteria by which trans-people's gender identities are recognized and their rights defined and protected.

Methods

Our data come from a textual analysis of newspaper coverage gathered from LexisNexis. Such a focus is warranted, as the media tend to both reflect and shape prevailing understandings (Gamson et al. 1992; Macdonald 2003). Investigating beliefs about an issue presented in the news media allows researchers to map out the existing dominant viewpoints within the marketplace of ideas, as news is a commodity for attracting audiences who can then be sold to advertisers (Gamson et al. 1992), and, as such, it has to make cultural sense to its audience (Best 2008). Mainstream journalists write stories that reflect commonsense understandings held by (college educated, middle-class, usually white and heterosexual) journalists and their similarly socially situated audience. While there is no single understanding of gender in our society, the dominant views are visible in the mainstream news.

Media scholars have demonstrated that the media do not only represent reality, they also participate in constructing it (Berns 2004; Gamson et al. 1992; Jansen 2002; Macdonald 2003). The mainstream news media do this by providing audiences with narratives, frames, and belief systems that shape interpretations of the world as well as actions within it. While media do not determine the audience viewpoint (Gamson et al. 1992), they greatly influence it, particularly for people with little preexisting knowledge of an issue (Berns 2004). Examining news coverage allows us to see what ideas might be disseminated to readers who had never before thought about transgender people changing their birth certificates, competing in sports, or seeking protection from employment discrimination.

To explore the criteria for determining gender in nonsexual contexts, we sought out instances in which biology-based and identity-based gender ideologies collided. As the visibility of transgender lives increased broadly in the 2000s, we centered our search in that decade. We looked for moments where who counts as a man or a woman was openly discussed, thus making the process of determining gender more visible. We identified five possible moments of ideological collision surrounding trans-people: sports inclusion, prison housing, inclusion of transgender children in schools, employment rights, and altering of government documents. All of these cases provided instances of cis-people grappling with how trans-people "fit" into previously unquestioned systems and locations. We chose not to examine schools or prisons because we wanted, respectively, all cases to have a comparative focus on adults and to not involve penal settings. Our three remaining cases generated substantial public debate and represented, on our initial selection, different issues: employment nondiscrimination laws, birth certificate alteration policies, and sports participation. We did not focus solely on cases of gender-segregated spaces; however, it is these locales that emerged as salient points of focus.

Birth certificate laws usually get amended with little fanfare. By contrast, a New York City proposal allowing people to change sex markers on their birth certificates without requiring genital surgery generated extensive media coverage. We gathered all the available stories that mentioned "New York" and "birth certificate" and included coverage of the proposed change in policy during 2006–2007, the time period when the amendment was proposed, discussed, and abandoned (a total of 42 articles).

Transgender employment nondiscrimination laws have been debated since the 1990s. Because we were interested in analyzing current criteria for determining gender, we limited our focus to a two-year period (January 1, 2009, to December 31, 2010). We searched for articles that mentioned "transgender" and "nondiscrimination" and were about trans-rights legislation. After a preliminary analysis of the articles, we also searched "bathroom bills," an often applied moniker. We compiled all news stories on the three bills proposed during this time: a federal bill and state-level bills in New Hampshire and Massachusetts (a total of 57 articles).

Since scholars have extensively analyzed most of the major controversies over trans-people in sports, we employ this literature in our analysis. Because this scholarship focuses almost exclusively on transwomen, we supplemented it with media coverage of two cases about transmen from 2009 to 2011: Kye Allums, a transman who played women's basketball, and "Will," a transman who played Australian men's football (a combined total of 92 articles).

We thematically coded each of the 191 articles for beliefs about gender, with a focus on gender determination criteria (such as chromosomes, genitals, or self-identity), and the types of spaces that generated panic (gender-integrated or gender-segregated). We each coded articles from all three of the cases, ensuring intercoder reliability through extensive discussions about themes. Through this preliminary analysis, we recognized the importance of gender-segregated social spaces to each of our three cases. Upon this analytic shift, we further coded the rationales offered in these moments of gender panic for blocking trans-people's access to gender-segregated spaces (such as safety, privacy, and fairness), the final criteria adopted for determining gender (biology-based, identity-based, none), and the gender of the trans-people at the center of these panics. This second wave of analysis revealed the greater policing of transwomen's access to women-only spaces, and the greater ability of biology-based criteria, rather than identity-based criteria, to quell gender panics.

Findings

Messages in news stories are rarely homogeneous (Gamson et al. 1992). To avoid accusations of biased coverage, journalists typically try to provide at least two sides to a story (Best 2008) that typically represent dominant understandings of a particular topic. In our cases, reporters regularly presented the perspectives of people who supported identity-based determination of gender as well as the views of people who positioned biological criteria as essential for determining gender. These inclusions suggest that, in the late 2000s, the identity-based model and the biology-based model represent the two most dominant and competing understandings of gender. An examination of these ideologies provides a deeper understanding of the sex/gender/sexuality system in the liberal moment of gender, the criteria for determining gender, and how gender determination (re)produces inequality.

Ideology Collision, Gender Panics, and Gender Naturalization Work

Modern athletic competition, like all gender-segregated spaces, rests on and reproduces an idea of two opposite genders (Lorber 1993). Because of its influence on other athletic organizations, we focus here on policies enacted by the International Olympic Committee (IOC) that determine under what circumstances and in what categories transgender and intersex athletes can compete. In the modern Olympics, almost all events are gender-segregated (Tucker and Collins 2009). To maintain this segregation, IOC officials have devised policies on coping with athletes who do not fit easily into this binary. This question of where to place transgender athletes first gained national attention in 1977, when the New York Supreme Court ruled that Dr. Renee Richards, a postoperative transsexual woman, could participate in the U.S. Women's Open Tennis Tournament because her testes had been removed and her body was physically "weakened" by the resulting loss of testosterone (Birrell and Cole 1990; Shy 2007). Following similar logic, in 2003 the IOC adopted the Stockholm Consensus, which allows trans-athletes to compete as the gender they identify as if they have undergone bodily modifications that "minimize gender related advantages" (Ljungqvist and Genel 2005). According to the IOC Medical Commission (2003), the criteria for appropriate transgender bodies are:

> Surgical anatomical changes have been completed, including external genitalia changes and gonadectomy.

Legal recognition of their assigned sex has been conferred by the appropriate official authorities.

Hormonal therapy appropriate for the assigned sex has been administered in a verifiable manner and for a sufficient length of time to minimize gender-related advantages in sport competitions.

In June 2012, the IOC added an additional set of criteria, stating that athletes competing as women cannot have a testosterone level "within the male range" unless it "does not confer a competitive advantage because it is non-functional" (IOC Medical and Scientific Department 2012), thus minimizing what is viewed as an unfair hormonal advantage. These explicit criteria allow the IOC to incorporate trans- and intersex athletes, and thus to validate the liberal moment of gender, without challenging the premise that modern competitive athletics rests on: the presumption that there are two genders and all athletes must be put into one of those two categories for competition.

These biology-based criteria quieted a slow-burning gender panic that resurfaced with each new case of a trans- or intersex athlete (for discussion of intersex athletes, see Buzuvis 2010; Dreger 2010; Fausto-Sterling 2000; Nyong'o 2010). These cases raised questions about whether or not it is fair for cis- and trans-people to compete against one another (Cavanagh and Sykes 2006). The answer hinged on which gender ideology is given primacy (i.e., fair to whom?). While trans-women might self-identify as women, people who subscribed to biology-based ideologies of gender view these athletes as males who carry a size and strength advantage over females. The official goal of the IOC policies is to be fair to all athletes, which means that trans-athletes could compete as the gender with which they identify, but only if they met the aforementioned criteria. With such explicit criteria, cis-gender people could have confidence that only transwomen who were as "weak" as cis-women were able to compete, a move that diffused gender panic and upheld the logic of gender segregation in the arena of sports.

In the New York birth certificate case, a policy proposal intended to improve the lives of transgender people set off a rapid gender panic. Since many trans-people do not have genital surgery, they are often unable to have a sex marker that reflects their self-identity and gender presentation on their official documents (Currah and Moore 2009). In 2006, the City of New York proposed legislation that validated identity-based determination of gender by removing the genital surgical requirement for a change of sex marker on the birth certificate if applicants were over 18 years of age, had lived as their desired gender for at least two years, and had documentation from medical and mental health professionals stating that their transitions were intended to be permanent. Under this amendment, trans-people were still regulated by the medical institution but their genital configurations would not determine their gender. The New York City Board of Health worked closely with other officials and trans-rights advocates in writing the new policy, and politicians and transgender activists lauded the amendment, which was, by all accounts, expected to pass (Caruso 2006b; Cave 2006a).

Journalists initially presented the amendment in positive terms (e.g., Caruso 2006a; Colangelo 2006; Finn 2006). However, the proposed policy resulted in an intensely negative public reaction. The Board of Health was inundated with calls and emails from people asking how this policy change would affect access to gender-segregated spaces, such as restrooms, hospital rooms, and prison blocks (Currah and Moore 2009). To quell the panic, the Board of Health withdrew the proposal and quickly amended it to maintain emphasis on genitals as the criteria for determining gender. Transgender people in New York could change their sex marker, but like the requirement to compete in the Olympics, they would have to provide proof of genital surgery. In this way, the Board of Health attempted to balance biology-based and identity-based gender models that had come into collision, doing the gender naturalization work of symbolically restoring the primacy of bodies (here, genitals) for determining gender while still validating the possibility for gender transitions.

The "transgender rights" bills we analyzed also resulted in gender panics by embracing identity-based determination of gender. At both the federal and state level, these bills typically offer protections for "gender identity and gender expression" or "transgender expression" in the realms of employment, housing, and public accommodations. In an attempt to make such protections widely inclusive, there is no definition of "expressions" or explicit bodily criteria for trans-people. The resulting gender panics center on this lack of definitional criteria. In response to the proposed bill in New Hampshire, some opponents worried that the bill "did not adequately define transgender individuals" (*The Lowell Sun* 2009). A similar argument was raised about the Massachusetts bill, with concerned citizens worrying that "transgender identity and expression" was too vague (Letter to the Editor 2009a) and created "dangerous ambiguity" over who was legally transgender (Prunier 2009) and therefore had access to men's or women's bathrooms. Highlighting this concern about bathroom access, one opponent in Massachusetts noted, "This bill opens the barn door to everybody. There is no way to know who of the opposite sex is using the [bathroom] facility for the right purposes" (Ring 2009). In these cases, what appears to critics as too much validation of identity-based determination of gender sets off panic, panic that is quelled if the bills do not pass into law. When the bills do pass, opponents continue to raise concerns about the potential for danger to women and children in public restrooms, a point we return to in the following sections.

By enforcing explicit bodily criteria for determining gender, the IOC and New York City policies shore up the fissures created in the strict two-category model of gender by the visibility of trans-people while also allowing for some degree of identity-based determination of gender. Similar to judicial rulings permitting name and sex marker changes on government documents (Meyerowitz 2002), policies about birth certificates and athletes work to balance liberal values of autonomy with the belief that there are two genders and that all people (trans or cis) can be put into one category or the other. A lack of bodily criteria, in contrast, appears as a threat to the gender

binary. An editorial opposing federal protections for trans-people highlights this fear clearly: "The Left seeks to obliterate the distinction between men and women. This distinction is considered to be a social construct.... For those of us who believe that the male-female distinction is vital to civilization, the Left's attempt to erase this distinction is worth fighting against" (Prager 2010). Similarly, Shannon McGinley, of the conservative Cornerstone Policy Research group, worried that the goal of transgender rights bills was "to create a genderless society" (Distaso 2009). These concerns illustrate our concept of "gender panic," as public debate centers on the necessity of culturally defending a rigid male–female binary that is simultaneously framed as stable and innate. These concerns further underscore the extensive naturalization work that goes into legitimating the current sex/gender/sexuality system. Yet, this work did not evenly center on gender-segregated spaces, or on all biological characteristics that could be used as criteria for determining gender. Rather, opposition gathered around "people with penises" in spaces designated as women-only.

Genitals = Gender: Determining Gender in Women-Only Spaces

In our three cases, concerned citizens and journalists posed many questions about what genitals would be allowed in which gender-segregated spaces. This overwhelming focus on genitalia as the determinant of gender is interesting when considered against other possible criteria. Within biology-based gender ideology, gender is determined at birth by doctors on the visible recognition of genitalia. However, such gender categorization is assumed by many to be the result of other, less visible, biological forces, namely, chromosomes and hormones. While genitalia and hormones can be modified, chromosomes are static—meaning, on some level, XY and XX could be the best criteria for maintaining a binary gender system. Within the transgender rights case, opponents to such bills occasionally drew on chromosomes to further their case for why such bills would be problematic. As one man wrote to a newspaper in Michigan: "Your DNA is proof of your genetic code and determines race [and] sex. . . . There is also one fact that transgender individuals cannot deny: your DNA proves if you are a man or a woman. It does not matter what changes you have made to your sexual organs" (Letter to the Editor 2009b). Yet, such responses comprise a very small part of the discourse in our cases.

That less weight is given to chromosomes in these cases of gender determination is interesting. In everyday interactions, chromosomes are poor criteria for gender attribution, because they are not visible (Kessler and McKenna 1978). Athletes can be tested for chromosomal makeup. Yet, the IOC did not include chromosomes as part of the criteria for competition, as such a requirement would bar trans-athletes from competition. Similarly, our other cases do not use chromosomes as gender determination criteria, because such rigid genetic criteria would effectively invalidate the possibility of gender transitions. Where we saw a call for chromosomal criteria was in cis-people's imagined interactions with trans-people, scenarios that sought to delegitimize calls for identity-based determination of gender. That chromosomes did not figure widely in policy decisions, in contrast, suggests that identity-based gender ideologies have gained some degree of cultural legitimacy. To balance both ideologies, institutions cannot use unchangeable criteria, such as chromosomes, to determine a person's gender.

Genitalia are the primary determiner of gender in all of our cases. Starting with the sports case, which has the most clearly defined criteria for determining gender, the IOC permits transwomen (who are assumed to have XY chromosomes) to compete as women as long as they undergo the removal of the testes and the penis.[4] While testes are a source of testosterone, which is a central concern in sports competition,[5] the IOC does not state why transwomen athletes must undergo a penectomy to compete as women, since penises themselves do not provide advantages in sports. Such a requirement may be partially due to deep cultural beliefs that a person with a penis cannot be a woman (Kessler and McKenna 1978), and so they cannot compete with women in athletics. Moreover,

this requirement may be a result of a widely held belief that people with penises present a danger to women, a question we take up later in this article.

This emphasis on determining gender through hormone levels and genitalia is applied only to athletes attempting to compete as women. If an athlete competing as a woman has her gender called into question (usually for performing "too well" for a woman), her hormone levels are tested for "irregularities." In contrast, people who want to compete as men (cis or trans) are allowed to inject testosterone if their levels are seen as lower than "those naturally occurring in eugonadal men" (Gooren and Bunck 2004, 451). Thus, in this sex/gender/sexuality system, testosterone is a right of people claiming the category of "men." Further, while no athlete with a penis can compete as a woman, athletes are not required to have a penis to compete as men. Highlighting this point, "Will," an Australian transman who played football on a men's team, was required to undergo a hysterectomy in order to change his sex marker, but he was not required to have phalloplasty (Stark 2009). Moreover, his use of testosterone was not seen as an unfair advantage because his levels did not exceed those of an average cis-gender man.

The heightened attention to the presence or absence of a penis in spaces marked as "women only" was reflected in all of our cases. In news stories about the New York City birth certificate policy and the transgender rights bills, opponents frequently hinged their concerns on "male anatomies" (Cave 2006b) or "male genitalia" (Kwok 2006) in women's spaces. A common imagined interaction that generated gender panic was transwomen with "male anatomies" being housed with female prisoners (Cave 2006b; Staff 2006; Weiss 2006; Yoshino 2006), or transwomen "who still have male genitalia" using women's bathrooms (Kwok 2006; Yoshino 2006). While several articles included interviews with transmen activists who emphasized how hard it would be for them as people with facial hair to be forced to use a women's restroom on the basis of the sex marker on their birth certificates, only one opponent cited in the same articles used the example of transmen in the bathroom rather than transwomen.[6] Thus, biology-based gender ideologies were more likely to be deployed when debating transgender access to women's spaces. Those debates suggest that it is penises rather than other potential biological criteria that are the primary determiner of gender because male anatomies are framed as sexual threats toward women in gender-segregated spaces.

Separate and Unequal: Reproducing Gender Inequality in Gender-Segregated Spaces

Women-only spaces generate the most concern in these moments of gender ideology collision. In the resulting gender panics, ideas about "fairness" and "safety" work to naturalize gender difference and to maintain unequal gender relations. In these moments of ideological collision, two persistent ideologies about womanhood are deployed to counter identity-based determination of gender: Women are weaker than men, and, as a result, women are always at (hetero)sexual risk. This construction produces "woman" as a "vulnerable subjecthood" (Westbrook 2008), an idea that what it is to be part of the category of woman is to be always in danger and defenseless.[7] Conversely, men, or more specifically, penises, are imagined as sources of constant threat to women and children, an idea that reinforces a construction of heterosexual male desire as natural and uncontrollable. Women-only spaces, then, can be framed as androphobic and, as a result, heterophobic, due to the assumed inability of women to protect themselves from men combined with the assumption that all men are potential rapists. These ideas carry enough cultural power to temper institutional validation of identity-based determination of gender. What people are attempting to protect in these moments of ideological collision, we suggest, is not just women, but also the binary logic that gender-segregated spaces are predicated on and (re)produce.

Within the sports case, the IOC focused on the issue of fairness when determining when a transwoman can compete against cis-women. Attempting to maintain both the values of identity-based determination and the logic of gender difference

that justifies gender-segregated athletic competitions, sports officials put transwomen athletes into a peculiar situation: In order to gain access to the chance to compete in tests of strength and endurance, they must first prove their weakness (Buzuvis 2010; Shy 2007). This equation of women with weakness also accounts for the regulation of women's, but not men's, sports: If women are inherently weak, they must be protected from competing with stronger bodies (e.g., men). Cis-men, in contrast, should not need such protection from people with XX chromosomes.

Gender panics around the issue of trans-athletes also focus on the question of safety. The United Kingdom's 2004 Gender Recognition Act, a law intended to grant more rights to transgender people, includes a provision that prohibits trans-athletes' competition in cases that endanger the "safety of competitors" (Cavanagh and Sykes 2006). Discussion of safety in this case revolved around regulating access to contact sports. Yet, during debate around this act, another meaning of safety surfaced. Lord Moynihan is reported as saying that "many people will be greatly concerned at the idea of themselves or their children being forced to share a changing room with a transsexual person" (Mcardle 2008, 46). The allusion is that transgender people present a sexual danger to vulnerable others, conflating transgenderism and sexual deviance.

This portrayal of transgender people as potential sexual dangers in gender-segregated spaces appeared repeatedly in our other two cases. People advocating biology-based determination of gender worried about protecting women and children, another group generally vested with vulnerable subjecthood, from sexual risk from people with penises who would, with the new policies, be legally able to enter women-only spaces. When opponents to the New York City birth certificate policy worried about "male anatomies" in women's prisons (Cave 2006b), they were hinting at the possibility that those "male anatomies" would sexually assault the women with whom they shared prison space. While most articles about the New York City proposal merely suggested this possibility, some were more explicit. An opinion piece argued that one of the dangers of the proposed law was "personal safety: Many communal spaces, like prison cells and public bathrooms, are segregated by sex to protect women, who are generally physically weaker than men, from assault or rape" (Yoshino 2006). Explaining his opposition to the transgender rights bill, New Hampshire Representative Robert Fesh similarly noted, "Parents are worried about their kids and sexual abuse" (Macarchuk 2009). In these imagined interactions, opponents to identity-based criteria for determining gender both rely upon and shore up an idea that women are uniquely susceptible to assault. Moreover, they position transwomen as dangerous, a perspective that is often used in other contexts to justify violence against them (Westbrook 2009).

Since the panics produced in these moments of ideology collision focus on the penis as uniquely terrifying, "gender panics" might more accurately be termed "penis panics." In these hypothetical interactions, opponents give penises the power to destroy the sanctity of women's spaces through their (presumed natural) propensity to rape. The imagined sexual threat takes three forms in the news stories we examined. Most commonly, the threat is stated in general terms, such as opponents claiming that passage of transgender rights bills in New Hampshire and Massachusetts would put "women and children at risk" (Love 2009) in public restrooms. Second, some opponents imagined cis-men pretending to be transwomen in order to gain access to women's restrooms for sexually nefarious purposes. Contesting the vague criteria of who counts as transgender, Representative Peyton Hinkle of New Hampshire stated his opposition to the bill by calling it an "invitation . . . to people with predatory tendencies to come and hide behind the fact that they are having a transgender experience" (Fahey 2009). A spokesperson for the Massachusetts Family Institute told a reporter that the anti-discrimination bill allowed sexual predators to enter women's restrooms under the "guise of gender confusion" (Nicas 2009). Finally, transwomen themselves (not cis-men pretending to be trans) are imagined as the potential threat. Dr. Paul McHugh, chair

of the psychiatry department at Johns Hopkins University, is reported to have written an email protesting the proposed New York City policy that stated: "I've already heard of a 'transgendered' man who claimed at work to be 'a woman in a man's body but is a lesbian' and who had to be expelled from the ladies' restroom because he was propositioning women there" (Cave 2006b). In these imagined interactions, transwomen have legal permission to enter gender-segregated spaces without the proper biological credentials. As such, their presence transforms a nonsexual space into a dangerously (hetero)sexual one. Within this heteronormative logic, all bodies with male anatomies, regardless of gender identity, desire female bodies, and many of them (enough to elicit concern from the public) are willing to use force to get access to those bodies.[8]

That these imagined sexual assaults occur only in women-only spaces is worth further analysis, as women share space with men daily without similar concerns. We suggest that women-only spaces generate intense androphobia because, by definition, these spaces should not contain bodies with penises. If women are inherently unable to protect themselves, and men (or, more specifically, penises) are inherently dangerous (Hollander 2001), the entrance of a penis into women's space becomes terrifying because there are no other men there to protect the women. The "safe" (read: gender-segregated) space is transformed into a dangerous, sexual situation by the entrance of an "improper body." These fears rely on and reproduce gender binarism, specifically the assumption of strong-weak difference in male/female bodies, as opponents assume that people who could be gaining access to women's space (people with penises) are inherently stronger than cis-women and easily able to overpower them.

This emphasis on the sexual threat of penises in women-only spaces shows that gender panics are not just about gender, but also about sexuality. In the sex/gender/sexuality system, all bodies are presumed heterosexual. This assumption makes gender-segregated spaces seem safe because they are then "sexuality-free zones." Because there are only two gender categories, gay men and lesbians must share gender-segregated spaces with heterosexual men and women, respectively, an entrance that is tolerated as long as such entrants demonstrate the appropriate visual cues for admittance and use the bathroom for the "right" purpose (waste elimination). The use of public restrooms for homosexual sex acts can, of course, create a panic (Cavanagh 2010). Gender-segregated spaces, then, can be conceived of as both homophobic and heterophobic, as the fear is about unwanted sexual acts in supposedly sex-neutral spaces. Unlike normative sexual interactions, where gender difference is required to make the interaction acceptable (Schilt and Westbrook 2009), in gender-segregated spaces, gender difference is a source of discomfort and potential sexual threat and danger. Rhetoric about women and children as inherently vulnerable to sexual threats taps into cultural anxieties about sexual predators and pedophiles, who are always imagined to be men (Levine 2002); such fears have been repeatedly successful in generating sex panics. Because unwanted sexual attention is seen as a danger to women and children, but rarely, if ever, as a danger to adult men (Vance 1984), men's spaces are not policed. This differential policing of gender-segregated spaces illustrates the cultural logics that uphold gender inequality and heteronormativity—two systems whose underlying logic necessitates male–female oppositeness.

Conclusion

In this article, we examine the process of determining gender. We argue that collisions of biology-based and identity-based ideologies in the liberal moment have produced a sex/gender/sexuality system where the criteria for determining gender vary across social spaces. Many people have long assumed that biological factors, such as chromosomes, are always the ultimate determiner of gender. Contrary to the dominant assumption, we suggest that the sex/gender/sexuality system is slowly changing. As it has encountered liberal values of self-determinism, the criteria for determining gender have shifted away from pure biological determinism. In nonsexual

gender-integrated spaces, identity can be used to determine gender, as long as that identity is as a man or a woman (Schilt and Westbrook 2009). By contrast, in gender-segregated spaces, a combination of identity and body-based criteria is used, allowing someone to receive cultural and institutional support for a change of gender only if they undergo genital surgery. Finally, in heterosexual interactions, biology-based criteria (particularly genitals) are used to determine gender (Schilt and Westbrook 2009).

While most cis-gender people keep the same classification in all spaces, transgender people may be given different gender classifications by social actors depending on the type of interaction occurring in the space. Thus, one could speak of a trans-person's "social gender," "sexual gender," and "sports (or other gender-segregated space) gender." To illustrate this point, Kye Allums, a trans-man who played college basketball on a woman's team, has a social gender of "man" and a sports gender of "woman." Within the criteria for trans-athletes, he can continue to play basketball with women as long as he does not take testosterone or have genital surgery (Thomas 2010), a modification that would change his sports gender from "woman" to "man." Another way to conceptualize this point is to say that access to gender-integrated social spaces is determined by identity while access to gender-segregated spaces is mostly determined by biology, a point we summarize in Table 1.

The criteria for gender determination vary across social spaces because of the different imagined purposes of interactions that should occur in these settings. Heterosexual encounters and gender-segregated spaces both justify and reproduce an idea of two opposite genders. In spaces in which a higher level of oppositeness is required from participants, visual and behavioral gender cues often are not considered sufficient for determining gender and, instead, the participants must also demonstrate bodily oppositeness. Because heterosexual interactions and gender-segregated spaces rely on (and reproduce) gender binarism, it is these spaces where validation of identity-based determination of gender produces panics and

TABLE I. Criteria for Determining Gender across Contexts

	Nonsexual, Gender-Integrated	Nonsexual, Gender-Segregated	Heterosexual
Trans-men	Identity-based criteria determine gender.	Identity-based criteria determine gender.	Biology-based criteria determine gender.
	Changes to genitalia are not typically required to establish legitimacy of their gender.	Changes to genitalia are not typically required to required to gain access to men's spaces.	Changes to genitalia required. This criterion is not typically enforced in a violent way.
Trans-women	Identity-based criteria determine gender.	A combination of identity-based and biology-based criteria determine gender.	Biology-based criteria determine gender.
	Changes to genitalia are more typically required to establish legitimacy of their gender.	Changes to genitalia are required to gain access to women's spaces.	Changes to genitalia required. This criterion is often enforced in a violent way.

biology-based gender ideologies reign. In contrast, validation of identity-based determination of gender is more likely to occur when it cannot be framed as endangering other people, particularly others seen as more worthy of protection than trans-people (cis-women and children). In gender-integrated workplaces, for example, coworkers may not feel endangered by working with a trans-man who has the "cultural genitals" to support his social identity as a man, such as facial hair, particularly if he identified himself as crossing from one side of the gender binary to the other (Schilt and Westbrook 2009). It is important to add, however, that, in these spaces, identity-based determination of gender is more likely to be accepted by others when the person in question is, in the social imagination, "penis free" (all trans-men as well as "post-op" trans-women), as the penis is culturally associated with power and danger. These attitudes have profound consequences for transgender rights.

The criteria for determining gender also differ for placement in the category of "man" or "woman." Here, we have focused on the criteria for accessing women-only spaces because it is those spaces that produced the most panic in our media sources and that have the clearest criteria for admission. This focus of cultural anxiety on trans-women is unsurprising. We have detailed how the mainstream media portrayed trans-women as dangerous to heterosexual men because they use their feminine appearance to trick men into homosexual encounters (Schilt and Westbrook 2009; Westbrook 2009). In these cases, it is again trans-women who are portrayed as dangerous, yet this time they are positioned as endangering women and children.

We do not take the lack of attention to trans-men in men-only spaces to mean that trans-men are more accepted by people who vocally oppose trans-women. In contrast, we suggest that trans-men and trans-women are policed differently. Transmen's perceived lack of a natural penis renders them, under the logic of vulnerable subjecthood, unable to be threatening (and, therefore, unlikely to generate public outcry). Cis-gender men, the group who would share a bathroom or locker room with trans-men, also are not seen in the public imagination as potential victims of sexual threat, as such an image is contradictory to cultural constructions of maleness and masculinity (Lucal 1995). Trans-men enter a liminal state, in some ways, as they cannot hurt men (making them women), but are not seen as needing protection from men (making them part of a "pariah femininity" [Schippers 2007] that no longer warrants protection). Thus, because of gender inequality, the criteria for the category "man" are much less strict than those for the category "woman," at least for access to gender-segregated spaces.

But why do genitals carry more weight in determining gender in these segregated spaces? Our research hints at three possible answers for further exploration. First, genitals are changeable criteria, unlike chromosomes, which allows for some validation of liberal values of self-determination. Second, male and female genitals are imagined to be opposite, so using them as the criteria for determining gender maintains a binaristic gender system. Finally, genitals play a central role in gender panics because gender and sexuality are inextricably intertwined. The social actors opposed to identity-based determination of gender assume that all bodies, regardless of gender identity, are heterosexual. Although genitals are not supposed to be used in interactions in gender-segregated spaces, a fear of their (mis)use drives the policing of bodies in those spaces, making sexuality a central force in deciding which criteria will be used to determine gender.

By using genitals as the criteria for determining gender, the sex/gender/sexuality system is able to adapt to new liberal ideals of self-determination and to withstand the threat that trans-people might pose to a rigid binary system of gender. Although the existence of transgender and genderqueer people is seen as capable of "undoing gender" (Deutsch 2007; Risman 2009), the binaristic gender system tends to adapt to and reabsorb trans-people (Schilt and Westbrook 2009; Westbrook 2010). Rather than being undone, gender is constantly "redone" (Connell 2010; West and Zimmerman 2009). Like all other norms and social systems, people create gender. Challenges to the gender system modify rather than break it. Gender crossing can receive some validation in the liberal moment, but only when a binary remains unquestioned. By providing criteria for who can transition and how they can do it, the sex/gender/sexuality system is both altered and maintained.

Notes

1. Following Kessler and McKenna (1978), we highlight the social construction of both "sex" and "gender" by using the term "gender" throughout this article, even in moments where most people use the term "sex" (e.g., "gender-segregated" rather than "sex-segregated"). We reserve "sex" for references to intercourse, unless using a specific term such as "sex marker".

2. We use the term "(hetero)sexuality" to highlight that when many social actors speak of "sexuality" they are inferring heterosexuality.

3. As sexuality and sexualization are social processes, it is difficult to draw a conceptual line between a sexual and nonsexual space. Workplaces, for example, can contain sexualized interactions, though the dominant understanding of a workplace might be nonsexual. We use this term to refer to settings in which the commonly agreed on purpose is nonsexual. Sexual interactions do, of course, occur in these settings, but many see such interactions as a violation of the expected purpose of these spaces.

4. It is notable that women athletes do not have to possess what would be considered female genitals in order to compete. The criteria for determining gender in sports are thus very similar to Kessler and McKenna's findings that "penis equals male but vagina does not equal female" (1978, 151) when determining gender.

5. This use of "sex hormones"—mainly the levels of testosterone—to determine gender emerged only in the sports case because of the belief that testosterone provides a competitive advantage.

6. The image of a trans-man in men-only spaces was referenced by opponents only once in our analysis. A conservative activist told a reporter that allowing "men" to go into women's bathrooms legally would create discomfort for women and put them at sexual risk. The reporter asked what bathroom transgender men should use, as their male appearance could also make cis-women uncomfortable in the bathroom. The activist replied, "They [trans-men] should use the women's bathroom, regardless of whom it makes uncomfortable because that's where they are supposed to go" (Ball 2009).

7. Often, it is actors with good intentions, such as antiviolence activists, who, in their attempt to protect a particular group, unintentionally (re)produce an idea that the group is constantly prone to attack and unable to protect themselves (Westbrook 2008).

8. The ability to harm others attributed to trans-people in these narratives should be

problematized. The trans-people described by biological determiners function as monstrous specters, so there is often little nuance in these portrayals of trans lives. By contrast, arguments made for trans-rights bills and for access to gender-segregated spaces often include descriptions of trans-people as victims of violence and harassment rather than as perpetrators.

References

Ball, Molly. 2009. Robocall distorts record. *Las Vegas Review-Journal,* 6 April.

Berns, Nancy. 2004. *Framing the victim: Domestic violence, media, and social problems.* Somerset, NJ: Transaction.

Best, Joel. 2008. *Social problems,* 1st edition. New York: Norton.

Birrell, Susan, and Cheryl L. Cole. 1990. Double fault: Renee Richards and the construction and naturalization of difference. *Sociology of Sport Journal* 7:1–21.

Buzuvis, Erin. 2010. Caster Semenya and the myth of a level playing field. *The Modern American* 6:36–42.

Caruso, David. 2006a. New York City to ease rules for records reflecting gender change. *The Associated Press,* 6 October.

Caruso, David. 2006b. New York City seeks to ease rules for official documents reflecting gender change. *The Associated Press,* 7 November.

Cavanagh, Sheila. 2010. *Queering bathrooms: Gender, sexuality, and the hygienic imagination.* Toronto, Ontario, Canada: University of Toronto Press.

Cavanagh, Sheila L., and Heather Sykes. 2006. Transsexual bodies at the Olympics: The International Olympic Committee's policy on transsexual athletes at the 2004 Athens Summer Games. *Body & Society* 12:75–102.

Cave, Damien. 2006a. New York plans to make gender personal choice. *The New York Times,* 7 November.

Cave, Damien. 2006b. No change in definition of gender. *The New York Times,* 6 December.

Colangelo, Lisa. 2006. Change of sex IDs on city docket. *New York Daily News,* 25 September.

Connell, Catherine. 2010. Doing, undoing, or redoing gender? Learning from the workplace experiences of trans-people. *Gender & Society* 24:31–55.

Connell, Raewyn. 1995. *Masculinities.* Berkeley: University of California Press.

Currah, Paisley, and Lisa Jean Moore. 2009. We won't know who you are: Contesting sex designations in New York City birth certificates. *Hypatia* 24:113–35.

Deutsch, Francine M. 2007. Undoing gender. *Gender & Society* 21:106–27.

Distaso, John. 2009. No to marriage, "bathroom bills." *New Hampshire Union Leader,* 24 April.

Dreger, Alice. 2010. Sex typing for sport. *Hastings Center Report* 40:22–24.

Fahey, Tom. 2009. Transgender rights in "bathroom bill." *New Hampshire Union Leader,* 15 March.

Fausto-Sterling, Anne. 2000. *Sexing the body: Gender politics and the construction of sexuality.* New York: Basic Books.

Finn, Robin. 2006. Battling for one's true sexual identity. *The New York Times,* 10 November.

Gamson, William A., David Croteau, William Hoynes, and Theodore Sasson. 1992. Media images and the social construction of reality. *Annual Review of Sociology* 18:373–93.

Goffman, Erving. 1977. The arrangement between the sexes. *Theory and Society* 4:301–31.

Gooren, Louis, and Mathijs Bunck. 2004. Transsexuals and competitive sports. *European Journal of Endocrinology* 151:425–29.

Hollander, Jocelyn A. 2001. Vulnerability and dangerousness: The construction of gender through conversation about violence. *Gender & Society* 15:83–109.

International Olympic Committee Medical Commission. 2003. Statement of the Stockholm Consensus on sex reassignment in sports. http://www.olympic.org/Assets/ImportedNews/Documents/en_report_905.pdf.

International Olympic Committee Medical and Scientific Department. 2012. IOC regulations on female hyperandrogenism. http://www.olympic.org/Documents/Commissions_PDFfiles/Medical_commission/2012-06-22-IOC-Regulations-on-Female-Hyperandrogenism-eng.pdf.

Jansen, Sue Curry. 2002. When the center no longer holds: Rupture and repair. In *Critical communication theory: Power, media, gender, and technology,* edited by Nick Couldry and James Curran. Lanham, MD: Rowman & Littlefield.

Kessler, Suzanne, and Wendy McKenna. 1978. *Gender: An ethnomethodological approach.* Chicago: University of Chicago Press.

Kwok, Stephan. 2006. N.Y. gender law not realistic. *Daily Trojan,* 10 November.

Letter to the Editor. 2009a. Seeking support against vaguely defined identities. *Sentinel & Enterprise,* 13 July.

Letter to the Editor. 2009b. Anti-discrimination ordinance would harm Kalamazoo County. *Kalamazoo Gazette,* 9 October.

Levine, Judith. 2002. *Harmful to minors.* Minneapolis: University of Minnesota Press.

Littleton v. Prange. 1999. No. 99-1214 (Tex. 18).

Ljungqvist, Arne, and Myron Genel. 2005. Transsexual athletes: When is competition fair? *Medicine and Sport* 366:S42-S43.

Lorber, Judith. 1993. Believing is seeing: Biology as ideology. *Gender & Society* 7:568–81.

Love, Norma. 2009. NH Senate committee rejects transgender plan. *The Associated Press,* 23 April.

Lowell Sun, The. 2009. Transgender rights bill passes in N.H. House. 8 April.

Lucal, Betsy. 1995. The problem with "battered husbands." *Deviant Behavior* 16:95–112.

Macarchuk, Alexis. 2009. N.H. transgender bill aims to extend protections. *University Wire,* 10 April.

Macdonald, Myra. 2003. *Exploring media discourse.* London: Arnold.

Mcardle, D. 2008. Swallows and amazons, or the sporting exception to the Gender Recognition Act. *Social & Legal Studies* 17:39–57.

Meadow, Tey. 2010. A rose is a rose: On producing legal gender classifications. *Gender & Society* 24:814–37.

Meyerowitz, Joanne. 2002. *How sex changed: A history of transsexuality in the United States.* Cambridge, MA: Harvard University Press.

Nicas, Jack. 2009. Downing backs transgender bill. *The Berkshire Eagle,* 20 February.

Nyong'o, Tavia. 2010. The unforgivable transgression of being Caster Semenya. *Women & Performance: A Journal of Feminist Theory* 20:95–100.

Prager, Dennis. 2010. Why activists connect men in dresses to same-sex marriage. *Creators Syndicate,* 31 May.

Prunier, Chanel. 2009. Transgender bill is misguided. *Telegram & Gazette,* 14 July.

Ring, Dan. 2009. Transgenders fighting for protection. *The Republican,* 15 July.

Risman, Barbara J. 2009. From doing to undoing: Gender as we know it. *Gender & Society* 23: 81–84.

Schilt, Kristen. 2010. *Just one of the guys? Transgender men and the persistence of gender inequality.* Chicago: University of Chicago Press.

Schilt, Kristen, and Laurel Westbrook. 2009. Doing gender, doing heteronormativity: "Gender normals," transgender people, and the social maintenance of heterosexuality. *Gender & Society* 23: 440–64.

Schippers, Mimi. 2007. Recovering the feminine other: Masculinity, femininity, and gender hegemony. *Theory & Society* 36:85–102.

Seidman, Steven. 1995. Deconstructing queer theory or the under-theorization of the social and the ethical. In *Social postmodernism: Beyond identity politics,* edited by Linda J. Nicholson and Steven Seidman. Cambridge, UK: Cambridge University Press.

Shy, Yael Lee Aura. 2007. Like any other girl: Male-to-female transsexuals and professional sports. *Sports Lawyers Journal* 14:95.

Staff. 2006. Facing facts Dec. 3-Dec. 9. *The New York Times,* 10 December.

Stark, Jill. 2009. I'm just an ordinary guy who wants to play footy. *Sunday Age,* 7 June.

Stryker, Susan. 2008. *Transgender history.* Seattle, WA: Seal Press.

Thomas, Katie. 2010. Transgender man is on women's team. *The New York Times,* 1 November.

Tucker, Ross, and Malcolm Collins. 2009. The science and management of sex verification in sport. *South African Journal of Sports Medicine* 21 (4): 147–50.

Vance, Carol. 1984. *Pleasure and danger: Exploring female sexuality.* New York: Routledge.

Weiss, Jillian Todd. 2006. NYC rejects birth certificate change regs. Transgender Workplace Diversity (blog), 5 December, 2006, http://transworkplace.blogspot.com.

West, Candace, and Don Zimmerman. 1987. Doing gender. *Gender & Society* 1:125–51.

West, Candace, and Don H. Zimmerman. 2009. Accounting for doing gender. *Gender & Society* 23:112–22.

Westbrook, Laurel. 2008. Vulnerable subjecthood: The risks and benefits of the struggle for hate crime legislation. *Berkeley Journal of Sociology* 52:3–24.

Westbrook, Laurel. 2009. Violence matters: Producing gender, violence, and identity through accounts of murder. Ph.D. diss., University of California, Berkeley, CA.

Westbrook, Laurel. 2010. Becoming knowably gendered: The production of transgender possibilities in the mass and alternative press. In *Transgender identities: Towards a social analysis of gender diversity,* edited by Sally Hines and Tam Sanger. London: Routledge.

Yoshino, Kenji. 2006. Sex and the city. *Slate Magazine,* 11 December.

The Gendered Family

The current debates about the "crisis" of the family—a traditional arrangement that some fear is collapsing under the weight of contemporary trends ranging from relaxed sexual attitudes, increased divorce, and women's entry into the labor force, to rap music and violence in the media—actually underscore how central the family is to the reproduction of social life—and to gender identity. If gender identity were biologically "natural," we probably wouldn't need such strong family structures to make sure that everything turned out all right. Yet, although the "typical" family of the 1950s television sitcom—breadwinner father, housewife/mother, and 2.5 happy and well-adjusted children—is the empirical reality for less than 10 percent of all households, it remains the cultural ideal against which contemporary family styles are measured.

In this section, three different articles examine the changing nature of the family. Caryn E. Medved and William K. Rawlins look at the role reversals in some contemporary heterosexual families, in which the woman is the breadwinner and the man is the stay-at-home dad. What happens to gender relations? Does this make families more egalitarian? Taking these questions further, Kathleen Gerson looks at what the next generation of families wants their lives to look like—and what they'll do if they can't have it. And what happens when the parents are "gender-equals"—that is, children are being raised by a gay or lesbian couple? It turns out that what children need is a lot of love, support, and time—and that those qualities know no gender or sexual orientation. Sarah Reed and her colleagues examine these same dynamics as they play out in the Black lesbian community.

At-Home Fathers and Breadwinning Mothers: Variations in Constructing Work and Family Lives

CARYN E. MEDVED AND WILLIAM K. RAWLINS

At times I used to dream about when they are older [and] I will be able to write; when they are older, the house will get cleaned lickety split . . . I do the dishes and I do the laundry and all the mundane household stuff [but] now I don't get to cuddle and watch Sesame Street.

The above excerpt is from an interview with Bob, an at-home father, reminiscing about the memorable times he used to spend with his daughters when they were younger. Bob is married to Julie, a senior manager working at a large firm in the Midwest. He continues, "There was always a realization between us that she was like the, I guess, the corporate person," and he humorously adds, "I have a lot of patience with kids, but with adults, less so." Alternative ways of composing and talking about work and family life as evidenced in Bob and Julie's story are slowly making their way into mainstream U.S. culture (Kershaw, 2009; Morgan, 2011; Stout, 2010). The number of couples reporting to be primarily or solely financially dependent on a wife's income range from 12% of women who earn more than 60% of the family's income to just under 3% who report being entirely dependent on a wife's earnings (Bureau of Labor Statistics, 2010; Raley, Mattingly, & Bianchi, 2006). The U.S. also saw a 200% increase in the number of reported at-home fathers between 1994 and 2005 (U.S. Census Bureau, 2005). Further, men were disproportionately affected early on during the recent recession as the most significant layoffs hit male-dominated industries (Şahin, Song, & Hobijn, 2010; see also Boushey, 2011). The Pew Research Center also

reports that women continue to outpace men in education and earnings growth (Fry & Cohn, 2010). Undoubtedly, substantial changes in the discourse and related practices of marriage and earning are underway.

Investigations of dual-earner couples' experiences have dominated work and family studies over the past few decades (e.g., Buzzanell, 1997; Hochschild, 1989; Hood, 1983; Medved, 2004; Potuchek, 1997; Risman & Johnson-Sumerford, 1998; Stone, 2007). This research documents the work and family choices and conflicts of dual-earner couples that now represent 47.8% of married couples in the U.S. (Bureau of Labor Statistics, 2011). Scholars also have turned their attention to alternative work and family arrangements including the experiences of: (a) at-home fathers (e.g., Doucet, 2004; Radin, 1988; Rochelen, Suizzo, Kelley, & Scaringi, 2008; Smith, 1998; Smith, 2009; Vavrus, 2002) and (b) breadwinning mothers (Drago, Black, & Wooden, 2005; Medved, 2009a; Meisenbach, 2010; Winslow-Bowe, 2006). Yet to our knowledge no significant efforts have been made to study the social construction and coordination of meaning and identity in the lives of *both husbands and wives* transposing post-World War II gendered marital work and family roles. We know little about *how* these supposed role reversing or reverse traditional couples do and/or undo gender through language and social interaction (Deutsch, 2007; West & Zimmerman, 1987). Illustrating the different ways these couples communicatively construct their unique approaches

Caryn E. Medved and William K. Rawlins, "At-Home Fathers and Breadwinning Mothers: Variations in Constructing Work and Family Lives," *Women & Language,* Vol. 34, No. 2 (September 2011), pp. 9–39. Reprinted by permission of *Women & Language.*

to work and family is this study's key contribution to the gender and communication literature; we provide a glimpse into varied examples of working out social change at the micro-level. Given that language and social interaction are crucial sites where the definitions and daily practices of masculinities and femininities along with their historic associations with the public and private spheres are reproduced, adapted, resisted and/or transformed, we are led to listen and learn from these couples' stories.

As a background for telling their stories, we first briefly review research on dual-earning couples' . . . professional women's workforce opting out, as well as stay-at-home fathering experiences. Second, we describe our theoretical approach to the study of gender and language (e.g., Deutsch, 2007; Ferree, Lorber, & Hess, 2000; Gerson & Piess, 1985; Potuchek, 1992). Third, we present our findings from exploratory, indepth interviews with ten at-home father and breadwinning mother couples. Specifically, we identify five homemaking-moneymaking stances among these couples: reversing, conflicting, collaborating, improvising, and sharing. We illustrate each of these five stances through a composite narrative, each developed from one of the couples' interview transcripts. Finally, we discuss our study's implications as well as future research directions. . . .

Review of Literature

. . .

Labor Force Decision Making and Opting Out

Stone (2007) found that while only a minority of professional women plan ahead to leave their careers for full-time motherhood, many exit due to frustration with both organizational as well as spousal flexibility and support, along with intensive mothering pressures (see also Hays, 1996; Medved & Kirby, 2005; Warner, 2005). Stone argues that these women do not make this choice lightly and voice concerns about likely problems with career re-entry in professional positions. Many fail to plan for potential unintended

consequences of financial dependency such as the possibility of divorce or husbands' job loss or disability (Bennetts, 2007). Gerson's (1985) arguments remain relevant as she contends that women's workforce decisions are products of: (a) "pushing" women out of the workforce (i.e., desires for traditional motherhood, lack of spousal assistance, lack of supportive work environments, falling career aspirations); as well as (b) "pulling" them into paid labor (i.e., career aspirations, ambivalence toward motherhood, financial necessity). She notes that "women [may] . . . resemble men who find themselves in jobs they would prefer to leave, except for one important difference . . . few men enjoy the traditional, although shrinking, female option of trading paid work for domestic work" (p. 19). Meaning construction in the lives of men (and their wives) who *do* trade career for domestic work is the focus of the present study. Further, we believe that to richly understand this inherently communicative process, we must investigate and juxtapose *both* men and women's interrelated accounts of labor force participation and exit. Just as life course theorists argue that work and family is constituted by "linked lives" (Elder, 1995), we argue that marital identities at times are also linked identities and must be explored as joint-constructions or co-constructions.

Stay-at-Home Fathering

Bridges, Etaugh, and Barnes-Farrell (2002) report that stay-at-home fathers are judged more harshly than stay-at-home mothers for ostensibly sacrificing their families' financial security. In other words, they are sanctioned for engaging in caregiving and *not* breadwinning per conventional gender expectations (Riggs, 1997). For their parts, working mothers are perceived as less communal (i.e., sensitive, warm, nurturing, and dedicated to family) and less effective as parents than fathers. Even so, Wentworth and Chell (2001) explain that "male cross-gender behavior is treated more harshly than female cross-gender behavior" (p. 640). They suggest "there is a stronger link between gender roles and perceived sexuality for men than for women" (p. 640). Although we must not forget that the sexuality of powerful career women is also challenged (Jamison, 1997), a man performing household labor or childcare may be perceived minimally as "less of a man," perhaps even threatening to children or homosexual (Murray, 1996). In an early study of primary caregiving fathers, Radin (1988) reported that men did not persist in at-home roles for extended periods of time due to gendered pressures to conform. Radin, however, found four commonalities among men who *did* remain in full-time caregiving roles for more than two years (versus reverting to traditional patterns) including: (a) viewing their own fathers as inattentive, (b) being in their 30s and/or with prior career experience, (c) enjoying the support of extended family members, and (d) having a small family. Rochlen and colleagues' (2008) work also found that men exit paid work when (a) their wives have a high value for career, (b) they see full-time parenting as an opportunity, and (c) caregiving aligns with their preference or personality. Both at-home mothering and fathering couples report similar levels of marital satisfaction, but women in either arrangement report higher levels of stress and exhaustion than men (Zimmerman, 2000).

In a study of 70 Canadian at-home fathers, Doucet (2004) reported that although stay-at-home fathers take on primary childcare responsibilities, they do not entirely forgo traditional masculine sources of work-related identity. At-home fathers report engaging in various kinds of work, including unpaid community work, part-time home-based employment, and self-provisioning work (e.g., landscaping, carpentry, woodworking, car repair). Doucet also found that among the various forms of masculinity displayed in at-home fathers' narratives, hegemonic forms of masculinity remained widespread (see also Vavrus, 2002). These men often mentioned feeling social pressure to earn and feeling isolated from the "real world" of paid labor, as well as the need to socialize with other men on common masculine conversational ground. Smith (1998) found that "hegemonic conceptions of who ought to be minding the children and house subvert or thwart [at-home father's] attempts to validate themselves and these practices" (p. 138).

In sum, we know that gender and power are intertwined with dual-career couples' negotiation of childcare, domestic labor, and labor force participation. Men's power and privilege in the home persists to a certain extent, despite women's increased contributions to household income. Yet lived moments of "undoing gender" cannot be discounted and warrant investigation (Deutsch, 2007). What is less well known is how couples engaging in gender atypical arrangements—particularly primary breadwinning mothers married to at-home fathers—come to understand, enact, and potentially resist or rework conventional gendered tasks and identities through language and social interaction. Given the relatively uncharted and exploratory nature of this study, we frame this investigation around one central research question: *How do stay-at-home fathers and breadwinning mothers articulate their stances toward moneymaking and homemaking?*

Doing, Undoing, and Reworking Gender

Gender operates on multiple, dynamic, and interdependent levels (e.g., Ashcraft & Mumby, 2003; Deutsch, 2007; Ferree, Lorber, & Hess, 2000; Gerson & Piess, 1985). We take up social constructionist and feminist arguments that the interactive and discursive expressions of gender are complexly intertwined with their structural and institutional manifestations (Deutsch, 2007; Holmer-Nadesan, 1996). Studying the discourse of these couples concurrently gives us (a) insight into their ongoing negotiations and coordination of gendered tasks and identities, as well as (b) examples of how available language shapes and is reshaped by what these couples see as possible performances of homemaking and moneymaking. We "do gender" in everyday discourse and related practices in the context of larger cultural and structural forces (West & Zimmerman, 1987). Equally important, we can *undo* and rework gender through our language and social interactions (Butler, 1990; Buzzanell, 1995; Denker, 2009; Medved, 2009b). We must not only explore the ways we perpetuate modern gendered assumptions about caregiving and wage-earning, but also the ways we resist and 'break the bowls' of gender (Lorber, 2005). We also need to pay attention to dissembling binaries; that is exploring the various enactments of gender in-between simply doing and undoing, public and private, or masculine and feminine (Connell, 1995; Deutsch, 2007; Geuss, 2003; Medved, 2007). Multiple masculinities and femininities exist as interdependent discourses, co-constructed identities, and lived experiences. Gender role prescriptions still exist although they are not as static or fixed as in the past. Instead, they persist in ongoing interplay with gendered identities, understandings of selves and as co-constructed processes in marital relationships (Sveningsson & Alversson, 2003). Sometimes gendered social change is subtle and can only be seen in small acts and words at the margins of our lived experiences. Further, fathering and housework are feminist issues (Silverstein, 1996) just as are women's access to and success in the workplace (Buzzanell, 1995). We embrace these theoretical assumptions about language and gender in the five stories below that (re)present varying gendered co-constructions of homemaking-moneymaking tasks and identities.

Investigative Practices

The texts examined in this study were collected through semi-structured interviews with eight married couples from a large metropolitan area and mid-sized town in the Midwest, and two couples from the east coast of the United States. Separate interviews were conducted with each husband and wife; sixteen of our interviews were conducted face-to-face and audio-recorded by one of the authors (Hertz, 1995). We interviewed four participants over the phone with two individuals' insights audio-taped and the others' preserved in detailed notes. Each interview lasted between one and two hours. All audio recordings were transcribed by a professional service, resulting in 495 typed pages.

Participants

All the stay-at-home fathering couples (SAHFC) were white, middle to upper-middle class, heterosexual couples with at-home fathers and breadwinning mothers, including one couple who had recently returned to a traditional arrangement. All were recruited through the authors' professional and social networks and flyers posted in local areas. Men volunteering to participate self-selected as a "stay-at-home" father. That is, they considered themselves primary childcare providers who had left full-time careers (or were on an extended hiatus) and were dependent on spousal income. While the label SAHFC is not ideal, it provides a clear description of what characteristics differentiate these couples from dual-career or traditional male breadwinning couples. In line with past research, these at-home fathers often still participated in part-time volunteer work or limited at-home paid labor (Doucet, 2004). On average, the couples had been married about 10 years (range = 5 to 18) with various numbers and ages of children (Appendix 1). The interviewed women's occupations included: management consultant, banker, lawyer, non-profit manager, online business manager, graduate student/program assistant, and sales manager. The amount of time these couples had spent in their current work and family arrangements averaged three years, ranging from three months to seven years. Given our goals, social constructionist underpinnings, and research question, we sought married couples who have lived this unique relational situation and were willing to share their stories. . . .

Five Homemaking-Moneymaking Stances

Before presenting the five stances, we briefly mention four factors that were commonly described as occasioning these ten couples' decisions to live as at-home fathering families (see also Doucet, 2004). First, both parents wanted their children to be raised in their own home by one or both of them; they wanted hands-on responsibility for their kids' daily lives. Second, except for one case of equal earnings, in every couple, the mother's paid work brought the family greater income and benefits than the father's earnings prior to his movement into full-time caregiving. Third, every father except one had greater flexibility in his work schedule than the mother, again, prior to his taking on full-time caregiving duties. A fourth occasioning factor is that of temperament. These men and women described the father's temperament as conducive to spending extended periods of time with their child(ren) and being relatively unthreatened by homemaking work and identities. We will return to these issues in our final discussion section, but for now, here are the stances.

Stance One: Reversing

We label this first stance *reversing* to indicate the performance of gender nontraditional homemaking and moneymaking tasks. Reversing, in this context, means to exchange duties though not necessarily to alter or transform their meanings and associated identities or eligibilities. Simply put, the sex of the person performing the task is reversed but its meaning stays intact in these couples' articulations. The couple illustrating the *reversing* stance had been married for eight years with a fifteen-month-old daughter. When Bethany was born, Scott and Alicia were both employed. Even so, Alicia observed, "When I was younger, I thought I'd have more children and be home. . . . The most important job you can do is stay at home." In Scott's words, "She wanted to take on that role." But they knew they could save money if she worked more after their daughter's birth because as a management consultant, "Alicia has always been the one who has made more in the relationship." Following Alicia's maternity leave, Scott had a five-month paid family leave; following this, Alicia quit her job to stay home full-time.

Home on leave with Bethany, Scott still tried doing work via email, occasionally taking her with him into the office, and attempting consulting and conference calls from home. He also tried to "squeeze work in" at night. Alicia remarked, "His ideas about what a father does were based on his father. . . . You always should have a job." Although he accomplished some work during his leave, he had an "identity crisis," according to Alicia. He felt tremendous anxiety about not staying connected with his occupation. It was "horrible," she said. "We idealized the idea of him being at home; we thought it seemed so great, but

it didn't work out that way." Meanwhile, Alicia's work was too challenging, mainly in relation to breastfeeding and travel. Her employer "tried" to accommodate her but, in Scott's words, "Alicia wanted to be home." She was ambivalent about work and felt guilty not being with her daughter. She would pump breast milk at work, and at night it was Scott's job to thaw the frozen bottles and feed Bethany. Alicia wanted Scott to have the chance to care for Bethany, but she also wanted to be a "mother."

Determining household tasks was a challenge for this couple when switching work roles. Steve asked: When the man is doing the more feminine chores, what happens to the more masculine tasks like raking leaves, etc.? Alicia said their negotiations over these issues became "his work versus my work but trying to keep Bethany in the forefront." She would "walk through the door" and start to care for their daughter, and from then on Scott would need to do his paid work. Due to exhaustion, "Later on we developed a list of who does what." Alicia said she always knew she would quit her job, it was a matter of when. And while Scott considers his time as an at-home father "a very profound experience," he thinks Bethany "needed" her mom at home and Alicia needed to be there. He's become more of a believer in a mother and child's biological connection and is devoting increasing amounts of time to his paying job.

Through this *reversing narrative*, we see a SAHFC organizing their activities and identities according to prescribed gender roles and traditionally gendered images of parenting, despite living in an alternative work arrangement (i.e., mother is primary earner and father is primary childcare provider). Homemaking work is described categorically and, by and large, as feminine or women's work; moneymaking work is viewed as a masculine or a predominantly male domain regardless of the sex of the person performing it. Becoming a SAHFC therefore involves transitory *role* reversals rather than the adoption of new identities; this stance still presupposes natural and gender-linked parenting roles. We term this stance "reversing" because the categorical reflections and identities associated with at-home parenting and outside-of-the-home moneymaking remain intact while often at odds with the gendered self-conceptions of the persons performing these labors. The commonsense notion of role reversal applies most straightforwardly here related to the husband's and wife's performances of unconventional duties without the reconfiguration of identities. Further, unequal eligibilities to perform homemaking and moneymaking roles persist based on traditionally determined societal gender alignments. As a result, this attempt to live according to preset—although reverse-gendered—duties and roles while still maintaining traditionally gendered personal identities and self-understandings was associated with a range of related tensions that rendered it a transitory option at best.

Stance Two: Conflicting

Stance two is termed *conflicting* in that couples articulate contradictory meanings for the performance of unconventional work and family tasks, identities, and eligibilities. The conflicting approach simultaneously reflects both openness and discontent with the division of task responsibilities. And, while their narratives acknowledge that elements of their identities and perceived eligibilities are different than gendered prescriptions, their meaning-making is fraught with tension. The SAHFC couple illustrating the *conflicting* stance had been married for eighteen years with a nine-year-old son and a seven-year-old daughter. Both Mike and Sue were employed full-time when their nanny of four years left. Mike said they already decided he would "back out of working full time" to "cover" their kids. With Sue's "higher earnings," Mike termed it "the path of least resistance ... also, optimizing the financial part" of their situation. For her part, Sue recalled she had just been unexpectedly laid off and was interviewing at the time; her husband " ... took a very pragmatic view as opposed to the more emotional view that I think I had at the time, where he's looking at it saying you're very marketable. . . . You need to go out there and find a job. Right? We've already committed to me being home. Right?"

Mike described "more blurred" distinctions between the family's parental roles for their children, "especially since they see that I'm still—when I'm home—I'm still working." He was proud of his "routine" and "groove" with the kids and that he was "the turn-to guy a lot of times when stuff is going on." Sue affirmed, "He's got good natural instincts to be taking care of the kids" and "has a great relationship with them." Yet she also revealed that "going to college, I assumed that I would work for a couple of years" to "pay off" her education and then she would "quit and I would be at home raising kids." Given their atypical work and family situation, however, she thought her kids would "grow up" with different attitudes toward women in the workplace, hoping they would be "more open-minded about what are some of the different options." At the same time she was trying to make sure "they don't get the message that [my paid] work is more important than them, even though I have to spend more of my time there."

Mike's biggest challenge as the at-home parent was "organizing everything," including the kids' chores, activities, and what is expected of them. Yet for him "the biggest other challenge" involved his own career issues, noting, "The part-time guy" has to accept "that one career role is gonna be subordinate to another." Mike's identity seemed strongly connected to his part-time paid work as a financial planning consultant. He frequently described "covering more of the kid stuff" in matter-of-fact terms and portrayed a traditional male's preoccupation with earning money despite protecting the needs of Sue's "full-time gig" and managing his schedule to do "the family thing in the afternoon" when the children returned home from school. Even so, he hoped that increasing his financial planning business would make it "much harder" for him to "flex" his time around everyone else's while equalizing his and Sue's incomes and time spent at home. Mike looked to the future and explained, "a year from now I hope that I say that it's much harder ... because my [work] demands have gone up." While "it works out pretty well" for now, Mike wanted more time for paid work.

Mike and Sue each described household chores as contested in traditionally gendered ways. Mike commented, "She's much more concerned about how clean the house is," and added, "She'll come home and be grumbly about the house being messy and no one will care about that but her." In turn, Sue observed, "I believe I have primary responsibility for dishes and laundry, but he would probably not agree." She continued, "Lately he's done a lot more laundry then he used to. In the past it was when I would come home and I'd lose it, the next day he'd do laundry, right? But, you know, he's kinda starting to see that pattern and wanting to avoid it." These accounts suggest disputed power arrangements where, besides being the primary income provider, the woman is somehow responsible for domestic matters. Sue remarked that often she "can't get this job done because I have to go off and do my other day job, right?"

Despite their shared perceptions of Mike's at-home parenting potential early in their marriage, Sue had not anticipated the consequences to her of their current family arrangement:

> We always knew that if and when we were to have kids . . . that he would be very good at staying home . . . But it was never real at that point, right? And I guess I had always grown up assuming— you know, I had a stay-at-home mom. . . . I assumed I would work for a couple of years to kind of pay off college, if you will, make it worth the while, you know, and then quit and I would be home raising the kids. I never really assumed that I'd be a long-term career woman.

In recent years she switched to a job "that has allotted me much more balance in my life, but I'm clearly not paid as much nor do I have as much advancement opportunity." She summarized, "I understand the rules of the game, but I don't like them, but yet I'm still there playing it." Mike contrasted Sue's identity needs with his, "She doesn't have the kind of attachment some people do to her job and her career in a self-esteem kind of standpoint . . . she doesn't identify herself as what she is. . . . It's not about her. . . . Like some people would say, like me." Mike repeatedly narrated a stereotypical vision blending the past and present of gendered predicaments in corporate America; many successful women want "to just get out of it" and are verbal about it. In contrast, he

believed that then and now dissatisfied men "hold more of that inside." Sue echoed these sentiments in describing their own arrangement's challenges, "So the biggest one that's probably—it's like the iceberg where I only see the little tip—is Mike's— Mike's self-esteem. And then, you know, the next one is just my emotional well-being." She depicted their situation in terms mirroring Mike's general discussion, "I think it weighs on him heavily to not be, you know, earning more money . . . and I think to some degree he's not gonna complain to me about anything that's going on in his life because I bring—I wear my stress on my sleeve, so why would he want to add to that?"

The narratives of couples we consider *conflicting* presuppose many facets of traditional feminine and masculine roles and subject positions associated with homemaking and moneymaking even as these couples worked together to negotiate alternative arrangements. To the extent that traditionally gendered discourses, roles, and identities implicitly or explicitly informed their alternative arrangements of parenting, housework, and/ or paid labor that challenged such regimes, they experienced conflict. These conflicts reflect inequities and asymmetrical eligibilities historically associated with gendered labor in the home, such as the woman working "a second shift." They also involve conflicted self-images derived from not being able to do what one had hoped to do or perceives one is supposed to do with one's time and talents as a traditionally gendered person/mother/ father. As such, neither partner feels fully reconciled to their domestic and paid labor-related identities even as they successfully manage their day-to-day routines.

Stance Three: Collaborating

The homemaking/moneymaking stance we call *collaborating* highlights an approach to work and family that recognizes existing gender prescriptions while, at the same time, expresses a desire to transcend these very same gendered work and family meanings. By collaborating, we mean that a SAHFC articulates an approach to work and life that both holds onto and lets go of conventional gendered meanings and practices. The couple whose story exemplifies the *collaborating* stance had been married for sixteen years with a seven-year-old son, Hank. Lisa and Ty each described their shared "conscious decision" to have a child and for Ty to stay home with him. Their rationale was based on Lisa's higher income and medical benefits from banking and the flexibility of Ty's paid work as a musician. Ty wryly framed his early realizations about doing full-time child-care in terms of gendered positions on knowledge, "It's not a hundred percent true, but men generally like to know or think they know what they're doing all the time. They avoid things that they don't know what they're doing, or they just pretend it doesn't exist." Even so, implicating himself, he described his own need to learn and address demands of childcare:

> So, when it comes to domestic stuff and baby stuff, it's so much easier to just say, I don't know anything about that. And you don't want to know anything about it. It's like if you don't know anything about it, nobody expects you to do it . . . I'm going to be here and if he throws up all over the place or has an explosion in a snowsuit and fills it up with poop, and you're out strolling around—you know, "Mommy, Mommy." There's no mommy there. It's just you.

He noted with gender-bending creativity, "For the biggest part of those early years, I was the man-mom."

For her part, Lisa sincerely felt that Ty "won the prize and got to stay home." Yet when asked how being the primary breadwinner affected their marriage, she replied, "Well, I don't know that it has affected it. That's always been my role. But I think it kind of works for us." She added, "Also I think Ty's not threatened by it. I think that some men have such an ego that they could never have a wife who is the breadwinner. They're too busy beating on their chests; they can't have someone else bringing home the bacon. But he's not that way." In terms of her paid work, Lisa mentioned liking "problem solving," creative challenges, and the opportunities to figure out numerical puzzles in the banking world. She was pleased about her self-sufficiency and her ability to provide income.

Even so, she also felt it was difficult to "feel like you're being a good parent and doing good at your job, I think. Especially the parent part. I just feel like I miss a lot. . . . There's not enough time and this child is growing up so fast." Because of her devotion to parenting, Lisa enjoyed her extended opportunities to be home with their son during her maternity leave and the two years she "worked from home." In fact, despite her second thoughts from a financial standpoint, she elected to spend the severance pay she was once awarded to support a full year at home taking care of Hank with Ty. Both parents emphasized choosing how they would live and being at home to raise their son over "materialistic" concerns.

The couple described household labor as equitably distributed based on personal preferences and availability. Ty explained that he enjoys cooking and would do that "regardless of anything." In his view other housework depended on Lisa's paid work, "on what had been going on with her on the job front and how exhausting or time consuming her job was." He described a period during Hank's early childhood, "that lasted about four years; she was gone before he woke up in the morning and got home sometimes in time just to go up and kiss him goodnight and maybe put him down at that point." At present, they have negotiated other patterns, "So, for instance, right now she does the laundry. She does grocery shopping. Although I do the day-to-day grocery shopping, she does the big grocery shopping. . . . She does more than half of the cleaning I would say, although I participate in that." Lisa's account of how they divided housework resonated closely with Ty's, "I think that it's determined a lot just by availability. . . . I think it's just more of what we need to do and who has the time to do it." She reflected, "I don't really think we've ever pointed a finger and said, 'Oh no, that's your job. You need to do it.' We've never done that. We've just kind of worked it out."

Like the other collaborating couples we interviewed, Ty and Lisa repeatedly expressed sensitivity to and respect for what the other was experiencing at various points by assuming identities and responsibilities of child-raising and breadwinning that often challenged traditionally gendered accounts. Their stories were sprinkled with bittersweet recognition of the limits their own negotiated choices placed upon their time and personally desired activities—but more often with ironically reflexive accounts of humorous situations that defied stereotyped options for parenting and occupational identities. Ty recalled how they mutually recognized "the sitcom moment" they found themselves reenacting with Lisa returning from the office just after Ty botched a dinner recipe at the end of his already trying day at home. He noted, "I'm not sure how couples deal with that 'cause it's kind of how does she come in and comfort me without it being patronizing? You know what I mean? How does the man blow off steam for something like the domestic travails of the day?"

Lisa and Ty each expressed summary satisfaction with the family and occupational arrangements they have accomplished together. Lisa stated, "I just think that we know it's not just one person's responsibility to raise a child or to have a home, or even working. . . . I just think that we know that we're a team and we know how important this child is to us and how important it is to him to have a stable, healthy, loving environment." In sum, like the other collaborating couples, Lisa and Ty expressed awareness of societal prescriptions for gender roles but were able to navigate jointly these rules in order to construct and minimize role-based tensions.

This narrative demonstrates how the *collaborating* stance involves a SAHFC acknowledging traditional feminine and masculine roles and subject positions associated with homemaking and moneymaking while negotiating collaboratively their own arrangements. These couples described gendered expectations for parents and breadwinners yet were able to distance themselves at times from the injunctions of traditionally gendered roles even as they were sensitive to their influence. At times, couples achieved this dual perspective through ironically appropriating gender-prescribed roles. They also portrayed themselves "as a team," emphasizing their equality and respect for their own choices and responsibilities. Such language seemed self-consciously to shape and reflect the couple's co-created discursive space, activities, and understandings of the risks and benefits of their ongoing choices. Consequently, their narratives embodied noticeably more acceptance and celebration of their mutual and individual contributions than conflict as well as a desire to surpass their current identities as at-home fathers and breadwinning mothers.

Stance Four: Improvising

A fourth stance that emerged from our readings of these texts articulates an approach to work and family life that attempts to improvise meaning without taking gender as the primary frame for tasks, identities, or eligibilities. The *improvising* stance disavows gendered assumptions and senses of self, at times replacing these assumptions with the language of personal preference or personality. The couple illustrating the *improvising* stance had been married for eight years with eight- and five-year-old daughters. Bob and Julie's first daughter required eye surgery and the couple was switching from breast- to bottle-feeding when Julie accepted a job with excellent benefits and exciting career prospects in a city where a renowned pediatric eye surgeon practiced. Bob left his job in a bookstore, and after their move, stayed home to care for their first child when Julie returned to work. Bob stated, "We were adamant that a stranger was not going to take care of our children." Julie added that "Bob was born to do this" and that "he has more patience." In contrast, she had always seen herself "working to get promoted" in a corporate job. Bob concurred that "there was always a realization between us that she was like the, I guess the corporate person. That is where her interests lie. That is what she is good at." He stated, "I have a lot of patience with kids, but with adults, less so . . . Julie loves kids, but playing 'super friends' for half an hour doesn't really appeal to her."

Traditionally gendered vocabularies and roles assumed minimal importance in this couple's descriptions of their family life and their respective identities. Rather, Bob spoke of himself and his domestic work in light of its specific demands, his own convictions, activities, and emotions. He related,

"I wanted kids, and it seemed very natural for me to be home with them. . . . Like I love taking care of them. I love being responsible."

Bob was ambivalent about their second child nearing school age. On one hand, he thought it may give him more time to finish renovating their home and to pursue writing. On the other, it marked a change in the childcare activities so important to his sense of self. He observed:

> At times I used to dream about when they are older I will be able to write; when they are older, the house will get done lickety split. But, you know, that time is such a—you know, I do the dishes and I do the laundry and all the mundane household stuff, [but] now I don't get to cuddle and watch *Sesame Street*. . . . And we still read, but that seems less, the more and more independent they get, the less and less it is with me.

At another point in the interview, he candidly noted the importance of full-time at-home fathering work to his identity, saying, "So much of your self esteem and your, how you look at yourself as an adult, . . . is your work in the world. What is it that you do? [T]hey are my job." For her part, Julie maintained, "Having kids hasn't changed my ambition." As senior manager of direct-to-consumer business at a large firm, she saw her operation as the "glue" between merchandising, the website and catalogue business, and the customers. The rewarding part of her job was that she could see quickly "the results of what they do." She wanted to continue to advance in her career.

Bob and Julie clearly divided their respective work responsibilities so that he performed most of the homemaking and Julie the moneymaking labor. Still, certain domestic issues have arisen between them that they both attributed respectfully to differing personal priorities rather than attributing these issues to gender-related power disparities, unspoken entitlements, or obligations. Although he disrupted their living space, Julie acknowledged that Bob's efforts to renovate their house on top of doing most of the housework and childcare involved "major, major" work. Even so, she said, "Sometimes I'd come home and household chores or dishes or dinner wasn't

done because he's been working on the house." At times, laundry and chores have been "issues" for her. She acknowledged Bob does the laundry, noting, "I think I've done one or two loads since we've been married." Yet sometimes she would be "frustrated" because items she wanted to wear to work weren't clean. She stated, "I want to be able to come home and relax." Often tired and stressed from work, she has learned there are things she can't control at home. Julie realized that Bob just has different priorities for his time than she does. Bob seemed to understand Julie's concerns and described these issues in similar terms, although from his perspective: "She will get frustrated. She comes home or she wants this one top and it is not washed. And she is like, 'Well, why haven't you done laundry?' And I am like, 'Well, we are not out of clothes.' She is like, 'Yeah, but . . . I want to wear it again.' I am like, 'Well, you have other clothes in your closet.' " For Bob, all of these tasks are part of his responsibility for "pretty much . . . everything at home." So his different priorities emerge from within the overall context of homemaking. He observed, "Yeah, and the housework for me is not as big a priority and honestly it is tough to find time. The kids will be like, 'Read me a story,' and the dishes are piled up." He added, "That is always my priority because I mean, it seems just natural to me, like what is more important washing dishes or your kid?"

The couple described their marriage as distinctive and involving friendship with open communication, equality, mutual support, and room for differences. Bob stated:

> Julie and I have, I would say, a very equal relationship. . . . We recognize that as good friends as we are and as much as we are working towards the same goals and everything, that we are different and there are times that those differences drive each other crazy. You know, differences in communication and outlook and that. But, we really have, I would say, remarkably few disagreements just because we try to avoid the miscommunication and things of that nature.

Julie succinctly characterized their marriage, "We're open and honest. We make sure that if something is bothering us, we tell each other. We're best friends." In her opinion, some of their friends "want to be us" since "they've come to know Bob and how we do things."

Their story embodies the *improvising* stance, which involves a SAHFC challenging and, at times actively disavowing, traditional feminine and masculine roles and subject positions associated with homemaking and moneymaking by mutually negotiating and performing alternative arrangements. These couples' descriptions of their expectations for themselves as parents and breadwinners actively displaced and refigured traditionally gendered roles and naturalized assumptions through fluid improvisation. They accepted their counter-stereotypical performance of tasks and mostly viewed this condition as non-problematic. Regarding each other as friends, they valued their subjective experiences and took for granted their equal and negotiated eligibilities to perform homemaking and moneymaking activities.

Stance Five: Sharing

Our final stance centers on *sharing* as constructed through the language of co-providing and co-caring. This stance reflects a consciousness for both creating new meanings and living work and family life differently. The couple exemplifying the *sharing* orientation to domestic and paid labor had been married for five years with a three-year-old son at the time of their interviews. Thomas self-selected to be interviewed because he considered himself equal to his wife as a primary childcare provider in their family. They moved to their present home in order for Sandra to pursue a doctorate, with Tom deciding to commence his doctoral studies soon after. In discussing their lives together, Tom observed, "We always envisioned being, you know, integrally related in our child's life. . . . And in a weird way we always envisioned both of us being fully working people and being parents as well." Even so, Sandra has perceived no familial models and little institutional support for their co-parenting efforts, placing most of the burdens on the two of them to develop their own practices and identities

as co-parents. She celebrated how Tom "purposefully" relinquished his identity as their primary breadwinner and saw the symbolic commitment to equality "most clearly manifested in the choice of our name. We took each other's last name."

They have had to pursue energetically their goals for themselves as scholars and their own standards as co-parents of their three-year-old son, Gary. Tom stated, "We're both the primary caregiver in the family." He described the negotiated and constantly evolving nature of their daily lives: "We don't have traditional work schedules. And so, I mean I'm certainly with Gary full-time. I'm with him multiple hours every day . . . sometimes I'll have class in the evening and Sandra's working from eight in the morning till ten at night at her job. So it's a really fluid, goofy schedule." Sandra echoed this depiction, noting that their requests for teaching assignments and course schedules always accommodate the other person. She called their efforts "schedule manipulation" accomplished for financial reasons, and "because we feel powerful doing what we're doing."

The spirit of shared power and cooperative adaptation permeated this couple's narratives as co-parents and homemakers. Tom related, "When he was first born . . . I would drive him to the university twice a day so he could breastfeed. And we would go sit on the edge of campus in our car. And that's when she and I would get to talk. Because we were committed to his breastfeeding and her being able to see him." Sandra observed, "A distinct quality between us is, well, I can say mutual respect." She declared that the "work" they have devoted together to "Gary first and then school" added a deep and edifying sense of friendship to their already loving marriage. She remarked, "And we have worked out the most intense friendship over this child that we're more intimate allies than I think we ever could have been."

The *sharing* narrative demonstrates considerable marital fluidity and responsiveness to each other's lived contingencies in organizing employment and childcare activities. Both individuals participated in wage-earning and care-providing and considered each other no less primary in either respect. Such a couple works consciously to sustain co-constructed values and identities for themselves as co-parents. Their shared participation in homemaking and moneymaking work occurs irrespective of gendered presuppositions or role-based discourses. There is continual negotiation of schedules and tasks arising from both persons' symmetrical eligibilities to embrace homemaking and moneymaking responsibilities. We term this stance "sharing" because of the necessarily common convictions and practices required to create and sustain this equal stance as active co-parents and co-providers in the face of numerous discourses, power arrangements, and social responses threatening its viability. The potential conflicts associated with this stance derive from the ongoing necessity of (re)negotiating the co-parents' own practices and identities, perceived time constraints, and cultivating legitimizing discourses for others who question their arrangement's integrity.

Discussion and Implications

In framing our study, we asked, *how do stay-at-home fathers and breadwinning mothers articulate their stances toward moneymaking and homemaking?* Analyzing our participants' discourses, we found these couples orchestrating their private and public lives differently depending on how they jointly framed tasks, identities, and role eligibilities. While some couples temporarily sojourned and retained traditionally gendered associations for their activities and selves, others keenly reconstituted historical alignments between femininity and care as well as masculinity and economic provision. Other couples relegated gender to a relatively minimal role in their articulations of daily life. We have (re)presented their diverse efforts through five stances: reversing, conflicting, collaborating, improvising, and sharing. Following Deutsch (2007), we adopt a perspective on "doing gender" (West & Zimmerman, 1987; West & Fenstermaker, 1995) that attempts to tease out not only how gender is perpetuated through language and social interaction but also how it is *adapted and even disassembled* in subtle and not so subtle ways. Further, across these five stances, we

vividly illustrate different micro-level approaches to "working out" social change with respect to work and family roles, identities and tasks. In our final section, we examine these stances more deeply with respect to the social construction of masculinities and femininities and its potential to segue into transformative social change, as well as directions for future research. Here we mainly focus on gender while recognizing that our insights are bound by class, race, and sexuality (Ferree, Lorber, & Hess, 2000; Johnson, 2001).

The language of "role reversal" has captured popular imagination with respect to stay-at-home fathers and breadwinning mothers (e.g., Harris, 2009). In some ways, the reversing stance exemplified by Scott and Alicia's early parenting experiences most straightforwardly depicts gender maintenance through both language and behaviors that appear to preserve traditional gendered assumptions of caregiving and paid employment. At the time of the interview, presupposed differences in biology and socialization seemed to trump the economics of their situation (assuming that earning more money is the valued economic outcome). Within a six-month period of time, Scott's identity crisis led to his move back into full-time paid employment. Like other professional women electing to opt out (Stone, 2007), Alicia's desire to "mother" and her difficulties managing work responsibilities motivated her shift into the central caregiver role. In the reversing stance, traditional distinctions remain between masculinity and public sphere participation as well as femininity and private sphere constructions.

While observing their reproduction of hegemonic forms of masculinity and femininity, we also must respect their situation's complexity and ongoing identity struggles. For most of their marriage, Alicia had earned more money than Scott; her role as primary wage-earner can be seen as part of women's growing structural access to workplace opportunities as well as Scott's willingness to embrace marriage as the secondary earner. Thus, during early marriage and the relatively short time of their reversal, they jointly constructed and lived moments of social change that cannot be discounted in their relational biography. And, while

Scott and Alicia reverted to conventional societal gendered roles, they ostensibly made this decision by choice. Future research needs to probe constructions of choice and/or agency with respect to marital work and life arrangements along with their political implications (see also Stone, 2007; Williams, 2000). Scott, for example, spoke of the profundity of his experience choosing to be home with his newborn daughter. While his time as an at-home father might have been relatively short, its personal and relational impact could be far-reaching. Perhaps Scott's caregiving experiences shifted his own understandings and/or performances of masculinity, regardless of his choice to return to paid employment. Further, other men in his workplace might have seen Scott take time off to care for his daughter and, as a result, considered this option in their own lives (Medved, Okimoto, & Ryan, 2010). The importance of role models as signaling or opening up social change must not be undervalued. We see in this first snapshot how existing gendered assumptions about work and family life can be reproduced through SAHFC's communication strategies, even in the context of reversing the performance of caring and earning duties while still holding out the potential for social change.

The conflicting stance illustrates how couples performing gender atypical duties can simultaneously experience the colliding forces of frustration *and* satisfaction, gender maintenance *and* resistance, as well as gender consciousness *and* a lack of gender awareness. These couples often articulated relational tensions or moments when the reality of their choices, duties, and identities clashed with how they wistfully thought their lives would progress, or the inflexibility of employment structures. For instance, like Sue, successful women's greater earning power may be framed as trapping couples (or individual wives or husbands) into enacting work and family lives that contradict or confuse their experiences of an authentic self. Sue's and Mike's narratives express both frustration about being constrained by Sue's ability to earn a greater income at the time of the interview as well as joy and competence in carrying out their respective tasks. She also noted Mike's discomfort over not contributing more significantly to the family income. This conflicting couple wanted the opportunity to change their arrangement but felt constrained by the conditions of their financial situation. Masculinities and femininities are portrayed in this stance as complex, contradictory, and dynamic constructions in relation to caring and earning.

Before we default to marking the conflicting stance as also simply perpetuating hegemonic forms of gender, we must recognize that conflict has always been part of social change—the very feelings of discomfort expressed by conflicting couples illustrate the social constructionist perspective in action. Unconventional gendered arrangements involving conflictual interactions can evidence social change, including real moments of relational renegotiation. Indeed, identity construction under such circumstances itself is a struggle at times; and, through Mike and Sue's (as well as all of our participants') words, we can see the struggle more vividly. Change at all levels isn't simply an either/or proposition, but a *process* of becoming or doing and undoing that we richly see in Mike and Sue's struggles and successes. Both the reversing and conflicting stances portray examples of difficult interactions occurring as these couples wrestle with shifting discourses and practices of work and family. The antagonistic sound of their conflicting narrative can be contrasted with another SAHFC story framing change as collaboration.

The collaborating stance illustrates the concurrent *holding onto* and *letting go* of masculinities and femininities in relation to homemaking and moneymaking. Ty's and Lisa's abilities both to acknowledge and parody traditional gendered assumptions about who "ought" to do particular tasks and how they "should" be performed provides an insightful example of the strategic use of irony in everyday talk and action (see also Risman & Johnson-Sumerford, 1998). As demonstrated by Trethewey (1999), irony is a "lived" strategy individuals may use in managing the "both/and" quality of life. Together, this couple bridged the exigencies of role eligibility and identity, often doing so communicatively in ways that allowed both historical constructions and current enactments of gender to co-exist. They did not seek resolution of this tension or wholesale transformation of gender but appeared to live with it and use it as a source of insight. Ty, for instance, insightfully invoked irony when he explained how he was both constrained by his understandings of appropriately masculine emotion yet also able to laugh when his well-planned dinner went awry in what he called a "sitcom" moment. Although not easy, he recognized the futility of holding tightly to this narrow view of being a man. Irony permitted Ty (and allows us) to see how seemingly incongruous alternatives (maintaining versus transforming gendered assumptions of care and paid labor) can actually co-exist in various ways.

While collaboration seems a sophisticated and gentile way to manage conflicting gendered selves, conventional masculinity and femininity remain part of the interpretive frame. The locus of conflict, or perhaps tension, in the collaborating stance seems to be more internal than relational, in contrast to the first two homemaking and moneymaking stances. Thus, we need to ask whether ironic collaboration can create enough "gender vertigo" to dismantle traditional forms of gender and power (Risman, 1999). Can irony sufficiently weaken the link between sex category and gendered divisions of labor? Or, to seriously affect social change, must masculinities and femininities be disassembled, fade into the background, or be degendered in interactions (Lorber, 2005)?

Case in point: the improvising stance as viewed through Bob and Julie's narrative seems to let go of gender accountability in their work and family lives. Following Deutsch (2007), we agree that "under some conditions, [gender] may be so irrelevant that it is not even accessed" (p. 116). Perhaps more realistically in the present analysis, we could say that gender assumed a less important role in Julie and Bob's communication about work and family life than it is often afforded. Bob articulated a sense of self and relationship with Julie grounded in the language of friendship, and Julie explained that Bob was born to be their daughter's

primary caregiver. Gender's assumed master status appears to be subsumed in their language of non-hierarchical relations, personal preference, and differing sex-typical abilities. Improvising couples didn't appear, actively or explicitly, to resist gender conventions; rather they seemed not to take them into account in their framing of work and family life. In the improvising stance, we see the undoing of gender most clearly through its relative absence. Bob and Julie minimized traditional masculinities and femininities in assigning duties and crafting selves. Even more interesting is their use of biological and/or natural language to justify *sex atypical* work and family roles. Bob is constructed as born to do caregiving and the more natural one to be at home full-time with their two girls. Most often, biological language is argued by gender theorists to only *reinforce* oppression and inequity between men and women. What are the personal or political implications of positioning some men as more natural caregivers than women (Silverstein, 1996)? And, does the absence of gendered discourse necessarily equate to its transgression? This stance portrays another way of framing and performing alternative forms of work and family life that raises fascinating questions about SAHFC arrangements and social change across identities, roles, institutions, and discourses.

Of course, the improvising stance comes with its own unique challenges. Tensions emerged, for instance, when Julie got frustrated that Bob did not do laundry the way she wanted it done; Bob retorted that it was his job and he would "do laundry like a guy." Although Bob still used gender to mark his performance of household labor, he owned the task as gender appropriate and even uniquely performed by men versus defining it as "woman's work." Here we see the language of equal role eligibilities producing relational tension (i.e., Julie wanted laundry done her way) but a very different type of tension is constructed than evidenced in discourses of unequal role eligibilities (i.e., if Sue perceived that women still need to perform the "second shift" of household labor). It is not the mere existence of tension that is most instructive about these couples' experiences, but the negotiated nature of these tensions as re-vealed through close examination of their dis-course. While clear divisions of labor existed, Bob and Julie's tensions arose from *how* work should be done rather than *who* should do particular kinds of work. The question then arises whether difference always means inequality (Deutsch, 2007). Bob and Julie's situation seems to illus-trate one example when differences, sex atypical as they are, do not seem to beget inequality. Does Bob's masculine identity rooted in the daily tra-vails of caregiving evidence maternal thinking (Ruddick, 1995) or changing norms of masculin-ity (Anderson, 2009; Morman & Floyd, 2002)? And, did Bob and Julie (as well as other couples participating in this study), at an earlier point in time, struggle differently with constructing their unconventional identities and, if so, how?

Finally, the sharing stance explicitly and con-sciously resists traditional masculinities and femininities in both word and deed while also contesting separate but equal allocations of labor. Empowerment through overt resistance is articu-lated in Tom and Sandra's account of sharing work and family tasks and identities, perhaps more so than in the other four stances. Here we see the post-feminist ideal of equal and fully participa-tive divisions of labor as well as external mark-ers of gender change such as taking each other's names (see also Risman & Johnson-Sumerford, 1998). Tensions arise in this stance due to the lack of role models and resistance to existing work and family structures. Here we see public attempts at reworking gender and creating new forms of language and behavior at the relational level. At the same time, Tom and Sandra also perform micro-acts of resistance by manipulating employ-ment structures to accommodate their desires to share work and family. Theirs is not an easy path; it is one fraught with challenges but expressed as empowering for both of them. Active resistance through gender consciousness is only one means of social change. Future research needs to explore effective and ineffective communication strate-gies and behavioral practices that aid SAHFCs in their attempts to realize potentially transforma-tive changes in social institutions (see also Kirby,

Golden, Medved, Jorgenson, & Buzzanell, 2003; Williams, 2000).

Conclusions and Next Steps

What can we learn from this study of variations in couples' homemaking and moneymaking stances? First, by documenting (and providing our inter-pretations of) the subtle differences in the per-formance and articulation of gender in the lives of these couples, we illustrate varieties of mascu-linities and femininities at play in their work and family lives. Scott, Mike, Ty, Bob, and Tom share with us shades and adaptations of masculinities, differentially caught up in interdependent webs of caregiving, wage earning, heterosexuality, and identity. Likewise, Alicia's enactment of being a woman, successful employee, wife and mother is but one rendering of femininity with similarities and differences from Sue, Lisa, Julie, and Sandra.

Second, the stories embodying these five homemaking-moneymaking stances reinforce that no one right way or single model for success in doing or undoing gender exists. A communi-cation approach to exploring gendered work and family social change recognizes the criticality of process over form or, at minimum, their intimate interaction. The key contribution of this study is to illustrate that ostensibly identical work and family arrangements are lived very differently when we dig deeper into the various ways SAHFCs com-municatively frame their work and family lives. We agree with Gerson's (2010) assertion that we must get "beyond drawing simple—and overly deterministic—associations between forms and outcome [but rather] we need to explore the forces that shape [work] and family" (p. 216), including often overlooked discursive, relational, and inter-actional forces.

Third, both the co-constructed and contextual natures of these performances come to the fore-front. Could Bob take on the identity of natural, full-time caregiver and gatekeeper of laundry without Julie's symmetrical performance as the determined, non-domestic career woman? If Tom wasn't willing to engage fully in caregiving, wage-earning, and identity transformation, could

Sandra claim her empowered shared marital identity? And, isn't Mike's identity struggle also part and parcel of Sue's struggles to craft a coherent, if only transient, sense of self? We believe that these narratives richly display how SAHFCs as relational partners co-construct a life and "participate together in the process of making sense of their local circumstances" (Bochner & Ellis, 1995, p. 201). These performances are also likely to change over time through the couples' ongoing negotiation of individually and mutually experienced contingencies emerging in their home and work lives. Today, more likely than in the past, families move in and out of assorted family forms and earning/caring arrangements, thereby making critical the present focus on processes of negotiation and renegotiation (Gerson, 2010).

Extending this line of scholarship beyond the issues outlined above, future research should investigate the experiences and attitudes of larger and more diverse samples of couples. We wonder what other stances (or modifications of the five offered in this analysis) might be developed through exploring a larger corpus of discourse and related data such as division of labor diaries or extensive participant-observation field notes. What additional tensions or struggles would their stories reflect? Over time, do couples living the conflicted stance ever articulate feeling reconciled or comfortable in their reversal? If not, (why) do they remain as SAHFC? When and why do reversing couples decide they need to make a change? Additional research also should include the voices of couples from an extensive socio-economic range and various racial and ethnic backgrounds. Choosing to stay-at-home may be a function of economics and not an option for many couples. We also know that historical and contemporary gender roles and identities in African American and Hispanic (Broman, 1991) marriages as well as gay and lesbian relationships (Moore, 2008) may differ at times from White and heterosexual Americans.

There are also important practical implications of this study. Couples also may use this

Appendix 1.
Participating Couples

Reversing	Conflicting	Collaborating	Improvising	Sharing
Scott/Alicia	Mike/Sue	Ty/Lisa	Bob/Julie	Tom/Sandra
Married: 8 yrs.	Married: 18 yrs.	Married: 16 yrs.	Married: 8 yrs.	Married: 5 yrs.
SAHFC: 5 mos.	SAHFC: 4 yrs.	SAHFC: 7 yrs.	SAHFC: 6 yrs.	SAHFC: 3 yrs.
Children: 2	Children: 2	Children: 1	Children: 2	Children: 1
	John/Liz	Matt/Ellen	Milt/Denise	
	Married: 14 yrs.	Married: 7 yrs.	Married: 12 yrs.	
	SAHFC: 4 yrs.	SAHFC: 1 yr.	SAHFC: 8 mos.	
	Children: 5	Children: 1	Children: 2	
		Jay/Gail		
		Married: 5 yrs.		
		SAHFC: 3 mos.		
		Children: 2		
		Tim/Annie		
		Married: 8 yrs.		
		SAHFC: 1 yr.		
		Children: 2		

information as a resource in their own decision-making. Couples must listen carefully to how spouses talk about the idea of transposing roles prior to making that decision or in the midst of related conflicts. Spouses might listen for ways husbands or wives talk about who they are or could be as earners or caregivers (identity adoption), their views on who should be doing particular types of work (role eligibility), and what types of work they see men and women legitimately doing (task responsibility). Keying into such language is not easy but might give couples one more tool to make good decisions or better diagnose the potential challenges or frustrations they may experience (or are experiencing) in taking on these types of arrangements.

In closing, our analysis of the five homemaking and moneymaking stances detailed in this study provides a unique glimpse into the diverse ways SAHFCs negotiate gendered tasks, identities, and roles related to caring and earning. In the midst of unconventional ways of composing their lives, these couples' narratives illustrate the variety of subtle and critical communicative processes that facilitate and constrain gendered social change. Their stories show us what it means to redraw the boundaries of our work and family lives.

References

Anderson, E. (2009). *Inclusive masculinity: The changing nature of masculinities.* New York, NY: Routledge.

Ashcraft, K. L., & Mumby, D. K. (2003). *Reworking gender: A feminist communicology of organization.* Thousand Oaks, CA: Sage.

Bennetts, L., (2007). *The feminine mistake: Are we giving up too much?* New York, NY: Hyperion.

Bochner, A. P., & Ellis, C. (1995). Telling and living: Narrative co-construction and the practices of interpersonal relationships. In W. Leeds-Hurwitz (Ed.), *Social approaches to communication* (pp. 201–213). New York, NY: The Guilford Press.

Boushey, H. (2011, January 25). The end of the mansession: Now it's the women who are the economy's big losers. *Slate Magazine.* Retrieved from http://www.slate.com

Bridges, J. S., Etaugh, C., & Barnes-Farrell, J. (2002). Trait judgments of stay-at-home and employed parents: A function of social role and/or shifting standards? *Psychology of Women Quarterly, 26,* 140–150.

Broman, C. L. (1991). Gender, work-family roles, and psychological well-being of blacks. *Journal of Marriage and Family, 53*(2), 509–521.

Bureau of Labor Statistics. (2011). *Employment characteristics of families summary.* Retrieved from http://www.bls.gov/news.release/famee.nro.htm

Bureau of Labor Statistics. (2010). Personal communication from Mary Bowler, Division of Labor Force Statistics. Washington D.C.

Butler, J. (1990). *Gender trouble: Feminism and the subversion of identity.* New York, NY: Routledge.

Buzzanell, P. M. (1995). Reframing the glass ceiling as a socially constructed process. Implications for understanding and change. *Communication Monographs, 4,* 327–354.

Connell, R. W. (1995). *Masculinities.* Berkeley, CA: University of California Press.

Denker, K. J. (2009) Doing gender in the academy: The challenges for women in the academic organization. *Women & Language, 32,* 103–112.

Deutsch, F. M. (2007). Undoing gender. *Gender & Society, 2,* 106–127.

Doucet, A. (2004). "It's almost like I have a job, but I don't get paid": Fathers at home reconfiguring work, care, and masculinity. *Fathering, 2,* 277–303.

Drago, R., Black, D., & Wooden, M. (2005). Female breadwinner families: Their existence, persistence, and sources. *Journal of Sociology, 41,* 343–362.

Elder, G. H., Jr. (1995). The life course paradigm: Social change and individual development. In P. Moen, G. H. Elder, Jr., & K. Lüscher (Eds.), *Examining lives in context: Perspectives on the ecology of human development* (pp. 101–139). Washington DC: APA Press.

Ferree, M. M., Lorber, J., & Hess, B. B. (2000). Introduction. In M.M. Ferree, J. Lorber, B. B. Hess (Eds.) *Revisioning gender* (pp. xv–xxxvi). Walnut Creek, CA: Altamira Press.

Fry, R., & Cohn, D. (2010, January 19). New economics of marriage: The rise of wives. Pew Center for Research. Retrieved from http://pewresearch.org/pubs/1466/economics-marriage-rise-of-wives

Gerson, K. (1985). *Hard choices: How women decide about work, career, and motherhood.* Berkley, CA: University of California Press.

Gerson, K. (2010). *The unfinished revolution: How a new generation is reshaping family, work, and gender in America.* New York, NY: Oxford University Press.

Gerson, K., & Peiss, J.M. (1985). Boundaries, negotiation, consciousness: Reconceptualizing gender relations. *Social Problems, 32,* 317–331.

Geuss, R. (2003). *Public goods, private goods.* Princeton, NJ: Princeton University Press.

Harris, D. (2009). Recession prompts gender role reversal. Retrieved from http://abcnews.go.com

Hays, S. (1996). *The cultural contradictions of motherhood.* New Haven, CT: Yale University Press.

Hertz, R. (1995). Separate but simultaneous interviewing of husbands and wives: Making sense of their stories. *Qualitative Inquiry, 1,* 429–451.

Hochschild, A. R. (1989). *The second shift: Working parents and the revolution at home.* New York, NY: Viking.

Holmer-Nadesan, M. (1996). Organizational identity and space of action. *Organizational Studies, 17,* 49–81.

Hood, J. C. (1983). *Becoming a two-job family.* New York, NY: Viking.

Jamison, K. H. (1997). *Beyond the double binds: Women and leadership.* New York, NY: Oxford University Press.

Johnson, F. (2001). Ideological undercurrents in the semantic notion of 'working mother.' *Women & Language, 24,* 21–28.

Kirby, E. L., Golden, A. A., Medved, C. E., Jorgenson, J., & Buzzanell, P. M. (2003). An organizational challenge to the discourse of work and family research: From problematics to empowerment. In P. Kalbfleish (Ed.), *Communication Yearbook 27* (pp. 1–43). Mahwah, NJ: Lawrence Erlbaum.

Kershaw, S. (2009, April 23). Mr. Moms (By Way of Fortune 500). *New York Times.* Retrieved from http://www.nytimes.com

Lorber, J. (2005). *Breaking the bowls: Degendering and feminist change.* New York, NY: Norton.

Medved, C. E. (2009a). Constructing breadwinning-mother identities: Moral, personal and political positioning. *Women's Studies Quarterly, 37,* 136–154.

Medved, C. E. (2009b). Crossing and transforming occupational and household gendered divisions of labor. C. Beck (Ed.), *Communication Yearbook 33* (pp. 300–341). New York, NY: Routledge.

Medved, C. E. (2007). Special Issue Introduction. Investigating family labor in communication studies: Threading across historical and contemporary discourses. *Journal of Family Communication, 7,* 225–243.

Medved, C. E. (2004). The everyday accomplishment of work and family: Accounting for practical actions and commonsense rules in everyday routines. *Communication Studies, 55,* 128–154.

Medved, C. E., & Kirby, E. L. (2005). Family CEOs: A feminist analysis of corporate mothering discourses. *Management Communication Quarterly, 18,* 435–478.

Medved, C. E., Okimoto, C., & Ryan, R. (2010). A qualitative analysis of explanations for the emergence of reverse traditional work and family arrangements. A paper presented at the Eastern Sociological Society Convention, Philadelphia, PA.

Meisenbach, R. J. (2010). The female breadwinner: Phenomenological experience and gendered identity in work/family spheres. *Sex Roles, 62,* 2–19.

Moore, M. R. (2008). Gendered power relations among women: A study of household decision making in Black, lesbian stepfamilies. *American Sociological Review, 73,* 335–356.

Morgan, C. (2011, Winter). Role reversal. *Rebel,* 65–70.

Morman, M. T., & Floyd, K. (2002). A 'changing culture of fatherhood': Effects on affectionate communication, closeness, and satisfaction in men's relationships with their fathers and their sons. *Western Journal of Communication, 66,* 395–412.

Murray, S. B. (1996). "We all love Charles": Men in child care and the social construction of gender. *Gender & Society, 10,* 368–385.

Potuchek, J. L. (1992). Employed wives' orientations to breadwinning: A gender theory analysis. *Journal of Marriage and the Family, 54,* 48–58.

Potuchek, J. L. (1997). *Who supports the family? Gender and breadwinning in dualearner marriages.* Stanford, CA: Stanford University Press.

Radin, N. (1988). Primary care giving fathers of long duration. In P. Bronstein & C. P Cowan (Eds.), *Fatherhood today: Men's changing role in the family* (pp. 127–143). New York, NY: John Wiley & Sons.

Raley, S. B., Mattingly, M. J., & Bianchi, S. M. (2006). How dual are dual-income couples? Documenting change from 1970 to 2001. *Journal of Marriage and the Family, 68,* 11–28.

Riggs, J. M. (1997). Mandates for mothers and fathers: Perceptions of breadwinners and care givers. *Sex Roles, 37,* 565–580.

Risman, B. J. (1999). *Gender vertigo: American families in transition.* New Haven, CT: Yale University Press.

Risman, B. J., & Johnson-Sumerford, D. (1998). Doing it fairly: A study of post-gender marriages. *Journal of Marriage and Family, 60,* 23–40.

Rochlen, A. B., Suizzo, M., Kelley, R. A., & Scaringi, V. (2008). "I'm just providing for my family:" A qualitative study of stay-at-home fathers. *Psychology of Men and Masculinity, 9,* 17–28.

Ruddick, S. (1995). *Maternal thinking: Towards a politics of peace.* Boston, MA: Beacon Press.

Şahin, A., Song, J., & Hobijn, B. (2010, February). *The unemployment gender gap during the current recession.* Federal Reserve Bank of New York. Retrieved from http://www.newyorkfed.org/research/economists/sahin/GenderGap.pdf

Silverstein, L. B. (1996). Fathering is a feminist issue. *Psychology of Women Quarterly, 20,* 3–37.

Smith, C. D. (1998). "Men don't do this sort of thing": A case study of the social isolation of househusbands. *Men and Masculinities, 1,* 138–172.

Smith, J. A. (2009). *The Daddy shift: How stay-at-home dads, breadwinning moms, and shared parenting are transforming the American family.* Boston, MA: Beacon Press.

Stone, P. (2007). *Opting out?: Why women really quit careers and head home.* Berkeley, CA: University of California Press.

Stout, H. (2010, September). What's the new status symbol for alpha women? A stay at home husband. *Marie Claire, 148, 150, 152.*

Sveningsson, S., & Alvesson, M. (2003). Managing managerial identities: Organizational fragmentation, discourse, and identity struggle. *Human Relations, 56,* 1163–1193.

Trethewey, A. (1999). Isn't it ironic: Using irony to explore the contradictions of organizational life. *Western Journal of Communication, 63,* 140–167.

U.S. Census Bureau (2005, September 21). SHP-1. Parents and children in stay-at-home parent family groups. Current Population Survey (CPS). Retrieved from www.census.gov

Varvus, M. D. (2002). Domesticating patriarchy: Hegemonic masculinity and television's "Mr. Mom." *Critical Studies in Media Communication, 19,* 352–375.

Warner, J. (2005). *Perfect madness: Mothering in the age of anxiety.* New York, NY: Penguin.

Wentworth, D. K., & Chell, R. M. (2001). The role of househusband and housewife as perceived by a college population. *The Journal of Psychology, 135,* 639–650.

West, C., & Zimmerman, D. (1987). Doing gender. *Gender & Society, 1,* 125–151.

West, C., & Fenstermaker, S. (1995). Doing difference. *Gender & Society, 9,* 8–37.

Wilkie, J. R., Ferree, M. M., & Ratcliff, K. S. (1998). Gender and fairness: Marital satisfaction in two-earner couples. *Journal of Marriage and the Family, 60,* 577–595.

Zvonkovic, A. M., Greaves, K. M., Schmiege, C. J., & Hall, L. D. (1996). The marital construction of gender through work and family decisions: A qualitative analysis. *Journal of Marriage and Family, 58,* 9.

Falling Back on Plan B: The Children of the Gender Revolution Face Uncharted Territory

KATHLEEN GERSON

Young adults today grew up with mothers who broke barriers in the workplace and parents who forged innovative alternatives to traditional marriage. These "children of the gender revolution" now face a world that is far different from that of their parents or grandparents. While massive changes in work and family arrangements have expanded their options, these changes also pose new challenges to crafting a marriage, rearing children, and building a career. Members of this new generation walk a fine line between their desire to achieve egalitarian, sharing relationships that can meld with satisfying work, and succumbing to the realities of gender conflict, fragile relationships, and uncertain job prospects. The choices they make will shape work and family life for decades to come.

Social forecasters have reached starkly different conclusions about what these choices will be. Some proclaim that the recent upturn in "opt-out" mothers foreshadows a wider return to tradition among younger women. Others believe the rising number of single adults foretells a deepening "decline of commitment" that is threatening family life and the social fabric. While there is little doubt that tumultuous changes have shaped the lives of a new generation, there is great disagreement about how. Does the diversification of families into two-earner, single-parent, and cohabiting forms represent a waning of family life or the growth of more flexible relationships? Will this new generation

integrate family and work in new ways, or will older patterns inexorably pull them back?

To find out how members of the first generation to grow up in these diversifying families look back on their childhoods and forward to their own futures, I conducted in-depth, life history interviews with a carefully selected group of young people between eighteen and thirty-two. These young women and men experienced the full range of changes that have taken place in family life, and most lived in some form of "nontraditional" arrangement at some point in their childhood. My interviews reveal a generation that does not conform to prevailing media stereotypes, whether they depict declining families or a return to strict gender divisions in caretaking and breadwinning.

In contrast to popular images of twenty- and thirty-somethings who wish to return to tradition or reject family life altogether, the young women and men I interviewed are more focused on *how well* their parents met the challenges of providing economic and emotional support than on *what form* their families took. Now making their own way in early adulthood, women and men share a set of lofty aspirations. Despite their varied family experiences, most hope to blend the traditional value of a lifelong relationship with the modern value of flexibly sharing work, child care, and domestic chores. In the best of all possible worlds, the majority would like to create a lasting marriage (or a "marriage-like" relationship) that allows them to balance home and work in a flexible, egalitarian way.

Yet young people are also developing strategies to prepare for "second-best" options in a world where time-demanding workplaces, a lack of child care, and fragile relationships may place their ideals out of reach. Concerned about the difficulty of finding a reliable and egalitarian partner to help them integrate work with family caretaking, most women see work as essential to their own and their children's survival, whether or not they marry. Worried about time-greedy workplaces, most men feel they must place work first and will need to count on a partner at home. As they prepare for second-best options, the differing fallback positions of "self-reliant" women and "neo-traditional" men may point to a new gender divide. But this divide does not reflect a new generation's highest aspirations for blending lifelong commitment and flexible, egalitarian sharing in their relationships.

Growing Up in Changing Families

Even though theorists and social commentators continue to debate the merits of various family forms, my interviewees did not focus on their family's "structure." Instead, I found large variation among children who grew up in apparently similar family types. Those who grew up in families with a homemaking mother and breadwinning father were divided in their assessments of this arrangement While a little more than half thought this was the best arrangement, close to half reached a different conclusion. When being a homemaker and out of the workforce appeared to undermine a mother's satisfaction, disturb the household's harmony, or threaten its economic security, the children concluded that it would have been better if their mothers had pursued a sustained commitment to work.

Many of those who grew up in a single-parent home also expressed ambivalence about their parents' breakups. Slightly more than half wished their parents had stayed together, but close to half believed that a breakup, while not ideal, was better than continuing to live in a conflict-ridden or silently unhappy home. The longer-term consequences of a breakup shaped the lessons children drew. If their parents got back on their feet and created better lives, children developed surprisingly positive outlooks on the decision to separate.

Those who grew up in a dual-earner home were the least ambivalent about their parents' arrangements. More than three-fourths believed that having two work-committed parents provided increased economic resources and also promoted marriages that seemed more egalitarian and satisfying. If the pressures of working long hours or coping with blocked opportunities and family-unfriendly workplaces took their toll, however, some children concluded that having overburdened, time-stressed caretakers offset these advantages.

In short, growing up in this era of diverse families led children to focus more on how well—or poorly—parents (and other caretakers) were able to meet the twin challenges of providing economic and emotional support rather than on its form. Even more important, children experienced family life as a dynamic process that changed over time. Since family life is best seen as a film, not a snapshot, the key to understanding young people's views lies in charting the diverse paths their families took.

Family Paths and Gender Flexibility

Families can take different paths from seemingly common starting points, and similar types of families can travel toward different destinations. When young adults reflect on their families, they focus on how their homes either came to provide stability and support or failed to do so. About a third of my interviewees reported growing up in a stable home, while a quarter concluded that their families grew more supportive as time passed. In contrast, just under one in ten reported living in a chronically insecure home, while a bit more than a third felt that family support eroded as they grew up. Why, then, do some children look back on families that became more supportive and secure, while others experienced a decline in their family's support?

Parents' strategies for organizing breadwinning and caretaking hold the key to understanding a family's pathway. Flexible strategies, which allowed mothers, fathers, and other caretakers to transcend rigid gender boundaries, helped families prevail in the face of unexpected economic and interpersonal crises. Inflexible responses, in contrast, left families ill-equipped to cope with eroding supports for a strict division in mothers' and fathers' responsibilities.

Rising Family Fortunes

The sources of expanding support differed by family situation, but all reflected a flexible response to unexpected difficulties. Sometimes marriages became more equal as demoralized mothers went to work and pushed for change or helped overburdened fathers. Josh, for example, reported that his mother's decision to go to work gave her the courage to insist that his father tackle his drug addiction.

> My parents fought almost constantly. Then my mom got a job. They separated for about five, six, seven months. Even though I was upset, I thought it was for the best. That's when (my dad) got into some kind of program and my mom took him back. That changed the whole family dynamic. We got extremely close. A whole new relationship developed with my father.

Chris recalled how his mother's job allowed his father to quit a dead-end job and train for a more satisfying career:

> Between 7th and 8th grade, my dad had a business which didn't work. It was a dead-end thing, and he came home frustrated, so my mom got him to go to school. It was hard financially, but it was good because he was actually enjoying what he was doing. He really flourished. A lot of people say, "Wow, your mom is the breadwinner, and that's strange." It's not. It is a very joint thing.

Parental breakups that relieved domestic conflict or led to the departure of an unstable parent also helped caretaking parents get back on their feet. Connie recounted how her mother was able to create a more secure home after separating from an alcoholic husband and finding a job that offered a steady income and a source of personal esteem:

> My father just sat in the corner and once in a while got angry at us, but [my mom]—I don't know if it was him or the money, but she didn't stand up for herself as much as I think she should. The tension with my dad never eased, and my mom had gotten sick with multiple bleeding ulcers. That was her real turning point. It was building inside of her to leave, 'cause she'd got a job and started to realize she had her own money . . . [She] became a much happier person. And because she was better, I was better. I had a weight taken off of me.

More stable and egalitarian remarriages could also give children the economic and emotional support they had not previously received. Having never known her biological father, Shauna recalled how her stepfather became a devoted caretaker and the "real" father she always wanted:

> At first, I was feeling it was a bad change because I wanted my mom to myself. Then my mom said, "Why don't you call him daddy?" The next thing I was saying "Daddy!" I remember the look on his face and his saying "She called me daddy!" I was so happy. After that, he's always been my dad, and there's never been any question about it. . . . [He] would get home before my mom, so he would cook the dinner and clean. My dad spoiled me for any other man, because this is the model I had.

When Isabella's parents divorced, her grandfather became a treasured caretaker:

> It's not like I didn't have a father, because my grandfather was always there. He was there to take me to after-school clubs and pick me up. I was sheltered—he had to take me to the library, wait till I finished all my work, take me home. I call him dad. Nobody could do better.

And when Antonio's single mother lost her job, his grandparents provided essential income that kept the family afloat:

> My mom and grandparents were the type of people that even if we didn't have [money], we was gonna get it. Their ideal is, "I want to give

you all the things I couldn't have when I was young." My grandparents and my mother thought like that, so no matter how much in poverty we were living, I was getting everything I wanted.

Despite their obvious differences, the common ingredient in these narratives is the ability of parents and other caretakers to reorganize child rearing and breadwinning in a more flexible, less gender-divided way. Mothers going to work, fathers becoming more involved in child rearing, and others joining in the work of family life—all of these strategies helped families overcome unexpected difficulties and create more economically secure, emotionally stable homes. Growing flexibility in how parents met the challenges of earning needed income and caring for children nourished parental morale, increased a home's financial security, and provided inspiring models of adult resilience. While children acknowledged the costs, they valued these second chances and gleaned lessons from watching parents find ways to create a better life. Looking back, they could conclude that "all's well that ends well."

Declining Family Fortunes

For some children, home life followed a downward slope. Here, too, the key to their experiences lay in the work and caretaking strategies of those entrusted with their care, but here gender inflexibility in the face of domestic difficulties left children with less support than they had once taken for granted. Faced with a father's abandonment or a stay-at-home mother's growing frustration, children described how their parents' resistance to more flexible strategies for apportioning paid and domestic work left them struggling to meet children's economic and emotional needs. Over time, deteriorating marriages, declining parental morale, and financial insecurity shattered a once rosy picture of family stability and contentment.

When parents became stuck in a rigid division of labor, with unhappy mothers and fathers ill-equipped to support the household, traditional marriages could deteriorate. Sarah explains how her mother became increasingly depressed and "over-involved" after relinquishing a promising career to devote all of her time to child rearing:

> When my sister was born, [my mom's] job had started up, career-wise, so she wasn't happy [but] she felt she had to be home. She had a lot of conflicts about work and home and opted to be really committed to family, but also resented it. . . . She was the supermom, but just seemed really depressed a lot of time . . . [It came] with an edge to it—"in return, I want you to be devoted to me." If we did something separate from her, that was a major problem. So I was making distance because I felt I had to protect myself from this invasion. . . . She thought she was doing something good to sacrifice for us . . . but it would have been better if my mother was happier working.

Megan recalls her father's mounting frustration as his income stagnated and he endured the complaints of a wife who expected him to provide a "better lifestyle":

> My mother was always dissatisfied. She wanted my father to be more ambitious, and he wasn't an ambitious man. As long as he was supporting the family, it didn't matter if it was a bigger house or a bigger car. Forty years of being married to a woman saying, "Why don't we have more money?"—I think that does something to your self-esteem.

Unresolved power struggles in dual-earner marriages could also cause problems, as wives felt the weight of "doing it all" and fathers resisted egalitarian sharing. Juggling paid and domestic work left Justin's mother exhausted, while a high-pressured job running a restaurant left his father with no time to attend nightly dinners or even Little League games. Justin describes the strain his parents experienced and its effect on him:

> I was slightly disappointed that I could not see my father more—because I understood but also because it depends on the mood he's in. And it got worse as work [went] downhill . . . [So] I can't model my relationship on my parents. My mother wasn't very happy. There was a lot of strain on her.

Harmful breakups, where fathers abandoned their children and mothers could not find new ways to support the family or create an identity beyond wife and mother, also eroded family support. Nina remembers how her father's disappearance, combined with her mother's reluctance to seek a job and create a more independent life, triggered the descent from a comfortable middle-class existence to one of abiding poverty:

> My mother ended up going on welfare. We went from a nice place to living in a really cruddy building. And she's still in the same apartment. To this day, my sister will not speak to my father because of what he's done to us.

Children (and their parents) sometimes lost the support of other caretakers. Shortly after Jasmine's father left to live with another woman and her mother fell into a deep depression, she suffered the loss of a "third parent" when her beloved grandmother died. Her grandmother's loss left her feeling especially bereft after her father's departure:

> It was so great when my parents were together and my grandmother was alive, so when she died, it was really hard. I lost [the money], and I lost her just being there. We were going through a real trauma in my whole family, so when [my father] left, it was like another death. I don't think it would have been any better if they'd stayed together, but my grandmother being alive would have been much more of a difference.

The events that propelled families on a downward track—including rising financial instability, declining parental involvement and morale, and a dearth of other supportive caretakers—share a common element. Whether parents faced marital impasses or difficult breakups, resistance to more flexible gender arrangements left them unable to sustain an emotionally or economically secure home. Their children concluded that all did *not* end well.

In sum, sustained parental support and economic security were more important to my informants than the form their families took. Since any family type holds potential pitfalls if parents do not or cannot prevail over the difficulties that arise, conventional categories that see families as static "forms" cannot account for the ways that families change as children grow to adulthood.

Instead, young women and men from diverse family backgrounds recounted how parents and other family members who transcended gender boundaries and developed flexible strategies for breadwinning and caretaking were better able to cope with marital crises, economic insecurities, and other unanticipated challenges.

A range of social trends—including the erosion of single-earner paychecks, the fragility of modern marriages, and the expanding options and pressures for women to work—require varied and versatile ways of earning and caring. These institutional shifts make gender flexibility increasingly desirable and even essential. Flexible approaches to work and parenting help families adapt, while inflexible ones leave them ill-prepared to cope with new economic and social realities.

Converging Ideals, Diverging Fallbacks

How do young adults use the lessons of growing up in changing families to formulate their own plans for the future? Women and men from diverse family backgrounds share a set of lofty aspirations. Whether or not their parents stayed together, more than nine out of ten hope to rear children in the context of a satisfying lifelong bond. Far from rejecting the value of commitment, almost everyone wants to create a lasting marriage or "marriage-like" partnership. This does not, however, reflect a desire for a traditional relationship. Most also aspire to build a committed bond where both paid work and family caretaking are shared. Three-fourths of those who grew up in dual-earner homes want their spouse to share breadwinning and caretaking, but so do more than two-thirds of those from traditional homes, and close to nine-tenths of those with single parents. While four-fifths of women want an egalitarian relationship, so do two-thirds of men. In short, most share an ideal that stresses the value of a lasting, flexible, and egalitarian partnership with considerable room for personal autonomy. Amy, an Asian American with two working parents, thus explains that:

> I want a fifty-fifty relationship, where we both have the potential of doing everything—both of

us working and dealing with kids. With regard to career, if neither has flexibility, then one of us will have to sacrifice for one period, and the other for another.

And Wayne, an African American raised by a single mother, expresses the essentially same hopes when he says that:

> I don't want the '50s type of marriage, where I come home and she's cooking. I want her to have a career of her own. I want to be able to set my goals, and she can do what she wants, too.

While most of my interviewees hope to strike a flexible breadwinning and caretaking balance with an egalitarian partner, they are also skeptical about their chances of achieving this ideal. Women and men both worry that work demands, a lack of child-rearing supports, and the fragility of modern relationships will undermine their aspirations to forge an enduring, egalitarian partnership. In the face of barriers to equality, most have concluded that they have little choice but to prepare for options that may fall substantially short of their ideals. Despite their shared aspirations, however, men and women face different institutional obstacles and cultural pressures, which are prompting divergent fallback strategies. If they cannot find a supportive partner, most women prefer self-reliance over economic dependence within a traditional marriage. Most men, if they cannot strike an equal balance between work and parenting, prefer a neo-traditional arrangement that allows them to put work first and rely on a partner for the lion's share of caregiving. In the event that Plan A proves unreachable, women and men are thus pursuing a different Plan B as insurance against their "worst case" fears. These divergent fallback strategies point toward the emergence of a new gender divide between young women, most of whom see a need for self-reliance, and young men, who are more inclined to retain a modified version of traditional expectations.

Women's Plan B

Torn between high hopes for combining work and family and worries about sustaining a lasting and satisfying partnership, young women are navigating uncertain waters. While some are falling back on domesticity, most prefer to find a more independent base than traditional marriage provides. In contrast to the media-driven message that young women are turning away from work and career in favor of domestic pursuits, the majority of my interviewees are determined to seek financial and emotional self-reliance, whether or not they also forge a committed relationship. Regardless of class, race, or ethnicity, most are reluctant to surrender their autonomy in a traditional marriage. When the bonds of marriage are so fragile, relying on a husband for economic security seems foolhardy. And if a relationship deteriorates, economic dependence on a man leaves few means of escape. Danisha, an African American who grew up in an inner-city, working-class neighborhood, and Jennifer, who was raised in a middle-class, predominantly white suburb, agree. Danisha proclaims that:

> Let's say that my marriage doesn't work. Just in case, I want to establish myself, because I don't ever want to end up, like, "What am I going to do?" I want to be able to do what I have to do and still be okay.

Jennifer concurs:

> I will have to have a job and some kind of stability before considering marriage. Too many of my mother's friends went for that—"Let him provide everything"—and they're stuck in a very unhappy relationship, but can't leave because they can't provide for themselves or the children they now have. So it's either welfare or putting up with somebody else's c—p.

Hoping to avoid being trapped in an unhappy marriage or left by an unreliable partner without a way to survive, almost three-fourths of women plan to build a non-negotiable base of self-reliance and an independent identity in the world of paid work. But they do not view this strategy as incompatible with the search for a life partner. Instead, it reflects their determination to set a high standard for a worthy relationship. Economic self-reliance and personal independence make it possible to resist "settling" for anything less than a satisfying, mutually supportive bond.

Women from all backgrounds have concluded that work provides indispensable economic, social, and emotional resources. They have drawn lessons about the rewards of self-reliance and the perils of domesticity from their mothers, other women, and their own experiences growing up. When the bonds of marriage are fragile, relying on a husband for economic security seems foolhardy. They are thus seeking alternatives to traditional marriage by establishing a firm tie to paid work, by redesigning motherhood to better fit their work aspirations, and by looking to kin and friends as a support network to enlarge and, if needed, substitute, for an intimate relationship. These strategies do not preclude finding a life partner, but they reflect a determination to set a high standard for choosing one. Maria, who grew up in a two-parent home in a predominantly white, working-class suburb, declares:

> I want to have this person to share [my] life with—[someone] that you're there for as much as they're there for you. But I can't settle.

And Rachel, whose Latino parents separated when she was young, shares this view:

> I'm not afraid of being alone, but I am afraid of being with somebody's who's a jerk. I want to get married and have children, but it has to be under the right circumstances, with the right person.

Maria and Rachel also agree that if a worthy relationship ultimately proves out of reach, then remaining single need not mean social disconnection. Kin and friends provide a support network that enlarges and, if needed, even substitutes for an intimate relationship. Maria explains:

> If I don't find [a relationship], then I cannot live in sorrow. It's not the only thing that's ultimately important. If I didn't have my family, if I didn't have a career, if I didn't have friends, I would be equally unhappy. [A relationship] is just one slice of the pie.

And Rachel concurs:

> I can spend the rest of my life on my own, and as long as I have my sisters and my friends. I'm okay.

By blending support from friends and kin with financial self-sufficiency, these young women are pursuing a strategy of autonomy rather than placing their own fate or their children's fate in the hands of a traditional relationship. Whether or not this strategy ultimately leads to marriage, it appears to offer the safest and most responsible way to prepare for the uncertainties of relationships and the barriers to men's equal sharing.

Men's Plan B

Young men face a different dilemma: Torn between women's pressures for an egalitarian partnership and their own desire to succeed—or at least survive—in time-demanding workplaces, they are more inclined to fall back on a modified traditionalism that contrasts vividly with women's search for self-reliance. While they do not want or expect to return to a 1950s model of fathers as the only breadwinner, most men prefer a modified traditionalism that recognizes a mother's right (and need) to work, but puts his own career first. Although Andrew grew up in a consistently two-income home, he distinguished between a woman's "choice" to work and a man's "responsibility" to support his family:

> I would like to have it be equal—just from what I was exposed to and what attracts me—but I don't have a set definition for what that would be like. I would be fine if both of us were working, but if she thought, "At this point in my life, I don't want to work," then it would be fine.

Because equality may prove to be too costly to their careers, seven out of ten men are pursuing a strategy that positions them as the main breadwinner, even if it allows for two working spouses. When push comes to shove, and the demands of work collide with the needs of children, this approach allows men to resist equal caretaking, even in a two-earner context. Like women, men from a range of family, class, and ethnic backgrounds fall back on neo-traditionalism. They favor retaining a clear boundary between a breadwinning father and a caretaking mother, even when she holds a paid job. This neo-traditional strategy stresses women's primary status as mothers and defines equality as a woman's "choice" to add work onto mothering.

By making room for two earners, this strategy offers the financial cushion of a second income, acknowledges women's desire for a life beyond the home, and allows for more involved fatherhood. Yet, by claiming separate spheres of responsibility for women and men, it does not challenge a man's position as the primary earner or undermine the claim that his work prospects should come first. Although James's mother became too mentally ill to care for her children or herself, Josh plans to leave the lion's share of caretaking to his wife:

> All things being equal, it [caretaking] should be shared. It may sound sexist, but if somebody's going to be the breadwinner, it's going to be me. First of all, I make a better salary, and I feel the need to work, and I just think the child really needs the mother more than the father at a young age.

Men are thus more likely to favor a fallback arrangement that retains the gender boundary between breadwinning and caretaking, even when mothers hold paid jobs. From young men's perspective, this modified but still gendered household offers women the chance to earn income and establish an identity at the workplace without imposing the costs of equal parenting on men. Granting a mother's "choice" to work supports women's claims for independence, but it does not undermine men's claim that their work prospects should come first. Acknowledging men's responsibilities at home provides for more involved fatherhood, but it does not envision domestic equality. And making room for two earners provides a buffer against the difficulties of living on one income, but it does not challenge men's position as the primary earner. Modified traditionalism thus appears to be a good compromise when the career costs of equality remain so high. New

economic insecurities, coupled with women's growing desire for equality, are creating dilemmas for men, even if they take a different form than the ones confronting women. Ultimately, however, men's desire to protect work prerogatives collides with women's growing desire for equality and need for independence.

Across the Gender Divide

In contrast to the popular images of a generation that feels neglected by working mothers, unsettled by parental breakups, and wary of equality, these life stories show strong support for working mothers, a focus on the quality of a relationship, and a shared desire to create lasting, flexible, and egalitarian partnerships. The good news is that most young women and men had largely positive experiences with mothers who worked and parents who strove for flexibility and equality. Those who grew up with a caring support network and sufficient economic security, whether in a single- or a two-parent household, did well. Young women and men both recounted how gender flexibility in breadwinning and caretaking helped their parents (and other caretakers) overcome such increasingly prevalent family crises as the loss of a father's income or the decline of a mother's morale. By letting go of rigid patterns that once narrowly defined women's and men's "proper" places in the family and the wider world, all kinds of families were able to overcome unexpected challenges and create more financially stable and emotionally supportive homes. And most, even among those who grew up in less flexible families, hope to build on the struggles and gains of their parents' generation by seeking equality and flexibility in their own lives.

The bad news, however, is that most young adults remain skeptical about their chances of achieving their ideals. Amid their shared desire to transcend gender boundaries and achieve flexibility in their own lives, young women and men harbor strong concerns that their aspirations will prove impossible to reach. Faced with the many barriers to egalitarian relationships and fearful that they will not find the right partner to help them integrate work with family caretaking, they are also preparing for options that may fall substantially short of their ideals. Reversing the argument that women are returning to tradition, however, these divergent fallback strategies suggest that a new divide is emerging between "self-reliant" women, who see work, an independent income, and personal autonomy as essential to their survival, and "neo-traditional" men, who grant women's "choice" to work but also feel the need and pressure to be a primary breadwinner.

While women are developing more innovative strategies than are men, the underlying story is one of a resilient, but realistic generation that has changed far more than the institutions it has inherited. Whether they grew up in a flexible home or one with more rigid definitions of women's and men's proper places, their hard-won lessons about the need for new, more egalitarian options for building relationships and caring for children are outpacing their ability to implement these goals.

Yet, young men and women still hope to reach across the divide that separates them. Aware that traditional job ladders and traditional marriages are both waning, they are seeking more flexible ways to build careers, care for families, and integrate the two. Convinced that the traditional career, defined by orderly steps up an organizational chart, is a relic of the past, most hope to craft a "personal career" that is not bound by a single employer or work organization. Most men as well as women are trying to redefine the "ideal worker" to accommodate the ebb and flow of family life, even if that means sacrificing some income for a more balanced life. They hope to create a shared "work-family" career that interweaves breadwinning and caretaking.

Growing up in changing families and facing uncertainty in their own lives has left this generation weary of rigid, narrowly framed "family values" that moralize about their personal choices or those of others. They are searching for a morality without moralism that balances an ethic of tolerance and inclusiveness with the core values of behaving responsibly and caring for others. The clash between self-reliant women and neo-traditional men may signal a new divide, but it stems from intensifying work-family dilemmas, not from a decline of laudable values.

Since new social realities are forcing young adults to seek new ways to combine love and work, the best hope for bridging gender divides lies in creating social policies that will allow twenty-first-century Americans to pursue the flexible, egalitarian strategies they want rather than forcing them to fall back on less desirable—and ultimately less workable—options. Whether the goal is equal opportunity or a healthy family landscape, the best family values can only be achieved by creating the social supports for gender flexibility in our communities, homes, and workplaces.

Good Gay Females and Babies' Daddies: Black Lesbian Community Norms and the Acceptability of Pregnancy

SARAH J. REED, ROBIN LIN MILLER, MARIA T. VALENTI, AND TINA M. TIMM

Introduction

Differential support exists for women pursuing motherhood as a function of where women fall in a socially constructed motherhood hierarchy. DiLapi's (1989) motherhood hierarchy delineates the degree of oppression faced by mothers who vary in the acceptability of their pregnancy. At the apex of her hierarchy is the ideal mother: the married, heterosexual woman. Her place at the top is established because she has correct sexual orientation and family form. Marginally appropriate mothers are those who are correct in either family form (i.e., bisexual, married mothers) or sexual orientation (i.e., single, heterosexual mothers). They encounter obstacles to pregnancy and parenthood, but not to the extent of inappropriate mothers. Those who are inappropriate mothers are incorrect in form and sexual orientation: lesbians. Lesbians encounter a multitude of legal, medical and social obstacles to pregnancy.

Within lesbian communities, differential value may be placed on motherhood and parenting. Lesbian communities often create strict expectations of behaviour (Lehavot, Balsam, and Ibrahim-Wells 2009) and lesbians who choose to parent may face cultural biases from within their community against parenting. In some communities, women who choose to mother face derision for having bought into heterosexist imperatives (Epstein 2002). These communities conceive of 'motherhood' and 'lesbianism' as mutually exclusive identities and having children may go against community norms. As Rothblum (2008) notes, 'Lesbian and bisexual women with children do not always find communities all that supportive' (73).

In contrast, children and parenting are highly valued among Blacks and Black culture serves as an important influence on women's views of family and motherhood (Collins 2000). Parenting is common among Black same-sex couples: California's 2000 Census data suggest that Black same-sex couples are over twice as likely as white same-sex couples to be living with children (Gates, Lau, and Sears 2006) and Black same-sex female couples are nearly as likely as Black heterosexual couples to be raising children (Ramos and Gates 2008).

Black lesbian communities often have gender identity norms that play a role in organising sexual and romantic life (Wilson 2009). As pregnancy and parenting are markedly gendered experiences, these norms may have a bearing on community views of motherhood. Black lesbian communities may thus have distinct pregnancy and parenting norms. There may be pressure for some to bear children, whereas others may be condemned. As DiLapi (1989) suggests, individual reproductive decisions are culturally mediated and influenced by social control and support. Cultural ideologies affect reproductive decisions and influence how those who bear children are treated.

Sarah J. Reed, Robin Lin Miller, Maria T. Valenti, and Tina M. Timm, "Good Gay Females and Babies' Daddies: Black Lesbian Community Norms and the Acceptability of Pregnancy," *Culture, Health, and Sexuality,* Vol. 13, No. 7 (August 2011), pp. 751–765. Copyright © 2011 by Taylor & Francis. Reprinted by permission of Taylor & Francis Ltd.

Group norms and expectations can thus facilitate, hinder or stigmatise reproduction.

Social Categorisation Theory

Social categorisation theory (SCT) provides one way to understand a community's pregnancy and parenting behaviour and beliefs. Social categorisation theory suggests that identity is embedded within groups that provide identity-relevant meanings (Turner et al. 1987). Social categorisation theory further postulates that in each group there are prototypic identities and that group members seek to behave as the prototypes (Turner 1999). People in a group with the most salient identities desire meeting prototypic expectations and salient identities are those that people are committed to that serve as a guide to behaviour (Stryker 1980). Self-verification occurs when behaviours match prototypic standards positively regarded by others in the group (Burke and Stets 1999) and is sought to gain group rewards and to avoid punishment associated with identity-behavioural discrepancies (Stets and Burke 2000).

The salience of an identity within a particular context may guide various social perceptions and behaviours. Young Black sexual minority youth have intersectional identities (Cole 2009) (e.g., age, race, sexual orientation), yet in settings where all identities are shared except gender identity, that identity may become salient and used to guide behaviour. That the participants in this study who are part of a racially homogeneous (Black identified) lesbian community have created a multitude of proscriptions related to sexual and gendered behaviour suggests these identities are salient. This analysis addresses the ways in which a community of young Black lesbians negotiate and construct identity vis-à-vis pregnancy and parenting. Through examination of the three aforementioned concepts related to SCT (i.e., prototypes, salience and self-verification), we will show how normative discourse in this community has tied 'appropriate' fertility behaviour to gendered bodies. Though SCT did not guide or delimit analysis, it provides one framework through which to view the ways in which pregnancy and parenting have implications for the gender identities of lesbians in this community.

Methods

Setting

The data for the current study are from an HIV-prevention research project conducted in partnership with a community-based organisation (CBO) catering to homeless and runaway lesbian, gay, bisexual and transgender youth; however, our research was conducted at the CBO's drop-in centre where youth come to socialise in a safe space. Our involvement in the project came at the bequest of the executive director who was concerned that there had been over 25 pregnancies to females frequenting the centre in the three years prior to the project. Exploration of pregnancy thus took place within the context of a study more broadly focused on sexual behaviour, as our intent was for the interviews to inform the adaptation of a culturally, developmentally appropriate HIV-prevention intervention. . . .

Participants

We completed 14 interviews. Five participants identified as femmes, five as studs and four as stemmes. As noted elsewhere, 'femme' is a term signifying a woman who is feminine in appearance, behaviour and relationship roles, whereas 'stud' is a term signifying a lesbian with a masculine presentation of self (Wilson 2009). 'Stemme' is term specific to this community—their gender presentation fluctuates. While participants were generally of a lower socio-economic background, only one noted that she had lived in the CBO's transitional living centre.

Our observations at the CBO and the interview data suggest that the youth frequenting the CBO conceived of themselves as a community. Prior to the interviews, we regularly 'hung out' at the drop-in centre to garner knowledge to inform the interview protocol. The same people regularly attended the drop-in centre and came more often to socialise than to eat dinner or attend programs. Nearly all attended in groups and many stayed until the facility closed—dancing, playing games, talking, and planning activities such as attending the city's Black pride parade or gay night at a local bar. They frequently referred to others who attended the drop-in space as their 'gay family', calling one another 'stud brothers' and 'gay mothers' (Reed 2010). This family construction is not surprising, given that within gay and lesbian communities, there is often an importance placed upon creating 'families of choice' (Dahlheimer and Feigal 1994). Participants were thus part of a Black lesbian, gay, bisexual and transgender community that they perceived as having familial qualities.

Among participants, half had been pregnant on at least one occasion (see Table 1) and all knew other adolescent lesbian or bisexual females who have been pregnant or birthed children. Those who planned their pregnancies engaged in sexual intercourse with males they called 'sperm donors' (Reed 2010). . . .

Results

Because of the impact of cultural norms and beliefs on the regulation of fertility, it is important to examine the cultural milieu in which participants resided and made reproduction and parenting decisions. As such, results first describe community sex and sexuality norms.

Gender Identity

'Femme means female' and femmes held themselves to conventional standards of feminine appearance and behaviour. In contrast, studs considered themselves to be like a 'guy', 'man' or 'boy'. Studs saw the terms 'man' and 'stud' as synonymous. When studs did acknowledge they were biologically female, they did not acknowledge feminine characteristics:

> AJ[1]: Studs are different than men 'cuz they're women.
> INTERVIEWER: Okay. How do they act differently than men?
> AJ: Studs don't act different than men. (age 20)

Being 'like a man' was equated with dominance in relationships and relational and community authority. As BJ (age 19) ardently stated while hitting the table, she's 'the dominant one', the 'one in control' within relationships.

Stemmes presented themselves one day as femme and another day as stud; as such, they were visibly unrecognisable unless they divulged their gender identity. Stemmes expose the amorphous nature of gender identity and are invisible— silenced, ostracised or prescribed a gender identity. Many participants refused to recognise that stemmes existed and instead described them as confused. As Shane (age 22) admitted: 'Sometimes they [studs and femmes] think that we're confused. We don't know what we want to be.' Stemmes show that personal identity claims were often at odds with community perceptions of identity.

Dating

Stud-femme dating was the norm in this community, as it was in the community studied by Wilson

TABLE 1. Participants' Pregnancy Experiences

Participants	Pregnancy age(s)	Pregnancy cause	Pregnancy outcome
Aisha	18	Planned	Birth
Ashley	16	Contraceptive failure	Birth
Aiyanna	15/15	Rape/planned	Abortion/birth
Aaliya	17	Contraceptive failure	Miscarriage
Shane	16/18	Rape/planned	Miscarriage/miscarriage
RJ	18	Planned	Stillborn
DJ	14	Unknown	Unknown

Note: Femmes are identified by names beginning with the letter A; Stemmes are identified by names beginning with the letter S; Studs are identified by initials.

(2009) in her analysis of Black lesbian sexual culture. Stemmes dated both femmes and studs, but often exhibited a preference for dating one or the other, they altered their behaviour and appearance often based on their relationship. Studs were uneasy at the thought of dating stemmes because they worried stemmes might 'switch up', which would upset the rules of who was allowed to date whom.

In stud-femme relationships, femmes considered stud partners as the 'man of the relationship', 'the backbone of the relationship' and acknowledged that their stud partners saw themselves as 'a straight guy'. As Aisha (age 20) explained, femmes thought of these relationships as heterosexual relationships: 'It's just like, a hetero, yeah a heterosexual relationship. Like you got your man, you got your woman. A stud is the man, femme is the woman.' Femmes desired that their partners 'have the swag of a man'. Studs desired to 'really portray the image of being the guy'.

Sexual Behaviour

Participants believed lesbians should not have sex with males and doing so was described as a violation of sexual identity because it was a misrepresentation of self. Studs should not have sex with males because community members perceived it as violating both their sexual and gender identity. If studs had sex with men, participants claimed or assumed that sex must have occurred before identifying as a stud. Studs such as AJ (age 20) were secretive about having had sex with men:

> I wouldn't be comfortable telling them [my friends] that I had sex with a guy. . . . Because I feel like, uh, it kinda interfered with me being a stud . . .

Occasionally, those who challenged sexual norms were physically threatened. Studs protected their space and identities through violence and threats, reinforcing their image as masculine and dominate. BJ (age 19) explained why 'something ain't right' about studs having sex with men:

> Because, look at a stud, like studs feel they hard body, like a male. And just to have sex with a

male, that is very like low tolerant in this community. . . . And if you sit up here and you go have sex with a man, you gonna get talked about. You gonna get hurt. . . . You gonna get popped.

Studs who violated gender identity proscriptions were liable to face losing their authority as studs, being shamed for having tarnished the group image and physical assault. Through protecting their identity and space through violence, threats and the perpetuation of gendered ideologies, studs maintained community stature and their masculine-based power.

Parenting Desires

All of the participants either were, or aspired to be, parents and all of the femmes and stemmes wanted to be biological mothers, if they were not biological mothers already. Those who became intentionally pregnant did so despite emotional discomfort, painful sex, flashbacks of rape and avowals never to have sex with men. However, although children and parenting were valued here as in other Black communities, motherhood was embraced and celebrated in the right circumstances, as gender identity, sexual behaviour and dating norms created corresponding standards for 'appropriate' reproductive behaviour.

Appropriate Motherhood

Given this normative community discourse, DiLapi's (1989) model provides a framework for considering the acceptability of parenting for the community of young Black lesbians described in this study. Femmes who pursued pregnancy within their exclusive same-sex partnerships were 'good gay females' and appropriate mothers. 'Dick dykes' who became pregnant outside of relationships and in an unplanned fashion were marginally appropriate mothers. Studs were described as inappropriate mothers. Young lesbians in this community who were pregnant or mothering received different levels of community support, depending upon where they fell in this motherhood hierarchy. Good gay mothers received the most communal and partner support, while studs received the least. Given that support was offered based on prescribed identity, stemmes could theoretically have been at any level, depending upon how others read their gender presentation. The next sections distinguish between good gay mothers, dick dykes and pregnant studs; the last section discusses studs' preference to be a non-biological parent.

Appropriate Mothers: Good Gay Females

Participants such as Shanequa (age 19) believed femmes planned their pregnancies, 'nine times out of ten'. Similarly, BJ (age 19) pointed out,' . . . most of the time if a femme come up pregnant, a real femme, it was planned. So the stud would be the daddy.' This last statement points to a belief femme pregnancies were planned within the context of a relationship with a stud. According to participant stories and site staff, femmes were the ones most often pregnant and who were most often biological mothers.

Femmes who planned their pregnancies were 'good gay females' who met their own, their partners' and their lesbian communities' parenting expectations. They earned cultural admiration and were the recipients of various forms of support throughout their pregnancies and after the birth of their child. When good gay females became pregnant, friends were simply 'curious' or 'puzzled' as to how they became pregnant, they were not treated violently, with disdain or as if they were not real lesbians or authentic femmes. They were given baby showers and treated 'nice' and with 'respect'. If they gave birth, friends flocked to help them care for their child.

These women were 'good', because they went about pregnancy in the socially acceptable way— through planning it with their partner. By doing so, femmes were not disregarding community ideologies. Femmes like Aisha (age 20) also saw part of their role in relationships as 'producin' for my family'. In having children, they could fulfil this role while providing identity verification for themselves and for their stud partners (see section on baby's daddies). They were being good femmes, in addition to meeting the expectations of a femme partner.

These young women were 'gay' because by the definition of some in their community, they could

no longer be true lesbians. To have sex with males for any reason required the revocation of one's lesbian identity. As Aiyanna (age 17) who became intentionally pregnant explained:

> AIYANNA: But, if they—if a person was to ask me what's my sexuality. I be like, 'I'm gay', 'cuz there's two differences between gay and lesbians. So I consider myself as gay, 'cuz I have been with a man.
> INTERVIEWER: Okay, so you wouldn't consider yourself lesbian, because . . .
> AIYANNA: No, lesbians are—that haven't been with a man. Period. At all. They still virgins.

Unlike dick dykes (see below) labelled by others, gay women who had intercourse with males to conceive proudly identified as gay.

Good gay females had to be 'females', which excluded studs and stemmes who were more masculine in their gender presentation from receiving the same support as appropriate mothers. For femmes, motherhood signified femininity. Due to their own gender beliefs and the gender norms of their community, femmes could most easily integrate motherhood with their gender identity.

Marginally Appropriate Mothers: Dick Dykes

Young women who have become pregnant unintentionally were 'nasty' dick dykes. Like stemmes who disrupted community ideologies, community members who claimed to be lesbians and had sex with males were prescribed an identity: dick dykes. Notably, this community considered the term 'dyke' as offensive, though elsewhere it has been re-appropriated. Nearly all participants discussed their own negative views of dick dykes or the negative ways in which the community treated dick dykes.

Participants typically used the term 'nasty' to describe sexual behaviours (e.g., anal sex) that they thought unfathomable or to describe physical conditions (e.g., genital sores) indicative of infection. When nasty was an adjective used to describe individuals, participants were referring to particular sub-groups they wished to avoid: people with sexually transmitted infections, sexually opportunistic males and dick dykes. Shanequa (age 19) explained attitudes towards pregnant dick dykes:

SHANEQUA: They think they nasty.

INTERVIEWER: Why do they think they're nasty?

SHANEQUA: Because, if a female come in here and say 'I'm a—I'm a lesbian', they not really expecting, if you're a lesbian, then why you should want a guy? . . . So I think they treat them a little different, but still care for them, 'cuz they're pregnant. But other than that, I think, they really treat them kinda different 'cuz they is pregnant, and they did say they were lesbian.

Dick dykes were less datable because they were thought more liable to cheat and there was added concern they may have sexually transmitted infections. Studs were particularly critical of women who become unintentionally pregnant, they taunted them while pregnant and ignored or ostracised them after they gave birth:

INTERVIEWER: Girls at the centre, that are pregnant, how are they treated?

RJ: Um, well some studs do look at them more differently. They feel like, you know, only if the studs know that the girl just been messing with the nigger, just to mess with him. But if the girl is pregnant and she got pregnant for her girlfriend, then they got to look at them different. Like that they know this girl just been messing with the guy just to mess with him and end up getting pregnant and want to have sex with girls too, and they look at them different.

INTERVIEWER: So do you think they have a more negative opinion of the person . . .

RJ: Yes.

INTERVIEWER: . . . who is just messing with a guy?

RJ: Negative. (age 24)

Unlike good gay females, this community did not respect or wish to emulate dick dykes. Dick dykes tarnished the image of lesbians who were not supposed to 'make a mistake and have a baby'.

They were also criticised for 'havin' babies for the wrong reasons'. Dick dykes made a mockery of the sexual essentialism upon which community ideologies were based.

Inappropriate Mothers: Studs

In contrast to community perceptions of femme pregnancy, young women had trouble believing studs would willingly become pregnant. The only stud who accepted the fact that another stud she knew had been pregnant believed that the stud's pregnancy had occurred before she identified as a stud:

> Well I really don't, I really don't put nothing against studs that have babies because it happens, you know. And some studs gonna have babies when they was 18 and they want to be a stud now when they 19. (RJ, age 24)

If a stud had a child, participants believed it must have it prior to labelling herself as a stud, just as studs must have had sex with males before identifying as a stud. The idea of a pregnant stud was at odds with studs' perceptions of their selves and each other. The idea of a stud having a biological child was difficult to fathom because of the way in which maternal identities were constructed in opposition to authentic stud identities.

Whereas motherhood is quintessentially feminine, studs disavowed femininity. They refused to feminise their appearances for any reason (Reed 2010) and prohibited others from touching them in ways that made their female anatomy salient (as substantiated by stud and femme descriptions of sexual roles). Pregnancy and birth could also bestow upon them vulnerability, a trait they attempted to hide or extinguish through their masculine presentation largely based around dominance and control. Traditional mothering would require reconfiguring their notion of stud to include that which was thought of as feminine.

For studs, mothering was a sexually transgressive act because their behaviour (e.g., sex with males) and role (e.g., mother) did not align with identity standards. As Epstein (2002) notes, 'Butch pregnancy and motherhood disrupt the notion of coherent butch identity' (97). Studs had a stake in maintaining a rigid notion of gender identity and sometimes resorted to violence to preserve their own identities and demonstrate authority. In one story recounted by CBO staff, a pregnant stud was beaten by other studs with a bike chain. A stud also described her own aggression towards a stud who gave birth:

> I was talkin' 'bout this one stud . . . I was just like 'uggg, you out here tryin' to play tough or play hard like you a man and you got, you just had a baby', Flat out, know what I'm sayin'? So, there was all some beef and stuff, like getting' feisty. Don't come on me like you a nigger, you tough, when you just laid down with a man. (BJ, age 19)

She was confused and disturbed by gender inconsistent behaviour. The stud mother still acted like 'a man' though she 'just had a baby'. Such gender inconsistent behaviour deprived 'stud' of its meaning as an identity. Failing to find this gender divergent behaviour problematic would call into question studs' masculine identity and the communal ideological beliefs situating them in a position of authority.

The only stud to become pregnant intentionally was RJ. She was dissatisfied with being a stud and already stripped of her authority because she did not 'really truly act like a boy'. She did not 'fit in' with other studs, 'live a stud life' or 'hang with a lot of studs' because she felt unaccepted by them. As she stated, 'a typical stud would not do the feminine things I would do'. For example, she described her mannerisms more like that of an effeminate gay man than a stud. Thus, pregnancy was less at odds with her self-perception and she had less to lose because she already did not fit.

Nonetheless, she was still uneasy about her decision to become pregnant. Unlike the femmes and stemmes who pursued pregnancy, she did not inform her girlfriend prior to attempting to become pregnant. Consequently, she was relatively alone throughout her pregnancy and miscarriage. She only informed a few individuals she was pregnant—none of whom were studs. Stud mothers must have been willing to confront a feminization of their physical appearance, a change in their stature in the community, possible discord

in their romantic relationships, violence and a disruption of gender identity relevant meaning.

Babies' Daddies

Whereas being pregnant contradicted studs' identity, being a 'baby's daddy' aligned with studs' gender scripts. Lesbian parents often assign names to their selves integrating their lesbianism and ethnicity (Oswald 2002). Becoming a baby's daddy allowed community members an expression of lesbianism, ethnicity and gender identity. This term further emphasises the salience of gender identity in this community.

Babies' daddies were the current or former partner of a child's biological mother or a close friend of the biological mother. The term suggested an ongoing relationship with the child's biological mother and responsibility for the child. In no instance was a femme described as a baby's daddy. As Alycia (age 16) explained, 'In the gay life, the stud plays the dad role'. All descriptions of a baby's daddy were permeated with traditionally masculine behaviours. Aisha (age 20) described the role of her stud partner in her child's life:

> She come home, she pay the bills . . . she bring the money home. That's daddy. You know, she take care of both of us, like, we do 50/50 but she in the long run, she still take care of me and the baby. You know, it's just daddy. Everything a man would do for his daughter, [name of partner] do for [name of child].

Being a baby's daddy provided studs with a rewarding role through which to enact masculinity. BJ (age 19) described the appeal of being a baby's daddy:

> I just think, I don't know. Just to fill out the rest of the blanks in our fantasies and our dreams and our mentalities of bein' a man. We got a little kid sayin' 'daddy this, daddy that', know what I'm sayin'?

Being a baby's daddy did not violate codes of gendered behaviour and bestowed upon studs an identity through which to enact masculinity.

Though babies' daddies tended to be studs, on rare occasions stemmes identified as a baby's daddy. However, stemmes did not derive as much meaning from the role. Instead, referring to themselves as babies' daddy was a way to signify to women that they were interested in dating them. As Shae (age 20) explained, stemmes referred to themselves as a baby's daddy, 'Because they love, or like, the women whose child it is.' For stemmes, one adopted the role to relate to the mother rather than to fulfil parenting desires per se. Stemmes joked about being a baby's daddy, whereas studs took the role seriously, talked about it in terms of responsibility and truly 'think of they self as daddy'. In either usage—either as a role or a relational device—the word implies a family identity, much like other same-sex couples who use last names to negotiate family identity (Suter, Daas, and Bergen 2008).

Stemmes did not actively seek the role of baby's daddy, whereas there is evidence that studs may. Understanding the significance of parenting to studs is therefore important because of the impact their parenting desires may have on their femme partners' reproductive decisions. Literature suggests that adolescent men's attitudes towards pregnancy are one of the best predictors of their girlfriends' attitudes towards pregnancy (Cowley and Tillman Farley 2001). Among older lesbians, having a partner who desires children motivates pregnancy willingness as well (Chabot and Ames 2004).

Studs in this community influenced their partners' pregnancy decisions. Three of five studs believed that studs planned pregnancies for their girlfriends. Studs like PJ (age 24) reported they have friends who 'make they girlfriends get pregnant for them'. Studs convinced their girlfriends to have a child because 'they feel they want to have kids, but they don't want to be the ones to produce'. Aiyanna (age 17), whose second pregnancy at age 15 occurred only months after having an abortion, described her decision to become pregnant as intricately tied to her stud partner's desire to parent. Her decision to have a child was made 'to have a child for her [my girlfriend]'. She reiterated this pregnancy rationale by stating that her pregnancy was an instance of 'me having it [a baby] for my girl'.

All femmes who sought pregnancy had permission from their stud partners to pursue pregnancy.

Stud partners played the role of 'decision maker', deciding whether the time was right for their partner to become pregnant. They granted permission for their femme partner to have sex with a male in order to become pregnant: the most rigid boundary police allowed for a bending of the rules. Although studs seemingly guided the pregnancy decision-making process, femmes who became pregnant did not see themselves as coerced by their partners to have children, instead, they viewed the choice to have children as one made together and indicative of their desire to have a family together (Reed 2010). Gendered practices were ultimately family practices.

In much the same way, family practices may also be gender practices. For studs, being a baby's daddy may have made their gender identity and their partner's gender identity more dichotomised. Pregnancy makes gender identities disparate because of the ways in which new roles accentuate femininity and masculinity (Burke and Cast 1997). Parenthood confers upon individuals more traditional gender roles and is the ultimate symbol of womanhood for women and manhood for men (Belsky and Kelly 1994). Even in same-sex relationships, a child magnifies gender differences (Chabot and Ames 2004) because parents are categorised as biological and non-biological parents set apart in terms of genetics and biology, social identification and legality.

Discussion

Though the focus of this paper has been on pregnancy and parenting, this study provides further evidence that gender identity norms influence relational scripts and behaviour in Black lesbian communities (Moore 2006; Wilson 2009). We have examined the ways in which lesbian pregnancy and parenting decisions in this community are influenced by community sexual and gender identity standards and, by extension, how pregnancy and parenting have implications for the sexual and gender identities of lesbians in this community. Thus, pregnancy and parenting allow for the contestation and affirmation of identity.

If viewed through the lens of SCT, this community creates group-based identity standards tying appropriate fertility behaviour to gendered bodies. Community members have a shared sense of inter-subjectivity and as such all perpetuate a cultural system outlining ideals for behaviour, including ideals for reproductive behaviour. Pregnancy guidelines are salient because they are intricately related to sexual and gender identity imperatives and community members perpetuate mothering hegemony through the regulation and punishment of lesbian maternal identities. There is pressure to abide by expectations related to pregnancy and parenting, perhaps even more so because the CBO is a place where lesbians come to feel accepted.

Lesbians in this community experience differential rewards and consequences if they are pregnant. Good gay females are prototypic mothers. Prototypic lesbians abstain from sex with males but pregnancy desires undermine their ability to meet this expectation given participants' limited socio-economic options. Thus, the community created a gender identity loophole: the prototypical femme abstains from sex with males unless seeking pregnancy with her partner's approval (e.g., good gay females) and the prototypical stud abstains from sex with males at all times (e.g., baby's daddy). People overtly defying the prototype (e.g., dick dykes) or who are prototypically marginal (e.g., stemmes) receive negative group appraisal or may even lose group membership, as happens when they are deprived of their ability to self-identify.

People in the same group and context do not have equally salient identities and for those with less salient identities, meeting prototypical standards is not as important (Ellestad and Stets 1998). People not attempting to live up to prototypic standards (as in the case of the pregnant stud) or who are not dismayed if inadvertently failing to live up to prototypic standards may have less salient identities. Those seen as studs by the community, but who not see themselves as studs, may violate stud codes, but it will matter less to them than it will to self-defined studs because their identities have been prescribed to them and are not a true reflection of their personal identities. Identity salience also accounts for the differential

importance stemmes and studs place on being a baby's daddy. Lesbians with salient masculine identities will be more likely to desire roles (e.g., baby's daddy) and behave in ways to assert that identity (Ellestad and Stets 1998). For these studs, being a baby's daddy expresses their gender identity. For some of these studs, compelling their femme partners to become pregnant provides self-verification. Regulating appropriate motherhood also provides a way to obtain self-verification. By re-appropriating others' identities, participants affirm their own; this is particularly true of studs whose control over community norms and their partner's sexual behaviour propagates their belief in their communal and relational authority. Communal policing is a way to create affirming sexual and gender identities. Thus, studs obtain gender identity self-verification both by supporting their femme partners' pregnancy desires as well as by enforcing the status quo within their community. Studs are constructing their identities and sexual selves within an 'overarching structure of heterosexual power' where they are largely socially devalued (Collins 2000, 131). The self-verification studs receive through parenting may be one of the few means through which they receive gender identity validation. Indeed, when other structural constraints limit their employment opportunities, cultural capital and other means through which to construct their identities, parenthood (and motherhood for femmes) may provide a measure of control and agency (Rolph 2008).

Notably, participants' socio-economic circumstances further shaped pregnancy and parenting experiences. Participants were aware that alternative contraceptive techniques existed and were one means through which to become pregnant without having sex with males (Donovan and Wilson 2008). Yet they acknowledged that such procedures were not economically feasible. Their pregnancy attempts thus place them at increased risk of HIV, for they are unable to afford safe pregnancy procedures and have access to high-risk (e.g., gay or bisexual male) sperm donors. For studs, having a biological child in this context requires both sex with males and a gender-incongruent nine-month pregnancy and birthing experience. Were alternative contraceptive techniques an option, it is unclear whether studs would be any more likely to desire bearing children. For alternative contraceptive techniques to be an option, studs would have to be in a profoundly different socio-economic circumstance, which would also likely affect their interpretation and construction of gender identity.

Given the significance and valuation of pregnancy and parenting in these participants' lives, our intervention approach was not one of pregnancy avoidance. Many people see adolescent motherhood as cause for concern, as a social problem, as something to be avoided (Breheny and Stephens 2010). Yet for this community, it is an important means of self-expression. As marginalised members of society, members of this community are often denied socially rewarding means of self-expression. Pregnancy and parenting allow them to create roles through which they may assert their identities and conserve element of those identities that contribute to a positive view of themselves. In this environment, valuing and pursuing parenting is an instrumental strategy. In affirming the value of lesbian parenting, they preserve motherhood and parenting as sites 'where Black women express and learn the power of self-definition' (Collins 2000, 183). To construct the intervention as pregnancy prevention would have been demeaning and alienating to many participants. Our intervention approach thus took a parenting preparedness and pregnancy safety approach that focused on partner dynamics and power sharing.

Limitations may have bearing on the findings of this study. Pregnancy was not the entire focus of the interviews, which, if it had been, may have resulted in richer categories. Similarly, data collection and analysis did not occur iteratively as is preferable in a grounded theory study (Charmaz 2006). A larger sample and having conducted analysis and interviews iteratively may also have led to more theoretically dense categories. Additionally, we recruited young women from a lesbian, gay, bisexual and transgender centre where they participate in a community organised around sexual and gender norms; many young

lesbian and bisexual females lack such a community. How young Black lesbians not connected to a community where these norms are enforced think about pregnancy and motherhood remains unknown and these results are not intended to be generalisable to other lesbian communities where different gender identity norms operate. We further recognise that experiences of motherhood are profoundly impacted by other aspects of these participants' identities such as their race/ethnicity and socio-economic status, however, the nature of the interviews did not permit us to conduct a more nuanced analysis of how these dynamics influence pregnancy and parenting aspirations.

Conclusion

. . . In a lesbian community in which there are not strict gender identity-based distinctions, pregnancy and parenting may be less likely to be sought to affirm gender identity. Further, in communities where there is not an ideological commitment to an assumption that feminine women mother, more masculine lesbians may become pregnant and will experience less resistance if they do so. In both of these instances, less constrained gender expectations may result in less gendered regulation of fertility.

Note

1. Participants are distinguished by names provided by the researchers. As is typical of studs, they are identified by initials. Femmes have been given names starting with A and stemmes have been given names starting with S.

References

Belsky, J., and J. Kelly. 1994. *The transition to parenthood*. New York: Delacorte Press.

Burke, P.J., and D.A. Cast. 1997. Stability and change in the gender identities of newly married couples. *Social Psychology Quarterly* 60: 277–90.

Burke, P.J., and J.E. Stets. 1999. Trust and commitment through self-verification. *Social Psychology Quarterly* 62: 347–66.

Breheny, M., and C. Stephens. 2010. Youth and disadvantage? The construction of teenage mothers in medical journals. *Culture, Health & Sexuality* 12: 307–22.

Chabot, J.M., and B.D. Ames. 2004. 'It wasn't let's get pregnant and go do it': Decision making in lesbian couples planning motherhood via donor insemination. *Family Relations* 53: 348–56.

Charmaz, C. 2006. *Constructing grounded theory: A practical guide through qualitative analysis.* Los Angeles: Sage.

Cole, E.R. 2009. Intersectionality and research in psychology. *American Psychologist* 64: 170–80.

Collins, P.H. 2000. *Black feminist thought: Knowledge, consciousness and the politics of empowerment.* New York: Routledge.

Cowley, C., and N.P. Tillman Farley. 2001. Adolescent girls' attitudes toward pregnancy: The importance of asking what the boyfriend wants. *Journal of Family Practice* 50: 603–7.

Dahlheimer, D., and J. Feigal. 1994. Community as family: The multiple-family contexts of gay and lesbian clients. In *Transitioning from individual to family counselling,* ed. C. Huber, 63–74. Alexandria, VA: American Counseling Association.

DiLapi, E.M. 1989. Lesbian mothers and the motherhood hierarchy. *Journal of Homosexuality* 18: 101–21.

Donovan, C., and A.R. Wilson. 2008. Imagination and integrity: Decision-making among lesbian couples to use medically provided donor insemination. *Culture, Health & Sexuality* 10: 649–65.

Ellestad, J., and J.E. Stets. 1998. Jealousy and parenting: Predicting emotions from identity theory. *Sociological Perspectives* 41: 639–68.

Epstein, R. 2002. Lesbian families. In *Voices: Essays on Canadian families,* ed. M.M. Lynn, 76–102. Toronto: Nelson Canada.

Gates, G., H. Lau, and R.B. Sears. 2006. Race and ethnicity of same-sex couples in California: Data from Census 2000. The Williams Institute. http://www.law.ucla.edu/williamsinstitute/publications/Race_and_ethnicity_of_same-sex_couples_in_california.pdf

Lehavot, K., K.F. Balsam, and G.D. Ibrahim-Wells. 2009. Redefining the American quilt: Definitions and experiences of community among ethnically diverse lesbian and bisexual women. *Journal of Community Psychology* 37: 439–58.

Moore, M.R. 2006. Lipstick or timberlands? Meanings of gender presentation in Black lesbian communities. *Journal of Women in Culture and Society* 32: 113–39.

Oswald, R.F. 2002. Resilience within the family networks of lesbians and gay men: Intentionality and redefinition. *Journal of Marriage and Family* 64: 374–83.

Ramos, C., and G.J. Gates. 2008. Census snapshot: California's Black lesbian, gay, bisexual and transgender population. The Williams Institute. http://www.law.ucla.edu/williamsinstitute/publications/BlackSnapshot.pdf

Reed, S.J. 2010. The pregnancy experiences and motivations of young Black women who have sex with women. Master's Thesis, Michigan State University.

Rolph, A. 2008. You've got to group up when you've got a kid: Marginalized youth women's accounts of motherhood. *Journal of Community and Applied Social Psychology* 18: 299–314.

Rothblum, E. 2008. Finding a large and thriving lesbian and bisexual community: The costs and benefits of caring. *Gay and Lesbian Issues and Psychological Review* 4: 69–79.

Stets, J.E., and P.J. Burke. 2000. Identity theory and social identity theory. *Social Psychology Quarterly* 63: 224–37.

Stryker, S. 1980. Identity salience and role performance. *Journal of Marriage and the Family* 4: 558–64.

Suter, E.A., K.L. Daas, and K.M. Bergen. 2008. Negotiating lesbian family identity via symbols and rituals. *Journal of Family Issues* 29: 26–47.

Turner, J.C. 1999. Some current issues in research on social identity and self-categorization theories. In *Social identity: Context, commitment, content,* ed. N. Ellemers, R. Spears, and B. Doosje, 6–34. Oxford: Blackwell.

Turner, J.C., M.A. Hogg, P.J. Oakes, S.D. Reicher, and M. Wetherell. 1987. *Rediscovering the social group: A self-categorization theory.* Oxford: Basil Blackwell.

Wilson, B.D.M. 2009. Black lesbian gender and sexual culture: Celebration and resistance. *Culture, Health & Sexuality* 11: 297–313.

6

The Gendered Classroom

Along with the family, educational institutions—from primary schools to secondary schools, colleges, universities, and professional schools—are central arenas in which gender is reproduced. Students learn more than the formal curriculum—they learn what the society considers appropriate behavior for men and women. And for adults, educational institutions are gendered workplaces, where the inequalities found in other institutions are also found.

From the earliest grades, students' experiences in the classroom differ by gender. Boys are more likely to interrupt, to be called upon by teachers, and to have any misbehavior overlooked. Girls are more likely to remain obedient and quiet and to be steered away from math and science.

Both contributions to this section are based on field research. The researchers sat down and talked with boys and girls about what they thought, how they understood both gender difference and gender inequality. Diane Reay takes on the new research on girls' aggression and finds that while both boys and girls can be mean and aggressive, there is a wider range of acceptable identities for girls than there may be for boys. Perhaps thanks to feminism, which did, after all, open up a wider array of possible futures for women, young girls have a wider range of identities from which to choose. Yet, Wayne Martino's portraits of middle schoolers are surprising in their gender conformity, especially for the boys. He finds that these discourses are what lie behind boys' difficulties in school, not some putative feminist agenda to keep boys down.

"Spice Girls," "Nice Girls," "Girlies," and "Tomboys": Gender Discourses, Girls' Cultures, and Femininities in the Primary Classroom

DIANE REAY

This article attempts to demonstrate that contemporary gendered power relations are more complicated and contradictory than any simplistic binary discourse of "the girls versus the boys" suggests (Heath, 1999). Although prevailing dominant discourses identify girls as "the success story of the 1990s" (Wilkinson, 1994), this small-scale study of a group of 7-year-old girls attending an inner London primary school suggests that, particularly when the focus is on the construction of heterosexual femininities, it is perhaps premature always to assume that "girls are doing better than boys." While girls may be doing better than boys in examinations, this article indicates that their learning in the classroom is much broader than the National Curriculum and includes aspects that are less favourable in relation to gender equity. Although masculinities are touched on in this article, this is only in as far as they relate to girls. This deliberate bias is an attempt to refocus on femininities at a time when masculinities appear to be an ever-growing preoccupation within education.

However, although the subjects of this research are 14 girls, the position the article takes is that femininities can only be understood relationally. There is a co-dependence between femininities and masculinities which means that neither can be fully understood in isolation from the other. The article therefore explores how a particular group of primary-aged girls is positioned, primarily in relation to dominant discourses of femininity but also in relation to those of masculinity. There is also an attempt to map out their relationships to transgressive but less prevalent discourses of femininity, which in a variety of ways construct girls as powerful. The findings from such a small-scale study are necessarily tentative and no generalised assertions are made about girls as a group. Rather, the aim is to use the girls' narratives and their experiences in school and, to a lesser extent, those of the boys, to indicate some ways in which the new orthodoxy, namely that girls are doing better than boys, does not tell us the whole story about gender relations in primary classrooms.

The last decade has seen a growing popular and academic obsession with boys' underachievement both in the UK and abroad (Katz, 1999; Smithers, 1999). However, as Lyn Yates points out, much of the "underachieving boys' discourse fails either to deal adequately with power or to see femininity and masculinity as relational phenomena" (Yates, 1997). For instance, within the explosion of concern with masculinities in academia, there has been little focus on the consequences for girls of "boys behaving badly." As Gaby Weiner and her colleagues argue:

> new educational discourses have silenced demands for increased social justice for girls and women characterised by increasing resistance to policies and practices focusing specifically on them. (Weiner et al., 1997, p. 15)

Diane Reay, "'Spice Girls,' 'Nice Girls,' 'Girlies,' and 'Tomboys': Gender Discourses, Girls' Cultures, and Femininities in the Primary Classroom," *Gender and Education*, Vol. 13, No. 2 (2001), pp. 153–166.

Jill Blackmore describes attempts by some male academics in Australia to develop programmes for boys which seek to depict boys as powerless in the face of the progress and success of feminism and girls, and, indeed, as victims of their own male psychology (Blackmore, 1999). Jane Kenway writes more broadly of "the lads' movement" in Australia; a general resurgence of concern that boys and men are getting an unfair deal (Kenway, 1995). In Britain, there has been a growing alarm about "boys doing badly" that preoccupies both mainstream and feminist academics alike (Epstein et al., 1998). What gets missed out in these current concerns is the specificity of the "failing boy" and the ways in which other groups of males continue to maintain their social advantage and hold on to their social power (Arnot et al., 1999; Lucey & Walkerdine, 1999). It is within this context of contemporary preoccupation with boys that this article attempts to problematise issues surrounding gender equity and, in particular, to challenge the view that in millennial Britain it is boys rather than girls who are relatively disadvantaged. . . .

Gender Discourses

Many writers on education have attempted to provide a variety of conceptual tools in order to understand educational contexts and processes (Ball, 1994; Maclure, 1994). A key debate amongst educational researchers has been between structuralist and post-structuralist approaches. Although often these two conceptual approaches are seen as opposing perspectives, in this article, I use and combine what I perceive to be the strengths of both positions to illuminate the ways in which girls both construct themselves, and are constructed, as feminine (see also, Walkerdine, 1991, 1997; Williams, 1997; Walkerdine et al., 2000 for similar approaches). As Davies et al. (1997) assert, power is both located in the structural advantage of individuals and also exercised partly through the construction of discourses.

Multiple discourses contribute not only to how researchers appreciate the conditions of childhood but also to how children come to view themselves (James et al., 1998). Post-structuralist feminists have explored extensively the ways in which different discourses can position girls (Davies, 1993; Hey, 1997; Walkerdine, 1997). It is important to recognise that there are many competing gender discourses, some of which have more power and potency than others for particular groups of girls (Francis, 1998). Such processes of discursive recognition, of feeling a better fit within one discourse than another (Francis, 1999), are influenced by social class. Similarly, gender discourses are taken up differentially by different ethnic groupings. It is also important to stress that girls can position themselves differently in relation to gender discourses according to the peer group context they find themselves in. For example, it soon became evident in my research that girls assume different positions depending on whether they are in single- or mixed-sex contexts. As Gee and his colleagues assert:

> There are innumerable discourses in modern societies: different sorts of street gangs, elementary schools and classrooms, academic disciplines and their sub-specialities, police, birdwatchers, ethnic groups, genders, executives, feminists, social classes and sub-classes, and so on and so forth. Each is composed of some set of related social practices and social identities (or positions). Each discourse contracts complex relations of complicity, tension and opposition with other discourses. (Gee et al., 1996, p. 10)

I found similar "complex relations of complicity, tension and opposition" in relation to the nexus of gender discourses that these girls draw on. Yet, any local discursive nexus is framed by a wider social context within which, as Valerie Hey (1997) points out, there is a lack of powerful public discourses for girls, leaving them caught between schooling which denies difference and compulsory heterosexuality which is fundamentally invested in producing it. If this gives the impression of a fluid situation in relation to how contemporary girls position themselves as female, there is also substantial evidence of continuities in which, at least for the girls in this research, conformist discourses continue to exert more power than transgressive or transformative ones.

Masculinities in the Classroom: Setting the Context

Although the main focus of this article is how gender discourses position girls at school, in order to understand femininities in this primary classroom, the ways in which masculinities are being played out cannot be ignored. I want to start with two short excerpts from boys. Josh and David, two white, middle-class, 7-year-old boys, interviewed each other about what they like most and least about being a boy:

> J: David, what do you like most about being a boy?
>
> D: Well, it must be that it's much easier to do things than being a girl, that's what I think. You get to do much better things.
>
> J: So you think you find being a boy more interesting than being a girl? Is that what you're saying?
>
> D: Yes because it's boring being a girl.
>
> J: OK, and what do you like least about being a boy?
>
> D: Well, I don't know, I can't think of anything.
>
> J: Well, can't you think really—there must be something.
>
> D: I'll think [long pause]. Well, it's easier to hurt yourself.
>
> D: OK What do you like most about being a boy?
>
> J: I'd probably say that it's better being a boy because they have more interesting things to do and it's more exciting for them in life I find.
>
> D: Yes, I see. What do you like least about being a boy?
>
> J: Ohh I'd probably say not being so attractive as girls probably I'd say they're much more attractive than boys.

Josh and David were the only middle-class boys in a Year 3 class of predominantly working-class children. Existing research has found that the culturally exalted form of masculinity varies from school to school and is informed by the local community (Skelton, 1997; Connolly, 1998). These two boys were adjusting to a predominantly working-class, inner-city peer group in which dominant local forms of masculinity were sometimes difficult for both to negotiate, but in particular, for David (for one thing, he did not like football). They both also found the low priority given to academic work among the other boys problematic. Even so, they were clear that it was still better being a boy.

Both boys, despite their social class positioning, were popular among the peer group. In particular, Josh commanded a position of power and status in the peer group which was virtually unchallenged (see also Reay, 1990). Sociogram data collected from all the children in the class positioned him as the most popular child, not only with the working-class boys in the class but also with the girls. David's positioning is more difficult to understand. His particular variant of middle-class masculinity was far less acceptable to his working-class peers than Josh's. He was studious and hated games. In the exercise where children drew and described their favourite playground activity, David sketched a single figure with a bubble coming out of his head with "thoughts" inside. He annotated it with "I usually like walking about by myself and I'm thinking." However, within the confines of the classroom, for much of the time, he retained both status and power, paradoxically through a combination of being male and clever. When the girls were asked to nominate two boys and two girls they would most like to work with, David was the second most popular male choice after Josh. However, he was the most popular choice with the other boys. The complex issues as to why these two boys were popular when their masculinities did not fit the dominant one within the male peer group are beyond the brief of this article. Rather, what is salient is the relevance of their positioning within the peer group for the group of girls who are the article's main protagonists.

Although the focus has been on "the others" within masculinity, black and white working-class boys (Willis, 1977; Sewell, 1997), it is the association of normativity with white, middle-class masculinity that seems most difficult for girls to challenge effectively. Disruptive, failing boys' behaviour has given girls an unexpected window of opportunity through which some variants of femininities can be valorised over specific pathologised masculinities, particularly within the arena of educational attainment. Both girls and boys were aware of discourses which position girls as more mature and educationally focused than boys and regularly drew on them to make sense of gender differences in the classroom (see also Pattman & Phoenix, 1999). What seems not to have changed is the almost unspoken acceptance of white, middle-class masculinity as the ideal that all those "others"—girls as well as black and white working-class boys—are expected to measure themselves against. Popular discourses position both masculinity and the middle classes as under siege, suggesting an erosion of both male and class power bases (Bennett, 1996; Coward, 1999). While there have been significant improvements in the direction of increasing equity, particularly in the area of gender, the popularity of Josh and David, combined with the uniform recognition among the rest of the peer group that they were the cleverest children in the class, suggests that popular discourses may mask the extent to which white, middle-class male advantages in both the sphere of education and beyond continue to be sustained.

However, 10 of the 12 boys were working class. The "failing boys" compensatory culture of aggressive "laddism" (Jackson, 1998) had already started to be played out at the micro-level of this primary classroom. The working-class, white and mixed race boys were more preoccupied with football than the academic curriculum (see also Skelton, 1999). When they were not playing football in the playground, they would often be surreptitiously exchanging football cards in the classroom. Alongside regular jockeying for position within the male peer group, which occasionally escalated into full-blown fights, there was routine, casual labelling of specific girls as stupid and dumb. The three Bengali boys at the bottom of this particular male peer group hierarchy compensated by demonising, in particular, the three middle-class girls. Their strategy echoes that of the subordinated youth in Wight's (1996) study, where in order to gain the approval and acceptance of their dominant male peers,

they endeavoured to become active subjects in a sexist discourse which objectified girls.

Sugar and Spice and All Things Nice?

3R had four identifiable groups of girls—the "nice girls," the "girlies," the "spice girls" and the "tomboys" (see Figure 1).

The latter two groups had decided on both their own naming as well as those of the "girlies" and the "nice girls," descriptions which were generally seen as derogatory by both girls and boys. "Girlies" and "nice girls" encapsulate "the limited and limiting discourse of conventional femininity" (Brown, 1998), and in this Year 3 class, although there was no simple class divide, the "nice girls" were composed of Donna, Emma and Amrit, the only three middle-class girls in 3R, plus a fluctuating group of one to two working-class girls. The "nice girls," seen by everyone, including themselves, as hard-working and well behaved, exemplify the constraints of a gendered and classed discourse which afforded them the benefits of culture, taste and cleverness but little freedom. Prevalent discourses which work with binaries of mature girls and immature boys and achieving girls and underachieving boys appear on the surface to be liberating for girls. However, the constraints were evident in the "nice girls'" self-surveillant, hypercritical attitudes to both their behaviour and their schoolwork; attitudes which were less apparent amongst other girls in the class. It would appear that this group of 7-year-old, predominantly middle-class girls had already begun to develop the intense preoccupation with academic success that other researchers describe in relation to middle-class, female, secondary school pupils (Walkerdine et al., 2000).

Contemporary work on how masculinities and femininities are enacted in educational contexts stresses the interactions of gender with class, race and sexuality (Mac an Ghaill, 1988; Hey, 1997; Connolly, 1998). Sexual harassment in 3R (a whole gamut of behaviour which included uninvited touching of girls and sexualised name-calling) was primarily directed at the "girlies" and was invariably perpetuated by boys who were subordinated within the prevailing masculine hegemony

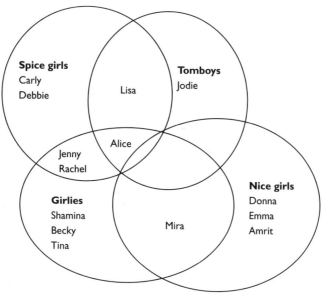

Figure 1. Girl Groups in 3R

either because of their race or social class. However, while sexual harassment was an infrequent occurrence, identifying the "nice girls" as a contaminating presence was not. In the playground, the three working-class Bengali boys were positioned as subordinate to the white and Afro-Caribbean boys; for example, they were often excluded from the football games on the basis that they were not skilful enough. These three boys constructed the "nice girls" as a polluting, contagious "other." They would regularly hold up crossed fingers whenever one of these girls came near them. As a direct result, the "nice girls" began to use the classroom space differently, taking circuitous routes in order to keep as far away from these boys as possible. Barrie Thorne (1993) found similar gender practices in which girls were seen as "the ultimate source of contamination." Like the girls in Thorne's research, the "nice girls" did not challenge the boys but rather developed avoidance strategies which further circumscribed their practices.

Being one of the "nice girls" had derogatory connotations for working-class girls as well as working-class boys. Alice, in particular, was adamant that she could not contemplate them as friends because they were "too boring," while in one of the focus

group discussions, Jodie, Debbie and Carly all agreed that "no one wants to be a nice girl." Their views reflect the findings of feminist research which position "being nice" as specific to the formulation of white, middle-class femininity (Jones, 1993; Griffin, 1995; Kenway et al., 1999). For a majority of the working-class girls in the class, being a "nice girl" signified an absence of the toughness and attitude that they were aspiring to.

This is not to construct the "nice girls" as passive in relation to other groups in the class. They often collaborated with Josh and David on classwork and were vocal about the merits of their approach to schoolwork over those of other girls in the class:

> EMMA: The other girls often mess around and be silly, that's why Alice and Lisa never get their work finished.
> DONNA: Yes we're more sensible than they are.
> EMMA: And cleverer.

However, the dominant peer group culture in the classroom was working class and, while this had little impact on the popularity of Josh and David, it did have repercussions for the status and social standing of the "nice girls" within the peer group.

"The limited and limiting discourse of conventional femininity" also had a powerful impact on the "girlies," a group of three working-class girls (two white and one Bengali). Kenway et al. (1999) write about "the sorts of femininities which unwittingly underwrite hegemonic masculinity" (p. 120). Certainly, the "girlies," with their "emphasised femininity" (Connell, 1987, p. 187), were heavily involved in gender work which even at the age of 7 inscribed traditional heterosexual relations. Paul Connolly (1998) describes the ways in which sexual orientation and relations defined through boyfriends and girlfriends seems to provide an important source of identity for young children. This was certainly the case for the "girlies." These girls were intensely active in the work of maintaining conventional heterosexual relationships through the writing of love letters, flirting and engaging in regular discussions of who was going out with who. They were far more active in such maintenance work than the boys.

Both the "girlies" and the "nice girls" were subject to "discourses of denigration" circulating among the wider peer group (Blackmore, 1999, p. 136). In individual interviews, many of the boys and a number of the other girls accounted for the "nice girls'" unpopularity by describing them as "boring" and "not fun to be with," while the "girlies" were variously described by boys as "stupid" and "dumb." While the boys were drawing on a male peer group discourse which positioned the "girlies" as less intelligent than they were, the "girlies" were far from "stupid" or "dumb." Although not as scholarly as the "nice girls," they were educationally productive and generally achieved more highly than their working-class male counterparts. Rather, the working-class discourse of conventional femininity within which they were enmeshed operated to elide their academic achievement within the peer group.

Discourses of conventional femininity also seemed to have consequences for the two Asian girls in the class. Amrit, who was Indian, was from a middle-class background while Shamina was Bengali and working class. Yet, both girls, despite their class differences, shared a high degree of circumscription in relation to the range of femininities available to them in the school context. As Shamina explained, "the spice girls and the tomboys are naughty. I am a good girl." In contrast to the other girls in the girls' focus group discussion, who all claimed to enjoy playing football, both Shamina and Amrit asserted that "football was a boys' game," and Amrit said, "It's not worth bothering with football. It's too boring. Me and my friends just sit on the benches and talk."

Heidi Mirza (1992) argues that the cultural construction of femininity among African-Caribbean girls fundamentally differs from the forms of femininity found among their white peers. In the case of Amrit and Shamina, there were substantial areas of overlap rather than fundamental differences. However, neither managed to carve out spaces in which to escape gender subordination from the boys in the ways that the "spice girls" and the "tomboys," both all-white groups, did. Racism and its impact on subjectivities may well be an issue here. Although it is impossible to make generalisations on the basis of two children, ethnicity, as well as class, appears to be an important consideration in the possibilities and performance of different femininities.

Membership of the "spice girls" revolved around two white, working-class girls, Carly and Debbie. Jenny, Rachel, Alice and Lisa were less consistently members of the group. Lisa and Alice would sometimes claim to be "tomboys" while Jenny and Rachel, when playing and spending time with the "girlies," and especially when Carly and Debbie were in trouble with adults in the school, would realign themselves as "girlies." Very occasionally, when she had quarrelled both with Carly and Debbie, and with Jodie, the one consistent tomboy among the girls, Alice too would reinvent herself as a "girlie."

Although there were many overlaps between both the practices and the membership of the "girlies" and the "spice girls," aspects of the "spice girls" interaction with the boys appeared to transgress prevailing gender regimes, while the "girlies'" behaviour followed a far more conformist pattern. Yet, the "spice girls" were, for much of the time, also active in constructing and maintaining traditional variants of heterosexuality. Their espousal of "girl power" did not exclude enthusiastic partaking of the boyfriend/girlfriend games. There was much flirting, letter writing, falling in and out of love and talk of broken hearts. However, they also operated beyond the boundaries of the "girlies'" more conformist behaviour when it came to interaction with the boys. Debbie and Carly, the most stalwart members of the "spice girls," both described the same activity—rating the boys—as their favourite playground game. As Carly explained, "you follow the boys around and give them a mark out of ten for how attractive they are."

The "spice girls" adherence to so-called girl power also allowed them to make bids for social power never contemplated by the "girlies" or the "nice girls." During a science lesson which involved experiments with different foodstuffs, including a bowl of treacle, Carly and Debbie jointly forced David's hand into the bowl because, as Carly asserted, "he is always showing off, making out he knows all the answers." This incident, which reduced David to tears and shocked the other children, served to confirm the class teacher in her view that the two girls "were a bad lot." The "girls with attitude" stance that Carly and Debbie so valued and their philosophy of "giving as good as they got" were reinterpreted by adults in the school as both inappropriate and counterproductive to learning. Paul Connolly (1998) points out that girls' assertive or disruptive behaviour tends to be interpreted more negatively than similar behaviour in boys, while Robin Lakoff (1975) has described how, when little girls "talk rough" like the boys do, they will normally be ostracised, scolded or made fun of. For the "spice girls," "doing it for themselves" in ways which ran counter to traditional forms of femininity resulted in them being labelled at various times by teachers in the staffroom as "real bitches," "a bad influence" and "little cows." The tendency Clarricoates found in 1978 for girls' misbehaviour to be "looked upon as a character defect, whilst boys' misbehaviour is viewed as a desire to assert themselves" was just as evident in teachers' discourses more than 20 years later.

Debbie and Carly were doubly invidiously positioned in relation to the "girls as mature discourse." They were perceived to be "too mature," as "far too knowing sexually" within adult discourses circulating in the school but they were also seen, unlike the boys and the majority of the girls in 3R, as "spiteful" and "scheming little madams" for indulging in behaviour typical of many of the boys. There were several incidents in the playground of sexual harassment of girls by a small group of boys. Most of the adults dismissed these as "boys mucking about." However, Carly and Debbie's attempts to invert regular processes of gender objectification, in which girls are routinely the objects of a male gaze, were interpreted by teachers as signs of "an unhealthy preoccupation with sex." Their predicament exemplifies the dilemma for girls of "seeking out empowering places within regimes alternatively committed to denying subordination or celebrating it" (Hey, 1997, p. 132). In this classroom, girls like Carly and Debbie seemed to tread a fine line between acceptable and unacceptable "girl power" behaviour. Overt heterosexuality was just about on the acceptable side of the line but retaliatory behaviour towards the boys was not.

Valerie Walkerdine (1997) describes how playful and assertive girls come to be understood as overmature and too precocious. Girls like Debbie and Carly, no less than the girls in Walkerdine's advertisements, occupy a space where girls have moved beyond being "nice" or "girlie." Rather, as sexual little women, they occupy a space where they can be bad. As Walkerdine points out, while it is certainly a space in which they can be exploited, it provides a space of power for little girls, although one which is also subject to discourses of denigration. The forms that denigration take are very different to those experienced by the "nice girls" or the "girlies" but become apparent in teachers' judgments of the two girls' behaviour.

"It's Better Being a Boy"— The Tomboys

The most intriguing case in my research was that of the "tomboys." The "tomboys" in Becky Francis's research study were depicted by another girl in the class as traitors to girlhood:

> Rather than rejecting the aspiration to maleness because it is "wrong" or "unnatural," Zoe argues that "girls are good enough," implying that her girlfriends want to be boys because they see males as superior, and that she is defending girlhood against this sexist suggestion. (Francis, 1998, p. 36)

As I have touched on earlier in the article, in 3R, there was a general assumption among the boys that maleness, if not a superior subject positioning, was a more desirable one. While, in particular the "spice girls," but also at various times both the "girlies" and "nice girls" defended girlhood against such claims, their stance was routinely undermined by the position adopted by the tomboys.

Jodie was the only girl in the class who was unwavering in her certainty that she was not a girl but a "tomboy," although a couple of the other girls in the class for periods of time decided that they were also "tomboys":

> JODIE: Girls are crap, all the girls in this class act all stupid and girlie.
> DIANE: So does that include you?
> JODIE: No, cos I'm not a girl, I'm a tomboy.

On the one hand, Jodie could be viewed as a budding "masculinised new woman at ease with male attributes" (Wilkinson, 1999, p. 37). Yet, her rejection of all things feminine could also be seen to suggest a degree of shame and fear of femininity. Jodie even managed to persuade Wayne and Darren, two of the boys in the class, to confirm her male status. Both, at different times, sought me out to tell me Jodie was "really a boy." It is difficult to know how to theorise such disruptions of normative gender positionings. Jodie's stance combines elements of resistance with recognition. She clearly recognised and responded to prevailing gender hierarchies which situate being male with having more power and status. Jodie appears to operate at the boundaries where femininity meets masculinity. She is what Barrie Thorne (1993) calls "active at the edges."

However, while Thorne reports that it was rarely used among her fourth and fifth graders, the term "tomboy" is frequently used in 3M as a marker of respect by both boys and girls. Being a "tomboy" seems to guarantee male friendship and male respect. Several of the working-class girls in the class, like Alice, appeared to move easily from taking up a position as a "tomboy" through to assuming a "girls with attitude" stance alongside Debbie and Carly to becoming a "girlie" and back again. One week Alice would come to school in army fatigues with her hair scraped back, the next, in Lycra with elaborately painted nails and carefully coiffured hair. However, Alice was unusual among the girls in ranging across a number of subject positions. For most of the girls, although they had choices, those choices seemed heavily circumscribed and provided little space for manoeuvre.

The regulatory aspects of the "girlies" and the "nice girls'" self-production as feminine were very apparent, yet the conformity of the "tomboys" to prevailing gender regimes was far more hidden. While it is important to recognise the transgressive qualities of identifying and rejecting traditional notions of femininity in Jodie's behaviour, the empowering aspects of being a "tomboy" also masked deeply reactionary features embedded in assuming such a gender position. Implicit in the concept of "tomboy" is a devaluing of traditional notions of femininity, a railing against the perceived limitations of being female. This is particularly apparent in Jodie's comments:

> JODIE: I don't really have any friends who are girls cos they don't like doing the things I like doing. I like football and stuff like that.
> DIANE: Don't girls like football?
> JODIE: Yeah, some of them, but they're no good at it.

Perhaps, in part, it is Jodie's obsession with football that contributes to her contradictory gender positionings. As Christine Skelton (1999) points out, there is a close association between football and hegemonic masculinities and, therefore, if Jodie is to be seen as "a football star," she needs to assume a male rather than a female subject positioning.

But there is another possible reading in which Jodie's preoccupation with football facilitates, rather than is the cause of, her flight from femininity.

Michelle Fine and Pat Macpherson define girls' identification with football as "both a flight from femininity . . . and an association of masculinity with fairness, honesty, integrity and strength" (Fine & Macpherson, 1992, p. 197). The girls in their study would call each other boys as a compliment: "Girls can be good, bad or—best of all—they can be boys" (p. 200) and this was definitely a viewpoint Jodie adhered to. Jodie's individualised resistance can be set alongside Carly and Debbie's joint efforts to disrupt prevailing gender orders among the peer group. Yet, paradoxically, Jodie, no less than the "girlies," seemed engaged in a process of accommodating the boys. The means of accommodation may differ but the compliance with existing gender regimes remains. Madeline Arnot (1982) writes of the ways in which boys maintain the hierarchy of social superiority of masculinity by devaluing the female world. In 3R, Jodie was also involved in this maintenance work. Although her practices are not rooted in subordination to the boys, she is still acquiescent in prevailing gender hierarchies. Her practices, no less than those of the "girlies" and the "nice girls," are confirmatory of male superiority.

Connell writes that "it is perfectly logical to talk about masculine women or masculinity in women's lives, as well as men's" (Connell, 1995, p. 163). However, so-called "masculine" girls do not seem to disrupt but rather appear to endorse existing gender hierarchies. All the girls at various times were acting in ways which bolstered the boys' power at the expense of their own. Even Jodie's performance of a surrogate masculinity works to cement rather than transform the gender divide. As a consequence, the radical aspects of transgressive femininities like those of Jodie's are undermined by their implicit compliance with gender hierarchies. Being one of the boys seems to result in greater social power but it conscripts Jodie into processes Sharon Thompson (1994) identifies as "raging misogyny." In my field notes, there are 16 examples of Jodie asserting that "boys are better than girls." Jodie's case is an extreme example of the ways in which girls' ventriloquising of the dominant culture's denigration of femininity and female relations can serve to disconnect them from other girls (Brown, 1998).

Conclusion

Performing gender is not straightforward; rather, it is confusing. The seduction of binaries such as male:female, boy:girl often prevents us from seeing the full range of diversity and differentiation existing within one gender as well as between categories of male and female. Both the girls and boys in 3R were actively involved in the production of gendered identities, constructing gender through a variety and range of social processes (Kerfoot & Knight, 1994). Yet, within this "gender work," social and cultural differences generate the particular toolkit of cultural resources individual children have available to them. There is a multiplicity of femininities and masculinities available in this primary classroom. But this is not to suggest that these children have myriad choices of which variant of femininity and masculinity to assume. They do not. Class, ethnicity and emergent sexualities all play their part, and constrain as well as create options.

Pyke argues that:

Hierarchies of social class, race and sexuality provide additional layers of complication. They form the structural and cultural contexts in which gender is enacted in everyday life, thereby fragmenting gender into multiple masculinities and femininities. (Pyke, 1996, p. 531)

Yet, despite the multiple masculinities and femininities manifested in 3R, there is evidence of hegemonic masculinity in this classroom no less than outside in the wider social world. Within such a context, it makes sense for girls to seek to resist traditional discourses of subordinate femininity. Yet, attempting to take up powerful positions through articulation with, and investment in, dominant masculinities serves to reinforce rather than transform the gender divide. As a consequence, the prevailing gender order is only occasionally disrupted, in particular by the "spice girls" through their sex play and objectification of a number of the boys and also, paradoxically, through their working-class status. Unlike the "nice girls" whose activities are circumscribed through being positioned by the boys as a contagious, polluting other, the "spice girls'" positioning as "rough" in relation to sensitive middle-class boys allows them to take up a "polluting" assignment (Douglas, 1966) and use it as a weapon to intimidate the boys.

The girls' struggle to make meaning of themselves as female constitutes a struggle in which gendered peer group hierarchies such as those in 3R position boys as "better" despite a mass of evidence to show they are neither as academically successful nor as well behaved as girls in the classroom. Peer group discourses constructed girls as harder working, more mature and more socially skilled. Yet, all the boys and a significant number of the girls, if not subscribing to the view that boys are better, adhered to the view that it is better being a boy. There are clearly confusions within the gender work in this classroom. To talk of dominant femininity is to generate a contradiction in terms because it is dominant versions of femininity which subordinate the girls to the boys. Rather, transgressive discourses and the deviant femininities they generate like Jodie's "tomboy" and Debbie and Carly's espousal of "girl power" accrue power in both the male and female peer group, and provide spaces for girls to escape gender subordination by the boys.

On the surface, gender relations in this classroom are continually churned up and realigned in a constant process of recomposition. But beneath, at a more subterranean level of knowing and making sense, both boys and girls seem to operate with entrenched dispositions in which being a boy is still perceived to be the more preferable subject positioning. Despite the contemporary focus, both within and without the classroom, on "girl power" (Arlidge, 1999), as Jean Anyon (1983) found almost 20 years ago, it appears that girls' subversions and transgressions are nearly always contained within, and rarely challenge, the existing structures. For much of the time, girls are "trapped in the very contradictions they would transcend." Girls' contestation may muddy the surface water of gender relations, but the evidence of this classroom indicates that the ripples only occasionally reach the murky depths of the prevailing gender order. Within both the localised and dominant discourses that these children draw on, being a boy is still seen as best by all the boys and a significant number of the girls.

Children may both create and challenge gender structures and meanings. However, for much of the time for a majority of the girls and boys in 3R, gender either operates as opposition or hierarchy or most commonly both at the same time. As Janet Holland and her colleagues found in relation to the adolescents in their study, the girls just as much as the boys in this class were "drawn into making masculinity powerful" (Holland et al., 1998, p. 30). The contemporary orthodoxy that girls are doing better than boys masks the complex messiness of gender relations in which, despite girls' better educational attainment, within this peer group, the prevalent view is still that it's better being a boy.

Despite the all-pervading focus on narrow, easily measured, learning outcomes in British state schooling, learning in classrooms is much wider than test results suggest. While test results indicate that girls are more successful educationally than boys, it appears that in this primary classroom girls and boys still learn many of the old lessons of gender relations which work against gender equity. Sue Heath (1999, p. 293) argues that there is a need for school-based work that sensitively addresses issues of gender identity and masculinities within a pro-feminist framework. There is also an urgent need for work that addresses the construction and performance of femininities.

References

Anyon, J. (1983) Intersections of gender and class: accommodation and resistance by working-class and affluent females to contradictory sex-role ideologies, in: S. Walker & L. Barton (Eds.) *Gender, Class and Education* (Lewes, Falmer Press).

Arlidge, J. (1999) Girl power gives boys a crisis of confidence, *Sunday Times*, 14 March.

Arnot, M. (1982) Male hegemony, social class and women's education, *Journal of Education*, 16, pp. 64–89.

Arnot, M., David, M. & Weiner, G. (1999) *Closing the Gender Gap: postwar education and social change* (Cambridge, Polity Press).

Ball, S. J. (1994) *Educational Reform* (Buckingham, Open University Press).

Bennett, C. (1996) The boys with the wrong stuff, *Guardian*, 6 November.

Blackmore, J. (1999) *Troubling Women: feminism, leadership and educational change* (Buckingham, Open University Press).

Brown, L. M. (1998) *Raising Their Voices: the politics of girls' anger* (Cambridge, MA, Harvard University Press).

Clarricoates, K. (1978) Dinosaurs in the classroom: a re-examination of some aspects of the "hidden" curriculum in primary schools, *Women's Studies International Forum*, 1, pp. 353–364.

Connell, R. W. (1987) *Gender and Power* (Sydney, Allen & Unwin).

———. (1995) *Masculinities* (Cambridge, Polity Press).

Connolly, P. (1998) *Racism, Gender Identities and Young Children* (London, Routledge).

Coward, R. (1999) The feminist who fights for the boys, *Sunday Times*, 20 June.

Davies, B. (1993) *Shards of Glass* (Sydney, Allen & Unwin).

Davies, P., Williams, J. & Webb, S. (1997) Access to higher education in the late twentieth century: policy, power and discourse, in: J. Williams (Ed.) *Negotiating Access to Higher Education* (Buckingham, Open University Press).

Douglas, M. (1966) *Purity and Danger: an analysis of concepts of pollution and taboo* (London, Routledge & Kegan Paul).

Epstein, D., Elwood, J., Hey, V. & Maw, J. (1998) *Failing Boys? Issues in Gender and Achievement* (Buckingham, Open University Press).

Fine, M. & Macpherson, P. (1992) Over dinner: feminism and adolescent female bodies, in: M. Fine (Ed.) *Disruptive Voices: the possibilities of feminist research* (Ann Arbor, MI, University of Michigan Press).

Francis, B. (1998) *Power Plays: primary school children's construction of gender, power and adult work* (Stoke-on-Trent, Trentham Books).

———. (1999) Modernist reductionism or post-structuralist relativism: can we move on? An evaluation of the arguments in relation to feminist educational research, *Gender and Education*, 11, pp. 381–394.

Heath, S. (1999) Watching the backlash: the problematisation of young women's academic success in 1990's Britain, *Discourse*, 20, pp. 249–266.

Hey, V. (1997) *The Company She Keeps: an ethnography of girls' friendship* (Buckingham, Open University Press).

Holland, J., Ramazanoglu, C., Sharpe, S. & Thomson, R. (1998) *The Male in the Head: young people, heterosexuality and power* (London, Tufnell Press).

Gee, J. P., Hull, G. & Lankshear, C. (1996) *The New Work Order* (London, Allen & Unwin).

Griffin, C. (1995) Absences that matter: constructions of sexuality in studies of young women friendship groups, paper presented at the *Celebrating Women's Friendship Conference*, Alcuin College, University of York, 8 April.

Jackson, D. (1998) Breaking out of the binary trap: boys' underachievement, schooling and gender relations, in: D. Epstein, J. Elwood, V. Hey & J. Maw (Eds.) *Failing Boys? Issues in Gender and Achievement* (Buckingham, Open University Press).

James, A., Jenks, C. & Prout, A. (1998) *Theorising Childhood* (Cambridge, Polity Press).

Jones, A. (1993) Becoming a "girl": post-structuralist suggestions for educational research, *Gender and Education*, 5, pp. 157–166.

Katz, A. (1999) Crisis of the "low can-do" boys, *Sunday Times*, 21 March.

Kenway, J. (1995) Masculinities in schools: under siege, on the defensive and under reconstruction, *Discourse*, 16, pp. 59–79.

Kenway, J. & Willis, S. with Blackmore, J. & Rennie, L. (1999) *Answering Back: girls, boys and feminism in schools* (London, Routledge).

Kerfoot, D. & Knight, D. (1994) Into the realm of the fearful: identity and the gender problematic, in: H. L. Radtke & H. J. Stam (Eds.) *Power/Gender: social relations in theory and practice* (London, Sage).

Lakoff, R. T. (1975) *Language and Woman's Place* (New York, Harper & Row).

Lucey, H. & Walkerdine, V. (1999) Boys' underachievement: social class and changing masculinities, in: T. Cox (Ed.) *Combating Educational Disadvantage* (London, Falmer Press).

Mac an Ghaill, M. (1988) *Young, Gifted and Black: student–teacher relations in the schooling of black youth* (Buckingham, Open University Press).

Maclure, M. (1994) Language and discourse: the embrace of uncertainty, *British Journal of Sociology of Education*, 15, pp. 283–300.

Mirza, S. H. (1992) *Young, Female and Black* (London, Routledge).

Pattman, R. & Phoenix, A. (1999) Constructing self by constructing the "other": 11–14 year old boys' narratives of girls and women, paper presented at the Gender and Education Conference, University of Warwick, 29–31 March.

Pyke, K. D. (1996) Class-based masculinities: the interdependence of gender, class and interpersonal power, *Gender & Society*, 10, pp. 527–549.

Reay, D. (1990) Working with boys, *Gender and Education*, 2, pp. 269–282.

Sewell, T. (1997) *Black Masculinities and Schooling: how black boys survive modern schooling* (Stoke-on-Trent, Trentham Books).

Skelton, C. (1997) Primary boys and hegemonic masculinities, *British Journal of Sociology of Education*, 18, pp. 349–369.

———. (1999) "A passion for football": dominant masculinities and primary schooling, paper presented to the British Educational Research Association Conference, University of Sussex, 2–5 September.

Smithers, R. (1999) Self-esteem the key for macho boys who scorn "uncool" school, *Guardian*, 16 March.

Thompson, S. (1994) What friends are for: on girls' misogyny and romantic fusion, in: J. Irvine (Ed.) *Sexual Cultures and the Construction of Adolescent Identities* (Philadelphia, PA, Temple University Press).

Thorne, B. (1993) *Gender Play: girls and boys in school* (Buckingham, Open University Press).

Walkerdine, V. (1991) *Schoolgirl Fictions* (London, Verso).

———. (1997) *Daddy's Girl: young girls and popular culture* (London, Macmillan).

Walkerdine, V., Lucey, H. & Melody, J. (2000) Class, attainment and sexuality in late twentieth-century Britain, in: C. Zmroczer & P. Mahony (Eds.) *Women and Social Class: international feminist perspectives* (London: UCL Press).

Weiner, G., Arnot, M. & David, M. (1997) Is the future female? Female success, male disadvantage and changing gender patterns in education, in: A. H. Halsey, P. Brown, H. Lauder & A. Stuart-Wells (Eds.) *Education: culture, economy and society* (Oxford, Oxford University Press).

Wight, D. (1996) Beyond the predatory male: the diversity of young Glaswegian men's discourses to describe heterosexual relationships, in: L. Adkins & V. Merchant (Eds.) *Sexualising the Social: power and the organisation of sexuality* (London, Macmillan).

Wilkinson, H. (1994) *No Turning Back: generations and the genderquake* (London, Demos).

———. (1999) The Thatcher legacy: power feminism and the birth of girl power, in: N. Walters (Ed.) *On the Move: feminism for a new generation* (London, Virago).

Williams, J. (Ed.) (1997) *Negotiating Access to Higher Education* (Buckingham, Open University Press).

Willis, P. (1977) *Learning to Labour: how working class kids get working class jobs* (Farnborough, Saxon House).

Yates, L. (1997) Gender equity and the boys debate: what sort of challenge is it? *British Journal of Sociology of Education*, 18, pp. 337–348.

Policing Masculinities: Investigating the Role of Homophobia and Heteronormativity in the Lives of Adolescent School Boys

WAYNE MARTINO

. . . How do adolescent boys fashion for themselves a particular form of subjectivity or masculinity? What practices do they engage in to decipher "who they are"? How are certain desires formed within a regime of knowledge-power relations that serve as an index of their masculinity? In other words, what enables the adolescent boy to recognize himself as a proper incumbent of certain categories of masculinity? (see also Coleman, 1990). . . .

The Research Method

The interviews included in this paper were part of my doctoral research into the construction of adolescent masculinities at a Catholic, co-educational high school in Perth, Western Australia. The school draws on a mainly white, middle-class population. Having been a teacher at the school and having taught many, though not all, of the boys interviewed, it was easy to find research participants. . . .

The fact that the researcher was acquainted with the boys in this study, however, might pose some concerns. While students might feel more comfortable with and trust a researcher they know with more personal information, they could also provide specific responses they think the researcher wants from them. Furthermore, some of the boys who had taken classes with the researcher might have acquired a vocabulary and an understanding with which to articulate specific issues. Consequently, the boys might be

more aware of the researcher's language use, tone, and inflection so that they could "read" the many meanings and intentions behind the questions posed to them. Despite these limitations, however, arguably certain benefits accrued by virtue of the researcher-participants classroom involvements in terms of the boys feeling comfortable and open to express their thoughts and opinions without the fear that their masculinity would be questioned. In fact, many of the boys stated that they would not have felt comfortable discussing their lives at school and their peer relationships with someone they did not know very well or like. . . .

Regulatory Practices and Peer Group Masculinities

At the school where this research was conducted, a dominant group consisting of approximately thirty boys regularly occupied a space on the oval where they played football (see Martino, 1999a). This group wielded considerable power and was identified as the "footballers." While it is important to avoid categorizing these boys as a homogenous group, it is important nonetheless to stress that all the boys interviewed identified them as a distinctive peer group—known as the "footballer/ surfie kind of guys." Thus, these boys had a recognizable identity and presence at the school and were perceived to wield power. This is not to deny,

Wayne Martino, "Policing Masculinities: Investigating the Role of Homophobia and Heteronormativity in the Lives of Adolescent School Boys," *Journal of Men's Studies*, Vol. 8, No. 2 (Winter 2000), pp. 213–236. Copyright © 2000 by the Men's Studies Press, LLC. Reprinted by permission of SAGE Publications.

though, that within the "footballers" there were hierarchies of power operating, as Steve testifies (see Martino, 1997, 1999a).

Steve,[1] a former member of the footballer group, rejected these boys because of the abusive treatment he received from them. Many of the "footballers" thought that Steve, who was a team captain, had a "big head" and consequently became a target for their abuse. What is interesting is that his own experiences of marginalization enabled him to reject the footballers' homophobic practices directed at other boys. When I ask him to explain his relations to other peer groups at school, he stated that "we don't hassle other people." This led him to describe the different groups he observed at school, while focusing on the power of the "footballers" to police other boys through practices of homophobic denigrations.

> STEVE: . . . there's sort of Smith and his mates [the "footballers"]—all their group . . . hangs around the oval. And then there's ours [Steve's group]. And a group that hangs around the basketball court. And then there's another group, [which] Smith's group thinks [are] "faggots."
>
> WM: They think who's a "faggot"?
>
> STEVE: The fourth group, which is Murray, Rob Murray, and Friedman.
>
> WM: So how do you know that they [Steve's group] think they're "faggots"?
>
> STEVE: 'Cause I used to hang around with them.
>
> WM: So they used to talk about them?
>
> STEVE: Yeah.
>
> WM: Why? What leads them to label them in that way, do you think?
>
> STEVE: Maybe because the other group they hang around—they're girls and boys. So they like sit around in a circle. They'll sit around with girls and everything whereas Smith and all that, they'd sit around [with] just boys and then the girls would be off somewhere else, so they used to think these guys had a bit of feminine side to 'em, so they'd tell them they're "poofters" or something like that.

> WM: What made them make that judgement—because the girls were there—they talked to girls?
>
> STEVE: I dunno. Well Ryan, he's got a sort of a "poofter" voice, which everyone picks up and gives him shit about.
>
> WM: And he's a part of that group?
>
> STEVE: Yeah . . . and then there's Friedman, well, he was, there was a rumor going around that he got kicked out, or he left X school because he got caught wanking himself or something like that—I'm not quite sure. So everyone labeled him as a "faggot." But I talk to him all the time, he's all right. We associate with this group all the time, so it's all right.
>
> WM: So you're saying these guys who talk and sit with the girls get treated badly by just that one group, by the "footballers"?
>
> STEVE: Yeah, they're teased, yeah.

What is interesting is that Ryan and Friedman are members of two distinct groups. Ryan has a small group of friends who are all girls, but Steve places him in the same group as the "handballers" (of which Friedman is a member)—those boys who are distinguished as "non-footballers"—who also sometimes sit and talk to girls during the break. Perhaps this is beside the point because Ryan, and other boys who form part of the "handballer" group, are targeted by the "footballers" on the basis of their assumed homosexuality. They are differentiated by the "footballers" on a number of counts, but primarily in terms of their engagement in handball and their association with girls. This leads them to be viewed as "having a bit of a feminine side to them" and forms the basis for attributions of homosexuality. Moreover, Ryan is considered to have a "poofy voice" and Friedman also has a reputation from a previous school because he "got caught wanking himself." This data draws attention to the regime of homophobic practices and strategies of surveillance that the powerful boys [footballers] use to police sex/gender boundaries. What is equally significant is Steve's questioning of these practices and his rejection of the rules for designating what constitutes appropriate or desirable masculinity as enacted through practices of homophobic othering and differentiation.

It is interesting, however, that Steve, while rejecting the abusive "footballers'" homophobic practices, also engages in homophobic discourse. For instance, he claims that despite the fact that Friedman was labeled a "faggot," "he was all right," and that he talked to him all the time, pointing to the role that Steve himself plays in policing his own masculinity within the limits prescribed by the norms of compulsory heterosexuality. This research, therefore, raises the issue of the need to investigate further these self-policing practices by probing boys' attitudes toward alternative sexualities and how Steve would feel if Dave were, in fact, gay.

Despite the limits of the normalizing practices in which Steve is negotiating and policing his own masculinity, his comments in relation to Dave appear to indicate that he is appealing to a sense of justice and to giving people "a fair go." This has implications for discussing issues of dominant forms of heterosexual masculinity with schoolboys that will be discussed later (see McLean, 1995).

Dave: Working at the Limits of Heterosexual Masculinities

Dave Friedman, the "handballer," who Steve mentioned above as being targeted by the "footballers," talks at length about the homophobic harassment he received at the hands of a particular group of boys while attending another school, a Catholic boys-only school. Interestingly, the "footballers" at the boys-only school are friends with Smith's footballers. So word spreads to his new school about his *reputation* as a "poofter" even before he arrives. And the reason he left the first school was due to escalating levels of homophobic harassment. What follows is Dave's account of life at the Catholic boys-only school.

> DAVE: There were these guys, and they hassled me . . . they targeted me and another guy . . . there might have been a couple of others, but it was largely associated with the fact that a lot of the things we did were perhaps

stereotypical of what they saw as being related to homosexuality.

> WM: Like?
>
> DAVE: Like at the time I did ballet, and the guy I knew, his posture and manner and everything he did was supposedly leading towards something such that they [footballers] suspect that he would turn out homosexual. So, they abused him for that, and me for that. I remember a couple of others, I can't remember what they did, but I remember distinctly that they were harassed for being homosexual. Well, they weren't, but they were seen as homosexual, whether they had a girlfriend or not, it was just that they paid no attention to sort of the facts.

Dave's attention is drawn to a regime of normalizing practices in which homophobic strategies are used against boys who are identified as homosexual on the basis of their posturing, manner, or activities like ballet. Thus, there are certain mannerisms and performative practices involving body posturing, as well as the kind of voice a boy has, which lead particular boys to be labeled as gay (see Nayak & Kehily, 1996; Walker, 1988). Furthermore, such practices are imbricated in the way that many boys learn to establish their masculinities, at the level of performativity, through processes of differentiation in which indicators of homosexuality are readily recognizable as markers of deviance from a heterosexual norm, and hence an appropriate masculinity (see Beckett, 1998; Connell, 1987, 1995; Epstein, 1994; McLean, 1996; Redman, 1996; Steinberg et al., 1997; Willis, 1977).

It is also important to note that Dave, like Steve, also engages in homophobic discourse or a form of heterosexism when he claims that boys were being harassed for being homosexual but then qualifies his comment by the assertion that they "weren't," which once again poses the question of how he would respond if they were. Would the homophobic taunting then be seen as legitimate? Once again this data points to the significant ways in which the marginalized boys also police and enact their masculinities within a regime of normalizing practices and compulsory heterosexuality.

However, what is interesting is the way that Dave develops an understanding of what motivates other boys to behave in this way. In fact, he uses the interview to try to account for the reasons as to why he is marginalized by the dominant group. Firstly, he attributes such practices to the bullies' own lack of confidence in themselves:

Socially . . . they stuck to one group, and they all drew on each other for support because I don't think they could have really survived on their own, and to get energy, I think, for confidence building. They didn't have any confidence [in] themselves, and they take pleasure in bringing other people down, tall poppy syndrome. They take other people down, which gives them a sense of satisfaction and everything, because the people they hang around with weren't really their friends. I really doubt that they were friends, but they were drawn together by a common sense of lower self-esteem, and they needed support and they drew themselves together, and they were able to profit from hurting other people.

Secondly, he attributes their behavior to innate drives or energies and lack of maturity. In fact, he mentions the influence of girls in quelling boys' tendency to display this kind of violence:

But a lot of boys didn't behave like that; they just went along with the leaders of the pack. A lot of them had influence from females from outside the school, which I think with them they reach a higher maturity at a younger age, so I think they did have influences there, but really I think with boys its in their own nature. You see boys grow up; you've got Adolf Hitler and that type of thing. They have a lot of energy in them that can be expelled either positively or negatively, and I think girls tend to be an energy that can nullify it, that if it is destructive they can stop it from going over the top. I mean because it is girls that make it seem as socially unacceptable; they condemn that type of behavior, like violent, real racist, prejudiced attitudes, that type of thing.

Here Dave tends to attribute the boys' behavior to innate drives that predispose them to act in violent ways. This is reinforced in his reference to the boys' energy that must be "expelled either positively or negatively." What is particularly interesting is that Dave explicitly mentions the role of girls in terms of their higher level of maturity that is implicitly tied to their tendency to "nullify" the violence that is enacted by boys against other boys. He appears to be drawing attention to the different norms for governing the conduct of girls who police boys' bullying practices through a condemnation of violent behaviors. This highlights the differences he encountered between the boys-only school and the coeducational school he now attends in terms of the varying levels and overt enactment of homophobic violence in each school setting. In fact, he appears to be suggesting that such a "culture" of violence was officially endorsed and socially sanctioned in the boys-only Catholic school he attended:

DAVE: I remember from, say, Year 5 that there were these very strong, very anti-homosexual feelings; everyone was very much against it. Maybe because, knowing that in the school, at this private Catholic school, the all-boys school, it was felt that obviously it was not socially acceptable and that it was very bad to feel like that. If you were a homosexual, it was very bad, it was against what society is meant to be. The values that they experienced, it said that homosexuals were just a lower form.

WM: So how did they know if someone was homosexual?

DAVE: No, they don't. They assume, if they like the person, they won't press it, if they don't like the person, which is usually the case, that is if they show any sign of weakness or compassion, then other people jump to conclusions and bring them down. So really it's a survival of the fittest. It's not very good to be sensitive. If you have no feeling and compassion or anything like that, you would survive in a place like that.

WM: It's not too good.

DAVE: This is my own personal point of view. Maybe it's a bit extremist, but it's just the way I see what happened to me in that environment. And now that I'm out of that environment, I've had a chance to analyze it and sort of observe it. I'm not viewing it with any emotions, but seeing it analytically—this is what they do and how they do it.

Thus Dave not only uses the confessional space of the interview as a form of therapy, but also as a means by which he is able to make some sense of his experiences. Here the regulatory behavior of the boys in terms of cutting down the "tall poppies" intersects with gendered regimes of practice in which particular forms of masculinity are regulated. Attention is drawn to a regime of bullying practices in which those boys who are sensitive or who display "any sign of weakness" risk becoming targets of homophobic violence at the hands of a "pack" of other boys who acquire and maintain a status at the top of a pecking order of masculinities (see Connell, 1987, 1995). This is highlighted in Dave's reference to the "survival of the fittest," which once again signals that he is drawing on a particular body of gendered knowledge that is grounded in a form of biological determinism to account for the behavior of his peers. Such behaviors, which involve enacting a form of power, are interpreted, in this particular case, as instances of boys publicly enacting and performing a stylized form of heterosexual masculinity (see Dixon, 1997; Epstein, 1997; Haywood, 1993; Nayak & Kehily, 1996; Parker, 1996; Redman, 1996; Skelton, 1997).

Many of the boys interviewed focused on the ways in which sexuality is used to police sex/gender boundaries and highlight some of the specific occasions on which it occurs in their peer groups. What is particularly interesting about Dave's final comment in the excerpt above is that it draws attention to how he is making sense of his experiences at his previous school. It is being physically removed from that environment, he indicates, which enables him to develop capacities for analyzing how particular modalities of power are operationalized within certain normalizing regimes of practice.

Dave is then asked about what life is like for him at his current school and whether he has experienced this kind of harassment there. While he claims that he has not encountered forms of

violence and abuse on the same level, he does mention how the "footballers," when he first came to the school, targeted him in this way. He talks about how the "footballers" knew some of the boys from his previous school and continued the homophobic abuse that his former peers had enacted against him. However, in this co-educational community, Dave highlights the extent to which the perpetration of such forms of violence was modified by the influence of the girls.

Despite the fact that levels of homophobic violence at his present school were not as great as in his previous educational setting, due primarily to what Dave considers girls' feminizing influence in a co-educational context, he still draws attention to the perpetration of such practices, particularly by the "footballers":

> WM: How did they give you crap?
> DAVE: It was again for my dancing. A lot of stuff like "ballet boy," I don't know; they were very unimaginative. Just a lot to do with being a woman; being homosexual was a big thing again because of dancing. That was the main problem!
> WM: Who was doing that here?
> DAVE: It was a large group at that time in Year 9. . . . I was condemned by that big group of footballers who had characters like Carl Roberts, Miles Teller, John Green and a few others.
> WM: So is that the big group on the oval?
> DAVE: Yeah.

Here Dave highlights the role of normalizing practices that involve designating ballet or dance as a feminized activity. Once again, the policing of heterosexual masculinities is framed in terms of identifying sex-inappropriate practices, which then form the basis for imputing homosexuality. It is not so much dance "itself" that poses a problem, but its *association* with the "feminine." This link is produced through a regime of practices that is imbricated in regulatory technologies of the gendered self (see Haywood, 1993; Laskey & Beavis, 1996; Mason & Tomsen, 1997; Martino, 1998b, Parker, 1996; Steinberg et al., 1997). What is emphasized by Dave and many of the boys interviewed is that the "footballers" perpetrated such sex-based harassment that functions as a means by which the latter are able to gain a "cool" or tough status as "masculine" subjects within a hierarchical peer group network (see Kessler et al., 1985; Mac an Ghaill, 1994; Walker, 1988; Willis, 1977). Thus, a certain demeanor, defined in these terms, becomes identifiable for the researcher as a particular stylized form of heterosexual masculinity that is embodied at the level of performativity (see Nayak & Kehily, 1996; Steinberg et al., 1997).

> WM: So how do you see that group on the oval?
> DAVE: I'd see them as a group that thinks themselves the most popular.
> WM: Popular? How are they popular?
> DAVE: Socially acceptable, I think, compared to the other groups whom they see as maybe inferior to them in their social acceptability.
> WM: What makes them popular do you think? Is it the things they do, their interests, the way you see them behaving?
> DAVE: I think it was for the boys their *masculinity*. . . . You had practically everyone in that group doing football, drinking beer, smoking, anything rebellious yet within the lines ruled by society as acceptable. They also talked about the women they had . . . they believed they had good looks . . . they ignored other people. I think this accounts for the whole group, they ignored others who were not in their rank, and they always kept to themselves. They considered themselves good looking and had a lot of girlfriend/boyfriend relationships, and having sex was big talk. The younger you were when you had it the first time, the better.

What is interesting is the normative ties that Dave establishes between the category of "masculinity" and a range of social practices. For Dave, displaying masculinity for these boys is linked to asserting publicly their heterosexuality by boasting about their sexual exploits with girls (see Hite, 1981; Holland, Ramazanoglu, & Sharpe, 1993; Kehily & Nayak, 1997; Wood, 1984). He also highlights the extent to which these boys bolstered such a stylized form of heterosexual masculinity through social practices that involved playing football, smoking, and drinking. On the basis of engaging in such practices and "having good looks," these boys were perceived to acquire a high-status masculinity.

Dave also mentions a group of popular girls who always talked about the "footballers" in their group and discusses their role in enforcing this model of masculinity:

> DAVE: The girls also talked about it [sex] by themselves and about the boys . . . they had top ten lists for the boys.
> WM: The girls had top ten lists?
> DAVE: Yeah, that group of popular girls, yeah. They judged the boys on good looks and their masculinity and how manly they were. It was sort of like you had the men as the roosters with them preening their feathers and going around the school kicking dirt into the face of other people and you had the girls watching to see who was the strongest, the most dominant. And the boys also would accept that male figure as the most manly of them all, the most socially acceptable, and they would look up to him. The girls would acknowledge that and also view him with the same attitude as the guys did, but it was constantly changing, though.

Here, Dave indicates how the practices of a group of girls contributed to the boys' acquisition of a particular stylized masculinity and, hence, social status. The girls' role in reinforcing a heterosexual masculinity is emphasized. Moreover, attention is drawn to the performative dimension of this masculinity by the comparison of the boys to "roosters preening their feathers." This is indicative of the boys posturing their bodies to establish a particular heterosexual masculinity that is on display, not only for the girls, but for other boys as well. The analogy is significant because it highlights the extent to which these boys learn to acquire a particular demeanor, which is readily recognizable and identifiable as an instance of displaying a stylized heterosexual masculinity (see Butler, 1990).

What is also important to note is that Dave's reference to the "footballers" as "kicking the dirt in the face of other people" describes another aspect of these boys' demeanor that is explainable in terms of their own sense of social superiority and embodied power over other boys:

WM: The "kicking of dirt in the face of other people," can you explain what you mean by that?

DAVE: I think that's more ignorance of other people. That those not in their group they pay no attention to and consider them not to be worthy of their attention. They're just totally ignored, and they feel that they don't need to interact with them at all or need to be with them at any time. . . . Also Manual Arts for these boys is a big thing, woodwork, metalwork, that type of thing, technical drawing . . . alcohol, sex, really manly things like ropemanship, callused hands, that type of thing, they find these things important . . . a lot of people are drawn into that category. You still have a lot of nice people who have a lot of potential who are drawn into this category. They're trying to be like that. I just really hope that they get out of it because a lot of people have potential in other areas, and they're wasting their time, I think.

The desirability of enacting such a form of heterosexual masculinity is further emphasized when Dave explains what he means when he describes these boys as *displaying their masculinity*:

WM: Can you talk to me about what you understand about displaying masculinity? Like you referred to that group of guys as having masculine attitudes. Can you explain what you mean by that?

DAVE: I'm not sure, but what I see as a *masculine* attitude is that they value certain things like bodily physical strength and attractiveness like they have to be physically attractive to the opposite sex as in they have to be very strong, handsome, charming . . . able to get attention of the opposite sex readily and easily whenever they wanted. They also have to be sport orientated, very sporty, very fit, able to do any sport and do it well. Intelligent, well it's not always good to not have a brain so they definitely want a bit of intelligence,

but they don't put too much emphasis on being brainy; it's more like not being too thick or stupid.

Dave's comments here draw attention to the stylized demeanor of the "footballers." The requirements for displaying a particular heterosexual masculinity are spelt out in terms of demonstrating physical strength, being able to attract the opposite sex readily, and engaging actively in sports. Moreover, Dave claims that boys need to balance not appearing too stupid, while avoiding presenting themselves as too intelligent, because both positions contravene the normalizing boundaries within which a high-status masculinity is enacted (see Gilbert & Gilbert, 1998; Martino, 1999b).

James: The Pervasive Role of Homophobic Practices

The effects of such practices in which sexuality is deployed as a means of policing gender boundaries for boys is also highlighted by James, aged 17, who had been harassed on the basis of his imputed homosexuality. In fact, his interview is used to describe a regime of social relations and practices in which heterosexual masculinities are policed through the deployment of homophobic strategies that are bodily and verbally enacted (see Butler, 1995; Flood, 1997; Mills, 1996; Nayak & Kehily, 1996; Ward, 1995). James had been the brunt of homophobic abuse and used the interview to make sense of why he had been targeted. He recounts a series of experiences involving encounters with various boys on the bus that he caught to and from school.

On his way to school one morning, a group of boys from one of the local high schools started calling James names. Initially, he was targeted as an "art boy" because he was carrying an art file. But the harassment escalated, and they began calling him "fag boy." Moreover, he claims that what exacerbated the harassment was the fact that one of his friends, Andrew, who always caught the bus with him, was a Year 9 boy, aged 14. He describes Andrew in the following way:

To me he is like my little brother because I don't have a little brother. He just comes over whenever he wants and does whatever he wants; he's good to be around. Even though people might think why hang around with a 14 year old, but I don't really care because he is like a good friend, and he like catches the bus. He always follows me around sometimes.

The homophobic harassment persisted, and Andrew also became implicated in the abuse that is directed at James, with their sexuality questioned. The boys at the back of the bus continued to target James and Andrew, calling them names and throwing objects at both. James indicated that he became very angry and tried to ignore the harassment. Eventually he took another bus to avoid being targeted. However, on this other bus, another group of Year 10 students from his own school started to harass him in much the same way as the previous group of boys.

In his interview, James questioned why he was the target of homophobic practices. He attempted to understand these boys' behavior.

I mean like I don't even know these people, and they call me "art boy" because I've got my file. No matter how many people are there at the bus stop, they always do it, no matter what, and I don't know why. I mean I don't know why these people insist on labeling, singling me out; they don't even know me. Maybe I look like a fag or something, or I deserve to be called a fag because I do art; hey, I just can't stand it. The thing that really irritates [me] is the fact that the bus is full of all these students from other schools as well and you can see them. They just look out for me, and they just go, "Yeah, those guys must be right!" They just look at you while the idiots at the back are abusing you, and they just look and think, "What's going on?" or you know, "Oh, yeah, he looks like a fag," or they just look at you blankly. They don't really give a shit, and you think one of them might turn around and say, you know, "What the hell are you doing that for? You don't even know him."

What is significant here again is James's deployment of homophobic discourse in self-monitoring and policing a particular form of hegemonic heterosexual masculinity. For instance, he makes the comment that maybe he deserves to be called "a fag" because he studies art, which raises issues about his own internalized homophobia. This data once again highlights the need for educators to develop strategies for questioning the role that homophobia plays in the regulation and formation of masculinities in the lives of boys at school.

James is also calling for support in a situation in which he feels quite helpless and angry. This call for help, which is underscored by an appeal to a sense of justice that he believes should motivate others to act on his behalf, is also reflected in his reference to the need for bus drivers to address the problem:

Almost every day when I catch the bus in the afternoon, I mean the bus I catch now in the afternoon, there is hardly anyone on it. I like to catch a bus; now when I go home from school I just like to be on my own. I hate it when there's groups of people coming my way. I get very intimidated because of all this shit. . . . I get really intimidated easily now . . . you think the bus driver might have done something like stop the bus and say don't do that; don't hang your heads out of the window. I mean one driver did, but it's never the same driver, but one driver did once, and I thought, "Oh, shit, they're going to get off and big mouth me or something and say, 'it's your fault, fag boy.'". . . It's that sort of shit that is bloody irritating; you know, just because I've got a file and I do art, I'm a fag boy. I mean, it's probably stupid in a way that we all consider them "cool." We don't actually think they're "cool," but because they're in their group with their friends, they think they're cool.

This interview with James draws attention to the regime of normalizing practices in which sex/gender boundaries are policed for adolescent boys.

Bruce: Practices of Self-Surveillance and the Gendered Dimension of Displaying Emotion

Bruce's interviews also highlight this regime of normalizing practices. He comments on the norms governing the public display of traditional forms of masculinity that emphasize the avoidance of communicating on an emotional level in peer group situations. He reads this capacity as "feminine" and claims that this is because girls are "more in touch with their emotions":

> Girls are kind of more open. I guess if guys . . . opened up to one another, . . . they might find out that they're all really the same, and that they could accept one another. Say, I open up my emotions to people, and some guys, still they'll reject you. They don't want you to say that the guy is in touch with his "feminine side," I guess. I say "feminine side" because females can get in touch with their emotions, and they're not afraid to talk about them, while a lot of guys are.

Here, Bruce identifies a particular mode of relating that is organized around quite specific norms for governing gender-specific conduct. On one level, he seems to be suggesting that enacting a particular currency of heterosexual masculinity involves an avoidance of emotions. This is reinforced through engaging in sexist practices as a principal mode of relating to other boys (see Easthope, 1986; Haywood, 1993; Holland et al., 1993; Parker, 1996; Segal, 1990; Simpson, 1994; Willis, 1977; Wood, 1984).

Bruce continues to elaborate on a generalized rule for behaving or relating, which he reads as an instance of heterosexual masculinity. The rule that boys should not show their emotions is also one that he identifies as constraining the way in which he would like to be able to relate to his male friends:

WM: So why do you think guys are afraid to express their emotions?

BRUCE: Rejection.

WM: Rejection from their friends?

BRUCE: Yeah, well I think it all comes back to rejection.

WM: What would they be rejected for, then? Why would they be rejected?

BRUCE: Um, for showing their emotions because this attitude of masculinity and this stereotype has been built up for so long, passed on from their fathers; it just keeps getting passed on generation after generation.

WM: So it's not really just a stereotype thing, is that what you're saying, that it's kind of quite "real"?

BRUCE: It's "real," definitely, with a lot of people. I'm not saying everyone's like that, but you will find a lot of it in most people. Even I must admit, um, I feel uncomfortable say, giving my best friend a big hug in front of other guys.

WM: Why?

BRUCE: Um, because that's not accepted by them; they reject that kind of idea of showing your emotions because you like this person, even though it's platonic. There's nothing sexual about it; it's just that you really like this person. You can't show that because it's like that's reserved for the opposite sex. You don't do that kind of thing; that's showing your emotions too much, and that's how we've been conditioned into being after so long, whereas females, they hug each other all the time. That's the way they are because they're friends and they like each other; they're not afraid to do that, and other females condone that. They don't reject it. So I guess there's a lot less prejudice when it comes to a showing of emotions in the female side than the male side; they're still very, I don't know, closed. They're like that little town on *Shame*, the little closed community within themselves. They're not allowed to show the real them; they have to hide that. I guess that could be attributed to years ago when the male was the breadwinner, the woman stayed at home, and that power that goes along with men and by showing your true emotions, that kind of doesn't. It doesn't reflect your power, I guess, you could say. One of the attitudes and emotions that go along with power is that you are very, you're hard, you're cold, you strive to achieve, you, um, I don't know, it's hard to express. Powerful people aren't usually real kind, friendly, open people if you know what I mean.

Bruce links boys' avoidance of expressing emotion to an "attitude of masculinity," which has been "passed on from their fathers." In so doing, he emphasizes the pivotal role of fathers and adult men in establishing norms for governing their son's behavior as gendered subjects. Moreover, what is significant is that Bruce has developed quite specific capacities for reading masculinity and is applying them to his own practices and those of other boys. For example, his reference to the Australian film, *Shame*, which dealt with the pack rape of a 16-year-old girl in an outback town, is pertinent in this respect. This film was studied in an English class conducted by the researcher where issues around masculinity were discussed at length. Bruce is drawing on these understandings to make sense of his own lived experiences of masculinity. He reiterates the extent to which specific norms govern regimes of practices for boys in terms of policing sex/gender boundaries (see Flood, 1997; Laskey & Beavis, 1996; McLean, 1996; Steinberg et al., 1997).

Conclusion

Foucault's work (1978, 1984, 1987) has been particularly useful in serving as an interpretive frame for analyzing the normalizing regimes of practice through which various masculinities are enacted. The data included in this paper have been used to draw attention to several boys' understanding and rejection of certain norms governing the production of a particular form of hegemonic heterosexual masculinity (Boulden, 1996; Butler, 1995; Epstein & Johnson, 1998; Frank, 1987; Martino, 1998b; McLean, 1996). It has also highlighted the powerful role that sexuality plays in terms of how these boys police and monitor their masculinities within heteronormative regimes of internalized homophobia. The willingness of these boys to question such norms on another level, however, appears to be related to their own active positioning against the "footballers," who are in the business of policing acceptable forms of masculinity through a regime of homophobic practices. It is important to highlight that not all Anglo-Australian boys necessarily embrace hegemonic masculinity in all its various forms. Dave, through his subjection to a regime of homophobic practices enacted by hegemonic boys at the schools he attended, demonstrates capacities for questioning these normalizing

practices. Steve, while not being a target of homophobic harassment himself, is also critical of the "footballers'" behavior because he, too, has been rejected and treated unfairly by them. Bruce, while not appearing to have been treated unfairly, is starting to reflect on what he perceives to be the limits and constraints imposed on him by a set of norms governing the production of hegemonic-heterosexual masculinity.

However, what needs to be highlighted is that these boys (except for Bruce), while questioning the homophobic practices of the "footballers," are themselves still caught up in normalizing regimes for policing heterosexual masculinity. This raises crucial questions about the pivotal role that sexuality plays in the formation and regulation of gendered subjectivity for all these boys.

The implications of this are significant in signaling a move forward in attempting to address issues of masculinity and homophobia in schools. As Britzman (1995) argues, crucial questions about how normality is constructed and naturalized need to be addressed in schools (see Martino, 1999b). In light of the research documented in this paper, it is indisputable that we have to find ways to help students to problematize the whole idea of what is considered to be natural and given and how we have come to understand ourselves in these terms. These questions, as illustrated in this paper, are directly related to how many boys come to understand themselves as appropriately masculine (see Epstein, 1998; Jackson, 1998; Martino, 1999a). However, the boys' willingness to talk about their experiences and issues of masculinity at school is noteworthy and may well serve as a platform for further addressing questions and issues of homophobia. Moreover, the whole idea of being treated fairly and with respect emerges as a strong force in these boys' accounts of their experiences at school. With Bruce, these issues are also present as he grapples with the regimes of compulsory heterosexuality that prescribe the limits of acceptable masculinity within peer group cultures at school (Mac an Ghail, 1994; Walker, 1988). In light of their comments, it would appear that addressing issues of masculinity within a social justice framework that appeals to students' sense of justice may well have productive consequences in addressing issues of power and masculinities in schools (see Nickson, 1996).

Several boys, however, claimed that they had never been given the opportunity to discuss such issues. As Shaun, another one of the interviewees claims, "There's no opportunity for guys to get down and think about what they're doing and why they are doing it and stuff like that."

This sentiment is also reiterated by Eric, who asserts that:

> . . . everything is seen as one type of male stereotype, but it's a particular version of masculinity. You have to be interested in sports, you have to like girls and all the rest of it, and it is always fed to you from day one, and you've never actually seen the other version of masculinity . . . and all of a sudden you just see this other version of masculinity, and you've never like, you know, through your education, you've never been told about it. . . .

In light of these comments that explicitly advocate the need for more open discussion about what constitutes masculinity, there are definite possibilities for engaging boys in actively exploring the impact and effects of heteronormative and homophobic currencies of masculinity on their lives. However, professional development for teachers and whole school approaches to dealing with gender issues are necessary in order to create a culture that is committed to interrogating those discourses that naturalize masculinity and in so doing present it as an unalterable given that is driven by "some kind of biological determinism" or essence (Jackson & Salisbury, 1996, p. 104; see also Gender Equity Taskforce, 1997; Gilbert & Gilbert, 1998; House of Representatives Standing Committee, 1994; Martino, 1998b). These discourses continue to be articulated in Australia within the popularist literature on boys (Biddulph, 1994, 1997) and, as Salisbury and Jackson (1996) argue, inform and shape many teachers' perceptions of boys' conduct in schools. In light of this and current research into boys and schooling, it is imperative that such interventions be executed in the best interests of both girls and boys. By opening spaces for discussion about masculinity and how it becomes normalized

in schools, it would appear, in light of what the boys have to say in this paper, that possibilities for successfully implementing a critical practice designed to encourage students to question the role that homophobia and heteronormativity play in their lives can be initiated. By appealing to students' sense of justice within a framework that stresses mutual respect and care for others, discussions can be conducted in schools that are designed to involve students in critically evaluating masculinities and their normalizing effects (Martino, 1995, 1998a).

Note

1. The boys' names used in this paper are pseudonyms. All names have been changed to ensure anonymity and to guarantee confidentiality.

References

Beckett, L. (1998). *Everyone is special: A handbook for teachers on sexuality education.* Brisbane: Association of Women Educators.

Biddulph, S. (1994). *Manhood.* Sydney: Finch Publishing.

Biddulph, S. (1997). *Raising boys.* Sydney: Finch Publishing.

Boulden, K. (1996). Keeping a straight face: Schools, students and homosexuality—Part 2. In L. Laskey & C. Beavis (Eds.), *Schooling and sexualities: Teaching for a positive sexuality* (pp. 175–185). Geelong: Deakin University for Education and Change.

Britzman, D. (1995). Is there a queer pedagogy? Or stop reading straight. *Educational Theory, 45,* 151–165.

Butler, J. (1990). *Gender trouble: Feminism and the subversion of identity.* London: Routledge.

Butler, J. (1995). The poof paradox: Homogeneity and silencing in three Hobart high schools. In L. Laskey & C. Beavis (Eds.), *Schooling and sexualities: Teaching for a positive sexuality* (pp. 131–149). Geelong: Deakin University for Education and Change.

Coleman, W. (1990). Doing masculinity/doing theory. In J. Hearn & D. Morgan (Eds.), *Men, masculinities and social theory* (pp. 186–199). London: Unwin Hyman.

Connell, R. W. (1995). *Masculinities.* Sydney: Allen & Unwin.

Connell, R. W. (1987). *Gender and power.* Cambridge: Polity Press.

Dixon, C. (1997). Pete's tool: Identity and sex-play in the design and technology classroom. *Gender and Education, 9,* 89–104.

Easthope, A. (1986). *What a man's gotta do: The masculine myth in popular culture.* London: Paladin.

Epstein, D. (1994). *Challenging lesbian and gay inequalities in education.* Buckingham & Philadelphia: Open University Press.

Epstein, D. (1997). Boyz' own stories: Masculinities and sexualities in schools. *Gender and Education, 9,* 105–115.

Epstein, D. (1998). Real boys don't work: "Underachievement," masculinity and the harassment of "sissies." In D. Epstein, J. Elwood, V. Hey, & J. Maw (Eds.), *Failing boys?* (pp. 96–108). Buckingham: Open University Press.

Epstein, D., & Johnson, R. (1998). *Schooling sexualities.* Buckingham: Open University Press.

Flood, M. (1997). *Homophobia and masculinities among young men (Lessons in becoming a straight man).* Paper presented at O'Connell Education Centre, Canberra, 22 April.

Foucault, M. (1978). *The history of sexuality: Volume 1.* (R. Hurley, Trans.). New York: Vintage.

Foucault, M. (1980). *Michel Foucault: Power/knowledge: Selected interviews and other writings 1972–1977.* C. Gordon (Ed.). Sussex: Harvester.

Foucault, M. (1984). Preface to *The history of sexuality,* Volume II. In P. Rabinow (Ed.), *The Foucault reader* (pp. 333–339). London: Penguin.

Foucault, M. (1988). Technologies of the self. In L. Martin, H. Gutman, & P. Hutton (Eds.), *Technologies of the self* (pp. 16–49). Amherst, MA: The University of Massachusetts Press.

Frank, B. (1987). Hegemonic heterosexual masculinity. *Studies in Political Economy, 24,* 159–170.

Gender Equity Taskforce. (1997). *Gender equity: A framework for Australian schools.* Canberra: Ministerial Council for Employment, Education, Training and Youth Affairs.

Gilbert, R., & Gilbert, P. (1998). *Masculinity goes to school.* Sydney: Allen & Unwin.

Haywood, C. (1993). *Using sexuality: An exploration into the fixing of sexuality to make male identities in a mixed sex sixth form.* Unpublished master's thesis, University of Warwick, UK.

Hite, S. (1981). *The Hite report on male sexuality.* New York: Knopf.

Holland, J., Ramazanoglu, C., & Sharpe, S. (1993). *Wimp or gladiator: Contradictions in acquiring masculine sexuality.* London: Tufnell Press.

House of Representatives Standing Committee. (1994). *Sticks and stones: Report on violence in Australian schools.* Canberra: Australian Government Publishing Service.

Jackson, D. (1998). Breaking out of the binary trap: Boys' underachievement, schooling and gender relations. In D. Epstein, J. Elwood, V. Hey, & J. Maw (Eds.), *Failing boys?* (pp. 77–95). Buckingham: Open University Press.

Jackson, D., & Salisbury, J. (1996). Why should secondary schools take working with boys seriously? *Gender and Education, 8,* 103–115.

Kehily, M., & Nayak, A. (1997). "Lads and laughter": Humor and the production of heterosexual hierarchies. *Gender and Education, 9,* 69–87.

Kessler, S., Ashenden, D., Connell, R., & Dowsett, G. (1985). Gender relations in secondary schooling. *Sociology of Education, 58,* 34–88.

Laskey, L., & Beavis, C. (1996). *Schooling and sexualities.* Geelong: Deakin University.

Mac an Ghaill, M. (1994). *The making of men.* Buckingham: Open University Press.

Martino, W. (1995). Deconstructing masculinity in the English classroom: A site for reconstituting gendered subjectivity. *Gender and Education, 7,* 205–220.

Martino, W. (1997). "A bunch of arseholes": Exploring the politics of masculinity for adolescent boys in schools. *Social Alternatives, 16,* 39–43.

Martino, W. (1998a). "Dickheads," "poofs," "try hards," and "losers": Critical literacy for boys in the English classroom, *English in Aotearoa, 35,* 31–57.

Martino, W. (1998b). "It's all a bit of a mess really!": Addressing homophobia in schools. In L. Becket (Ed.), *Everyone is special!* (pp. 33–39). Brisbane: Association of Women Educators.

Martino, W. (1999a). "Cool boys," "party animals," "squids," and "poofters": Interrogating the dynamics and politics of adolescent masculinities in school. *British Journal of the Sociology of Education, 20*(2), 239–263.

Martino, W. (1999b). "It's ok to be gay": Interrupting straight thinking in the English classroom. In W. Letts & J. Sears (Eds.), *Queering elementary education* (pp. 137–149). Colorado: Rowan & Littlefield.

Mason, G., & Tomsen, S. (1997). *Homophobic violence*. Sydney: The Hawkins Press.

McLean, C. (1996). Men, masculinity and heterosexuality. In L. Laskey & C. Beavis (Eds.), *Schooling and sexualities: Teaching for a positive sexuality* (pp. 25–35). Geelong: Deakin University, Centre for Education and Change.

McLean, C. (1995). "What about the boys?" *South Australian Education of Girls and Female Students' Association Journal, 4*(3), 15–25.

Mills, M. (1996). "Homophobia kills": A disruptive moment in the educational politics of legitimization. *British Journal of Sociology of Education, 17*(3), 315–326.

Nayak, A., & Kehily, M. (1996). Playing it straight: Masculinities, homophobias and schooling. *Journal of Gender Studies, 5*(2), 211–230.

Nickson, A. (1996). Keeping a straight face: Schools, students and homosexuality—Part 1. In L. Laskey & C. Beavis (Eds.), *Schooling and sexualities: Teaching for a positive sexuality* (pp. 161–174). Geelong: Deakin University for Education and Change.

Parker, A. (1996). The construction of masculinity within boys' physical education. *Gender and Education, 8*(2), 114–157.

Redman, P. (1996). Curtis loves Ranjit: Heterosexual masculinities, schooling and pupils' sexual cultures. *Educational Review, 48*(2), 175–182.

Rich, A. (1980). Compulsory heterosexuality and lesbian experience. *Signs, 54*, 631–60.

Segal, L. (1990). *Slow motion: Changing masculinities, changing men*. London: Virago Press.

Simpson, M. (1994). *Male impersonators: Men performing masculinity*. New York: Routledge.

Skelton, C. (1997). Primary boys and hegemonic masculinities. *British Journal of the Sociology of Education, 18*(3), 349–369.

Steinberg, D. L., Epstein, D., & Johnson, R. (1997). *Border patrols: Policing the boundaries of heterosexuality*. London: Cassell.

Walker, J. C. (1988). *Louts and legends*. Sydney: Allen & Unwin.

Ward, N. (1995). "Pooftah," "wanker," "girl": Homophobic harassment and violence in schools. In *Girls & boys: Challenging perspective, building partnerships. Proceedings of the Third Conference of the Ministerial Advisory Committee on Gender Equity* (pp. 82–93). Brisbane: Ministerial Advisory Committee on Gender Equity.

Willis, P. (1977). *Learning to labour: How working class kids get working class jobs*. Westmead: Saxon House.

Wood, J. (1984). Groping towards sexism: Boys' sex talk. In A. McRobbie & M. Nava (Eds.), *Gender and generation* (pp. 54–84). London: Macmillan.

The Gender of Religion

The first time people put in an appearance in the Bible, it's gendered. "Male and female created He them" is the ungrammatical but somehow authoritative way the King James Bible puts it in Genesis (1:27). And this has always been a justification for a divinely ordained binary division between males and females.

But how can we be so sure? After all, it doesn't say "male *or* female"—as if one had to be only one and not the other. In fact, it might even mean that "He" created each of us as "male and female"—a divinely inspired androgyny.

We needn't necessarily subscribe to these positions to recognize two important things about religion and its relation to gender. First, religion, itself, at least in the Western world, is preoccupied with gender (Eastern religions are far less obsessed with gender). Indeed, prescribing the proper relationships between women and men is one of the Bible's chief preoccupations. And, second, that all such prescriptive elements are subject to multiple interpretations.

The institutional articulation of proper interpretations of doctrine—the fact that religious "experts" tell us what these rather vague prescriptive notions actually mean in everyday life—makes these timeless Biblical truths quite responsive to immediate, concrete, historical needs. For centuries, the institution of the church used certain Biblical passages to justify the utter subordination of women.

Whether articulated by Dan Brown or feminist theologians, the Biblically inspired but utterly political persecution of independent women is an indelible stain on the history of religious institutions. Stephanie Sequino provides a bird's-eye view of the relationship between gender inequality and religion.

Each generation finds the texts it needs to justify the world as that generation finds it. Today, as the formerly fixed prescriptions of the proper relationships between women and men are being challenged everywhere in the world, new generations of the observant are pointing to different, if equally canonical, texts to justify their position. John P. Bartowski and Jen'nan Ghazal Read compare Evangelical and Muslim women's view of gender and identity.

Whether in doctrine or in institutional practices, women's second-class status has generated significant resistance from women. And yet, ironically, women are far more religious than men, far more likely to go to church, and far more likely to say that God has a place in daily conversations. Just as the institution of religion is gendered, so too are the individuals who are religious. Gendered people navigate gendered institutions, and J. Edward Sumerau explores the ways in which different groups of religious women and men navigate these institutions.

Help or Hindrance? Religion's Impact on Gender Inequality in Attitudes and Outcomes

STEPHANIE SEGUINO

Introduction

Despite progress in some areas, gender inequality persists globally in key areas, such as income, education, economic security, and gender-related violence. Increased attention has been directed at the contribution of institutions to the perpetuation of gender stratification in recent years (Cavalcanti & Tavares, 2007; Guiso, Sapienza, & Zingales, 2003; Morrisson & Jütting, 2005; Sen, 1999, 2007). A good deal of evidence indicates that formal religious institutions, which shape cultural norms, social rules, and behaviors, have a measurable impact on the rigidity of gender roles and attitudes (Inglehart & Norris, 2003). There is little research, however, on whether those gender inequitable attitudes contribute to unequal outcomes for women.

Why might gender attitudes, induced by religious and other institutions, have a tangible effect on gender inequality in well-being? Embedded norms and stereotypes shape everyday behaviors and decision-making, ranging from choices about whether to lay off a woman or a man during economic downturns; to educate daughters or sons when money is scarce; or to promote a man or a woman into a managerial position. Credentials influence these decisions, of course. Objective external constraints are also part of the decision-making process (will an education increase a boy's income more than a girl's?). But in each case, the decision-maker inevitably assesses credentials through the lens of an internal gender ranking rule, influenced by external social conditions and the norms and stereotypes embedded in culture. That ranking rule is a reflection of an underlying set of power relations that are an enactment of the degree of gender stratification a society will tolerate.

Economists have sought to explain gender inequalities in wages, producing a large body of research that finds roughly 20–30% of wage gaps cannot be accounted for by gender-related productivity differences (Weichselbaumer & Winter-Ebmer, 2005). The unexplained portion of gender wage gaps has been attributed to discrimination, but economists have not progressed very far in empirically identifying the mechanisms that account for discriminatory decision-making. It is plausible that at least some of the unexplained one-third of gender wage gaps and other forms of measured gender inequality can be traced to institutions—including religious institutions—that contribute to gender hierarchal attitudes.

This paper seeks to shed light on two aspects of the role of institutions in perpetuating inequality. First, we evaluate the data to assess the contribution of religious institutions to the perpetuation of gender ideology, norms, and stereotypes, and thus social attitudes that legitimate gender inequality in social, economic, and political spheres. We do this using cross-country data on gender attitudes from the World Values Survey (WVS). The survey data permit

Stephanie Seguino, "Help or Hindrance? Religion's Impact on Gender Inequality in Attitudes and Outcomes," *World Development*, Vol. 39, No. 8 (2011), pp. 1308–1321. Reprinted with permission from Elsevier.

an assessment of the effect of individuals' degree of religiosity and their religious denomination on attitudes toward gender equality. The gender attitude questions concern rigidity of gender identity, women's roles as mothers and workers, and beliefs about gender hierarchy in employment, education, and politics. We take this analysis one step further to explore whether differences in religiosity of citizens can explain cross-country variation in objective measures of gender equality in well-being.

Religion, Religiosity, Gender

The role of religion in perpetuating norms that promote gender inequitable attitudes is complex because religious institutions themselves are not monolithic. A wide variety of voices are in evidence in religious organizations, even if dominated by hierarchical authorities. Through internal debates and struggles, religious doctrines, norms, and rules can change over time, albeit at a relatively slow pace. In hierarchical structures, however, a dominant factor in shaping gender attitudes is the views held by those at the top of the religious structure at any given point in time.

There are several explanations for why the gender norms that religious institutions instill might be gender inequitable. The first relates to religiosity as a response to economic insecurity and the second underscores the role of hierarchy in formal institutions. With regard to the former, the intensity of religious beliefs has been posited to be a response to economic insecurity and the stage of economic development (Norris & Inglehart, 2004). Assuming the link between religion and economic security is valid, we might anticipate that individuals under stress have a need for clear, rigid rules, including behavioral norms. Further, in such circumstances, survival instincts elevate the goal of high fertility in the face of excessive infant and adult mortality rates. In such a scenario, attitudes toward gender roles may be rigid and dichotomous in response to a struggle for economic survival.

The organizational structures that characterize most major religions may be a second factor. To varying degrees, the dominant organized religions have access to and control over material resources, and as such, exercise power to create and maintain social norms that perpetuate structures of power to preserve their control. Elite groups tend to capture power in institutions, and thus, patriarchal dominance in the economic sphere is likely to be replicated in religious organizations. Seen in this light, religious institutions may reflect patriarchal[1] values in order to buttress the economic, social, and political power of males to the disadvantage of women (Kardam, 2005; Norris & Inglehart, 2004; Sen, 2007). Whatever their other roles, such as solace and even social support, if religious institutions inculcate gender norms and rules that disadvantage women, they may hinder policy efforts aimed at closing gender gaps in important areas, such as education and employment.

Where norms that embody gender hierarchy and rigid roles dominate the social landscape, the heterosexual family and women's primary role as (unpaid) caretaker are emphasized. Divorce, abortion, and homosexuality contradict the social roles prescribed for women (and by implication, delineate separate roles for men) and tend to be viewed unfavorably. Further, sons tend to be more valued than daughters in patriarchal contexts.

If organized religions in their current state do indeed perpetuate gender inequitable attitudes, we might expect that people who exhibit higher degrees of religiosity hold more gender inequitable attitudes. An important question is whether the incidence of gender unequal attitudes in a country translates into gender inequality of outcomes. In other words, is there evidence that gender inequality in measures of well-being is more pronounced in countries exhibiting a greater degree of religiosity?

It is useful to consider why religiosity and dominant religion might have an impact not only on attitudes but also on real economic outcomes. Two transmission mechanisms exist. First, at the micro level, gender unequal attitudes act as a "stealth" factor, shaping everyday decisions. Employers' choices on whom to hire and whom to lay off are affected by norms regarding who in the gender hierarchy is most deserving of a job. Families make decisions on which family member should undertake paid labor or unpaid caring labor. We, therefore, might anticipate that insofar as religiosity affects norms and attitudes, there will be consequent measurable effects at the country level on gender gaps in education, the sex ratio, and shares of the labor force, to name a few.

The second transmission mechanism is the effect of religious attitudes on a government's distribution of resources (for example, for education and health care) and regulation, such as enactment and enforcement of anti-discrimination legislation in employment, and rules on access to loans, inheritance, and property ownership. In countries with dominant religions that are gender inequitable, it is possible that gender outcomes are worsened through the government channel as well.

An individual's religious denomination may influence gender norms and outcomes, implying that some religions could be more patriarchal than others. However, whether any one organized religion is more patriarchal than others is an empirical question on which there is as yet no consensus. Psacharopoulos and Tzannatos (1989) find that Muslims, Hindus, and Catholics have lower female labor force participation rates than other religions and the non-religious. Islam has been identified as significantly more patriarchal than other dominant religions on such measures as education and life expectancy (Baliamoune-Lutz, 2007; Dollar & Gatti, 1999; Fish, 2002; Forsythe & Korzeniewicz, 2000) although some recent empirical evidence challenges that view (Donno & Russet, 2004; Noland, 2005).

The debate is clearly not yet resolved. Nevertheless, these findings suggest that in addition to a person's religiosity, religious denomination may also influence gender attitudes. Based on this discussion, we hypothesize that the greater the degree of religiosity a person exhibits, the more likely s(he) is to hold gender inequitable attitudes. We make no theoretical predictions *vis-à-vis* the effect of a person's adherence to a particular religious denomination.

It is important to note that we are not able to precisely identify causality from religiosity to gender attitudes although we can assess correlation. This reflects the understanding that religiosity is itself a produced social condition, linked to, for example, the size of the welfare state, cultural value patterns, historical conditions, and social divisions that might lead to religious identification as a form

of group solidarity (Verweij, Ester, & Nauta, 1997). There are thus feedback loops between broader cultural, economic, and social conditions that manifest in religious formations.

Empirical Analysis Of Religiosity And Gender Attitudes

. . . While the amount of data appears daunting to digest, the results are in fact quite straightforward and unambiguous with regard to the effect of religiosity on gender attitudes. For all gender attitudes questions, the importance of religion in the individual's life is positively associated with gender inequitable attitudes. . . .

All denominations are associated with more gender inequitable attitudes relative to the "no religious affiliation" group on at least some of the questions. Most religious denominations are associated with restrictive attitudes on abortion and divorce compared to the "no religion" reference group. It is notable that religious denomination, more generally, has only a limited effect on attitudes in response to the prompts *It is a problem if women have more income than their husbands; Men make better political leaders;* and *A university education is more important for a boy than girl.* No major religious denomination stands out as being significantly more strongly associated with gender inequitable attitudes than the others. It is notable, however, that Protestants, Buddhists, and Hindus hold significantly more gender inequitable attitudes than the non-religious on 4 out of 9 of gender attitudes questions, more than the remaining major denominations.

We turn now to the control variables, which are themselves of independent interest. On all but one question, men hold significantly more unequal gender attitudes than women, after controlling for differences in education, age, income, and religion. These results highlight an interesting contradiction in women's collective identities as women and religious persons, given that they are on average more religious than men.[2]

Older individuals hold more gender inequitable attitudes than the young on average. This may reflect the impact of a trend toward more gender equitable attitudes globally. With women's increased labor force participation in many countries, it is possible that the young hold more gender equitable attitudes because they see mothers and other adult women taking on a wider array of roles in society, including in paid work. This is consistent with social role theory, which argues that gender attitudes are strongly impacted by children's observation of the gender roles of parents and other adults (Eagly & Diekman, 2003).

As expected, education contributes to gender-equalizing attitudes. Individuals from higher income households also hold more gender equitable attitudes, an effect that is significantly positive for all but one gender attitude question. Interestingly, household income level is not positively correlated with degree of approval of women as single mothers, suggestive of the way that gender roles are modified as the need for two household incomes rises.

Contribution of Religiosity to Gender Outcomes

We now turn to an exploration of religiosity's relationship with objective measures of gender equality via the effect on gender attitudes and views on the role of religion in government. It is useful to reiterate the possible transmission mechanisms from religion to gender outcomes. Insofar as religions inculcate attitudes that promote a gender hierarchy and rigid gender roles with women as caretakers, there can be direct effects in everyday behavior that disadvantage women. Women may feel pressure to quit work when they have children. Employers may hire or promote men over women. Parents may invest more resources in boys than girls.

An indirect effect is the influence of religious attitudes on government policies. The stronger the belief that religion should guide government decisions, the more likely we are to observe gender inequitable policies, rules, and distribution of resources, contributing to gender inequality in material well-being. Figure 1 describes pathways by which the effects of religiosity are transmitted to gender outcomes, with arrows indicating the direction of causality and hypothesized signs of the relationships noted. . . .

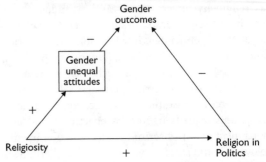

Figure 1. Religiosity Impacts on Gender and Well-Being Outcomes

To summarize, the empirical results provide overwhelming statistical evidence that the gender attitudes index has a negative and significant effect on all measures of gender equality in well-being. The results are robust across seven measures of gender equality in well-being and statistical techniques that take into account possible endogeneity of several explanatory variables.[3] The results imply that religiosity has an independent association (if not causality) with gender outcomes, via its effect on shaping gender norms and stereotypes. The transmission of this effect is not determined by the country's level of development.

Conclusion

Two questions about the persistence of gender inequality continue to reverberate. Why do societies persistently invest less in female well-being than male? And why, even when women reach adult life with equal abilities, do they fare so poorly in labor markets, in political representation, and in gaining access to positions where they have a seat at the table as decision-makers?

This paper seeks to shed light on those questions by investigating the impact of religiosity on attitudes toward gender equality. We find that religiosity is indeed strongly linked to gender inequitable beliefs. Not only religion matters, of course. The gender gap in attitudes is wide, with men showing evidence of holding more inequitable gender attitudes than women. Perhaps more heartening in terms of the potential for public policy to promote greater equality, we also found that individuals with higher levels of education and income showed evidence of holding more gender equitable views. This evidence implies that apart from its intrinsic value and role in stimulating growth, broad-based education is tied to social and institutional change on the macro level.

We find overwhelming statistical evidence that the effect of religiosity extends beyond attitudes to negatively impact several measures of gendered well-being outcomes, even after controlling for *per capita* GDP and level of development. We also found that higher-income countries perform better on some measures of gender equality, such as female-to-male population ratios, education ratios, female share of professional and technical jobs, and skilled health personnel attending births. But for several indicators—women's share of the labor force, maternity leave compensation, and the Social Watch's Gender Equality Index—higher *per capita* GDP does not give robust evidence of ameliorating women's status, suggesting that more interventionist policies may be required.

In this study, no one religion stands out as consistently more gender inequitable in its effects than all the others. This contrasts with several macrolevel studies that have examined the role of religion with a focus on Islam (Baliamoune-Lutz, 2007; Dollar, 1999; Forsythe & Korzeniewicz, 2000). The empirical evidence presented here implies that dominant religions—and not exclusively Islam—have varying effects on gender attitudes and outcomes, some positive, some negative. The emphasis in previous research placed on any one religion, therefore, seems misplaced—or at least, is not fully illuminating with regard to the effect on gender attitudes and outcomes. Of greater significance, however, is the finding that once we control for the individual's religion, we find that religiosity itself—the intensity of religious belief and the frequency of religious participation—is consistently negatively correlated with gender attitudes and outcomes.

We may infer from these results that religiosity contributes to and perpetuates hierarchical gender ideology, norms, and stereotypes. Gender norms are difficult to change. Progressively advancing the participation of women in decision-making roles and in labor market participation, however, can hasten positive change. There is some evidence that increases in women's share of employment promote gender equitable norms and stereotypes (Seguino, 2007). Similarly, evidence from India shows that political affirmative action can reduce gender bias in attitudes (Beaman, Chattopadhyay, Duflo, Pande, & Topalova, 2008). This suggests that greater efforts to increase women's paid employment—through such policies as paid parental leave, subsidized child care, and affirmative action in employment—could serve as a fulcrum for gender equitable change, along with reservation policies (quotas) on political lists to increase political participation.

There are other potential countervailing forces to those social institutions that would hinder advancement of the goal of gender equality. Academic research identifying the beneficial impact of gender equality and women's organizations that advocate for gender sensitivity in public sector spending, for example, can play a role in shaping government policies and resource distribution.

It does not appear, however, from this analysis, that religious institutions as currently structured provide a pathway for amelioration of women's unequal status. Even if in hard times, religious organizations offer women solace and some material support, the net effect on women's well-being would appear to be negative, based on the empirical results presented in this paper. These results suggest the wisdom of scrutinizing the impact on gender equality of aid funneled through religious organizations. Donors may find that religious nongovernmental organizations have a weaker record in improving women's relative well-being than non-religious organizations.

That said, religious institutions themselves are susceptible to change, albeit slow, and internal groups show evidence of advocating for progressive change. Examples abound. At a recent conference in Kuala Lumpur, Muslim women, frustrated with the patriarchal interpretation of Islamic text, met to come up with ways to demand equal rights for women (Tavernise, 2009). In the United States, Catholics for Choice and Catholics for Gay Marriage are activist groups working to change church norms and rules on homosexuality, abortion, and contraception. Formal religious institutions offer an organizational framework within which women's groups can operate, and this may lead to more rapid change than could have been imagined decades ago when gender outcomes were more unequal and global communication more limited.

Notes

1. The term patriarchy refers to a gender hierarchical system, recognizing, however, that patriarchy takes many different forms across countries and over time.

2. Based on data from all waves of the World Values Survey (WVS), 62% of men say religion is important or very important in their lives while 71% of women so identify.

3. Some studies link the degree of religiosity (inversely) to the level of development (for example, Inglehart & Norris, 2003) and, in turn, religiosity has been argued to influence the level of development (see Guiso et al., 2003). To address this, we ran another set of 3SLS [three - stage least squares] regressions with religiosity measures included as explanatory variables in the GDP regression and GDP an explanatory variable in a fourth equation estimating the determinants of religiosity (in addition to equations for gender well-being equality, GDP, and the gender attitudes index), controlling for variations in the degree of economic insecurity—infant mortality, death rates, immunization rates, and access to clean water. The gender attitudes index coefficients continued to be negative and statistically significant at the 1% level with the exception of the percentage of births attended by skilled health personnel. We ran one final set of regressions, controlling for a summary measure of gender institutions from the Jütting, Dayton-Johnson, Dreschler, and Morrisson (2008) Gender, Institutions, and Development (GID) database. Those authors provide evidence that an index of gender practices has a negative effect on gender equality in outcomes. In our regressions, the GID variable was negative and significant while the gender attitudes index retained its sign and significance in most regressions (results available on request).

References

Baliamoune-Lutz, M. (2007). Globalisation and gender inequality: Is Africa different? *Journal of African Economies, 16*(2), 301–348.

Beaman, L., Chattopadhyay, R., Duflo, E., Pande, R., & Topalova, P. (2008). *Powerful women: Does exposure reduce prejudice?* Massachusetts Institute of Technology Department of Economics working paper no. 08-14 and John F. Kennedy School of Government Faculty research paper no. RWP08-37.

Cavalcanti, T. & Tavares, J. (2007). *The output cost of gender discrimination: A model-based macroeconomic estimate.* Working paper, University of Cambridge and Universidade Nova de Lisboa.

Dollar, D. & Gatti, R. (1999). *Gender inequality, income and growth: Are good times good for women?* Policy research report on gender and development working paper series no. 1.

Donno, D., & Russett, B. (2004). Islam, authoritarianism, and female empowerment: What are the linkages? *World Politics, 56*(4), 582–607.

Eagly, A., & Diekman, A. (2003). The malleability of sex differences in response to changing social roles. In L. Aspinwall, & U. Staudinger (Eds.), *A psychology of human strengths: Fundamental questions and future directions for a positive psychology* (pp. 103–115). Washington, DC: American Psychological Association.

Fish, M. S. (2002). Islam and authoritarianism. *World Politics, 55*(1), 4–37.

Forsythe, N., & Korzeniewicz, R. P. (2000). Gender inequalities and economic growth: A longitudinal evaluation. *Economic Development and Cultural Change, 48*(3), 573–617.

Guiso, L., Sapienza, P., & Zingales, L. (2003). People's opium? Religion and economic attitudes. *Journal of Monetary Economics, 50*(1), 225–282.

Inglehart, R., & Norris, P. (2003). *Rising tide: Gender equality and cultural change around the world.* Cambridge, UK: Cambridge University Press.

Kardam, N. (2005). *Gender and institutions: Creating an enabling environment.* Paper presented at UN Division of the Advancement of Women Expert Group Meeting, Bangkok, Thailand, November 8–11, 2005.

Jütting, J., Dayton-Johnson, J., Dreschler, D., & Morrisson, C. (2008). Measuring gender inequality. *Journal of Human Development, 9*(1), 65–86.

Morrisson, C., & Jütting, J. (2005). Women's discrimination in developing countries: A new data set for better policies. *World Development, 33*(7), 1065–1081.

Noland, M. (2005). Religion and economic performance. *World Development, 33*(8), 1215–1232.

Norris, P., & Inglehart, R. (2004). *Sacred and secular: Religion and politics worldwide.* Cambridge, UK: Cambridge University Press.

Psacharopoulos, G., & Tzannatos, Z. (1989). Female labor force participation: An international perspective. *World Bank Research Observer, 4*(2), 187–201.

Seguino, S. (2007). Plus ça change? Evidence on global trends in gender norms and stereotypes. *Feminist Economics, 13*(2), 1–28.

Sen, A. (1999). *Development as freedom.* New York: Anchor Books.

Sen, G. (2007). Informal institutions and gender equality. In J. Jütting, D. Drechsler, S. Bartsch, & I. de Soysa (Eds.), *Informal institutions: How social norms help or hinder development* (pp. 49–72). Paris, France: OECD.

Tavernise, S. (2009). *In quest for equal rights, Muslim women's meeting turns to Islam's tenets.* New York Times, February 16.

Verweij, J., Ester, P., & Nauta, R. (1997). Secularization as an economic and cultural phenomenon. *Journal of the Scientific Study of Religion, 36*(2), 309–324.

Weichselbaumer, D., & Winter-Ebmer, R. (2005). A meta-analysis of the international gender wage gap. *Journal of Economic Surveys, 19*(3), 479–511.

Veiled Submission: Gender, Power, and Identity Among Evangelical and Muslim Women in the United States

JOHN P. BARTKOWSKI AND JEN'NAN GHAZAL READ

Introduction

During the past decade, a wealth of published studies have illuminated devout women's affiliation with conservative religious communities such as evangelical Protestantism and Orthodox Judaism (Ammerman 1987; Bartkowski 1999, 2001a; Beaman 2001; Brasher 1998; Davidman 1993; Gallagher and Smith 1999; Griffith 1997; Ingersoll 1995; Manning 1999; McNamara 1985; Pevey, Williams, and Ellison 1996; Rose 1987; Sherkat 2000; Smith 2000; Stacey 1990; Stacey and Gerard 1990; Stocks 1997). Given America's religious pluralism, such studies provide important insight into women's diverse motivations for affiliating with theologically conservative religious traditions. Yet, despite the prominence of religious diversity in the U.S., little research has compared the experiences of conservative religious women across faith traditions.

One noteworthy exception to this general pattern of neglect is Christel Manning's book, *God Gave Us the Right* (1999). Manning compares religious experiences among women affiliated with three different faith traditions—evangelical

John P. Bartkowski and Jen'nan Ghazal Read, "Veiled Submission: Gender, Power, and Identity Among Evangelical and Muslim Women in the United States," *Qualitative Sociology,* Vol. 26, No. 1 (Spring 2003), pp. 71–92. Copyright © 2003 by Human Sciences Press, Inc. With kind permission from Springer Science and Business Media.

Protestantism, Orthodox Judaism, and conservative Catholicism. Manning's investigation reveals that conservative religious women are all confronted with the task of negotiating gender. However, her comparative account also highlights the distinctive strategies that women across these three faith traditions employ to negotiate their gender identities and family relationships. Each of these three faith traditions provides women with different cultural resources for negotiating gender. For example, evangelical women's social practices are informed by biblical dictates about appropriate gender relations and conservative Protestant notions of individual moral accountability before God. Orthodox Jewish women negotiate their gender identities by wrestling with cultural mandates concerning Passover preparation and dominant interpretations of the Torah, and conservative Catholic women grapple with papal edicts about women's place in the Church and the relevance of Mary (in Catholic circles, the revered mother of Jesus) to their identities as Catholic women.

Our study extends the scope of such comparative investigations by contrasting gender relations across two of the most distinctive, robust, and fastest-growing religious traditions in the U.S. today—evangelical Protestantism and Islam. (See Finke and Stark 1992; Iannaccone 1994; Roof and McKinney 1987; Smith 1998; Stark and Finke 2000 on evangelical distinctiveness and growth. See Bagby, Perl, and Froehle 2001; Esposito 1998; Haddad 1991; Read 2002 and 2003 for related work on Islam.) In both evangelical Protestantism and Islam, religious women negotiate their identities in light of cultural prescriptions concerning appropriate gender relations. Throughout this study, we attempt to connect women's strategies for gender identity negotiation to the specific cultural repertoire provided by each of these distinct faith traditions. Our study is therefore informed by the conceptualization of religion as a cultural repertoire—a dynamic "tool kit"—as distinct from theories that construe religion as a static, top-down social institution (Ammerman 2003; Bartkowski 1999, 2001a; Manning 1999; Pattillo-McCoy 1998; Smith 1998, 2000. See Griswold 1994;

Swidler 1986; Williams 1995 for general reviews). Affiliation with a faith community provides adherents with exposure to influential ideologies (e.g., theological edicts, gender-family norms) and distinctive social resources (e.g., sacred scripture, faith-based social networks, community status) (Ammerman 1997; Becker 1999; Becker and Eiesland 1997; Ebaugh and Chafctz 2000; Warner and Wittner 1998). As such, religious actors are capable of using the repertoire of their faith tradition in strategic, creative, and sometimes subversive ways to meet the practical demands of everyday life. Malleable cultural repertoires enable religious adherents to remain engaged with broader social trends, such as changing gender norms in society at large. In this way, religious affiliation has an influential, but not determinative, impact on the values, practices, and identities of grassroots adherents (Ammerman 2003). The women we interview therefore engage actively in boundary work—i.e., strategies by which they draw distinctions between their identities as religious believers and "others" situated outside their religious communities (cf. Lamont 1992, 2000; Lamont and Fournier 1992; Nippert-Eng 1996). While these general insights are now readily accepted by cultural sociologists, new empirical comparisons among religious groups further clarify the unique forms of boundary work and identity negotiation that take place in particular faith communities.

Guided by this aim, we begin our investigation by reviewing current debates on the status of women among evangelical and Islamic elites. We analyze popular books written by leading evangelical and Muslim commentators—traditionalists and feminists, respectively—who provide advice to women within each of these religious subcultures. After outlining these debates, we turn to in-depth interviews with evangelical and Muslim women to demonstrate how they draw on their distinct cultural repertoires to negotiate their identities. By highlighting patterns of convergence and distinction across these religious subcultures, we expand scholarly knowledge concerning gender identity negotiation among different types of conservative religious women.

Elite Debates Over The Status of Women: Traditionalism and Feminism in Two Religious Subcultures

We begin our comparative analysis of gender in evangelicalism and Islam with the acknowledgment that gender ideologies within each of these religious subcultures are hotly contested.[1] Feminist critiques of gender traditionalism have established themselves within the elite discourse of both these religious communities. Consequently, the gender discourse promulgated by evangelical and Islamic elites is fragmented—broadly, along the lines of traditionalist versus feminist viewpoints (Bartkowski 2001a; Read and Bartkowski 2000).

Wifely Submission Versus Mutual Submission: Evangelical Gender Debates

Within evangelical Protestantism, elite debates over the status of women hinge on the question of submission, and the precise meaning of biblical references to this concept (Bartkowski 1997, 1999, 2000, 2001a; Bartkowski and Xu 2000; Bartkowski, Wilcox, and Ellison 2000; Ellison and Bartkowski 2002). Traditionalist evangelicals champion the ideology of wifely submission, namely, the idea that wives should defer to their husbands in family decision-making (e.g., Dobson 1991; LaHaye 1976; Pride 1985). They give interpretive primacy to biblical passages that seem to mandate wifely submission, including Ephesians 5:22: "Wives, submit to your husbands as to the Lord. For the husband is the head of the wife as Christ is the head of the Church, his body, of which he is the Savior. Now as the church submits to Christ, so also wives should submit to their husbands in everything."

Many traditionalist evangelical advice authors cast the wife as an "executive vice-president" whose input may be solicited, but need not be heeded, by her husband in family decision-making. Despite her vice-presidential status, the devout evangelical wife is charged with carrying out her husband's presidential decisions even if she disagrees with them. Ironically, evangelical authors argue that women will find "liberation" in a patriarchal family structure because they need not concern themselves with taking final responsibility for domestic decisions.

Such reassurances have not, however, placated evangelical feminists (also known as biblical feminists). As an increasingly visible faction within evangelical Protestantism, biblical feminists contend that the Bible mandates not wifely submission, but rather "mutual submission" between wives and husbands (e.g., Follis 1981; Scanzoni and Hardesty 1992. See Bartkowski 2001a, ch. 4). Within their advice manuals, evangelical feminists conceive of the husband and wife as a "team." And rather than alluding to hierarchical metaphors (e.g., president/vice-president), evangelical feminists conceive of marriage as an equilateral triangle with spouses at the base corners and Jesus Christ, the divine head of the spousal relationship, at the top (e.g., Gabriel 1993, p. 94). Pointing to biblical passages that talk about Christian believers "submitting to one another" (Ephesians 5:21), evangelical feminists argue that mutual submission is more authentically Christian because both spouses recognize that they must follow Jesus Christ's model of self-sacrifice and other-centeredness in family decision-making. These critics challenge patriarchal interpretations of the Bible, which they paint as sexist misreadings of God's instructions for family life.

Elite Debates over the Islamic Veil: Sign of Devotion or Tool of Oppression?

Similar disputes between traditionalists and feminists have emerged in contemporary Islam (Read and Bartkowski 2000). However, given the distinctive features of the Islamic cultural repertoire, Muslim gender debates turn not on notions of submission but rather on the meaning of the veil (i.e., *hijab*) for Islamic women. The all-male Islamic clergy (variously called faghihs, imams, muftis, mullahs, and ulamas) prescribe veiling as a custom in which good Muslim women should engage, and justify their pro-veiling stance on a number of grounds (Al-Swailem 1995; Afshar 1985; Philips and Jones 1985; Siddiqi 1983). First, they argue that men's sexuality can be ignited through unregulated social contact with women. They contend that the purpose of the veil is to regulate such social contact and "protect [a woman's] virtue and to safeguard her chastity from lustful eyes and covetous hands" (Siddiqi 1983, p. viii; see also

Al-Swailem 1995, pp. 27–29; Philips and Jones 1985, pp. 39–46).

Traditionalist Muslim elites also see the veil as a symbol of the Muslim woman's unflagging obedience to Islamic principles. In an effort to legitimate their pro-veiling viewpoint, these commentators highlight a series of passages in the Qur'an that seem to support this religious practice. One of these scriptural verses urges women "not [to] display their beauty and adornments" but rather to "draw their head cover over their bosoms and not display their ornament" (S. 24:31). Two other popular verses read as follows: "And when you ask them [the Prophet's wives] for anything you want, ask them from before a screen (*hijab*); that makes for greater purity for your hearts and for them" (S. 33:53); "O Prophet! Tell your wives and daughters and the believing women that they should cast their outer garments over themselves, that is more convenient that they should be known and not molested . . ." (S. 33:59).

In recent years, however, feminist critiques of *hijab* have challenged these traditional Islamic interpretations of the Qur'an (Al-Marayati 1995; Mernissi 1991; Shaheed 1994, 1995; see Read and Bartkowski 2000). Fatima Mernissi (1987, 1991), the most prominent Muslim feminist and author of several popular books on *hijab,* is highly critical of traditionalist Muslims who judge women's devotion to Islam by their wearing of the veil. Mernissi argues that the veil is used to "censure and punish" Muslim women, and asks: "How did [Islamic] tradition succeed in transforming the Muslim woman into that submissive, marginal creature who buries herself and only goes out into the world timidly and huddled in her veils? Why does the Muslim man need such a mutilated companion?" (Mernissi 1991, p. 194).

Like evangelical feminists, Muslim feminists generate critical readings of the Qur'an designed to undermine traditionalist scriptural interpretations on which Muslim clergy often base their pro-veiling decrees. Muslim feminists are quick to point out that the Qur'an never directly instructs women to wear a veil and refers obscurely to a "curtain," not *hijab*. To bolster their critiques, Islamic feminists emphasize the importance of the "occasions of revelation" (*asbab nuzul al-Our'an*), which refer to the specific, historical circumstances under which Qur'anic passages were revealed (Mernissi 1991, pp. 87–88, 92–93: see Sherif 1987). They surmise that the veil verse (S. 33:53) was intended solely for the wives of Muhammed, not for all Muslim women. Finally, opponents of *hijab* cite several verses in the Qur'an that invoke images of gender egalitarianism, including one passage that refers to the "vast reward" Allah has prepared for both "men who guard their modesty and women who guard their modesty" (S. 33:35).

In sum, then, gender is a site of ideological contestation among both evangelical elites and Muslim luminaries. Within both of these religious subcultures, gender debates pit defenders of traditionalism against feminist critics of the religious status quo. Yet, despite the common form of this gender conflict (traditionalism versus feminism), the content of these debates differs significantly. Within evangelicalism, women's submission emerges as the core point of ideological dispute, and among Muslim elites the meaning of *hijab* and the propriety of wearing the veil emerge as primary points of conflict.

Gender And Power at the Grassroots: Identity Negotiation Among Evangelical and Muslim Women

. . . [O]ur sample is composed of women with traditional religious convictions (those who advocate wifely submission and those who veil, respectively) and women with non-traditional beliefs (evangelical advocates of mutual submission and unveiled Muslim women). All of these women are devout—i.e., active in their faith and self-identified as highly religious. All of the evangelical women are married, as are the majority of Muslim women in our sample. Every woman in our sample, evangelical and Muslim, shares a common social status in that they are well-educated, middle- and upper-class women. The ages of evangelical women range from 20 to 73, with a mean age of 35. Muslim women interviewed for this study range in age from 20 to 55, with a mean age of 33. Interviews with evangelical women were audiotaped and transcribed, while interviews with Muslim women were recorded with handwritten notes and expanded into detailed transcripts immediately following each interview. Both sets of transcribed interviews were analyzed in light of the key theoretical constructs and sensitizing concepts discussed above—i.e., the character of religiously-based cultural repertoires and the process of identity negotiation. . . .

Embracing Religious Traditionalism: Wifely Submission and Veiling

When asked about the meaning of the term submission, several of the evangelical women in our study voiced orthodox sensibilities. These women typically began by describing their standpoint in terms of the dominant evangelical gender discourse (i.e., husband headship and wifely submission). The language of submission enables these women to draw boundaries between themselves and other women with more secular and individualistic orientations toward self and family. Interestingly, however, once these women had highlighted their prima facie support for gender traditionalism, they began to qualify their patriarchal commitments.

Veronica, a young married evangelical woman, provides an explanation of wifely submission that is quite common among respondents committed to this ideal. However, her commentary is laced with equally common qualifications. The qualifications articulated by Veronica reveal the complex character of her viewpoint, one that is traditional at first blush, but also defies this one-dimensional category.

When asked about the meaning of submission, Veronica engages in a strategic form of boundary work that emphasizes women's empowerment through submission to their husbands. Articulating this fine-grained distinction, she says:

> Basically, I think in a Christian sense [submission] would be [concerned with] the role of the woman to not always buck horns with the man and fight his . . . [she pauses momentarily] . . . not really his authority, because he doesn't have authority over me—but [not] to fight his lead in the

marriage. Philip feels like such a man when I say, "How do you want to do this?" Do you know what I'm saying? He feels big. It definitely helps [men] when they know that they have someone to protect. It puts a lot of responsibility on them, but it makes them act better. So I guess that is how I would define submission. It's not just, "Whatever you say, honey, beat me." That's not at all what I'm saying. [Rather, it is] just not to buck horns always and constantly be fighting or nagging. You let him do this. If you want to talk about something, you can talk about it. But not continuously.

Several evangelical women interviewed are like Veronica and embrace the idea of wifely submission. Given the traditionalist boundary work in which they are engaged, these women face two difficult dilemmas. First, how can the submissive wife retain her sense of self-efficacy in a cultural climate that privileges rights-based individualism as the social standard against which men and, increasingly, women are measured?[2] In many respects, the privileged status of expressive individualism in America—the revered right of the individual to pursue her own ends (Bellah et al. 1985, 1992; Williams 1999)—lends itself to equating subordinate women with doormats. Second, how can the submissive wife avoid becoming resentful or envious of her husband's power? One strategy that wives can use to overcome both the doormat and power envy problems is purely rhetorical in character. Along with other women who embrace wifely submission, Veronica critiques the notion of hierarchy implied in the word submission. As she notes, Philip takes the "lead" in their marriage but he does not exercise "authority over" her. At first glance, these fine-grained distinctions might appear to be mere hair-splitting. Yet, evangelical women committed to the principle of wifely submission draw important distinctions between a wife's obligation to fall in line under an autocratic ruler and her choice to follow his benevolent leadership. Being trampled under foot, much like a doormat, is rejected in favor of "choosing" to submit.

Second, evangelical women who support wifely submission are quick to point out that women are not inferior because they submit to their husbands.

In fact, accounts like Veronica's suggest just the opposite. Veronica argues that it is men's deficiencies, rather than women's inferiority, that make wifely submission central to a harmonious marriage. She says: "Philip feels like such a man when I say, 'How do you want to do this?' . . . He feels big. It definitely helps [men] when they know that they have someone to protect. It puts a lot of responsibility on them, but it makes them act better."

The idea that weakness in men, not women, makes wifely submission necessary is widely held by evangelical women who support the principle of wifely submission.[3] Angela is a women's Bible study instructor in Veronica's evangelical church. During her women's Bible study, Angela describes the male ego alternatively as "soft," like an under inflated balloon, and "leaky," in Angela's own words, "like a bucket with holes in it." This soft and leaky male ego is in constant need of a woman's deference through the practice of wifely submission. Far from being passive doormats, many evangelical women who support wifely submission portray themselves as active strategists who have generously decided to defer to husbands whose fragile egos could not withstand the onslaught of women's overt assertiveness.

Finally, in a more practical sense, evangelical women who defend wifely submission argue that the proper application of this concept necessitates negotiation, discussion, and compromise. Although Veronica clearly relinquishes final-say power to Philip—you don't "buck horns always," you "let him do this"—she says that discussion and negotiation are certainly part of the process. Other wives were careful to make this point as well. Among such women, discussions among spouses are considered not just an option but are thought to be the only proper place from which to begin the decision-making process within the home. In this way, these women's views depart from those of leading evangelicals. The tidy ideological prescriptions found in evangelical advice manuals briefly mention, but largely gloss over, the need for spousal discussion in marital decision-making. Yet, in everyday life, discussion, negotiation, and compromise become paramount if couples are to resolve conflicts effectively.

Like evangelical advocates of wifely submission, many of our veiled Muslim respondents discuss the meaning of *hijab* in terms consistent with the orthodox Islamic position on this subject. Many veiled women see *hijab* as a symbol of devotion to Allah (i.e., God), and several cite scriptural edicts interpreted to support this religious practice. Huneeya, a respondent in her early 20s, explains: "I wear the *hijab* because the Qur'an says it's better [for women to be veiled]." In a telling point of convergence with the evangelical language of patriarchy, Mona comments: "The veil represents submission to God." Mona proceeds to explain that men are forced to respect women in *hijab* because it is a sign of their unwavering religious devotion. Masouda contends that the veil is a "symbol of worship" used by pious Muslim women to show their devotion to Allah and the Prophet Muhammed.

When compared with orthodox evangelical proponents of wifely submission, however, the immigrant status of the veiled Muslim women and the distinctiveness of their cultural practice invest *hijab* with more far-reaching implications. Living in a non-Muslim, Western environment, many of the veiled respondents come to rely on Islamic women's friendship networks that form around the veil. Najette succinctly states, "The veil lets you identify that you're a Muslim woman . . . when people see you, they know you're Muslim and you feel secure." Hannan goes on to explain that *hijab* serves to unify Muslims, saying that because "Muslim people know I am Muslim . . . they greet me in Arabic." Masouda also recounts this shared sense of community: "You know if you see a veiled woman here in town that she is Muslim." Aisha similarly maintains: "The veil differentiates Muslim women from other women. When you see a woman in *hijab*, you know she's a Muslim." In keeping with Islamic prescriptions for women to "wear" their religious convictions for all to see, these veiled respondents find comfort in the cultural and ethnic distinctiveness that the veil affords them.

This is not to say, however, that gender is irrelevant to the practice of veiling. Several of our veiled respondents defend the practice of veiling by enlisting arguments about essential gender difference. Just as some evangelical women advocate wifely submission "for men's sake," veiling is often seen as a corrective for masculine foibles, including men's apparent lack of sexual restraint. Enlisting a gendered and sexualized theodicy (i.e., a religious explanation for evil), Sharadda states: "Islam is natural and men need some things naturally. If we abide by these needs [and veil accordingly], we will all be happy. If the veil did not exist, many evil things would happen. Boys would mix with girls, which will result in evil things." Among other veiled respondents, veiling is justified by notions of gender difference that have less to do with men's flaws and more to do with women's inherently redeeming attributes. Hannan describes what she perceives to be women's distinctive attributes and their connection to the veil: "Women are like diamonds; they are so precious. They should not be revealed to everyone—just to their husbands and close kin." These womanly characteristics are believed to be protected by *hijab*.

Like their evangelical counterparts, these respondents are not merely reproducing the rhetoric of gender difference advanced by Muslim elites. Rather than simply wearing the veil to "save" men from their uncontrollable sexuality, many claimed that the *hijab* actually serves to liberate women from the private sphere and allows them to pursue various public sphere activities. Several of our veiled respondents participate in the paid labor force, attend co-educational institutions, and belong to various social and civic organizations. To many of these respondents, the *hijab* is a great equalizer that enables women to intermingle with and work alongside of men. As Hannan says: "Women who wear the *hijab* are not excluded from society. They are freer to move around in society because of it." Rabbab echoes this view, and claims that "taking away the *hijab* would make women have to fight to be taken seriously [in public settings] . . . With *hijab*, men take us more seriously." Somewhat ironically, Masouda alludes to the relative privilege of veiled women compared to American women: "The veil serves to distract people away from women's bodies— something that doesn't happen here in the U.S."

Like some evangelical women who feel liberated by submission to their husbands, these women argue that the veil frees them to participate in public activities from which they might otherwise be excluded.

Devout but Non-Traditional: Egalitarian Evangelical and Muslim Women

As noted . . . , feminist criticisms that have emerged within evangelical and Muslim quarters have created space for women who reject the dominant discourse of patriarchy within these faith traditions. In our interviews with evangelical and Muslim women, we noticed that such non-traditionalism is readily apparent at the grassroots of these religious communities as well, despite it being the marginalized definition of gender. To be sure, few of these women use the word "feminist" to describe their viewpoint (cf. Manning 1999). But their ideas certainly resonate with those articulated by leading feminists within their respective faith traditions.

Within evangelicalism, these convictions are manifested among women who unflinchingly invoke the term "mutual submission" to define marital decision-making prescribed in the Bible. Rose, an evangelical wife in her late 40s, situates her vision of gender within the ideology of mutual submission:

> Well, first of all, my understanding of what those passages in Ephesians say is that [husbands and wives] are mutually submissive. So, I am to submit to him, but he also is to submit to me. Again, I think it just goes back to that teamwork thing. We are mutually submissive to each other. But submission to me is not [pause] . . . I mean, that [word] gets negative [reactions]. When people say "submit," it's like, "Ugh, that's terrible." I don't think it is. I don't think it is at all. I think being willing to sacrifice what you want for the people around you is a very noble thing . . . That's strength. It's not weakness. You know, a lot of people don't see it that way. But I think it's mutual. I think we are to submit to each other, is my understanding of it. That's the way it's always been taught when they teach it in church. That's what we've been taught. It's mutual submission to each other.

Rose proceeds to form an equilateral triangle with her thumbs and forefingers to illustrate her view of a good Christian marriage. Not unlike the triangular metaphor invoked by egalitarian evangelical commentators (Gabriel 1993, p. 94), she envisions Christ at the top and the two spouses—equal teammates—at the base corners.

This egalitarian image is consistent with those articulated by other evangelical women who embrace the principle of mutual submission. The commentary of Heather, also a middle-aged wife and mother, is akin to that of Rose. Heather explains that submission means "to come alongside someone. And in that, to me, when I think of somebody coming alongside, whether it's to encourage you or to hold you accountable, I don't see that as a dominating type of submission. There's someone there because they want what's best for you."

In response to her remarks, Heather is asked: "And what role, if any, does submission play in your marital relationship?" She laughs, responding:

I just don't submit. No. You know, I guess I should also say that I think that it's such a two-way thing. If I was married to someone who told me I had to do certain things, I would not be very submissive under the definition of what most people see as submission. You know, I see my husband as the most encouraging person in all of life. Somebody who, whether it's work-related or home, as a general rule does anything possible to help me to excel and to do better . . . But I see [submission] more as walking alongside than I see it as beneath or in any way under him.

Such ardent defenses of mutual submission beg a vexing question: How is it that women like Veronica and Rose are able to get along with another with such seemingly disparate views of submission between them? Recall that Veronica embraces the orthodox standpoint of wifely submission, which implies a husband-wife hierarchy. Rose, on the other hand, is an advocate of the egalitarian principle of mutual submission, in which there is no place for marital hierarchy. Interestingly, these two women are not only associated with the same religious subculture—evangelical

Protestantism—they are members of the very same evangelical church in central Texas—an Evangelical Free Church (see Bartkowski 2001a). How is it that one church can accommodate women with such divergent views about gender? In this particular church, family ministers invoke both traditional and egalitarian images of Christian family life, often blending together such terms as wifely submission and mutual submission in sermons and Bible studies. In a more general sense, ideological flexibility within evangelicalism *writ large* facilitates compatibility among women with divergent views. Within this religious subculture, terms such as "submission" are used to construct boundaries that distinguish evangelical wives from women in mainstream American culture (Bartkowski 2001a; Bartkowski, Wilcox, and Ellison 2000; Gallagher and Smith 1999; Manning 1999; Smith 1998, 2000). When submission is understood in this broad sense as a marker of cultural distinctiveness, both Veronica and Rose would agree that submission is unfortunately not manifested in the non-evangelical marriages of the American mainstream.

Beyond this general point of agreement between women like Veronica and Rose, elite evangelical debates over submission provide the evangelical cultural repertoire with immense flexibility—essentially, interpretive "wiggle-room." While submission is clearly an evangelical cultural tool, the meaning of this term is flexible enough within this religious subculture to accommodate the broadly traditional sensibilities of Veronica and the more progressive convictions of Rose (Bartkowski 2001a). When they hear the word "submission" from the pulpit in their local congregation, Veronica and Rose are both likely to interpret this term as "selflessness," "yielding," and "respect," which is how many of the evangelical women interviewed in our study describe this term. Evangelical debates over this term allow both women to understand it differently—that is, as the wife's responsibility (Veronica) or as the couple's mutual obligation (Rose)—without challenging their shared commitment to evangelical Christianity. Discursive debates among evangelical elites help to facilitate ideological diversity at the grassroots of this religious subculture.

Like non-traditional evangelical women who advocate mutual submission, many of the unveiled Muslim women we interviewed draw on themes from the anti-veiling discourse to justify their decision not to veil. Their accounts often reiterate Islamic feminist arguments that the veil is used as a patriarchal tool of oppression, imposed on Muslim women because men refuse to tame their own sexual impulses. Najwa clearly conveys this belief: "Men can't control themselves, so they make women veil." Rabeeya similarly argues that Muslim women are expected to veil because "Middle Eastern men get caught up in beauty. The veil helps men control themselves." When asked about the significance of the veil in Muslim societies, Fozia states emphatically: "The veil is used to control women." Unlike their veiled counterparts who see *hijab* as God-ordained, the unveiled women link the veil to men's desires to control women and unwillingness to manage their own sexuality.

Also in keeping with Islamic feminist views, several of the unveiled respondents challenge the conflation of religiosity, cultural identity, politics, and the veil. Recall that Islamic feminists are highly critical of the clergy's attempts to link Muslim women's religious responsibilities with *hijab,* arguing instead that the origins of the veil predate Islam. Articulating these same arguments, several of the unveiled respondents seek to sever the veil from its religious and political ties. Drawing boundaries that define the veil as a cultural (i.e.. ethnic) symbol rather than a religious icon, Samiya contends, "The veil is a dress that is culturally significant, not religiously." Fozia focuses on the politicized meaning of the veil: "Women are made to believe that the veil is religious. In reality, it's all political"; and Fatima agrees: "The veil is definitely political. It is used by men as a weapon to differentiate us from Westerners."

Isolating *hijab*'s political and cultural foundations allows these unveiled women to draw boundaries that cast them as more moderate than women whose religious devotion, in their view, has been manipulated by religious elites for political gain. Mah'ha, a 45-year-old woman, articulates a common complaint among the unveiled women regarding the politicization of Islam, "The veil is

(now) sanctioned by religion. It used to be a choice." Many of the unveiled women claim that their religious commitment and ethnic pride are manifested in ways that do not include the practice of veiling, including daily prayer and study of the Qur'an. And they are quick to point out that Islamic piety does not hinge on the veil. Samiya, a 38-year-old unveiled woman, says as much: "Muslim society doesn't exist on the veil. Without the veil, you would still be Muslim." Amna concurs, "If the veil didn't exist in Muslim societies, it would really affect the sexual and social atmosphere more than the religious." In sum, the unveiled women in our study feel that a Muslim woman can be true to her cultural and religious heritage without wearing *hijab.*

Contested understandings of the veil among Muslim women articulated above beg the same question as that which we raised concerning evangelical women. How do veiled and unveiled Muslim women view their sisters whose cultural practices do not conform to their own? Are relationships among these women antagonistic, as one might expect from the public and highly distinctive nature of this cultural practice? Unlike the evangelical women featured above (all of whom are affiliated with the same central Texas evangelical church), the Muslim women in our study do not all attend the same mosque. Yet, like their evangelical counterparts, these Muslim women are able to emphasize cultural similarity with all of their Islamic sisters. And, where differences emerge, women on both sides of this *hijab*-inspired divide build bridges to sisters whose orientation toward the veil is different than their own.

At times, such empathy is a product of terribly complicated boundary work. Resistance to *hijab* among Americans, and even Westernized Arabs, makes many veiled women empathize with their sisters who opt against wearing the veil. Huneeya, for example, disclosed personal difficulties she faced with her family because of her decision to wear *hijab*: "I wear the *hijab* because the Qur'an says it's better, [but] my family is against *hijab*. They think it is against modernity." Similarly, Najette appreciated why some Muslim women choose not to veil, claiming that many Americans who do not understand the practice of veiling consider her "weird." Many of the veiled respondents were also quick to defend their unveiled sisters' piety, focusing on the importance of religious *beliefs* as well as practices. When asked what being a good Muslim entails, Masouda and Rabbab, both of whom veil, responded that one's "attitude toward God" is the most important aspect. Another veiled respondent went so far as to say, "*Hijab* is not so important for being a good Muslim. Other things are more important, like having a good character and being honest."

Unveiled Muslim women also manifested empathy toward the practice of veiling. Like their veiled counterparts, the unveiled women defended their veiled sisters' choices on a number of grounds. First, several respondents imply that it would be wrong to criticize veiled women for wearing *hijab* when it is men—specifically, male Muslim elites—who are to blame for the existence and pervasiveness of the veil in Islamic culture. Amna, who does not veil, adopts a conciliatory tone toward women who do. She concedes that "the veil helps women in societies where they want to be judged solely on their character and not on their appearance." Since many of the unveiled respondents construe *hijab* to be a product of *patriarchal* oppression and assorted *masculine* hang-ups (e.g., struggles with sexuality, a preoccupation with domination and control), veiled women cannot legitimately be impugned for wearing *hijab*.

Second, many of the unveiled respondents are willing to concede that, despite their own critical views of the veil, *hijab* serves as an important cultural marker for Islamic women other than themselves. When asked about the role of the veil among Muslim women she knows in the United States, Rabeeya recognizes that many of her veiled Islamic sisters who currently live in America "want to feel tied to their culture even when they are far away from home." As a devout Islamic woman living in a predominantly Christian society, Rabeeya is able to empathize with other Muslim women residing in the United States who veil in order to shore up their cultural identity. The fact that she emphasizes her cultural

distinctiveness in other ways does not lead her to dismiss Islamic sisters who don the veil.

So, consistent with the civility expressed among orthodox and non-traditional evangelical women, several of the unveiled women in our study express tolerance and empathy for their sisters in *hijab*. At one time or another in the past, several of these unveiled women had even donned the veil themselves. Two of the unveiled respondents, for example, are native Iranians who are currently living in the United States. When these women return to Iran, they temporarily wear the veil. Najwa, one of these women, explains: "As soon as we cross the Iranian border, I go to the bathroom on the airplane and put on the *hijab*." Given such personal experiences, women like Najwa are critical of the veil as a religious icon but are unwilling to look down on Islamic women who wear *hijab*.

In sum, evangelical and Muslim women creatively negotiate the mandates of their faith to produce religious subcultures that are at once distinctive and flexible. Women in both of these religious traditions engage in boundary work that distinguishes them, albeit in different ways, from mainstream American values. Boundary-drawing strategies differ across these two religions because each faith tradition provides a distinctive repository of cultural tools for doing so. Moreover, within each faith tradition, the challenges associated with crafting a religious identity differ depending on these women's gender convictions and practices. Traditional women explain their conservative sensibilities and practices in a way that counters the risk of being branded as "backwards" and "out of step" with contemporary social norms. Non-traditional evangelical and Muslim women distance themselves from the "excessive" conservatism of their faith tradition. Yet, these women must take care to affirm their religious devotion, thereby defining their faith as genuine and authentic despite their own progressive values.

Conclusion

This study began by comparing elite discursive disputes over gender within evangelical Protestantism and Islam. While leading evangelicals debate biblical references to women's submission, Muslim luminaries dispute the meaning of the veil to Islamic womanhood. We then explored the culturally distinctive strategies of identity negotiation employed by evangelical and Muslim women living in central Texas. Women from both of these communities engage in boundary work, drawing on religious resources to craft distinctive identities that selectively appropriate values from the American cultural mainstream.

Evangelical women are confronted with the task of negotiating their identities in light of conservative Protestant disputes over submission. The women interviewed here generally align themselves with a traditionalist ideology (wifely submission) or an egalitarian viewpoint (mutual submission). However, these same women articulate more guarded, measured viewpoints that permit them to function effectively in a heterogeneous religious subculture where believers may disagree about the practice of godly womanhood within the home. In a similar fashion, veiled and unveiled Muslim women we interviewed have well-defined beliefs about the meaning of the veil. In general, veiled Muslim respondents defended their wearing of *hijab* as consistent with the mandates of the Qur'an. The veil also takes on special meaning given the Middle Eastern culture from which these women have emigrated. For their part, unveiled women were critical of *hijab,* which they viewed as a tool of patriarchal oppression and an inaccurate gauge of Muslim women's devotion to Islam. And yet, like their evangelical counterparts, these disparate groups of Muslim women demonstrate empathy toward their sisters who engage in divergent cultural practices.

Women affiliated with both of these religious subcultures are negotiating their social marginality as they grapple with questions of gender identity. The general acceptance of egalitarian gender ideologies in American culture during the last several decades gives the evangelical discourse of wifely submission an anachronistic cast. Given the apparent connection between wifely submission and an "unenlightened" patriarchal era that has been eclipsed by feminist liberation, evangelical women who embrace husband-headship take great

pains to disentangle wifely submission and patriarchal oppression. Conservative Protestant women who embrace mutual submission have considerably less "explaining to do" to non-evangelicals because their convictions are more closely aligned with egalitarian gender ideals. Yet, both groups of evangelical women mark themselves as distinct from mainstream American culture by embracing the concept of submission in the face of broader social support for expressive individualism (cf. Bellah et al. 1985, 1992; Williams 1999), a rights-based ideology that rejects submission in any form. Whatever their stance on the question of submission, evangelical women highlight its virtues. Given Christian mandates for believers' selflessness and other-centeredness, submission critiques a broader cultural climate in which liberation is equated with selfishly "looking out for number one."

Turning to our Muslim respondents, Islam provides a sense of sisterhood (a feminized *ummah*) to women within this religious subculture regardless of their orientation toward the veil. In part, this sisterhood is fostered by the marginalization of Islam from the Christocentric cultural mainstream in the United States. Because some of these women don *hijab* and others eschew it, these women disagree about the meaning of the veil and its place in Islam. And yet, as émigrés to the U.S., the Muslim women in our study are all cultural and religious outsiders in a country that is often hostile toward their religion. It is their shared liminal status that forges for them close social bonds. Given their shared status as strangers in a foreign land, an individual Muslim woman's "choice" to wear *hijab* or to abstain from doing so is seen as less important than her devotion to Islam, Allah, and the Prophet Muhammed. In light of their common social circumstances, these women avoid becoming preoccupied with the veil and instead generate tolerance and respect for the diverse cultural manifestations of Islam.

Several implications emerge from our investigation. First, a decade of studies involving evangelical and Orthodox Jewish women have revealed that conservative religious culture is not simply produced from "above" through the rhetoric of elites. Our study extends previous investigations by (1) examining the contours of elite gender debates in conservative religious communities; (2) expanding this line of inquiry to a new cultural domain (Islam); and (3) drawing detailed comparisons between women affiliated with two religious traditions that have heretofore escaped comparison. Transmitted through interpretive communities in local churches and mosques, elite evangelical and Muslim discourses have carved out a range of standpoints for women affiliated with each of these religious subcultures. Nevertheless, the respondents in our study are unique and indispensable contributors to cultural production within their faith traditions. To be sure, the women in this study value the cultural repertoire their faith traditions afford them, and a portion of the resources in this repertoire emanate from the mouths and pens of religious elites. Yet at the same time, these women's social circumstances are often at odds with the voices of elites in these religious subcultures. As such, the women that we interviewed actively negotiate and refashion their religious identities (Ammerman 2003). Like women in other conservative religious traditions, devout evangelical and Muslim women exhibit a remarkable degree of agency in crafting religious identities. And these women's religious identities are forged through the creative application of their specific faith commitments and cultural tools to meet the particular demands of their life circumstances.

In fact, even the most traditional elements of these two conservative religions often end up serving progressive ends. In evangelical homes where commitments to wifely submission hold sway, this theological concept often gives way to egalitarian practices (Bartkowski 2001a; Bartkowski, Wilcox, and Ellison 2000; Bartkowski and Xu 2000; Gallagher and Smith 1999). Co-parenting and joint decision-making are more common in evangelical homes than in secular and mainline religious households (Bartkowski and Xu 2000; Lundquist and Smith 1998). And the practice of veiling emancipates Muslim women from the constraints commonly connected with conservative religions. Veiling, a traditional practice

reinforcing gender difference, can actually promote equal opportunity for Muslim women where co-educational schooling and paid employment are concerned (Read and Bartkowski 2000). Moreover, veiling liberates Muslim women from America's oppressive beauty culture and the objectifying male gaze that accompanies it. In both faith traditions, then, commitments to religious orthodoxy and gender difference frequently serve emancipatory ends.

Second, our comparative investigation reveals that evangelical and Muslim women use markedly different cultural resources to craft their religious and gender identities. Quite notably, evangelical women have the opportunity to "pass" as "regular" women with mainstream values in a way that Muslim women would find more difficult. It is the language and ideology of submission that identifies evangelical women in terms of their distinct religious convictions. And, to quote a telling adage, such convictions need not be worn on one's sleeve. And yet, in a quite literal sense, the cultural practice of veiling places the religious convictions of Islamic women on their sleeves. Gender traditionalism within the Muslim cultural repertoire is manifested through more visible and practical means than such privatized, diffuse ideological convictions such as submission. So, whereas evangelical women can more fully participate in America's cultural mainstream through strategic silence, Muslim women's commitment to veiling is more public and therefore less negotiable. The wearing of *hijab*—and, in a categorical sense, a woman either wears the veil or does not—highlights Muslim women's more "extreme" cultural distinctiveness. Engaging in this social practice "gives away" the religious, ethnic, and national identity of the veiled Muslim woman to all persons with whom she comes into contact.

Although clear-cut comparisons between material and non-material culture have fallen out of favor in recent years, this distinction is indeed relevant when considering women's status within these two different religious traditions. We have argued that evangelicalism and Islam are both "big-tent" religions with flexible, wide-ranging cultural repertoires. Both religious communities create space for women with traditional gender convictions and their non-traditional counterparts. However, evangelical women are probably much more capable of finessing the traditional/non-traditional divide through boundary work that is largely discursive in character. Rhetorical redefinitions of submission, if carefully crafted, can help to bring evangelical women together, regardless of their support for or opposition to gender traditionalism. Yet, it is much more difficult to finesse embodied cultural practices that are not reducible to discourse (Bartkowski 2001b). Such is the case with veiling. In contrast to the non-material theology of submission stands the materiality of *hijab*. The veil clearly marks Islamic women who wear it, and places unveiled Muslim women in the position of explaining why they do not do so.

Beyond this substantive disparity, the symbolic meanings rendered through these cultural tools are remarkably different as well. The veil is a multifaceted cultural tool in a way that submission is not. The practice of veiling identifies a Muslim woman not just by her religious status or gender convictions, but also underscores her distinctive ethnic and national identities. As a multifaceted cultural tool capable of carrying many different cultural meanings simultaneously, the veil can be likened to a Swiss army knife. A Swiss army knife is a composite of various tools that, taken together, can serve many different functions, such as cutting wood, opening cans, and tightening screws, to name a few. In just this way, the veil is a multidimensional cultural tool that is capable of marking many different social statuses, such as religious affiliation, ethnic identity, and national origin.

A very different tool metaphor comes to mind in considering the evangelical discourse of submission. When comparing the gender discourse used by traditional and non-traditional Protestant women, the evangelical ideology of submission functions like a crescent wrench. A crescent wrench is a tool that performs a single function, namely, loosening or tightening nuts and bolts. Despite its singular function, a crescent wrench is malleable such that it can be adjusted to fit nuts and bolts of many different sizes. As a cultural crescent

wrench, evangelical definitions of submission can be "adjusted" along a wide-ranging continuum to fit women with traditional commitments (wifely submission) and those with more egalitarian beliefs (mutual submission). Beyond these polarized settings, the crescent wrench ideology of submission can even be adjusted to a "mid-range setting" to de-emphasize traditionalism/egalitarianism in favor of seemingly ungendered concepts like "selflessness," "respect," and "other-centeredness."

This study has sought to chart the points of convergence and divergence between two religious traditions that have heretofore escaped comparison. Drawing on interviews with evangelical and Muslim women, we have shown how the cultural repertoires of evangelicalism and Islam lend themselves to gender negotiations that are similar in form but quite different in content. In the end, this study adds to a now sizable body of research on gender negotiation among women in conservative religious communities. Our encapsulation of this overall finding as "veiled submission," communicated in the title of our study, suggests that there is more complexity and negotiation in such communities than first meets the eye. Yet, beyond this basic contribution, our inquiry underscores the need to move beyond the particularistic emphasis of so many previous studies in favor of investigations with a comparative focus across distinct faith traditions. As American religious groups wrestle with the challenge of thriving in a multicultural environment, sociologists would be well served to explore how the cultural repertoires of different faith communities influence their adherents while affecting the prospects for interfaith dialogue on issues of common concern.

Notes

1. Consistent with cultural transmission arguments, we assume no direct link between this elite advice literature and members of these faith communities. Rather, we argue that elite viewpoints are transmitted to believers through social and religious networks (Bartkowski 2001a).

2. We cannot fully address the relationship between gender, religion, and individualism here. In many respects, individualism draws its force

from hegemonic masculinity (Connell 1987, 1995). Capable personhood becomes defined as the embodiment of traditional masculine qualities—autonomy, self-direction, and independence—a standard against which both men and women, husband and wife, are measured. Communitarians argue that religious commitment and affiliation with other "communities of memory" provide a critical corrective to the excesses of utilitarian individualism in the home and society at large (Bahr and Bahr 2001; Bellah et al. 1985).

3. In other religious traditions, men's deficiencies are defined differently and lead to different cultural practices. For example, cultural notions about men's roving eyes and distractible nature are sometimes enlisted to support segregated seating in Orthodox Jewish synagogues (see Davidman 1993, Manning 1999 for treatments of gender in Orthodox Jewish settings).

References

Afshar, H. (1985). The legal, social and political position of women in Iran. *International Journal of the Sociology of Law*, 13, 47–60.

Al-Marayati, L. (1995). Voices of women unsilenced—Beijing 1995 focus on women's health and issues of concern for Muslim women. *UCLA Women's Law Journal*, 6, 167.

Al-Swailem, A. A. (1995). Introduction. In H. Abdullah, *A comparison between veiling and unveiling* (pp. 10–15). Riyadh, Saudi Arabia: Dar-us-Salam Publications.

Ammerman, N. T. (1987). *Bible believers: Fundamentalists in the modern world*. New Brunswick: Rutgers University Press.

Ammerman, N. T. (1997). *Congregation and community*. New Brunswick: Rutgers University Press.

Ammerman, N. T. (2003). Religious identities and religious institutions. In Michele Dillon (Ed.), *Handbook of sociology of religion* (pp. 207–224). New York: Cambridge University Press.

Bagby, I., Perl, P. M., & Froehle, B. T. (2001). The mosque in America: A national portrait. Report from the Mosque Study Project 2000. Washington, DC: Council on American-Islamic Relations. Available on-line at http://www.cair-net.org/mosquereport/.

Bahr, H. M., & Bahr, K. S. (2001). Families and self-sacrifice: Alternative models and meanings for family theory. *Social Forces*, 79, 1231–1258.

Bartkowski, J. P. (1997). Debating patriarchy: Discursive disputes over spousal authority among evangelical family commentators. *Journal for the Scientific Study of Religion*, 36, 393–410.

Bartkowski, J. P. (1999). One step forward, one step back: "Progressive traditionalism" and the negotiation of domestic labor within evangelical families. *Gender Issues*, 17, 40–64.

Bartkowski, J. P. (2000). Breaking walls, raising fences: Masculinity, intimacy, and accountability among the Promise Keepers. *Sociology of Religion*, 61, 33–53.

Bartkowski, J. P. (2001a). *Remaking the godly marriage: Gender negotiation in evangelical families*. New Brunswick, NJ: Rutgers University Press.

Bartkowski, J. P. (2001b). Faithfully embodied: Religious identity and the body. Paper presented at the annual meetings of the Society for the Scientific Study of Religion. Columbus, Ohio.

Bartkowski, J. P., Wilcox, W. B., & Ellison, C. G. (2000). Charting the paradoxes of evangelical family life: Gender and parenting in conservative protestant households. *Family Ministry*, 14, 9–21.

Bartkowski, J. P., & Xu, X. (2000). Distant patriarchs or expressive dads? The discourse and practice of fathering in conservative protestant families. *Sociological Quarterly*, 41, 465–485.

Beaman, L. G. (2001). Molly Mormons, Mormon feminists and moderates: Religious diversity and the LDS church. *Sociology of Religion*, 62, 65–86.

Becker, P. E. (1999). *Congregations in conflict: Cultural models of local religious life*. New York: Cambridge University Press.

Becker, P. E., & Eiesland, N. L. (Eds.) (1997). *Contemporary American religion: An ethnographic reader*. Walnut Creek, CA: AltaMira Press.

Bellah, R. N., Madsen, R., Sullivan, W. M., Swidler, A., & Tipton, S. M. (1985). *Habits of the heart: Individualism and commitment in American life*. Berkeley: University of California Press.

Bellah, R. N., Madsen, R., Sullivan, W. M., Swidler, A., & Tipton, S. M. (1992). *The good society*. New York: Vintage.

Brasher, B. (1998). *Godly women: Fundamentalism and female power*. New Brunswick, NJ: Rutgers University Press.

Connell, R. W. (1987). *Gender and power: Society the person, and sexual politics.* Stanford, CA: Stanford University Press.

Connell, R. W. (1995). *Masculinities: Knowledge, power, and social change.* Cambridge: Polity Press.

Davidman, L. (1993). *Tradition in a rootless world: Women turn to Orthodox Judaism.* Berkeley: University of California Press.

Dobson, J. (1991). *Straight talk: What men need to know, what women should understand* (revised and expanded). Dallas: Word.

Ebaugh, H. R., & Chafetz, J. S. (2000). *Religion and the new immigrants.* Walnut Creek. CA: AltaMira Press.

Ellison, C. G., & Bartkowski, J. P. (2002). Evangelical Protestantism and the household division of labor among married couples. *Journal of Family Issues, 23,* 950–985.

Esposito, J. L. (1998). Muslims in America or American Muslims. In Y. Y. Haddad & J. L. Esposito (Eds.), *Muslims on the Americanization path?* (pp. 3–17). Atlanta: Scholars Press.

Finke, R., & Stark, R. (1992). *The churching of America, 1776–1990: Winners and losers in our religious economy.* New Brunswick, NJ: Rutgers University Press.

Follis, A. B. (1981). *"I'm not a women's libber, but . . ." and other confessions of a Christian feminist.* Nashville: Abingdon.

Gabriel, G. (1993). *Being a woman of God* (revised and expanded edition). Nashville: Thomas Nelson.

Gallagher, S. K., & Smith, C. (1999). Symbolic traditionalism and pragmatic egalitarianism: Contemporary evangelicals, families, and gender. *Gender and Society, 13,* 211–233.

Griffith. R. M. (1997). *God's daughters: Evangelical women and the power of submission.* Berkeley: University of California Press.

Griswold, W. (1994). *Cultures and societies in a changing world.* Boston: Pine Forge Press.

Haddad. Y. Y. (1991). Introduction. In Y. Y. Haddad (Ed.), *The Muslims of America* (pp. 3–12). Oxford: Oxford University Press.

Iannaccone, L. R. (1994). Why strict churches are strong. *American Journal of Sociology, 99,* 1180–1211.

Ingersoll, J. J. (1995). Which tradition, which values? "Traditional family values" in American Protestant fundamentalism. *Contention, 4,* 91–103.

LaHaye, B. (1976). *The spirit-controlled woman.* Eugene, OR: Harvest House.

Lamont, M. (1992). *Money, morals, and manners: The culture of the French and American upper-middle class.* Chicago: University of Chicago Press.

Lamont, M. (2000). *The dignity of working men: Morality and the boundaries of race, class, and immigration.* New York: Russell Sage Foundation.

Lamont, M. & Fournier, M. (Eds.) (1992). *Cultivating differences: Symbolic boundaries and the making of inequality.* Chicago: University of Chicago Press.

Lundquist, M. & Smith, C. (1998). The triumph of ambivalence: American evangelicals on sex roles and marital decision-making. Paper presented at the annual meeting of the Society for the Scientific Study of Religion, Montreal, Quebec, Canada.

Manning. C. (1999). *God gave us the right: Conservative Catholic, evangelical Protestant, and Orthodox Jewish women grapple with feminism.* New Brunswick. NJ: Rutgers University Press.

McNamara, P. H. (1985). Conservative Christian families and their moral world: Some reflections for sociologists. *Sociological Analysis, 46,* 93–99.

Mernissi, F. (1987). *Beyond the veil* (revised edition). Bloomington: Indiana University Press.

Mernissi, F. (1991). *The veil and the male elite: A feminist interpretation of women's rights in Islam.* M. J. Lakeland (Trans.). New York: Addison-Wesley Publishing Company.

Nippert-Eng, C. E. (1996). *Home and work: Negotiating boundaries through everyday life.* Chicago: University of Chicago Press.

Patillo-McCoy, M. (1998). Church culture as a strategy of action in the black community. *American Sociological Review, 63,* 767–784.

Pevey, C., Williams, C. L., & Ellison, C. G. (1996). Male God imagery and female submission: Lessons from a Southern Baptist ladies' Bible class. *Qualitative Sociology, 19,* 173–193.

Philips. A. A. B., & Jones, J. (1985). *Polygamy in Islam.* Riyadh, Saudi Arabia: International Islamic Publishing House.

Pride, M. (1985). *The way home: Beyond feminism, back to reality.* Westchester, IL: Crossway Books.

Read, J. G. (2002). Challenging myths of Muslim women: The influence of Islam on Arab-American women's labor force participation. *Muslim World, 96,* 19–38.

Read, J. G. (2003). The sources of gender role attitudes among Christian and Muslim Arab-American women. *Sociology of Religion*, 69, 207–202.

Read, J. G., & Bartkowski, J. P. (2000). To veil or not to veil? A case study of identity negotiation among Muslim women in Austin, Texas. *Gender and Society*, 14, 395–417.

Roof, W. C., & McKinney, W. (1987). *American mainline religion: Its changing shape and future.* New Brunswick, NJ: Rutgers University Press.

Rose, S. D. (1987). Women warriors: The negotiation of gender in a charismatic community. *Sociological Analysis*, 48, 245–258.

Scanzoni. L. D., & Hardesty, N. A. (1992). *All we're meant to be: Biblical feminism for today* (third revised edition). Grand Rapids, MI: William B. Eerdmans Publishing Company.

Shaheed, F. (1994). Controlled or autonomous: Identity and the experience of the network, women living under Muslim laws. *Signs*, 19, 997–1019.

Shaheed, F. (1995). Networking for change: The role of women's groups in initiating dialogue on women's issues. In M. Afkhami (Ed.), *Faith and freedom: Women's human rights in the Muslim world* (pp. 78–98). Syracuse, NY: Syracuse University Press.

Sherif, M. H. (1987). What is hijab? *The Muslim World*, 77, 151–163.

Sherkat, D. E. (2000). "That they be keepers of the home": The effect of conservative religion on early and late transitions into housewifery. *Review of Religious Research*, 41, 344–358.

Siddiqi, M. I. (1983). *Islam forbids free mixing of men and women.* Lahore, Pakistan: Kazi.

Smith, C. (1998). *American evangelicalism: Embattled and thriving.* Chicago: University of Chicago Press.

Smith, C. (2000). *Christian America? What evangelicals really want.* Berkeley: University of California Press.

Stacey, J. (1990). *Brave new families.* New York: Basic Books.

Stacey, J., & Gerard, S. E. (1990). "We are not doormats": The influence of feminism on contemporary evangelicals in the United States. In F. Ginsberg & A. L. Tsing (Eds.), *Uncertain terms: Negotiating gender in American culture* (pp. 98–117). Boston: Beacon Press.

Stark, R. & Finke, R. (2000). *Acts of faith: Explaining the human side of religion.* Berkeley: University of California Press.

Stocks, J. (1997). To stay or to leave? Organizational legimacy in the struggle for change among evangelical feminists. In P. E. Becker & N. L. Eiesland (Eds.), *Contemporary American religion: An ethnographic reader* (pp. 99–119). Walnut Creek, CA: AltaMira Press.

Swidler, A. (1986). Culture in action: Symbols and strategies. *American Sociological Review*, 51, 273–286.

Warner, R. S. & Wittner, J. G. (Eds.) (1998). *Gatherings in diaspora: Religious communities and the new immigration.* Philadelphia: Temple University Press.

Williams, R. H. (1995). Constructing the public good: Social movements and cultural resources. *Social Problems*, 42, 124–144.

Williams, R. H. (1999). Visions of the good society and the religious roots of American political culture. *Sociology of Religion*, 60, 1–34.

"That's What a Man Is Supposed to Do": Compensatory Manhood Acts in an LGBT Christian Church

J. EDWARD SUMERAU

An emerging line of research shows that lesbian, gay, bisexual, and transgendered (LGBT) Christians face significant conflict between their sexual and religious identities (McQueeney 2009; Moon 2004; Thumma 1991; Wilcox 2003, 2009; Wolkomir 2006). Implications of these studies include that LGBT Christians draw on the "cultural toolkits" (Swidler 1986) of Christian and queer culture to create "safe spaces" for the processes of ideological, identity, and emotion work necessary for resolving their identity conflicts. They also suggest gay men are more likely to face such conflict (Rodriguez and Ouellette 2000a), and LGBT Christian organizations often become male dominated in terms of leadership, culture, and demographics over time (Wilcox 2009). While these studies have invigorated our understanding of LGBT Christian culture, they have thus far left the "politics of masculinity" (Messner 1997) among gay Christian men unexplored. How do gay Christian men construct identities as men, and what consequences do these actions have for the reproduction of inequality?

I examine these questions through an ethnographic study of a southeastern LGBT Christian organization. Specifically, I analyze how a group of gay Christian men, responding to sexist, heterosexist, and religious stigma, as well as the acquisition of a new pastor, constructed "compensatory manhood acts," which refer to acts whereby subordinated men signify masculine selves by emphasizing elements of hegemonic masculinity (Schrock and Schwalbe 2009). In so doing, I synthesize and extend analyses of LGBT Christian cultures and

masculinities by demonstrating how gay Christian men signify masculine selves, and the consequences these actions have for the reproduction of inequality. Importantly, it is not my intention to generalize my findings to the larger population of LGBT Christian churches. Rather, I use the data from this case to elaborate strategies of compensatory manhood acts subordinated groups of men may use in various social settings when they seek to compensate for their subordination in relation to other men and signify masculine selves (see Schwalbe et al. 2000).

The Social Construction of Masculinities

Over the past three decades, sociologists have demonstrated that men construct, enact, and negotiate a wide variety of masculinities shaped by both their social locations within interlocking systems of oppression, and local, regional, and global conceptions of what it means to be a man (see, e.g., Connell and Messerschmidt 2005; Messner 1997; Schrock and Schwalbe 2009). Rather than as a physical or personality trait embedded within male bodies, these studies conceptualize masculinities as collective forms of practice, belief, and interaction, which reproduce the subordination of women to men, and some men to others. These studies also show how the social construction of masculinities reproduces sexism (Kimmel 1996), heterosexism (Pascoe 2007), classism (Eastman and Schrock 2008), racism (Chen 1999), and ageism (Slevin and Linneman 2010). Overall, these studies

---

J. Edward Sumerau, "'That's What a Man Is Supposed to Do': Compensatory Manhood Acts in an LGBT Christian Church," *Gender & Society*, Vol. 26, No. 3 (June 2012), pp. 461–487. Copyright © 2012 by J. Edward Sumerau. Reprinted by permission of SAGE Publications.

suggest that understanding the reproduction of large-scale systems of inequality requires interrogating the social construction of masculinities.

Interrogating masculinities requires analyzing how men signify masculine selves. Following Goffman (1977), this process involves the dramaturgical work men do to establish and affirm the identity man (see also West and Zimmerman 1987). We may thus conceptualize masculine selves as the result of putting on a convincing "manhood act" (Schwalbe 2005). Schrock and Schwalbe (2009, 289) define "manhood acts" as "the identity work males do to claim membership in the dominant gender group, to maintain the social reality of the group, to elicit deference from others, and to maintain privileges vis-à-vis women." Whereas the elements of a convincing manhood act may vary historically and culturally and across different social settings, Schrock and Schwalbe (2009) argue that all such acts aim to signify a masculine self by exerting control over and resisting being controlled by others (see also Johnson 2005).

Interrogating masculinities, however, also requires making sense of "hegemonic masculinity" (Connell 1987, 1995; Connell and Messerschmidt 2005), or the most honored way to be a man in a given cultural or historical context. Even though very few men may enact the most honored version of manhood in a given culture or time, the hegemonic ideal typically carries enough symbolic weight to pervade the entire culture and provide the yardstick by which all performances of manhood are judged (Chen 1999; Connell 1987; Schrock and Schwalbe 2009). As Erving Goffman (1963, 128) observed:

> In an important sense there is only one unblushing male in America: a young, married, white, urban, northern, heterosexual, Protestant father of college education, fully employed, of good complexion, weight, and height, and a recent record in sports. Every American male tends to look out upon the world from this perspective.

As such, all blushing males, such as the gay men at the heart of this study, may feel the need to find ways to compensate for their subordination vis-à-vis the hegemonic ideal.

Historically, one strategy of compensation available to subordinated groups of men living within systems of oppression and privilege is the imitation of the hegemonic ideal (Connell 1995; Johnson 2005; Kimmel 1996). Since such systems are dominated by, identified with, and centered on the most honored way of being a man (Johnson 2005), this requires enacting and/or affirming the beliefs, values, characteristics, and practices of hegemonic masculinity (Chen 1999; Connell 1995; Kimmel 1996). At times, these men may engage in "compensatory manhood acts"—emphasizing and/or exaggerating elements of hegemonic masculinity to compensate for their subordination and signify masculine selves (Schrock and Schwalbe 2009).

Previous research has documented compensatory manhood acts in many social contexts. Some of the men in Snow and Anderson's (1987, 1362) study of the homeless, for example, used "fanciful identity assertions" to define their future or ideal selves as sexual, desirable, and powerful men capable of possessing female trophies. As one man stated, "Chicks are going to be all over us when we come back into town with our new suits and Corvettes. We'll have to get some cocaine too. Cocaine will get you women every time." Similarly, ethnographers have shown how male racial minorities (Anderson 1999; Chen 1999; Ferguson 2001), poor and working-class men (Eastman and Schrock 2008; MacLeod 1995; Schrock and Padavic 2007), and female-to-male transsexuals (Schilt 2006; Schilt and Westbrook 2009) engage in exaggerated displays of masculinity to compensate for their subordination in relation to the hegemonic ideal. In each case, subordinated men unable to enact the most honored form of manhood engage in compensatory manhood acts to differentiate themselves from women, and bolster their claims to privileges conferred on men in a patriarchal society.

Researchers have also documented how some men who identify as gay reject heterosexuality as an index of manhood while emphasizing conventional notions of masculinity. Specifically, these studies have shown how gay men compensate for their subordination and signify masculine selves by emphasizing larger bodies and muscularity

(Hennen 2005), athletic ability (Anderson 2011), sexual risk-taking (Collins 2009; Green and Halkitis 2006), brotherhood and the devaluation of women (Yeung and Stombler 2000; Yeung, Stombler, and Wharton 2006), the punishment of male performances of femininity (Asencio 2011), youthfulness (Slevin and Linneman 2010), and expressions of "macho" fashion (Mosher, Levitt, and Manley 2006). Similarly, Wolkomir (2009, 507) showed how gay men in mixed-orientation marriages emphasized their ability to provide for their wives and children: "A man takes care of his wife and family, and I could still do that." Whether they stressed physical, sexual, or paternal prowess, gay men in each of these studies emphasized elements of the hegemonic ideal to signify creditable masculine selves.

Previous research has also revealed the importance of evaluating socially constructed notions of Christian manhood. Sociologists of religion, for example, have shown how heterosexual Christian men redefine notions of male headship and spousal authority (Bartkowski 2001; Gallagher and Smith 1999) and make sense of competing discourses of instrumental and affective masculinity (Bartkowski and Xu 2000; Gallagher and Wood 2005) by drawing on a combination of Christian and hegemonic notions of masculine authority. Similarly, scholars have revealed how heterosexual men in Christian subcultures (Wilkins 2009) and conservative Christian movements (Heath 2003; Robinson and Spivey 2007) emphasize immutable differences between women and men to reproduce masculine privilege. Whereas these studies suggest heterosexual Christian men may interpret manhood in a variety of ways, they also reveal that these efforts rely heavily on differentiating Christian men from women and other men.

Studies of gay Christian men, however, have generally neglected masculinities. Rather, these studies typically focus on how gay Christian men manage the emotional (Wolkomir 2006) and identity-based (Thumma 1991) dilemmas surrounding sexual and religious identity integration. When researchers have incorporated gender into their analyses, they have limited their focus to how notions of Black (McQueeney 2009; Pitt 2010) and Latino (Rodriguez and Ouellette 2000b) masculinities impact strategies of identity integration. Instead of evaluating the impact of gender on identity integration, the present study examines how gay Christian men draw on gendered, sexual, and religious discourses to construct compensatory manhood acts.

Finally, it is important to note that sociologists have tied the accomplishment of compensatory manhood acts to the reproduction of inequality (Schrock and Schwalbe 2009). Studies have shown, for example, how working-class men use violence to maintain control over women in heterosexual relationships (Pyke 1996). Similarly, researchers have shown how African American (Anderson 1999), working-class (MacLeod 1995), and homosexual (Yeung, Stombler, and Wharton 2006) men construct compensatory manhood acts in ways that unintentionally reproduce their own subordination. Although the gay Christian men I studied are in some ways unique, their example reveals how the construction of compensatory manhood acts is not only about resisting subordination but is also a means through which men may claim organizational power.

Setting and Method

Data for this study derive from participant observation in a church affiliated with the United Fellowship of Metropolitan Community Churches (UFMCC). The UFMCC is an international denomination composed of more than 300 congregations. It promotes an inclusive doctrine based on "the recognition of the inherent value of each individual regardless of sexual orientation, race, class, gender, gender identification, age, or abilities" (UFMCC 2009). The church examined here developed in 1993 when LGBT Christians who felt excluded by churches in their community formed two Bible study groups. Over the next 15 years, these groups expanded into a regular church that purchased its own property and held weekly services.

My involvement with Shepherd Church (all names are pseudonyms) began when I contacted their office and explained my interest in studying the organization. At the time, I was seeking a setting to study the development of local religious and LGBT organizations over time. The representative I spoke with explained that since they were currently without a pastor, I would need to propose my research interests to the board. At their next board meeting, I introduced myself as a bisexual, white, atheist male raised in a working-class Baptist home, and presented members with a proposal for my study, professional references, and some articles I wrote while working as a journalist. Two weeks later, the members granted my request to study the church.

Over the next 36 months, I observed and participated in worship services (190), board meetings (30), Bible studies (45), choir practices (10), outreach efforts (5), and social events (105) with members of Shepherd Church. I also collected newsletters, newspaper pieces, emails, hymnals, pamphlets, and publications by the congregation and the denomination. On average, I spent about one to three hours with members during each visit conducting informal interviews before and after each activity. Throughout my fieldwork, I tape-recorded every meeting and took shorthand notes whenever possible. Afterward, I used these resources to compose detailed field notes, transcribed audio recordings in full, and took notes on any materials gathered in the field (for gender and sexual demographics in Shepherd Church over time, see Table 1).

I also conducted 20 life history interviews with members of the church. Interviews lasted between three and four hours, and I tape-recorded and transcribed each one in full. Apart from using an interview guide that consisted of a list of orienting questions about members' religious and social background and involvement in the church, the interviews were unstructured. My sample consisted of eight white lesbian women, two African American lesbian women, and ten white gay men including the new pastor. Each respondent held informal and/or formal positions of power in the church at some point during my study. All respondents held middle- and upper-middle-class jobs, and all but one had been raised in Protestant churches.

It is important to note that the racial and class characteristics of Shepherd Church may have played a role in the men's construction of masculinities (for race and class demographics in Shepherd Church, see Table 2). Although studies of LGBT Christians have thus far left the construction of race, class, and gender identities unexplored, they have found that cultural notions of race, class, and gender impact the identity integration strategies of Christian sexual minorities (see, e.g., McQueeney 2009; Pitt 2010; Rodriguez and Ouellette 2000b). In the case of Shepherd Church, the congregation was mostly white (88%) and middle- to upper-middle-class (90%) prior to the arrival of the pastor. These men's construction of compensatory manhood acts may well have benefited from their locations in privileged racial and class categories.

TABLE 1. Gender and Sexual Characteristics of Shepherd Church over Time

Demographic Category	Subgroup Characteristics	Population at Time of Pastor's Arrival	Population One Year after Pastor's Arrival
Women	Lesbian	59 (60%)	15 (33%)
	Transsexual	3 (3%)	0 (0%)
	Heterosexual	4 (4%)	0 (0%)
	Total	66 (67%)	15 (33%)
Men	Gay	25 (26%)	30 (67%)
	Transsexual	3 (3%)	0 (0%)
	Bisexual	2 (2%)	0 (0%)
	Heterosexual	2 (2%)	0 (0%)
	Total	32 (33%)	30 (67%)
Total church	Total	98 (100%)	45 (100%)

TABLE 2. Race and Class Characteristics of Shepherd Church over Time

Race/Ethnic Category	Social Class Category	Population at Time of Pastor's Arrival	Population One Year after Pastor's Arrival
White	Upper class	12 (12%)	3 (7%)
	Middle class	58 (59%)	17 (38%)
	Lower class	18 (18%)	18 (40%)
	Total	88 (90%)	38 (84%)
Black	Middle class	2 (2%)	1 (2%)
	Lower class	3 (3%)	5 (11%)
	Total	5 (5%)	6 (13%)
Hispanic	Middle class	1 (1%)	1 (2%)
	Lower class	4 (4%)	0 (0%)
	Total	5 (5%)	1 (2%)
Total church	Total	98 (100%)	45 (100%)

Regional and religious factors may also have impacted the compensatory strategies of these men. Their surrounding community, for example, consisted of a minimal LGBT public presence, well-organized local and state anti-gay political groups, and a religious atmosphere dominated by conservative Protestants. Further, the vast majority of these men were raised in the southeast and came from conservative Protestant backgrounds. In a similar fashion, the newly acquired pastor was a white, middle-class man raised in the Southern Baptist tradition, and had, prior to openly coming out as gay, held prominent positions in conservative Baptist churches in Virginia. These men's construction of compensatory manhood acts may thus have been influenced by their collective regional and religious interpretations of Christian manhood. . . .

Problematizing Gay Christian Manhood

Prior to the arrival of the new pastor, women and men ran Shepherd Church in an egalitarian manner (see, e.g., Sumerau 2010; Sumerau and Schrock 2011). Specifically, they took turns leading worship services and Bible studies, holding formal positions of power, and delivering sermons and musical performances. Further, they stressed equal representation, sought to include all members in organizational decisions, and affirmed racial, gendered, classed, and sexual diversity in the church, thereby collectively establishing an LGBT Christian space that was growing in terms of population and finances at the time of the pastor's arrival.

During this period of rapid growth, the vast majority of members expressed concerns about being taken seriously in the larger religious community. Specifically, they believed they needed to acquire the services of an ordained pastor in order to be a legitimate church. As a result, they began holding meetings and conference calls with the denomination. In response, the denomination selected three candidates, and the members had the opportunity to either veto or approve each candidate. Importantly, all three candidates were white, middle-class, gay men raised and trained in conservative Protestantism. After vetoing the first two candidates, the congregation approved and installed the final candidate.

The new pastor, however, brought a different image for the church. Specifically, he emphasized notions of Christian manhood predicated on masculine authority (see, e.g., Bartkowski 2001). As he explained to a group of men during his first week in the church:

I think you have done well here with the lesbians running things, but inclusive doesn't mean anything goes. This is still a Christian church, and that means we have to act accordingly, and be responsible Christian men. Like a father does with his children, each of you needs to be the strong, dependable blocks we build this church on, and, like in a family, you have to model this behavior for the rest of the church.

Similar to members of the Promise Keepers (Heath 2003), the new pastor viewed masculine authority as a central element of both Christian manhood and a truly Christian organization.

The new pastor's arrival thus facilitated a dramatic transformation in Shepherd Church. Specifically, most of the gay men collaborated with the pastor to construct compensatory manhood acts. Four of the gay men, the majority of the lesbian women (44 of 59), and all of the bisexual, heterosexual, and transgendered women and men, however, began departing the organization in the months following the pastor's arrival. Rather than conform to the new "politics of masculinity" (Messner 1997) in the church, they formed a new Bible study group where they continued to promote their egalitarian version of Christianity.

It is important to note that the pastor's notion of Christian manhood may have been especially salient to the gay men at Shepherd Church because of painful experiences each of them faced in the course of their lives. Raised in conservative Christian churches, they all learned from an early age to base their sense of themselves as good people on their ability to be Christian men. Their development of homosexual identities, however, placed these claims in jeopardy. As a result, they experienced feelings of guilt, shame, and fear. As Michael recalled:

> I was supposed to grow up and be a man—be responsible for a wife and a family and my church. How was I supposed to do that? I remember feeling like my life was over. I had heard what those gay people were like; I wasn't like that: I was a good Christian man.

For Michael and the other gay men, being a Christian man was a "moral identity" (Katz 1975; McQueeney 2009). Each of these attributes signified his worth, character, and value as a person. Being gay, however, created the possibility that he was not a good person.

The men's experiences were especially traumatic because their identification as homosexuals violated what they believed were valid scriptural interpretations of the sanctity of heterosexual marriage and traditional, complementary gender roles (see Ammerman 1987; Bartkowski 2001). Specifically, most conservative Christian churches defined homosexuals as sinners and abominations in the eyes of God. As Marcus explained one morning after church:

> Growing up you heard about "those gay people" and how they were ruining the world, but it didn't really sink in until I realized I was one of "those people." Then, whoa man, I spent so many nights crying, praying and asking why God would do this to me. Why did I have to be damned? Why couldn't I be good, just why?

For Marcus and the others, identifying as gay was similar to receiving a death sentence, and deemed their Christian identities invalid. As others have noted (see, e.g., Wilcox 2003), they joined an LGBT church in search of a "safe space" to express their Christian *and* sexual identities.

Their painful experiences, however, were not limited to their sexual and religious identities. Raised in conservative Christian churches, they also learned from an early age that God's will is expressed in a divine mandate requiring women's submission and men's leadership for the promotion of an ideal Christian society (see also Wolkomir 2006). Specifically, they learned that real men headed churches and families by leading, protecting, and providing for their wives, children, and fellow Christians (Ammerman 1987). As Micah noted:

> I still get it every time I go home: "When you going to grow up and be a man, boy?" and "What kind of man don't have no wife or kids?" Oh, and "When you goin' to grow out of the gay stuff?" It's hard sometimes because that's what a man is supposed to do right—raise a family, take care of a wife. What does that say about me?

For Micah and many others, identifying as homosexual generated a direct attack on their manhood. Similar to men in "bear" groups (Hennen 2005) and gay fraternities (Yeung, Stombler, and Wharton 2006), they sought to claim masculine selves denied to them in the larger social world. In the following sections, I examine how the new pastor and the gay men who remained at Shepherd Church accomplished this by constructing compensatory manhood acts.

Constructing Gay Christian Manhood

What follows is an analysis of how the gay men at Shepherd Church constructed compensatory manhood acts. First, I examine how they constructed compensatory manhood acts by emphasizing paternal stewardship over the church and the LGBT community. Specifically, this strategy involved defining themselves as fatherly guides and financial providers. Then, I show how they constructed compensatory manhood acts by stressing emotional control and inherent rationality to differentiate themselves from women and effeminate men. Finally, I analyze how they constructed compensatory manhood acts by defining intimate relationships in a Christian manner, thus emphasizing responsible sexual conduct, monogamy, and immutable sexual natures. While these strategies allowed them to signify masculine selves, they also reproduced the superiority of men at the expense of women and sexual minorities.

Emphasizing Paternal Stewardship

On his arrival, the new pastor stressed resisting stereotypical depictions of homosexual men as selfish and irresponsible children. As he stated in his first sermon, the members of Shepherd Church could resist such stereotypes by being good stewards of their church:

> We all know how others try to clobber us gay guys by saying we're anti-family or irresponsible children who only want to play. Well, we know different, and part of our job as men is to show the world we are good providers and leaders in our communities.

Importantly, the gay men at Shepherd Church were already intimately familiar with these cultural depictions of homosexual men. As Troy explained during one Bible Study:

> You know how they see us, right? They talk about us like we're kids. We're too busy doing our makeup and partying to raise a family or support our partners or any of the other things real men do with their time or, more likely, with their money.

Seeking to refute such depictions, they constructed compensatory manhood acts by emphasizing paternal stewardship. Specifically, they defined themselves as fatherly guides and financial providers for women and other sexual minorities.

These gay men constructed identities as Christian men by defining themselves as fatherly guides providing the necessary leadership for their communities to survive. This tactic involved defining other sexual minorities as children requiring supervision. As Matthew noted:

> It's like being a father to your own kids. Many of these folks that come here and to other community events are fresh out of the closet, and, like children, they have no clue how to look out for themselves. That's where we come in. We can come to them like parents, provide them with the wisdom and experience we have, and they'll be better for it.

In a similar fashion, Tommy explained, during a Bible study, "Well, it's understandable that a lot of these little ones don't realize all the fighting and struggles we went through building this community. They just need some good fatherly teaching." Echoing others, Matthew and Tommy emphasized the importance of sharing the "wisdom and experience" they possessed with the "kids" or "children" that "have no clue" how to exist within an LGBT community. Similar to members of the Promise Keepers (Heath 2003), they constructed compensatory manhood acts by defining themselves as fatherly guides capable of providing for less informed others.

The gay men at Shepherd Church also constructed compensatory manhood acts by defining women as selfish creatures in need of fatherly guidance. As Micah noted:

> It's not a bad thing, just how they are, but the lesbians jumping beds and relationships so often that they often lose sight of what matters. It's just how they are. We have to kind of pick up the slack. It's not that they're bad people, but they need some strong guidance.

Similarly, Dante observed, "It's not a lesbian thing, I don't think. My mom's that way. Women are kind of flighty, I guess, and that's okay because, like in a family, the men can make sure things run smooth." Echoing others, Dante and Micah defined "women" as "kind of flighty" and in need of the guidance "men" could provide. Similar to gay men in mixed-orientation marriages (Wolkomir 2009), they defined women as subordinates in need of their guidance and direction.

After the pastor's arrival, these gay men also began defining themselves as financial providers. Specifically, this strategy involved differentiating between male providers and others:

> Tommy says, "I think it's important to remember this is our church, and we have a responsibility to take care of it." Speaking up, Maria says, "Well, anyone can help with the cleaning. Alice and I have been doing it the last couple weeks, and it's important." The Pastor holds out his hand, and says, "That is good work ya'll are doing, Maria, but more importantly, like the check John and Michael put in this morning, is the financial well-being of the church. I mean, we can worship in some dirt, but we need for all of us to come together to take care of finances and be real stewards for our father's house."

In moments like this, they defined "financial" provision as the primary form of Christian stewardship. Whereas "anyone" could "help with the cleaning," they downplayed these traditionally feminine activities and emphasized the "financial well-being" of the church.

Importantly, the gay men at Shepherd Church often explicitly invoked gender when discussing financial provision without women around. As Marcus explained, "Well, it's a man job to bring in the money, and so it's okay that the lesbians don't

kick in as much cash, but it's disappointing sometimes, but that's what men are supposed to do, right?" Marcus and others defined bringing in money as an activity that "men are supposed to do" while asserting that "the lesbians" often did not do so anyway. Similarly, they often defined financial provision as an essential element of manhood. As the Pastor observed, "It's important to recognize women trying to contribute, but it's more important to make sure the men understand it's their job, their responsibility, their calling from God." Echoing leaders of the ex-gay movement (Robinson and Spivey 2007), the pastor defined financial provision as a "calling," a "responsibility," and a "job" men receive from God, and emphasized "making sure the men understand" God's plan. On the contrary, congregational logs revealed that women often contributed more money than men. Importantly, none of the men ever mentioned this. In a culture where breadwinning is interpreted as evidence of a masculine self (see Kimmel 1996), the men may have ignored this information to preserve their compensatory manhood acts from possible challenges.

Overall, the gay men at Shepherd Church constructed compensatory manhood acts by emphasizing paternal stewardship over the church and the larger LGBT community. In so doing, however, they reproduced cultural notions of male supremacy by defining women and other sexual minorities as irresponsible children incapable of taking care of themselves (see Kimmel 1996). Similar to leaders of the ex-gay Christian movement (Robinson and Spivey 2007), men active in the Promise Keepers (Heath 2003), and gay men in mixed-orientation marriages (Wolkomir 2009), they constructed identities as men by reproducing the supremacy of fatherly guidance, male headship, and breadwinning. As such, their compensatory manhood acts reproduced the elevation of men at the expense of women and sexual minorities.

Stressing Emotional Control and Inherent Rationality

On his arrival, the new pastor also stressed resisting stereotypical depictions of homosexual men as overly emotional and effeminate. As he stated in the first Bible study I attended where only men were present, the gay men at Shepherd Church could resist such stereotypes by controlling their emotions and drawing on their inherent rationality:

It's important to talk about how we go about handling our emotions during these changing times. As men, we all know that the media seems to guess we are all weepy and girly like women, but we know, probably better than most, that our Father blessed us with an inherent rationality that we can draw on in times of struggle, and it's important for us all to do this and keep our emotions in check as we make necessary changes for the church.

Importantly, the gay men at Shepherd Church were already well versed in the importance of emotional control. As Michael noted in an interview:

Sometimes, life can be hell. People will be really nasty when they hear you're a gay. Sissy, wimp, and fag are, like, words, but fists and damnation leave some deep marks. As a man, it's hard to control your feelings and deal with the pain; it's hard, but it's important.

Similarly, Troy recalled, "It was like in high school, if you lost control, even for a second let a tear slip, or your voice crack, you were automatically a queeny bitch." Seeking to refute depictions of overly emotional, effeminate homosexual men, they constructed compensatory manhood acts by stressing emotional control and inherent rationality.

These gay men constructed identities as men by stressing emotional control. This strategy often involved making references to Biblical figures that suffered unfairly while remaining composed and faithful to God. As the pastor argued during one Bible study:

"Now, you have to remember that it wasn't easy," the pastor says while Tommy passes the candy jar around the table. "I mean, Paul had it rough, and he could have sat down on the edge of the cliff and cried "Woe is me!" I don't think anyone would have blamed him, just like no one might blame some of us after the discrimination our people have faced." As he finishes speaking, four men offer "amens." Smiling, the pastor continues,

"What we have to remember, like Paul did, is that God is with us, and we will be okay and make it through if we don't give up, don't give in. Part of that is keeping our emotions, our grief, our tears in check—there is no time for tears when you're working for God!"

Similarly, Daniel noted, "It's like a fight, you can't wimp out like some sissy or little girl. When things are hard, and they can be really hard, you just have to have faith and fight on." Echoing these sentiments, Jamie observed, "We all learned crying and whining is for queens. Real men have to stand up, not take stuff from bigots and idiots." As these statements reveal, the gay men at Shepherd Church defined emotional control as central to manhood, and the expression of emotions as something that only a "sissy or little girl" would do. Similar to mixed-martial arts fighters (see Vaccarro, Schrock, and McCabe 2011), these men thus constructed compensatory manhood acts by defining the expression of emotions as inherently unmanly.

They also constructed compensatory manhood acts by explicitly defining emotional display as feminine and differentiating themselves from women. As Donny stated:

"The way those women were just a-crying, I can't imagine acting like that," he says while nudging my arm. Puzzled, I ask, "You do realize Manny was crying as loud as any of the women?" Smiling, he responds, "I said 'those women,' didn't I? You've met Manny before, if that ain't a true-blue queen I don't know who is, probably has more right to the title 'woman' than any of the others with all the whining and carrying on he does."

Similarly, Martin explained after a worship service, "I swear, those queens, the lesbian ones and the gay ones, give us such a bad name. Look at them crying over photos and such, you wouldn't catch me dead doin' that, damn girls." Echoing Donny and others, Martin considered that "crying" in the presence of others was something that "damn girls" and "queens" did, which gave real gay men a "bad name." Further, as Donny's comments suggest, this type of behavior could disqualify males from the identity "man." Similar to some men in batterer intervention programs (Schrock and Padavic 2007), these gay men constructed compensatory manhood acts by defining emotional control as masculine and emotional expression as feminine.

These gay men also constructed identities as men by stressing inherent rationality. Specifically, they stressed the rational nature of men while accusing lesbians of falling victim to emotions. The following field note provides a typical example:

> Troy turns to James and I, and says, "You hear Jamie saying there's a new sheriff in town now that he's on the board," and James responds, "Well, I don't know what you think, but I got to say, good, it's just like bringing in the pastor. We need real leadership, no more of this lesbian drama and funny business. We need to focus on what really matters and how we can grow as a church." Chuckling and handing me a drink, Troy says, "Well, I can agree there. Sometimes they just, I don't know, things get so heated, so crazy, it seems like we need to make decisions with more composure or something."

Similarly, the pastor noted, "I don't know. I've dealt with lesbians before, but these just seem to take everything so personal. Real decision making needs to leave all those feelings at the door." As these examples reveal, these gay men stressed leaving "feelings" and "personal" concerns out of the "real decision making" while equating female leadership with "drama," "funny business," and "heated" or "crazy" decision making lacking "composure." Similar to how lawyers (Pierce 1995) define rationality as masculine, they constructed compensatory manhood acts by suggesting they, and not women, possessed the inherent rationality necessary to lead the church.

Further, they claimed men's inherent rationality made them naturally more suited for leadership. As Tommy noted, "Men are just built to make decisions, like my own talents for taking care of things; that's just something inside me." Similarly, Martin noted, "I think sometimes the drama gets the best of women, but it's not their fault, they're not built like us, and that's just how it is. Men just seem to know how to handle the important stuff." Micah also observed, "Sometimes I think maybe God did just make us different. I know a lot of people have left because they liked it better with the ladies running things, but it seems so much smoother, like a well-oiled machine now." These gay men thus stressed their own inherent ability to lead, and defined their God-given rationality as greater than the "drama" of the "ladies." Similar to how ex-gay Christian advocates define masculinity as a God-given good to rationalize the use of intervention therapies (Robinson and Spivey 2007), they constructed identities as men by symbolically positioning themselves above supposedly irrational women.

The gay men at Shepherd Church thus constructed compensatory manhood acts by stressing emotional control and inherent rationality. Similar to men in batterer intervention programs (Schrock and Padavic 2007), law firms (Pierce 1995), gay and ex-gay Christian support groups (Wolkomir 2006), ex-gay ministries (Robinson and Spivey 2007), and mixed-martial arts groups (Vaccarro, Schrock, and McCabe 2011), they constructed identities as men by reproducing a long-held cultural mandate that "real men" control their emotions (see Kimmel 1996). Whereas these strategies allowed them to construct identities as men, they relied on depictions of women as emotionally unstable and incapable of leadership, reproducing the subordination of women by perpetuating stereotypical depictions of immutable differences between feminine and masculine emotional subjectivity (see Schwalbe et al. 2000).

Defining Intimate Relationships in a Christian Manner

On his arrival, the new pastor also emphasized resisting cultural depictions of homosexual men as sexually promiscuous. As he told a group of men at the first fellowship dinner he attended, they could accomplish this by following Christian principles:

> As gay men, we have to be careful about our relationships. There are those out there just looking to clobber us and call us sickos, but if we model respectable, Christian, monogamous, and committed relationships, in time those same people will welcome us into the fold like states that have begun to recognize gay marriages.

Importantly, these gay men were already acutely aware of these issues. As Barney explained:

> It's all over the place, this silly belief that all we do is screw and screw and screw. Now, don't get me wrong, I'm a man so I definitely like to screw. But we're not all roaming around looking in every corner for a piece of tail—that's just crazy!

Seeking to refute such depictions, these gay men constructed compensatory manhood acts by defining intimate relationships in a Christian manner. Although they could have interpreted Christian principles regarding intimate relationships in a variety of ways (see Gallagher and Wood 2005), they defined Christian intimacy in ways that symbolically positioned themselves above supposedly promiscuous lesbians, bisexuals, and polyamorous others (see also Wilkins 2009).

The gay men at Shepherd Church constructed compensatory manhood acts by emphasizing responsible sexual conduct. This was especially true for single men, and men who had recently come out of the closet. Typically, they focused on using protection and viewing sex as part of a quest for a long-term relationship. As the new pastor explained in an interview:

> Like any other man, the boys coming out of the closet feel like they gotta get their numbers up. But what's important for them to know is it's not about being gay, it's about becoming responsible gay Christian men. It's not about who you sleep with, but how you do it. It's about building relationships, healthy exchanges between caring adults that could lead to more than a hook-up, and it's about being safe.

Similarly, Martin noted during a social gathering, "Oh, we can be as nasty as anyone, but the point is finding that special someone, not just out doing everything for the sake of doing it." As these illustrations reveal, these gay men emphasized forming "healthy, committed, adult relationships" that "could possibly lead" to something more serious, and "being safe" in regard to diseases and hook-ups. At the same time, they echoed elements of hegemonic masculinity by asserting that, "like any other man," all gay men would naturally seek to "get their numbers up."

Since single men were in much shorter supply in the church, the primary way these gay men constructed compensatory manhood acts involved emphasizing monogamy. Similar to some conservative Christian interpretations of heterosexual marriage (see Bartkowski 2001), this strategy involved defining monogamous homosexuality as the ultimate expression of God's will. Specifically, church members began holding holy unions, relationship workshops, couples retreats, and major anniversary festivities for committed couples after the arrival of the new pastor. As Michael observed during an anniversary celebration, "One thing about being back in the church is the opportunity to live right, settle down with a partner, and make a home together just like God intends." Similarly, Dante explained during a Bible study, "The whole point of this life, or the way I read the Bible, is to find someone special, someone you feel fits you right, and build a committed relationship." Echoing other men in the church as well as many heterosexual Christians, these gay men constructed compensatory manhood acts by defining monogamy as the way to "live right," and "the whole point of this life" according to the "Bible."

Whereas the dual emphasis on responsible sexual conduct and homosexual monogamy challenged dominant Christian conceptions of homosexuality, gay men at Shepherd Church also constructed compensatory manhood acts by using these discourses to denigrate promiscuity on the part of lesbian, gay, and bisexual others. The following field note excerpt offers an example:

> Barney asks, "So what does a lesbian bring to a second date?" I say, "What?" Chuckling erupts as Barney says, "A moving van," and slaps me on the back. Allan adds, "Don't get me wrong, the lesbian drama is a lot of fun, but sometimes I wish they would grow up." Patrick adds, "Well, it's just weird, the way women hop from relationship to relationship, from bed to bed; makes me wonder if there is something about the cunt that causes all the heterosexual adultery out there." Grinning at the laughter, he continues, "Men just aren't like that, we get around and then find a partner; women just go crazy, on to the next every two weeks or so. It's freakin' scary!" Softly,

Martin adds, "It's just un-Christian, I think, and maybe that's why they have so many troubles, the lot of them."

In exchanges like these, gay men denigrated lesbians for failing to obtain long-term monogamous relationships. While these men were obviously aware of stereotypical depictions of lesbians, they reinterpreted such depictions to proclaim their own superiority. Rather than simply as an example of getting their numbers up, they defined lesbian serial monogamy as evidence of immaturity and immorality. Similarly, many men expressed dismay and even disgust at the dating practices of lesbians. As Troy explained, "It's just odd, hopping around the way they do. It's just unseemly, and it makes the rest of us look bad." Echoing others, Troy felt the way lesbians "hop from relationship to relationship, from bed to bed" made gay men "look bad," and, like Patrick and Martin, he felt the way "women just go crazy" was "just unseemly" and "un-Christian." Similar to how some boys use language to turn girls into props for signifying heterosexuality (Pascoe 2007) and some female rugby players use notions of femininity to distance themselves from lesbians (Ezzell 2009), these men used their definition of monogamy to turn lesbians into props for constructing compensatory manhood acts.

These gay men also constructed compensatory manhood acts by emphasizing immutable sexual natures. Specifically, this strategy involved defining bisexual and polyamorous desires as a sign of weakness or an inability to accept one's sexuality. As Micah explained in an interview:

In my experience, bisexuality doesn't exist. Don't get me wrong, I messed with a girl or two before I accepted that I was gay. But I feel like bisexual is just for before they realize if they are gay or straight. I think you're just born one way or another.

For Micah and many others, bisexuality was not a possibility. Most of the men felt they had been "born" gay, and just did not "realize" it until a certain point in their lives. As the pastor observed: "Bisexuality is tricky; I mean, I was just talking to Dana and, I don't know, sometimes I think ya'll need to get off the fence, but other times I don't know."

Echoing the pastor, these gay men often spoke of bisexual and polyamorous others as "on the fence" or "in between" sexualities. Similar to many Christian treatments of homosexuality (see Moon 2004), they sanctified immutable sexual natures by dismissing alternate sexual desires and practices.

Because of the emphasis on immutable sexualities, bisexual and polyamorous members often faced the same conflicts lesbian women and gay men face in other churches. As Dana, a bisexual man, noted, "They're as bad as the Baptists. They want me to join the opposite team, but it's the same damn message—narrow-minded bullshit." Further, many gay men spoke of "accepting your God-given sexuality" and your "sexual nature." As Martin noted at a gathering:

I think people need to be honest with themselves. We're all born gay or straight. We all know this. God doesn't mention other options in the Bible, and why should we expect otherwise? The point is to find a partner, a companion, a lover, and how are you supposed to do that playing both sides of the field? It seems weird to associate with the bisexuals, and poly-whatevers in politics. It makes the rest of us look like freaks.

Echoing Christian notions of immutable sexual natures, Martin and others stressed an obligation to follow the sexual design laid down by "God" in the "Bible," and to recognize that "we're all born gay or straight" so we should not "expect otherwise" or "associate" with "bisexuals," "poly-whatevers," or other "freaks." Similar to ex-gay Christian depictions of homosexuals and feminists (Robinson and Spivey 2007), these gay men constructed compensatory manhood acts by differentiating themselves from unnatural deviants unwilling to submit to the demands of God.

In sum, the gay men at Shepherd Church constructed compensatory manhood acts by defining intimate relationships in a Christian manner. In so doing, however, they reproduced narrow definitions of sexuality often used to justify the subordination of sexual minorities in mainstream Christianity (see, e.g., Wilcox 2009; Wolkomir 2006). Further, they accomplished this by turning women into scapegoats, and symbolically positioning the sexual desires of gay men above those of lesbians, bisexuals, and polyamorous people. As such, their construction of compensatory manhood acts ultimately reproduced sexist and heterosexist notions of sexuality.

Conclusion

The gay men at Shepherd Church learned from an early age to base their perceptions of themselves as good people on their ability to be Christian men. Their development of homosexual identities, however, placed these claims in jeopardy. While they could have rejected dominant notions of manhood, as they all once had and those who left the church continued to do, the arrival of a new pastor provided them with an opportunity to go in a different direction. As a result, they worked with the pastor to construct compensatory manhood acts—emphasizing elements of hegemonic masculinity to compensate for their subordination and signify masculine selves. Specifically, they did so by emphasizing paternal stewardship, stressing emotional control and inherent rationality, and defining intimate relationships in a Christian manner.

While their construction of compensatory manhood acts allowed them to successfully compensate for their subordination and signify masculine selves, it also reproduced cultural notions that facilitate the subordination of women and alternative sexualities. By characterizing women as overly emotional and incapable of handling leadership positions, for example, they reproduced conventional gendered discourses used to justify masculine authority in occupational (Padavic 1991), religious (Robinson and Spivey 2007), and legal (Pierce 1995) settings. Similarly, their promotion of immutable sexual natures reproduced rhetoric (see, e.g., Moon 2004) used to deny equal rights to LGBT people. Whereas religious researchers have sought to understand why LGBT churches tend to become male dominated in terms of leadership, demographics, and culture (see, e.g., Wilcox 2009), these findings reveal that part of this answer may lie in the "politics of masculinity" (Messner 1997) promoted in these social settings.

These findings also support research on the impact of cultural notions of masculinity on gay Christian men (see, e.g., McQueeney 2009; Pitt 2010; Rodriguez and Ouellette 2000b), and extend this research by revealing how gay Christian men draw on conventional notions of gender, sexuality, and religion to construct compensatory manhood acts. Specifically, the gay Christian men at Shepherd Church drew on notions of Christian manhood to deflect cultural stigma against homosexual men, fashion creditable masculine selves, and claim gender-based privilege in their local organization. Similar to leaders of conservative Christian groups, such as the Promise Keepers (Heath 2003) and the ex-gay ministries (Robinson and Spivey 2007), they promoted a "politics of masculinity" (Messner 1997) characterized by the elevation of men at the expense of women and other sexual minorities. Whereas researchers have generally treated LGBT and conservative Christian groups as purely oppositional forces (see, e.g., Wolkomir 2006), the case of Shepherd Church suggests that in some cases these organizations may share more similarities than previously thought. These findings thus reveal the importance of examining and comparing the social construction of masculinities in specific religious settings.

These findings also extend previous treatments of compensatory manhood acts by drawing our attention to the ways subordinated men may use such actions to claim power over women and effeminate men. Whereas previous studies have shown how subordinated men construct compensatory manhood acts to claim power over women in intimate relationships (Pyke 1996), they have generally focused on how such actions unintentionally reproduce subordinated men's *own* disadvantage (see, e.g., Anderson 1999; MacLeod 1995; Yeung, Stombler, and Wharton 2006). The gay Christian men at Shepherd Church, however, constructed compensatory manhood acts in ways that explicitly defined women and other sexual minorities as inferior beings. While these actions did in fact reproduce cultural notions that facilitate the oppression of gay men, they also reproduced societal patterns of gender inequality by justifying the superiority of men within the context of their church. These findings thus reveal the importance of addressing not only how subordinated men compensate for their disadvantage at the societal level but also how such actions may ultimately result in the oppression of women and sexual minorities in local settings.

These findings also reveal the necessity of examining how subordinated men construct compensatory manhood acts in ways that simultaneously deflect stigma *and* claim organizational power over women. Whereas previous studies of subordinated men generally focus on *either* attempts to deflect stigma or efforts to claim privileges over women, the case of Shepherd Church reveals that these may often be interrelated results of the construction of compensatory manhood acts. Further, examples of this interrelation may be seen in many arenas where subordinated men seek to resist controlling images while bolstering claims to male privilege. African American men during the Civil Rights movement, for example, sought to de-stigmatize cultural notions of Black men while devaluing the contributions of African American women (see, e.g., Collins 2000). In a similar fashion, poor and working-class men may fashion themselves as hard workers while denigrating women who enter their occupational domains (see, e.g., Padavic 1991). Unraveling the ways subordinated men may accomplish these interrelated goals, however, requires asking questions beyond the scope of the present study. Researchers could, for example, examine how subordinated men accomplish these goals in nonreligious settings, such as social movement organizations, occupations, and schools. Further, researchers could examine what role women might play in the construction of compensatory manhood acts as well as the ways women may resist such acts. Finally, researchers should explore the ways that cultural notions of race, class, age, and/or nationality might play a role in these actions.

These findings also demonstrate the importance of examining when and where subordinated men are more likely to engage in strategies of compensation. Previous studies have, for example, conceptualized men's strategies of compensation as—seemingly automatic—responses to marginalization vis-à-vis the hegemonic ideal (see, e.g., Connell and Messerschmidt 2005; Schrock and Schwalbe 2009). In the case of Shepherd Church, however, all the gay men experienced marginalization in relation to the most honored form of manhood, and yet none of them constructed compensatory manhood acts prior to the arrival of the new pastor. Rather than merely a reaction to religious and/or sexual marginalization, their construction of compensatory manhood acts relied on the establishment of organizational leadership conducive to the elevation of men at the expense of women. Whereas future research may reveal important variations, these findings suggest that subordinated men may be more likely to construct compensatory manhood acts when they find themselves in settings where organizational leaders promote and affirm masculine authority and privilege (see also Dellinger 2004).

To fully understand the reproduction of gender and sexual inequality, we must analyze how subordinated men construct identities as men and the consequences of these actions (Schrock and Schwalbe 2009). Specifically, this will require critically investigating how men who belong to marginalized social groups interpret notions of manhood as well as the factors that lead some men to act in ways that reproduce the elevation of men at the expense of women and sexual minorities. As the case of Shepherd Church reveals, the construction of compensatory manhood acts relies on both the adoption of notions of male supremacy and organizational conditions conducive to the subordination of women. Unraveling and comparing the variations in compensatory manhood acts and, more generally, the multitude of ways men collaborate to signify, interpret, and affirm the oppression of women and sexual minorities, may deepen our understanding of the reproduction of inequality as well as possibilities for social change.

References

Ammerman, Nancy T. 1987. *Bible believers: Fundamentalists in the modern world*. New Brunswick, NJ: Rutgers University Press.

Anderson, Elijah. 1999. *Code of the Street: Decency, violence and the moral life of the inner city*. New York: Norton.

Anderson, Eric. 2011. Updating the outcome: Gay athletes, straight teams, and coming out in educationally based sports teams. *Gender & Society* 25:250–68.

Asencio, Marysol. 2011. Locas, respect, and masculinity: Gender conformity in migrant Puerto Rican gay masculinities. *Gender & Society* 25: 335–54.

Bartkowski, John. 2001. *Remaking the Godly marriage: Gender negotiation in evangelical families.* New Brunswick, NJ: Rutgers University Press.

Bartkowski, John, and Xiaohe Xu. 2000. Distant patriarchs or expressive dads? The discourse and practice of fathering in conservative Protestant families. *Sociological Quarterly* 41:465–85.

Chen, Anthony S. 1999. Lives at the center of the periphery, lives at the periphery of the center: Chinese American masculinities and bargaining with hegemony. *Gender & Society* 13:584–607.

Collins, Dana. 2009. "We're there and queer": Homonormative mobility and lived experience among gay expatriates in Manila. *Gender & Society* 23:465–93.

Collins, Patricia Hill. 2000. *Black feminist thought: Knowledge, consciousness, and the politics of empowerment.* New York: Routledge.

Connell, R. W. 1987. *Gender and power.* Stanford, CA: Stanford University Press.

Connell, R. W. 1995. *Masculinities.* Los Angeles: University of California Press.

Connell, R. W., and James W. Messerschmidt. 2005. Hegemonic masculinity: Rethinking the concept. *Gender & Society* 19:829–59.

Dellinger, Kirsten. 2004. Masculinities in "safe" and "embattled" organizations: Accounting for pornographic and feminist magazines. *Gender & Society* 18:545–66.

Eastman, Jason T., and Douglas P. Schrock. 2008. Southern rock musicians' construction of white trash. *Race, Gender & Class* 15:205–19.

Ezzell, Matthew B. 2009. "Barbie dolls" on the pitch: Identity work, defensive othering, and inequality in women's rugby. *Social Problems* 56:111–31.

Ferguson, Ann Arnett. 2001. *Bad boys: Public schools in the making of Black masculinity.* Ann Arbor: University of Michigan Press.

Gallagher, Sally K., and Christian Smith. 1999. Symbolic traditionalism and pragmatic egalitarianism: Contemporary evangelicals, family, and gender. *Gender & Society* 13:211–33.

Gallagher, Sally K., and Sabrina L. Wood. 2005. Godly manhood going wild?: Transformations in conservative Protestant masculinity. *Sociology of Religion* 66:135–60.

Goffman, Erving. 1963. *Stigma: Notes on the management of spoiled identity.* Englewood Cliffs, NJ: Prentice-Hall.

Goffman, Erving. 1977. The arrangement between the sexes. *Theory and Society* 4:301–31.

Green, Adam I., and Perry N. Halkitis. 2006. Crystal methamphetamine and sexual sociality in an urban gay subculture: An elective affinity. *Culture, Health & Sexuality* 8:317–33.

Heath, Melanie. 2003. Soft-boiled masculinity: Renegotiating gender and racial ideologies in the Promise Keepers movement. *Gender & Society* 17:423–44.

Hennen, Peter. 2005. Bear bodies, bear masculinity: Recuperation, resistance, or retreat? *Gender & Society* 19:25–43.

Johnson, Allan G. 2005. *The gender knot: Unraveling our patriarchal legacy.* Philadelphia: Temple University Press.

Katz, Jack. 1975. Essences as moral identities: Verifiability and responsibility in imputations of deviance and charisma. *American Journal of Sociology* 80:1369–90.

Kimmel, Michael. 1996. *Manhood in America: A cultural history.* New York: Free Press.

MacLeod, Jay. 1995. *Ain't no makin' it: Aspirations and attainment in a low-income neighborhood.* Boulder, CO: Westview.

McQueeney, Krista. 2009. "We are God's children, y'all": Race, gender, and sexuality in lesbian-and-gay-affirming congregations. *Social Problems* 56:151–73.

Messner, Michael A. 1997. *The politics of masculinities: Men in movements.* Thousand Oaks, CA: Sage.

Moon, Dawne. 2004. *God, sex, and politics: Homosexuality and everyday theologies.* Chicago, IL: University of Chicago Press.

Mosher, Chad M., Heidi M. Levitt, and Eric Manley. 2006. Layers of leather: The identity formation of Leathermen as a process of transforming meanings of masculinity. *Journal of Homosexuality* 51:93–123.

Padavic, Irene. 1991. The re-creation of gender in a male workplace. *Symbolic Interaction* 14:279–94.

Pascoe, C. J. 2007. *Dude, you're a fag: Masculinity and sexuality in high school.* Berkeley: University of California Press.

Pierce, Jennifer. 1995. *Gender trials: Emotional lives of contemporary law firms.* Berkeley: University of California Press.

Pitt, Richard N. 2010. "Still looking for my Jonathan": Gay Black men's management of religious and sexual identity conflicts. *Journal of Homosexuality* 57:39–53.

Pyke, Karen D. 1996. Class-based masculinities: The interdependence of gender, class, and interpersonal power. *Gender & Society* 10:527–49.

Robinson, Christine M., and Sue E. Spivey. 2007. The politics of masculinity and the Ex-Gay movement. *Gender & Society* 21:650–75.

Rodriguez, Eric M., and Suzanne C. Ouellette. 2000a. Gay and lesbian Christians: Homosexual and religious identity integration in the members and participants of a gay-positive church. *Journal for the Scientific Study of Religion* 39:333–47.

Rodriguez, Eric M., and Suzanne C. Ouellette. 2000b. Religion and masculinity in Latino gay lives. In *Gay masculinities*, edited by Peter M. Nardi. Thousand Oaks, CA: Sage.

Schilt, Kristen. 2006. Just one of the guys? How transmen make gender visible at work. *Gender & Society* 20:465–90.

Schilt, Kristen, and Laurel Westbrook. 2009. Doing gender, doing heternormativity: "Gender normals," transgender people, and the social maintenance of heterosexuality. *Gender & Society* 23:440–64.

Schrock, Douglas, and Michael Schwalbe. 2009. Men, masculinity, and manhood acts. *Annual Review of Sociology* 35:277–95.

Schrock, Douglas P., and Irene Padavic. 2007. Negotiating hegemonic masculinity in a batterer intervention program. *Gender & Society* 21:625–49.

Schwalbe, Michael. 2005. Identity stakes, manhood acts, and the dynamics of accountability. In *Studies in symbolic interaction, number 28*, edited by Norman Denzin. New York: Elsevier.

Schwalbe, Michael, Sandra Godwin, Daphne Holden, Douglas Schrock, Shealy Thompson, and Michelle Wolkomir. 2000. Generic processes in the reproduction of inequality: An interactionist analysis. *Social Forces* 79:419–52.

Slevin, Kathleen F., and Thomas J. Linneman. 2010. Old gay men's bodies and masculinities. *Men and Masculinities* 12:483–507.

Snow, David, and Leon Anderson. 1987. Identity work among the homeless: The verbal construction and avowal of personal identities. *American Journal of Sociology* 92:1336–71.

Sumerau, J. Edward. 2010. Constructing an inclusive congregational identity in a metropolitan community church. Unpublished master's thesis, Florida State University, Tallahassee.

Sumerau, J. Edward, and Douglas P. Schrock. 2011. "It's important to show your colors": Counter-heteronormative embodiment in a metropolitan community church. In *Embodied resistance: Breaking the rules, challenging the norms*, edited by Chris Bobel and Samantha Kwan. Nashville, Tennessee: Vanderbilt University Press.

Swidler, Ann. 1986. Culture in action: Symbols and strategies. *American Sociological Review* 51:273–86.

Thumma, Scott. 1991. Negotiating a religious identity: The case of the gay evangelical. *Sociological Analysis* 52:333–47.

UFMCC (United Fellowship of Metropolitan Community Churches). 2009. Mission statement, press kit, and informational bulletins. http://www.mcchurch. org (accessed summer 2009).

Vaccarro, Christian, Douglas P. Schrock, and Janice McCabe. 2011. Managing emotional manhood: Fighting and fostering fear in mixed martial arts. *Social Psychology Quarterly*, 74: 414–437.

West, Candace, and Don Zimmerman. 1987. Doing gender. *Gender & Society* 1:125–51.

Wilcox, Melissa. 2003. *Coming out in Christianity: Religion, identity, and community*. Bloomington: Indiana University Press.

Wilcox, Melissa M. 2009. *Queer women and religious individualism*. Bloomington: Indiana University Press.

Wilkins, Amy C. 2009. Masculinity dilemmas: Sexuality and intimacy talk among Christians and Goths. *Signs* 34:343–68.

Wolkomir, Michelle. 2006. *Be not deceived: The sacred and sexual struggles of gay and ex-gay Christian men*. New Brunswick, NJ: Rutgers University Press.

Wolkomir, Michelle. 2009. Making heteronormative reconciliations: The story of romantic love, sexuality, and gender in mixed-orientation marriages. *Gender & Society* 23:494–519.

Yeung, King-To, and Mindy Stombler. 2000. Gay and Greek: The identity paradox of gay fraternities. *Social Problems* 47:134–52.

Yeung, King-To, Mindy Stombler, and Renee Wharton. 2006. Making men in gay fraternities: Resisting and reproducing multiple dimensions of hegemonic masculinity. *Gender & Society* 20:5–31.

The Gendered Workplace

Perhaps the most dramatic social change in industrial countries in the twentieth century has been the entry of women into the workplace. The nineteenth-century ideology of "separate spheres"—the breadwinner husband and the home-maker wife—has slowly and steadily evaporated. While only 20 percent of women and only 4 percent of married women worked outside the home in 1900, more than three-fourths did so by 1995, including 60 percent of married women. In the first decade of the next century, 80 percent of the new entrants into the labor force will be women, minorities, and immigrants.

Despite the collapse of the doctrine of separate spheres—work and home—the workplace remains a dramatically divided world, where women and men rarely do the same jobs in the same place for the same pay. Occupational sex segregation, persistent sex discrimination, wage disparities—all these are problems faced by working women. Paula England provides a bird's-eye overview of where workplace equality has proved most successful and those areas in which women's progress is stalled.

Even women who are seeking to get ahead by entering formerly all-male fields frequently bump into the "glass ceiling"—a limit on how high they can rise in any organization. On the other hand, men who do "women's work"—taking occupations such as nurse, nursery school teacher, librarian—not only avoid the glass ceiling but actually glide up a "glass escalator"—finding greater opportunities at the higher, better paying levels of their professions than women. Adia Harvey Wingfield makes clear that the glass escalator is also a racialized ride—and that men of color may have a different set of experiences entirely.

Finally, Robin Ely and her colleagues look at the deleterious effects of traditional gender stereotypes in the workplace—first with the dangers (and lower profits) of hypermasculinity and second with the way these stereotypes hold women back.

The Gender Revolution: Uneven and Stalled

PAULA ENGLAND

We sometimes call the sweeping changes in the gender system since the 1960s a "revolution." Women's employment increased dramatically (Cotter, Hermsen, and England 2008); birth control became widely available (Bailey 2006); women caught up with and surpassed men in rates of college graduation (Cotter, Hermsen, and Vanneman 2004, 23); undergraduate college majors desegregated substantially (England and Li 2006); more women than ever got doctorates as well as professional degrees in law, medicine, and business (Cotter, Hermsen, and Vanneman 2004, 22–23; England et al. 2007); many kinds of gender discrimination in employment and education became illegal (Burstein 1989; Hirsh 2009); women entered many previously male-dominated occupations (Cotter, Hermsen, and Vanneman 2004, 10–14); and more women were elected to political office (Cotter, Hermsen, and Vanneman 2004, 25). As sweeping as these changes have been, change in the gender system has been uneven—affecting some groups more than others and some arenas of life more than others, and change has recently stalled. My goal in this article is not to argue over whether we should view the proverbial cup as half empty or half full (arguments I have always found uninteresting) but, rather, to stretch toward an understanding of why some things change so much more than others. To show the uneven nature of gender change, I will review trends on a number of indicators. While the shape of most of the trends is not in dispute among scholars, the explanations I offer for the uneven and halting nature of change have the status of hypotheses rather than well-documented conclusions.

I will argue that there has been little cultural or institutional change in the devaluation of traditionally female activities and jobs, and as a result, women have had more incentive than men to move into gender-nontraditional activities and positions. This led to asymmetric change; women's lives have changed much more than men's. Yet in some subgroups and arenas, there is less clear incentive for change even among women; examples are the relatively low employment rates of less educated women and the persistence of traditionally gendered patterns in heterosexual romantic, sexual, and marital relationships.

I also argue, drawing on work by Charles and Bradley, that the type of gender egalitarianism that did take hold was the type most compatible with American individualism and its cultural and institutional logics, which include rights of access to jobs and education and the desideratum of upward mobility and of expressing one's "true self" (Charles 2011; Charles and Bradley 2002, 2009). One form this gender egalitarianism has taken has been the reduction of discrimination in hiring. This has made much of the gender revolution that has occurred possible; women can now enter formerly "male" spheres. But co-occurring with this gender egalitarianism, and discouraging such integration is a strong (if often tacit) belief in gender essentialism—the notion that men and women are innately and fundamentally different in interests and skills (Charles 2011; Charles and

Paula England, "The Gender Revolution: Uneven and Stalled," *Gender & Society*, Vol. 24, No. 2 (2010), pp. 149–166. Copyright © 2010 by Sociologists for Women in Society. Reprinted by permission of SAGE Publications.

Bradley 2002, 2009; Ridgeway 2009). A result of these co-occurring logics is that women are most likely to challenge gender boundaries when there is no path of upward mobility without doing so, but otherwise gender blinders guide the paths of both men and women.

Devaluation of "Female" Activities and Asymmetric Incentives for Women and Men to Change

Most of the changes in the gender system heralded as "revolutionary" involve women moving into positions and activities previously limited to men, with few changes in the opposite direction. The source of this asymmetry is an aspect of society's valuation and reward system that has not changed much—the tendency to devalue and badly reward activities and jobs traditionally done by women.

Women's Increased Employment

One form the devaluation of traditionally female activities takes is the failure to treat child rearing as a public good and support those who do it with

state payments. In the United States, welfare reform took away much of what little such support had been present. Without this, women doing child rearing are reliant on the employment of male partners (if present) or their own employment. Thus, women have had a strong incentive to seek paid employment, and more so as wage levels rose across the decades (Bergmann 2005). As Figure 1 shows, women's employment has increased dramatically. But change has not been continuous, as the trend line flattened after 1990 and turned down slightly after 2000 before turning up again. This turndown was hardly an "opt-out revolution," to use the popular-press term, as the decline was tiny relative to the dramatic increase across 40 years (Kuperberg and Stone 2008; Percheski 2008). But the stall after 1990 is clear, if unexplained.

Figure 1 also shows the asymmetry in change between men's and women's employment; women's employment has increased much more than men's has declined. There was nowhere near one man leaving the labor force to become a full-time homemaker for every woman who entered, nor did men pick up household work to the extent women

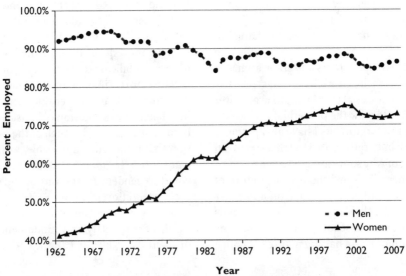

Figure 1. Percentage of U.S. Men and Women Employed, 1962–2007
Source: Cotter, Hermsen, and Vanneman (2009).
Note: Persons are considered employed if they worked for pay anytime during the year. Refers to adults aged 25 to 54.

added hours of employment (Bianchi, Robinson, and Milkie 2006). Men had little incentive to leave employment.

Among women, incentives for employment vary. Class-based[1] resources, such as education, affect these incentives. At first glance, we might expect less educated women to have higher employment rates than their better-educated peers because they are less likely to be married to a high-earning man. Most marriages are between two people at a similar education level (Mare 1991), so the less educated woman, if she is married, typically has a husband earning less than the husband of the college graduate. Her family would seem to need the money from her employment more than the family headed by two college graduates. Let us call this the "need for income" effect. But the countervailing "opportunity cost" factor is that well-educated women have more economic incentive for employment because they can earn more (England, Garcia-Beaulieu, and Ross 2004). Put another way, the opportunity cost of staying at home is greater for the woman who can earn more. Indeed, the woman who did not graduate from high school may have potential earnings so low that she could not even cover child care costs with what she could earn. Thus, in typical cases, for the married college graduate, her own education encourages her employment, while her husband's high earnings discourage it. The less educated woman typically has a poor husband (if any), which encourages her employment, while her own low earning power discourages her employment.[2] It is an empirical question whether the "need for income" or "opportunity cost" effect predominates.

Recent research shows that the opportunity-cost effect predominates in the United States and other affluent nations. England, Gornick, and Shafer (2008) use data from 16 affluent countries circa 2000 and show that, in all of them, among women partnered with men (married or cohabiting), those with more education are more likely to be employed. Moreover, there is no monotonic relationship between partner's earnings and a woman's employment; at top levels of his income, her employment is deterred. But women whose male partners are at middle income levels are more

likely to be employed than women whose partners have very low or no earnings, the opposite of what the "need for income" principle suggests.

In the United States, it has been true for decades that well-educated women are more likely to be employed, and the effect of a woman's own education has increased, while the deterring effect of her husband's income has declined (Cohen and Bianchi 1999). For example, in 1970, 59 percent of college graduate women, but only 43 percent of those with less than a high school education, were employed sometime during the year. In 2007, the figures were 80 percent for college graduates and 47 percent for less than high school (the relationship of education and employment was monotonic such that those with some college and only high school were in between college graduates and high school dropouts) (figures are author's calculation from data in Cotter, Hermsen, and Vanneman 2009).[3]

Women Moving into "Male" Jobs and Fields of Study

The devaluation of and underpayment of predominantly female occupations is an important institutional reality that provides incentives for both men and women to choose "male" over "female" occupations and the fields of study that lead to them. Research has shown that predominantly female occupations pay less, on average, than jobs with a higher proportion of men. At least some of the gap is attributable to sex composition because it persists in statistical models controlling for occupations' educational requirements, amount of skill required, unionization, and so forth. I have argued that this is a form of gender discrimination—employers see the worth of predominantly female jobs through biased lenses and, as a result, set pay levels for both men and women in predominantly female jobs lower than they would be if the jobs had a more heavily male sex composition (England 1992; Kilbourne et al. 1994; England and Folbre 2005). While the overall sex gap in pay has diminished because more women have moved into "male" fields (England and Folbre 2005), there is no evidence that the devaluation of occupations because they are filled with women has diminished (Levanon, England, and Allison 2009). Indeed, as U.S. courts have interpreted the law, this type of between-job discrimination is not even illegal (England 1992, 225–51; Steinberg 2001), whereas it is illegal to pay women less than men in the same job, unless based on factors such as seniority, qualifications, or performance. Given this, both men and women continue to have a pecuniary incentive to choose male-dominated occupations. Thus, we should not be surprised that desegregation of occupations has largely taken the form of women moving into male-dominated fields, rather than men moving into female-dominated fields.

Consistent with the incentives embedded in the ongoing devaluation of female fields, desegregation of fields of college study came from more women going into fields that were predominantly male, not from more men entering "female" fields. Since 1970, women increasingly majored in previously male-dominated, business-related fields, such as business, marketing, and accounting; while fewer chose traditionally female majors like English, education, and sociology; and there was little increase of men's choice of these latter majors (England and Li 2006, 667–69). Figure 2 shows the desegregation of fields of bachelor's degree receipt, using the index of dissimilarity (D), a scale on which complete

segregation (all fields are all male or all female) is 100 and complete integration (all fields have the same proportion of women as women's proportion of all bachelor's degrees in the given year) is 0. It shows that segregation dropped significantly in the 1970s and early 1980s, but has been quite flat since the mid-1980s. Women's increased integration of business fields stopped then as well (England and Li 2006).

Women have also recently increased their representation in formerly male-dominated professional degrees, getting MDs, MBAs, and law degrees in large numbers. Women were 6 percent of those getting MDs in 1960, 23 percent in 1980, 43 percent in 2000, and 49 percent in 2007; the analogous numbers for law degrees (JDs) were 3, 30, 46, and 47 percent, and for MBAs (and other management first-professional degrees), 4, 22, 39, and 44 percent (National Center for Education Statistics 2004–2008). There was no marked increase in the proportion of men in female-dominated graduate professional programs such as library science, social work, or nursing (National Center for Education Statistics 2009).

As women have increasingly trained for previously male-dominated fields, they have also integrated previously male-dominated occupations in management and the professions in large numbers

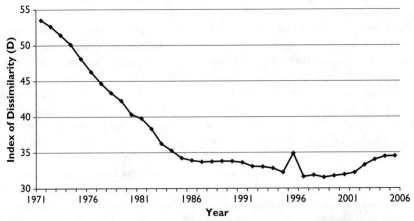

Figure 2. Sex Segregation of Fields of Study for U.S. Bachelor Degree Recipients, 1971–2006
Source: Author's calculations from the National Center for Education Statistics (NCES) 1971–2003 and NCES 2004–2008.

(Cotter, Hermsen, and Vanneman 2004, 10–13). Women may face discrimination and coworker resistance when they attempt to integrate these fields, but they have a strong pecuniary incentive to do so. Men lose money and suffer cultural disapproval when they choose traditionally female-dominated fields; they have little incentive to transgress gender boundaries. While some men have entered female-intensive retail service jobs after losing manufacturing jobs, there is little incentive for voluntary movement in this direction, making desegregation a largely one-way street.

What about employers' incentives? There is some debate about whether, absent equal employment legislation, employers have an incentive to engage in hiring and placement discrimination or are better off simply hiring gender-blind (for debate, see Jackson 1998; England 1992, 54–68). Whichever is true, legal enforcement of antidiscrimination laws has imposed some costs for hiring discrimination (Hirsh 2009), and this has probably reduced discrimination in hiring, contributing to desegregation of jobs.

The "Personal" Realm

"The personal is political" was a rallying cry of 1960s feminists, urging women to demand equality in private as well as public life. Yet conventions embodying male dominance have changed much less in "the personal" than in the job world. Where they have changed, the asymmetry described above for the job world prevails. For example, parents are more likely to give girls "boy" toys such as Legos than they are to give dolls to their sons. Girls have increased their participation in sports more than boys have taken up cheerleading or ballet. Women now commonly wear pants, while men wearing skirts remains rare. A few women started keeping their birth-given surname upon marriage (Goldin and Shim 2004), with little adoption by men of women's last names. Here, as with jobs, the asymmetry follows incentives, albeit nonmaterial ones. These social incentives themselves flow from a largely unchanged devaluation of things culturally defined as feminine. When boys and men take on "female" activities, they often

suffer disrespect, but under some circumstances, girls and women gain respect for taking on "male" activities.

What is more striking than the asymmetry of gender change in the personal realm is how little gendering has changed at all in this realm, especially in dyadic heterosexual relationships. It is still men who usually ask women on dates, and sexual behavior is generally initiated by men (England, Shafer, and Fogarty 2008). Sexual permissiveness has increased, making it more acceptable for both heterosexual men and women to have sex outside committed relationships. But the gendered part of this—the double standard—persists stubbornly; women are judged much more harshly than men for casual sex (Hamilton and Armstrong 2009; England, Shafer, and Fogarty 2008). The ubiquity of asking about height in Internet dating Web sites suggests that the convention that men should be taller than their female partner has not budged. The double standard of aging prevails, making women's chances of marriage decrease with age much more than men's (England and McClintock 2009). Men are still expected to propose marriage (Sassler and Miller 2007). Upon marriage, the vast majority of women take their husband's surname. The number of women keeping their own name increased in the 1970s and 1980s but little thereafter, never exceeding about 25 percent even for college graduates (who have higher rates than other women) (Goldin and Shim 2004). Children are usually given their father's surname; a recent survey found that even in cases where the mother is not married to the father, 92 percent of babies are given the father's last name (McLanahan forthcoming). While we do not have trend data on all these personal matters, my sense is that they have changed much less than gendered features of the world of paid work.

The limited change seen in the heterosexual personal realm may be because women's incentive to change these things is less clear than their incentive to move into paid work and into higher-paying "male" jobs. The incentives that do exist are largely noneconomic. For example, women may find it meaningful to keep their birth-given surnames and give them to their children, and they probably enjoy sexual freedom and initiation, especially if they are not judged adversely for it. But these noneconomic benefits may be neutralized by the noneconomic penalties from transgressing gender norms and by the fact that some have internalized the norms. When women transgress gender barriers to enter "male" jobs, they too may be socially penalized for violating norms, but for many this is offset by the economic gain.

Co-occurring Logics of Women's Rights to Upward Mobility and Gender Essentialism

I have stressed that important change in the gender system has taken the form of women integrating traditionally male occupations and fields of study. But even here change is uneven. The main generalization is shown by Figure 3, which divides all occupations by a crude measure of class, calling professional, management, and nonretail sales occupations "middle class," and all others "working class" (including retail sales, assembly

work in manufacturing, blue-collar trades, and other nonprofessional service work). Using the index of dissimilarity to measure segregation, Figure 3 shows that desegregation has proceeded much farther in middle-class than working-class jobs. Middle-class jobs showed dramatic desegregation, although the trend lessened its pace after 1990. By contrast, working-class jobs are almost as segregated as they were in 1950! Women have integrated the previously male strongholds of management, law, medicine, and academia in large numbers. But women have hardly gained a foothold in blue-collar, male-dominated jobs such as plumbing, construction, truck driving, welding, and assembly in durable manufacturing industries such as auto and steel (Cotter, Hermsen, and Vanneman 2004, 12–14). This is roughly the situation in other affluent nations as well (Charles and Grusky 2004). This same class difference in trend can be seen if we compare the degree of segregation among those who have various levels of education; in the United States, sex segregation declined much more dramatically since 1970 for

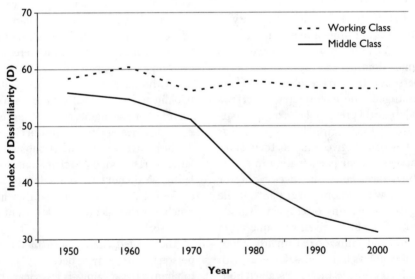

Figure 3. Sex Segregation of Middle-Class and Working-Class Occupations in the United States, 1950–2000

Source: Cotter, Hermsen, and Vanneman (2004, 14).

Note: Middle-class occupations include professional, management, and nonretail sales. All others are classified as working-class occupations.

college graduates than any other group (Cotter, Hermsen, and Vanneman 2009, 2004, 13–14).

Why has desegregation been limited to high-level jobs? The question has two parts: why women did not integrate blue-collar male jobs in significant numbers, and why women did integrate professional and managerial jobs in droves. Why one and not the other? Many factors were undoubtedly at work,[4] but I will focus on one account, which borrows from Charles and Bradley (Charles 2011; Charles and Bradley 2002, 2009). In the United States and many Western societies today, a certain kind of gender egalitarianism has taken hold ideologically and institutionally. The logic is that individuals should have equal rights to education and jobs of their choice. Moreover, achievement and upward mobility are generally valued. There is also a "postmaterialist" aspect to the culture which orients one to find her or his "true self." The common ethos is a combination of "the American dream" and liberal individualism. Many women, like men, want to "move up" in earnings and/or status, or at least avoid moving down. But up or down relative to what reference group? I suggest that the implicit reference group is typically those in the previous generation (or previous birth cohorts) of one's own social class background and one's own sex. For example, women might see their mothers or aunts as a reference, or women who graduated with their level of education ten years ago. Persons of the same-sex category are the implicit reference group because of strong beliefs in gender essentialism, that notion that men and women are innately and fundamentally different (Charles 2011; Ridgeway 2009). While liberal individualism encourages a commitment to "free choice" gender egalitarianism (such as legal equality of opportunity), ironically, orienting toward gender-typical paths has probably been encouraged by the emerging form of individualism that stresses finding and expressing one's "true self." Notions of self will in fact be largely socially constructed, pulling from socially salient identities. Because of the omnipresent nature of gender in the culture (Ridgeway 2009; West and Zimmerman 1987), gender often becomes the most available material from which to construct aspirations and

may be used even more when a job choice is seen as a deep statement about self (Charles and Bradley 2009).

Given all this, I hypothesize that if women can move "up" in status or income relative to their reference group while still staying in a job typically filled by women, then because of gender beliefs and gendered identities, they are likely to do so. If they cannot move up without integrating a male field, and demand is present and discrimination not too strong, they are more likely to cross the gender boundary. Applying this hypothesis, why would women not enter male blue-collar fields? To be sure, many women without college degrees would earn much more in the skilled blue-collar crafts or unionized manufacturing jobs than in the service jobs typically filled by women at their education levels—jobs such as maid, child care worker, retail sales clerk, or assembler in the textile industry. So they have an economic incentive to enter these jobs. But such women could also move "up" to clerical work or teaching, higher status and better paying but still traditionally female jobs. Many take this path, often getting more education.

In contrast, consider women who assumed they would go to college and whose mothers were in female-dominated jobs requiring a college degree like teacher, nurse, librarian, or social worker. For these women, to move up in status or earnings from their reference group options requires them to enter traditionally male jobs; there are virtually no heavily female jobs with higher status than these female professions. These are just the women, usually of middle-class origins, who have been integrating management, law, medicine, and academia in recent decades. For them, upward mobility was not possible within traditional boundaries, so they were more likely to integrate male fields.

In sum, my argument is that one reason that women integrated male professions and management much more than blue-collar jobs is that the women for whom the blue-collar male jobs would have constituted "progress" also had the option to move up by entering higher-ranking female jobs via more education. They thus had options for upward mobility without transgressing gender boundaries not present for their middle-class sisters.

Even women entering male-typical occupations, however, sometimes choose the more female-intensive subfields in them. In some cases, ending up in female-intensive subfields results from discrimination, but in others it may result from the gender essentialism discussed above. An example is the movement of women into doctoral study and into the occupation of "professor." This development brought women into a new arena. But within this arena, there was virtually no desegregation of fields of doctoral study from 1970 on (England et al.2007, 32).[5] Women have gone from being only 14 percent of those who get doctorates in 1971 to nearly half. But, conditional on getting a doctoral degree, neither women nor men have changed the fields of study they choose much (England et al. 2007). This can be seen in Figure 4, which shows the percentage women were of nine large fields of study in each year from 1971 to 2006. The percentage female in every field went up dramatically, reflecting the overall increase in women getting doctorates. But the rank order of fields in their percentage female changed little. The fields

with the highest percentage of women today are those that already had a high percentage of women decades ago relative to other fields.

What explains the failure of fields of doctoral study—and thus academic departments—to desegregate? Following the line of argument above, I suggest that the extreme differentiation of fields of academic study allowed many women moving "up" to doctoral study and an academic career to do so in fields that seemed consistent with their (tacitly gendered) notions of their interests and "true selves." Women academics in the humanities and social sciences thus find themselves in the more female subunits (disciplines) of a still largely male-dominated larger unit (the professorate).

Conclusion

Change in the gender system has been uneven, changing the lives of some groups of people more than others and changing lives in some arenas more than others. Although many factors are at play, I have offered two broad explanations for the uneven nature of change.

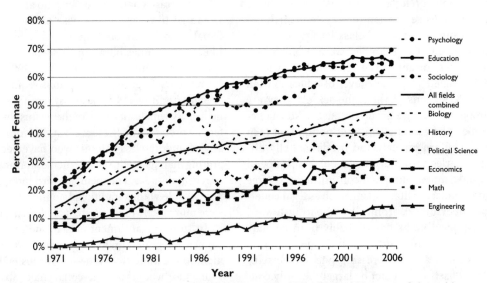

Figure 4. Percentage of All Doctoral Degree Recipients Who Were Women in Selected Large Fields, 1971–2006
Source: Author's calculations from the National Center for Education Statistics (NCES) 1971–2003 and NCES 2004–2008.
Note: All fields combined refers to all fields of doctoral study, not only the nine fields shown here. Engineering refers to doctoral degrees in E.E. Psychology excludes clinical psychology.

First, I argued that, because of the cultural and institutional devaluation of characteristics and activities associated with women, men had little incentive to move into badly rewarded, traditionally female activities such as homemaking or female-dominated occupations. By contrast, women had powerful economic incentives to move into the traditionally male domains of paid employment and male-typical occupations; and when hiring discrimination declined, many did. These incentives varied by class, however; the incentive to go to work for pay is much stronger for women who can earn more; thus employment levels have been higher for well-educated women. I also noted a lack of change in the gendering of the personal realm, especially of heterosexual romantic and sexual relationships.

Second, I explored the consequences of the co-occurrence of two Western cultural and institutional logics. Individualism, encompassing a belief in rights to equal opportunity in access to jobs and education in order to express one's "true self," promotes a certain kind of gender egalitarianism. It does not challenge the devaluation of traditionally female spheres, but it encourages the rights of women to upward mobility through equal access to education and jobs. To be sure, this ideal has been imperfectly realized, but this type of gender egalitarianism has taken hold strongly. But co-occurring with it, somewhat paradoxically, are strong (if tacit) beliefs in gender essentialism—that men and women are innately and fundamentally different in interests and skills (Charles 2011; Charles and Bradley 2002, 2009; Ridgeway 2009). Almost no men and precious few women, even those who believe in "equal opportunity," have an explicit commitment to undoing gender differentiation for its own sake. Gender essentialism encourages traditional choices and leads women to see previous cohorts of women of their social class as the reference point from which they seek upward mobility. I concluded that the co-occurrence of these two logics—equal opportunity individualism and gender essentialism—make it most likely for women to move into nontraditional fields of study or work when there is no possible female field

that constitutes upward mobility from the socially constructed reference point. This helps explain why women integrated male-dominated professional and managerial jobs more than blue-collar jobs. Women from working-class backgrounds, whose mothers were maids or assemblers in nondurable manufacturing, could move up financially by entering blue-collar "male" trades but often decide instead to get more education and move up into a female job such as secretary or teacher. It is women with middle-class backgrounds, whose mothers were teachers or nurses, who cannot move up without entering a male-dominated career, and it is just such women who have integrated management, law, medicine, and academia. Yet even while integrating large fields such as academia, women often gravitate toward the more female-typical fields of study.

As sociologists, we emphasize links between parts of a social system. For example, we trace how gender inequality in jobs affects gender inequality in the family, and vice versa (England and Farkas 1986). Moreover, links between parts of the system are recognized in today's prevailing view in which gender is itself a multilevel system, with causal arrows going both ways from macro to micro (Risman 2004). All these links undoubtedly exist, but the unevenness of gender-related change highlights how loosely coupled parts of the social system are and how much stronger some causal forces for change are than others. For example, because it resonated with liberal individualism well, the part of the feminist message that urged giving women equal access to jobs and education made considerable headway and led to much of what we call the gender revolution. But even as women integrated employment and "male" professional and managerial jobs, the part of feminism challenging the devaluation of traditionally female activities and jobs made little headway. The result is persistently low rewards for women who remain focused on mothering or in traditionally female jobs and little incentive for men to make the gender revolution a two-way street.

While discussing the uneven character of gender change, I also noted that the type of gender change with the most momentum—middle-class women entering traditionally male spheres—has recently stalled (Cotter, Hermsen, and Vanneman 2004, 2009). Women's employment rates stabilized, desegregation of occupations slowed down, and desegregation of fields of college study stopped. Erosion of the sex gap in pay slowed as well (Cotter, Hermsen, and Vanneman 2009). While the reason for the stalling is unclear, like the unevenness of change, the stalling of change reminds us how contingent and path-dependent gender egalitarian change is, with no inexorable equal endpoint. Change has been as much unintended consequence of larger institutional and cultural forces as realization of the efforts of feminist organizing, although the latter has surely helped.[6] Indeed, given the recent stalling of change, future feminist organizing may be necessary to revitalize change.

Notes

1. In this article, I use the term *class* to cover both categoric notions of class and gradational notions of socioeconomic position. Often I use education or occupation as imperfect but readily available indicators of class.

2. A complementary hypothesis about why employment rates are lower for less educated women is that, compared to women with more education, they place a higher value on motherhood and find less intrinsic meaning in the jobs they can get. In this vein, Edin and Kefalas (2005) argue that low-income women place a higher value on motherhood because they have so few alternative sources of meaning. However, Ferree (1976) found that working-class women were happier if employed; they worked for the money but also gained a sense of competence, connectedness, and self-determination from their jobs. McQuillan et al. (2008) find that neither education nor careerism is associated with the value placed on motherhood. Overall, there is no clear conclusion on class differences in how women value motherhood and jobs.

3. Women's employment is higher at higher education levels, but it is not clear if the gender gap in employment is less at higher education levels. This is because men's employment is also affected by education. For example, in 2007, 94 percent of men with a college education, but only 74 percent of those with less than high school, were employed sometime during the year (Cotter, Hermsen, and Vanneman 2009). How gender inequality in employment varies by education depends on the metric used to measure inequality. Inequality is smaller at high education levels if the ratio of women's to men's proportion employed is used, but not if the difference between men's and women's log odds of employment is used (author calculations from Cotter, Hermsen, and Vanneman 2009; results not shown).

4. One important additional factor is that blue-collar male jobs have been contracting (Morris and Western 1999), so integrating them would have been more difficult even if women had wanted to do so. Moreover, male coworkers may fight harder to harass and keep women out of blue-collar than professional and managerial jobs; lacking class privilege, blue-collar men may feel a stronger need than more privileged men to defend their gender privilege. Finally, it is possible that the Equal Employment Opportunity Commission had an institutional bias toward bringing cases challenging discrimination in high-level managerial and professional positions, particularly when they became concerned with the "glass ceiling." This could explain why Burstein (1989) found more discrimination cases in high-level jobs.

5. England et al. (2007) showed no nontrivial change in segregation of doctoral degrees through 2002. Using the same source (National Center for Education Statistics 2004–2007), I have computed the index of dissimilarity, which shows that the lack of change continued through 2006 (results not shown).

6. Risman (2009) reminds us that that our own teaching has probably had an effect on keeping feminism alive, as today's young feminists often say that the college classroom was where they began to identify as feminists.

References

Bailey, Martha J. 2006. More power to the pill: The impact of contraceptive freedom on women's life cycle labor supply. *Quarterly Journal of Economics* 121:289–320.

Bergmann, Barbara. 2005. *The economic emergence of women.* 2nd ed. New York: Basic Books.

Bianchi, Suzanne, John P. Robinson, and Melissa A. Milkie. 2006. *Changing rhythms of American family life.* New York: Russell Sage Foundation.

Burstein, Paul. 1989. Attacking sex discrimination in the labor market: A study in law and politics. *Social Forces* 67:641–65.

Charles, Maria. 2011. A world of difference: International trends in women's economic status. *Annual Review of Sociology* 37:355–371.

Charles, Maria, and Karen Bradley. 2002. Equal but separate: A cross-national study of sex segregation in higher education. *American Sociological Review* 67:573–99.

Charles, Maria, and Karen Bradley. 2009. Indulging our gendered selves: Sex segregation by field of study in 44 countries. *American Journal of Sociology* 114:924–76.

Charles, Maria, and David B. Grusky. 2004. *Occupational ghettos: The worldwide segregation of women and men.* Stanford, CA: Stanford University Press.

Cohen, Philip N., and Suzanne M. Bianchi. 1999. Marriage, children, and women's employment: What do we know? *Monthly Labor Review* 122:22–31.

Cotter, David A., Joan M. Hermsen, and Paula England. 2008. Moms and jobs: Trends in mothers' employment and which mothers stay home. In *American families: A multicultural reader,* 2nd ed., edited by Stephanie Coontz, with Maya Parson and Gabrielle Raley, 379–86. New York: Routledge.

Cotter, David A., Joan M. Hermsen, and Reeve Vanneman. 2004. *Gender inequality at work.* New York: Russell Sage Foundation.

Cotter, David A., Joan M. Hermsen, and Reeve Vanneman. 2009. End of the gender revolution website. http://www.bsos.umd.edu/socy/vanneman/ endofgr/default.html (accessed December 14, 2009).

Edin, Kathryn, and Maria Kefalas. 2005. *Promises I can keep: Why poor women put motherhood before marriage.* Berkeley: University of California Press.

England, Paula 1992. *Comparable worth: Theories and evidence.* New York: Aldine.

England, Paula, Paul Allison, Su Li, Noah Mark, Jennifer Thompson, Michelle Budig, and Han Sun. 2007.

Why are some academic fields tipping toward female? The sex composition of U.S. fields of doctoral degree receipt, 1971–2002. *Sociology of Education* 80:23–42.

England, Paula, and George Farkas. 1986. *Households, employment, and gender: A social, economic, and demographic view.* New York: Aldine.

England, Paula, and Nancy Folbre. 2005. Gender and economic sociology. In *The handbook of economic sociology,* edited by N. J. Smelser and R. Swedberg, 627–49. New York: Russell Sage Foundation.

England, Paula, Carmen Garcia-Beaulieu, and Mary Ross. 2004. Women's employment among Blacks, whites, and three groups of Latinas: Do more privileged women have higher employment? *Gender & Society* 18 (4): 494–509.

England, Paula, Janet C. Gornick, and Emily Fitzgibbons Shafer. 2008. Is it better at the top? How women's employment and the gender earnings gap vary by education in sixteen countries. Paper presented at the 2008 annual meeting of the American Sociological Association.

England, Paula, and Su Li. 2006. Desegregation stalled: The changing gender composition of college majors, 1971–2002. *Gender & Society* 20:657–77.

England, Paula, and Elizabeth Aura McClintock. 2009. The gendered double standard of aging in U.S. marriage markets. *Population and Development Review* 35:797–816.

England, Paula, Emily Fitzgibbons Shafer, and Alison C. K. Fogarty. 2008. Hooking up and forming romantic relationships on today's college campuses. In *The gendered society reader,* 3rd ed., edited by Michael Kimmel and Amy Aronson, 531–46. New York: Oxford University Press.

Ferree, Myra Marx. 1976. Working-class jobs: Paid work and housework as sources of satisfaction. *Social Problems* 23 (4): 431–41.

Goldin, Claudia, and Maria Shim. 2004. Making a name: Women's surnames at marriage and beyond. *Journal of Economic Perspectives* 18:143–60.

Hamilton, Laura, and Elizabeth A. Armstrong. 2009. Gendered sexuality in young adulthood: Double binds and flawed options. *Gender & Society* 23:589–616.

Hirsh, C. Elizabeth. 2009. The strength of weak enforcement: The impact of discrimination charges on sex and race segregation in the workplace. *American Sociological Review* 74 (2): 245–71.

Jackson, Robert Max. 1998. *Destined for equality: The inevitable rise of women's status.* Cambridge, MA: Harvard University Press.

Kilbourne, Barbara Stanek, Paula England, George Farkas, Kurt Beron, and Dorothea Weir. 1994. Returns to skills, compensating differentials, and gender bias: Effects of occupational characteristics on the wages of white women and men. *American Journal of Sociology* 100:689–719.

Kuperberg, Arielle, and Pamela Stone. 2008. The media depiction of women who opt out. *Gender & Society* 2:497–517.

Levanon, Asaf, Paula England, and Paul Allison. 2009. Occupational feminization and pay: Assessing causal dynamics using 1950–2000 census data. *Social Forces* 88:865–92.

Mare, Robert D. 1991. Five decades of educational assortative mating. *American Sociological Review* 56:15–32.

McLanahan, Sara. Forthcoming. Children in fragile families. In *Families in an unequal society,* edited by Marcia Carlson and Paula England. Stanford, CA: Stanford University Press.

McQuillan, Julia, Arthur L. Greil, Karina M. Shreffler, and Veronica Tichenor. 2008. The importance of motherhood among women in the contemporary United States. *Gender & Society* 22:477–96.

Morris, Martina, and Bruce Western. 1999. Inequality in earnings at the close of the twentieth century. *Annual Review of Sociology* 25:623–57.

National Center for Education Statistics. 1971–2003. *Digest of education statistics.* Washington, DC: Government Printing Office.

National Center for Education Statistics. 2004–2008. Table numbers by year: 2004: 253, 2005: 252, 2006: 58, 2007: 264, 2008: 279. http://nces.ed.gov/programs/digest (accessed December 14, 2009).

Percheski, Christine. 2008. Opting out? Cohort differences in professional women's employment rates from 1960 to 2000. *American Sociological Review* 73:497–517.

Ridgeway, Cecilia L. 2009. Framed before we know it: How gender shapes social relations. *Gender & Society* 23:145–60.

Risman, Barbara J. 2004. Gender as a social structure: Theory wrestling with activism. *Gender & Society* 18:429–50.

Risman, Barbara J. 2009. From doing to undoing: Gender as we know it. *Gender & Society* 23:81–84.

Sassler, Sharon, and Amanda Miller. 2007. Waiting to be asked: Gender, power and relationship progression among cohabiting couples. Presented at the annual meeting of the American Sociological Association, New York, August.

Steinberg, Ronnie J. 2001. Comparable worth in gender studies. In *International encyclopedia of the social and behavioral sciences,* vol. 4, edited by Neil J. Smelser and Paul B. Baltes. Cambridge: Cambridge University Press.

West, Candace, and Donald H. Zimmerman. 1987. Doing gender. *Gender & Society* 1:125–51.

Racializing the Glass Escalator: Reconsidering Men's Experiences with Women's Work

ADIA HARVEY WINGFIELD

Sociologists who study work have long noted that jobs are sex segregated and that this segregation creates different occupational experiences for men and women (Charles and Grusky 2004). Jobs predominantly filled by women often require "feminine" traits such as nurturing, caring, and empathy, a fact that means men confront perceptions that they are unsuited for the requirements of these jobs. Rather than having an adverse effect on their occupational experiences, however, these assumptions facilitate men's entry into better paying, higher status positions, creating what Williams (1995) labels a "glass escalator" effect.

The glass escalator model has been an influential paradigm in understanding the experiences of men who do women's work. Researchers have identified this process among men nurses, social workers, paralegals, and librarians and have cited its pervasiveness as evidence of men's consistent advantage in the workplace, such that even in jobs where men are numerical minorities they are likely to enjoy higher wages and faster promotions (Floge and Merrill 1986; Heikes 1991; Pierce 1995; Williams 1989, 1995). Most of these studies implicitly assume a racial homogenization of men workers in women's professions, but this supposition is problematic for several reasons. For one, minority men are not only present but are actually overrepresented in certain areas of reproductive work that have historically been dominated by white women (Duffy 2007). Thus, research that focuses

primarily on white men in women's professions ignores a key segment of men who perform this type of labor. Second, and perhaps more important, conclusions based on the experiences of white men tend to overlook the ways that intersections of race and gender create different experiences for different men. While extensive work has documented the fact that white men in women's professions encounter a glass escalator effect that aids their occupational mobility (for an exception, see Snyder and Green 2008), few studies, if any, have considered how this effect is a function not only of gendered advantage but of racial privilege as well.

In this article, I examine the implications of race–gender intersections for minority men employed in a female-dominated, feminized occupation, specifically focusing on Black men in nursing. Their experiences doing "women's work" demonstrate that the glass escalator is a racialized as well as gendered concept.

Theoretical Framework

In her classic study *Men and Women of the Corporation*, Kanter (1977) offers a groundbreaking analysis of group interactions. Focusing on high-ranking women executives who work mostly with men, Kanter argues that those in the extreme numerical minority are tokens who are socially isolated, highly visible, and adversely stereotyped. Tokens have difficulty forming relationships with colleagues and often are excluded from social

Adia Harvey Wingfield, "Racializing the Glass Escalator: Reconsidering Men's Experiences with Women's Work," *Gender & Society*, Vol. 23, No. 1 (February 2009), pp. 5–26. Copyright © 2009 by Sociologists for Women in Society. Reprinted by permission of SAGE Publications.

networks that provide mobility. Because of their low numbers, they are also highly visible as people who are different from the majority, even though they often feel invisible when they are ignored or overlooked in social settings. Tokens are also stereotyped by those in the majority group and frequently face pressure to behave in ways that challenge and undermine these stereotypes. Ultimately, Kanter argues that it is harder for them to blend into the organization and to work effectively and productively, and that they face serious barriers to upward mobility.

Kanter's (1977) arguments have been analyzed and retested in various settings and among many populations. Many studies, particularly of women in male-dominated corporate settings, have supported her findings. Other work has reversed these conclusions, examining the extent to which her conclusions hold when men were the tokens and women the majority group. These studies fundamentally challenged the gender neutrality of the token, finding that men in the minority fare much better than do similarly situated women. In particular, this research suggests that factors such as heightened visibility and polarization do not necessarily disadvantage men who are in the minority. While women tokens find that their visibility hinders their ability to blend in and work productively, men tokens find that their conspicuousness can lead to greater opportunities for leadership and choice assignments (Floge and Merrill 1986; Heikes 1991). Studies in this vein are important because they emphasize organizations—and occupations— as gendered institutions that subsequently create dissimilar experiences for men and women tokens (see Acker 1990).

In her groundbreaking study of men employed in various women's professions, Williams (1995) further develops this analysis of how power relationships shape the ways men tokens experience work in women's professions. Specifically, she introduces the concept of the glass escalator to explain men's experiences as tokens in these areas. Like Floge and Merrill (1986) and Heikes (1991), Williams finds that men tokens do not experience the isolation, visibility, blocked access to social networks, and stereotypes in the same ways that women tokens do.

In contrast, Williams argues that even though they are in the minority, processes are in place that actually facilitate their opportunity and advancement. Even in culturally feminized occupations, then, men's advantage is built into the very structure and everyday interactions of these jobs so that men find themselves actually struggling to remain in place. For these men, "despite their intentions, they face invisible pressures to move up in their professions. Like being on a moving escalator, they have to work to stay in place" (Williams 1995, 87).

The glass escalator term thus refers to the "subtle mechanisms in place that enhance [men's] positions in [women's] professions" (Williams 1995, 108). These mechanisms include certain behaviors, attitudes, and beliefs men bring to these professions as well as the types of interactions that often occur between these men and their colleagues, supervisors, and customers. Consequently, even in occupations composed mostly of women, gendered perceptions about men's roles, abilities, and skills privilege them and facilitate their advancement. The glass escalator serves as a conduit that channels men in women's professions into the uppermost levels of the occupational hierarchy. Ultimately, the glass escalator effect suggests that men retain consistent occupational advantages over women, even when women are numerically in the majority (Budig 2002; Williams 1995).

Though this process has now been fairly well established in the literature, there are reasons to question its generalizability to all men. In an early critique of the supposed general neutrality of the token, Zimmer (1988) notes that much research on race comes to precisely the opposite of Kanter's conclusions, finding that as the numbers of minority group members increase (e.g., as they become less likely to be "tokens"), so too do tensions between the majority and minority groups. For instance, as minorities move into predominantly white neighborhoods, increasing numbers do not create the likelihood of greater acceptance and better treatment. In contrast, whites are likely to relocate when neighborhoods become "too" integrated, citing concerns about property values and racialized ideas about declining neighborhood quality (Shapiro 2004). Reinforcing, while at the same time tempering, the findings of research on men in female-dominated occupations, Zimmer (1988, 71) argues that relationships between tokens and the majority depend on understanding the underlying power relationships between these groups and "the status and power differentials between them." Hence, just as men who are tokens fare better than women, it also follows that the experiences of Blacks and whites as tokens should differ in ways that reflect their positions in hierarchies of status and power.

The concept of the glass escalator provides an important and useful framework for addressing men's experiences in women's occupations, but so far research in this vein has neglected to examine whether the glass escalator is experienced among all men in an identical manner. Are the processes that facilitate a ride on the glass escalator available to minority men? Or does race intersect with gender to affect the extent to which the glass escalator offers men opportunities in women's professions? In the next section, I examine whether and how the mechanisms that facilitate a ride on the glass escalator might be unavailable to Black men in nursing.[1]

Relationships with Colleagues and Supervisors

One key aspect of riding the glass escalator involves the warm, collegial welcome men workers often receive from their women colleagues. Often, this reaction is a response to the fact that professions dominated by women are frequently low in salary and status and that greater numbers of men help improve prestige and pay (Heikes 1991). Though some women workers resent the apparent ease with which men enter and advance in women's professions, the generally warm welcome men receive stands in stark contrast to the cold reception, difficulties with mentorship, and blocked access to social networks that women often encounter when they do men's work (Roth 2006; Williams 1992). In addition, unlike women in men's professions, men who do women's work frequently have supervisors of the same sex. Men workers can thus enjoy a gendered bond with their supervisor in the context of a collegial work environment. These factors often converge, facilitating men's

access to higher-status positions and producing the glass escalator effect.

The congenial relationship with colleagues and gendered bonds with supervisors are crucial to riding the glass escalator. Women colleagues often take a primary role in casting these men into leadership or supervisory positions. In their study of men and women tokens in a hospital setting, Floge and Merrill (1986) cite cases where women nurses promoted men colleagues to the position of charge nurse, even when the job had already been assigned to a woman. In addition to these close ties with women colleagues, men are also able to capitalize on gendered bonds with (mostly men) supervisors in ways that engender upward mobility. Many men supervisors informally socialize with men workers in women's jobs and are thus able to trade on their personal friendships for upward mobility. Williams (1995) describes a case where a nurse with mediocre performance reviews received a promotion to a more prestigious specialty area because of his friendship with the (male) doctor in charge. According to the literature, building strong relationships with colleagues and supervisors often happens relatively easily for men in women's professions and pays off in their occupational advancement.

For Black men in nursing, however, gendered racism may limit the extent to which they establish bonds with their colleagues and supervisors. The concept of gendered racism suggests that racial stereotypes, images, and beliefs are grounded in gendered ideals (Collins 1990, 2004; Espiritu 2000; Essed 1991; Harvey Wingfield 2007). Gendered racist stereotypes of Black men in particular emphasize the dangerous, threatening attributes associated with Black men and Black masculinity, framing Black men as threats to white women, prone to criminal behavior, and especially violent. Collins (2004) argues that these stereotypes serve to legitimize Black men's treatment in the criminal justice system through methods such as racial profiling and incarceration, but they may also hinder Black men's attempts to enter and advance in various occupational fields.

For Black men nurses, gendered racist images may have particular consequences for their relationships with women colleagues, who may view Black men nurses through the lens of controlling images and gendered racist stereotypes that emphasize the danger they pose to women. This may take on a heightened significance for white women nurses, given stereotypes that suggest that Black men are especially predisposed to raping white women. Rather than experiencing the congenial bonds with colleagues that white men nurses describe, Black men nurses may find themselves facing a much cooler reception from their women coworkers.

Gendered racism may also play into the encounters Black men nurses have with supervisors. In cases where supervisors are white men, Black men nurses may still find that higher-ups treat them in ways that reflect prevailing stereotypes about threatening Black masculinity. Supervisors may feel uneasy about forming close relationships with Black men or may encourage their separation from white women nurses. In addition, broader, less gender-specific racial stereotypes could also shape the experiences Black men nurses have with white men bosses. Whites often perceive Blacks, regardless of gender, as less intelligent, hardworking, ethical, and moral than other racial groups (Feagin 2006). Black men nurses may find that in addition to being influenced by gendered racist stereotypes, supervisors also view them as less capable and qualified for promotion, thus negating or minimizing the glass escalator effect.

Suitability for Nursing and Higher-Status Work

The perception that men are not really suited to do women's work also contributes to the glass escalator effect. In encounters with patients, doctors, and other staff, men nurses frequently confront others who do not expect to see them doing "a woman's job." Sometimes this perception means that patients mistake men nurses for doctors; ultimately, the sense that men do not really belong in nursing contributes to a push "*out* of the most feminine-identified areas and *up* to those regarded as more legitimate for men" (Williams 1995, 104). The sense that men are better suited for more masculine jobs means that men workers are often assumed to be more able and skilled than their women counterparts. As Williams writes (1995, 106), "Masculinity is often associated with competence and mastery," and this implicit definition stays with men even when they work in feminized fields. Thus, part of the perception that men do not belong in these jobs is rooted in the sense that, as men, they are more capable and accomplished than women and thus belong in jobs that reflect this. Consequently, men nurses are mistaken for doctors and are granted more authority and responsibility than their women counterparts, reflecting the idea that, as men, they are inherently more competent (Heikes 1991; Williams 1995).

Black men nurses, however, may not face the presumptions of expertise or the resulting assumption that they belong in higher-status jobs. Black professionals, both men and women, are often assumed to be less capable and less qualified than their white counterparts. In some cases, these negative stereotypes hold even when Black workers outperform white colleagues (Feagin and Sikes 1994). The belief that Blacks are inherently less competent than whites means that, despite advanced education, training, and skill, Black professionals often confront the lingering perception that they are better suited for lower-level service work (Feagin and Sikes 1994). Black men in fact often fare better than white women in blue-collar jobs such as policing and corrections work (Britton 1995), and this may be, in part, because they are viewed as more appropriately suited for these types of positions.

For Black men nurses, then, the issue of perception may play out in different ways than it does for white men nurses. While white men nurses enjoy the automatic assumption that they are qualified, capable, and suited for "better" work, the experiences of Black professionals suggest that Black men nurses may not encounter these reactions. They may, like their white counterparts, face the perception that they do not belong in nursing. Unlike their white counterparts, Black men nurses may be seen as inherently less capable and therefore better suited for low-wage labor than a professional, feminized occupation such as nursing. This perception of being less qualified means that they also may not be immediately assumed to be better suited for the higher-level, more masculinized jobs within the medical field.

As minority women address issues of both race and gender to negotiate a sense of belonging in masculine settings (Ong 2005), minority men may also face a comparable challenge in feminized fields. They may have to address the unspoken racialization implicit in the assumption that masculinity equals competence. Simultaneously, they may find that the racial stereotype that Blackness equals lower qualifications, standards, and competence clouds the sense that men are inherently more capable and adept in any field, including the feminized ones.

Establishing Distance from Femininity

An additional mechanism of the glass escalator involves establishing distance from women and the femininity associated with their occupations. Because men nurses are employed in a culturally feminized occupation, they develop strategies to disassociate themselves from the femininity associated with their work and retain some of the privilege associated with masculinity. Thus, when men nurses gravitate toward hospital emergency wards rather than obstetrics or pediatrics, or emphasize that they are only in nursing to get into hospital administration, they distance themselves from the femininity of their profession and thereby preserve their status as men despite the fact that they do "women's work." Perhaps more important, these strategies also place men in a prime position to experience the glass escalator effect, as they situate themselves to move upward into higher-status areas in the field.

Creating distance from femininity also helps these men achieve aspects of hegemonic masculinity, which Connell (1989) describes as the predominant and most valued form of masculinity at a given time. Contemporary hegemonic masculine ideals emphasize toughness, strength, aggressiveness, heterosexuality, and, perhaps most important, a clear sense of femininity as different from and subordinate to masculinity (Kimmel 2001; Williams 1995). Thus, when men distance

themselves from the feminized aspects of their jobs, they uphold the idea that masculinity and femininity are distinct, separate, and mutually exclusive. When these men seek masculinity by aiming for the better paying or most technological fields, they not only position themselves to move upward into the more acceptable arenas but also reinforce the greater social value placed on masculinity. Establishing distance from femininity therefore allows men to retain the privileges and status of masculinity while simultaneously enabling them to ride the glass escalator.

For Black men, the desire to reject femininity may be compounded by racial inequality. Theorists have argued that as institutional racism blocks access to traditional markers of masculinity such as occupational status and economic stability, Black men may repudiate femininity as a way of accessing the masculinity—and its attendant status—that is denied through other routes (hooks 2004; Neal 2005). Rejecting femininity is a key strategy men use to assert masculinity, and it remains available to Black men even when other means of achieving masculinity are unattainable. Black men nurses may be more likely to distance themselves from their women colleagues and to reject the femininity associated with nursing, particularly if they feel that they experience racial discrimination that renders occupational advancement inaccessible. Yet if they encounter strained relationships with women colleagues and men supervisors because of gendered racism or racialized stereotypes, the efforts to distance themselves from femininity still may not result in the glass escalator effect.

On the other hand, some theorists suggest that minority men may challenge racism by rejecting hegemonic masculine ideals. Chen (1999) argues that Chinese American men may engage in a strategy of repudiation, where they reject hegemonic masculinity because its implicit assumptions of whiteness exclude Asian American men. As these men realize that racial stereotypes and assumptions preclude them from achieving the hegemonic masculine ideal, they reject it and dispute its racialized underpinnings. Similarly, Lamont (2000, 47) notes that working-class Black men in the United States and France develop a "caring self" in which they emphasize values such as "morality, solidarity, and generosity." As a consequence of these men's ongoing experiences with racism, they develop a caring self that highlights work on behalf of others as an important tool in fighting oppression. Although caring is associated with femininity, these men cultivate a caring self because it allows them to challenge racial inequality. The results of these studies suggest that Black men nurses may embrace the femininity associated with nursing if it offers a way to combat racism. In these cases, Black men nurses may turn to pediatrics as a way of demonstrating sensitivity and therefore combating stereotypes of Black masculinity, or they may proudly identify as nurses to challenge perceptions that Black men are unsuited for professional, white-collar positions.

Taken together, all of this research suggests that Black men may not enjoy the advantages experienced by their white men colleagues, who ride a glass escalator to success. In this article, I focus on the experiences of Black men nurses to argue that the glass escalator is a racialized as well as a gendered concept that does not offer Black men the same privileges as their white men counterparts.

Data Collection and Method

I collected data through semistructured interviews with 17 men nurses who identified as Black or African American. Nurses ranged in age from 30 to 51 and lived in the southeastern United States. Six worked in suburban hospitals adjacent to major cities, six were located in major metropolitan urban care centers, and the remaining five worked in rural hospitals or clinics. All were registered nurses or licensed practical nurses. Six identified their specialty as oncology, four were bedside nurses, two were in intensive care, one managed an acute dialysis program, one was an orthopedic nurse, one was in ambulatory care, one was in emergency, and one was in surgery. The least experienced nurse had worked in the field for five years; the most experienced had been a nurse for 26 years. I initially recruited participants by soliciting attendees at the 2007 National Black Nurses Association annual meetings and then used a snowball sample to create the remainder of the data set. All names and identifying details have been changed to ensure confidentiality (see Table 1).

I conducted interviews during the fall of 2007. They generally took place in either my campus office or a coffee shop located near the respondent's home or workplace. The average interview lasted about an hour. Interviews were tape-recorded and transcribed. Interview questions primarily focused on how race and gender shaped the men's experiences as nurses. Questions addressed respondents' work history and current experiences in the field, how race and gender shaped their experiences as nurses, and their future career goals. The men discussed their reasons for going into nursing, the reactions from others on entering this field, and the particular challenges, difficulties, and obstacles Black men nurses faced. Respondents also described their work history in nursing, their current jobs, and their future plans. Finally, they talked about stereotypes of nurses in general and of Black men nurses in particular and their thoughts about and responses to these stereotypes. I coded the data according to key themes that emerged: relationships with white patients versus minority patients, personal bonds with colleagues versus lack of bonds, opportunities for advancement versus obstacles to advancement.

The researcher's gender and race shape interviews, and the fact that I am an African American woman undoubtedly shaped my rapport and the interactions with interview respondents. Social desirability bias may compel men to phrase responses that might sound harsh in ways that will not be offensive or problematic to the woman interviewer. However, one of the benefits of the interview method is that it allows respondents to clarify comments diplomatically while still giving honest answers. In this case, some respondents may have carefully framed certain comments about working mostly with women. However, the semistructured interview format nonetheless enabled them to discuss in detail their experiences in nursing and how these experiences are shaped by race and gender. Furthermore, I expect that shared racial status also facilitated a level of

TABLE 1. Respondents

Name	Age	Specialization	Years of Experience	Years at Current Job
Chris	51	Oncology	26	16
Clayton	31	Emergency	6	6
Cyril	40	Dialysis	17	7
Dennis	30	Bedside	7	7 (months)
Evan	42	Surgery	25	20
Greg	39	Oncology	10	3
Kenny	47	Orthopedics	23	18 (months)
Leo	50	Bedside	20	18
Ray	36	Oncology	10	5
Ryan	37	Intensive care	17	11
Sean	46	Oncology	9	9
Simon	36	Oncology	5	5
Stuart	44	Bedside	6	4
Terrence	32	Bedside	10	6
Tim	39	Intensive care	20	15 (months)
Tobias	44	Oncology	25	7
Vern	50	Ambulatory care	7	7

comfort, particularly as respondents frequently discussed issues of racial bias and mistreatment that shaped their experiences at work.

Findings

The results of this study indicate that not all men experience the glass escalator in the same ways. For Black men nurses, intersections of race and gender create a different experience with the mechanisms that facilitate white men's advancement in women's professions. Awkward or unfriendly interactions with colleagues, poor relationships with supervisors, perceptions that they are not suited for nursing, and an unwillingness to disassociate from "feminized" aspects of nursing constitute what I term *glass barriers* to riding the glass escalator.

Reception from Colleagues and Supervisors

When women welcome men into "their" professions, they often push men into leadership roles that ease their advancement into upper-level positions. Thus, a positive reaction from colleagues is critical to riding the glass escalator. Unlike white men nurses, however, Black men do not describe encountering a warm reception from women colleagues (Heikes 1991). Instead, the men I interviewed find that they often have unpleasant interactions with women coworkers who treat them rather coldly and attempt to keep them at bay. Chris is a 51-year-old oncology nurse who describes one white nurse's attempt to isolate him from other white women nurses as he attempted to get his instructions for that day's shift:

She turned and ushered me to the door, and said for me to wait out here, a nurse will come out and give you your report. I stared at her hand on my arm, and then at her, and said, "Why? Where do you go to get your reports?" She said, "I get them in there." I said, "Right. Unhand me." I went right back in there, sat down, and started writing down my reports.

Kenny, a 47-year-old nurse with 23 years of nursing experience, describes a similarly and particularly painful experience he had in a previous job where he was the only Black person on staff:

> [The staff] had nothing to do with me, and they didn't even want me to sit at the same area where they were charting in to take a break. They wanted me to sit somewhere else. . . . They wouldn't even sit at a table with me! When I came and sat down, everybody got up and left.

These experiences with colleagues are starkly different from those described by white men in professions dominated by women (see Pierce 1995; Williams 1989). Though the men in these studies sometimes chose to segregate themselves, women never systematically excluded them. Though I have no way of knowing why the women nurses in Chris's and Kenny's workplaces physically segregated themselves, the pervasiveness of gendered racist images that emphasize white women's vulnerability to dangerous Black men may play an important role. For these nurses, their masculinity is not a guarantee that they will be welcomed, much less pushed into leadership roles. As Ryan, a 37-year-old intensive care nurse says, "[Black men] have to go further to prove ourselves. This involves proving our capabilities, *proving to colleagues that you can lead,* be on the forefront" (emphasis added). The warm welcome and subsequent opportunities for leadership cannot be taken for granted. In contrast, these men describe great challenges in forming congenial relationships with coworkers who, they believe, do not truly want them there.

In addition, these men often describe tense, if not blatantly discriminatory, relationships with supervisors. While Williams (1995) suggests that men supervisors can be allies for men in women's professions by facilitating promotions and upward mobility, Black men nurses describe incidents of being overlooked by supervisors when it comes time for promotions. Ryan, who has worked at his current job for 11 years, believes that these barriers block upward mobility within the profession:

> The hardest part is dealing with people who don't understand minority nurses. People with their biases, who don't identify you as ripe for promotion. I know the policy and procedure, I'm familiar with past history. So you can't tell me I can't move forward if others did. [How did you deal with this?] By knowing the chain of command, who my supervisors were. Things were subtle. I just had to be better. I got this mostly from other nurses and supervisors. I was paid to deal with patients, so I could deal with [racism] from them. I'm not paid to deal with this from colleagues.

Kenny offers a similar example. Employed as an orthopedic nurse in a predominantly white environment, he describes great difficulty getting promoted, which he primarily attributes to racial biases:

> It's almost like you have to, um, take your ideas and give them to somebody else and then let them present them for you and you get no credit for it. I've applied for several promotions there and, you know, I didn't get them. . . . When you look around to the, um, the percentage of African Americans who are actually in executive leadership is almost zero percent. Because it's less than one percent of the total population of people that are in leadership, and it's almost like they'll go outside of the system just to try to find a Caucasian to fill a position. Not that I'm not qualified, because I've been master's prepared for 12 years and I'm working on my doctorate.

According to Ryan and Kenny, supervisors' racial biases mean limited opportunities for promotion and upward mobility. This interpretation is consistent with research that suggests that even with stellar performance and solid work histories, Black workers may receive mediocre evaluations from white supervisors that limit their advancement (Feagin 2006; Feagin and Sikes 1994). For Black men nurses, their race may signal to supervisors that they are unworthy of promotion and thus create a different experience with the glass escalator.

Strong relationships with colleagues and supervisors are a key mechanism of the glass escalator effect. For Black men nurses, however, these relationships are experienced differently from those described by their white men colleagues.

Black men nurses do not speak of warm and congenial relationships with women nurses or see these relationships as facilitating a move into leadership roles. Nor do they suggest that they share gendered bonds with men supervisors that serve to ease their mobility into higher-status administrative jobs. In contrast, they sense that racial bias makes it difficult to develop ties with coworkers and makes superiors unwilling to promote them. Black men nurses thus experience this aspect of the glass escalator differently from their white men colleagues. They find that relationships with colleagues and supervisors stifle, rather than facilitate, their upward mobility.

Perceptions of Suitability

Like their white counterparts, Black men nurses also experience challenges from clients who are unaccustomed to seeing men in fields typically dominated by women. As with white men nurses, Black men encounter this in surprised or quizzical reactions from patients who seem to expect to be treated by white women nurses. Ray, a 36-year-old oncology nurse with 10 years of experience, states,

> Nursing, historically, has been a white female's job [so] being a Black male it's a weird position to be in. . . . I've, several times, gone into a room and a male patient, a white male patient has, you know, they'll say, "Where's the pretty nurse? Where's the pretty nurse? Where's the blonde nurse?" . . . "You don't have one. I'm the nurse."

Yet while patients rarely expect to be treated by men nurses of any race, white men encounter statements and behaviors that suggest patients expect them to be doctors, supervisors, or other higher-status, more masculine positions (Williams 1989, 1995). In part, this expectation accelerates their ride on the glass escalator, helping to push them into the positions for which they are seen as more appropriately suited.

(White) men, by virtue of their masculinity, are assumed to be more competent and capable and thus better situated in (nonfeminized) jobs that are perceived to require greater skill and proficiency. Black men, in contrast, rarely encounter patients (or colleagues and supervisors) who

immediately expect that they are doctors or administrators. Instead, many respondents find that even after displaying their credentials, sharing their nursing experience, and, in one case, dispensing care, they are still mistaken for janitors or service workers. Ray's experience is typical:

> I've even given patients their medicines, explained their care to them, and then they'll say to me, "Well, can you send the nurse in?"

Chris describes a somewhat similar encounter of being misidentified by a white woman patient:

> I come [to work] in my white uniform, that's what I wear—being a Black man, I know they won't look at me the same, so I dress the part—I said good evening, my name's Chris, and I'm going to be your nurse. She says to me, "Are you from housekeeping?" . . . I've had other cases. I've walked in and had a lady look at me and ask if I'm the janitor.

Chris recognizes that this patient is evoking racial stereotypes that Blacks are there to perform menial service work. He attempts to circumvent this very perception through careful self-presentation, wearing the white uniform to indicate his position as a nurse. His efforts, however, are nonetheless met with a racial stereotype that as a Black man he should be there to clean up rather than to provide medical care.

Black men in nursing encounter challenges from customers that reinforce the idea that men are not suited for a "feminized" profession such as nursing. However, these assumptions are racialized as well as gendered. Unlike white men nurses who are assumed to be doctors (see Williams 1992), Black men in nursing are quickly taken for janitors or housekeeping staff. These men do not simply describe a gendered process where perceptions and stereotypes about men serve to aid their mobility into higher-status jobs. More specifically, they describe interactions that are simultaneously raced *and* gendered in ways that reproduce stereotypes of Black men as best suited for certain blue-collar, unskilled labor.

These negative stereotypes can affect Black men nurses' efforts to treat patients as well. The men

I interviewed find that masculinity does not automatically endow them with an aura of competency. In fact, they often describe interactions with white women patients that suggest that their race minimizes whatever assumptions of capability might accompany being men. They describe several cases in which white women patients completely refused treatment. Ray says,

> With older white women, it's tricky sometimes because they will come right out and tell you they don't want you to treat them, or can they see someone else.

Ray frames this as an issue specifically with older white women, though other nurses in the sample described similar issues with white women of all ages. Cyril, a 40-year-old nurse with 17 years of nursing experience, describes a slightly different twist on this story:

> I had a white lady that I had to give a shot, and she was fine with it and I was fine with it. But her husband, when she told him, he said to me, I don't have any problem with you as a Black man, but I don't want you giving her a shot.

While white men nurses report some apprehension about treating women patients, in all likelihood this experience is compounded for Black men (Williams 1989). Historically, interactions between Black men and white women have been fraught with complexity and tension, as Black men have been represented in the cultural imagination as potential rapists and threats to white women's security and safety—and, implicitly, as a threat to white patriarchal stability (Davis 1981; Giddings 1984). In Cyril's case, it may be particularly significant that the Black man is charged with giving a shot and therefore literally penetrating the white wife's body, a fact that may heighten the husband's desire to shield his wife from this interaction. White men nurses may describe hesitation or awkwardness that accompanies treating women patients, but their experiences are not shaped by a pervasive racial imagery that suggests that they are potential threats to their women patients' safety.

This dynamic, described primarily among white women patients and their families, presents a picture of how Black men's interactions with clients are shaped in specifically raced and gendered ways that suggest they are less rather than more capable. These interactions do not send the message that Black men, because they are men, are too competent for nursing and really belong in higher-status jobs. Instead, these men face patients who mistake them for lower-status service workers and encounter white women patients (and their husbands) who simply refuse treatment or are visibly uncomfortable with the prospect. These interactions do not situate Black men nurses in a prime position for upward mobility. Rather, they suggest that the experience of Black men nurses with this particular mechanism of the glass escalator is the manifestation of the expectation that they should be in lower-status positions more appropriate to their race and gender.

Refusal to Reject Femininity

Finally, Black men nurses have a different experience with establishing distance from women and the feminized aspects of their work. Most research shows that as men nurses employ strategies that distance them from femininity (e.g., by emphasizing nursing as a route to higher-status, more masculine jobs), they place themselves in a position for upward mobility and the glass escalator effect (Williams 1992). For Black men nurses, however, this process looks different. Instead of distancing themselves from the femininity associated with nursing, Black men actually embrace some of the more feminized attributes linked to nursing. In particular, they emphasize how much they value and enjoy the way their jobs allow them to be caring and nurturing. Rather than conceptualizing caring as anathema or feminine (and therefore undesirable), Black men nurses speak openly of caring as something positive and enjoyable.

This is consistent with the context of nursing that defines caring as integral to the profession. As nurses, Black men in this line of work experience professional socialization that emphasizes and values caring, and this is reflected in their statements about their work. Significantly, however, rather than repudiating this feminized component of their jobs, they embrace it. Tobias, a 44-year-old oncology nurse with 25 years of experience, asserts:

> The best part about nursing is helping other people, the flexibility of work hours, and the commitment to vulnerable populations, people who are ill.

Simon, a 36-year-old oncology nurse, also talks about the joy he gets from caring for others. He contrasts his experiences to those of white men nurses he knows who prefer specialties that involve less patient care:

> They were going to work with the insurance industries, they were going to work in the ER where it's a touch and go, you're a number literally. I don't get to know your name, I don't get to know that you have four grandkids, I don't get to know that you really want to get out of the hospital by next week because the following week is your birthday, your 80th birthday and it's so important for you. I don't get to know that your cat's name is Sprinkles, and you're concerned about who's feeding the cat now, and if they remembered to turn the TV on during the day so that the cat can watch *The Price Is Right*. They don't get into all that kind of stuff. OK, I actually need to remember the name of your cat so that tomorrow morning when I come, I can ask you about Sprinkles and that will make a world of difference. I'll see light coming to your eyes and the medicines will actually work because your perspective is different.

Like Tobias, Simon speaks with a marked lack of self-consciousness about the joys of adding a personal touch and connecting that personal care to a patient's improvement. For him, caring is important, necessary, and valued, even though others might consider it a feminine trait.

For many of these nurses, willingness to embrace caring is also shaped by issues of race and racism. In their position as nurses, concern for others is connected to fighting the effects of racial inequality. Specifically, caring motivates them to use their role as nurses to address racial health disparities, especially those that disproportionately affect Black men. Chris describes his efforts to minimize health issues among Black men:

> With Black male patients, I have their history, and if they're 50 or over I ask about the prostate exam and a colonoscopy. Prostate and colorectal death is so high that that's my personal crusade.

Ryan also speaks to the importance of using his position to address racial imbalances:

> I really take advantage of the opportunities to give back to communities, especially to change the disparities in the African American community. I'm more than just a nurse. As a faculty member at a major university, I have to do community hours, services. Doing health fairs, in-services on research, this makes an impact in some disparities in the African American community. [People in the community] may not have the opportunity to do this otherwise.

As Lamont (2000) indicates in her discussion of the "caring self," concern for others helps Chris and Ryan to use their knowledge and position as nurses to combat racial inequalities in health. Though caring is generally considered a "feminine" attribute, in this context it is connected to challenging racial health disparities. Unlike their white men colleagues, these nurses accept and even embrace certain aspects of femininity rather than rejecting them. They thus reveal yet another aspect of the glass escalator process that differs for Black men. As Black men nurses embrace this "feminine" trait and the avenues it provides for challenging racial inequalities, they may become more comfortable in nursing and embrace the opportunities it offers.

Conclusions

Existing research on the glass escalator cannot explain these men's experiences. As men who do women's work, they should be channeled into positions as charge nurses or nursing administrators and should find themselves virtually pushed into the upper ranks of the nursing profession. But without exception, this is not the experience these Black men nurses describe. Instead of benefiting from the basic mechanisms of the glass escalator, they face tense relationships with colleagues, supervisors' biases in achieving promotion, patient stereotypes that inhibit caregiving, and a sense of comfort with some of the feminized aspects of their jobs. These "glass barriers" suggest that the glass escalator is a racialized concept as well as a gendered one. The main contribution of this study is the finding that race and gender intersect to determine which men will ride the glass escalator. The proposition that men who do women's work encounter undue opportunities and advantages appears to be unequivocally true only if the men in question are white.

This raises interesting questions and a number of new directions for future research. Researchers might consider the extent to which the glass escalator is not only raced and gendered but sexualized as well. Williams (1995) notes that straight men are often treated better by supervisors than are gay men and that straight men frequently do masculinity by strongly asserting their heterosexuality to combat the belief that men who do women's work are gay. The men in this study (with the exception of one nurse I interviewed) rarely discussed sexuality except to say that they were straight and were not bothered by "the gay stereotype." This is consistent with Williams's findings. Gay men, however, may also find that they do not experience a glass escalator effect that facilitates their upward mobility. Tim, the only man I interviewed who identified as gay, suggests that gender, race, and sexuality come together to shape the experiences of men in nursing. He notes,

> I've been called awful things—you faggot this, you faggot that. I tell people there are three Fs in life, and if you're not doing one of them it doesn't matter what you think of me. They say, "Three Fs?" and I say yes. If you aren't feeding me, financing me, or fucking me, then it's none of your business what my faggot ass is up to.

Tim's experience suggests that gay men—and specifically gay Black men—in nursing may encounter particular difficulties establishing close ties with straight men supervisors or may not automatically be viewed by their women colleagues as natural leaders. While race is, in many cases, more obviously visible than sexuality, the glass escalator effect may be a complicated amalgam of racial, gendered, and sexual expectations and stereotypes.

It is also especially interesting to consider how men describe the role of women in facilitating—or denying—access to the glass escalator. Research on white men nurses includes accounts of ways white women welcome them and facilitate their advancement by pushing them toward leadership positions (Floge and Merrill 1986; Heikes 1991; Williams 1992, 1995). In contrast, Black men nurses in this study discuss white women who do not seem eager to work with them, much less aid their upward mobility. These different responses indicate that shared racial status is important in determining who rides the glass escalator. If that is the case, then future research should consider whether Black men nurses who work in predominantly Black settings are more likely to encounter the glass escalator effect. In these settings, Black men nurses' experiences might more closely resemble those of white men nurses.

Future research should also explore other racial minority men's experiences in women's professions to determine whether and how they encounter the processes that facilitate a ride on the glass escalator. With Black men nurses, specific race or gender stereotypes impede their access to the glass escalator; however, other racial minority men are subjected to different race or gender stereotypes that could create other experiences. For instance, Asian American men may encounter racially specific gender stereotypes of themselves as computer nerds, sexless sidekicks, or model minorities and thus may encounter the processes of the glass escalator differently than do Black or white men (Espiritu 2000). More focus on the diverse experiences of racial minority men is necessary to know for certain.

Finally, it is important to consider how these men's experiences have implications for the ways the glass escalator phenomenon reproduces racial and gendered advantages. Williams (1995) argues that men's desire to differentiate themselves from women and disassociate from the femininity of their work is a key process that facilitates their ride on the glass escalator. She ultimately suggests that if men reconstruct masculinity to include traits such as caring, the distinctions between masculinity and femininity could blur and men "would not have to define masculinity as the negation of femininity" (Williams 1995, 188). This in turn could create a more equitable balance between men and women in women's professions. However, the experiences of Black men in nursing, especially their embrace of caring, suggest that accepting the feminine aspects of work is not enough to dismantle the glass escalator and produce more gender equality in women's professions. The fact that Black men nurses accept and even enjoy caring does not minimize the processes that enable *white* men to ride the glass escalator. This suggests that undoing the glass escalator requires not only blurring the lines between masculinity and femininity but also challenging the processes of racial inequality that marginalize minority men.

Note

1. I could not locate any data that indicate the percentage of Black men in nursing. According to 2006 census data, African Americans compose 11 percent of nurses, and men are 8 percent of nurses (http://www.census.gov/compendia/statab/tables/08s0598.pdf). These data do not show the breakdown of nurses by race and sex.

References

Acker, Joan. 1990. Hierarchies, jobs, bodies: A theory of gendered organizations. *Gender & Society* 4:139–58.

Britton, Dana. 1995. *At work in the iron cage.* New York: New York University Press.

Budig, Michelle. 2002. Male advantage and the gender composition of jobs: Who rides the glass escalator? *Social Forces* 49 (2): 258–77.

Charles, Maria, and David Grusky. 2004. *Occupational ghettos: The worldwide segregation of women and men.* Palo Alto, CA: Stanford University Press.

Chen, Anthony. 1999. Lives at the center of the periphery, lives at the periphery of the center: Chinese American masculinities and bargaining with hegemony. *Gender & Society* 13:584–607.

Collins, Patricia Hill. 1990. *Black feminist thought.* New York: Routledge.

——. 2004. *Black sexual politics.* New York: Routledge.

Connell, R. W. 1989. *Gender and power.* Sydney, Australia: Allen and Unwin.

Davis, Angela. 1981. *Women, race, and class.* New York: Vintage.

Duffy, Mignon. 2007. Doing the dirty work: Gender, race, and reproductive labor in historical perspective. *Gender & Society* 21:313–36.

Espiritu, Yen Le. 2000. *Asian American women and men: Labor, laws, and love.* Walnut Creek, CA: AltaMira.

Essed, Philomena. 1991. *Understanding everyday racism.* New York: Russell Sage.

Feagin, Joe. 2006. *Systemic racism.* New York: Routledge.

Feagin, Joe, and Melvin Sikes. 1994. *Living with racism.* Boston: Beacon Hill Press.

Floge, Liliane, and Deborah M. Merrill. 1986. Tokenism reconsidered: Male nurses and female physicians in a hospital setting. *Social Forces* 64:925–47.

Giddings, Paula. 1984. *When and where I enter: The impact of Black women on race and sex in America.* New York: HarperCollins.

Harvey Wingfield, Adia. 2007. The modern mammy and the angry Black man: African American professionals' experiences with gendered racism in the workplace. *Race, Gender, and Class* 14 (2): 196–212.

Heikes, E. Joel. 1991. When men are the minority: The case of men in nursing. *Sociological Quarterly* 32:389–401.

hooks, bell. 2004. *We real cool.* New York: Routledge.

Kanter, Rosabeth Moss. 1977. *Men and women of the corporation.* New York: Basic Books.

Kimmel, Michael. 2001. Masculinity as homophobia. In *Men and masculinity,* edited by Theodore F. Cohen. Belmont, CA: Wadsworth.

Lamont, Michelle. 2000. *The dignity of working men.* New York: Russell Sage.

Neal, Mark Anthony. 2005. *New Black man.* New York: Routledge.

Ong, Maria. 2005. Body projects of young women of color in physics: Intersections of race, gender, and science. *Social Problems* 52 (4): 593–617.

Pierce, Jennifer. 1995. *Gender trials: Emotional lives in contemporary law firms.* Berkeley: University of California Press.

Roth, Louise. 2006. *Selling women short: Gender and money on Wall Street.* Princeton, NJ: Princeton University Press.

Shapiro, Thomas. 2004. *Hidden costs of being African American: How wealth perpetuates inequality.* New York: Oxford University Press.

Snyder, Karrie Ann, and Adam Isaiah Green. 2008. Revisiting the glass escalator: The case of gender segregation in a female dominated occupation. *Social Problems* 55 (2): 271–99.

Williams, Christine. 1989. *Gender differences at work: Women and men in non-traditional occupations.* Berkeley: University of California Press.

———. 1992. The glass escalator: Hidden advantages for men in the "female" professions. *Social Problems* 39 (3): 253–67.

———. 1995. *Still a man's world: Men who do women's work.* Berkeley: University of California Press.

Zimmer, Lynn. 1988. Tokenism and women in the workplace: The limits of gender neutral theory. *Social Problems* 35 (1): 64–77.

Rethink What You "Know" About High-Achieving Women

ROBIN J. ELY, PAMELA STONE, AND COLLEEN AMMERMAN

As researchers who have spent more than 20 years studying professional women, we have watched with interest the recent surge in attention paid to women's careers, work-family conflict, and the gender gap in leadership. Among the most visible contributions to this public conversation have been Anne-Marie Slaughter's 2012 *Atlantic* article "Why Women Still Can't Have it All" and Sheryl Sandberg's book *Lean In,* both of which ignited fierce public debate.

A lot of ink has been spilled on these topics, and both individuals and organizations have focused on gender gaps in business and other sectors. Can anything more be said? The 50th anniversary of the admission of women to Harvard Business School's MBA program inspired us to find out—specifically, to learn what HBS graduates had to say about work and family and how their experiences, attitudes, and decisions might shed light on prevailing controversies.

We trained our analytical lens on these graduates for two reasons. First, attending a top-tier business school is a reasonable indication of high levels of achievement, talent, ambition, and promise, and by looking at men and women who graduated from the same school, we had a level playing field for gender comparisons. Second, HBS graduates are trained to assume leadership positions, so their attitudes and experiences—interesting in their own right—shape the policies, practices, and unwritten rules of their organizations.

We surveyed more than 25,000 HBS graduates altogether; in this article we focus on MBAs, by far the largest proportion. Because we are primarily

Robin J. Ely, Pamela Stone, and Colleen Ammerman, "Rethink What You 'Know' About High-Achieving Women," *Harvard Business Review,* Vol. 92, No. 12 (December 2014), pp. 101–109. Copyright © 2014 by Harvard Business Publishing; all rights reserved. Reprinted with permission.

interested in the experiences of those who are still in the workplace, we report on Baby Boomers (ages 49–67), Generation X (ages 32–48), and Millennials (ages 26–31), also known as Generation Y. What our survey revealed suggests that the conventional wisdom about women's careers doesn't always square with reality.

Do Men and Women Want the Same Things?

The highly educated, ambitious women and men of HBS don't differ much in terms of what they value and hope for in their lives and careers. We asked them to tell us how they defined success when they graduated from HBS and how they define it now, and they gave similar responses. Career-related factors figured prominently in their early definitions of success: Men and women mentioned job titles, job levels, and professional achievements at roughly the same rates.

When reflecting on how they define success today, both men and women cited career-related factors less often—unless they were Millennials, who mentioned those factors with about the same frequency across time. (This is unsurprising, given that only a few years have elapsed since they graduated, and most of their working lives are still ahead of them.) Today, however, family happiness, relationships, and balancing life and work, along with community service and helping others, are much more on the minds of Generation X and Baby Boomers. Two examples are illustrative. A woman in her forties, who left HBS about 20 years ago, told us: "For me, at age 25, success was defined by career success. Now I think of success much differently: Raising happy, productive children, contributing to the world around me, and pursuing work that is meaningful to me." These sentiments were echoed by a man in his fifties, for whom success early on was "becoming a highly paid CEO of a medium-to-large business." And today? "Striking a balance between work and family and giving back to society." Indeed, when we asked respondents to rate the importance of nine career and life dimensions, nearly 100%, regardless of gender, said that "quality of personal and family relationships" was "very" or "extremely" important.

With regard to career importance, men and women were again in agreement. Their ratings of key dimensions of professional life, such as "work that is meaningful and satisfying" and "professional accomplishments," were the same, and the majority said that "opportunities for career growth and development" were important to them, with women actually rating them slightly higher.

These results indicate that Harvard MBAs aimed for and continue to value fulfilling professional and personal lives. Yet their ability to realize them has played out very differently according to gender. Among those graduates who are employed full-time, men are more likely to have direct reports, to hold profit-and-loss responsibility, and to be in senior management positions. Setting aside those measures of success, since not everyone aspires to them, we found that women are less satisfied with their careers. Whereas about 50% to 60% of men across the three generations told us

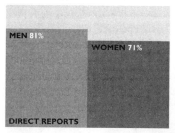
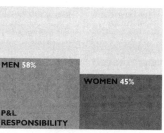
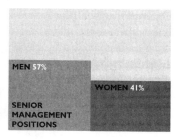

Figure 1. Who Has Been Given High-Level Responsibilities?
Source: Robin J. Ely, Pamela Stone, and Colleen Ammerman.
Note: Among HBS graduates working full-time, men were significantly more likely than women to have direct reports, profit-and-loss responsibility, and positions in senior management.

they were "extremely satisfied" or "very satisfied" with their experiences of meaningful work, professional accomplishments, opportunities for career growth, and compatibility of work and personal life, only 40% to 50% of women were similarly satisfied on the same dimensions.

Given the gender gap in career outcomes, gaps in career satisfaction and in successfully combining work and family are unsurprising. A deeper analysis revealed that some prevailing beliefs about why women's progress has stalled are unsupported. We also found that certain expectations regarding how couples will distribute career and family responsibilities may contribute to women's stymied goals and lesser satisfaction.

Are Women Opting Out?

The pull of child rearing has long been a dominant explanation for the small proportion of women in corporate boardrooms, C-suites, partnerships, and other seats of power. For years before Lisa Belkin's 2003 *New York Times Magazine* cover story added the term "opt out" to the cultural lexicon, senior executives were assuming that high-potential women who quit their jobs were leaving to care for their families. In the early 1990s Mike Cook, then the CEO of Deloitte & Touche, thought this was why only 10% of partner candidates in his firm were women, even though Deloitte had been hiring equal numbers of men and women for the preceding 10 years. But when Cook convened a task force to look behind the numbers, he learned that more than 70% of the women who had left the firm were still employed full-time one year later. Fewer than 10% were out of the workforce to care

for young children. The vast majority of female employees who left Deloitte did not jettison (or even pause in) their careers; they simply went to jobs elsewhere. (For more details, see our colleague Rosabeth Moss Kanter's case "A Hole in the Pipeline," written with Jane Roessner.)

Fast-forward 20 years, and this mistaken thinking persists. Despite the fact that men and women actually have pretty similar career priorities, the belief that women value career less is widespread. We found that 77% of HBS graduates overall—73% of men and 85% of women—believe that "prioritizing family over work" is the number one barrier to women's career advancement. (We saw essentially the same numbers when we restricted the analysis to graduates who are in top management positions and when we included Executive Education graduates, suggesting that this conviction packs some punch.)

As one alumna in her mid-thirties noted, a key factor is still "deep-rooted attitudes that a woman should be the primary caregiver, so it is 'understood' that her career may have to take a backseat for a while as similar male colleagues move ahead at a more rapid pace."

But here's the kicker: It simply isn't true that a large proportion of HBS alumnae have "opted out" to care for children. When we asked Gen X and Baby Boom women (who are most likely to have children under 18 living with them today) about their current status, we learned essentially what Mike Cook's task force did: *Only 11% are out of the workforce to care for children full-time.* The figure is even lower (7%) for women of color. (In that group, black and South Asian women are at the lowest end of the spectrum, at just 4%.)

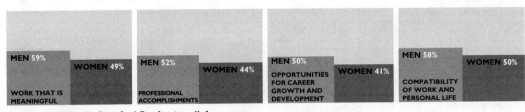

Figure 2. Who Is Satisfied Professionally?
Source: Robin J. Ely, Pamela Stone, and Colleen Ammerman.
Note: Men were significantly more satisfied than women on four key dimensions.

Seventy-four percent of Gen X alumnae are working full-time, as are 52% of Baby Boom alumnae (some of whom, like their male counterparts, have retired or are cutting back on their hours), and they average 52 hours a week. When we saw how few women were out of the workforce, we wondered whether those who were might have been disproportionately less likely to respond to the survey. But a number of checks turned up no evidence of response bias.

Even for HBS women who *are* currently out of the workforce to care for children, "opting out" is not an accurate description of their experience. Our survey data and other research suggest that when high-achieving, highly educated professional women leave their jobs after becoming mothers, only a small number do so because they prefer to devote themselves exclusively to motherhood; the vast majority leave reluctantly and as a last resort, because they find themselves in unfulfilling roles with dim prospects for advancement. The message that they are no longer considered "players" is communicated in various, sometimes subtle ways: They may have been stigmatized for taking advantage of flex options or reduced schedules, passed over for high-profile assignments, or removed from projects they once led. One alumna, now in her late fifties, recalled, "I left my first job after being 'mommy-tracked' when I came back from maternity leave."

Another, in her forties, said, "The flexible part-time roles I have taken [while raising my child] . . . have never been intellectually fulfilling." A third told us that even finding such a role proved impossible: "I thought success would be combining career and family successfully at the same time. I thought I could scale back to part-time, and I'd ramp back up as the kids grew . . . [But my] industry offered few if any professional part-time positions." Yet another recounted leaving the workforce in response to unfulfilling work: "I last quit three years ago because I could not seem to get new challenges and became bored by the work. I had great reviews and the company liked me. There appeared to be preconceived notions about part-time women wanting less challenging work, off track, when I was seeking the more challenging

work, on some sort of track. And being part-time took me out of the structured review and promotion ladder."

Do Family Responsibilities Push Women Out of the Leadership Pipeline?

We also wanted to consider how taking time off for parenting might affect the trajectory of women's careers. We asked survey respondents about *any* breaks they had taken over the course of their careers and learned that 28% of Gen X and 44% of Baby Boom women had at some point taken a break of more than six months to care for children, compared with only 2% of men across those two generations.

Time out of the workforce *could* account for the fact that women are less likely to be in senior positions. After all, it's often argued that because being in senior leadership is directly tied to years of professional experience, women are less likely to be in those roles precisely because they are more likely to have taken such breaks. So we delved deeper, with controls for variables such as age, industry, sector, and organization size, analyzing a range of factors related to family status and parenting, looking for a link to women's lesser representation in top management. But we found no connections. We considered not only whether graduates had gone part-time or taken a career break to care for children, but also the number of times they had done so. We asked about common career decisions made to accommodate family responsibilities, such as limiting travel, choosing a more flexible job, slowing down the pace of one's career, making a lateral move, leaving a job, or declining to work toward a promotion. Women were more likely than men to have made such decisions—but again, none of these factors explained the gender gap in senior management. In fact, both men and women in top management teams were typically *more* likely than those lower down in the hierarchy to have made career decisions to accommodate family responsibilities. We even looked at whether simply being a parent— aside from any career changes or decisions related to parenting—made a difference. It did not.

Again and again, our core finding—HBS alumnae have not attained senior management positions at the same rates as men—persisted.

We don't think these findings—which are, frankly, surprising—are the final word on the subject. Indeed, they suggest that we need much more nuanced data about how professional men and women navigate their family and career decisions and how their lives unfold if we are to understand the impact that family responsibilities have on both women's and men's careers. We don't mean to suggest that no relationship exists between individuals' choices regarding work and family and their career outcomes. But what is clear is that the conventional wisdom doesn't tell the full story. We will explore this more deeply in subsequent surveys, and we hope other researchers will take up this question too.

Are Women's and Men's Expectations for Work and Family at Odds?

We also wanted to better understand the gender gaps we found in satisfaction with career and with the combining of work and the rest of life, so we looked at what respondents told us about their expectations when they launched their post-HBS careers and what they had experienced in the years since. Ultimately, we uncovered some disconnects that may illuminate why women and men are not equally fulfilled.

More than half the men in Generation X and the Baby Boom said that when they left HBS, they expected that their careers would take priority over their spouses' or partners'. The vast majority

(83%) of the graduates in these generations reported being married, and because we don't have reliable data on sexual orientation, we assume that their partners are of the opposite sex. Thus we call this expectation "traditional," to denote an arrangement whereby the man's career takes precedence over the woman's. Notably, this expectation was less prevalent among men of color than among white men. Forty-eight percent of the former—compared with 39% of white men—anticipated that their spouses' careers would be of equal importance. Meanwhile, the vast majority of women across racial groups and generations anticipated that their careers would rank equally with those of their partners. (Only 7% of Gen X and 3% of Baby Boom women, and even fewer of their male counterparts, expected that the woman's career would take priority over the man's—an arrangement we call "progressive.")

Most graduates went on to lead fairly traditional lives on this score. Close to three-quarters of Gen X and Baby Boom men reported that their careers had indeed taken precedence—more than had originally expected this arrangement. Meanwhile, many women's expectations for career equality were disappointed. Though majorities of Gen X and Baby Boom women reported that they were in egalitarian or progressive partnerships, the remainder found that their careers took lower priority. That figure—40%—is almost double the proportion who left HBS expecting a traditional arrangement. This outcome varied significantly among racial groups, with black women being the least likely to end up with a partner whose career took precedence.

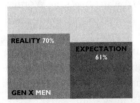 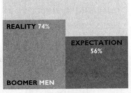 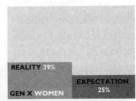 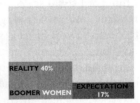

Figure 3. Different Expectations—and Results—Regarding "Traditional" Career Priority
Source: Robin J. Ely, Pamela Stone, and Colleen Ammerman.
Note: A strong majority of men expected to be in "traditional" partnerships, in which their careers would take precedence. Their expectations were actually exceeded. A distinct minority of women expected their partners' careers to take precedence, but for about 40% of them, that's exactly what happened.

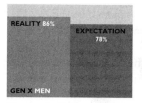
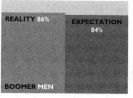
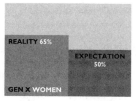
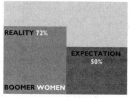

Figure 4. Different Expectations—and Results—Regarding "Traditional" Child Care
Source: Robin J. Ely, Pamela Stone, and Colleen Ammerman.
Note: A large majority of men expected their partners to take primary responsibility for child care. Those expectations were met and exceeded. (Across the two generations, black men's expectations and reality were somewhat lower, at 68% and 72%.) Half the women expected to take primary responsibility for raising children, and more than two-thirds of them actually did so. (Among black women, however, 53% were the primary caregivers.)

We had asked a parallel set of questions about child care: How had graduates who were expecting to have partners and children (91%) anticipated dividing child care responsibilities when they left HBS, and how did they actually divide them? Across the board, we found expectations on this dimension to be much more traditional than those regarding career priority. At the time they graduated from HBS, more than three-quarters of men expected that their partners would do the lion's share of child care. Black men were somewhat less likely to expect such an arrangement. Meanwhile, about half the women expected that they would take on the majority of this work. Latinas were the least likely, at 40%, to have expected to shoulder most of the child care.

These expectations about child care may help to explain the more traditional career arrangements of graduates who had expected otherwise. About half the women who had egalitarian career expectations also assumed that they would perform most of the child care in their families. But if women are primarily responsible for child care, their careers are more likely to become secondary in importance to their partners', perhaps helping to explain their lesser career satisfaction.

Ultimately, more-traditional arrangements did win out. Healthy majorities of Gen X and Baby Boom women took responsibility for most of the child care in their families. Even higher percentages of Gen X and Baby Boom men reported having spouses who did so. Black men and women were the least likely to have a traditional arrangement;

their numbers were lower by roughly 15 to 20 percentage points.

So although a much larger proportion of women expected a traditional division of child care responsibilities than expected a traditional career priority, men and women sharply diverged on both dimensions. Women were more likely to have egalitarian expectations—and to see their expectations dashed. As we've also seen, men *are* more successful in their careers, which no doubt plays a role in the difference between expectations and reality as many women watch their partners' careers take off and eclipse their own.

Whatever the explanation, this disconnect exacts a psychic cost—for both women and men. Women who started out with egalitarian expectations but ended up in more-traditional arrangements felt less satisfied with how their careers have progressed than did women who both expected and experienced egalitarian partnerships at home. And in general, women tended to be less satisfied than men with their career growth—except for those whose careers and child care responsibilities were seen as equal to their partners'. Conversely, men who expected traditional arrangements but found themselves in egalitarian relationships were less satisfied with their career growth than were their peers in more-traditional arrangements, perhaps reflecting an enduring cultural ideal wherein men's work is privileged. Indeed, traditional partnerships were linked to higher career satisfaction for men, whereas women who ended up in such arrangements were less satisfied, regardless of their original expectations.

The Millennials Are Rising—Is Change on the Way?

It is tempting to think that people launching their careers today will change the game. After all, it was only a few generations ago that women were barred from higher education and many professions. Won't gender parity develop with the passage of time? Unfortunately, we don't think it's quite that simple, given what we heard from Millennial MBAs. What these men and women expect at this early stage in their careers and lives looks as incompatible—and unrealistic—as it was for earlier generations.

It's not that things have stayed the same. Among HBS graduates, Millennial men are somewhat less likely than older men to expect their careers to take precedence. They're also less likely to expect that their partners will do the majority of child care: A third anticipate doing an equal share, as compared with 22% of Gen X men and 16% of Baby Boom men. (This generation looks different in other ways, as well: When we asked Millennials to define success today, they cited job titles, being in the C-suite, and similar status concerns less often than did older generations.)

Nevertheless, like their predecessors, the youngest men have expectations more traditional than those of their female peers. Whereas three-quarters of Millennial women anticipate that their careers will be at least as important as their partners', half the men in their generation expect that their own careers will take priority. And whereas two-thirds of Millennial men expect that their partners will handle the majority of child care, just under half—42%—of Millennial women expect that they themselves will do so.

We can't help noting that 42% is still a sizable proportion, and these young women may find—as Gen X and Baby Boom women apparently did—that shouldering most of the child rearing hinders equal career importance. Only 10% of the Millennial graduates have children, and they are still early in their careers, so we do not yet know how these mismatched expectations will ultimately play out. But if previous generations are any indication, change won't occur soon.

Overcoming Myths and Changing Reality

At a certain point the belief that a woman's primary career obstacle is *herself* became conventional wisdom, for both women and men. From "opting out" to "ratcheting back," the ways we talk about women's careers often emphasize their willingness to scale down or forgo opportunities, projects, and jobs. The very premise seems to be that women value career less than men do, or that mothers don't want high-profile, challenging work.

Yet framing the conversation like this doesn't reflect reality—at least not for HBS women, and not, we'd venture, for many other highly educated, career-oriented women. Alumnae set out from HBS placing considerable value on achievement and fulfillment at work and on having careers that are valued as much as their partners' are. Life outside work, including family relationships, is also important to them—just as it is to men. So why do we see a gender gap in top management even in this high-achieving group? The answer doesn't seem to be that women have simply left the workforce, because very few are caring for children full-time. Nor does it seem that women's (or men's) efforts to accommodate personal and family obligations, such as by working less than full-time or making lateral career moves, explain why women are less likely to be in top management.

Our findings call for more-comprehensive organizational solutions to address gender disparities in career achievement. Companies need to provide adequate entry points to full-time work for women who have, for instance, recently been on a part-time schedule or taken a career break. Our results make equally clear that companies need to move beyond regarding flextime and other "family-friendly" policies as sufficient for retaining and developing high-potential women. Women *are* leaning in. Most women who have achieved top management positions have done so while managing family responsibilities—and, like their male counterparts, while working long hours. Women want *more* meaningful work, *more* challenging assignments, and *more* opportunities for career growth. It is now time, as Anne-Marie Slaughter has pointed out, for *companies* to lean in, in part by considering how they can institutionalize a level playing field for all employees, regardless of gender or caregiver status.

Companies need to be vigilant about unspoken but powerful perceptions that constrain women's opportunities. The misguided assumption that high-potential women are "riskier" hires than their male peers because they are apt to discard their careers after parenthood is yet another bias women confront. As one 30-year-old alumna reported, "I have thought about going to interviews without my [wedding and engagement] rings on so that an interviewer doesn't get a preconceived notion of my dedication based upon where I might be in my life stage."

Admittedly, wading into this territory is difficult and emotionally fraught. Decisions about family life and relationships are always deeply personal. "Lean in" is a rallying cry for women trying to navigate the workplace, but our survey results make us think that Sheryl Sandberg's other slogan—"Make your partner a real partner"—is every bit as crucial, and perhaps more apt for young, achievement-oriented women who aspire to have meaningful, fully valued careers. The fact that HBS alumnae are finding themselves in relationships in which their careers are subordinate to their partners' more often

than they anticipated strikes us as meaningful. Our findings indicate that ending up in less-egalitarian partnerships is disappointing—perhaps especially so when a career has stalled. In fact, women may be doing more and more child care because their careers have hit a wall, leading them to default to a support role in which their jobs are secondary. Meanwhile, men feel pressured to demonstrate their family devotion by performing as breadwinners, even when that means more time away from home. In our research we heard from many men who feel harshly judged by their companies and the culture at large for wanting to spend less time at work and more with their kids. One 42-year-old alumnus reported, "I struggle with balancing family and work life, and so far my reputation is suffering both at work and at home."

In the end, we found not just achievement and satisfaction gaps between men and women, but a real gap between what women expect as they look ahead to their careers and where they ultimately land. The men and women who graduate from HBS set out with much in common—MBAs, high ambitions, and preparation for leadership. Perhaps it's time for more-candid conversations—at home, at work, and on campus—about how and why their paths unfold so differently.

Unmasking Manly Men

ROBIN J. ELY AND DEBRA MEYERSON

What can managers in white-collar firms learn from roughnecks and roustabouts on an offshore oil rig? That extinguishing macho behavior is vital

to achieving top performance. That's a key finding from our study of life on two oil platforms, during which we spent several weeks over the course of

19 months living, eating, and working alongside crews offshore.

Oil rigs are dirty, dangerous, and demanding workplaces that have traditionally encouraged displays of masculine strength, daring, and technical prowess. But over the past 15 years or so the platforms we studied have deliberately jettisoned their hard-driving, macho cultures in favor of an environment in which men admit when they've made mistakes and explore how anxiety, stress, or lack of experience may have caused them; appreciate one another publicly; and routinely ask for and offer help. These workers shifted their focus from proving their masculinity to larger, more compelling goals: maximizing the safety and well-being of coworkers and doing their jobs effectively.

The shift required a new attitude toward work, which was pushed from the top down. If you can't expose errors and learn from them, management's thinking went, you can't be safe or effective. Workers came to appreciate that to improve safety and performance in a potentially deadly environment, they had to be open to new information that challenged their assumptions, and they had to acknowledge when they were wrong.

Their altered stance revealed two things: First, that much of their macho behavior was not only unnecessary but actually got in the way of doing their jobs; and second, that their notions about what constituted strong leadership needed to change. They discovered that the people who used to rise to the top—the "biggest, baddest roughnecks," as one worker described them—weren't necessarily the best at improving safety and effectiveness. Rather, the ones who excelled were mission-driven guys who cared about their fellow workers, were good listeners, and were willing to learn.

Over the 15-year period these changes in work practices, norms, perceptions, and behaviors

were implemented company-wide. The company's accident rate declined by 84%, while productivity (number of barrels produced), efficiency (cost per barrel), and reliability (production "up" time) increased beyond the industry's previous benchmark.

But the changes had an unintended effect as well. The men's willingness to risk a blow to their image—by, for example, exposing their incompetence or weakness when necessary in order to do their jobs well—profoundly influenced their sense of who they were and could be as men. No longer focused on affirming their masculinity, they felt able to behave in ways that conventional masculine norms would have precluded.

If men in the hypermasculine environment of oil rigs can let go of the macho ideal and improve their performance, then men in corporate America might be able to do likewise. Numerous studies have examined the costs of macho displays in contexts ranging from aeronautics to manufacturing to high tech to the law. They show that men's attempts to prove their masculinity interfere with the training of recruits, compromise decision quality, marginalize women workers, lead to civil- and human-rights violations, and alienate men from their health, feelings, and relationships with others. The price of men's striving to demonstrate their masculinity is high, and both individuals and organizations pay it.

The problem lies not in traditionally masculine attributes per se—many tasks require aggressiveness, strength, or emotional detachment—but in men's efforts to prove themselves on these dimensions, whether in the hazardous setting of an offshore oil platform or in the posh, protected surroundings of the executive suite. By creating conditions that focus people on the real requirements of the job, rather than on stereotypical images believed to equate with competence, organizations can free employees to do their best work.

The Gender of Politics
and the Politics of Gender

The realm of the political—of states and governments, welfare and warfare, taxes and services, elected and electorate—has always been gendered. What governments *do* is gendered—whether it is diplomacy with other nations, engaging in warfare, or administering justice and collecting revenues (all considered masculine) as opposed to ensuring fairness in the legal and political process, spending on social services, health care, education, or families and providing a social safety net—that is, *caring* for its citizens (all coded as feminine).

Just as political institutions are gendered, so too are the politicians and those who elect them. Voters are categorized into smaller constituencies, and gender turns out to be an increasingly important one. Women not only represent more than half the electorate, but an increasingly independent one. Did you know that a century ago, the campaign against woman suffrage argued that allowing women to vote would be unfair to single men? You see, we believe in "one man, one vote" but allowing women to vote would be like giving married men two votes, since those critics couldn't conceive that a woman could possibly even consider voting differently than her husband!

The essays in this section approach the gender of politics at all these levels. Richard York and Shannon Elizabeth Bell provide a more general overview of the interplay between gender and politics. And the article by Victoria L. Brescoll examines what we might call the micro-politics of gender, how language styles factor into women's political position.

Life Satisfaction Across Nations: The Effects of Women's Political Status and Public Priorities

RICHARD YORK AND SHANNON ELIZABETH BELL

Introduction

What are the societal goals behind economic growth? Ostensibly, expansion of the economy is aimed at improving people's lives. Measures of economic affluence, such as the Gross Domestic Product (GDP) per capita, are commonly used as indicators of quality of life of people in nations. However, the connection between GDP per capita and quality of life is not straightforward (Diener, Helliwell, and Kahneman, 2010).[1] In fact, some activists and scholars have argued that GDP is "utterly unrelated to the well-being of a community" (Waring quoted in Nash, 1995) because the levels of inequality, poverty, health, educational attainment, and environmental conditions in a nation are not reflected in the GDP (Waring, 1999). The recognition of the limitations of economic measures for gauging a nation's living conditions and overall well-being has spread widely. Increasingly, scholars and activists are calling for a shift toward measuring societal well-being using indicators that assess not only people's physical conditions, including their health, but also how people themselves evaluate their own well-being (Diener et al., 2010; New Economics Foundation. 2009). Focusing on more direct measures of well-being has the advantage of allowing us to ask the question of *whether* economic growth and other indicators of economic development actually improve people's lives, rather than assuming that they do *a priori*. This type of approach also opens up the possibility of assessing how a variety of other factors, such as social inequalities, affect the ways in which people experience their lives. To help further our understanding of the factors that influence the well-being of people, our aim here is to assess the effects of women's representation in the political sphere, affluence as measured by GDP per capita, and other factors on the average self-reported life satisfaction of people across nations.

How societies work to improve people's lives has important implications for the environment. A considerable body of research has established that some of the hallmarks of modernity and development—economic growth, urbanization, and the globalization of markets, among other factors—are associated with a rising tide of environmental problems, historically unprecedented in scale and diversity (Jorgenson and Clark, 2012; Rosa et al., 2004; York et al., 2003). Scholars have found that those nations considered to be the most "developed" by these types of criteria typically have high levels of environmental impact relative to the standard of living of their people (Dietz et al., 2009, 2012; Knight and Rosa, 2011; New Economics Foundation, 2009). Furthermore, there is growing evidence that while increasing the quantity of material possessions, economic growth has not necessarily improved people's lives (Blanchflower and Oswald, 2011; Diener et al., 2010; Leiserowitz et al., 2005). In fact, empirical work has established that high levels of consumption of energy and other

Richard York and Shannon Elizabeth Bell, "Life Satisfaction Across Nations: The Effects of Women's Political Status and Public Priorities," *Social Science Research*, Vol. 48 (2004), pp. 48–61. Copyright © 2014 by Elsevier. Reprinted with permission from Elsevier.

natural resources are not closely connected with the quality of life of people in societies (Mazur and Rosa, 1974; Rosa, 1997; Seaford, 2011). There are quite a number of so-called "less-developed countries" (LDCs) where people live long lives and report high levels of life satisfaction, while having relatively small ecological footprints (New Economics Foundation, 2009; Seaford, 2011).

In light of the many environmental problems the world faces, finding ways to improve people's lives without increasing their material affluence is critical for the future of our planet. Thus, there is a need to assess which societal factors show promise for improving people's well-being without relying on increasing resource consumption. We maintain that important insights into this effort can be found in the work of feminist scholars who argue that greater gender equality and a reorientation of social priorities can improve people's quality of life without the environmental consequences associated with common modes of economic growth (Waring, 1999). Here we aim to assess the effects of various factors on the average subjective well-being of people in nations, focusing especially on gender equality in national parliaments.

To put our research in context, we first present a brief overview of research on cross-national differences in well-being. We then briefly review research on the connections between gender relationships and quality of life, presenting some of the reasons why we may expect there to be a connection between women's political representation and the well-being of the populace. We then explain our analysis and present our findings.

Cross-National Differences in Well-Being

There is a large body of cumulative scholarly work on the factors that influence people's well-being, examining both individual level factors and societal level factors (Blanchflower and Oswald, 2011; Diener and Lucas, 2000; Diener et al., 2010; Veenhoven, 2005). Here we focus on the literature examining average differences across nations, since that is the level of our own analysis.

Many analyses have focused on the extent to which material affluence, typically measured as per capita GDP or GNP, is connected with subjective well-being. While there is a diversity of findings, an assessment of the research overall suggests that people in more affluent nations tend to report higher levels of life satisfaction than people in poor nations, but the association is fairly weak (Blanchflower and Oswald, 2011; Diener and Lucas, 2000). In particular, the cross-sectional pattern, broadly speaking, suggests a relationship of diminishing returns, where the association of life satisfaction with higher income is clearest when comparing nations with very low income to those with moderate levels of income, but there is not a clear difference in life satisfaction between nations with moderate levels of income and those which are highly affluent (Blanchflower and Oswald. 2011; Diener et al., 2010; Seaford, 2011). Additionally, while the cross-sectional pattern suggests that affluence matters to some degree, analyses of time-series data have not found compelling evidence to suggest that economic growth increases life satisfaction within nations (Blanchflower and Oswald, 2011).

Political and social factors have been shown to affect average subjective well-being in nations. In particular, the average well-being of people is generally higher in nations where democracy and democratic participation, personal freedom, and individualism are strong (Frey and Stutzer, 2000; Helliwell and Huang, 2008; Veenhoven, 1999; Welsch, 2003). Well-being is also higher in nations with low economic inequality (Veenhoven, 2005; Winkelmann and Winkelmann, 2010). Additionally, well-being appears to be greater in nations with higher levels of public spending, particularly on health care, and more developed welfare states (Kotakorpi and Laamen, 2010; Pacek and Radcliff, 2008).

Related to the research on subjective well-being, there is an important body of literature in sociology examining the connection between military development and physical well-being (commonly indicated by life expectancy). Dixon and Moon (1986) and Moon and Dixon (1985) found that military spending was associated with lower physical well-being in nations, whereas democracy was connected with higher well-being. Similarly, Jenkins and Scanlan (2001) and Scanlan and Jenkins (2001) found that military spending and arms imports reduced food security and increased child hunger in nations. Since there is an established connection between physical well-being, particularly as indicated by life expectancy, and subjective well-being (Di Tella and MacCulloch, 2008), it is reasonable to expect that military spending will affect subjective well-being. Furthermore, a number of scholars have identified an inverse relationship between military spending and spending on social protection programs, health care, and environmental protection (Waring, 1999; Sivard, 1996; Mazurana and McKay, 2001; Winter et al., 2001). Unsurprisingly, nations that spend more money on wars and military arms have less to spend on programs aimed at improving the health and welfare of the citizenry. As Mukherjee and Waring (2012) argue, nations with well-developed social assistance programs aimed at shielding vulnerable populations from threats to livelihood—including poverty, discriminatory treatment, and a lack of access to basic services like health care or nutrition—are better able to cope with crises, such as the recent global financial crisis, which has put severe strains on people living in many nations throughout the world.

Gender Equality and Quality of Life

While high levels of military spending and the resulting insufficiencies in social assistance programs can have dire consequences for the health and welfare of a country's citizenry, there are also other factors that contribute to lower levels of well-being and life satisfaction within nations. One significant, but understudied, factor is gender equality. In fact, there is a clear association between women's empowerment and a number of quality-of-life outcomes, including those connected to health, reproduction, education, and the environment, which are manifested at various levels of society. While the focus of our analysis is on the nation, and particularly on women's equality in political representation, it is important to understand how women's empowerment affects well-being at the household and community levels as well, since these have consequences that aggregate

to the national level. Thus, in order to explain why it is reasonable to hypothesize that gender equality may improve average subjective well-being in nations, below we offer a review of the research on the effects of gender equality at the household and community levels before discussing the research that suggests a relationship between gender equality and the well-being of nations.

The Household

Research studies conducted around the world suggest an association between women's empowerment and better health, nutrition, and educational outcomes at the household level. Women's empowerment has been linked to higher rates of infant and child survival, health, and well-being (Caldwell and Caldwell, 1993; Jejeebhoy, 1995; Kishor, 2000). There are a number of reasons for these better health outcomes. For one, when women experience greater autonomy at the household level, they are more likely to utilize methods of family planning with their partners (Dyson and Moore, 1983; Basu, 1992; Balk, 1994; Morgan and Niraula, 1995; Gwako and Moogi, 1997; Schuler et al., 1997; Hindin, 2000). Women who have agency over their sexuality and the power to make reproductive choices are more likely to delay when they begin to bear children, leave more time between births, and have fewer children overall; all of these factors are associated with lower rates of infant, child, and maternal morbidity and mortality (Hobcraft, 2000; United Nations, 1994).

Additionally, there is evidence that when women have more control over the household budget, a larger fraction of the family's income and resources is devoted to children's nutrition, education, and health (Quisumbing and Maluccio, 1999; Duflo, 2003; Smith et al., 2003). There is also evidence that when women have increased access to credit, there is a larger impact on children's school enrollment, child nutrition, and long-term food security than when men borrow money (Pitt and Khandker, 1998; Coleman, 2004; Hazarika and Guha-Khasnobis, 2008). Women's ownership of land is also important. For example, in her study of child health in Nepal, Allendorf (2007) found that young children of women who owned land were significantly less likely to be malnourished than children whose mothers worked on family-owned land or whose families were landless. In short, "a very large body of research from many countries around the world confirms that putting more income in the hands of women yields beneficial results for child nutrition, health, and education . . . empowering women is a well-proven strategy for improving children's well-being" (Food and Agriculture Organization of the United Nations, 2011, p. 9).

The Community

Women's empowerment does not just contribute to the well-being of the household; it also impacts the larger community in significant ways. For example, women's sexual and reproductive agency is essential to stemming the spread of HIV/AIDS. According to Farmer (1996), numerous studies reveal that most of the women in the U.S. who are at high risk of HIV infection know that condoms can prevent transmission of the virus; however, many are simply unable to insist that their partners use them. One such study of African-American women in Los Angeles found that condom usage was much lower among couples when the woman depended on her male partner for rent money (Farmer, 1996). As Francisco and Antrobus (2009) assert, "no amount of education can protect a woman from exposure to the virus if she cannot negotiate safe sex" (p. 163).

Women who have the freedom to act within the public sphere can effect important changes to improve the well-being of their communities. It is well-documented that women make up the bulk of the leadership and membership of grassroots environmental justice organizations in the United States (Cable, 1992; Brown and Ferguson, 1995; Kaplan, 1997; Naples, 1998; Bell, 2013) and have initiated various other social justice causes, such as struggles for welfare, organized labor, health care, and employment rights (Norris and Cyprès, 1996; Seitz, 1995, 1998; Maggard, 1987, 1990, 1999; Hall, 1986; Scott, 1995; Giesen, 1995; Weiss, 1993). This pattern also holds true for many community-based social change efforts in LDCs, such as India, Afghanistan, Peru, and the Tibet Autonomous

Region of China, among many others (Taylor-lde and Taylor, 2002; Taylor et al., 2012). Numerous scholars have found that women's leadership in such grassroots efforts is often tied to their identities as mothers. Naples (1992, 1998) describes this "activist mothering" among urban Latina and African American women community workers, who view motherhood as a role that extends beyond caring for their biological or legal children into the wider community. In the context of Black communities, Patricia Hill Collins (1990) similarly describes women who view themselves as "othermothers"—women who believe that their mothering practices include social activism.

While women may be driven to community activist work because of their identities as mothers and protectors, the social activism of men, by contrast, may be impeded by masculine identities. For instance, Bell and Braun (2010) find that while women in the Appalachian coalfields call on their socially-sanctioned roles as mothers and protectors to defend their communities from irresponsible mining practices, the "coal-mining identity" held by many men living in the region serves as a barrier to men's willingness to become involved in environmental justice activism. This is a pattern likely replicated in other regions where there is a "community economic identity" (Bell and York, 2010) associated with a polluting or destructive industry. In many cases, women are far more willing to stand up against unjust industry practices and fight for the rights of their communities because they do not experience the same employment loyalties or peer pressure that the men in these communities feel. Thus, when women have the freedom to initiate and participate in civic life—including social protest or activist work—important social change directed at improving quality of life may be more likely to occur.

The National Level

Through its effects at the household and community levels, and through processes that emerge within larger social aggregates, gender equality also has effects on the well-being of national populations. For instance, within the context of LDCs, Lee (2000) found that nations with smaller gaps between women's and men's educational levels experience longer life expectancies for both genders. Furthermore, cross-national analyses by both Caldwell (1986) and Lee (2000) reveal that the single most important factor for reducing mortality rates in LDCs is increasing female education. This finding is especially pronounced among children, and numerous studies corroborate this phenomenon. For instance, in an examination of the World Fertility Survey, Caldwell (1989) found that the children of uneducated Peruvian women experienced a death rate that was almost seven times greater than the children of Venezuelan women with seven years of education. Similarly, on the other side of the world in Asia, the children of uneducated Nepalese women experienced a mortality rate that was almost 15 times higher than the children of Malaysian women with seven or more years of education.

In addition to the above literature linking gender equality with objective measures of well-being within nations, there is also some evidence suggesting a relationship between gender equality and life satisfaction as a subjective measure of well-being. Countering the assumption that increasing gender equality is a "zero-sum game" wherein "women gain while men lose," Bjørnskov et al. (2007: 2) found in their cross-national analysis of 66 nations that both women *and* men reported higher levels of life satisfaction in societies with less gender discrimination within the political realm.

The mechanism by which greater gender equality improves the well-being of a given society may be tied to the higher number of women in the parliaments of those nations. There is evidence suggesting that women parliamentarians tend to have greater concern with grassroots politics than their male counterparts (Norris, 1996; Devlin and Elgie, 2008) and thus may be more likely to legislate based on the well-being of the citizenry, rather than what will benefit industries or corporations. Corroborating this supposition, Wängnerud's (2009) review of the literature on women in the parliaments of established democracies reveals that women parliamentarians tend to lean more toward the left than men and they also tend to be more likely to support policies that are concerned with environmental protection, social policy, affirmative actions, and policies that could be characterized as representing "women's interests," such as family policy, care for the elderly, and health care. Similarly, Powley (2006) found that in Rwanda's parliament, women (who, between 2003 and 2008 occupied 48.75% of the seats in the lower half of parliament, and now occupy 64%) have intensely advocated for increased government spending on healthcare and education, particularly early childhood education.[2] Regarding environmental outcomes, carbon dioxide emissions per capita are lower in nations where there is a higher proportion of women in parliament (Ergas and York, 2012) and, likewise, nations with higher proportions of women parliamentarians are also more likely to ratify environmental treaties (Norgaard and York, 2005).

Due to the above noted effects of women's empowerment on conditions at the household, community, and national levels, it is reasonable to expect that women's status in a nation may be connected with the quality of life experienced by people in that nation. Here, we empirically assess whether the relationship between gender equality and quality of life suggested by the above discussion—one where higher status for women in the political sphere is associated with greater life satisfaction among the population—is an accurate characterization of the pattern across nations of the world. . . .

Discussion and Conclusion

The results of our analysis, taken as a whole, are clearly consistent with the relationships hypothesized by many feminists. As Waring (1999, 2009) and others have suggested, women's political status is associated with higher levels of life satisfaction. Additionally, public priorities, as indicated by government spending, also have important effects, as is indicated by our findings about the effects of military and healthcare spending. Military spending is associated with lower levels of subjective well-being, pointing to the costs associated with the war industry. In contrast, healthcare spending is positively associated with life satisfaction.

This finding is quite striking when taking into account that life expectancy is included in our models, where we found it to have a substantial positive effect. Thus, health care spending has an effect above and beyond whatever it contributes to lengthening people's lives. This is likely because many health problems that diminish people's quality of life do not necessarily shorten their lives. But, also, we suspect this association exists because healthcare spending is correlated with more general government efforts to address the well-being of the public, in particular through social assistance programs designed to protect a nation's people from economic and social ruin during times of crisis.

As striking as our findings regarding factors that do significantly affect life satisfaction are the factors which we found to not have significant effects on life satisfaction. It is noteworthy that our analysis did not establish a clear connection between life satisfaction and either GDP per capita or the ecological footprint per capita. These findings undermine the widely held assumption that economic growth and high levels of consumption are necessary to improve people's quality of life. This is, in fact, good news, in light of the environmental impacts of affluent lifestyles.

The fact that we did not find a connection between democracy and life satisfaction is noteworthy, and may be disheartening to those advocating transitions to democracy in non-democratic nations. This non-finding suggests that, perhaps, it is not so much the presence of democracy in and of itself that leads to life satisfaction, but rather it matters what actions governments take to improve the lives of their publics. Of course, democracy is a multifaceted concept, and perhaps different measures of democracy, as they become available, when analyzed may suggest that some aspects of democracy are important for life satisfaction while others are not.

Arguably, the most notable finding from our study, and the one that is our focus here, and therefore worth returning to for further discussion, is that women's representation in parliament has a significant effect on general life satisfaction within nations. Despite the scant attention gender representation in politics has received in past studies of life satisfaction at the cross-national level, this finding should actually not be surprising in light of the evidence of women parliamentarians' propensity toward supporting policies aimed at improving social welfare and environmental protection (Wängnerud, 2009; Norgaard and York, 2005; Ergas and York, 2012). In order to illustrate the substantive meaning of the statistical findings, below we offer vignettes on Norway and Greece to explore the connections between women's political representation and quality of life in specific contexts. We focus on these two nations for illustrative purposes because they have important similarities, while contrasting starkly on some key analytic factors. These are two nations with much in common on the surface—they are both classified as possessing a "very high human development" ranking by the United Nations Human Development Index, are considered to be "High-Income" members of the OECD by the World Bank, and both are in Western Europe. However, among the so-called "More Developed Countries" (MDCs) in our analysis, these two nations fell at opposite ends of the spectrum in terms of levels of life satisfaction and levels of women's participation in parliament.

Of the nations in our analysis, Norway has the second highest level of average life satisfaction (8.1 on a 10 point scale) and the second largest percentage of women in parliament (36.5%) for the time period we examined. Greece, on the other hand, had one of the lowest levels of life satisfaction (6.8) and one of the lowest percentages of women parliamentarians (8%) among the MDCs[3] in our analysis. As shown in Table 2, which provides data collected by the OECD Better Life Index, Norway and Greece are strikingly different on a number of measures related to education, employment, income, and environmental factors that influence well-being and life satisfaction. In Norway, 81% of 25–64 year olds have earned the equivalent of a high school degree, compared to only 65% of Greeks in the same age range. On average, Norwegians work 30% fewer hours per year than Greeks (1426 h of work per year in Norway compared to 2032 h of work per year in Greece).

TABLE 2. Norway and Greece compared on indicators of well-being, 2013

	Norway	Greece
High School Degree Equivalent Completion Rate among people ages 25–64	81%	65%
Employment Rate among people ages 25–64	Over 75%	56%
Average number of hours spent working per year	1426	2032
Average household net adjusted disposable income	31,459 USD	20,440 USD
Air pollution, measured by PM-10 (particulate matter)	15 micrograms per cubic meter	31 micrograms per cubic meter
Percent of people who state they are satisfied with their water quality	96%	69%
Percent of people stating they know someone they could rely on during a time of need	93%	81%

Source: OECD Better Life Index, 2013.

In addition, environmental quality is markedly better in Norway compared with Greece. Air pollution in Greece is more than twice as high as it is in Norway (31 micrograms of particulate matter per cubic meter in Greece, compared to 15 micrograms of particulate matter per cubic meter in Norway), and while 96% of Norwegians state that they are satisfied with their water quality, only 69% of Greeks make the same claim. Community life is also quite different in the two nations. In Norway, 93% of people state that they know someone they could rely on in a time of need, compared to only 81% of people in Greece. On the more widely-accepted measures of well-being—income and employment—the differences between the two nations are equally stark. While over 75% of individuals in Norway between the ages of 25 and 64 are employed, only 56% of people in the same age range are employed in Greece. Furthermore, the average household net adjusted disposable income in Norway is 31,459 USD, while it is just 20,440 USD in Greece.

Of course, the last two statistics—employment and income—are particularly low in Greece because of the recent economic crisis of 2009, which occurred after the time period examined in our analysis. In fact, Greece is currently enduring the most severe economic crisis it has seen since World War II (Petmesidou, 2013). However, it is important to note that in 2005, well before the financial crisis, Norway still had a much higher labor force participation rate, and significantly lower unemployment rate than Greece (4.4% unemployment in

Norway verses 9.8% unemployment rate in Greece in 2005) (United Nations, 2014).

Numerous scholars have shown that, counter to the popular narrative that the economic crisis in Greece was a result of its "excessive" social welfare programs, in actuality, Greece's social spending has fallen below the average of other nations in Western Europe (Matsaganis, 2012). In fact, some scholars argue that Greece actually *underspent* in social protection programs (Petmesidou, 2013, 2006), and this may be part of the story of why the economic crisis has had such a devastating impact on so many of Greece's citizens. For, as Mukherjee and Waring (2012) note, the nations with more extensive social assistance programs have been better able to cope with the financial crisis. Indeed, as Matsaganis (2012) and others have argued, "a recession, (even a 'Great' one) should not overly trouble a well-designed system of protection. Mitigating the social effects of economic crises is what . . . . modern welfare states were created for" (p. 413). It is important to underscore the fact that the impact of this crisis has been disproportionately felt among the more vulnerable people of Greece, indicating an ineffective, and unequal, welfare state. As Petmesidou (2013) argues, "Well before the onset of the crisis, there was extensive unmet need" that was the result of a social welfare program that

> sustained a divide between some fairly well protected social groups (enjoying access to the formal labor market and clientelistic networks), and a

number of deprived social groups (the precariously employed, particularly in the underground economy; old-age people with no rights to social insurance or with insufficient coverage; unqualified young persons; the long-term unemployed and others) (p. 602).

As Ferrera (1996, p. 21) has argued, the Southern European model of welfare (including Greece, Portugal, Spain, and Italy) has major holes in the social safety net for some segments of the population, while providing "unparalleled peaks of generosity" for certain protected and more powerful groups in society. This unequal coverage meant that when the economic crisis hit, its impact was "inversely related to political power," such that the least powerful groups suffered the greatest increases in poverty (Matsaganis, 2012, p. 412).

Norway's social programs, on the other hand, follow a different model (the Nordic Model) and are universal, meaning that they do not disproportionately benefit certain, more powerful segments of the population as they do in Greece. In fact, as Norgaard and York (2005) assert, "The achievement of equality between classes and sexes has been an expressed central aim of government policy [in Norway] since the 1940s" (p. 516). Studies on the effectiveness of the different European social welfare programs in reducing individual risks associated with poverty, illness, disability, unemployment, and old age indicate that the Nordic Model is significantly more successful at protecting the well-being of citizens than the brand of social welfare implemented in Mediterranean states, like Greece (Sapir, 2006; Põder and Kerem, 2011). Specifically, the Nordic Model has the highest level of wealth redistribution in its social welfare program. This model is aimed at reducing income inequality and poverty through redistributing wealth by implementing taxes and transfers. In addition, this model includes other protections, such as generous and extensive unemployment benefits, that the Mediterranean model does not offer (Sapir, 2006). Sapir's (2006) study found that countries in the European Union[4] following the Nordic Model live within a system that "delivers both efficiency and equity," while the Mediterranean model followed by Greece "delivers neither efficiency nor equity" (p. 380). Thus, Norwegians enjoy both high employment rates and low poverty rates, while Greeks experience low employment rates and high poverty rates, and as Sapir's (2006) work reveals, this pattern held even before the economic crisis hit.

Importantly, through our analysis we found that the nations following the Nordic Model of social welfare (Norway, Sweden, Denmark, and Finland) also had the highest percentage of women in parliament (ranging from 43% in Sweden to 36.2% in Finland), while Greece and Italy, which follow the Mediterranean Model, had some of the lowest percentages of women in parliament among the MDCs in our analysis (8% in Greece and 11.2% in Italy). Thus, this comparison provides further support for the notion that women parliamentarians tend to be more likely to support programs aimed at social welfare, which in turn help improve public well-being.

However, our findings suggest there is more to the story of the connection between women's political participation and life satisfaction than simply that women are more likely to support social welfare programs and environmental protection. Recall that we controlled for two of the hypothesized routes by which gender differences could matter. As noted previously, Waring (1999) suggests that women are less likely to support military spending and more likely to support health care, which is consistent with the respective negative and positive correlations between these two factors and women's political representation, as shown in the bivariate correlations . . . Thus, women's political power appears to matter for life satisfaction above and beyond gender differences in support for government spending priorities. While more research is needed to further unravel this association, it may be tied to the fact that nations with greater representation of women in positions of political power also tend to be more egalitarian. Political representation is not entirely independent of other forms of empowerment, and in fact is positively correlated with other indicators of women's status (see, for example, Nugent and Shandra, 2009).

Our analysis and discussion highlight the potential benefits to societies of increasing women's political status. One route to increasing women's participation in parliament is to institute quotas for women in parliament, much in the way that Rwanda and a number of other nations have done. After a genocide that wiped out more than half a million lives and orphaned hundreds of thousands of children, Rwanda had a non-functional economy and government. As Wilber (2011) argues, women were at the forefront of rebuilding the nation, forming the Forum of Rwandan Women Parliamentarians (FFRP) in 1996. The first organization "to cross party lines in a country sharply and dangerously split," the FFRP provided an opportunity "to amplify women's voices in a newly shared agenda" (Wilber, 2011). These strong female voices undoubtedly played a significant role in influencing the inclusion of a provision in Rwanda's new constitution, adopted in 2003, that reserves "thirty per cent of posts in decision making organs" for women (Republic of Rwanda, 2003, 2013, Article 9 [4]). In the ten years following the establishment of this quota, larger and larger numbers of women have been elected to parliament, far beyond the seats that are reserved for them. In 2008, 56% of the seats in the Chamber of Deputies went to women, making Rwanda the first country[5] to surpass 50% women in a lower house of parliament (Wilber, 2011). In the 2013 election, Rwanda beat its own record, and now women hold 64% of the seats in the Chamber of Deputies and 40% of the seats in the Senate (Republic of Rwanda, 2003, 2013). While, as noted above, there is likely a lag in the effects of women's participation in parliament on the well-being and life satisfaction of a nation's residents, recent research in the area of Rwandan politics suggests that the well-being of Rwandans, particularly women and children, may be on the rise. For instance, in 2006 the Rwandan parliament passed a gender-based violence bill that was introduced by the FFRP. By criminalizing wife-beating, this bill was ground-breaking legislation in a society where violence against women has been "commonplace and unnamed" (Wilber, 2011). In addition, women parliamentarians in Rwanda have been found to consult with their constituents on how best to allocate funding for projects in communities and to invite the participation of civil society in shaping policies (Wilber, 2011). A fruitful area for future research in this realm will be to follow the levels of life satisfaction in Rwanda, and other nations instituting gender quotas, over time.

There are clearly multiple factors that influence the average life satisfaction of people in nations, and no one factor alone is overwhelmingly determinative. However, of these factors, women's political representation seems to be important as are the public spending priorities of governments. Our results taken as a whole point to the heartening conclusion that the escalation of resource consumption and continuing economic growth may not be necessary to improve subjective well-being. Rather, improving gender equality, at least in the political sphere, and focusing spending priorities on increasing the level of people's health, instead of military development, may be a potential route toward bolstering the quality of life in a society.

Notes

1. The cited work is an edited volume, with chapters by various authors. Our reference is specifically to the general summary remarks made by the editors in the introduction based on their overall assessment of the various works in the volume, as well as the extensive literature on cross-national differences in well-being, but also more generally to the content of the volume, which has several chapters addressing various aspects of cross-national differences in subjective well-being.

2. However, due to the fact that women's representation in the Rwandan parliament is relatively recent, the policy outcomes have not always reflected these women parliamentarians' priorities.

3. While there were a number of LDCs that fell below Greece on both scales, we wanted to choose a comparator country that was as similar as possible to Norway so as to make it a fair comparison.

4. While Norway is not a member of the European Union, and so is not included in Sapir's analysis, its social welfare program follows the Nordic Model of the EU nations of Denmark, Sweden,

and Finland. Thus, by extension, Sapir's findings should be considered true for Norway as well.

5. Rwanda does not rank as the leading country in our analysis due to the fact that the data for our study is the average of the percent of women in parliaments between 1997 and 2005.

References

Allendorf, Keera, 2007. Do women's land rights promote empowerment and child health in Nepal? World Dev. 35 (11), 1975–1988.

Basu, Alaka M., 1992. Culture, The Status of Women and Demographic Behavior. Clarendon Press, Oxford.

Balk, Deborah, 1994. Individual and community aspects of women's status and fertility in rural Bangladesh. Popul. Stud. 48 (1), 21–45.

Bell, Shannon Elizabeth, 2013. Our Roots Run Deep as Ironweed: Appalachian Women and the Fight for Environmental Justice. University of Illinois Press, Chicago and Urbana.

Bell, Shannon Elizabeth, Braun, Yvonne A., 2010. Coal, identity, and the gendering of environmental justice activism in central Appalachia. Gend. Soc. 24(6), 794–813.

Bell, Shannon Elizabeth, York, Richard, 2010. Community economic identity: the coal industry and ideology construction in West Virginia. Rural Soc. 75 (1), 111–143.

Blanchflower, David G., Oswald, Andrew J., 2011. International happiness: a new view on the measure of performance. Acad. Manage. Perspect. 25 (1), 6–22.

Bjørnskov, Christian, Dreher, Axel, Fischer, Justina A.V., 2007. On Gender Inequality and Life Satisfaction: Does Discrimination Matter? SSE/EFI Working Paper Series in Economics and Finance, No. 657. <http://www.hdl.handle.net/10419/56302> (retrieved 23.03.14).

Brown, P., Ferguson, F.I.T., 1995. 'Making a big stink': women's work, women's relationships, and toxic waste activism. Gend. Soc. 9 (2), 145–172.

Cable, Sherry, 1992. Women's social movement involvement: the role of structural availability in recruitment and participation processes. Soc. Quart. 33 (1), 35–50.

Caldwell, John, 1986. Routes to low mortality in poor countries. Popul. Dev. Review 12 (2), 171–220.

Caldwell, John C., 1989. Mass Education as a Determinant of Mortality Decline. In: Caldwell, John C., Gigi Santow (Eds.), Selected Readings in Cultural, Social, and Behavioral Determinants of Health. Canberra: Australian National University Health Transition Centre, pp. 103–111.

Caldwell, John C., Caldwell, Pat, 1993. Women's position and child mortality and morbidity in less developed countries. In: Federici, Nora, Mason, Karen O., Sogner, Solvi (Eds.). Women's Position and Demographic Change. Clarendon Press, Oxford, pp. 122–139.

Coleman, Isobel, 2004. The payoff from women's rights. For. Affairs 83 (3), 80–95.

Collins, Patricia Hill, 1990. Black Feminist Thought: Knowledge, Consciousness, and the Politics of Empowerment. Routledge, New York.

Devlin, Claire, Elgie, Robert, 2008. The effect of women's representation in parliament: the case of Rwanda. Parliament. Affairs 61 (2), 237–254.

Diener, Ed, Helliwell, John F., Kahneman, Daniel (Eds.), 2010. International Differences in Well-being. Oxford University Press, Oxford, UK.

Diener, Ed, Lucas, Richard E., 2000. Explaining differences in societal levels of happiness: relative standards, need fulfillment, culture, and evaluation theory. J. Happiness Stud. 1, 41–78.

Dietz, Thomas, Rosa, Eugene A., York, Richard, 2012. Environmentally efficient well-being: is there a kuznets curve? Appl. Geogr. 32 (1). 21–28.

Dietz, Thomas, Rosa, Eugene A., York, Richard, 2009. Environmentally efficient well-being: rethinking sustainability as the relationship between human well-being and environmental impacts. Human Ecol. Rev. 16 (1), 114–123.

Di Tella, Rafael, MacCulloch, Robert J., 2008. Gross national happiness as an answer to the Easterlin paradox? J. Dev. Econ. 86, 22–42.

Dixon, William J., Moon, Bruce E., 1986. The military burden and basic human needs. J. Conflict Resolut. 30 (4), 660–684.

Duflo, Esther, 2003. Grandmothers and granddaughters: old age pension and intra-household allocation in South Africa. World Bank Econ. Rev. 17, 1–25.

Dyson, Tim, Moore, Mick, 1983. On kinship structure, female autonomy, and demographic behaviour in India. Popul. Dev. Rev. 9 (1), 35–60.

Ergas, Christina, York, Richard, 2012. Women's status and carbon dioxide emissions: a quantitative cross-national analysis. Soc. Sci. Res. 41 (4), 965–976.

Farmer, Paul, 1996. Women, poverty, and AIDS. In: Farmer, P., Connors, M., Simmons. J. (Eds.), Women, Poverty, and AIDS: Sex, Drugs, and Structural Violence. Common Courage Press, Monroe, ME, pp. 3–38.

Ferrera, M., 1996. The Southern Model of Welfare in Social Europe. J. Eur. Social Policy 6 (1). 17–37.

Food and Agriculture Organization of the United Nations, 2011. The State of Food and Agriculture: Women In Agriculture: Closing the Gender Gap for Development. Rome: FAO of the UN.

Francisco, Gigi, Antrobus, Peggy, 2009. Mainstreaming trade and millennium development goals? In: Salleh, A. (Ed.), Eco-sufficiency and Global Justice: Women Write Political Ecolog. Pluto Press, New York, pp. 157–164.

Frey, Bruno S., Stutzer, Alios, 2000. Happiness, economy, and institutions. Econ. J. 110, 918–938.

Giesen, Carol A.B., 1995. Coal Miners' Wives: Portraits of Endurance. The University Press of Kentucky, Lexington. KY.

Gwako, Edwins Laban Moogi, 1997. Conjugal power in rural Kenya families: its influence on women's decisions about family size and family planning practices. Sex Roles 36 (3–4), 127–147.

Hall, Jacquelyn Dowd, 1986. Disorderly women: gender and labor militancy in the Appalachian south. J. Am. History 73 (2), 354–382.

Hazarika, G., Guha-Khasnobis, B., 2008. Household access to microcredit and children's food security in rural Malawi: A gender perspective. IZA Discussion Paper No. 3793. Bonn, Germany: Institute for the Study of Labor.

Helliwell, John, Huang, Haifang, 2008. How's your government? International evidence linking good government and well-being. Br. J. Polit. Sci, 38. 595–619.

Hindin, Michelle J., 2000. Women's autonomy, women's status and fertility-related behavior in Zimbabwe. Popul. Res. Policy Rev. 19. 255–282.

Hobcraft, John, 2000. The consequences of female empowerment for child well-being: a review of concepts, issues and evidence in a post-Cairo context, In: Presser, Harriet B., Sen, Gita (Eds.), Women's Empowerment and Demographic Processes: Moving Beyond Cairo. International studies in demography, Oxford University Press, Oxford, pp. 159–185.

Jejeebhoy, Shireen J., 1995. Women's Education, Autonomy, and Reproductive Behaviour: Experience from Developing Countries. Clarendon Press, Oxford.

Jenkins, J. Craig, Scanlan, Stephen J., 2001. Food security in less developed countries, 1970 to 1990. Am. Sociol. Rev. 66 (5), 718–744.

Jorgenson, Andrew K., Clark, Brett, 2012. Are the economy and the environment decoupling? A comparative international study, 1960–2005. Am. J. Sociol. 118, 1–44.

Kaplan, Temma, 1997. Crazy for Democracy: Women in Grassroots Movements. Routledge, New York.

Kishor, Sunita, 2000. Empowerment of women in Egypt and links to the survival and health of their infants. In: Presser, Harriet B., Sen, Gita (Eds.). Women's Empowerment and Demographic Processes: Moving Beyond Cairo. Oxford University Press, New York.

Knight, Kyle, Rosa, Eugene A., 2011. The environmental efficiency of well-being: a cross-national analysis. Soc. Sci. Res. 40, 931–949.

Kotakorpi, Kaisa, Laamen, Jani-Petri, 2010. Welfare state and life satisfaction: evidence from public health care. Economica 77, 565–583.

Lee, Matthew R., 2000. Modernization, gender equality, and mortality rates in less developed countries. Sociol. Spectrum 20 (2), 195–220.

Leiserowitz, Anthony A., Kates, Robert W., Parris, Thomas M., 2005. Do global attitudes and behaviors support sustainable development? Environment 47 (9), 23–38.

Matsaganis, Manos, 2012. Social policy in hard times: the case of Greece. Crit. Soc. Policy 32 (3). 406–421.

Mazur, Allan, Rosa, Eugene A., 1974. Energy and life-style. Science 186. 607–610.

Mazurana, Dyan, McKay, Susan, 2001. Women, girls, and structural violence: a global analysis. Ch. 1. In: Christie, D.J., Wagner, R.V., Winter, D.A. (Eds.), Peace, Conflict, and Violence: Peace Psychology for the 21st Century. Prentice-Hall, Englewood Cliffs. NJ.

Maggard, Sally Ward, 1987. Women's participation in the brookside coal strike: militance, class, and gender in Appalachia. Frontiers 9 (3), 16–21.

Maggard, Sally Ward, 1999. Gender contested: women's participation in the brookside coal strike.

In: West, Guida, Blumberg, Rhoda Lois (Eds.), Women and Social Protest. Oxford University Press, New York, pp. 75–98.

Maggard, Sally Ward, 1999. Coalfield women making history. In: Billings, Dwight B., Norman, Gurney, Ledford. Katherine (Eds.). Back Talk From Appalachia: Confronting Stereotypes. The University Press of Kentucky, Lexington.

Moon, Bruce E., Dixon, William J., 1985. Politics, the state, and basic human needs: a cross-national study. Am. J. Polit. Sci. 29 (4), 661–694.

Morgan, S. Philip, Niraula, Bhanu B., 1995, Gender inequality and fertility in two Nepali villages, Popul. Dev. Rev. 21 (3), 541–561.

Mukherjee, Anit, Waring, Marilyn, 2012. Social Protection: A Question of Delivering on Rights and Services. Discussion Paper 13. London: Commonwealth Secretariat. <http://marilynwaring .com/DP_13_social_protection.pdf> (retrieved 28.03.14).

Naples, Nancy A., 1992. Activist mothering: cross-generational continuity in the community work of women from low-income urban neighborhoods. Gend. Soc. 6, 441–463.

Naples, Nancy A., 1998. Grassroots Warriors: Activist Mothering. Community Work, and The War on Poverty. Routledge, New York.

Nash, Terre, 1995. Who's Counting? Marilyn Waring on Sex, Lies and Global Economics. National Film Board of Canada. <http://www.nfb.ca/film/ whos_counting>.

New Economics Foundation, 2009. The Happy Planet Index 2.0. London: NEF.

Norgaard, Kari, York, Richard, 2005. Gender equality and state environmentalism. Gend. Soc. 19 (4), 506–522.

Norris, Pippa, 1996. Women politicians: transforming Westminster? Parliament. Affairs 49 (1), 89–102.

Norris, Randall, Cyprès, Jean-Philippe, 1996. Women of Coal. University Press of Kentucky, Lexington, KY.

Nugent, Colleen, Shandra, John M., 2009. State environmental protection efforts, women's status, and world polity. Org. Environ. 22 (2), 208–229.

OECD Better Life Index, 2013. <http://www .oecdbetterlifeindex.org/> (accessed 31.03.14).

Pacek, Alexander C., Radcliff, Benjamin, 2008. Welfare policy and subjective well-being across nations: an individual-level assessment. Soc. Indic. Res. 89. 179–191.

Petmesidou, Maria, 2006. Social care services: 'Catching up' amidst high fragmentation and poor initiatives for change. In: Petmesidou, M., Mossialos, E. (Eds.), Social Policy Developments in Greece. Ashgate, Aldershot, pp. 318–357.

Petmesidou, Maria, 2013. Is social protection in Greece at a crossroads? Eur. Soc. 15 (4), 597–616.

Pitt, Mark M., Khandker., Shahidur R., 1998. The impact of group-based credit programs on poor households in Bangladesh: does the gender of participants matter? J. Polit. Econ. 106 (5), 958–996.

Põder, Kaire, Kerem, Kaie, 2011. Social models in a European comparison: convergence or divergence? East. Eur. Econ. 49 (5), 55–74.

Powley, Elizabeth, 2006. Rwanda: The Impact of Women Legislators on Policy Outcomes Affecting Children and Families. Working Paper. UNICEF, Division of Policy and Planning. Retrieved April 4, 2014 from http://www.unicef .org/policyanalysis/files/Rwanda_the_impact_ of_women_legislators.pdf.

Quisumbing, Agnes R., Maluccio, John A., 1999. Intrahousehold allocation and gender relations: New empirical evidence. Policy Research Report on Gender and Development. Working Paper Series, No. 2. The World Bank Development Research Group/Poverty Reduction and Economic Management Network. <http://www.worldbank .org/gender/prr> (retrieved 19.05.12).

Republic of Rwanda, 2003. The constitution of the Republic of Rwanda. <http://www.rwandahope .com/constitution.pdf> (accessed 02.04.14).

Republic of Rwanda, 2013. Women win 64% of seats in parliamentary elections, maintaining number one spot worldwide. Government of the Republic of Rwanda Website. <http://www.gov.rw/Women-win-64-of-seats-in-parliamentary-elections-maintaining-number-one-spot-worldwide> (accessed 02.04.14).

Rosa, Eugene A., 1997. Cross national trends in fossil fuel consumption, societal well-being and carbon releases. In: Stern. P.C., Dietz. T., Ruttan. V.W., Socolow, R.H., Sweeney, J.L. (Eds.), Environmentally Significant Consumption: Research directions. National Academy Press, Washington, DC, pp. 100–109.

Rosa, Eugene A., York, Richard, Dietz, Thomas, 2004. Tracking the anthropogenic drivers of ecological impacts. Ambio 33 (8), 509–512.

Sapir, André, 2006. Globalization and the reform of European social models. J. Common Market Stud. 44 (2), 369–390.

Scanlan, Stephen J., Jenkins, J. Craig, 2001. Military power and food security: a cross-national analysis of less-developed countries. 1970–1990. Int. Stud. Quart. 45 (1), 159–187.

Schuler, Sidney Ruth, Hashemi, Syed Mesbahuddin, Riley, Ann P., 1997. The influence of changing roles and status in Bangladesh's fertility transition: evidence from a study of credit programs and contraceptive use. World Dev. 25 (4), 563–575.

Scott, Shaunna L., 1995. Two Sides to Everything: The Cultural Construction of Class Consciousness in Harlan County, Kentucky. State University of New York Press, Albany, NY.

Seaford, Charles, 2011. Time to legislate for the good life. Nature 477, 532–533.

Seitz, Virginia Rinaldo, 1995. Women, Development, and Communities for Empowerment in Appalachia. State University of New York. Albany, NY.

Seitz, Virginia Rinaldo, 1998. Class, gender, and resistance in the Appalachian coalfields. In: Naples, Nancy A. (Ed.). Community Activism and Feminist Politics: Organizing Across Race, Class, and Gender. Routledge, New York.

Sivard, Ruth Leger, 1996. World Military and Social Expenditures, 1996, 16th ed. World Priorities Inc., Washington, DC.

Smith, Lisa C., Ramakrishnan, Usha, Ndiaye, Aida, Haddad, Lawrence J., Martorell, Reynaldo, 2003. The importance of women's status for child nutrition in developing countries (Research Report No. 131). Washington, DC: International Food Policy Research Institute.

Taylor, Daniel C., Taylor, Carl E., Taylor, Jesse O., 2012. Empowerment on an Unstable Planet. Oxford University Press, Oxford.

Taylor-Ide, Daniel, Taylor, Carl E., 2002. Just and Lasting Change: When Communities Own their Futures. Johns Hopkins University Press, Baltimore, MD.

United Nations, 1994. "The Health Rationale for Family Planning: Timing of Births and Survival." ST/ESA/SER.A/141. New York: United Nations Department for Economic and Social Information Analysis, Population Division.

United Nations, 2014. World Statistics Pocketbook, United Nations Statistics Center. Country Level Data: Norway and Greece. <http://data.un.org/CountryProfile.aspx> (accessed 01.04.14).

Veenhoven, Ruut, 1999. Quality of life in individualistic society: a comparison of 45 nations in the early 1990s. Soc. Indic. Res. 48, 157–186.

Veenhoven, Ruut, 2005. Inequality of happiness in nations, J. Happiness Stud. 6, 351–355.

Wängnerud, Lena, 2009. Women in parliaments: descriptive and substantive representation. Annu. Rev. Pol. Sci. 12, 51–69.

Waring, Marilyn, 1999. Counting for Nothing: What Men Value and What Women are Worth, second ed. University of Toronto Press, Toronto.

Waring, Marilyn, 2009. Policy and the measure of woman. In: Salleh. A. (Ed.), Eco-sufficiency and Global Justice: Women Write Political Ecology. Pluto Press, Berlin, pp. 165–179.

Weiss, Chris, 1993. Appalachian women fight back: organizational approaches to nontraditional job advocacy. In: Fisher, Stephen L. (Ed.), Fighting Back in Appalachia: Traditions of Resistance and Change. Temple University Press, Philadelphia, PA, pp. 151–164.

Welsch, Heinz, 2003. Freedom and rationality as predictors of cross-national happiness patterns: the role of income as a mediating variable. J. Happiness Stud. 4, 295–321.

Wilber, Roxanne, 2011. Lessons from Rwanda: How women transform governance. Solutions. 2(2). <http://www.thesolutionsjournal.com/node/887> (accessed 02.04.14).

Winkelmann, Liliana, Winkelmann, Rainer, 2010. Does inequality harm the middle class? Kyklos 63, 301–316.

Winter, Deborah Du Nan, Philisuk, Marc, Houck, Sara, Lee, Matthew, 2001. Understanding militarism: money, masculinity, and the search for the mystical. Ch. 12. In: Christie. D.J., Wagner, R.V., Winter, D.A. (Eds.), Peace, Conflict, and Violence: Peace Psychology for the 21st Century. Prentice-Hall, Englewood Cliffs, NJ.

York, Richard, Rosa, Eugene A., Dietz, Thomas, 2003. Footprints on the earth: the environmental consequences of modernity. Am. Sociol. Rev. 68 (2), 279–300.

Who Takes the Floor and Why: Gender, Power, and Volubility in Organizations

VICTORIA L. BRESCOLL

Given its centrality to psychology, impression formation, and interpersonal interactions, the study of volubility—the total amount of time spent talking in group contexts—has generated a considerable amount of research over the last fifty years. Individuals mostly base their judgments of others' traits (e.g., how dominant they are) or states (e.g., whether they are a manager or a subordinate) on others' verbal and nonverbal behaviors. Thus how much an individual talks in interpersonal interactions is a key way in which we not only draw inferences about that person but also in how we interact with him or her.

Moreover, interpersonal communication—whether verbal or nonverbal—has a direct impact on the way that status and power hierarchies are built, maintained, and changed. For example, research by Bales and his colleagues showed that power hierarchies are formed largely based on how much members participate in the group (Bales, 1950; Bales et al., 1951); the more an individual verbally participates, the more likely that individual will be seen as having power. Therefore, volubility not only plays an important role in establishing power hierarchies but also in communicating one's power to others (Mast, 2002).

Overall, two main factors have emerged as central to understanding volubility in organizations: power and gender (Coates, 1986; James and Drakich, 1993; Tannen, 1993; Locke and Hauser, 1999).

Identifying the unique contributions of each of these factors, however, has been somewhat elusive. Past research has typically examined the emergent relationships between power and volubility (e.g., the correlation between talking time and reported measures of dominance) but has not manipulated power independent of gender (see James and Drakich, 1993, for a review). In most social contexts, women have less power than men, and as a result, power and gender are naturally confounded (Dovidio et al., 1988; Sidanius and Pratto, 1999). Therefore, on the basis of previous research it is difficult to identify the unique effects of power on volubility independent of preexisting trait variables, such as gender, and the extent to which power has equivalent effects on men and women's volubility in organizations.

The present studies attempt to address these issues by examining the independent effects of power and gender on volubility, as well the potential interaction. Study 1 examined the relationship between volubility, power, and gender using archival data from the U.S. Senate, a real-world organization in which power varied independently of gender. Study 2 was a laboratory experiment that independently manipulated power for both men and women and examined the resulting effects on volubility. Study 3 then examined whether powerful women are correct in assuming that they will incur backlash as a result of talking more than others.

Victoria L. Brescoll, "Who Takes the Floor and Why: Gender, Power, and Volubility in Organizations," *Administrative Science Quarterly*, Vol. 56, No. 4 (2012), pp. 622–641. Copyright © 2012 by Victoria L. Brescoll. Reprinted by permission of SAGE Publications.

The Effects of Power and Gender on Volubility

The Effects of Power on Volubility

Here, power is defined in terms of control over resources (e.g., Keltner, Gruenfeld, and Anderson, 2003; Thibaut and Kelley, 1959) and what is frequently referred to as "social power," which highlights an individual's capacity to influence and control the behavior of others (e.g., Overbeck and Park, 2001; Galinsky, Gruenfeld, and Magee, 2003). A large literature has established that experimental manipulations of power have a number of important psychological consequences. For example, power increases a person's likelihood of engaging in approach-type behaviors (Keltner, Gruenfeld, and Anderson, 2003), such as expressing more confidence in their own ideas (Galinsky et al., 2008), taking risks (Anderson and Galinsky, 2006), and taking action to accomplish their goals (Galinsky, Gruenfeld, and Magee, 2003). Such increases in agency have been linked to more general increases in perceptions of control (Fast et al., 2009). Past research has found that experimental manipulations of power have a similar effect on both men and women. Furthermore, previous research on volubility has generally assumed that power should increase volubility, regardless of gender (see Mast, 2002, for a review). This relationship between volubility and power may exist because the amount of attention that is paid to an individual in social groups is directly related to that individual's ability to control the behavior or opinions of others (Fiske, 2010). When an individual is higher in power than the other members of the group, he or she may feel licensed to demand the attention of others (Locke, 1998; Mast, 2002). In turn, others may allow that individual to talk for a disproportionately longer amount of time, perhaps to signal deference or to avoid negative consequences that may result from failing to do so (Fiske, 2010).

Several studies in the communications literature have found that volubility is positively related to leadership and dominance in new groups (for meta-analyses, see Stein and Heller, 1979; Mullen, Salas, and Driskell, 1989; Mast, 2002). For example, Schmid Mast (2001) examined all-male and all-female small-group discussions and found a relationship between talking time and ratings of dominance reported by other group members. As discussed above, however, a limitation of past research in this area is that these studies have not independently manipulated power, instead observing the emergent relationships between power and volubility in a group context (e.g., Kimble and Musgrove, 1988; Palmer, 1989; Linkey and Firestone, 1990; Ng, Brooke, and Dunne, 1995). This point is critical because, as noted by several researchers, men disproportionately occupy positions of social, political, and economic power relative to women (e.g., Basow, 1986). Moreover, these power differences may often be reflected in patterns of communication, as strong parallels have been observed between interactions among individuals with high and low power and interactions among men and women (Henley, 1977). Therefore, to assess the extent to which power and gender may independently contribute to volubility (or potentially interact), it is necessary to manipulate power for both men and women directly or examine contexts in which power varies independently of gender.

Nevertheless, one relatively straightforward prediction from these literatures is that power should have a main effect on both men and women's talking time in organizations: in general, high-power individuals should talk more than low-power individuals, regardless of gender, because power licenses those individuals to talk for a greater amount of time relative to other individuals in the group:

> **Hypothesis 1:** There will be a main effect of power on volubility such that individuals who are higher on objective measures of power will speak for a longer time than individuals who are lower on objective measures of power.

The Effects of Gender on Volubility

At the same time, a great deal of research has established that women are less likely than men to engage in aggressive or dominant behaviors (Eagly and Steffen, 1986; Archer, 2009). For example, in small group contexts, women are less likely to engage in nonverbal displays such as chin thrusts as well as verbal displays, such as initiating speech (Dovidio et al., 1988). Similarly, women are less likely than men to emerge as a leader (Eagly and Karau, 1991), initiate negotiations (Bowles, Babcock, and Lai, 2007), and behave aggressively (Eagly and Steffen, 1986; Archer, 2009). Conversely, women are more likely than men to engage in low-power displays, such as smiling (LaFrance, Hecht, and Paluck, 2003) and maintaining eye contact when an interaction partner is speaking (Swim, 1994).

These basic gender differences, many of which have been confirmed via meta-analyses, can be explained in terms of social role theory (Eagly and Steffen, 1984, 2000). Social role theory states that because men and women occupy different social roles, they behave in predictably different ways in line with these roles. Specifically, because women are more likely than men to be in nurturing roles (e.g., mother, caretaker), they may behave in ways that are more communal and less aggressive. Another explanation for such gender differences focuses on men's greater levels of testosterone relative to women, which is associated with greater aggression and dominance (Dabbs and Dabbs, 2000).

Therefore, it may be that, overall, women are less voluble than men in organizations simply because they are less likely to engage in behaviors that are dominant or aggressive, which may include talking more than others in a group setting. In other words, research on gender differences makes a distinct prediction from the power literature in suggesting a main effect of gender on volubility: in general, men will talk more than women, regardless of individual differences in power:

> **Hypothesis 2:** There will be a main effect of gender on volubility such that men will speak for a longer time than women.

The Interaction Between Gender and Power on Volubility

A third possibility is that power has a different effect on men and women's volubility. It may be that while men show a strong positive relationship between talking time and power, women show no such effect (or a much weaker one) for at least two reasons. The first stems from the different ways men and women approach leadership and power

(Yoder and Kahn, 1992; Eagly and Carli, 2007). Some research has found that women lead (i.e., enact their power) in a more democratic, non-hierarchical fashion than men (Helgelsen, 1995), while men are more sensitive to and more comfortable with hierarchy (Pratto et al., 1997) and may behave in ways that reinforce their position in the hierarchy (e.g., talking more when they have power). In contrast, women may talk to establish and maintain relationships with others (Maltz and Borker, 1982; Coates, 1986; Edelsky, 1993; Gayle, Preiss, and Allen, 1994; Mast, 2002) and therefore would be likely to speak for the same amount of time as their counterparts, regardless of their power.

An alternative explanation, which predicts the same interaction pattern, has to do with women's potential fear of backlash (i.e., social and economic penalties). The status incongruity hypothesis proposes that women, by dint of their mere categorization as women, are assumed to be low in power (Rudman et al., 2012). Therefore when women engage in power-seeking behavior (i.e., power displays), their behavior is judged to be incongruent with their gender, and as a result, women may incur backlash from both male and female perceivers (Rudman, 1998; Heilman and Okimoto, 2007; Brescoll and Uhlmann, 2008). In turn, women's fear of encountering backlash may deter them from engaging in power displays (Rudman et al., 2012). For example, fear of backlash has been shown to explain women's failure to self-promote (Moss-Racusin and Rudman, 2010) and engage in aggressive negotiations (Amanatullah and Morris, 2010). With respect to volubility, though men may be quite sensitive to power hierarchies and associated displays of power, such as talking more than others, even high-power women may avoid dominating a conversation, group meeting or other public setting for fear of experiencing negative consequences (Tannen, 1993).

> **Hypothesis 3:** There will be an interactive effect between gender and power on volubility such that men will show a strong positive relationship between power and volubility, while women will show no such effect (or a much weaker one).

Thus past research makes a number of predictions regarding the effects of power on volubility for men and women, with one literature predicting a main effect of power, another predicting a main effect of gender, and a third predicting an interaction effect. As noted above, this issue is further complicated by the fact that in most social contexts, power and gender are confounded (Dovidio et al., 1988; Sidanius and Pratto, 1999) and in previous research on volubility, power and gender have not been manipulated independently. Therefore the present studies sought to test the predictions outlined above in contexts in which both men and women's power independently varied along quantifiable dimensions. Study 1 tested these hypotheses using field data from U.S. senators. Additionally, two laboratory experiments (Studies 2 and 3) were conducted to establish the causal direction of the effects of power on volubility, as well as the underlying mechanisms.

Study 1: Gender and Volubility in the United States Senate

Study 1 examined the relationship between volubility and gender and power using archival data from the United States Senate. Specifically, I measured the total amount of time that each senator spent speaking on the Senate floor for the entirety of two different congressional sessions (2005 and 2007) with two different political parties in control (the Republican party in 2005 and the Democratic party in 2007).

This data set was selected for a number reasons. First, although almost all organizations have a formal or informal power hierarchy of some kind, it can be extremely difficult, if not impossible, to quantify that hierarchy. Unlike Congress, most organizations do not have publicly available data that would allow such a detailed quantification. Because the Senate is a public organization whose activity is officially documented by law (via C-SPAN, the *Congressional Record,* etc.), however, most senatorial behavior is observable and therefore subject to study. Second, unlike almost any other organization, the U.S. Senate (via the *Congressional Record* and C-SPAN) keeps records not just of every word that is uttered in the Senate but

also of other nonverbal (e.g., smiling, gesturing) and verbal behaviors (e.g., the topics that senators are talking about, whether they use visual aids in their presentation). Finally, this data source is high in ecological validity in that the senators were unaware that anyone was conducting a study on their speaking behavior.

This field study provides the first examination of the relationship between volubility and gender and power in a real-world organization. For example, perhaps among individuals who are generally low in power in society overall (e.g., college undergraduates), the effects of power on volubility are quite different from real-world contexts in which there is considerable variability in the amount of power that individuals hold in their organization. Moreover, these data provided an important opportunity to examine the unique effects of power and gender on volubility, as power could be measured independently from gender in this context. . . .

Discussion

With respect to the hypotheses, the results from Study 1 showed a main effect of power on volubility. This result seems to favor hypothesis 1, that power licenses individuals to speak for disproportionately longer amounts of time in organizations. But the results also indicated an interaction between power and gender on volubility. Although this interaction effect was marginally significant, it is important to note that the number of female senators (N = 14) was small, which affected the statistical power of the study. Furthermore, the correlations between power and gender lend support to this interaction in that, for male senators, the correlation between power and gender was highly significant for both years, whereas for female senators, the correlation was not significant in either year.

This interaction result supports hypothesis 3, that power differentially affects speaking time for men and women, which may occur either because men and women have different motives for speaking within an organization, reflecting hierarchical relationships versus establishing rapport with others, or because women are concerned about the potential backlash stemming from appearing to talk too much. In contrast, there was no main effect of gender on volubility, and therefore hypothesis 2 was not supported by this study. Additionally, it is important to note that in this sample, men and women did not differ in their overall level of power, which is consistent with the notion that this particular data set was unique in its ability to disentangle the effects of power and gender.

Although the results are thought-provoking, this study was correlational and therefore could not address questions about the direction of the effect, such as whether power causes men to talk more or whether talking disproportionately more than others leads men to gain power. In the case of the Senate, it seems likely that power increases volubility, rather than the other way around. An individual senator can obtain power in many ways, including fundraising, making behind-the-scenes deals with other members of Congress, etc. Therefore, given the multiple routes to obtaining power in the Senate, it seems unlikely that merely talking more on the Senate floor would cause an individual senator to gain power in any significant way. Nevertheless, Study 2, a controlled experiment, was conducted to test the causal relationship between power and volubility and further explore the interaction between gender and power on volubility as well as the underlying reasons for it.

Study 2: Experimental Manipulation of Power

Results from the U.S. Senate data indicated an interaction between power and gender on volubility. Specifically, male senators showed a strong positive relationship between power and speaking time, while female senators did not. One question surrounds the causal direction of this effect: does power in fact cause men to increase their volubility? To examine this, Study 2 experimentally manipulated power for male and female participants and measured the resulting effects on volubility.

A second question concerns the underlying reasons why power may have different effects for men than for women. As outlined in the introduction, one explanation of this interaction is that while men are more comfortable with hierarchy (Offerman and Schrier, 1985) and will actively engage in behaviors that communicate their power to others, women are likely to enact their power in a more democratic, non-hierarchical fashion (Helgelsen, 1995). Thus men may behave in ways that reinforce their position in the hierarchy, whereas women may talk to establish rapport with others and therefore would be likely to talk for the same amount of time as their female counterparts, regardless of their power (Maltz and Borker, 1982; Coates, 1986; Edelsky, 1993; Gayle, Preiss, and Allen, 1994; Mast, 2002).

An alternative explanation, however, is that high-power women are not as voluble as their male counterparts because they are concerned about the potential backlash that may result from talking too much. Rudman and colleagues' (2012) status incongruity hypothesis proposes that women are assumed to be low in power, and therefore women may incur "backlash" when they engage in power-seeking behavior (Okimoto and Brescoll, 2010). In turn, fear of backlash may lead high-power women to avoid talking disproportionately longer than others for fear of experiencing negative consequences.

These competing hypotheses can be distinguished in two ways. The first method is via different predictions about the overall level of talking time as a function of gender and high versus low power. Specifically, an explanation based on women's desire to establish rapport with others predicts that, relative to men, high-power women should reduce their talking time while low-power women should increase their talking time. Therefore, women, regardless of power, will talk for the same amount of time, which should be less than high-power men and more than low-power men. In contrast, an explanation based on fear of backlash predicts that only high-power women will regulate their volubility, such that their talking time should be equivalent to low-power women as well as low-power men (which should all be less than high-power men). In short, a rapport explanation predicts that both low- and high-power women will adjust their talking time, relative to men, whereas a fear of backlash explanation predicts that only high-power women will adjust their talking time, relative to men.

A second means of testing these competing hypotheses is to explicitly measure the desire to establish rapport and fear of backlash and conduct mediation analyses to determine which underlying construct explains the differential effects of power on volubility for high-power men versus high-power women. Moss-Racusin and Rudman (2010) recently developed a fear of backlash scale, which has been shown to explain women's failure to self-promote. Thus, in Study 2, participants completed Moss-Racusin and Rudman's (2010) scale to assess fear of backlash as well as additional items specific to talking time. A second scale was also developed to measure the extent to which talking time was explained by a desire to establish rapport with others. . . .

Discussion

Results from Study 2 demonstrated that independently manipulating power has different effects on men's and women's reported volubility. As observed in the Senate data from Study 1, male participants in Study 2 showed a significant positive effect of power on volubility, whereas female participants did not. This result is important because it replicates the interaction effect in a different population and organizational context and also establishes a causal link between increases in power and subsequent effects on volubility (for men).

Moreover, the particular pattern of results in Study 2 sheds light on the underlying reasons for this interaction effect. Only high-power women appeared to adjust their volubility such that their reported talking time was equivalent to low-power women as well as low-power men. This pattern is consistent with predictions stemming from a fear-of-backlash explanation and is distinct from the predictions based on differences in wanting to establish rapport. The fear-of-backlash explanation was further supported in mediation analyses. In short, though women did express a greater desire than men to establish rapport, only fear of backlash mediated the differential effects of power on volubility for high-power men versus high-power women.

A remaining question from this study concerns the extent to which self-reported measures of

volubility map onto actual behavior. Given that the results of Study 2 were consistent with the actual behaviors exhibited by senators in Study 1, there is good reason to believe that the same interaction pattern should be replicated in an experimental context measuring actual talking behavior, though future research should examine this issue directly.

Study 3: Is Fear of Backlash Justified?

Studies 1 and 2 found an interaction between gender and power on volubility such that men show a strong positive relationship between power and volubility, while women show no such effect. The results of Study 2 demonstrated that this difference is explained by women's concern about incurring backlash from appearing to talk too much. The goal of Study 3 was to examine whether this fear of backlash is in fact justified: Are high-power women evaluated negatively when they talk disproportionately more than others?

A second question concerns the source of potential backlash. This is a nuanced point about the nature of backlash effects. One interpretation is that men judge highly voluble women negatively because (in general) men are higher in power and therefore perceive women's power displays as a threat to their own power. In other words, it may be that women talk less solely because they are concerned about negative evaluations from male perceivers. A tenet of the status incongruity hypothesis, however, is that backlash stems from the more general incongruity between existing gender hierarchies and behaviors that display power. This theory predicts that both male and female perceivers should be equally likely to show backlash effects (Rudman et al., 2012) and thus should have equivalent negative evaluations of increased volubility in high-power women. . . .

Discussion

Results from this study are informative for multiple reasons. First, these results suggest that high-power women are in fact justified in their concern that they will experience backlash from being highly voluble: a female CEO who talked disproportionately longer than others was rated as significantly less competent and less suitable for leadership than a male CEO who was reported as speaking for the same amount. Second, this effect did not interact in any way with participant gender in that both male and female participants were equally likely to exhibit backlash effects. This result lends further support to the status incongruity hypothesis and the notion that backlash effects result in beliefs about existing gender hierarchies that are shared among both male and female perceivers (Rudman et al., 2012).

Two additional findings emerged from these data. Specifically, a high-power woman who talked much less than others was judged as equally competent/deserving of leadership as a high-power man who talked much more than others. Similarly, a high-power male who talked much less than others was judged to be equally incompetent/undeserving of leadership as the high-power female who talked much more. Though speculative, this result suggests that the prescriptions for powerful men's and women's talking behavior may be much more comprehensive than originally hypothesized (i.e., powerful men *should* display their power, while powerful women *should not*).

General Discussion

The results of three studies revealed a number of novel findings about the nature of power, gender, and volubility in organizations. Study 1 utilized data from the U.S. Senate, a real-world organization, and found a significant relationship between power and volubility on the Senate floor. This effect, however, was qualified by a marginal interaction between power and gender, such that male senators showed a significant relationship between power and volubility, while female senators did not.

Study 2 built on these findings using an experimental design in which power was directly manipulated. Consistent with the Senate data, there was a significant positive effect of power on volubility for male participants but not for female participants. Thus this experiment replicated the interaction effect found in Study 1 while also demonstrating a causal link between power and subsequent increases in volubility for men.

Furthermore, Study 2 helped to identify the underlying reasons for this difference between men and women. The results suggested that women do not show an effect of power on volubility because they are concerned about the potential backlash that may result from appearing to talk too much. Examination of the specific pattern of data revealed that only high-power women adjusted their volubility such that their reported talking time was virtually identical to low-power women and low-power men, a pattern that is consistent with a fear-of-backlash explanation, rather than an explanation based on differences in men and women's desire to establish rapport. Additionally, subsequent measures indicated that while women did express a greater desire to establish rapport than men, only fear of backlash mediated the differential effects of power on volubility for high-power men versus high-power women.

Study 3 then examined whether powerful women are justified in their fear of experiencing backlash. Results showed that a female CEO who talked disproportionately longer than others in an organizational setting was rated as significantly less competent and less suitable for leadership than a male CEO who talked for an equivalent amount of time. Importantly, this effect was found among both male and female perceivers, which lends further support to the status incongruity hypothesis and the idea that backlash effects result from beliefs about existing gender hierarchies that are shared among both men and women (Rudman et al., 2012). Study 3 also revealed that a male CEO who was low in volubility was seen as less competent and suitable for leadership than his highly voluble male counterpart, while a female CEO who was low in volubility was equally competent and deserving of leadership as a highly voluble male CEO. Though future research is necessary to explore this issue further, such a finding raises the interesting possibility that the expectations that individuals should behave in ways that conform to existing gender hierarchies may apply equally to women and men—a hypothesis that naturally follows from the status incongruity hypothesis but one that has received little attention in the backlash literature. . . .

Conclusion

When Hillary Rodham Clinton began her campaign for the Senate in New York State in 1999, one of the first things she did was to embark on a very well-publicized "listening tour." She spent valuable political months visiting nearly every county in New York State. Obviously, she needed to win over voters in a state in which she had only resided for a matter of months. But more than that, the listening tour clearly signaled that she was going to listen and *not* talk at the voters—i.e., stay relatively silent while they told her what they needed from a senator. And, ironically, when Clinton engaged in a low-power behavior (i.e., listening rather than talking), she was given a great deal of power by virtue of being elected to office.

The present studies shed some light on why Clinton's strategy was successful and perhaps why a male politician might not engage in a similar "listening tour," but beyond this particular example, these data suggest that even "regular" women without political experience are acutely aware of the fact that talking more than others at work may not be a successful way to communicate their power to others. From the vantage of psychological processes, this result highlights an instance in which power does not appear to have an equivalent effect on men and women's behavior, and from the vantage of women's ability to achieve success within an organization, it suggests that existing power hierarchies may be quite difficult for women to navigate and may require some creative strategies that may work better for them than for men.

References

Amanatullah, E. T., and M. W. Morris 2010 "Negotiating gender roles: Gender differences in assertive negotiating are mediated by women's fear of backlash and attenuated when negotiating on behalf of others." Journal of Personality and Social Psychology, 98: 256–267.

Anderson, C., and A. D. Galinsky 2006 "Power, optimism, and risk-taking." European Journal of Social Psychology, 36: 511–536.

Archer, J. 2009 "Does sexual selection explain human sex differences in aggression?" Behavioral and Brain Sciences, 32: 249–311.

Bales, R. F. 1950 Interaction Process Analysis: A Method for the Study of Small Groups. Cambridge, MA: Addison-Wesley.

Bales, R. F., F. L. Strodtbeck, T. M. Mills, and M. E. Roseborough 1951 "Channels of communication in small groups." American Sociological Review, 16: 461–468.

Basow, S. A. 1986 Gender Stereotypes: Traditions and Alternatives, 2d ed. Monterey, CA: Brooks/Cole.

Bowles, H. R., L. Babcock, and L. Lai 2007 "Social incentives for gender differences in the propensity to initiate negotiation: Sometimes it does hurt to ask." Organizational Behavior and Human Decision Processes, 103: 84–103.

Brescoll, V., and E. L. Uhlmann 2008 "Can angry women get ahead? Status conferral, gender, and workplace emotion expression." Psychological Science, 19: 268–275.

Coates, J. 1986 Women, Men and Language. London and New York: Longman.

Dabbs, J. M., Jr., and M. G. Dabbs 2000 Heroes, Rogues, and Lovers: Testosterone and Behavior. New York: McGraw-Hill.

Dovidio, J. F., C. E. Brown, K. Heltman, S. L. Ellyson, and C. F. Keating 1988 "Power displays between women and men in discussions of gender-linked topics: A multichannel study." Journal of Personality and Social Psychology, 55: 580–587.

Eagly, A. H., and L. Carli 2007 Through the Labyrinth: The Truth About How Women Become Leaders. Cambridge, MA: Harvard Business School Press.

Eagly, A. H., and S. J. Karau 1991 "Gender and the emergence of leaders: A meta-analysis." Psychological Bulletin, 60: 685–710.

Eagly, A. H., and V. J. Steffen 1984 "Gender stereotypes stem from the distribution of women and men into social roles." Journal of Personality and Social Psychology, 46: 735–754.

Eagly, A. H., and V. J. Steffen 1986 "Gender and aggressive behavior: A meta-analytic review of the social psychological literature." Psychological Bulletin, 100: 309–330.

Eagly, A. H., and V. J. Steffen 2000 "Gender stereotypes stem from the distribution of women and men into social roles." In C. Stangor (ed.), Stereotypes and Prejudice: Key Readings: 142–160. Philadelphia: Psychology Press.

Edelsky, C. 1993 "Who's got the floor?" In D. Tannen (ed.), Gender and Conversational Interaction: 189–224. New York: Oxford University Press.

Fast, N. J., D. H. Gruenfeld, N. Sivanathan, and A. D. Galinsky 2009 "Illusory control: A generative force behind power's far-reaching effects." Psychological Science, 20: 502–508.

Fiske, S. T. 2010 "Interpersonal stratification: Status, power, and subordination." In S. T. Fiske, D. T. Gilbert, and G. Lindzey (eds.), Handbook of Social Psychology, 5th ed.: 941–982. Hoboken, NJ: Wiley.

Galinsky, A. D., D. H. Gruenfeld, and J. C. Magee 2003 "From power to action." Journal of Personality and Social Psychology, 85: 453–466.

Galinsky, A. D., J. C. Magee, D. H. Gruenfeld, J. A. Whitson, and K. A. Liljenquist 2008 "Power reduces the press of the situation: Implications for creativity, conformity, and dissonance." Journal of Personality and Social Psychology, 95: 1450–1466.

Galinsky, A. D., J. C. Magee, E. Inesi, and D. H. Gruenfeld 2006 "Power and perspectives not taken." Psychological Science, 17: 1068–1074.

Gayle, B. M., R. W. Preiss, and M. Allen 1994 "Gender differences and the use of conflict strategies." In L. H. Turner and H. M. Sterk (eds.), Differences that Make a Difference: Examining the Assumptions in Gender Research: 13–26. Westport, CT: Bergin & Garvey.

Heilman, M. E., and T. G. Okimoto 2007 "Why are women penalized for success at male tasks?: The implied communality deficit." Journal of Applied Psychology, 92: 81–92.

Helgelsen, S. 1995 The Female Advantage: Women's Ways of Leadership. New York: Doubleday.

Henley, N. M. 1977 Body Politics: Power, Sex, and Nonverbal Communication. Englewood Cliffs, NJ: Prentice-Hall.

James, D., and J. Drakich 1993 "Understanding gender differences in amount of talk: A critical review of research." In D. Tannen (ed.), Gender and Conversational Interaction: 281–317. New York: Oxford University Press.

Keltner, D., D. H. Gruenfeld, and C. Anderson 2003 "Power, approach, and inhibition." Psychological Review, 110: 265–284.

Kimble, C. E., and J. I. Musgrove 1988 "Dominance in arguing mixed-sex dyads: Visual dominance patterns, talking time, and speech loudness." Journal of Research in Personality, 22: 1–16.

LaFrance, M., M. A. Hecht, and E. L. Paluck 2003 "The contingent smile: A meta-analysis of sex differences in smiling." Psychological Bulletin, 129: 305–334.

Linkey, H. E., and I. J. Firestone 1990 "Dyad dominance composition effects, nonverbal behaviors, and influence." Journal of Research in Personality, 24: 206–215.

Locke, J. L. 1998 The De-voicing of Society: Why We Don't Talk to Each Other Anymore. New York: Simon & Schuster.

Locke, J. L., and M. Hauser 1999 "Sex and status effects on primate volubility: Clues to the origin of vocal languages?" Evolution and Human Behavior, 20: 151–158.

Maltz D. N., and R. A. Borker 1982 "A cultural approach to male-female miscommunication." In J. J. Gumperz (ed.), Language and Social Identity: 196–216. New York: Cambridge University Press.

Mast, M. 2002 "Dominance as expressed and inferred through speaking time: A meta-analysis." Human Communication Research, 28: 420–450.

Moss-Racusin, C., and L. Rudman 2010 "Disruptions in women's self-promotion: The backlash avoidance model." Psychology of Women Quarterly, 34: 186–202.

Mullen, B., E. Salas, and J. E. Driskell 1989 "Salience, motivation, and artifact as contributions to the relation between participation rate and leadership." Journal of Experimental Social Psychology, 25: 545–559.

Ng, S. H., M. Brooke, and M. Dunne 1995 "Interruption and influence in discussion groups." Journal of Language and Social Psychology, 14: 369–381.

Offerman, L. R., and P. E. Schrier 1985 "Social influence strategies: The impact of sex, role, and attitudes towards power." Personality and Social Psychology Bulletin, 11: 286–300.

Okimoto, T., and V. L. Brescoll 2010 "The price of power: Power-seeking and backlash against female politicians." Personality and Social Psychology Bulletin, 36: 923–936.

Overbeck J. R., and B. Park 2001 "When power does not corrupt: Superior individuation processes among powerful perceivers." Journal of Personality and Social Psychology, 81: 549–565.

Palmer, M. T. 1989 "Controlling conversations: Turns, topics, and interpersonal control." Communication Monographs, 56: 1–18.

Pratto, F., L. M. Stallworth, J. Sidanius, and B. Siers 1997 "The gender gap in occupational role attainment: A social dominance approach." Journal of Personality and Social Psychology, 72: 37–53.

Rudman, L. A. 1998 "Self-promotion as a risk factor for women: The costs and benefits of counter-stereotypical impression management." Journal of Personality and Social Psychology, 74: 629–645.

Rudman, L. A., J. E. Phelan, S. Nauts, and C. A. Moss-Racusin 2012 "Status incongruity and backlash toward female leaders: Defending the gender hierarchy motivates prejudice against female leaders." Journal of Experimental Social Psychology, 48: 165–179.

Schmid Mast, M. 2001 "Gender differences and similarities in dominance hierarchies in same-gender groups based on speaking time." Sex Roles, 34: 547–556.

Sidanius, J., and F. Pratto 1999 Social Dominance: An Intergroup Theory of Social Hierarchy and Oppression. New York: Cambridge University Press.

Stein, R. T., and T. Heller 1979 "An empirical analysis of the correlations between leadership status and participation rates reported in the literature." Journal of Personality and Social Psychology, 37: 1993–2002.

Swim, J. K. 1994 "Perceived versus meta-analytic effect sizes: An assessment of the accuracy of gender stereotypes." Journal of Personality and Social Psychology, 66: 21–36.

Tannen, D. 1993 "The relativity of linguistic strategies: Rethinking power and solidarity in gender and dominance." In D. Tannen (ed.), Gender and Conversational Interaction: 165–185. New York: Oxford University Press.

Thibaut, J. W., and H. H. Kelley 1959 The Social Psychology of Groups. New York: Wiley.

Yoder, J. D., and A. S. Kahn 1992 "Toward a feminist understanding of women and power." Psychology of Women Quarterly, 16: 381–388.

The Gendered Media

Do the media *cause* violence, or do the media simply reflect the violence that already exists in our society? Think of how many times we have heard variations of this debate: Does gangsta rap or violent video games or violent movies or violent heavy metal music lead to increased violence? Does violent pornography lead men to commit rape? Or do these media merely remind us of how violent our society already is?

And how do the various media contribute to our understanding of gender? What role do the various media play in the maintenance of gender difference or gender inequality?

Like other social institutions, the media are a gendered institution. The media (1) reflect already existing gender differences and gender inequalities, (2) construct those very gender differences, and (3) reproduce gender inequality by making those differences seem "natural" and not socially produced in the first place. Part of its function of maintaining inequality is to first create the differences, and then to attempt to conceal its authorship so that those differences seem to flow from the nature of things.

Media reflect already existing gender differences and inequalities by targeting different groups of consumers with different messages that assume prior existing differences. In a sense, women and men don't use or consume the same media—there are women's magazines and men's magazines, chick flicks and action movies, chick lit and lad lit, pornography and romance novels, soap operas and crime procedurals, guy video games and girl video games, blogs, and 'zines—and, of course, advertising that is intricately connected to each of these different formats. As with other institutions, there are "his" and "hers" media.

The essays in this part explore the media as a gendered set of institutions, and they also discuss the way the media are a socializing agent that genders people through media representations. Alicia Summers and Monica K. Miller look at the changing portrayals of women in video games. Alexander K. Davis and his colleagues look at the construction of masculinity in reality television, especially on makeover shows. And Lindsey Wotanis and Laura McMillan focus on one YouTube performer to show the gendered environment in which women and men interact online.

From Damsels in Distress to Sexy Superheroes: How the Portrayal of Sexism in Video Game Magazines Has Changed in the Last Twenty Years

ALICIA SUMMERS AND MONICA K. MILLER

The early days of game consoles such as Nintendo are probably best remembered by games such as *Mario Brothers* and *Zelda*. These adventure games portrayed the heroic tale of the brave male character that was on a perilous quest to rescue a princess. The games provided fun for the whole family, and, as a side effect, sent women's quest for equality back to medieval times, where the knight in shining armor had to rescue the damsel in distress. The sexist portrayal of the male as the hero and the female as the victim is typical of traditional gender role attitudes. Although many Americans hold more feminist than traditional gender role attitudes, many still endorse more traditional attitudes (N. Zoe Hilton, Grant T. Harris, and Marnie E. Rice 2003). Yet, times have changed since those early games and so too has the gaming empire. Female characters such as Lara Croft (*Tomb Raider*) have become main characters and heroes in games. The rise of female heroes and feature roles demonstrates a step forward in equality, but at what price? Characters such as Lara Croft are often portrayed in tight, revealing clothing, or as disproportionately curvaceous, essentially creating a heroine who is also a sexual object. Although these examples are merely anecdotal, they do encourage a closer examination of the portrayal of females in video games.

Video games are a popular form of media, earning more than $25 billion a year (Entertainment Software Association 2012). In the US, nearly every household has at least one gaming device (i.e., PC, smartphone, video game console) and almost 50 percent have an average of two dedicated gaming consoles (Entertainment Software Associate 2012). Youths are even more likely to engage in game play with estimates of 87 percent of eight to seventeen year olds playing video games (David Walsh, Douglas Gentile, Erin Walsh, Nat Bennett, Brad Robideau, Monica Walsh, Sarah Strickland, et al. 2005). Multiple gaming consoles (e.g., Nintendo, PlayStation, Xbox) mean multiple gaming options. In correspondence with these consoles are video game magazines. Each console has its own officially licensed magazine in which it describes and advertises its new games, often portraying current games available, and describing the plot and characters within the game. These magazines reach a large number of readers. *Xbox*, for example, achieved a circulation rate of 67,097 copies per month in 2008 (Future Publishing 2008).

Thousands of youths every year are exposed to video game characters within these games. Players may look to these characters to determine appropriate behaviors and roles, similarly to how individuals use other forms of media to learn roles

Alicia Summers and Monica K. Miller, "From Damsels in Distress to Sexy Superheroes: How the Portrayal of Sexism in Video Game Magazines Has Changed in the Last Twenty Years," *Feminist Media Studies*, Vol. 14, No. 6 (2014), pp. 1028–1040. Copyright © 2014 by Taylor & Francis. Reprinted by permission of Taylor & Francis Ltd.

and behaviors (Darcy H. Granello 1997). If game characters are portrayed in a stereotypic or sexist fashion, it may impact how youths view women. Therefore, it is important to understand how female characters in video games are portrayed and how this portrayal may have changed over the years. The current analysis seeks to examine this issue by focusing specifically on female characters, in the hopes of determining how video game magazines have changed in their portrayal of women over time.

Portrayal of Women in the Media

Several studies have examined the portrayal of women in a variety of media types (Lynn J. Jaffe and Paul D. Berger 1994; Katharina Lindner 2004; Jennifer L. Paff and Hilda Buckley Lakner 1997; Nancy F. Russo, Lynn Feller, and Patrick H. DeLeon 1982). A common theme that has emerged is that women are often portrayed in a stereotypic fashion. In the 1970s, sex role stereotypes were commonly observed in the media, with women being more likely to be portrayed inside the home and males more likely to be portrayed outside the home (Jaffe and Berger 1994). Women were also more likely to be doing household chores, while males were more likely to be playing sports or doing professional (work-related) activities (Jaffe and Berger 1994). A content analysis of advertising images of women from the 1970s found that women were often portrayed in demeaning stereotypic roles such as being dependent on males, doing demeaning household chores, and being submissive and unintelligent (Russo, Feller, and DeLeon 1982). Further analyses of advertising in magazines found that the female gender role portrayal did not change from 1950 to 1994, with females typically portrayed in stereotypic feminine roles (Paff and Lakner 1997). Another study, which focused on women in magazines, confirmed that the stereotypic portrayal of women has changed little from 1955 to 2002 (Lindner 2004). This research indicates that women are often stereotyped in the media. Some of the more recent research, however, has discovered a different theme.

Several more recent studies on the portrayal of women in the media have found that women are often portrayed as sex objects (Nicole R. Krassas, Joan M. Blauwkamp, and Peggy Wesselink 2003; Donna Rouner, Michael D. Slater, and Melanie Domenici-Rodríguez 2003; Julie M. Stankiewicz and Francine Rosselli 2008). One content analysis of almost two thousand advertisements, from more than fifty popular US magazines, found that more than half of the advertisements that contained women portrayed them as sex objects (Stankiewicz and Rosselli 2008). Further, about 3 percent of portrayals showed women as aggressive sexual objects, while almost 10 percent showed women as sexualized and victims. Another study found that, in men's magazines, women are more likely than men to be portrayed as sex objects (Krassas, Blauwkamp, and Wesselink 2003). Beer advertisements also typically portray very sexist, negative, and stereotypic images of females (Rouner, Slater, and Domenech-Rodríguez 2003).

In sum, these media studies indicate that women are often portrayed in stereotypical gender roles. The most current studies have found that women are also portrayed as sexual objects, who are sometimes aggressors or victims. These studies largely looked at advertisements for products listed in men's or women's magazines. Such advertisements would not necessarily have reason to portray women as aggressors or victims, whereas video games may be more likely to portray women in such a fashion because the women in the games may, in fact, be aggressors or victims. Thus, video game magazines may be quite different from advertisements for other products.

Portrayal of Women in Video Games and Video Game Magazines

Video games and video game magazines, as increasingly popular forms of media, have also been studied to determine how females are being portrayed (Berrin Beasley and Tracy Collins Standley 2002; Melinda C. R. Burgess, Stephen Paul Stermer, and Stephen R. Burgess 2007; Tracy L. Dietz 1998; Karen E. Dill and Kathryn P. Thill 2007; James D. Ivory 2006; Monica K. Miller and Alicia Summers 2007; Shirley Matile Ogletree and Ryan Drake 2007; Erica Scharrer 2004; Christine Ward Gailey 1993). Although these studies represent a variety of methodologies and data sources, they all have examined the portrayal of females in video games.

Typical gender stereotypes in earlier video game studies noted female characters in need of rescue (Ward Gailey 1993). One study found that, in 21 percent of the games, women were portrayed as a victim or damsel in distress (Dietz 1998). Another popular theme is that female characters are less common than male characters (Ivory 2006), with male characters in some studies outnumbering females by three or four to one (Burgess, Stermer, and Burgess 2007; Scharrer 2004).

Studies of the portrayal of female video game characters, as with portrayals in other forms of media, have also shown a tendency for women to be sexualized. Early studies found few sexual themes and only 28 percent of females portrayed as sex objects (Dietz 1998; Ward Gailey 1993). More recent games, on the other hand, have shown an increasing number of female characters who are portrayed as sex objects. Female characters are more likely to wear more revealing attire (Beasley and Collins Standley 2002; Miller and Summers 2007; Scharrer 2004) than male characters. They are also more likely than male characters to be portrayed as sexy (Beasley and Collins Standley 2002; Burgess, Stermer, and Burgess 2007; Dill and Thill 2007; Ivory 2006; Miller and Summers 2007).

Recent female video game characters were not only found to be sexy, but also aggressive. One study found that 40 percent of female characters were both sexualized and aggressive compared to less than 1 percent of male characters (Dill and Thill 2007). A second study also found more pairings of sexiness and aggression among female characters than among male characters (Burgess, Stermer, and Burgess 2007). This was not true of earlier studies, which found women were not aggressive (Dietz 1998).

In sum, female video game characters, as represented in games and magazines, are often portrayed as sex objects. In the most current studies women characters are also aggressive. Such studies are of importance because the media portrayals can affect players' attitudes and behaviors toward women.

Why Study Female Portrayal in the Media

Media can play a large role in the socialization of youth (Gayle R. Bessenoff 2006; Sandra L. Calvert, Tracy Kondla, Karen A. Ertel, and Douglas S. Meisel 2001; Granello 1997; Kyra Lanis and Katherine Covell 1995; L. Monique Ward, Edwina Hansbrough, and Eboni Walker 2005). Prior research has indicated that the media can influence perceptions of gender identity (Calvert et al. 2001), self-esteem, and body image (Bessenoff 2006). Individuals also may look to media, such as popular television dramas, in order to gain a better understanding of relationship dynamics, which may influence their own behaviors in a relationship (Granello 1997). Perhaps most importantly, the media may influence sex role attitudes of both males and females (Lanis and Covell 1995; Ward, Hansbrough, and Walker 2005). Females who view certain types of music videos have been shown to have an increased endorsement of traditional sex role attitudes, as compared to those who did not watch the videos (Ward, Hansbrough, and Walker 2005). Similarly, males who view media in which a woman is presented as a sex object are more likely to engage in sex role stereotyping and accept rape myths (Lanis and Covell 1995). These studies clearly indicate that the media can influence an individual's perceptions of appropriate gender roles.

Like other forms of media, so too video games may inform sex role attitudes. A video game follow up study examined the attitudes of forty-nine freshmen, asking them to describe male and female characters. They described male characters as powerful, aggressive, hostile, and athletic, while the female video game characters were described as provocatively dressed, having a curvaceous figure, thin, sexual, and aggressive (Dill and Thill 2007). Their perceptions of the video game characters mostly matched the way characters were portrayed in the game. This may influence their perception of "real" males and females, as viewing images of women portrayed as sex objects has been shown to be related to the endorsement of certain gender stereotypes (L. Monique Ward and Kimberly Friedman 2006; Ward, Hansbrough, and Walker 2005), such as viewing women as sex objects (Jochen Peter and Patti M. Valkenburg 2007).

In sum, it appears that the portrayal of women in video games could impact the gender stereotypes and sex role attitudes of game players. This is particularly important because the portrayal of women in media appears to have changed over time. While early studies indicate women being portrayed in a stereotypical fashion typically associated with traditional gender roles, more recent studies have found women portrayed as sexual objects. This change in the portrayal of women may be best explained by a closer examination of sexism.

Hostile and Benevolent Sexism

Sexism has typically been defined by attitudes or behaviors that are based on traditional sex role stereotyping (Peter Glick and Susan T. Fiske 1997). In 1997, this definition was challenged by the proposition that sexism can refer to a broader variety of phenomena than just stereotyping. The concept of ambivalent sexism arose from the theory that sexism can take different forms (Glick and Fiske 1997). Glick and Fiske proposed that ambivalent sexism includes two distinct forms of sexism—hostile and benevolent sexism. Benevolent sexism endorses more traditional attitudes toward women, particularly paternalistic, protective attitudes toward women. Hostile sexism, on the other hand, endorses attitudes and behaviors that exploit women as sexual objects through the expression of derogatory characteristics of women. Both are built on the notion of male power, although they come from different perspectives. Hostile sexism seeks to justify male power through the objectification of women. It also views women as power seeking and using their sexuality to gain advantage. Benevolent sexism is considered a more positive form of sexism that encourages male power through the ascription of traditional gender roles and the need for men to protect women. Individuals may hold both benevolent and hostile sexist attitudes, thus the term ambivalent sexism (Glick and Fiske 1997).

Research on ambivalent sexism has examined men's sexism toward females, by providing participants with vignettes depicting various behaviors on behalf of the female. Results indicate that men expressed increased hostile sexism and decreased benevolent sexism towards a female character that portrayed promiscuous (negative) behavior, and showed more benevolent sexism toward characters who showed the positive trait of chasteness and portrayed traditional gender roles (Chris G. Sibley and Marc Stewart Wilson 2004). This study suggests that sexism plays a role in how characters are viewed. Thus, the portrayal of characters in a sexist manner may likewise impact the sexist attitudes of the individual viewing the character.

Study Overview

Previous research on video games has consistently failed to examine the portrayal of women over time. Most of the research that has been conducted has examined recent games (Beasley and Collins Standley 2002; Dietz 1998), recent video game advertisements (Scharrer 2004), recent Internet reviews of the game (Ivory 2006), or recent video game articles (Miller and Summers 2007). They have also primarily focused on specific gender differences (e.g., aggressiveness of males versus females) at a given point in time, rather than examining specific, stereotypic traits across time. The current study seeks to fill a research gap by examining the portrayal of sexism in video game magazines over the past twenty years. This will be accomplished by analyzing female characters in video game magazine articles. Two main research questions are posited to address the role of sexism. Has the portrayal of female characters changed over time in terms of benevolent sexism? Has the portrayal of female characters changed over time in terms of hostile sexism?

Hypotheses

Several hypotheses are postulated to address the research questions. Hypothesis 1 predicts that the portrayal of female characters in a benevolent sexist way will have reduced over time. Benevolent sexism, as indicated above, includes traditional gender role attitudes for women, a sense of protective paternalism, a desire for intimacy, and complementary gender differentiation where women are perceived as more moral or pure than men (Glick and Fiske 1997). Therefore, changes in benevolent sexism will be exhibited based on the following specific predicted changes:

Hypothesis 1a. There will be fewer princesses in more recent game articles. Princesses typically fall into the more traditional gender role for women. As princesses are conceptualized as a more traditional gender role, holding with benevolent sexism, the reduction of these characters in newer games would indicate a trend toward less benevolent sexism.

Hypothesis 1b. The female characters will be less likely to be portrayed as needing rescue in new game articles. Needing rescue portrays protective paternalism, an important aspect of benevolent sexism.

Hypothesis 1c. The female characters will be less likely to be portrayed as helpless in newer game articles. Helplessness, like needing rescue, portrays protective paternalism in that women need to be helped by men.

Hypothesis 1d. The female characters will be less likely to be portrayed as innocent in newer game articles. This item represents the complementary gender differentiation aspect of benevolent sexism as innocence is synonymous with purity.

Hypothesis 2 postulates that the portrayal of female characters in a hostile sexist way will have increased over time. Hostile sexism is nearly the opposite of benevolent sexism. Hostile sexism endorses the exploitation of women as sexual objects and the idea of dominant paternalism, where men have the power and women do not. The portrayal of hostile sexism in the game is therefore operationalized according to the following specific hypotheses:

Hypothesis 2a. Female video game characters will increase in sexiness over time. Sexiness of the character portrays the women as a sexual object.

Hypothesis 2b. Female video game characters will wear more revealing clothing in more recent game articles. As with sexiness ratings, the revealing nature of a female character's clothing is indicative of her role as a sexual object.

Method

Sample

A convenience sample of game articles from *Xbox, PlayStation,* and *Nintendo Power* magazines were selected from the years 1988–2007. Researchers searched libraries and Internet sources (e.g., eBay) for back issues of the magazines and ordered a large sample, paying special attention to early *Nintendo* magazines, as a large sample of these was required to capture the early game characters. Researchers also purchased currently available copies of the gaming magazines for the years 2005, 2006, and 2007. These magazines were chosen because they are the official gaming magazines of the corresponding popular gaming consoles Xbox, PlayStation, and Nintendo. The popularity of these magazines is apparent with circulations numbering in the hundreds of thousands. Game articles were chosen if they contained at least one full page of text and photographs and if there was enough information (i.e., information or pictures in text about the character) to code the characters. Some characters were not selected because they were never distinctly portrayed (e.g., there were no images of the character). All female characters discussed and pictured in the article were coded. . . .

Results

A total of 223 female characters from 175 game magazine articles were coded from the years 1988–2007. The sample was missing characters from 1992, 1995, 1997, and 1998, but the remaining years averaged fourteen characters per year. A series of linear and logistic regression analyses examined Hypothesis 1, which predicted that the portrayal of benevolent sexism will have reduced over time. The second series of regression analyses examined Hypothesis 2, which predicted that the portrayal of hostile sexism will have increased over time.

Hypothesis 1. Benevolent Sexism over Time

The purpose of Hypothesis 1 was to examine the portrayal of female characters over time in terms of benevolent sexism. Hypotheses 1b, 1c, and 1d were generally supported, while hypothesis 1a approached, but did not reach, statistical significance (see figure 1).

Hypothesis 1a

It was predicted that there would be fewer princesses in more recent games. A logistic regression analysis examined the changes in princess characters over time. Although the number of princess characters did decrease over time (20 percent of characters in 1988 and 0 percent of characters in 2007), the difference did not quite achieve statistical significance.

Hypothesis 1b

It was predicted that female characters would be less likely to be portrayed as needing rescue in newer game articles. A logistic regression analysis revealed that the percentage of female characters needing rescue significantly decreased over time. The percentage of female characters being rescued peaked in 1991 (69 percent) and dropped down to 0 for the years 2005–2007.

Hypothesis 1c

It was predicted that female characters would be less likely to be portrayed as helpless in newer game articles. Helplessness, like needing rescue, portrays protective paternalism in that women need to be helped by men. This hypothesis was generally supported. Helpless was indicated by ratings on an eight-point scale ranging from a low point of zero (*not at all helpless*) to a high point of seven (*extremely helpless*). As predicted, helplessness ratings decreased consistently between time periods. With the highest ratings of helplessness occurring in 1989 and 1991 and the lowest occurring in 2006.

Hypothesis 1d

Finally, it was predicted that female characters would be less likely to be portrayed as innocent in newer game articles. As indicated above, innocence was coded from zero (*not at all innocent*) to seven (*extremely innocent*). A linear regression revealed a significant decrease in innocence over time. The year 1991 had the most innocent characters and 2006 had the least innocent characters.

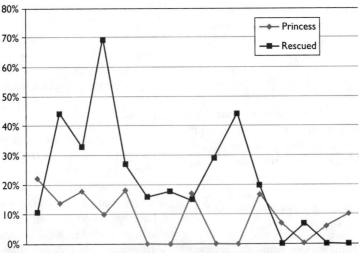

Figure 1. Changes in Female Characters' Roles Over Time
Note: This figure portrays the percentage of characters that are portrayed as a princess or needing rescue over time. The lines begin with characters from 1988 and range to characters from games in 2007 (with a few missing years in-between).

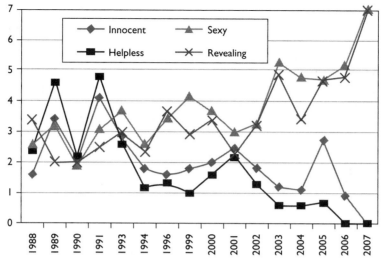

Figure 2. Changes in Female Characters Over Time
Note: This figure portrays the scale ratings of female characters in terms of their innocence, helplessness, sexiness, and revealing clothing over time. The scale ranges from zero (*not at all*) to seven (*extremely*). The lines begin with characters from 1988 and range to characters from games in 2007 (with a few missing years in-between).

Hypothesis 2. Changes in Hostile Sexism

The purpose of Hypothesis 2 was to examine the portrayal of female characters over time in terms of hostile sexism. It was predicted that video game characters would demonstrate an increase in hostile sexist portrayal over time (see figure 2).

Hypothesis 2a

It was predicted that female video game characters would increase in sexiness over time. This hypothesis was supported. Female characters showed a consistent trend of increased sexiness over time. The lowest sexiness score was in 1990 and the highest was in 2007.

Hypothesis 2b

It was predicted that female video game characters would wear more revealing clothing in more recent game articles. The more revealing the attire, the more the individual is shown as a sexual object. The overall revealingness of the characters' attire increased significantly over time. Female characters in 1989 had the lowest revealing scores compared to later years where revealing reached an average of more than 4.0, with the highest in 2003.

Discussion

The current study demonstrates a changing trend in the portrayal of female characters in video games, at least as they are portrayed in magazines, in the last twenty years. No more are females princesses who need to be rescued; now, they are often sexualized and dressed in revealing clothes. As a princess, they were portrayed in a benevolent, yet stereotypic manner. In early games, females were put on a pedestal, considered pure and innocent, and needed the hero (a male, of course) to rescue them. In more modern games, this is rarely the case. The females are often the heroes of the game. They are sexy and often portrayed as a sexual object. In short, there has been a vast change from a benevolent sexism to a hostile sexism portrayal of female characters as represented in video game magazines. This sexist shift may impact attitudes, which have very real consequences outside the game arena.

These portrayals of women may impact how males view women. As noted above, several studies have shown that portraying women as sex objects may encourage negative attitudes toward women (Lanis and Covell 1995; Ward, Hansbrough, and

Walker 2005). Beyond that, it may have implications for how women view themselves. Women who were exposed to sexist ads often viewed their body as larger, creating a greater divergence between what they viewed as their real compared to their ideal body (Howard Lavine, Donna Sweeney, and Stephen H. Wagner 1999), which can lower their self-esteem (Sarah K. Murnen, Linda Smolak, J. Andrew Mills, and Lindsey Good 2003).

This portrayal may also impact other attitudes, of both males and females. Both hostile and benevolent sexism have been shown to impact how individuals see the victim in rape cases (Dominic Abrams, G. Tendayi Viki, Barbara Masser, and Gerd Bohner 2003). Hostile sexism, in particular, is often correlated with rape myth acceptance (Kristine M. Chapleau, Debra L. Oswald, and Brenda L. Russell 2007). If new games portray women in a fashion that is consistent with hostile sexism, it may lead youths to adopt these sexist attitudes, which can be detrimental to their perception of real women in the real world.

Limitations

A few limitations of the current study should be considered. First, the study is not a random sample of all video game magazines. As back issues from the last twenty years were needed, it was not financially or logistically possible to obtain all issues for each magazine. It is possible that the magazines that were acquired and included in the study were somehow different from other magazines from the same years, although the researchers have little reason to believe this is so.

Second, data coding was not always clear-cut. The newer gaming magazines, particularly *Xbox* and *PlayStation,* often gave less detail about the games than the older *Nintendo* magazines. This means that older characters often had more data (i.e., less missing data) than some of the newer characters coded. Coding was further complicated by the fact that many of the newer games are more complex, sometimes allowing the player to create their own character, including body type and costume. This means that the characters shown (and coded) may not reflect the actual playable character that was made.

Finally, the coding was done in magazines, not the games themselves. Therefore, it is possible, although unlikely, that the portrayal of the character in the game differed from the portrayal of the character in the magazine which was advertising the game. Game play may have resulted in a richer dataset, which would provide a better look at the portrayal of females. Despite these limitations, coding resulted in an abundant dataset which had sufficient information for the desired analyses.

Conclusion

Video games, as with other forms of media, may have a serious impact on the attitudes of youths who view and play them. This study examined video game magazine short articles about the games, with few pictures and text. If female characters are portrayed in this fashion merely in advertising the game, then one can only imagine how they are depicted in the actual game. Further, players will not be exposed to a short article, they will be exposed to hours of game play, continuously bombarded with images of women portrayed as sexual objects. If this portrayal affects their sex role attitudes, they may exhibit hostile sexism (consistent with the portrayal they have observed) and view women as sexual objects, who seek power over men.

Future research should seriously consider this issue and begin a more in-depth exploration of how women are portrayed, as well as how this portrayal affects youths. As with other media studies, it will be important to examine game play and sex role attitudes following exposure to the sexist portrayal of video game females, in order to determine if, and how much of an impact these portrayals actually have. From here, researchers can determine if the portrayal of female characters can be beneficial or harmful to the developing ideals of youth.

References

Abrams, Dominic, G. Tendayi Viki, Barbara Nasser, and Gerd Bohner. 2003. "Perceptions of Stranger and Acquaintance Rape: The Role of Benevolent and Hostile Sexism in Victim Blame and Rape Proclivity." *Journal of Personality and Social Psychology* 84 (1): 111–125.

Beasley, Berrin, and Tracy Collins Standley. 2002. "Shirts vs. Skins: Clothing as an Indicator of Gender Role Stereotyping in Video Games." *Mass Communication and Society* 5 (3): 279–293.

Bessenoff, Gayle R. 2006. "Can the Media Affect Us? Social Comparison, Self-discrepancy, and the Thin Ideal." *Psychology of Women Quarterly* 30 (3): 239–251.

Burgess, Melinda C. R., Steven Paul Stermer, and Stephen R. Burgess. 2007. "Sex, Lies, and Video Games: The Portrayal of Male and Female Characters on Video Game Covers." *Sex Roles* 57 (5–6): 419–433.

Calvert, Sandra L., Tracy Kondla, Karen A. Ertel, and Douglas S. Meisel. 2001. "Young Adults' Perceptions and Memories of a Televised Woman Hero." *Sex Roles* 45 (1/2): 31–52.

Chapleau, Kristine M., Debra L. Oswald, and Brenda L. Russell. 2007. "How Ambivalent Sexism toward Women and Men Support Rape Myth Acceptance." *Sex Roles* 57 (1–2): 131–136.

Dietz, Tracy L. 1998. "An Examination of Violence and Gender Role Portrayals in Video Games: Implications for Gender Socialization and Aggressive Behavior." *Sex Roles* 38 (5/6): 425–442.

Dill, Karen E., and Kathryn P. Thill. 2007. "Video Game Characters and the Socialization of Gender Roles: Young People's Perceptions Mirror Sexist Media Depictions." *Sex Roles* 57 (11–12): 851–864.

Entertainment Software Association. 2012. *Essential Facts About the Computer and Video Game Industry*. Washington, DC: Author.

Future Publishing. 2008. "ABCs: Future announces half-year results for 17 titles." Accessed September 3, 2012. http://www.futureplc.com/2008/08/14/abcs-future-announces-half-year-results-for-17-titles/

Glick, Peter, and Susan T. Fiske. 1997. "Hostile and Benevolent Sexism: Measuring Ambivalent Sexist Attitudes toward Women." *Psychology of Women Quarterly* 21 (1): 119–135.

Granello, Darcy Haag. 1997. "Using Beverly Hills, 90210 to Explore Developmental Issues in Female Adolescents." *Youth & Society* 29 (1): 24–53.

Hilton, N. Zoe, Grant T. Harris, Marnie E. Rice. 2003. "Adolescents' Perceptions of the Seriousness of Sexual Aggression: Influence of Gender, Traditional Attitudes, and Self-reported Experience." *Sexual Abuse: A Journal of Research and Treatment* 15: 201–214.

Ivory, James D. 2006. "Still a Man's Game: Gender Representation in Online Reviews of Video Games." *Mass Communication and Society* 9 (1): 103–114.

Jaffe, Lynn, J., and Paul D. Berger. 1994. "The Effect of Modern Female Sex Role Portrayals on Advertising Effectiveness." *Journal of Advertising Research* 34 (4): 32–42.

Krassas, Nicole R., Joan M. Blauwkamp, and Peggy Wesselink. 2003. "'Master Your Johnson': Sexual Rhetoric in *Maxim* and *Stuff* Magazines." *Sexuality & Culture* 7 (3): 98–119.

Lanis, Kyra, and Katherine Covell. 1995. "Images of Women in Advertisements: Effects on Attitudes Related to Sexual Aggression." *Sex Roles* 32 (9–10): 639–649.

Lavine, Howard, Donna Sweeney, and Stephen H. Wagner. 1999. "Depicting Women as Sex Objects in Television Advertising: Effects on Body Dissatisfaction." *Personality and Social Psychology Bulletin* 25 (8): 1049–1058.

Lindner, Katharina. 2004. "Images of Women in General Interest and Fashion Magazine Advertisements from 1955 to 2002." *Sex Roles* 51 (7/8): 409–421.

Miller, Monica K., and Alicia Summers. 2007. "Gender Differences in Video Game Characters' Roles, Appearances, and Attire as Portrayed in Video Game Magazines." *Sex Roles* 57 (9–10): 733–742.

Murnen, Sarah K., Linda Smolak, J. Andrew Mills, and Lindsey Good. 2003. "Thin, Sexy Women and Strong, Muscular Men: Grade-school Children's Responses to Objectified Images of Women and Men." *Sex Roles* 49 (9/10): 427–437.

Ogletree, Shirley Matile, and Ryan Drake. 2007. "College Students' Video Game Participation and Perceptions: Gender Differences and Implications." *Sex Roles* 56 (7–8): 537–542.

Paff, Jennifer L., and Hilda Buckley Lakner. 1997. "Dress and the Female Gender Role in Magazine Advertisements of 1950–1994: A Content Analysis." *Family and Consumer Sciences Research Journal* 26 (1): 29–58.

Peter, Jochen, and Patti M. Valkenburg. 2007. "Adolescents' Exposure to a Sexualized Media Environment and Their Notions of Women as Sex Objects." *Sex Roles* 56 (5–6): 381–395.

Rouner, Donna, Michael D. Slater, and Melanie Domenech-Rodríguez. 2003. "Adolescent Evaluation of Gender Role and Sexual Imagery in Television Advertisements." *Journal of Broadcasting and Electronic Media* 47 (3): 435–454.

Russo, Nancy F., Lynn Feller, and Patrick H. DeLeon. 1982. "Sex Role Stereotypes in Television Advertising: Strategies for Change in the 80's." *Academic Psychology Bulletin* 4: 117–135.

Scharrer, Erica. 2004. "Virtual Violence: Gender and Aggression in Video Game Advertisements." *Mass Communication and Society* 7 (4): 393–412.

Sibley, Chris G., and Marc Steward Wilson. 2004. "Differentiating Hostile and Benevolent Sexist Attitudes toward Positive and Negative Sexual Female Subtypes." *Sex Roles* 51 (11–12): 687–696.

Stankiewicz, Julie M., and Francine Rosselli. 2008. "Women as Sex Objects and Victims in Print Advertisements." *Sex Roles* 58 (7–8): 579–589.

Walsh, David, Douglas Gentile, Erin Walsh, Nat Bennett, Brad Robideau, Monica Walsh, Sarah Strickland, and David Mcfadden. 2005. "Tenth Annual MediaWise® Video and Computer Game Report Card." Accessed December 12, 2005. http://www.mediafamily.org/research/report_vgrc_2005.shtml

Ward, L. Monique, and Kimberly Friedman. 2006. "Using TV as a Guide: Associations between Television Viewing and Adolescent's Sexual Attitudes and Behaviors." *Journal of Research on Adolescence* 16 (1): 133–156.

Ward, L. Monique., Edwina Hansbrough, and Eboni Walker. 2005. "Contributions of Music Video Exposure to Black Adolescents' Gender and Sexual Schemas." *Journal of Adolescent Research* 20 (2): 143–166.

Ward Gailey, Christine. 1993. "Mediated Messages: Gender, Class, and Cosmos in Home Video Games." *The Journal of Popular Culture* 27 (1): 81–98.

Own It! Constructions of Masculinity and Heterosexuality on Reality Makeover Television

ALEXANDER K. DAVIS, LAURA E. ROGERS, AND BETHANY BRYSON

Introduction

In less than 60 minutes, a reality makeover show can transform a sad, unfulfilled, plain-Jane housewife into a beaming, self-confident starlet—and transfix audiences in the process. Such transformations are infamous among feminist scholars and social scientists for directing symbolic violence toward women, as they promote largely unattainable ideals of female beauty. However, many makeover programs feature male contestants, and existing scholarship does not direct adequate analytical attention to the meaning of men's makeovers. In this paper, we ask: are male images equally oppressive, or do they escape the pressure to achieve unattainable perfection?

Alexander K. Davis, Laura E. Rogers, and Bethany Bryson, "Own It! Constructions of Masculinity and Heterosexuality on Reality Makeover Television," *Cultural Sociology*, Vol. 8, No. 3 (2014), pp. 258–274. Copyright © 2014 by Alexander K. Davis, Laura E. Rogers, and Bethany Bryson. Reprinted by permission of SAGE Publications.

Existing work on male contestants in the makeover genre offers tentative support to both sides of this puzzle. Some analyses support the oppression hypothesis, finding that men on makeover programs are subject to treatment identical to that of women (e.g. Weber, 2009). All contestants are required to hand themselves over to makeover experts, and that subjection causes them to occupy a passive and feminized position, regardless of gender. Other analyses support the possibility of escape, arguing that the presence of men on makeover shows actually signals the flexibility of contemporary masculinity (e.g. Feasey, 2008). Rather than valorizing a single version of masculinity, the makeover process demonstrates that a variety of masculinities can all lead to an improved life.

To arbitrate between these contradictory possibilities, we consider *both* female and male contestants in the same analysis. Unlike the existing sociological literature on the makeover genre, which typically devotes attention to only women or only men, this approach allows us to understand the ways in which makeover programs package gender as a *relational system* (Connell, 1987). In so doing, we find that makeover shows do not merely provide instructions for producing femininity or masculinity on their own terms; instead, makeover programs actively construct and define femininity and masculinity in relation to each other as oppositional categories that fuel a system of compulsory heterosexuality (Rich, 1980) and the patriarchal power that underlies it. For male contestants in particular, the makeover process offers an opportunity to engage in what Schrock and Schwalbe (2009) term "manhood acts": concerted efforts to enact hierarchies of gendered power and claim membership in the privileged gender group.

In the sections that follow, we offer a theoretical context for these empirical issues with a review of the existing literatures on makeover television programming, gender in the media, and the sociology of masculinities. We provide a brief description of our methodological approach, and we conduct our analysis in three parts: the linking of personal and professional success to a heightened display of femininity or masculinity, the importance of male privilege and power to the makeover process, and the centrality of heterosexual relationships to makeover definitions of a successful life. We conclude with a recapitulation of our findings and their implications for theories of gender inequality more broadly.

Literature Review

Meaning-making on Reality Makeover Television

Television is a primary source of cultural information in the contemporary United States (Giroux, 1994). Though small-screen audiences are no longer conceptualized as "cultural dopes" who passively internalize media messages without consciously processing them (Hall, 1981; Radway, 1984; Schudson, 1989), television persists in the sociological literature as an important source of cultural beliefs, ideologies, and values (Gamson et al., 1992; Gerbner et al., 2002; Grindstaff and Turow, 2006). Unusually potent in this regard is the genre known as "reality television". While there is ongoing debate about what constitutes an accurate definition of reality television due to the constant expansion and development of new program offerings (Montemurro, 2008), scholarly work about the genre—regardless of the operational definition used—indicates that reality television is an especially potent transmitter of cultural messages to television viewers[1] (Wright et al., 1995; Gamson, 1998; Grindstaff, 2002).

Three characteristics collude to make reality programs unusually effective in reaching and influencing their audiences. First, reality television makes a discursive claim by definition to be "real" or reflect "reality" in its most genuine form. The ancestry of the modern-day reality genre can be traced back to the emergence of television as a consumer product, but only recently has the genre begun to be advertised explicitly as a "genuine" or "authentic" representation of reality outside the television screen (Friedman, 2002; Holmes and Jermyn, 2004). In other words, reality television is unique in the extent to which it brings "ordinary" people into focus and purports to offer a candid look into their everyday experiences. Second, overt emotional expression is central to reality television programming. Deeply affective moments in which reality stars engage in confession, exhibitionism, and emotional revelation are necessary means to shoring up semblances of "authenticity" (Biressi and Nunn, 2005; Skeggs and Wood, 2012). This combination of relatable characters and emotional vulnerability captures the attention of viewers and induces them to recognize reality television themes in their own lives. Third, reality television programs craft ambiguous and permeable boundaries between shows and real life. This spillover keeps audiences engaged through their phones or computers when episodes of reality programs are not currently airing, but more importantly to producers, it enables a more undetectable insertion of commercial messages into television programs themselves. This deliberate, profit-driven strategy helps to ensure the continued financial success of many popular reality shows (Murray and Ouellette, 2004).

Within the unwieldy collection of programs that comprises reality television, the makeover subgenre best exemplifies this commercial tendency. The strategic acquisition of goods, services, and skills are clearly linked to the promise of a better life in each and every makeover script. This is the linchpin around which makeover shows turn: if there are problems with one's life, they can all be remediated with proper attention to one's appearance and self-fashioning (Lancioni, 2010). However, underlying these messages about the possibilities of positive life transformation are deeper messages about status, value, and social class. The political logic of makeover shows is not simply an abstract quest toward self-actualization in all aspects of a contestant's life; rather, the ultimate goal is often to make a contestant more successful in the labor market (Ouellette and Hay, 2008). Numerous scholars have identified this as evidence that only one form of capital carries value on makeover programs, and that form is a narrowly-defined set of high-status symbols and messages used to convey middle-class legitimacy (Skeggs and Wood, 2012). Thus, as makeover programs inscribe normative class regimes onto the bodies of the contestants being transformed, they likewise reinforce their relevance to broader cultural narratives about what constitutes a valuable life.

Gender Performance, Embodied Oppression and Media Images

Alongside social class, gender occupies a prominent position within the cultural messages that reality makeover shows disseminate. Much like the analyses of class-based messages described in the preceding section, theories about the place of gender on television emphasize the oppressive subtext lurking beneath banal messages about happiness and fulfillment. For decades, scholars across disciplines have documented the ways in which representations of gender in the media negatively and disproportionately impact women. Research has repeatedly shown that the television medium persists in generating unrealistic portrayals of women's lives and reducing them to feminine stereotypes and caricatures (e.g. Press, 1991; Wolf, 1991; Cavender et al., 1999).

Recent content analyses of reality television identify makeover programs as unusually problematic in this regard, as they employ a range of rhetorical strategies to hide the systematic devaluation of women. Some point to narratives of identity, in which one's "inner beauty" must be brought out through interventions ranging from surgery to wardrobe overhauls (e.g. Banet-Weiser and Portwood-Stacer, 2006; Heyes, 2007). Others note that stories of empowerment mask the painful realities of cosmetic surgery, which is overwhelmingly advertised to and sought by women (e.g. Tait, 2007). Regardless of the details of each script, it is well established that makeover shows promote the "ideal female body" as a commodity that can be obtained by finding the right haircut, the right clothes, and the right plastic surgeon (Gallagher and Pecot-Hebert, 2007; Harrison, 2003; Deery, 2004; Pitts-Taylor, 2007). In doing so, makeover programs reproduce three social problems. First, they reify the notion that a woman's worth hinges on how she uses and fashions her body (Skeggs, 2001; McRobbie, 2004). Second, in presenting bodies as individual problems with individual solutions, makeover shows do nothing to contest broader normative constructions of femininity (Frith et al., 2010). Third, in emphasizing improving the self via improving the body, makeover shows make the performative character of social class and gender invisible and thus cause such middle-class visions of femininity to seem natural and essential to an "authentic" self (Weber, 2009).

There exists much less analytic attention to the presence of male contestants in the makeover genre, and when men and masculinity are considered, a dazzling array of interpretations ensues. One subset of authors treats the appearance of men on makeover programs as identical to women, as the class- and gender-based proscriptions embedded in makeover scripts do damage to female and male contests alike (e.g. Franco, 2008; Weber, 2009). A second subset argues that makeover programs open up new possibilities for contemporary manhood. In these accounts, makeover images of men enable more flexible approaches to masculinity than were previously possible (e.g. Feasey, 2008). A final subset understands the same messages about masculinity as a new iteration of familiar hierarchies of gendered value. For them, reality scripts and contestants themselves go to great lengths to reassert the boundary between a desirable form of commercialized masculinity and other, more marginal masculinities (e.g. Carroll, 2008; Broomfield, 2011; Quail, 2011) or the specter of homosexuality (e.g. Papacharissi and Fernback, 2008; Shugart, 2008; Johnson, 2010). Given this variety of incompatible accounts, we thus ask: do male makeover contestants indeed experience the same oppressive treatment imposed on women, do they signal positive changes for gender culture writ large, or do they represent something else altogether?

Men, Masculinity and Heteronormativity

Sociological theories of masculinity offer tentative purchase on this puzzle. Of central importance to such work is the concept of "hegemonic masculinity", defined loosely as a normative and idealized set of social practices designed to maintain dominance on the basis of gender (Connell, 1987, 1995). Although the paradigm has been revised since its inception, two primary themes have remained salient. First, multiple masculinities exist, and they exist in hierarchical relation to one another

(Connell and Messerschmidt, 2005). Though definitions of those masculinities are predicated on other social categories and can change over time, they always function in relation to whichever form of masculinity is dominant in a given social context (Hennen, 2008). Moreover, there are typically tremendous rewards, both social and economic, to enacting a more privileged form of masculinity (Logan, 2010). Second, heterosexuality is a critical dividing line between dominant masculinities and subordinated masculinities. Boundary work to maintain that line can be literal, as is often the case when straight men direct discrimination and harassment at gay men. However, it can also be a symbolic act, designed to thwart off accusations of homosexuality, whether real (Kimmel and Mahler, 2003) or jokingly imagined (Pascoe, 2007).

Newer contributions refocus attention on one of the original driving factors for sociological attention to masculinity: better understanding the reproduction of gender inequality. This return to a "gender relations" (Connell, 1987) approach emphasizes the ways in which femininity and masculinity are co-constructed in social action as unequal social categories. That is, masculinity becomes defined as whatever actions in a given cultural milieu ensure a dominant position for men and a subordinate position for women. Schrock and Schwalbe (2009) name such actions "manhood acts" and define them as what men[2] "do to create, maintain, and claim membership in a dominant gender group" (p. 281). This concept retains the flexibility of the multiple masculinities literature, as manhood acts "can vary historically and culturally" (p. 280), but it also re-centers gender inequality, as manhood acts are "inherently about upholding patriarchy" (p. 287). Heterosexuality, too, remains an important nexus of domination in this understanding of masculinity, but it becomes more than a mere method of control used by men against other men. Rather, "women become props that men use to affirm a heterosexual identity" (p. 288) and uphold their privileged social position. In short, attempting to theorize masculinity on its own terms is a necessarily incomplete approach; a more adequate conceptualization of men and masculinity must also account for femininity, patriarchal dominance, and the heterosexual matrix that binds all of these entities together (see also Schippers, 2007).

Drawing from these ideas, we suggest that what is at stake for men on reality makeover shows is learning how to successfully showcase their privileged social position over other men and, more importantly, over women. The appearance of men in the makeover subgenre thus does not offer promising evidence of egalitarian social transformation but instead cements a vision of male dominance—and male-dominated heterosexuality—as required for the optimally-fulfilling life which the makeover narrative promises to men and women alike. . . .

Data and Methods

In order to investigate these issues, we transcribed and coded five episodes of each of the five most well-known reality makeover shows airing from 2002 to 2008. In addition to popularity and availability, our series selection criteria required that the shows complete transformations in single episodes and that contestants *not* compete with each other for access to makeover tools (including cash). Thus, the shows we selected were: *What Not to Wear* (WNTW), *How to Look Good Naked* (HTLGN), *Tim Gunn's Guide to Style* (TGGS), *Extreme Makeover* (EM) and *Queer Eye for the Straight Guy* (QE). We transcribed each episode in our sample by typing collectively into instant messaging software. At the beginning of each episode, we assigned ourselves one or more characters whose lines we would type. The instant messaging software, then, collected all the parts of our 'conversation' into a single document containing the script of each show.

To code our data, we made an initial deductive pass through the transcripts, coding phrases from the data based on themes from the literature described above: self, gender, and the market. As we recorded key phrases from every show under these headers, we did so freehand in colored marker on a coding sheet that allowed us to arrange unmatched phrases inductively in clusters that related to each other. At the same time, we also used different colors to indicate other information, such as the gender of the contestant. In addition, we marked out spaces for new themes as they emerged. As these new ideas began appearing they needed to be coded in relation to the hypothesized categories. We used axial coding methods (Corbing and Strauss, 1990) in order to account for relationships among coding categories, strategies of action and interaction, causal relationships, and outcomes. Our final pass through the data was to do selective and theoretical coding. We passed this coding work back and forth to ensure inter-coder reliability and discussed discrepancies as a group.

Analysis and Discussion

Gender Normativity: Diagnosing Failures of Femininity or Masculinity

Each of the five shows opens with a brief introduction to the contestant(s) and an appraisal of the personal or professional shortcomings that mark the current state of their lives. This quickly evolves into a pointed assessment of contestants' current bodies, wardrobes, or self-concepts and almost always relies upon explicitly gendered language. Many of these critiques describe the need to uncover a hidden femininity or masculinity lurking beneath surface deficiencies. The hosts of TGGS and WNTW often describe their female contestants as having "beautiful" bodies or "great figures" that are being hidden from view by wardrobe defects, while friends and family members of QE contestants often opine, as one man's sister did, that their loved one is "a handsome guy, and it doesn't really show" (QE2). Equally salient, though, are attempts to curb contestants' organic bodily displays and preferred modes of dress. While cultivating an underlying femininity or masculinity is a goal stated at the outset of numerous makeovers, gendered excesses which project the wrong sort of feminine or masculine visage are also frequent targets. Mike, for instance, exemplifies many male contestants on EM when he complains of the self-consciousness he feels when unclothed: "With a shirt off, you can see that I have a lot of fur on my back" (EM3).

The most egregious offenses are the ways in which any evidence of masculinity is identified as a problem for female contestants, while the same goes for femininity in male contestants. Innumerable female contestants are plucked, tweezed, and otherwise professionally depilated on seemingly every inch of their skin aside from the top of their heads,[3] while the most notable change to men is the opposite. For Eric, his long hair "worn in a ponytail" (QE5) is an obstacle to his plans to propose to his girlfriend, and for Wayne, a friend believes that "he would probably attract a whole new group of people" (QE2) if he were to discard his similarly long locks. In one unusually stark example, Valerie's friend Ann confesses to the cameras that her "masculine look has plagued her since childhood", and Valerie herself joins in to add that her "nose would be alright for a man" (EM2). Likewise, as Mike expresses his wishes about his desired makeover, he focuses in on his chest as an area of immediate concern. While his fiancée, who is undergoing a makeover at the same time, longs for breast augmentation surgery, Mike says, "I'd like a boob job, myself. I'd like to lose mine" (EM3). Thus, the messages about gender on makeover programs seek to discipline contestants' "natural" proclivities in order to excavate an idealized femininity or masculinity—and one that is wholly free of the other.

Underlying this comparable treatment of men and women, however, are striking gender differences in the rationales offered for seeking life transformation. Consistent with much existing feminist critique of the makeover genre, female contestants are expected to view looking good and flaunting their bodies as worthy ends in and of themselves. Hosts Stacy and Clinton of WNTW ask questions like, "You are tiny under there! Why would you lose all that weight and not want to show it off?" (WNTW2) or wonder aloud if they can "force out the sexy star underneath this army of oversized clothes" (WNTW1). In contrast, critiques of male contestants are much more often tied to forms of prestige, status and, above all, wealth. Eric is described in the early moments of his makeover as "practically an executive at his job right now", but his problem is that "he just needs to fit the part a bit more" (QE5). Thus, for men, what is at stake in the makeover process is being able to secure the social power that should be theirs or, at the very least, cultivate a heightened

masculinity that can compensate for their perceived lack of social power.

Masculine Dominance: Re-centering Privilege Through the Makeover Process

As each program progresses from naming contestants' problems to actively rectifying them, gender differences in the treatment of contestants multiply dramatically. While talk with female contestants tends to obfuscate the financial dimensions[4] of their makeovers, instead favoring explanations about how and why to showcase particular bodily attributes, the conversations shared between makeover hosts and male contestants foreground social standing. For instance, QE contestant Jeff Lubie says of himself, "Little Jeffie's gotta grow up and move on" (QE4), and the theme of updating his appearance and surroundings to look like a mature adult recurs throughout the remainder of the episode. The narrative arc in that single episode reflects a broader trend observable in the vast majority of transformations made to the lives of male contestants: instead of being instructed in how to flaunt their physical characteristics,[5] men undergo revisions of their personal presentations and environment that allow them to look as if they possess greater status and wealth.

On QE, contestants begin the work of the makeover with a series of confessions to the panel of hosts, and they typically articulate economic concerns as paramount in their willingness to undergo the process ahead of them. For some contestants, like Todd, being unable to adequately manage their personal finances feels like an obstacle to personal fulfillment. He talks openly about "want[ing] a career and want[ing] a career goal", and finds it "pretty frustrating" to not have them. He continues, "The bank of mom and dad is very good to me. They're always there for me, but I have to say that I hate it. I feel very guilty" (QE1). For other contestants, monetary concerns interfere with their ability to move forward in their romantic relationships. Eric, who wants to propose to his girlfriend, recounts to the QE hosts that "getting a divorce destroyed my finances" and that he needs help to figure out "where my money is going and how to grow it a little bit more" (QE5).

Contestants often look distraught when verbalizing these sentiments, and high-school student Ronnie epitomizes that discomfort when he brings up his girlfriend, saying, "She's paying for everything for the prom, and it makes me feel, like, really awkward" (QE3). Given a cultural standard of masculinity in which wealth is an important signifier of status and success (Kimmel, 2005), these comments reflect a generalized desire on the part of male makeover contestants to recoup or achieve the economic markers of manhood that they do not currently possess.

Contestants are not alone in expressing such fiscal concerns; hosts also comment on deficiencies of wealth, whether real or perceived. In some cases, this linguistic contrast between female and male makeover participants can be as simple as a single word. Linda, one mom nominated for a mini-makeover, has her hair dyed and cut alongside her daughter into a style described succinctly as "hot", whereas in the same episode Steve receives a similar dye-and-cut procedure into something more "distinguished" (EM1). Lengthier comments reflect similar differences. During one episode of EM, Geri hears tips about how to negotiate her "fuller bustline", using "plunging v-neck tops" to give her "just a hint of sex appeal and the perfect amount of coverage", but her husband Ethan receives a much more detailed education about "classic Italian men's tailoring, luxurious leathers, supple cashmeres" (EM5), and their usefulness for evenings out on the town. Thus, while women are inundated with shortcuts to look curvier and/or thinner, men experience opportunities to absorb cultural capital alongside the more overt visual markers of status each makeover program provides. As a result, makeovers provide male contestants with an opportunity to engage in what Schrock and Schwalbe (2009) call manhood acts: behaviors organized around "claiming privilege, eliciting deference, and resisting exploitation" (p. 281) that ensure their membership in the dominant gender group.

For some men, including Ethan, ensuring an appropriate aesthetic distinction between work attire and evening attire is their goal. In response to the first outfit he tries on, his personal shopper instantly opines, "It's definitely different than your uniform" (EM5), and the chasm between his work uniform and his new wardrobe subsequently becomes a recurring theme in their interactions. Personal care and grooming are also identified as important methods of distancing men's appearances from the work they do. Much is made of Riley's hands during his mini-makeover. Because he works in a motorcycle shop during the day, his makeover team immediately hones in on his inadequate fingernail care: "Your nails should always be clean. One of the most unattractive things for a man is for them to have dirt under their nails" (EM1). What is most notable about these two particular interactions is that the actual spending of money is de-emphasized. Nail care is a profoundly inexpensive life change when compared to the average makeover[6] on EM, and Ethan is even told outright, "All you have to do is invest in one great piece of clothing that makes you feel good. It can be a jacket, the shoes, anything. You don't have to spend thousands" (EM5). In other words, amidst an emphasis on knowledge and skill acquisition in men's makeovers, the *appearance* of status and wealth can trump the actual possession of such qualities.

The ownership of actual wealth, however, does remain crucial to men's makeover narratives, and this is most apparent in the unusually class-inflected transformation of WNTW contestant Eddie. Within moments of the show's start, a voiceover announces that Eddie's "charity case style" is "poached from thrift stores". Hosts Stacy and Clinton echo this sentiment within moments of meeting him, announcing that "your friends and family think . . . you look like a guy without a job. Or without a home." For Eddie, at issue is not merely that he looks like a "vandal" or like he might "kidnap a child"; his problem is located in the actual amount of his income he spends on clothes each year. After he recounts that he spends "about forty bucks" at thrift shops at the beginning of each season "and then, like, twenty for the summer", Stacy replies, "I think that's the lowest number I've ever heard for an entire wardrobe." The cash-focused "shift from thrift" theme of his episode persists until his final conversation with the hosts, in which they re-emphasize how important it is for him "to have nice, high-quality stuff" (WNTW5) in his wardrobe. But as his wife's amazement and tears make clear at the end of that episode, embedded in men's lessons about how to augment their social status are deeper lessons about learning to perform the most potent manhood act of all: compulsory heterosexuality.

Compulsory Heterosexuality: Evidence of Successfully-Reconstructed Masculinity

As countless feminist scholars have asserted, both within sociology (e.g. Connell, 1987; Pierce, 1995; Schrock and Schwalbe, 2009) and in other fields (e.g. Chodorow, 1978; Rich, 1980; Butler, 1990), heterosexuality is the most definitional characteristic of masculine gender performance. Unsurprisingly, then, the most commonly invoked litmus test for personal success in the makeover genre is heterosexual romance. Many male contestants seek out or are nominated for makeover interventions either because they are currently failing at that test or wish to re-enter the dating pool after a long period of being single. Wayne's long hair described above is but one item in a laundry list of concerns that are keeping him single, including an outdated wardrobe and "the ugliest wallpaper I've ever seen in my life" (QE2). Similarly, widower Art describes himself as having "the soul of a thirty-year-old and the body of a seventy-year-old". His EM hopes involve rectifying the signs of age on his body so that he can find "the right person" to be with him for the rest of his life (EM1). Others are looking to take a next step in their existing romantic relationships—usually a marriage proposal—or to bring the spark back to their marriages. Riley's wife nominates him for a mini-makeover because she's "never seen him in a suit and tie" and dreams of "being with somebody who just stepped out of GQ" (EM2).

These comments become much more obviously pernicious when compared to the sorts of justifications made by and for female contestants' heterosexual relationships. For many women, the critiques they issue toward themselves and hear from show hosts mimic this concern for heterosexual love and relationships, but they are much more often centered on the men in their lives than themselves. While men like Riley and WNTW contestant Eddie agree under pressure to acquiesce to their wives' makeover nominations, women express feeling tremendous guilt for the current state of their bodies, wardrobes, and lives. For instance, Val says of herself, "I'm a woman, but I just don't think I look enough like one", and she goes on to add, "I'm married to this wonderful man, and I almost feel like I have cheated him out of a wife" (EM2). A voiceover introduction on HTLGN describes contestant Shannon's problems as rooted in "spending her overpacked days in an icky mommy uniform of t-shirts and jeans", and that same voiceover links those clothing choices directly to her inability to be adequately "physical with her husband" (HTLGN2). Even more dramatic differences ensue when children are discussed. Male contestants' children will often collude in makeover commentary but rarely discussed as beneficiaries of their fathers' makeovers. In contrast, having children is almost universally cited as a reason for female contestants to change. In trying to get Ali to agree to his advice, Tim Gunn says of her cleavage, "You're now married, and you have [children] Remy and Sky. It's time to put away the big guns" (TGGS2). Likewise, Carson says to Shannon, "You're not ever gonna be some sort of skinny supermodel, and that's okay. You're a mom. You've got bigger priorities than walking down runways and looking hungry" (HTLGN2). In all of these cases, female contestants need makeovers to better enact heterosexual, male-centric lives, in which they can be better wives to their husbands and, for Ali and Shannon, better mothers[7] to their children.

Potent messages about male dominance and heterosexual romance also populate intangible parts of men's makeovers. For Wayne, a new haircut, new wardrobe, and new wallpaper collectively take up less screen time than does his interaction with a dating expert who describes herself as "man's best friend". She tells him that "the way to attract a woman is to be totally, rivetingly confident" and that he must "get used to the fact that you are hot". In her instruction about nonverbal behavior, she becomes even more explicit about how he should take charge with women: she encourages him to "undress" her with his eyes, and when a woman meets his glance from across the room, he is taught to "take her" without hesitation. If he masters such principles, she promises that "every woman" (QE2) will want him. Art receives analogous wisdom from the dating expert he speaks with on EM. She notes that he walked into the room to meet her looking "down on himself and insecure" and tells him that "nobody wants to see some schlump; they want to see a king" before sending him back out to re-enter more confidently. In addition to instructions about "consistently look[ing] at their eyes" and "smiles mean[ing] everything to a woman", she also remarks that dominance is necessary to attract women, saying, "You are a man. You need to take control." Her suggestions for how to accomplish that include taking a woman to a familiar restaurant, paying for the meal, and half-standing "out of the chair to show respect for them leaving". In fact, the connection between social status and heterosexual attractiveness does not remain tacit for Art: his dating expert notes that "class and money" (EM4) are crucial for securing female attention.

This theme of male dominance within heterosexual relationships emerges yet again as makeovers come to a close. As Todd makes progress toward his weight loss goal, he makes direct eye contact with the camera and announces, "I'm starting to feel these [his biceps, to which he points] right here, so ladies, watch out, 'cause the new Todd Eastern is coming for you!" (QE1). In doing so, he echoes the assertiveness that Art and Wayne are told they must cultivate to be romantically successful. Comparing QE contestant Eric's marriage proposal to EM contestant Mary's experience further highlights the extent to which male dominance appears crucial to successful makeovers. Much is made of Eric's passion for medieval re-enactment, including his plan "to go to court" and ask his "lady for her hand in marriage" (EM5). During his episode, he is shown asking her father for her hand in marriage, which includes an explicit promise to take care of her for the rest of his life. Mary, on the other hand, is fully on the receiving end of patriarchal expectations. Her boyfriend

flies to the EM premises to propose, saying, "Change your name, take mine. All you got to do is say yes." She subsequently describes his proposal during her reveal as "all of her dreams coming true" (EM3), and the first thing she squeals to her gaggle of students upon her return to work as a teacher is that she's engaged to be married. In short, while a heteronormative resolution is requisite for all contestants, logics of romantic success inform the content of that resolution differently for men and for women. While makeover shows encourage men to claim elevated social status in their new or improved relationships, women's transformations largely earn them subordinate roles in comparable relationships.

Nowhere is that more evident than in each contestant's final reveal to friends and family. The monetary cost of men's makeovers is a central device around which their stories are structured, especially when it comes to learning how to properly spend money on others. For Jeff, the quintessential manhood act in his makeover journey is not a wardrobe overhaul or ridding his apartment of its "tube socks and beer" smell. Instead, he aims to change from a man who had "never given her flowers, never bought her jewelry" into the "romantic", "marrying-type" (QE4) able to execute the perfect marriage proposal. Over the course of his episode, he receives an education about diamonds, and he selects an extravagant necklace and engagement ring worth $10,000 for his soon-to-be fiancée. Ronnie, who had such palpable discomfort with his girlfriend covering the cost of their prom, is provided with a set of diamond earrings for his mother and a Tiffany charm bracelet for his girlfriend. Even Eric, who has the unusual fortune of meeting with a financial advisor on camera during the filming of his episode, learns that spending money on his partner is an ideal conduit for showing his love and appreciation to her. In addition to designing a custom engagement ring for her, he also receives advice about how to actualize their "number one dream" (QE5) of saving for a house. These final gestures and gifts serve as final evidence that each makeover man has evolved into a properly masculine figure, able to spend money in ways that either attract women or cement their existing heterosexual relationships.

As a result, men are not alone in their production of manhood acts on reality makeover shows. Women on makeover shows are also critically important producers of manhood acts—whether they function as the evidence that a male contestant's makeover was successful or they themselves are made over and therefore come to occupy a subsidiary position in a heterosexual relationship. In sum, then, men on makeover shows are neither as feminized nor as flexibly masculine as previous scholarship suggests. Instead, their presence as contestants reifies existing ideologies of gender inequality in which social status is a requisite component of masculinity, deference to men is a requisite component of femininity, and a male-dominated heterosexuality is a requisite component of both.

Conclusion and Implications

Thus, for both female and male contestants, we find that much of the makeover process *appears* similar. Plot lines identify the problems preventing contestants from reaching their true potential, prescribe and carry out costly interventions to fix those obstacles, and reveal the 'one true self' lying dormant the entire time. Amidst this focus on shopping and self-transformation, the makeover process induces contestants to highlight bodily gender cues and learn gender-specific skills so that they can maximize their success at romance, work, and self-esteem. As a result, makeover shows actively portray heightened femininity or heightened masculinity as necessary for a more successful life, and they conceal the performative character of gender (Butler, 1990) by describing contestants' femininity or masculinity as a hidden characteristic that can be uncovered with the "right" attitude, clothes, haircut, or surgical interventions.

However, we also find that made-over men and women are treated in categorically different ways. Consistent with existing feminist critiques of makeover shows, the women in our sample are indicted for not properly displaying their bodies. They learn how the modifications offered through surgery, shopping, and attitude adjustments can

allow them to embody a more objectified, more sexualized, and thus more successful self. This treatment defines the social worth of women almost solely by their physical characteristics. In contrast, male contestants are counseled about the virtues of luxury goods and their use as evidence of social status. The same sorts of surgical and shopping interventions that contribute to oppression for women actually *amplify* social power and privilege for men by linking their newfound masculinity to the promise of more money, better jobs, and greater influence. Because of this, we argue that makeover shows help their male contestants perform "manhood acts" (Schrock and Schwalbe, 2009): concerted efforts to (re)establish hierarchies of gendered power and membership in the privileged gender group. Thus, makeover shows promulgate unidimensional and limiting images of how to "do" gender (West and Zimmerman, 1987) for both men and women, but these differences in rationale ultimately imbue men with agency and power that is not equally applied to women.

Moreover, makeover hosts and scripts routinely position heterosexual romantic success—in which those unequal opposites attract—as the ultimate goal of locating one's "true" self. Contestants' failed pasts inevitably involve not displaying enough skin or status to attract desirable partners, and their imagined futures revolve around the promise that uncovering their normatively-gendered selves will lead to more (heterosexual) dates and more serious (heterosexual) relationships. For male contestants in particular, this foregrounding of heterosexual romance helps "compensate" for and distance themselves from the perceived effeminacy or homosexuality of their makeover experience (Johnson, 2010). Thus, rather than oppressing men or opening up unlimited possibilities for expressing masculinity, we find that the treatment of men on makeover shows reproduces and contributes to broader cultural ideologies of a "natural" and seemingly desirable gender order in which men are the most powerful, women experience considerable oppression, and heterosexual relationships continue to be the most important metric for measuring a self-actualized life.

While the popularity of reality makeover shows is waning, the roles of gender oppression and compulsory heterosexuality undoubtedly remain important in many other reality formats. Future research should devote attention to current and emerging reality formats, carefully exploring the relationship between gender ideologies and definitions of life success portrayed in newer programs. Especially important would be directing empirical questioning to the presence of queer contestants, both in newer iterations of the makeover genre and in other reality formats. On one hand, their presence may reduce heteronormative imperatives for reality contestants, but on the other hand, they may be subject to the same sorts of normalizing messages about romance and happiness as their straight counterparts are. Although it would certainly be useful to catalog the content of those other formats, future research should also study audiences, asking how viewers make sense of the gendered and sexual messages in the reality genre and import them (or not) into their own lives and imagined futures. Such work would be crucial to better understanding the real-world ramifications of the gender inequality and compulsory heterosexuality so often depicted in reality programming and outlined in this paper.

Notes

1. Hill (2005) and Sender (2012) find in their audience studies that viewers are not uncritical absorbers of the messages transmitted through reality television, but they do work media messages about selfhood into their own self-concepts and understandings of everyday life.
2. Also central to recent theorizing is the notion that men are not alone in negotiating masculinity. Much empirical research focuses on women instead of men, highlighting the ways in which they enact masculinity themselves (e.g. Moore, 2006) or define themselves in ways that uphold male dominance (e.g. Ezzell, 2009).
3. Such a focus is unsurprising, given the salience of body hair as a marker of femininity and heteronormativity for women (see Fahs, 2011).
4. Given the voluminous literature about the portrayal of women on makeover shows (outlined in

our review of the literature), we do not discuss the treatment of female contestants in our sample at length in this section.
5. Men and women alike largely lack the cultural scripts necessary to talk at length about men's bodies (see Eck, 2003), which could be an obstacle to direct conversation about the physical/visual dimensions of men's makeover interventions.
6. Estimates calculated off of real episodes of the program suggest that each extreme makeover costs tens of thousands of dollars (Dixon, 2007).
7. Such observations in the makeover genre are consistent with broader cultural expectations for women's sole devotion to family and childcare (see Blair-Loy, 2003; Hays, 1998).

References

Banet-Weiser S and Portwood-Stacer L (2006) "I just want to be me again!": Beauty pageants, reality television and post-feminism. *Feminist Theory* 7: 255–72.

Biressi A and Nunn H (2005) *Reality TV: Realism and Revelation*. London: Wallflower Press.

Blair-Loy M (2003) *Competing Devotions: Career and Family among Women Executives*. Cambridge, MA: Harvard University Press.

Broomfield MA (2011) Policing masculinity and dance reality television: What gender noncomformity can teach us in the classroom. *Journal of Dance Education* 11(4): 124–128.

Butler J (1990) *Gender Trouble: Feminism and the Subversion of Identity*. New York: Routledge.

Carroll H (2008) Men's soaps: Automotive television programming and contemporary working-class masculinities. *Television & New Media* 9(4): 263–283.

Cavender G, Bond-Maupin L and Jurik NC (1999) The construction of gender in reality crime TV. *Gender & Society* 13: 643–63.

Chodorow N (1978) *The Reproduction of Mothering*. Berkeley, CA: University of California Press.

Connell RW (1987) *Gender and Power*. Palo Alto, CA: Stanford University Press.

Connell RW (1995) *Masculinities*. Cambridge: Polity Press.

Connell RW and Messerschmidt JW (2005) Hegemonic masculinity: Rethinking the concept. *Gender & Society* 19(6): 829–859.

Corbin JM and Strauss A (1990) Grounded theory research: Procedures, canons, and evaluative criteria. *Qualitative Sociology* 13(1): 3–21.

Deery J (2004) Reality TV as advertisement. *Popular Communication* 2: 1–20.

Dixon WW (2007) Hyperconsumption in reality television: The transformation of the self through televisual consumerism. *Quarterly Review of Film and Video* 25(1): 52–63.

Eck BA (2003) Men are much harder: Gendered viewing of nude images. *Gender & Society* 17: 691–710.

Ezzell MB (2009) "Barbie dolls" on the pitch: Identity work, defensive othering, and inequality in women's rugby. *Social Problems* 56(1): 111–31.

Fahs B (2011) Dreaded "otherness": Heteronormative patrolling in women's body hair rebellions. *Gender & Society* 25(4): 451–472.

Feasey R (2008) *Masculinity and Popular Television*. Edinburgh: Edinburgh University Press.

Franco JL (2008) "Extreme makeover": The politics of gender, class, and cultural identity. *Television & New Media* 9: 471–486.

Friedman J (ed.) (2002) *Reality Squared: Televisual Discourse on the Real*. New Brunswick, NJ: Rutgers University Press.

Frith H, Raisborough J and Klein O (2010) C'mon girlfriend: Sisterhood, sexuality and the space of the benign in makeover TV. *International Journal of Cultural Studies* 13(5): 471–489.

Gallagher AH and Pecot-Hebert L (2007) "You need a makeover!": The social construction of female body image in "A Makeover Story", "What Not to Wear", and "Extreme Makeover". *Popular Communication* 5: 57–79.

Gamson J (1998) *Freaks Talk Back: Tabloid Talk Shows and Sexual Nonconformity*. Chicago, IL: University of Chicago Press.

Gamson WA, Croteau D, Hoynes W and Sasson T (1992) Media images and the social construction of reality. *Annual Review of Sociology* 18: 373–93.

Gerbner G, Gross L, Morgan M, Signorielli N and Shanahan J (2002) Growing up with television: Cultivation processes. In: Bryant J and Zillmann D (eds) *Media Effects: Advances in Theory and Research*. Mahwah, NJ: Lawrence Erlbaum Associates.

Giroux HA (1994) *Disturbing Pleasures: Learning Popular Culture*. New York: Routledge.

Grindstaff L (2002) *The Money Shot: Trash, Class, and the Making of TV Talk Shows*. Chicago, IL: University of Chicago Press.

Grindstaff L and Turow J (2006) Video cultures: Television sociology in the "new TV" age. *Annual Review of Sociology* 32: 103–25.

Hall S (1981) Notes on deconstructing "the popular". In: Samuel R (ed.) *People's History and Socialist Theory*. London: Routledge & Kegan Paul, 227–40.

Harrison K (2003) Television viewers' ideal body proportions: The case of the curvaceously thin woman. *Sex Roles* 48: 255–64.

Hays S (1998) *The Cultural Contradictions of Motherhood*. New Haven, CT: Yale University Press.

Hennen P (2008) *Faeries, Bears, and Leathermen: Men in Community Queering the Masculine*. Chicago: University of Chicago Press.

Heyes CJ (2007) Cosmetic surgery and the televisual makeover: A Foulcauldian feminist reading. *Feminist Media Studies* 7: 17–32.

Hill A (2005) Reality TV: Performance, authenticity, and television audiences. In: Wasko J (ed.) *A Companion to Television*. Oxford: Blackwell Publishing.

Holmes S and Jermyn D (2004) *Understanding Reality Television*. New York: Routledge.

Johnson P (2010) She just called you a metro: Rating masculinity on reality television. In: Lancioni J (ed.) *Fix Me Up: Essays on Television Dating and Makeover Shows*. Jefferson, NC: McFarland.

Kimmel MS (2005) *Manhood in America: A Cultural History*. New York: Free Press.

Kimmel MS and Mahler M (2003) Adolescent masculinity, homophobia, and violence: Random school shootings, 1982–2001. *American Behavioral Scientist* 46(10): 1439–1458.

Lancioni J (ed.) (2010) *Fix Me Up: Essays on Television Dating and Makeover Shows*. Jefferson, NC: McFarland.

Logan TD (2010) Personal characteristics, sexual behaviors, and male sex work: A quantitative approach. *American Sociological Review* 75(5): 679–704.

McRobbie AA (2004) Notes on "What not to wear" and post-feminist symbolic violence. *The Sociological Review* 52: 97–109.

Montemurro B (2008) Toward a sociology of reality television. *Sociology Compass* 2(1): 84–106.

Moore MR (2006) Lipstick or Timberlands? Meanings of gender representation in black lesbian communities. *Signs* 32(1): 113–139.

Murray S and Ouellette L (eds) (2004) *Reality TV: Remaking Television Culture*. New York: New York University Press.

Ouellette L and Hay J (2008) *Better Living through Reality TV: Television and Post-Welfare Citizenship*. Malden, MA: Blackwell Publishing.

Papacharissi Z and Fernback J (2008) The aesthetic power of the Fab 5: Discursive themes of homonormativity in *Queer Eye for the Straight Guy*. *Journal of Communication Inquiry* 32(4): 348–367.

Pascoe CJ (2007) *Dude, You're a Fag: Masculinity and Sexuality in High School*. Berkeley, CA: University of California Press.

Pierce JL (1995) *Gender Trials: Emotional Lives in Contemporary Law Firms*. Berkeley, CA: University of California Press.

Pitts-Taylor V (2007) *Surgery Junkies: Wellness and Pathology in Cosmetic Culture*. New Brunswick, NJ: Rutgers University Press.

Press AL (1991) *Women Watching Television: Gender, Class, and Generation in the American Television Experience*. Philadelphia, PA: University of Pennsylvania Press.

Quail C (2011) Nerds, geeks, and the hip/square dialectic in contemporary television. *Television & New Media* 12(5): 460–482.

Radway JA (1984) *Reading the Romance: Women, Patriarchy, and Popular Literature*. Chapel Hill: University of North Carolina Press.

Rich A (1980) Compulsory heterosexuality and lesbian existence. *Signs* 5(4): 631–60.

Schippers M (2007) Recovering the feminine other: Masculinity, femininity, and gender hegemony. *Theory & Society* 36(1): 85–102.

Schrock D and Schwalbe M (2009) Men, masculinity, and manhood acts. *Annual Review of Sociology* 35: 277–95.

Schudson M (1989) How culture works: Perspectives from media studies on the efficacy of symbols. *Theory & Society* 18: 153–80.

Sender K (2012) *The Makeover: Reality Television and Reflexive Audiences*. New York: New York University Press.

Shugart H (2008) Managing masculinities: The metrosexual moment. *Communication and Critical/Cultural Studies* 5(3): 280–300.

Skeggs B (2001) The toilet paper: Femininity, class and mis-recognition. *Women's Studies International Forum* 24(3/4): 295–307.

Skeggs B and Wood H (2012) *Reacting to Reality Television: Performance, Audience and Value*. New York: Routledge.

Tait S (2007) Television and the domestication of cosmetic surgery. *Feminist Media Studies* 7: 119–135.

Weber BR (2009) *Makeover TV: Selfhood, Citizenship, and Celebrity*. Durham, NC: Duke University Press.

West C and Zimmerman DH (1987) Doing gender. *Gender & Society* 1: 125–163.

Wolf N (1991) *The Beauty Myth: How Images of Beauty Are Used against Women*. New York: W. Morrow.

Wright JC, Huston AC, Truglio R, Fitch M, Smith E and Piemyat S (1995) Occupational portrayals on television: Children's role schemata, career aspirations, and perceptions of reality. *Child Development* 66: 1706–18.

Performing Gender on YouTube: How Jenna Marbles Negotiates a Hostile Online Environment

LINDSEY WOTANIS AND LAURIE MCMILLAN

Introduction

In February 2012, only nine of the fifty most-subscribed YouTube channels featured female performers, and only one of these female-led channels was ranked in the top ten. This underrepresentation of women suggests that gender matters on YouTube, but *how* gender matters is not clear. While some studies point to males spending more time on video-sharing sites such as YouTube (Mary Madden 2009; Heather Molyneaux, Susan O'Donnell, Kerri Gibson, and Janice Singer 2008, 4), other statistics find the opposite (Brian Chappell 2012), and still other research suggests that males and females are equally represented in terms of viewership (Kathleen Moore 2011) and content creation (Lee Rainie, Joanna Brenner, and Kristen Purcell 2012). No matter which picture is most accurate, none accounts for the paucity of female YouTubers ranked in the top fifty most-subscribed channels.

A possible answer for the gender imbalance may be found in qualitative research and anecdotal reports on YouTube suggesting that although video-sharing environments potentially can create "a participatory model of culture" that includes "multiple voices and an expanded flow of information" (Douglas Kellner and Gooyong Kim 2009, 2–3), such an ideal is rarely achieved. Indeed, rather than operating democratically in ways that offer males and females similar opportunities, YouTube videos may be subject to "surveillance, judgment, and evaluation—practices signaling

consumer agency but simultaneously disciplining and constituting subjects" (Sarah Banet-Weiser 2011, 288). The literature suggests that much of this disciplining is sexist and gendered, affecting female participants to a greater extent than male participants (Azy Barak 2005; Jodi Biber, Dennis Doverspike, Daniel Baznik, Alana Cober, and Barbara A. Ritter 2002; Susan Herring, Kirk Job-Sluder, Rebecca Scheckler, and Sasha Barab 2002; Clancy Ratliff 2007). Still, despite observations of problematic interactions, scholars also regularly focus on users who participate in YouTube as a way of being heard and building community (Patricia G. Lange 2007b, 2007c; Roger Saul 2010). As a whole, then, the literature points to YouTube as a site that can potentially both reinscribe and challenge gender inequities.

In order to contribute to research on gender dynamics on YouTube, this study focuses on the most-subscribed female YouTuber, Jenna Mourey (whose YouTube channel is titled JennaMarbles). The study was conducted in two parts. The first part investigated the degree to which Mourey's YouTube reception could be understood as misogynistic and hostile. Comments posted to videos served as a primary measurement of community reaction to the content and performer. To target the effects of performer gender on reception, comments on Mourey's top-ten videos in February 2012 were compared to viewer comments on the top-ten videos of a male counterpart: Ryan Higa

Lindsey Wotanis and Laurie McMillan, "Performing Gender on YouTube: How Jenna Marbles Negotiates a Hostile Online Environment," *Feminist Media Studies*, Vol. 14, No. 6 (2014), pp. 912–928.

(whose YouTube channel is titled Nigahiga). Mourey and Higa are close in age (twenty-six and twenty-two years old, respectively), have similar comedic styles, and seem to target similar teen and young adult audiences. The categorization and analysis of comments on these two channels—one featuring a female and the other featuring a male performer—ultimately offered quantitative evidence that supports earlier findings of hostility toward women on YouTube. Evidence of misogyny directed toward Mourey, the most successful female YouTube performer, suggests the seriousness of hostility toward women on video-sharing sites and provides a framework for the next part of this analysis.

The second part of the study thus focused on the content and style of Mourey's video oeuvre in order to contribute to research on YouTubers who successfully negotiate a hostile environment. While Mourey's popularity is certainly not based on one factor, her tendency to perform gender extremes—both masculine and feminine roles—is an ongoing feature of her videos. Gender performances and parody in Mourey's videos operate at both implicit and explicit levels, allowing her to simultaneously critique and benefit from traditional gender roles. This two-part study of gender on YouTube thus both supports research describing harsh responses to women on video-sharing sites and offers one YouTube performer's strategy for achieving success in this environment.

Review of the Literature

YouTube as Hostile Space

Video-sharing takes place across the internet, and commercial sites such as Vimeo, NetFlix, and Hulu are on the rise. YouTube is a prime medium to study because it is currently the most active video-sharing site and because users not only view but also create and comment on video content. YouTube has grown exponentially since its launch in the spring of 2005, with more than eight hundred million unique users visiting the site each month (Statistics 2012). Paul Haridakis and Gary Hanson (2009) found that YouTube is a uniquely social medium (330), so it is not surprising that

YouTube has created "Community Guidelines" by which users are expected to abide. The guidelines defend free speech while addressing a range of problematic behaviors not permitted, including violence, abuse, hate speech, harassment, and sexually explicit content (YouTube Community Guidelines). Users can report instances of community guideline violations by flagging videos, which are then reviewed. When videos violate community guidelines, YouTube will remove them; repeat offenders are supposedly banned from the site.

However, YouTube does not explicitly address violations of community guidelines that occur in comments responding to videos. All users can flag comments as spam, but other community violations fall to individual channel owners to address. When posting a video, YouTubers may disable or screen comments; they can also delete comments posted to their videos. Still, even though many YouTube performers say they have been "emotionally hurt" by comments exhibiting "hating behavior," these same performers often choose not to moderate comments at all because more viewer interaction on a site is likely to increase popularity (Patricia G. Lange 2007a, 25). The result is that the site claims to have no tolerance for "hate speech" and other abusive behaviors, but many users still make comments that even to an untrained eye are violations of YouTube policies.

YouTube thus has a reputation as a site full of "abusive comments," a situation which is "exacerbated by anonymity (so that there are few disincentives to behave badly) and scale (so that it becomes difficult to keep up with policing and moderating comments)" (Jean Burgess and Joshua Green 2009, 96). Comments may be used as a tool to value some YouTube performers and condemn others. With such a self-governing system, it may be no surprise that, on YouTube, the most popular videos and channels represent "far less racial diversity than broadcast network television" (John McMurria 2006). While some "minority content . . . circulates on YouTube" and *may* reach a niche audience, "there's little or no chance that such content will reach a larger viewership" (Henry Jenkins 2009, 124).

YouTube performers may be targeted not only on the basis of race and other social markers but also in terms of gender. Awareness of women being harassed on vlogs has prompted the question, "Is this new technology producing new social relations—or a rerun of old-style social relations with which we are all too familiar?" (Toby Miller 2009, 427). As Herring et al. (2002), Molyneaux et al. (2008), and Ratliff (2007) show, gender often plays a role in social dynamics on YouTube. For example, in her research on videos featuring teen and tween girls, Banet-Weiser (2011) found that the young performers "are judged and gain value according to how well the girls producing [the videos] fit normative standards of femininity" (288–289). Comments thus police the behavior and representation of girls in terms of gendered norms. Such reception is not confined to the videos of young girls, but, rather, "sexist and often abusive comments" are a part of YouTube culture—so commonplace that even "prominent female YouTubers have to contend with" such reception (Burgess and Green 2009, 96).

Danielle Keats Citron (2009) finds that the public tends to trivialize the harm that "cyber gender harassment" can inflict. Often victims are portrayed "as overly sensitive complainers" while those inflicting harassment are treated "as juvenile pranksters" (Citron 2009, 375–376). Other times the problem is minimized because people believe it is simply part of the online world that "victims can ignore or defeat with counterspeech," advancing the argument that those who are unable to deal with the problem should just abandon online interactions (Citron 2009, 375–376). Such sentiments end up "discouraging women from reporting cyber gender harassment and preventing law enforcement from pursuing cyber-harassment complaints" (375–376). Furthermore, such harassment can have deep and long-lasting effects on women, and in many ways shut them out of online communities:

> [Cyber gender harassment] discourages them from writing and earning a living online. It interferes with their professional lives. It raises their vulnerability to offline sexual violence. It brands them as incompetent workers and inferior sexual objects. The harassment causes considerable emotional distress. Some women have committed suicide. (Citron 2009, 375)

Online harassment is likely to discourage women from creating video content that may be shared on YouTube, ultimately silencing voices that could benefit others.

YouTube Possibilities

Despite recognition of misogyny and other forms of hostile reception, scholars point to ways YouTube has been utilized by nonprofessionals to share viewpoints that may be excluded from traditional mainstream media outlets. To some degree, independent YouTubers gain popularity as they use the kinds of strategies that are outlined on YouTube's "Creator Playbook." This free online resource is designed to help content creators make decisions that will optimize views and subscriber-numbers on the video-sharing site. It includes advice on topics such as creating a coherent channel, using cross-promotion and social media to build a viewing community, and reaching out to viewers for feedback (Creator Playbook). Jenna Mourey, Ryan Higa, and other YouTube performers who have achieved high numbers of subscribers tend to utilize such strategies, though the success of Mourey and Higa came before the Playbook was first published in 2011.

As helpful as the Creator Playbook may be in detailing strategies connected with channel success, it does not provide suggestions for content creators who are subjected to a hostile or threatening reception through viewer comments. The guide also does not acknowledge that women or members of other social groups facing offline social injustices may need advice about handling online interactions where such injustices may be mirrored or exacerbated. In other words, the Creator Playbook treats YouTube performers as if they all have equal opportunities for success, even though qualitative studies—as well as the list of most-subscribed channels—suggest that this is not the case.

In considering useful strategies for women and others facing a hostile reception on YouTube, then, it is necessary to look beyond the general advice offered in the Creator Playbook. However, most of the literature focusing on the use of YouTube to challenge social hierarchies focuses on content creators whose impact is limited, with the scholarship itself aiming to draw attention to YouTube content that is not widely viewed. Among these studies, scholars note challenges to dominant paradigms of masculinity (Peter Lehman 2007), debates about gender in Islam from Muslim and non-Muslim women (Farida Vis, Liesbet Van Zoonen, and Sabina Mihelj 2011), the use of intimacy to promote social change (Lange 2007c), and media production by Black teen girls to negotiate their identities (Carla E. Stokes 2010). While the positive impact of even limited viewership of such videos should not be minimized, these types of studies are not able to offer insights about successfully negotiating hostile reception in ways that are likely to address the gender imbalance on the list of most-subscribed YouTubers.

The most helpful study of a YouTube performer who has been successful in terms of views and subscriptions despite a somewhat marginal social position is Saul's (2010) study of KevJumba. A Chinese American teenage YouTuber who often receives racist comments on his videos, KevJumba uses parody to skillfully manage negative comments. However, Saul points out that in doing so, KevJumba "sometimes seems to paradoxically reinscribe the marginalizing discourses of adolescence that he otherwise skillfully contests" (470). While Saul's study addresses ethnicity rather than gender issues, his findings complement studies of performance and parody in feminist circles.

Attention to gender performance and parody is rooted in Judith Butler's landmark text, *Gender Trouble: Feminism and the Subversion of Identity* (1990). Butler argues that feminists should not attempt to find "a point of view outside of constructed identities" (187); instead, feminists should "locate strategies of subversive repetition enabled by those constructions" (188) in order to contest problematic markers of gendered identity. In other words, repetition and parody can be strategically used to disrupt normative gender roles. Such work is important, for as Judith Butler points out in

Undoing Gender (2004), "a normative conception of gender can undo one's personhood" (1). Parody has the potential to challenge normative conceptions, as parody "seeks to transform its audience's consciousness so that it can no longer view the object of parody in the same way ever again" (Susan Burgess 2011, 130).

Butler's ideas of performativity and parody have been extended (Judith Halberstam 1998; Carrie Paechter 2010) and applied, especially in the analysis of pop culture icons such as Madonna and Lady Gaga (Banet-Weiser 2011; Alexander Cho 2009; Alyx Vesey 2009). In such analyses, researchers find varying degrees of success whereby performers help their own voices to be heard by operating within dominant paradigms, while they also promote positive social change by exaggerating—and thus challenging—accepted norms. These performance strategies highlight the way a person may be "constituted by norms and dependent on them" while also trying "to live in ways that maintain a critical and transformative relation to" these norms (Butler 2004, 4).

Altogether, then, research that offers useful strategies for negotiating a hostile YouTube environment while simultaneously increasing viewership and making a potentially positive impact is limited. Resources such as the Creator Playbook offer a general overview of useful strategies without considering barriers to success that content creators from certain social groups might encounter. Scholarship on videos that feature performers from marginalized groups, on the other hand, rarely include those with large viewership. The exception is a study of KevJumba, a YouTuber from a marginalized group who encounters hostility and yet has gained a large viewership. KevJumba's approach is connected to feminist articulations of performance and parody. That strategy is the most fruitful context for examining the work of Jenna Mourey and her ability to rise to the top of the YouTube rankings despite the negative feedback female performers tend to receive on YouTube.

About Jenna Marbles

"She has more Facebook fans than Jennifer Lawrence, more Twitter followers than Fox News and more Instagram friends than Oprah" (Amy O'Leary 2013). At the time the data for this research were collected (February 2012), "Jenna Marbles'" channel ranked number one on the list of most-subscribed female YouTube channels and number ten (and the only female channel) on the list of the fifty most-subscribed YouTube channels (VidStatsX). The performer's real name is Jenna Mourey; she is a twenty-six-year-old native of Rochester, NY, who currently resides in California. She earned a Master's degree in sports psychology from Boston University.

Mourey joined YouTube on February 16, 2010 and in three short years has been labeled "the woman with 1 billion clicks" by *The New York Times* (O'Leary 2013). Her first video—a short silent "film" about her now-famous dog "Marbles"—is nothing like her current, more popular videos, which often feature Mourey in front of her camera, providing commentary on or parody of various topics such as relationships, social behavior, and popular culture. For example, Mourey's first viral video, "How to trick people into thinking you're good looking," is a "mock-torial" for women about how to groom themselves. The video has had more than fifty-one million views.

Mourey has produced more than 145 videos, the majority of which resemble her very first viral video. She has amassed millions of subscribers—8,795,816 as of May 15, 2013 (quadruple the number of subscribers since the time of the data collection in February 2012)—and she has more than one billion video views. And, those numbers rise rapidly and earn Mourey a pay day. Because she has monetized her channel, allowing advertising on her videos, sources estimate that Mourey may have earned anywhere from $500,000 to $1 million since she joined YouTube (iJaredTV). These figures do not include income Mourey has generated from the sale of JennaMarbles Merch, products such as tee shirts associated with her channel.

This success has transformed Mourey into an "American entertainer and YouTube personality" (Jenna Marbles). She has been featured in articles by ABC News (Andrea Canning 2011) and *The New York Times* (Jennifer Conlin 2011; O'Leary 2013). She's also professionalizing "to handle the deluge

of endorsement requests and fan mail," with recent hires including "a personal assistant, a business manager, her mother, and a soon-to-be-hired chief technical officer" (O'Leary 2013). Currently, Mourey uploads a new video to her YouTube channel every Wednesday.

About Ryan Higa

In order to evaluate the effect of gender on viewer comments, comparing Mourey's comments with a similar male YouTube performer was important. Ryan Higa was the most appropriate match. Higa joined YouTube in 2006 and started the channel "Nigahiga" with friends Sean Fujiyoshi, Tim Enos, and Tarynn Nago (Ryan Higa a). According to Higa, the name of the channel has Japanese origins; "niga" means "rant" in Mandarin (Tonya TKO 2008). At the time the data for this research were collected (February 2012), "Nigahiga" ranked number two on the list of most-subscribed YouTube channels (VidStatsX). Unlike Mourey, Higa has two YouTube channels. On "Nigahiga," Higa posts videos on a variety of topics that are comedic in nature and often provide pop-culture parody. On "HigaTV," which he launched in 2011 as his "personal YouTube channel," Higa posts a variety of "behind-the-scenes" and "bloopers" footage compiled in the making of the videos posted to "Nigahiga." For the purpose of this study, researchers analyzed videos and comments from Higa's primary (and more popular) channel, "Nigahiga."

Higa was born in Hilo, Hawaii on June 6, 1990. The twenty-two-year-old YouTuber dropped out of college at UNLV, with his parents' blessing, to pursue his burgeoning YouTube success (Nigahiga 2013). Though many of his videos feature him solo, plenty of others include collaborations with friends and other YouTube stars, including KevJumba.

Higa has published 152 videos on "Nigahiga," where he also has amassed 8,051,136 subscribers as of April 2013, with more than 1.4 billion video views. "HigaTV," where Higa has published only thirty-eight videos as of May 2013, is newer and far less popular, with just more than a million subscribers and fifty-three million video views. Like Mourey, Higa sells merchandise and has monetized

Types of Comments	Jenna Mourey's Videos N = 919	Ryan Higa's Videos N = 888
Critical/Hostile comments (total)	18%	4%
content or personality	9%	3%
sexist/racist or sexually aggressive	9%	1%
Supportive comments (total)	82%	96%
content or personality	75%	94%
physical appearance	7%	2%

Figure 1. Comment Results

his site, earning a paycheck for every click on his videos. In addition, Higa has made appearances on several television and web series (Ryan Higa b), including SupahNinjas on Nickelodeon. . . .

Findings

Mourey Receives More Critical/Hostile Comments Than Higa

The majority of responses to the videos of both Ryan Higa and Jenna Mourey are supportive (96 percent and 82 percent, respectively). However, Mourey receives critical/hostile feedback more than four times as often as Higa (4 percent for Higa, 18 percent for Mourey) (see Figure 1).

Furthermore, the kind of critical/hostile feedback and the kind of supportive feedback differ for the two performers. Of the 4 percent critical/hostile feedback Ryan Higa receives, 3 percent of the comments focus on the video content or on Higa's personality. Most of these responses come from viewers who are offended by Higa's videos. In one of his top-ten videos, "How to be Emo," Higa parodies emo lifestyles, which some viewers deem offensive. For example, one fan responds, "this is the only video of yours that i don't like. i'm a self-harmer, and it's really offensive" [sic] (yoursexytomato). Similarly, in a video that uses song lyrics to parody a conversation leading to domestic violence between Chris Brown and Rihanna, the critical comments tend to focus on domestic violence being a serious issue and not an appropriate subject for humor.

The other 1 percent of critical/hostile feedback Higa receives is categorized as racist. A Hawaiian of mixed descent, Higa has Asian features and a distinct accent. A typical racist comment is "Why the fuck are you famous? Your english is bad just like ur acting . . ." [sic] (Steelheartftw). Such comments suggest that even the most popular YouTube performers are subject to harsh and inappropriate responses from viewers at times.

In comparison, Mourey's critical/hostile feedback is not only more common but also more often includes hater remarks and inappropriate sexual comments. Half of Mourey's critical/hostile feedback focuses on her video content or personality, while the other half includes sexually explicit or aggressive comments. Typical examples of hater feedback on Mourey's videos include, "No even remotely funny. What is more pathetic is that people found humor in it" [sic] (yankee9123) and "she's not much to look at and she's not even funny" (slickrickyy69). Mourey's viewers are unlike Higa's viewers in that they do not seem to be offended by her videos.

Comments categorized as sexually explicit are distinct from hater comments because hater feedback argues that the performer offers nothing of value at all. Sexually explicit feedback, on the other hand, suggests that the value of the performer is in her status as a sexual object or potential sexual partner for the viewer, effectively ignoring the content of the video performance and the personality of the YouTube performer.

This relegation of the YouTube performer to the domain of sexual object is what makes such feedback critical and hostile. An example of a less aggressive comment is: "JennaMarbles, why tan or use self tanner when you can get some color inside of you" (DarkLascivious). A slightly more aggressive comment is "I'd like to grind my cock against you ass . . ." [sic]. Some of the sexually explicit comments are directed to other (male) viewers rather than addressing Mourey, such as "any guy on here not wanna bang the hell outta her?" (nocupsinvan). Whether the sexually explicit comments speak to Mourey or *about* Mourey, the effect is to objectify her. Higa does not receive *any* comments in this vein. While it might be argued that the racist comments directed at Higa are similar to the sexual comments responding to Mourey's videos, the numbers are much greater for Mourey, signaling a more hostile reception.

While both performers receive a lot of positive feedback on the content of their videos and their personalities, 7 percent of the commentary directed at Mourey focuses on her physical appearance in complimentary ways, while only 2 percent of the commentary about Higa compliments his physical appearance. In Higa's case, positive comments about his physical appearance are most likely to appear on his Twilight spoof because he appears as a "hot vampire."

Overall, as top YouTube performers, both Higa and Mourey receive an overwhelming amount of positive feedback. Still, the critical/hostile responses they receive differ greatly in amount and type: Mourey receives more critical/hostile feedback, and this feedback tends to consist of hater commentary and explicit sexual remarks.

Videos Successfully Employ Performance Strategies

Despite the fair amount of critical/hostile comments she typically receives, Mourey continues to post videos to her channel each week, and her popularity continues to grow. In her videos, which are usually composed of social commentary or parody, Mourey employs a variety of performance strategies that mock traditional gender roles and stereotypes yet simultaneously reinforce them.

Mourey mocks traditional gender roles and stereotypes through her use of explicit gender performance, which includes female and male varieties. Explicit gender performance here is understood to mean exaggerated examples of gendered behavior that are performed purposefully and directly labeled (often in the videos' titles) by

Mourey as representing "girl" or "boy" behaviors. For instance, in her top-ten videos (See Appendix 1), Mourey explicitly performs gender in seven of the videos analyzed. One of these parodies "boy" behavior ("What Boys Do on the Internet"), while the other six explicit performances of gender focus on "girl" behavior in various settings or situations.

While Mourey's parodies mock gender stereotypes, she often employs them to her own advantage. In "How To Get Ready For A Date," Mourey mocks women who change their appearance and behavior—in essence, objectifying themselves—to win over a potential mate. Yet, to demonstrate her point, Mourey objectifies herself by wearing a tight, pink dress with black high heels and using lots of makeup and accessories, thus embodying the very stereotype she is trying to dispel. In this way, she is making her desired point yet also creating a situation that draws in potential viewers through her use of a "sexy girl" or objectified appearance.

In other videos, like "What Girls Do In The Car" and "What Girls Do On The Internet," Mourey performs a skit in which she plays the role of the "every girl" and parodies how she behaves in these varying situations. In this way, she is drawing on what might be considered normative female behaviors and using them in performative ways that parody such conventions. For example, she refers to the stereotype that women are bad drivers when she says, "I almost hit a cone," in "What Girls Do In The Car." In the same video, she applies lipstick while looking in the rearview mirror and saying in a sing-song voice to herself, "touchy-upy, touchy-upy." In such instances, Mourey fits Butler's (1990) suggestion that extreme gender performances tend to reveal everyday ways that gender performance occurs.

In "What Girls Do On The Internet," Mourey refers to women's tendencies to self-deprecate. As she pretends to look at a website on her computer, she says, in voiceover, "Oh, look at that girl's butt. Her butt looks so good. Why can't my butt look like that?" Later in the video, she revisits the subject when her character gets hungry. "I'm so hungry. Oh, I want a cake. No, no, no. Think of your butt. Think of your butt," her character's conscience mutters.

Mourey not only embodies "femaleness" in her appearance, but also in her manner of speech and behavior in these two parody scenarios, which highlight many of the social and cultural challenges women deal with daily. In these examples, those challenges include dealing with perceptions about female intelligence and driving ability as well as negotiating ideas of body image and beauty.

Mourey also performs male gender explicitly in videos like "What Boys Do On The Internet" and also "What Boys Do In The Car" (though the latter was not in her top ten as of February 2012). In these videos, Mourey ties up her long, blonde hair and hides it beneath a baseball cap. She dresses in male attire and paints a curly black mustache on her face. She talks in a more masculine voice and employs mannerisms and speech patterns that could be considered "typical," if not exaggerated, behaviors of men. For example, in "What Boys Do On The Internet," Mourey imitates a man as he surfs the web, looking for sports statistics on ESPN.com first, then quickly making his way to sites containing pornography, at which point Mourey proceeds to simulate male masturbation. In this way, she also serves to highlight male cultural stereotypes as understood through a female perspective.

Yet, beyond these examples of overt gendered performance, Mourey also employs implicit masculine and feminine characteristics and behaviors in almost every one of her videos. Implicit gender performance refers to patterns of speech, behavior, and appearance that are not directly labeled as male or female conventions.

Implicit gender performance is first noticeable in an introductory video screen, which Mourey has used to brand her videos since March 30, 2011. In this introduction, Mourey is seen posing in football pads with a bare midriff, her long blonde hair worn down, and eye black under her eyes. Right from the start, Mourey is projecting an objectified, sexual appeal while simultaneously appearing as "tough" or "masculine" by her chosen attire (and lack thereof).

Furthermore, Mourey typically has a "potty mouth." She frequently uses foul language and sometimes, in doing so, uses an elevated volume of speech. Mourey has roots in Rochester and Boston, and while she does not use a pronounced accent from either of these locations, she tends to employ the "tough guy" manner of speech that might be considered typical or representative of men in these northeastern cities.

Mourey also frequently uses implicit female performance. Mourey almost always appears in full makeup in her videos and her hair is usually combed neatly. Exceptions to this sometime include videos when she is engaging in parody and purposefully manipulating her appearance to suit the skit, as in "What Girls Do In The Bathroom In The Morning," which is not included in the top-ten category. She also frequently wears low-cut tops, and is usually shown only from the waist up in the video frame; such framing highlights her physical appearance.

Additionally, at the end of nearly every video, Mourey invites viewers to subscribe to her channel, where she "puts out new videos every Wednesday . . . yeah!" She says this to viewers in a very feminine, high-pitched, baby-talk voice. She also tends to speak to her dogs, Marbles and Kermit, using this voice whenever they appear in the videos. This kind of speech is often linked to women and is representative of female gender performance.

Discussion

Mourey receives more critical/hostile feedback than Higa. Furthermore, the *kind* of feedback differs. Mourey receives more hater commentary. Both critical/hostile and supportive feedback on Mourey's videos regularly objectify her, with the critical/hostile feedback characterized by sexually explicit and aggressive comments and the supportive feedback consisting of compliments regarding Mourey's physical appearance. The kind of harassment that many researchers note in online environments is thus evident when viewer responses to Mourey's and Higa's videos are compared.

Some of these differences might be attributed to the varying content of Mourey's and Higa's YouTube performances. Mourey discusses gender roles and draws direct attention to her body and appearance more often than Higa, which some might argue accounts for the difference in feedback. However, this content difference should not lead to the hater feedback directed at Mourey; it is a fallacy to assume that drawing attention to the body is an invitation for sexually aggressive comments. Even when considering the content differences in Mourey's and Higa's videos, then, analysis of the comments responding to their videos shows that hostile and objectifying comments tend to be more plentiful for Mourey. These reception differences seem connected to the gender of the YouTube performers.

In response to this environment, Mourey's use of gender performance and parody works to her advantage, especially when she executes such performance explicitly; doing so renders her akin to a character. Her on-screen behaviors, mode of dress, style and cadence of speech, and video content have become patterned over time and therefore expected by viewers in much the same way that audiences expect well-developed characters in other popular media to act in each new performance. These performance strategies allow Mourey to trademark herself; when she breaks from the mold, viewers often make comments about the fact that she has strayed from her typical performance.

Though Mourey appears to be savvy in her execution of each style of gendered performance, she still falls into the traps of traditional gender norms. She appeals to viewers by presenting herself in a very feminine, often objectified, manner even in the instances where she is rebuking the norm with her parodies. The fact that her videos receive more sexually-explicit comments than those of Higa suggests that many viewers watch her videos simply to gaze (Laura Mulvey 1975). This suggests that women on YouTube are treated in much the same way as women in other media platforms (Jennifer Siebel Newsom 2011), raising the question of whether YouTube is suited to women seeking to have their voices heard.

Conclusions

This study of gender in the YouTube environment supports research describing harsh responses to women in online venues (Barak 2005; Biber et al. 2002; Citron 2009; Herring et al. 2002; Ratliff 2007) and offers one YouTube performer's approach to sharing her own voice within this environment; the success of her gendered performance allows Mourey to continue critiquing culture through the production of YouTube videos, while earning a paycheck in the process.

Our findings show that the top female YouTuber receives more negative responses to her videos than her male counterpart. These responses, some of which have a harshly critical or sexually-aggressive tone, create a hostile environment within which Mourey and other members of non-dominant groups operate. Mourey successfully uses performance strategies to negotiate a hostile online environment and, as a result, is meeting with social and financial success. She utilizes both explicit and implicit male and female behaviors in her videos to attract and keep audiences comprising men and women. Her performance serves as a means to capitalize on cultural norms of gender while simultaneously critiquing them.

YouTube and other social media platforms are fertile ground for gender studies and can teach us about recognizing hostile online environments, addressing cyber gender harassment, and coping with both. Mourey provides one example of how women can use gender performance strategies to their advantage to achieve success within video-sharing environments. Future studies of other women like her can suggest additional strategies women can employ to their advantage on YouTube and other social media platforms.

Furthermore, the gender imbalance on YouTube, with only 18 percent of the top most-subscribed channels in February 2012 featuring females, mirrors the representation of women in leadership roles across professional realms, including politics, corporate settings, the entertainment industry, and education (Leslie Bennetts 2012; Martha M. Lauzen 2012; Jennifer E. Manning and Colleen J. Shogan 2012; Rachel Soares, Baye Cobb, Ellen Lebow, Hannah Winsten, Veronica Wojnas, and Allyson Regis 2011; "Women CEOs" 2011). Such consistent imbalances suggest widespread issues. As a space consisting of videos and written text, YouTube lends itself to direct textual analysis that is more difficult when studying gender in various professional contexts. However, future research connecting gender issues across online and offline contexts may be most productive in identifying strategies and interventions that encourage female leadership and the inclusion of diverse voices in professional and popular realms.

References

Banet-Weiser, Sarah. 2011. "Branding the Post-feminist Self: Girls' Video Production and YouTube." In *Mediated Girlhoods: New Explorations of Girls' Media Culture,* edited by Mary Celest Kearney, 277–294. New York: Peter Lang.

Barak, Azy. 2005. "Sexual Harassment on the Internet." *Social Science Computer Review* 23 (1): 77–92.

Bennetts, Leslie. 2012. "Women and the Leadership Gap." *The Daily Beast,* May 5. http://www.thedailybeast.com/newsweek/2012/03/04/the-stubbom-gender-gap.html

Biber, Jodi, Dennis Doverspike, Daniel Baznik, Alana Cober, and Barbara A. Ritter. 2002. "Sexual Harassment in Online Communications: Effects of Gender and Discourse Medium." *Cyber-Psychology & Behavior* 5 (1): 33–42.

Burgess, Jean, and Joshua Green. 2009. *YouTube: Online Video and Participatory Culture.* Cambridge: Polity.

Burgess, Susan. 2011. "YouTube on Masculinity and the Founding Fathers: Constitutionalism 2.0." *Political Research Quarterly* 64 (1): 120–131.

Butler, Judith. 1990. *Gender Trouble: Feminism and the Subversion of Identity.* New York: Routledge.

Butler, Judith. 2004. *Undoing Gender.* New York: Routledge.

Canning, Andrea. 16 Aug. 2011. "The Anti-dirty Dance: Teens Say No to Grinding." *ABC News,* http://abcnews.go.com/US/jenna-marbles-anti-dirty-dance-teens-grinding/story?id=14314828#.UFzchoJXGqwc

Chappell, Brian. 31 July. 2012. "2012 Social Network Analysis Report: Demographic, Geographic and Search Data Revealed." *Ignite Social Media,* http://www.ignitesocialmedia.com/social-media-stats/2012-social-network-analysis-report/#Youtube

Cho, Alexander. 7 Aug. 2009. "Lady Gaga, Balls-out: Recuperating Queer Performativity." *Flow,* 10. http://flowtv.org/2009/08/lady-gaga-balls-out-recuperating-queer-performativityalexandercho-flow-staff/

Citron, Danielle Keats. 2009. "Law's Expressive Value in Combating Cyber Gender Harassment." *Michigan Law Review* 108: 373–415.

Conlin, Jennifer. 2011. "Rendering Grinders Toothless." *New York Times,* August 12. http://www.nytimes.com/2011/08/14/fashion/with-grinding-an-unwanted-advance-at-the-dance.html?_=1&adxnnl=1&adxnnlx=1348262989-knKV6ottVwlagH/obERpCg&

Creator Playbook. n.d. *YouTube,* https://www.youtube.com/yt/playbook/

Halberstam, Judith. 1998. *Female Masculinity.* Durham, NC: Duke University Press.

Haridakis, Paul, and Gary Hanson. 2009. "Social Interaction and Co-viewing with YouTube: Blending Mass Communication Reception and Social Connection." *Journal of Broadcasting & Electronic Media* 53 (2): 317–335.

Herring, Susan, Kirk Job-Sluder, Rebecca Scheckler, and Sasha Barab. 2002. "Searching for Safety Online: Managing "Trolling" in a Feminist Forum." *The Information Society* 18 (5): 371–384.

iJaredTV. 29 June. 2012. "How Much Money Does JennaMarbles Make on YouTube 2012." http://www.youtube.com/watch?v=jk2IQ10sNPU

Jenkins, Henry. 2009. "What Happened before YouTube." In *YouTube: Online Video and Participatory Culture,* edited by Jean Burgess and Joshua Green, 109–125. Cambridge: Polity.

Jenna Marbles. n.d. *Wikipedia.com,* http://en.wikipedia.org/wiki/Jenna_Marbles

Kellner, Douglas, and Gooyong Kim. 2009. "YouTube, Critical Pedagogy, and Media Activism: An Articulation." http://pages.gseis.ucla.edu/faculty/kellner/essays/2009_Kellner-Kim_UT_Politics%20and%20PedagogyFINAL%20April%2009.pdf

Lange, Patricia G. 31 March 2007a. "Commenting on Comments: Investigating Responses to Antagonism on YouTube." *Society for Applied Anthropology Conference,* http://sfaapodcasts.files.wordpress.com/2007/04/update-apr-17-lange-sfaa-paper-2007.pdf

Lange, Patricia G. 2007b. "Publicly Private and Privately Public: Social Networking on YouTube." *Journal of Computer-Mediated Communication* 13 (1): 361–380.

Lange, Patricia G. 2007c. "The Vulnerable Video Blogger: Promoting Social Change through Intimacy." *The Scholar and Feminist Online* 5 (2): 1–5. http://sfonline.barnard.edu/blogs/lange_01.htm

Lauzen, Martha M. 2012. "The Celluloid Ceiling: Behind-the-Scenes Employment of Women on the Top 250 Films of 2011." *Center for the Study of Women in Television and Film,* http://womenintvfilm.sdsu.edu/files/2011_Celluloid_Ceiling_Exec_Summ.pdf

Lehman, Peter. 2007. "You and Voyeurweb: Illustrating the Shifting Representation of the Penis on the Internet with User-generated Content." *Cinema Journal* 46 (4): 108–116.

Lindlof, Thomas R., and Bryan C. Taylor. 2002. *Qualitative Communication Research Methods.* 2nd ed. Thousand Oaks, CA: Sage.

Madden, Mary. 2009. "The Audience for Online Video Sharing Sites Shoots Up." *Pew Internet,* http://www.pewinternet.org/Reports/2009/13-The-Audience-for-Online-VideoSharing-Sites-Shoots-Up/2-Demographics/Online-video-viewing-has-grown-across-all-age-groups.aspx

Manning, Jennifer E., and Colleen J. Shogan. 26 Nov. 2012. "Women in the United States Congress, 1917–2012." *Congressional Research Service.* http://www.fas.org/sgp/crs/misc/RL30261.pdf

Mcmurria, John. 2006. "The YouTube Community." *Flow TV,* 5. http://flowtv.org/2006/10/the-youtube-community-2/

Miller, Toby. 2009. "Cybertarians of the World Unite: You Have Nothing to Lose But Your Tubes!" In *The YouTube Reader,* edited by Pelle Snickars, and Patrick Vonderau, 424–440. Stockholm: National Library of Sweden.

Molyneaux, Heather, Susan O'Donnell, Kerri Gibson, and Janice Singer. 2008. "Exploring the Gender Divide on YouTube: An Analysis of the Creation and Reception of Vlogs." *American Communication Journal* 10 (2): 1–14.

Moore, Kathleen. 26 July 2011. "71% of Online Adults Now Use Video-sharing Sites." *Pew Internet,* http://www.ignitesocialmedia.com/social-media-stats/2012-social-network-analysis-report/#Youtube

Mulvey, Laura. 1975. "Visual Pleasure and Narrative Cinema." *Screen* 16 (3): 6–18.

Newsom, Jennifer Siebel. 2011. *Miss Representation,* Film.

Nigahiga. 10 April. 2013. "Draw My Life—Ryan Higa." *YouTube,* http://www.youtube.com/watch?v=KPmoDYayoLE

O'Leary, Amy. 12 April 2013. "The Woman with 1 Billion Clicks, Jenna Marbles." *The New York Times,* http://www.nytimes.com/2013/04/14/fashion/jennamarbles.html?pagewanted=all&_r=0

Paechter, Carrie. 2010. "Tomboys and Girly-girls: Embodied Femininities in Primary Schools." *Discourse: Studies in the Cultural Politics of Education* 31 (2): 221–235.

Rainie, Lee, Joanna Brenner, and Kristen Purcell. 13 Sept 2012. "Photos and Videos as Social Currency Online." *Pew Internet,* http://www.ignitesocialmedia.com/social-media-stats/2012-social-network-analysis-report/#Youtube

Ratliff, Clancy. 2007. "Attracting Readers: Sex and Audience in the Blogosphere." *The Scholar and Feminist Online* 5 (2): 1–4.

Ryan Higa. (a) IMBD. http://www.imdb.com/name/nm3090514/

Ryan Higa. (b) Wikipedia. http://en.wikipedia.org/wiki/Ryan_Higa

Saul, Roger. 2010. "KevJumba and the Adolescence of YouTube." *Educational Studies* 46 (5): 457–477.

Soares, Rachel, Baye Cobb, Ellen Lebow, Hannah Winsten, Veronica Wojnas, and Allyson Regis. 2011. "2011 Catalyst Census: *Fortune* 500 Women Board Directors." *Catalyst,* http://www.catalyst.org/file/533/2011_fortune_500_census_wbd.pdf

Statistics. 2012. "YouTube." http://www.youtube.com/t/press_statistics

Stokes, Carla E. 2010. ""Get on My Level": How Black American Adolescent Girls Construct Identity and Negotiate Sexuality on the Internet." In *Girl Wide Web 2.0: Revisiting Girls, the Internet, and the Negotiation of Identity,* edited by Sharon R. Mazzarella, 45–67. New York: Peter Lang.

Tonya Tko. 30 Nov. 2008. "NigaHiga Explains Name, Happy Slip, Kev Jumba & TonyaTko -Amazing Asians vol 1." *YouTube,* http://www.youtube.com/watch?v=blAWuc-3_08#t=01m29s

Vesey, Alyx. 3 May. 2009. "Lady Gaga—Not Buying It." *Feminist Music Geek,* http://feministmusicgeek.com/2009/05/03/lady-gaga-not-buying-it/

Vidstatsx. n.d., http://vidstatsx.com/collage/top-100

Vis, Farida, Liesbet Van Zoonen, and Sabina Miheli. 2011. "Women Responding to the Anti-Islam Film Fitna: Voices and Acts of Citizenship on YouTube." *Feminist Review* 97 (1): 110–129.

Women CEOs. 2011. *CNN Money,* http://money.cnn.com/magazines/fortune/fortune500/2011/womenceos/

YouTube Community Guidelines. n.d., http://www.youtube.com/t/community_guidelines

Appendix 1: Jenna Marbles Top Ten Videos as of 2/4/2012

Jenna Marbles

YouTube: http://www.youtube.com/user/JennaMarbles/videos?sort=p&view = u

Facebook: http://www.facebook.com/pages/Jenna-Mourey/311917224927

Twitter: http://twitter.com/Jenna_Marbles

Blog: http://jennamarblesblog.com/

Joined YouTube: February 16, 2010

2,284,676 subscribers

340,469,769 video views

TABLE A1.

Ranking	Title of video	Number of views	Date posted	Length (min:sec)
1	"How To Trick People into Thinking You're Good Looking"	35,692,165	July 9, 2010	2:37
2	"How To Avoid Talking To People You Don't Want To Talk To"	18,218,246	February 15, 2011	2:47
3	"What I Would Have Done In Cancun"	14,007,416	March 9, 2011	5:42
4	"What Girls Do In The Car"	13,715,458	September 28, 2011	1:48
5	"What Girls Do On The Internet"	9,826,352	June 15, 2011	2:35
6	"How To Get Ready For A Date"	8,927,003	July 20, 2011	3:06
7	"How Lady Gaga Writes A Song"	8,898,805	July 21, 2010	2:08
8	"White Girls At The Club"	8,604,197	September 21, 2011	5:59
9	"What Nicki Minaj Wants In A Man"	8,484,291	May 20, 2011	2:40
10	"What Boys Do On The Internet"	7,876,804	June 22, 2011	2:22

Appendix 2: Nigahiga's Top Ten Videos as of 2/4/12

TABLE A2.

Ranking	Title of video	Number of views	Date posted	Length (min:sec)
1	"How To Be Gangster"	33,601,494	November 4, 2007	5:24
2	"The iPod Human"	32,967,451	November 10, 2007	1:53
3	"How To Be Ninja"	32,437,508	July 25, 2007	5:35
4	"Nice Guys"	30,437,508	May 31, 2011	2:50
5	"How To Be Emo"	28,503,041	November 24, 2007	4:54
6	"The ShamWOOHOO!"	23,940,026	April 10, 2009	0:47
7	"Why Chris Brown Beat Rihanna"	23,067,782	March 2, 2009	2:04
8	"Daily Life of Rustin Hieber"	19,895,287	February 22, 2011	4:56
9	"Movies In Minutes *Twilight*"	19,681,347	January 21, 2009	4:11
10	"The Ninja Glare"	19,122,513	August 14, 2008	3:47

PART III

Gendered Intimacies

"Man's love is of man's life a thing apart," wrote the British Romantic poet, Lord Byron. "'Tis woman's whole existence." Nowhere are the differences between women and men more pronounced than in our intimate lives, our experiences of love, friendship, and sexuality. It is in our intimate relationships that it so often feels like men and women are truly from different planets.

The very definitions of emotional intimacy bear the mark of gender. But there are signs of gender convergence. Women, it appears, find themselves more interested in pursuing explicitly sexual pleasures, despite their "Venutian" temperament that invariably links love and lust. Beth A. Quinn navigates that always-controversial gray zone between "girl-watching" and intrusive harassment in a way that enables us to understand better how street harassment is not designed to engage women but to intimidate them. Diane Felmlee and her colleagues examine the emerging transformation of friendship from the *Harry Met Sally* days. M. Paz Galupo and her colleagues look at friendship dynamics among transgendered people. And guys, it turns out, according to research by Peggy Giordano and her colleagues, are pretty committed to ideals of romantic love—still. Take that, Lord Byron. Thing apart, indeed.

Sexual Harassment and Masculinity: The Power and Meaning of "Girl Watching"

BETH A. QUINN

Confronted with complaints about sexual harassment or accounts in the media, some men claim that women are too sensitive or that they too often misinterpret men's intentions (Bernstein 1994; Buckwald 1993). In contrast, some women note with frustration that men just "don't get it" and lament the seeming inadequacy of sexual harassment policies (Conley 1991; Guccione 1992). Indeed, this ambiguity in defining acts of sexual harassment might be, as Cleveland and Kerst (1993) suggested, the most robust finding in sexual harassment research.

Using in-depth interviews with 43 employed men and women, this article examines a particular social practice—"girl watching"—as a means to understanding one way that these gender differences are produced. This analysis does not address the size or prevalence of these differences, nor does it present a direct comparison of men and women; this information is essential but well covered in the literature.[1] Instead, I follow Cleveland and Kerst's (1993) and Wood's (1998) suggestion that the question may best be unraveled by exploring how the "subject(ivities) of perpetrators, victims, and resistors of sexual harassment" are "discursively produced, reproduced, and altered" (Wood 1998, 28).

This article focuses on the subjectivities of the perpetrators of a disputable form of sexual harassment, "girl watching." The term refers to the act of men's sexually evaluating women, often in the company of other men. It may take the form of a verbal or gestural message of "check it out," boasts of sexual prowess, or explicit comments about a woman's body or imagined sexual acts. The target may be an individual woman or group of women or simply a photograph or other representation. The woman may be a stranger, coworker, supervisor, employee, or client. For the present analysis, girl watching within the workplace is centered.

The analysis is grounded in the work of masculinity scholars such as Connell (1987, 1995) in that it attempts to explain the subject positions of the interviewed men—not the abstract and genderless subjects of patriarchy but the gendered and privileged subjects embedded in this system. Since I am attempting to delineate the gendered worldviews of the interviewed men, I employ the term "girl watching," a phrase that reflects their language ("they watch girls").

I have chosen to center the analysis on girl watching within the workplace for two reasons. First, it appears to be fairly prevalent. For example, a survey of federal civil employees (U.S. Merit Systems Protection Board 1988) found that in the previous 24 months, 28 percent of the women surveyed had experienced "unwanted sexual looks or gestures," and 35 percent had experienced "unwanted sexual teasing, jokes, remarks, or questions." Second, girl watching is still often normalized and trivialized as only play, or "boys will be boys." A man watching girls—even in his workplace—is frequently accepted as a natural and commonplace activity, especially if he is in the presence of other men.[2] Indeed, it may be required (Hearn 1985). Thus, girl watching sits on

Beth A. Quinn, "Sexual Harassment and Masculinity: The Power and Meaning of 'Girl Watching,'" *Gender & Society*, Vol. 16, No. 3 (June 2002), pp. 386–402. Copyright © 2002 by Sociologists for Women in Society. Reprinted by permission of SAGE Publications.

the blurry edge between fun and harm, joking and harassment. An understanding of the process of identifying behavior as sexual harassment, or of rejecting this label, may be built on this ambiguity.

Girl watching has various forms and functions, depending on the context and the men involved. For example, it may be used by men as a directed act of power against a particular woman or women. In this, girl watching—at least in the workplace—is most clearly identified as harassing by both men and women. I am most interested, however, in the form where it is characterized as only play. This type is more obliquely motivated and, as I will argue, functions as a game men play to build shared masculine identities and social relations.

Multiple and contradictory subject positions are also evidenced in girl watching, most notably that between the gazing man and the woman he watches. Drawing on Michael Schwalbe's (1992) analysis of empathy and the formation of masculine identities, I argue that girl watching is premised on the obfuscation of this multiplicity through the objectification of the woman watched and a suppression of empathy for her. In conclusion, the ways these elements operate to produce gender differences in interpreting sexual harassment and the implications for developing effective policies are discussed.

Previous Research

The question of how behavior is or is not labeled as sexual harassment has been studied primarily through experimental vignettes and surveys.[3] In both methods, participants evaluate either hypothetical scenarios or lists of behaviors, considering whether, for example, the behavior constitutes sexual harassment, which party is most at fault, and what consequences the act might engender. Researchers manipulate factors such as the level of "welcomeness" the target exhibits and the relationship of the actors (supervisor-employee, coworker-coworker).

Both methods consistently show that women are willing to define more acts as sexual harassment (Gutek, Morasch, and Cohen 1983; Padgitt

and Padgitt 1986; Powell 1986; York 1989; but see Stockdale and Vaux 1993) and are more likely to see situations as coercive (Garcia, Milano, and Quijano 1989). When asked who is more to blame in a particular scenario, men are more likely to blame, and less likely to empathize with, the victim (Jensen and Gutek 1982; Kenig and Ryan 1986). In terms of actual behaviors like girl watching, the U.S. Merit Systems Protection Board (1988) survey found that 81 percent of the women surveyed considered "uninvited sexually suggestive looks or gestures" from a supervisor to be sexual harassment. While the majority of men (68 percent) also defined it as such, significantly more men were willing to dismiss such behavior. Similarly, while 40 percent of the men would not consider the same behavior from a coworker to be harassing, more than three-quarters of the women would.

The most common explanation offered for these differences is gender role socialization. This conclusion is supported by the consistent finding that the more men and women adhere to traditional gender roles, the more likely they are to deny the harm in sexual harassment and to consider the behavior acceptable or at least normal (Gutek and Koss 1993; Malovich and Stake 1990; Murrell and Dietz-Uhler 1993; Popovich et al. 1992; Pryor 1987; Tagri and Hayes 1997). Men who hold predatory ideas about sexuality, who are more likely to believe rape myths, and who are more likely to self-report that they would rape under certain circumstances are less likely to see behaviors as harassing (Murrell and Dietz-Uhler 1993; Pryor 1987; Reilly et al. 1992).

These findings do not, however, adequately address the between-group differences. The more one is socialized into traditional notions of sex roles, the more likely it is for both men and women to view the behaviors as acceptable or at least unchangeable. The processes by which gender roles operate to produce these differences remain underexamined.

Some theorists argue that men are more likely to discount the harassing aspects of their behavior because of a culturally conditioned tendency to misperceive women's intentions. For example, Stockdale (1993, 96) argued that "patriarchal norms create a sexually aggressive belief system in some people more than others, and this belief system can lead to the propensity to misperceive." Gender differences in interpreting sexual harassment, then, may be the outcome of the acceptance of normative ideas about women's inscrutability and indirectness and men's role as sexual aggressors. Men see harmless flirtation or sexual interest rather than harassment because they misperceive women's intent and responses.

Stockdale's (1993) theory is promising but limited. First, while it may apply to actions such as repeatedly asking for dates and quid pro quo harassment,[4] it does not effectively explain motivations for more indirect actions, such as displaying pornography and girl watching. Second, it does not explain why some men are more likely to operate from these discourses of sexual aggression contributing to a propensity to misperceive.

Theoretical explanations that take into account the complexity and diversity of sexual harassing behaviors and their potentially multifaceted social etiologies are needed. An account of the processes by which these behaviors are produced and the active construction of their social meanings is necessary to unravel both between- and within-gender variations in behavior and interpretation. A fruitful framework from which to begin is an examination of masculine identities and the role of sexually harassing behaviors as a means to their production.

Method

I conducted 43 semistructured interviews with currently employed men and women between June 1994 and March 1995. Demographic characteristics of the participants are reported in Table 1. . . .

TABLE I. Participant Demographic Measures

Variable	Men		Women		Total	
	n	%	n	%	n	%
Student participants and referrals	6	33	12	67	18	42
Racial/ethnic minority	2	33	2	17	4	22
Mean age	27.2		35		32.5	
Married	3	50	3	25	6	33
Nontraditional job	1	17	4	33	5	28
Supervisor	0	0	6	50	6	33
Some college	6	100	12	100	18	100
Acme participants	12	48	13	52	25	58
Racial/ethnic minority	2	17	3	23	5	20
Mean age	42.3		34.6		38.6	
Married	9	75	7	54	16	64
Nontraditional job	0	0	4	31	4	16
Supervisor	3	25	2	15	5	20
Some college	9	75	9	69	18	72
All participants	18	42	25	58	43	100
Racial/ethnic minority	4	22	5	20	9	21
Mean age	37.8		34.9		36.2	
Married	12	67	10	40	22	51
Nontraditional job	1	6	8	32	9	21
Supervisor	3	17	8	32	11	26
Some college	15	83	21	84	36	84

Findings: Girl Watching as "Hommo-Sexuality"

[They] had a button on the computer that you pushed if there was a girl who came to the front counter.... It was a code and it said "BAFC"—Babe at Front Counter.... If the guy in the back looked up and saw a cute girl come in the station, he would hit this button for the other dispatcher to [come] see the cute girl.

—*Paula, police officer*

In its most serious form, girl watching operates as a targeted tactic of power. The men seem to want everyone—the targeted woman as well as coworkers, clients, and superiors—to know they are looking. The gaze demonstrates their right, as men, to sexually evaluate women. Through the gaze, the targeted woman is reduced to a sexual object, contradicting her other identities, such as that of competent worker or leader. This employment of the discourse of asymmetrical heterosexuality (i.e., the double standard) may trump a woman's formal organizational power, claims to professionalism, and organizational discourses of rationality (Collinson and Collinson 1989; Gardner 1995; Yount 1991).[5] As research on rape has demonstrated (Estrich 1987), calling attention to a woman's gendered sexuality can function to exclude recognition of her competence, rationality, trustworthiness, and even humanity. In contrast, the overt recognition of a man's (hetero)sexuality is normally compatible with other aspects of his identity; indeed, it is often required (Connell 1995; Hearn 1985). Thus, the power of sexuality is asymmetrical, in part, because being seen as sexual has different consequences for women and men.

But when they ogle, gawk, whistle and point, are men always so directly motivated to disempower their women colleagues? Is the target of the gaze also the intended audience? Consider, for example, this account told by Ed, a white, 29-year-old instrument technician.

When a group of guys goes to a bar or a nightclub and they try to be manly....A few of us always found [it] funny [when] a woman would walk by and a guy would be like, "I can have her." [pause] "Yeah, OK, we want to see it!" [laugh]

In his account—a fairly common one in men's discussions—the passing woman is simply a visual cue for their play. It seems clear that it is a game played by men for men; the woman's participation and awareness of her role seem fairly unimportant.

As Thorne (1993) reminded us, we should not be too quick to dismiss games as "only play." In her study of gender relations in elementary schools, Thorne found play to be a powerful form of gendered social action. One of its "clusters of meaning" most relevant here is that of "dramatic performance." In this, play functions as both a source of fun and a mechanism by which gendered identities, group boundaries, and power relations are (re)produced.

The metaphor of play was strong in Karl's comments. Karl, a white man in his early thirties who worked in a technical support role in the Acme engineering department, hoped to earn a degree in engineering. His frustration with his slow progress—which he attributed to the burdens of marriage and fatherhood—was evident throughout the interview. Karl saw himself as an undeserved outsider in his department and he seemed to delight in telling on the engineers.

Girl watching came up . . . Like many of the men I interviewed, his first reaction was to muse about premenstrual syndrome and clothes. When I inquired about the potential social effects of the transformation (by asking him, Would it "be easier dealing with the engineers or would it be harder?") he haltingly introduced the engineers' "game."

KARL: Some of the engineers here are very [pause] they're not very, how shall we say? [pause] What's the way I want to put this? They're not very, uh [pause] what's the word? Um. It escapes me.

RESEARCHER: Give me a hint?

KARL: They watch women but they're not very careful about getting caught.

RESEARCHER: Oh! Like they ogle?

KARL: Ogle or gaze or [pause] stare even, or [pause] generate a commotion of an unusual nature.

His initial discomfort in discussing the issue (with me, I presume) is evident in his excruciatingly formal and hesitant language. The aspect of play, however, came through clearly when I pushed him to describe what generating a commotion looked like: "'Oh! There goes so-and-so. Come and take a look! She's wearing this great outfit today!' Just like a schoolboy. They'll rush out of their offices and [cranes his neck] and check things out." That this is as a form of play was evident in Karl's boisterous tone and in his reference to schoolboys. This is not a case of an aggressive sexual appraising of a woman co-worker but a commotion created for the benefit of other men.

At Acme, several spatial factors facilitated this form of girl watching. First, the engineering department is designed as an open-plan office with partitions at shoulder height, offering a maze-like geography that encourages group play. As Karl explained, the partitions offer both the opportunity for sight and cover from being seen. Although its significance escaped me at the time, I was directly introduced to the spatial aspects of the engineers' game of girl watching during my first day on site at Acme. That day, John, the current human resources director, gave me a tour of the facilities, walking me through the departments and offering informal introductions. As we entered the design engineering section, a rhythm of heads emerged from its landscape of partitions, and movement started in our direction. I was definitely aware of being on display as several men gave me obvious once-overs.

Second, Acme's building features a grand stairway that connects the second floor—where the engineering department is located—with the lobby. The stairway is enclosed by glass walls, offering a bird's eye view to the main lobby and the movements of visitors and the receptionists (all women). Robert, a senior design engineer, specifically noted the importance of the glass walls in his discussion of the engineers' girl watching.

There's glass walls around the upstairs right here by the lobby. So when there's an attractive young female...someone will see the girl in the area and

they will go back and inform all the men in the area. "Go check it out." [laugh] So we'll walk over to the glass window, you know, and we'll see who's down there.

One day near the end of my stay at Acme, I was reminded of his story as I ventured into the first-floor reception area. Looking up, I saw Robert and another man standing at the top of the stairs watching and commenting on the women gathered around the receptionist's desk. When he saw me, Robert gave me a sheepish grin and disappeared from sight.

Producing Masculinity

I suggest that girl watching in this form functions simultaneously as a form of play and as a potentially powerful site of gendered social action. Its social significance lies in its power to form identities and relationships based on these common practices for, as Cockburn (1983, 123) has noted, "patriarchy is as much about relations between man and man as it is about relations between men and women." Girl watching works similarly to the sexual joking that Johnson (1988) suggested is a common way for heterosexual men to establish intimacy among themselves.

In particular, girl watching works as a dramatic performance played to other men, a means by which a certain type of masculinity is produced and heterosexual desire displayed. It is a means by which men assert a masculine identity to other men, in an ironic "hommo-sexual" practice of heterosexuality (Butler 1990).[6] As Connell (1995) and others (Butler 1990; West and Zimmerman 1987) have aptly noted, masculinity is not a static identity but rather one that must constantly be reclaimed. The content of any performance—and there are multiple forms—is influenced by a hegemonic notion of masculinity. When asked what "being a man" entailed, many of the men and women I interviewed triangulated toward notions of strength (if not in muscle, then in character and job performance), dominance, and a marked sexuality, overflowing and uncontrollable to some degree and natural to the male "species." Heterosexuality is required, for just as the label "girl" questions a man's claim to masculine power, so does the label "fag" (Hopkins 1992; Pronger 1992).

I asked Karl, for example, if he would consider his sons "good men" if they were gay. His response was laced with ambivalence; he noted only that the question was "a tough one."

The practice of girl watching is just that—a practice—one rehearsed and performed in everyday settings. This aspect of rehearsal was evident in my interview with Mike, a self-employed house painter who used to work construction. In locating himself as a born-again Christian, Mike recounted the girl watching of his fellow construction workers with contempt. Mike was particularly disturbed by a man who brought his young son to the job site one day. The boy was explicitly taught to catcall, a practice that included identifying the proper targets: women and effeminate men.

Girl watching, however, can be somewhat tenuous as a masculine practice. In their acknowledgment (to other men) of their supposed desire lies the possibility that in being too interested in women the players will be seen as mere schoolboys giggling in the playground. Taken too far, the practice undermines rather than supports a masculine performance. In Karl's discussion of girl watching, for example, he continually came back to the problem of men's not being careful about getting caught. He referred to a particular group of men who, though "their wives are [pause] very attractive—very much so," still "gawk like schoolboys." Likewise, Stephan explained that men who are obvious, who "undress [women] with their eyes" probably do so "because they don't get enough women in their lives. Supposedly." A man must be interested in women, but not too interested; they must show their (hetero)sexual interest, but not overly so, for this would be to admit that women have power over them.

The Role of Objectification and (Dis)Empathy

As a performance of heterosexuality among men, the targeted woman is primarily an object onto which men's homosocial sexuality is projected. The presence of a woman in any form—embodied, pictorial, or as an image conjured from words—is required, but her subjectivity and active participation are not. To be sure, given the ways the discourse of asymmetrical sexuality works, men's actions may result in similarly negative effects on the targeted woman as that of a more direct form of sexualization. The crucial difference is that the men's understanding of their actions differs. This difference is one key to understanding the ambiguity around interpreting harassing behavior.

When asked about the engineers' practice of neck craning, Robert grinned, saying nothing at first. After some initial discussion, I started to ask him if he thought women were aware of their game ("Do you think that the women who are walking by...?"). He interrupted, misreading my question. What resulted was a telling description of the core of the game:

> It depends. No. I don't know if they enjoy it. When I do it, if I do it, I'm not saying that I do. [big laugh]...If they do enjoy it, they don't say it. If they don't enjoy it—wait a minute, that didn't come out right. I don't know if they enjoy it or not [pause]; that's not the purpose of us popping our heads out.

Robert did not want to admit that women might not enjoy it ("that didn't come out right") but acknowledged that their feelings were irrelevant. Only subjects, not objects, take pleasure or are annoyed. If a woman did complain, Robert thought "the guys wouldn't know what to say." In her analysis of street harassment, Gardner (1995, 187) found a similar absence, in that "men's interpretations seldom mentioned a woman's reaction, either guessed at or observed."

The centrality of objectification was also apparent in comments made by José, a Hispanic man in his late 40s who worked in manufacturing. For José, the issue came up when he considered the topic of compliments. He initially claimed that women enjoy compliments more than men do. In reconsidering, he remembered girl watching and the importance of intent.

> There is [pause] a point where [pause] a woman can be admired by [pause] a pair of eyes, but we're talking about "that look." Where, you know, you're admiring her because she's dressed nice, she's got a nice figure, she's got nice legs.

But then you also have the other side. You have an animal who just seems to undress you with his eyes and he's just [pause], there's those kind of people out there too.

What is most interesting about this statement is that in making the distinction between merely admiring and an animal look that ravages, José switched subject position. He spoke in the second person when describing both forms of looking, but his consistency in grammar belies a switch in subjectivity: you (as a man) admire, and you (as a woman) are undressed with his eyes. When considering an appropriate, complimentary gaze, José described it from a man's point of view; the subject who experiences the inappropriate, violating look, however, is a woman. Thus, as in Robert's account, José acknowledged that there are potentially different meanings in the act for men and women. In particular, to be admired in a certain way is potentially demeaning for a woman through its objectification.

The switch in subject position was also evident in Karl's remarks. Karl mentioned girl watching while imagining himself as a woman in the gender reversal question. As he took the subject position of the woman watched rather than the man watching, his understanding of the act as a harmless game was destabilized. Rather than taking pleasure in being the object of such attention, Karl would take pains to avoid it.

So with these guys [if I were a woman], I would probably have to be very concerned about my attire in the lab. Because in a lot of cases, I'm working at a bench and I'm hunched over, in which case your shirt, for example, would open at the neckline, and I would just have to be concerned about that.

Thus, because the engineers girl watch, Karl feels that he would have to regulate his appearance if he were a woman, keeping the men from using him in their game of girl watching. When he considered the act from the point of view of a man, girl watching was simply a harmless antic and an act of appreciation. When he was forced to consider the subject position of a woman, however, girl watching was something to be avoided or at least carefully managed.

When asked to envision himself as a woman in his workplace, like many of the individuals I interviewed, Karl believed that he did not "know how to be a woman." Nonetheless, he produced an account that mirrored the stories of some of the women I interviewed. He knew the experience of girl watching could be quite different—in fact, threatening and potentially disempowering—for the woman who is its object. As such, the game was something to be avoided. In imagining themselves as women, the men remembered the practice of girl watching. None, however, were able to comfortably describe the game of girl watching from the perspective of a woman and maintain its (masculine) meaning as play.

In attempting to take up the subject position of a woman, these men are necessarily drawing on knowledge they already hold. If men simply "don't get it"—truly failing to see the harm in girl watching or other more serious acts of sexual harassment—then they should not be able to see this harm when envisioning themselves as women. What the interviews reveal is that many men—most of whom failed to see the harm of many acts that would constitute the hostile work environment form of sexual harassment—did in fact understand the harm of these acts when forced to consider the position of the targeted woman.

I suggest that the gender reversal scenario produced, in some men at least, a moment of empathy. Empathy, Schwalbe (1992) argued, requires two things. First, one must have some knowledge of the other's situation and feelings. Second, one must be motivated to take the position of the other. What the present research suggests is that gender differences in interpreting sexual harassment stem not so much from men's not getting it (a failure of the first element) but from a studied, often compulsory, lack of motivation to identify with women's experiences.

In his analysis of masculinity and empathy, Schwalbe (1992) argued that the requirements of masculinity necessitate a "narrowing of the moral self." Men learn that to effectively perform masculinity and to protect a masculine identity, they must, in many instances, ignore a woman's pain and obscure her viewpoint. Men fail to exhibit empathy with women because masculinity precludes them from taking the position of the feminine other, and men's moral stance vis-à-vis women is attenuated by this lack of empathy.

As a case study, Schwalbe (1992) considered the Thomas-Hill hearings, concluding that the examining senators maintained a masculinist stance that precluded them from giving serious consideration to Professor Hill's claims. A consequence of this masculine moral narrowing is that "charges of sexual harassment…are often seen as exaggerated or as fabricated out of misunderstanding or spite" (Schwalbe 1992, 46). Thus, gender differences in interpreting sexually harassing behaviors may stem more from acts of ignoring than states of ignorance.

The Problem with Getting Caught

But are women really the untroubled objects that girl watching—viewed through the eyes of men—suggests? Obviously not; the game may be premised on a denial of a woman's subjectivity, but an actual erasure is beyond men's power! It is in this multiplicity of subjectivities, as Butler (1990, ix) noted, where "trouble" lurks, provoked by "the unanticipated agency of a female 'object' who inexplicably returns the glance, reverses the gaze, and contests the place and authority of the masculine position." To face a returned gaze is to get caught, an act that has the power to undermine the logic of girl watching as simply a game among men. Karl, for example, noted that when caught, men are often flustered, a reaction suggesting that the boundaries of usual play have been disturbed.[7]

When a woman looks back, when she asks, "What are you looking at?" she speaks as a subject, and her status as mere object is disturbed. When the game is played as a form of hommo-sexuality, the confronted man may be baffled by her response. When she catches them looking, when she complains, the targeted woman speaks as a subject. The men, however, understand her primarily as an object, and objects do not object.

The radical potential of sexual harassment law is that it centers women's subjectivity, an aspect prompting Catharine MacKinnon's (1979) unusual hope for the law's potential as a remedy. For men engaged in girl watching, however, this subjectivity

may be inconceivable. From their viewpoint, acts such as girl watching are simply games played with objects: women's bodies. Similar to Schwalbe's (1992) insight into the senators' reaction to Professor Hill, the harm of sexual harassment may seem more the result of a woman's complaint (and law's "illegitimate" encroachment into the everyday work world) than men's acts of objectification. For example, in reflecting on the impact of sexual harassment policies in the workplace, José lamented that "back in the '70s, [it was] all peace and love then. Now as things turn around, men can't get away with as much as what they used to." Just whose peace and love are we talking about?

Reactions to Anti-Sexual Harassment Training Programs

The role that objectification and disempathy play in men's girl watching has important implications for sexual harassment training. Consider the following account of a sexual harassment training session given in Cindy's workplace. Cindy, an Italian American woman in her early 20s, worked as a recruiter for a small telemarketing company in Southern California.

> [The trainer] just really laid down the ground rules, um, she had some scenarios. Saying, "OK, would you consider this sexual harassment?" "Would you…" this, this, this? "What level?" Da-da-da. So, um, they just gave us some real numbers as to lawsuits and cases. Just that "you guys better be careful" type of a thing.

From Cindy's description, this training is fairly typical in that it focuses on teaching participants definitions of sexual harassment and the legal ramifications of accusations. The trainer used the common strategy of presenting videos of potentially harassing situations and asking the participants how they would judge them. Cindy's description of the men's responses to these videos reveals the limitation of this approach.

> We were watching [the TV] and it was [like] a studio audience. And [men] were getting up in the studio audience making comments like "Oh well, look at her! I wouldn't want to do that to her either!" "Well, you're darn straight, look at her!"

Interestingly, the men successfully used the training session videos as an opportunity for girl watching through their public sexual evaluations of the women depicted. In this, the intent of the training session was doubly subverted. The men interpreted scenarios that Cindy found plainly harassing into mere instances of girl watching and sexual (dis)interest. The antiharassment video was ironically transformed into a forum for girl watching, effecting male bonding and the assertion of masculine identities to the exclusion of women coworkers. Also, by judging the complaining women to be inferior as women, the men sent the message that women who complain are those who fail at femininity.

Cindy conceded that relations between men and women in her workplace were considerably strained after the training ("That day, you definitely saw the men bond, you definitely saw the women bond, and there was a definite separation"). The effect of the training session, rather than curtailing the rampant sexual harassment in Cindy's workplace, operated as a site of masculine performance, evoking manly camaraderie and reestablishing gender boundaries.

To be effective, sexual harassment training programs must be grounded in a complex understanding of the ways acts such as girl watching operate in the workplace and the seeming necessity of a culled empathy to some forms of masculinity. Sexually harassing behaviors are produced from more than a lack of knowledge, simple sexist attitudes, or misplaced sexual desire. Some forms of sexually harassing behaviors—such as girl watching—are mechanisms through which gendered boundaries are patrolled and evoked and by which deeply held identities are established. This complexity requires complex interventions and leads to difficult questions about the possible efficacy of any workplace training program mandated in part by legal requirements.

Conclusion

In this analysis, I have sought to unravel the social logic of girl watching and its relationship to the question of gender differences in the interpretation of sexual harassment. In the form analyzed here,

girl watching functions simultaneously as only play and as a potent site where power is played. Through the objectification on which it is premised and in the nonempathetic masculinity it supports, this form of girl watching simultaneously produces both the harassment and the barriers to men's acknowledgment of its potential harm.

The implications these findings have for antisexual harassment training are profound. If we understand harassment to be the result of a simple lack of knowledge (of ignorance), then straightforward informational sexual harassment training may be effective. The present analysis suggests, however, that the etiology of some harassment lies elsewhere. While they might have quarreled with it, most of the men I interviewed had fairly good abstract understandings of the behaviors their companies' sexual harassment policies prohibited. At the same time, in relating stories of social relations in their workplaces, most failed to identify specific behaviors as sexual harassment when they matched the abstract definition. As I have argued, the source of this contradiction lies not so much in ignorance but in acts of ignoring. Traditional sexual harassment training programs address the former rather than the latter. As such, their effectiveness against sexually harassing behaviors born out of social practices of masculinity like girl watching is questionable.

Ultimately, the project of challenging sexual harassment will be frustrated and our understanding distorted unless we interrogate hegemonic, patriarchal forms of masculinity and the practices by which they are (re)produced. We must continue to research the processes by which sexual harassment is produced and the gendered identities and subjectivities on which it poaches (Wood 1998). My study provides a first step toward a more process-oriented understanding of sexual harassment, the ways the social meanings of harassment are constructed, and ultimately, the potential success of antiharassment training programs.

Notes

1. See Welsh (1999) for a review of this literature.
2. For example, Maria, an administrative assistant I interviewed, simultaneously echoed and critiqued

this understanding when she complained about her boss's girl watching in her presence: "If he wants to do that in front of other men...you know, that's what men do."

3. Recently, more researchers have turned to qualitative studies as a means to understand the process of labeling behavior as harassment. Of note are Collinson and Collinson (1996), Giuffre and Williams (1994), Quinn (2000), and Rogers and Henson (1997).

4. Quid pro quo ("this for that") sexual harassment occurs when a person with organizational power attempts to coerce an individual into sexual behavior by threatening adverse job actions.

5. I prefer the term "asymmetrical heterosexuality" over "double standard" because it directly references the dominance of heterosexuality and more accurately reflects the interconnected but different forms of acceptable sexuality for men and women. As Estrich (1987) argued, it is not simply that we hold men and women to different standards of sexuality but that these standards are (re)productive of women's disempowerment.

6. "Hommo" is a play on the French word for man, *homme*.

7. Men are not always concerned with getting caught, as the behavior of catcalling construction workers amply illustrates; that a woman hears is part of the thrill (Gardner 1995). The difference between the workplace and the street is the level of anonymity the men have vis-à-vis the woman and the complexity of social rules and the diversity of power sources an individual has at his or her disposal.

References

Bernstein, R. 1994. Guilty if charged. *New York Review of Books*, 13 January.

Buckwald, A. 1993. Compliment a woman, go to court. *Los Angeles Times*, 28 October.

Butler, J. 1990. *Gender trouble: Feminism and the subversion of identity*. New York: Routledge.

Cleveland, J. N., and M. E. Kerst. 1993. Sexual harassment and perceptions of power: An underarticulated relationship. *Journal of Vocational Behavior* 42 (1): 49–67.

Cockburn, C. 1983. *Brothers: Male dominance and technological change*. London: Pluto Press.

Collinson, D. L., and M. Collinson. 1989. Sexuality in the workplace: The domination of men's sexuality. In *The sexuality of organizations*, edited by J. Hearn and D. L. Sheppard. Newbury Park, CA: Sage.

———. 1996. "It's only Dick": The sexual harassment of women managers in insurance sales. *Work, Employment & Society* 10 (1): 29–56.

Conley, F. K. 1991. Why I'm leaving Stanford: I wanted my dignity back. *Los Angeles Times*, 9 June.

Connell, R. W. 1987. *Gender and power*. Stanford, CA: Stanford University Press.

———. 1995. *Masculinities*. Berkeley: University of California Press.

Estrich, S. 1987. *Real rape*. Cambridge, MA: Harvard University Press.

Garcia, L., L. Milano, and A. Quijano. 1989. Perceptions of coercive sexual behavior by males and females. *Sex Roles* 21 (9/10): 569–77.

Gardner, C. B. 1995. *Passing by: Gender and public harassment*. Berkeley: University of California Press.

Giuffre, P., and C. Williams. 1994. Boundary lines: Labeling sexual harassment in restaurants. *Gender & Society* 8:378–401.

Guccione, J. 1992. Women judges still fighting harassment. *Daily Journal*, 13 October, 1.

Gutek, B. A., and M. P. Koss. 1993. Changed women and changed organizations: Consequences of and coping with sexual harassment. *Journal of Vocational Behavior* 42 (1): 28–48.

Gutek, B. A., B. Morasch, and A. G. Cohen. 1983. Interpreting social-sexual behavior in a work setting. *Journal of Vocational Behavior* 22 (1): 30–48.

Hearn, J. 1985. Men's sexuality at work. In *The sexuality of men*, edited by A. Metcalf and M. Humphries. London: Pluto Press.

Hopkins, P. 1992. Gender treachery: Homophobia, masculinity, and threatened identities. In *Rethinking masculinity: Philosophical explorations in light of feminism*, edited by L. May and R. Strikwerda. Lanham, MD: Littlefield, Adams.

Jensen, I. W., and B. A. Gutek. 1982. Attributions and assignment of responsibility in sexual harassment. *Journal of Social Issues* 38 (4): 121–36.

Johnson, M. 1988. *Strong mothers, weak wives*. Berkeley: University of California Press.

Kenig, S., and J. Ryan. 1986. Sex differences in levels of tolerance and attribution of blame for sexual harassment on a university campus. *Sex Roles* 15 (9/10): 535–49.

MacKinnon, C. A. 1979. *The sexual harassment of working women.* New Haven, CT: Yale University Press.

Malovich, N. J., and J. E. Stake. 1990. Sexual harassment on campus: Individual differences in attitudes and beliefs. *Psychology of Women Quarterly* 14 (1): 63–81.

Murrell, A. J., and B. L. Dietz-Uhler. 1993. Gender identity and adversarial sexual beliefs as predictors of attitudes toward sexual harassment. *Psychology of Women Quarterly* 17 (2): 169–75.

Padgitt, S. C., and J. S. Padgitt. 1986. Cognitive structure of sexual harassment: Implications for university policy. *Journal of College Student Personnel* 27:34–39.

Popovich, P. M., D. N. Gehlauf, J. A. Jolton, J. M. Somers, and R. M. Godinho. 1992. Perceptions of sexual harassment as a function of sex of rater and incident form and consequent. *Sex Roles* 27 (11/12): 609–25.

Powell, G. N. 1986. Effects of sex-role identity and sex on definitions of sexual harassment. *Sex Roles* 14: 9–19.

Pronger, B. 1992. Gay jocks: A phenomenology of gay men in athletics. In *Rethinking masculinity: Philosophical explorations in light of feminism,* edited by L. May and R. Strikwerda. Lanham, MD: Littlefield Adams.

Pryor, J. B. 1987. Sexual harassment proclivities in men. *Sex Roles* 17 (5/6): 269–90.

Quinn, B. A. 2000. The paradox of complaining: Law, humor, and harassment in the everyday work world. *Law and Social Inquiry* 25 (4): 1151–83.

Reilly, M. E., B. Lott, D. Caldwell, and L. DeLuca. 1992. Tolerance for sexual harassment related to self-reported sexual victimization. *Gender & Society* 6:122–38.

Rogers, J. K., and K. D. Henson. 1997. "Hey, why don't you wear a shorter skirt?" Structural vulnerability and the organization of sexual harassment in temporary clerical employment. *Gender & Society* 11:215–38.

Schwalbe, M. 1992. Male supremacy and the narrowing of the moral self. *Berkeley Journal of Sociology* 37:29–54.

Stockdale, M. S. 1993. The role of sexual misperceptions of women's friendliness in an emerging theory of sexual harassment. *Journal of Vocational Behavior* 42 (1): 84–101.

Stockdale, M. S., and A. Vaux. 1993. What sexual harassment experiences lead respondents to acknowledge being sexually harassed? A secondary analysis of a university survey. *Journal of Vocational Behavior* 43 (2): 221–34.

Tagri, S., and S. M. Hayes. 1997. Theories of sexual harassment. In *Sexual harassment: Theory, research and treatment,* edited by W. O'Donohue. New York: Allyn & Bacon.

Thorne, B. 1993. *Gender play: Girls and boys in school.* Buckingham, UK: Open University Press.

U.S. Merit Systems Protection Board. 1988. *Sexual harassment in the federal government: An update.* Washington, DC: Government Printing Office.

Welsh, S. 1999. Gender and sexual harassment. *Annual Review of Sociology* 1999:169–90.

West, C., and D. H. Zimmerman. 1987. Doing gender. *Gender & Society* 1: 125–51.

Wood, J. T. 1998. Saying makes it so: The discursive construction of sexual harassment. In *Conceptualizing sexual harassment as discursive practice,* edited by S. G. Bingham. Westport, CT: Praeger.

York, K. M. 1989. Defining sexual harassment in workplaces: A policy-capturing approach. *Academy of Management Journal* 32:830–50.

Yount, K. R. 1991. Ladies, flirts, tomboys: Strategies for managing sexual harassment in an underground coal mine. *Journal of Contemporary Ethnography* 19:396–422.

Gender Rules: Same- and Cross-Gender Friendship Norms

DIANE FELMLEE, ELIZABETH SWEET, AND H. COLLEEN SINCLAIR

Introduction

Interaction among friends constitutes one of the arenas in which social norms regarding gender shape people's behavior on a routine basis, and in everyday settings. A number of norms or "rules" for friendship are endorsed cross-culturally (Argyle and Henderson 1984), and these normative expectations that men and women hold for their friends often differ by gender (see meta-analysis by Hall 2011). Yet most prior studies did not utilize experimental methods to examine gender differences in friendship norms, nor did they investigate the extent to which such differences depended on the gender composition of the friendship. It seems likely that certain friendship rules will vary, contingent on whether a male is evaluating the behavior of a female, versus a male, friend. Further, extant research seldom provided the social context for determining the importance of a particular friendship norm, nor has it examined reactions to norm violations, as opposed to just the importance of the norm. The main purpose of this study was to examine the degree to which women and men differed in their expectations for same- and cross-gender friendships. To this end, we investigated the reactions of a sample of U.S. college students to vignettes in which a friend of the same, or the "opposite," gender violated basic friendship norms. The review of literature is limited to U.S. undergraduate samples, unless otherwise noted. Yet the presence of several, emerging studies based on other countries (e.g., Argyle and Henderson 1984; Halatsis and Christakis 2009; Lenton and Webber 2006) demonstrates that this topic possesses cross-cultural relevance.

A related question concerning friendship, "Can heterosexual men and women be friends?" has received perennial attention within the scholarly literature (e.g, Booth and Hess 1974; O'Meara 1989; Werking 1997). Some studies point to the serious challenges facing such friendships (O'Meara 1989), while others emphasize the viability of such bonds (Monsour 2002). However, a query that extends beyond the age-old debate regarding platonic affiliation between the genders is the one we address here: how does gender shape friendship expectations in the first place? In other words, to what extent are there important, normative rules and expectations that govern platonic associations among and between women and men? Answers to this question are useful in developing a deeper understanding of the role of gender in framing informal affiliations in our society.

The Rules of Friendship

According to Argyle and Henderson (1984), a number of rules, or social norms, characterize friendships, several of which were endorsed by samples of adults from various cultures, including Britain, Italy, Hong Kong, and Japan. Argyle and Henderson identified 21 highly endorsed rules for same-gender friendships. The rules fell into several categories, including expectations regarding intimacy, exchange, involvement with third parties, and coordination of behavior (e.g., a friend should keep a confidence, friends should stand up

Diane Felmlee, Elizabeth Sweet, and H. Colleen Sinclair, "Gender Rules: Same- and Cross-Gender Friendship Norms," *Sex Roles*, Vol. 66, No. 7 (April 2012), pp. 518–529. Copyright © 2012 by Springer Science+Business Media. Reprinted with kind permission from Springer Science and Business Media.

for one another). Findings also suggested that when such rules were broken, friendships suffered and sometimes were terminated. Although rules for cross-gender friendships were not investigated, Argyle and Henderson, as well as subsequent researchers, have examined gender differences in the expectations one holds of friendships. We turn now to the review of the literature on gender and friendship.

Gender and Friendship

Friendship often differs for men and women (Sheets and Lugar 2005, Russian and American sample). Women place higher value on their relationships and their connectedness to others than do men. For example, there is a good deal of evidence that women are more likely than men to describe themselves in terms of relatedness to others, whereas men describe themselves more often in terms of their independence from others (e.g., Cross and Madson 1997; Guimond et al. 2006). In self photographs, women depicted themselves in socially connected ways, but men's self-photographs emphasized their separateness (Clancey and Dollinger 1993). Men and women's notions of interdependence also contrast, such that women place greater stress on the relational aspects of interdependence (Gabriel and Gardner 1999).

Not only do women appear to define themselves more in terms of their relationships, but evidence suggests that the quality of their associations varies from that of men. When it comes to relating, men and women appear to display distinct styles. Women's friendships are characterized by more intimacy, self-disclosure, and emotional support (for a meta-analysis, see Reis 1998; see also Baumgarte and Nelson 2009; Fehr 2004), whereas those of men's friendship tend to be more agentic and instrumental, focusing on shared activities (Fox et al. 1985; Rubin 1985). Such differences lead to the conclusion that women's friendships are "face-to-face" while those of men are "side-by-side" (Wright 1982). However, Duck and Wright (1993) note that some of these gender discrepancies may reflect variance in the overarching importance of friend relationships to women and men, with women, as noted above, identifying relationships as more central to their self-concept (Cross and Madson 1997).

Gender and Friendship Norms

Given the evidence showing gender differences in the importance of and approach to relationships, it seems likely that men and women hold discrepant standards for their friendships. Research suggests that women expect more of their friends than do men, especially when it comes to rules governing emotional support and disclosure (Argyle and Henderson 1984). A recent meta-analysis (Hall 2011) noted that studies find that friendship expectations are indeed higher for females than for males with regard to communion (e.g., intimacy), solidarity (e.g., mutual activities), symmetrical reciprocity (e.g., loyalty), and overall friendship expectations, but lower than those for males for expectations of agency (e.g., friend's wealth, status). According to Hall (2011), the findings support evolutionary theory (e.g., Bleske and Buss 2000), suggesting that females develop elevated communion expectations due to their relatively extensive investment in offspring, and their need to maintain female coalitions to assist in rearing children.

An alternative theoretical explanation for differences between men and women in friendship centers upon the social and cultural context of gender. Friendship represents a significant social relational arena for the enactment of cultural messages and beliefs regarding gender. People "do gender" while engaging with their friends (West and Zimmerman 1987), and friendship represents a place where gender ideology and inequality are enacted on a regular basis. Contemporary gender stereotypes contain messages that frame women as more communal in their relationships, and men as more instrumental and more agentic (Eagly et al. 2000). Women are thought to be nicer but less competent (Fiske et al. 2002). Girls also are encouraged to value interconnectedness and nurturance more highly than are boys (Chodorow 1978; Gilligan 1982). Parents, peers, social institutions, and the mass media foster cooperation and emotional support among girls, whereas boys are led to be more competitive, independent, and aggressive (e.g., Thome 1986). These stereotypical beliefs about gender form a cultural frame through which people come to understand themselves and others, which then shapes how people behave in particular relational contexts (Ridgeway 2009). The influence of cultural stereotyping and the social construction of gender persists throughout life, and messages that encourage warmth and nurturance on the part of women do not end with childhood.

Cross-Gender Friendships

Cultural messages provide scripts for how men and women should interact with each other, and therefore, not only gender, but the gender composition of a friendship influences a platonic relationship. Women and men regularly face a host of media images that romanticize and sexualize their routine encounters and confront an array of societal expectations and constraints that make a rewarding friendship with someone of the "opposite sex" challenging (Baumgarte 2002). Yet males and females now routinely interact within environments that bring them into close contact, such as in college, the labor force, and other societal institutions. Cultural scripts have yet to catch up with the times, however, and models of men and women relating in a platonic context are rarer than those of them interacting in sexualized situations, even within friendships (Baumgarte 2002; Hughes et al. 2005).

To date, research on norms within friendships has focused on norms within same-gender friendships. The concept of cross-gender friendship represents a relatively new historical phenomenon in our society (e.g., Monsour 2002). The novelty of platonic ties between men and women, as compared with marital and same-gender friendships, makes it less likely that there are clear, established cultural expectations for these affiliations. In particular, they lack cultural scripts and obvious role models to use in guiding social interaction (O'Meara 1989). Given the paucity of information on the rules and scripts of cross-gender bonds, we believe it important to examine whether these friendships possess different norms from their same-gender counterparts. Thus, in addition to examining how friendship norms might differ by gender, we investigated beliefs about cross-gender friendship and whether male-female friendships were held to different standards than those within the same gender.

Heterosexual, cross-gender friendships tend to enhance people's lives and shape views of the self and others (Monsour 2002), and they provide benefits common to same-gender relationships, such as social support. Male-female friendships also afford unique advantages, such as an "insider perspective" of the other gender (Monsour 2002; Werking 1997). Cross-gender pairs face a number of serious social challenges, as well, including a lack of social support, the presumption by others of sexual involvement, missing cultural role models, and gender inequality (O'Meara 1989; West et al. 1996). Self-disclosure is lower in friendships between men and women than in those within the same gender, among both Americans and Japanese (Kito 2005). Moreover, people can be more demanding in their preferences for traits in a cross-gender, as opposed to a same-gender, friend (Sprecher and Regan 2002) and may have higher normative expectations for such friendships.

Issues related to sexuality and gender also influence male-female friendships. Men perceive a greater sexual interest from women in cross-gender encounters than reported by the women themselves (Henningsen et al. 2006), including among friends (Koenig et al. 2007). Men view sex with a cross-gender friend as more beneficial than do women (Bleske and Buss 2000) and rate sexual attraction and a desire for sex as more important reasons for forming a cross-gender friendship (Bleske-Rechek and Buss 2001). Sexual attraction remains a challenge for cross-gender friendships, according to a recent study of Greek participants, although it does not necessarily result in termination of an existing bond (Halatsis and Christakis 2009).

Friendship rules also suggest that attraction constitutes a potential problem for friends. One widely endorsed rule (Argyle and Henderson 1984), for example, maintains that friends should not have intimate contact that could be construed as sexual. Yet the particular gender composition of a pair of friends is apt to influence assessments of this norm. Certain cross-gender pairs, for example, may not endorse fully the norm against physical intimacy, especially in the present social climate where "hooking up" with acquaintances and "friends with benefits" are becoming increasingly common (Bogle 2008). Men, too, are apt to view physical intimacy from a cross-gender friend more positively than women, because of the value they place on sexual attraction in such ties. When it involves same-gender pairs, demonstrations of physical affection between women are more accepted than between men (Lewis 1978). In men's friendships, displays of intimacy in general are less common due to gender norms about masculinity and emotional restraint (Bank and Hansford 2000; Lewis 1978). Yet, due to homophobia, demonstrations of physical affection between men are particularly taboo (Bank and Hansford 2000; Lewis 1978). As a result, American heterosexual men and women would likely respond quite differently to intimate contact—even of the potentially benign variety such as being greeted by a kiss—when it comes from a same-gender, rather than a cross-gender, friend. Thus, women may disapprove of a violation of the physical intimacy norm from a cross-gender friend, whereas men will likely regard the physical intimacy norm encroachment as particularly inappropriate within-gender.

In addition to exploring the role of gender in evaluations of within- and between-gender friendship norms, we study general attitudes towards female-male affiliations by examining whether most participants believe such bonds are possible. Recent research documents the percentage of cross-gender friends among college students, with estimates varying between 25% (for both U.S. and Russian samples; Sheets and Lugar 2005), 30–35% (Reeder 2003), and 30–42% (Lenton and Webber 2006). Yet relatively few studies explore the broader question regarding beliefs as to whether or not men and women can be friends. Attitudes toward cross-gender friendship are important to examine, because they act as a barometer for social change regarding relations between the genders. Certain individuals might lack the opportunity to easily develop a friendship with someone of the other gender, for instance, but the fact that they approve of such a relationship remains meaningful.

Attitudes towards female-male friendship also are relevant for our purposes, because they might influence evaluations of same- and cross-gender friendship norms.

Summary of the Current Study

We gathered data from a sample of U.S. college students to compare men's and women's perceptions of norms in same- and cross- gender friendship. Participants responded to whether they felt that men and women could be friends, and they evaluated vignettes in which the behavior of a friend was designed to challenge one of seven basic friendship rules. The gender of the friend was varied experimentally within-subjects. . . .

First, we hypothesized that women would be more disapproving than men of a friend who challenged the rules of emotional closeness and trust, because of the significance women assign to these dimensions of friendship. Second, we expected people would be more disapproving of a male, as opposed to a female, friend who behaved in ways that could have sexual connotations, especially when that physical intimacy occurred between men, due to the virulence of homophobia towards males (Kimmel 1994). Additional interactions between gender of participant and gender of friend were explored, but given the rarity of examinations of norms in cross-gender friendships, hypotheses other than the one regarding physical intimacy were not advanced.

Summary of Research Questions and Hypotheses

RQ1: Do people believe that cross-gender friendships are possible, and does gender influence these beliefs?

RQ2: What are the differences in the overall, approval levels of the reactions to the norm violations, and do these differ by gender?

H1: Women will disapprove more than men of a friend who violates norms of emotional closeness and trust in friendships.

H2: Males will receive more disapproval in an interaction that has possible sexual connotations, particularly if the interaction is between men. . . .

Method

Participants

The participants consisted of 263 college students (195 female, 68 male), ranging between 18–25 years. Five participants over the age of 25 and one homosexual participant were dropped from the analysis, because they represented potential outliers. Their inclusion did not affect our main findings. The average age was 19.7 years and the sample was 42.3% White, 27% Asian, 9.3% Latino, 3.3% Black, and 12% other ethnicities. Approximately 97% of the students were single. The surveys were distributed during class in four large, introductory social science courses at a west coast university. . . .

Materials

Stimulus Materials: Vignettes

Research subjects read seven vignettes involving a person described as their friend and rated the appropriateness of the behavior in each situation. Vignettes varied randomly between-subjects as to whether the friend described was male or female. Type of norm violated was varied within-subject, such that each participant received seven mini-vignettes to evaluate. Respondents were given the following instructions: "Here are several questions involving friends. For each scenario, you are asked to give your opinion concerning the appropriateness of the behavior of your friend."

The vignette format (e.g., Alves and Rossi 1978; Hughes 1998) had the advantage that it allowed for the direct experimental manipulation of the independent variable (friend gender) with a relatively subtle manipulation (i.e., the use of either masculine or feminine names and pronouns). It also allowed us to provide a social context for a particular friendship rule, thus making judgments of violations of those rules more salient than when simply listing a rule (e.g., "friends should keep confidences") and having participants rate its importance (Finch 1987). Unlike in a traditional survey design, there was less worry about the risk of bias in estimates that could occur due to the omission of covariates (Maxwell and Delaney 2004), such as structural factors that influence friendship (Adams and Blieszner 1998; Blieszner and Adams 1992). . . .

Results

Can Women and Men Be Friends?

First we examined responses to the question (RQ1): Can men and women be friends? According to the great majority of our sample (81.6%), the answer was yes. Only 2.3% of the sample responded "no," men and women cannot be friends, with another 16.2% reporting "maybe." There were significant gender differences in the three-category response pattern. . . . (Women: 80.5% yes, 18.5% maybe, 2% no, Men: 84.5% yes, 9.9% maybe, 5.6% no.) In a dichotomous classification of responses, in which the "maybe" replies were combined with the few cases of "no," (yes versus maybe/no), the significant gender difference abated. . . . Part of the gender difference in the trichotomous classification appears to reside in the tendency of females, as compared to males, to respond more cautiously with an answer of "maybe." . . .

Exploring Norm Rankings

We examined whether certain norm violations were more acceptable than others (RQ 2). . . .

The results revealed significant differences in the perceived appropriateness of various norm violations and underscore the diverse nature of the norms studied here. . . . An interaction of gender and norms shows that differences in the ranking of the appropriateness of the norms varied by gender. . . . Note that the general pattern as to which norm violation was less appropriate than others did not really differ between men and women, but rather women appeared to have clearer delineations than men about what is, and is not, acceptable. For men, a number of the norm violations were not significantly different from one another in their perceived appropriateness (23.8% of the comparisons). In contrast, for women almost all of the means for the scenarios were significantly different from one another, with only one comparison between mean approval (4.8%) failing to differ significantly (i.e., means for "won't confide" and "surprise visit"). . . .

Hypothesis Testing: Gender and Reacting to Norm Violations

Next, we examined whether perceptions of norm violations differed by gender of the perceiver and gender of the hypothetical friend. . . . This analysis allowed us to examine both main effect differences in how men and women judged norm violations as well as how men and women were judged as friends. Further, the interaction between participant's gender and friend's gender allowed us to examine same-gender vs. cross-gender friendship differences. . . .

Looking at . . . analyses for participant gender, men and women differed significantly in how acceptable it was for friends to cancel plans, give kisses, and fail to stand up for each other. Specifically, women . . . expressed more disapproval than men . . . of a friend who cancels plans with them for a date, . . . , in support of H1. "Flaking is a pet peeve," reported one young woman. Another pointed out that "friendship supersedes boyfriends." A third remarked: "It's never cool to ditch someone for somebody else." In contrast, an approving young man noted: "Can't blame him for wanting to get laid. At least he told me a day in advance."

Women also viewed a friend failing to stand up for them as more inappropriate than did men, as predicted (H1) . . . Women were less upset, on the other hand, about the possibility of receiving a kiss . . . In addition, there was a tendency for women to be more disapproving of a friend who broke a confidence as well as one who failed to confide his or her feelings, although findings were marginal. . . .

Figure 1 displays significant, and marginally significant, gender differences in the mean approval of the scenarios. Here we see clearly the tendency for women's evaluations of violations to be less approving than those of men for all the vignettes, except for that of the Kiss.

Male and female friends were regarded differently for telling secrets and giving kisses. Although telling secrets was the worst of the violations in a friendship, women . . . were judged more harshly than men . . . for telling secrets. . . . Women were particularly critical of other women breaking their

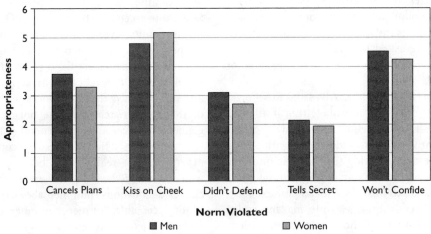

Figure 1. Significant and Marginal Differences in How Men and Women View Violations of Friendship Norms

Note: Solid bars indicate that gender differences between men and women on the first three categories of norm violations were all significant . . . Light bars with dark borders indicate marginal differences . . . for perceptions of telling secrets and failing to confide. No significant gender differences existed for reactions to surprise visits or friends staying over. Higher scores indicate that the norm violation was deemed more acceptable than norm violations with lower means (scores could range from 0–7).

trust, since the lowest mean across all conditions was in women evaluating female friends who breached a confidence, as illustrated by one young female participant, who said: "Trust should not be broken. . . ."

In contrast, men were judged more harshly than women for giving kisses . . . However, this gender difference, and the main effect of participant gender on perceptions of being greeted with a kiss, were both qualified by an interaction. Post hoc comparisons show that generally a kiss on the cheek from a woman is acceptable for either gender. Both male and female participants rated a woman's expression of affection as fine . . . However, the appropriateness of a man kissing anyone on the cheek, especially by another man, was viewed as borderline, if not clearly, inappropriate. . . .

As expected (H2), people appeared to be less suspicious of female friends than they were of male friends who interacted in ways that could be viewed as expressions of sexual or romantic attraction. The findings provided support for our hypothesis that males would be less accepting of a male friend who behaved in a manner that could be interpreted as a display of homosexuality. As one young man pointed out: "My guy friends and I don't kiss." Whereas, a typical female participant, on the other

hand, noted approvingly: "What are friends for?" This interaction effect is displayed in Figure 2.

Perceptions of other norm violations did not differ by gender. Further, even when controlling for responses to "can men and women be friends" and race of the participant . . . the pattern of the results obtained here remained the same. . . .

Discussion

The main purpose of this study was to investigate differences between men and women in the degree to which they approved of various violations of friendship norms in same-gender friendships and cross-gender friendships. Gender affected the normative evaluations of behavior in our findings, similar to previous experimental research with different samples (Felmlee and Muraco 2009; Muraco 2005). In all but two of the seven vignettes, there were significant (or in two cases, marginally significant), effects of gender, and/or friend's gender. The findings tended to provide support for our hypotheses regarding gender and friendship norms. Women were significantly more critical of violations of friendship rules than were men, in particular when a friend canceled plans or failed to defend them publicly (H1). Women also

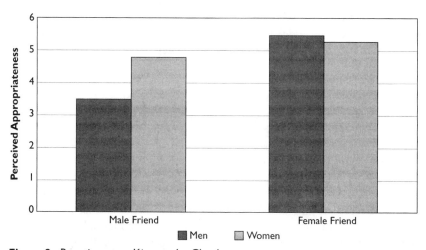

Figure 2. Reactions to a Kiss on the Cheek
Note: Higher scores indicate that the norm violation was deemed more acceptable than norm violations with lower means (scores could range from 0–7). . . . Only means within the female friend condition did not differ significantly.

disapproved more of someone who told a secret or failed to confide, findings that were of marginal significance. In other words, women tended to have relatively high expectations for their friendships, whether with other women or men, results consistent with those of studies on ideal friendship standards and expectations (Elkins and Peterson 1993; Hall 2011).

The central role women place on intimacy and communication within their close friendships may lead them to have relatively stringent expectations for those bonds. Societal processes reward females for being intimate and communicative from childhood on, and help to construct norms for the feminine gender that center around these themes. Yet there remain important social structural bases for gender differences in expectations as well. Men typically have higher status and power in our society than women (Fiske 2009), suggesting that they can afford to be more easy-going in their friendships. On the other hand, supportive relationships have a greater impact on women's well-being than that of men (Kenler et al. 2005; adult, twin sample). Given women's relatively lower economic standing and social power (Fiske 2009), they may rely more on supportive relationships, and their need for informal ties may result in greater demands and expectations for these crucial bonds.

The gender of a friend had a significant effect on behavioral appraisals in two situations. Women who betrayed a confidence were judged significantly more harshly than were men. Female friends were held to higher standards than were their male counterparts, it appears, perhaps because women are expected to place greater value on their intimate connections in the first place. Furthermore, a man who bestowed a "big kiss" in a friendly greeting received significantly lower levels of support than did a woman (H2). In other words, it is more acceptable for women to express physical affection with a friend than it is for men (Hays 1985). Kissing someone in a greeting represents a behavior that could be construed as romantic or sexual, especially when initiated by a man. These findings demonstrate that certain friendship expectations vary not only by the gender of the person making the assessment but also by the gender of the friend.

The least positive reactions to the "kiss on the cheek" scenario were reported by men for male friends who kissed them in a greeting (H2), suggesting that societal homophobia plays a major part in shaping such responses. A few females expressed similar homophobic, or heterosexist, sentiments, including one who noted that a kiss from a female was great, as long as it was "ONLY on the cheek, nowhere else." In her response, she distanced herself from the devalued identity of a lesbian, similar to the distance several heterosexual men placed between themselves and the label of "gay male." Men may feel particular pressure to disassociate themselves from such a label because homophobia, and the more general fear of being seen as unmanly, remains deeply fundamental to the construction of manhood (Kimmel 1994).

The significant interaction effect in the Kiss vignette provided support for our hypothesis that situations in which sexual connotations were involved would yield evidence of unique cross-gender versus same-gender expectations (H2). Here we saw that men's judgments differed significantly, depending on whether the kiss was bestowed by a same-gender or a cross-gender friend.

Several of the findings are particularly noteworthy because they were derived on the basis of a subtle gender manipulation involving only names and pronouns. For example, although both women and men viewed breaking a confidence as a serious norm violation, a woman who told a secret was evaluated particularly severely. This judgment was made simply due to the use of a feminine name and pronoun in the vignette description. People of both genders also evaluated a man less positively than a woman who kissed them, once again on the basis of the type of name and pronoun alone. Thus, even a subtle manipulation of gender in a behavioral description can trigger gender stereotypes and expectations.

Although the gender differences we found appeared robust and noteworthy, the magnitude of these variations should not be overstated. Women did indeed disapprove more of several violations of friendship norms, but that did not mean that men *approved* of such violations. Neither men nor women endorsed a friend who cancelled plans, for example, but women objected more strongly. Likewise, both genders censured a friend who failed to stand up for them, but women were more intense in their reaction. More generally, women's mean ratings of the various vignettes appeared to be more extreme than those of men . . . but the relative order of the ranking of the average reactions did not vary by gender. Both men and women found a request to stay over to be the most acceptable, for instance, and that of disclosing a confidence to be particularly problematic. It is not the case that men held one set of friendship expectations and women an entirely separate set. Furthermore, there were no gender differences or trends in responses to two vignettes, those of the stay over and surprise visit. In other words, gender discrepancies were not inevitable, and those that did occur differed by degree rather than by kind.

The gender trends in the data underscore the argument that social context remains a particularly powerful influence on the normative evaluations of interpersonal interactions on the part of women and men (e.g., Felmlee 1999; Goffman 1979). The findings reinforce the argument that gender represents an ongoing social construction shaped by the context in which interaction occurs, rather than a fixed socialized role or a psychological predisposition (e.g., Deaux and Major 1987; Frieze et al. 1991; Messner 2000). The responses of the participants often reflect predominate cultural beliefs regarding relational behavior among men and women (Ridgeway and Correll 2004) and as such may echo ideological stereotypes rather than the lived reality of actual friendship behavior (Walker 1994).

We found little evidence of unique, social scripts for cross-gender friendships, at least with respect to the types of friendship behavior examined here. With only one, exception, that of the Kiss vignette discussed earlier, there were no significant cross-gender interaction effects in the assessments of behavior that challenged basic friendship rules. For example, people did not disapprove significantly more of a same-gender, as opposed to a cross-gender, friend who betrayed a secret. The important norm suggesting that friends should keep confidences remained as salient in one type of bond as the other. These findings align with the conclusions of others that the meaning of intimacy is more similar than different in cross- and same-gender friendships (Monsour 1992). They also provide support for the argument that cross-gender ties lack clear, shared cultural scripts (e.g., O'Meara 1989). Given the frequent, significant effect of gender in these vignettes, the results suggest that in the contexts examined here, gender expectations "trump" those of cross-gender. When no cultural guides exist for cross-gender ties, then people invoke instead well-known, cultural gender schemas.

Friendship Between Women and Men

Another goal of our study was to investigate responses to the classic question: Can men and women be friends? Our participants, whether male or female, overwhelmingly responded in the affirmative (81.6%). Only a small minority of individuals (2.3%) said "no," men and women cannot be friends. These findings stand in contrast to those of earlier studies in which people focused more on the existing barriers to cross-gender friendship (e.g., Bell 1981). There also were gender differences in the responses, with women, for example, more likely to respond "maybe." Perhaps women expressed greater caution when answering this question, because they were more concerned than men with the threat of sexual attraction challenging the platonic nature of such a friendship.

The question we posed about the viability of cross-gender friendship differed from the more common question addressed in previous research, which ascertained whether respondents actually had such a friendship. It may have been easier in our study to be supportive of such ties in the abstract. We also allowed participants to define, for themselves, what was meant by a "friendship between men and women," because we wanted an intuitive approach to answering the question. This flexibility in interpretation likely generated more approval than if we had provided a definition. Nevertheless, the fact that such a large majority of our sample advocated cross-gender friendships implies that substantial, societal shifts in attitudes have resulted in the general acceptance of such associations among young, U.S. adults.

Limitations, Future Directions, and Conclusions

There are several limitations to the current study. The sample is restricted to college students, and our information is from only one time point. Future research would benefit from longitudinal data gathered from more representative samples with a broader age range. Another limitation concerns the use of a single item measure to examine the level of appropriateness of the behavior in the friendship vignettes, although each vignette also included an open-ended response. A multiple item scale would have provided a more reliable measure and represents a task for future research.

In conclusion, the gender differences in our results are modest, but at the same time, they remain remarkably robust and predictable with respect to both same- and cross-gender friendships. For example, as hypothesized, women were more disapproving of the actions of a friend that challenged expectations of intimacy and trust, whereas men were particularly unenthusiastic in response to an expression of physical intimacy from a male friend. Females, as compared to males, also appeared to hold higher, and more discerning, expectations of their friends in general. Thus, certain, basic gender discrepancies in close relationships regarding intimacy remain surprisingly foreseeable, and structural and societal changes have yet to erase these discrepancies. At the same time, the fact that such a large proportion of our sample (81.6%) believed in the viability of cross-gender friendships suggests that the attitudes of both men and women toward platonic ties are becoming more liberal than in previous eras, at least for this subgroup. The widespread acceptance of these relationships may be one reason that reactions to the vignettes were frequently shaped by gender, but almost never by cross-gender effects. Future research needs to examine further these intriguing patterns in the associations between gender and the salient bonds of friendship.

References

Adams, R. G., & Blieszner, R. (1998). Structural predictors of problematic friendship in later life. *Personal Relationships, 5*, 439–447. doi:10.1111.j. 1475–6811.1998.tb00181.x.

Alves, W. M., & Rossi, P. H. (1978). Who should get what? Fairness judgments of the distribution of earnings. *The American Journal of Sociology, 84*, 541–564. doi:10.1086/226826.

Argyle, M., & Henderson, M. (1984). The rules of friendship. *Journal of Social and Personal Relationships, 1*, 211–237. doi:10.1177/0265407584012005.

Bank, B. J., & Hansford, S. L. (2000). Gender and friendship: Why are men's best same-sex friendships less intimate and supportive? *Personal Relationships, 7*, 63–78. doi:10.1111/j.1475-6811.2000. tb00004.x.

Baumgarte, R. (2002). Cross-gender friendship: The troublesome relationship. In R. Goodwin & D. Cramer (Eds.), *Inappropriate relationships* (pp. 103–124). Mahwah: Lawrence Erlbaum Associates.

Baumgarte, R., & Nelson, D. W. (2009). Preference for same-versus cross-sex friendships. *Journal of Applied Social Psychology, 39*, 901–917. doi:10.1111/ j.1559-1816.2009.00465.x.

Bell, R. R. (1981). *Worlds of friendship*. Beverly Hills: Sage Publications, Inc.

Bleske, A. L., & Buss, D. M. (2000). Can men and women be just friends? *Personal Relationships, 7*, 131–151. doi:10.1111/j.1475-6811.2000.tb00008.x.

Bleske-Rechek, A. L., & Buss, D. M. (2001). *Personality and Social Psychology Bulletin, 27*, 1310–1323. doi:10.1177/01461672012710007.

Blieszner, R., & Adams, R. G. (1992). *Adult friendship*. Newbury Park: Sage.

Bogle, K. (2008). *Hooking up: Sex, dating, and relationships on campus*. New York: NYU Press.

Booth, A., & Hess, E. (1974). Cross-sex friendship. *Journal of Marriage and the Family, 36*, 38–47. doi:10.2307350992.

Chodorow, N. (1978). *The reproduction of mothering: Psychoanalysis and the sociology of gender*. Berkeley: University of California Press.

Clancey, S. M., & Dollinger, S. J. (1993). Photographic depictions of the self: Gender and age differences in social connectedness. *Sex Roles, 29*, 477–495. doi:10.1007/BF00289322.

Cross, S. E., & Madson, L. (1997). Models of the self: Self-construals and gender. *Psychological Bulletin, 122*, 5–37. doi:10.1037/0033-2909.122.1.5.

Deaux, K., & Major, B. (1987). Putting gender into context: An interactive model of gender-related behavior. *Psychological Review, 94,* 369–389. doi:10.1037/0033-295X.94.3.369.

Duck, S., & Wright, P. H. (1993). Reexamining gender differences in same-gender friendships: A close look at two kinds of data. *Sex Roles, 28,* 709–727. doi:10.1007/BF00289989.

Eagly, A. H., Wood, W., & Diekman, A. B. (2000). Social role theory of sex differences and similarities: A current appraisal. In T. Ecked & H. M. Trautner (Eds.), *The developmental social psychology of gender* (pp. 123–174). Mahwah: Erlbaum.

Elkins, L. E., & Peterson, C. (1993). Gender differences in best friendships. *Sex Roles, 29,* 497–508. doi:10.1007/BF00289323.

Fehr, B. (2004). Intimacy expectations in same-sex friendships: A prototype interaction-pattern model. *Journal of Personality and Social Psychology, 86,* 265–284. doi:10.1037/0022-3514.86.2.265.

Felmlee, D. H. (1999). Social norms in same-and cross-gender friendships. *Social Psychology Quarterly, 62,* 53–67. doi:10.2307/2695825.

Felmlee, D., & Muraco, A. (2009). Gender and friendship norms among older adults. *Research on Aging, 31,* 318–344. doi:10.1177/0164027508330719.

Finch, J. (1987). Research Note: The vignette technique in survey research. *Sociology, 21,* 105–114. doi:10.1177/0038038587021001008.

Fiske, S. T. (2009). Interpersonal stratification: Status, power, and subordination. In S. T. Fiske, D. T. Gilbert & G. Lindzey (Eds.), *Handbook of social psychology,* 5th Ed. (pp. 941–982). Hoboken, NJ: Wiley.

Fiske, S. T., Cuddy, A. J. C., Glick, P., & Xu, J. (2002). A model of (often mixed) stereotype content: Competence and warmth respectively follow from perceived status and competition. *Journal of Personality and Social Psychology, 82,* 878–902. doi:10.1037/0022-3514.82.6.878.

Fox, M., Gibbs, M., & Auerbach, D. (1985). Age and gender dimensions of friendship. *Psychology of Women Quarterly, 9,* 489–502. doi:10.1111/j.1471-6402.1985.tb00898.x.

Frieze, I. H., Sales, E., & Smith, C. (1991). Considering the social context in gender research. *Psychology of Women Quarterly, 15,* 371–392. doi:10.1111/j.1471-6402.1991.tb00414.x.

Gabriel, S., & Gardner, W. L. (1999). Are there "his" and "hers" types of interdependence? The implications of gender differences in collective versus relational interdependence for affect, behavior, and cognition. *Journal of Personality and Social Psychology, 77,* 642–655. doi:10.1037/0022-3514.77.3.642.

Gilligan, C. (1982). *In a different voice: Psychological theory and women's development.* Cambridge: Harvard University Press.

Goffman, E. (1979). *Gender advertisements.* New York: Harper & Row.

Guimond, S., Chatard, A., Martinot, D., Crisp, R. J., & Redersdorff, S. (2006). Social comparison, self-stereotyping, and gender differences in self-construals. *Journal of Personality and Social Psychology, 90,* 221–242. doi:10.1037/0022-3514.90.2.221.

Halatsis, P., & Christakis, N. (2009). The challenge of sexual attraction within heterosexuals' cross-sex friendship. *Journal of Social and Personal Relationships, 26,* 919–937. doi:10.1177/0265407509345650.

Hall, J. A. (2011). Sex differences in friendship expectations: A meta-analysis. *Journal of Social and Personal Relationships.* doi:10.1177/0265407510386192.

Hays, R. B. (1985). A longitudinal study of friendship development. *Journal of Personality and Social Psychology, 48,* 909–924. doi:10.1037/0022-3514.48.4.909.

Henningsen, D. D., Henningsen, M. L. M., & Valde, K. S. (2006). Gender differences in perceptions of women's sexual interest during cross-sex interactions: An application and extension of cognitive valence theory. *Sex Roles, 54,* 821–829. doi:10.1007/s11199-006-9050-y.

Hughes, R. (1998). Considering the vignette technique and its application to a study of drug injecting and HIV risk and safer behaviour. *Sociology of Health & Illness, 20,* 381–400. doi:10.1111/1467-9566.00107.

Hughes, M., Morrison, K., & Asada, K. J. K. (2005). What's love got to do with it? Exploring the impact of maintenance rules, love attitudes, and network support on friends with benefits relationships. *Western Journal of Communication, 69,* 49–66. doi:10.1080/10570310500034154.

Kenler, K. S., Myers, J., & Prescott, C. A. (2005). Sex differences in the relationship between social support and risk for major depression: A longitudinal study of opposite-sex pairs. *The American Journal of Psychiatry, 162,* 250–256. doi:10.1176/appi.ajp.162.2.250.

Kimmel, M. S. (1994). Masculinity as homophobia: Fear, shame and silence in the construction of gender identity. In H. Broad & M. Kaufman (Eds.), *Theorizing masculinities* (pp. 119–141). Thousand Oaks: Sage.

Kito, M. (2005). Self-disclosure in romantic relationships and friendships among American and Japanese college students. *Journal of Social Psychology, 145,* 127–140. doi:10.3200/SOCP.145.2.127-140.

Koenig, B. L., Kirkpatrick, L. E., & Ketelaar, T. (2007). Misperception of sexual and romantic interests in opposite-sex friendships: Four hypotheses. *Personal Relationships, 14,* 411–429. doi:10.1111/j.1475-6811.2007.00163.x.

Lenton, A. P., & Webber, L. (2006). Cross-sex friendships: Who has more? *Sex Roles, 54,* 809–820. doi:10.1007s11199-006-9048-5.

Lewis, R. A. (1978). Emotional intimacy among men. *Journal of Social Issues, 34,* 108–121. doi:10.1111/j.1540-4560.1978.tb02543.x.

Maxwell, S. E., & Delaney, H. D. (2004). *Designing experiments and analyzing data: A model comparison perspective.* Mahwah: Lawrence Erlbaum Associates.

Messner, M. A. (2000). Barbie girls versus sea monsters: Children constructing gender. *Gender and Society, 14,* 765–784. doi:10.1177/089124300014006004.

Monsour, M. (1992). Meanings of intimacy in cross- and same-sex friendships. *Journal of Social and Personal Relationships, 9,* 277–295. doi:10.1177/0265407592092007.

Monsour, M. (2002). *Women and men as friends: Relationships across the life span in the 21st century.* Mahwah: Lawrence Erlbaum.

Muraco, A (2005). Heterosexual evaluations of hypothetical friendship behavior based on sex and sexual orientation. *Journal of Social and Personal Relationships, 22,* 587–605. doi:10.1177/0265407505054525.

O'Meara, J. D. (1989). Cross-sex friendship: Four basic challenges of an ignored relationship. *Sex Roles, 21,* 525–543. doi:10.1007/BF00289102.

Reeder, H. M. (2003). The effect of gender role orientation on same-and cross-sex friendship formation. *Sex Roles, 49,* 2003. doi:10.1023/A:1024408913880.

Reis, H. T. (1998). Gender differences in intimacy and related behaviors: Context and process. In D. L. Canary & K. Dindia (Eds.), *Sex differences and similarities in communication* (pp. 203–231). Mahway: Erlbaum.

Ridgeway, C. L. (2009). Framed before we know it: How gender shapes social relations. *Gender and Society, 23,* 145. doi:10.1177/0891243208330313.

Ridgeway, C. L., & Correll, S. J. (2004). Unpacking the gender system: A theoretical perspective on gender beliefs and social relations. *Gender and Society, 18,* 510–531. doi:10.1177/0891243204265269.

Rubin, I. B. (1985). *Just friends: The role of friendship in our lives.* New York: Harper & Row.

Sheets, V. L., & Lugar, R. (2005). Friendship and gender in Russia and the United States. *Sex Roles, 51,* 131–140. doi:10.1007/s11199-005-1200.0.

Sprecher, S., & Regan, P. C. (2002). Liking some things (in some people) more than others: Partner preferences in romantic relationships and friendships. *Journal of Social and Personal Relationships, 19,* 463–481. doi:10.1177/0265407502019004048.

Thorne, B. (1986). Girls and boys together . . . but mostly apart: Gender arrangements in elementary schools. In W. Hartup & Z. Rubin (Eds.), *Relationships and development* (pp. 167–184). Hillsdale: Erlbaum.

Walker, K. (1994). Men, women, and friendship: What they say, what they do. *Gender and Society, 8,* 246–265. doi:10.1177/089124394008002007.

Werking, K. (1997). *We're just good friends: Women and men in nonromantic relationships.* New York: Guilford.

West, C., & Zimmerman, D. H. (1987). Doing gender. *Gender and Society, 1,* 125–151. doi:10.1177/0891243287001002002.

West, L., Anderson, J., & Duck, S. (1996). Crossing the barriers to friendships between men and women. In J. Wood (Ed.), *Gendered relationships* (pp. 111–127). Mountain View: Mayfield.

Wright, P. H. (1982). Men's friendships, women's friendships and the alleged inferiority of the latter. *Sex Roles, 8,* 1–20. doi:10.1007/BF00287670.

Transgender Friendship Experiences: Benefits and Barriers of Friendships Across Gender Identity and Sexual Orientation

M PAZ GALUPO, L ANDREW BAUERBAND, KIRSTEN A GONZALEZ, D BRIENNE HAGEN,

SHANDELLE D HETHER, AND TIANA E KRUM

The present research investigates the benefits and barriers of friendships for transgender individuals and provides a unique contribution to the friendship literature by considering friendship from a transgender lens. In addition to providing an in-depth exploration of how friends' gender identity and sexual orientation impact transgender individuals' perception of friendship, this research can also serve as a model for understanding the negotiation of transgender identities within a social context outside of the traditional psycho-medical literature that serves to problematize transgender experience.

Few studies have focused on understanding transgender friendship experience. Lesbian, gay, bisexual and transgender (LGBT) friendship research which largely emphasizes sexual minority experience, however, provides a useful initial framework from which to conceptualize the social context of transgender friendship experience.

LGBT Friendship Research: Framing Transgender Friendship Experiences

LGBT friendship research has largely focused on understanding friendships that form between individuals within the larger LGBT community. Friendships are considered to have increased importance for gender and sexual minorities as friendship is emphasized during times of social change and is particularly salient for individuals when their identity is at odds with social norms (Weeks, 1995). LGBT friendship is often characterized as providing a unique type of familial support (Hines, 2007; Nardi, 1992; Weinstock, 2000) where friendships function as "families of choice" (Weston, 1991) and serve to buffer gender and sexual minorities from social isolation or rejection associated with homophobia and transphobia.

Friendships are often characterized as social networks that comprise both general LGBT (Esterberg, 1997; Tillman-Healy, 2001) and transgender (Hines, 2007) communities. Connection to the larger LGBT community is one way that individuals can positively experience their transgender identity (Riggle et al., 2011). As part of a larger interview study on transgender identity and relationships Hines (2007) stresses the significance of friendships between transgender individuals. In particular, transgender friends offer support, have similar experiences, and share knowledge with one another. While providing support and having similar experiences are regarded as characteristics of friendship in general (Duck, 1991; Rawlings, 1992), Hines' (2007) participants described these benefits primarily in relation to decisions and experiences surrounding transitioning and/or in ways that are specific to transgender experience. Transgender friends were also seen

M. Paz Galupo, L. Andrew Bauerband, Kirsten A. Gonzalez, D. Brienne Hagen, Shandelle D. Hether, and Tiana E. Krum, "Transgender Friendship Experiences: Benefits and Barriers of Friendships Across Gender Identity and Sexual Orientation," *Feminism and Psychology*, Vol. 24, No. 2 (2014), pp. 193–215. Copyright © 2014 by the authors. Reprinted by permission of SAGE Publications.

as providing needed counseling that was unavailable from the traditional health care system. Hines' (2007) research provides a beginning point for conceptualizing transgender friendship and highlights the ways that friendship experience is shaped by minority status and inequalities. Benefits of friendships with other transgender individuals were largely seen as filling in the gaps of support and services not otherwise provided by traditional family, friends, and institutions.

Although her work provides a focus on transgender experience, Hines (2007) did not address barriers to friendships with transgender individuals or explore friendship experiences with friends across different identities. Additional research is necessary to provide a more comprehensive understanding of transgender friendship experiences. Although the LGBT friendship literature has focused most directly on sexual minority friendships, it has often assumed a similar context for understanding transgender experience. It will be important, therefore, to understand how transgender friendships are both similar to and different from sexual minority friendships.

Past research has suggested that lesbians and gay men form the majority of their friendships with same-sex individuals who also identify with the LGBT community (Galupo, 2007a, 2009). These within community friendships are seen as having unique benefits as they may provide a sense of shared experience, an avenue for processing minority status, and an opportunity for experiencing equity not easily achieved in other friendships where sexual orientation and or sex differences require negotiation (Berger, 1982; Nardi, 1999; Stanley, 1996). Having same orientation friends has also been related to psychological adjustment (Berger, 1982). While lesbians and gay men may find a unique type of support through same-orientation friendships, bisexual women and men may be less likely to do so as they are less likely to have a friend with the same (bisexual) identity as themselves (Galupo, 2007a).

Research on sexual minority friendships with individuals in the LGBT community has largely focused on the benefits of such friendships while research that examines friendships between LGBT

and heterosexual individuals has primarily considered the barriers to friendship development. Initial research on the topic suggested that lesbian and gay male friendships outside the LGBT community are tenuously constructed around a number of barriers. Barriers include the stigma of having a sexual minority friend, sexual tension, and reduced comfort in disclosing personal information especially as it relates to sexual minority experience (O'Boyle and Thomas, 1996; Price, 1999). Although bisexual individuals are more likely to have cross-orientation friendships with heterosexual individuals (Galupo, 2007a), these friendships exist at the cost of bisexual identity where issues related to bisexual identity are less likely to be acknowledged within the friendship (Galupo et al., 2004; Galupo, 2007b).

Benefits of friendships outside the LGBT community have also been considered. For example, sexual minority women report that through their friendships with heterosexual women they gain an understanding that acceptance from heterosexuals is possible, gain an objective perspective in their lives, are able to break down stereotypes, and experience increased closeness and trust within the friendship accompanying sexual orientation disclosure (Galupo and St. John. 2001). Muraco (2006) discusses ways in which friendships with heterosexual individuals can function as "intentional families" for both sexual minority and heterosexual friends.

Although gender identity has not been systematically addressed in the LGBT friendship research, aspects of the past literature may prove relevant for understanding transgender friendship experiences. Inherent in the way the literature approaches LGBT friendship is with an acknowledgement and understanding of the power and inequalities that exist across sexual orientation identity. Using a similar approach, the consideration of friendship for transgender individuals both within and outside the LGBT community will likely yield an understanding of the ways power and inequality operate around gender identity. Additionally, LGBT friendship research has considered the friendships of sexual minorities by examining patterns across sexual orientation, sex, and race

(Galupo, 2007a, 2009). However, this research has neglected to extend to gender identity either by considering how sexual minority friendships are experienced across gender identity, or by considering the friendships of individuals who identify as transgender. Importantly, there has not been an acknowledgement within the LGBT friendship literature that some sexual minority individuals may also identify as transgender, and vice versa.

Feminist Intersectional Theory: Researching Transgender Experience and Friendship

Feminist intersectional theory emphasizes the importance of examining relationships among social identities as intersecting categories of oppression and inequality (Collins, 2000; Crenshaw, 1991; hooks, 1984; McCall, 2005). This theoretical framework originally critiqued both gender- and race-based research for failing to acknowledge individuals living at the intersections of the two. Initially focused on race, class, and gender, more recent conceptualizations are inclusive of sexual orientation, specifically addressing the role of homophobia and heterosexism in the lives of women and racial minorities (Anzaldua, 1990; King, 1990; Trujillo, 1991).

Recently intersectional theory has been extended to understand transgender experience (Futty, 2010; Hines, 2010b; Monro and Richardson, 2010; Nagoshi and Brzuzy, 2010) and this literature can inform an intersectional approach to researching transgender friendship experience. Central to the inclusion of transgender within an intersectional framework is an acknowledgment of dimensions of inequality and power that surround cultural meanings of gender and gender identity. Viewing gender identity within intersectional theory shifts the focus from the "unnatural" and "abnormal" conceptualizations of transgender that are traditionally highlighted by psycho-medical perspectives, while making visible and subjective non-transgender identities. Recent use of the term cisgender to refer to non-transgender experience emphasizes this focus (Futty, 2010). Understanding gender identity across transgender/cisgender experience, then, allows a comparative dimension which invites exploration of cisgender experience. It also allows a discussion of cisgender privilege in ways that are analogous to other systems of privilege (Serano, 2007).

Researching transgender experiences within an intersectional framework is ideal for a number of reasons. It potentially allows for: (1) a comparative approach across transgender and cisgender identities; (2) a disaggregation of sexual and gender minority experience, as not all transgender individuals are comfortable being considered within the larger LGBT community (Fassinger and Arseneau, 2007); (3) a systematic comparison across sexual orientation and gender identity which can serve to highlight the similarities and differences in the way the two operate. Attending to differences is important as the two are often conflated in the research literature (Hines, 2010a). Attending to similarities allows for an understanding of how gender and sexual minorities operate as non-normative identities, and is particularly highlighted when making comparisons across normative (cisgender/heterosexual) and non-normative (transgender/sexual minority) identities; and (4) an understanding of how experiences differ among individuals who identify as transgender. This is important as not all transgender individuals see their experiences as similar to others who identify under the transgender umbrella (Monro and Richardson, 2010).

Studying friendship, in particular, provides additional application of intersectional theory as a means for interrogating transgender experience. Because intersectional theory provides a lens for considering institutionalized inequalities as they relate to social interactions (Zinn and Dill, 2000) and because expression and negotiation of identities vary across social context (Galupo, 2011), friendship provides an ideal location from which to explore intersections of identity between two or more individuals. In particular, past research has focused on friendships that exist across social categories (cross-race, cross-orientation, cross-gender) as an avenue for exploring intersectionality (Galupo, 2009; Galupo & Gonzalez, 2013; Muraco, 2006, 2012). A similar approach could be usefully applied for understanding transgender individuals' experience of friendship as it shifts in relation to friends' sexual orientation and gender identity.

Statement of the Problem

The present research explores transgender friendship experience in the United States. Based on participant responses to open-ended questions, we focus our analysis on understanding transgender friendship with transgender, cisgender, sexual minority, and heterosexual individuals. We explore the benefits and barriers to transgender friendship across gender identity and sexual orientation of the friend.

Utilizing an intersectional methodology, the present research allows for comparisons of transgender friendship experiences across friends' gender identity (transgender and cisgender) and sexual orientation (sexual minority and heterosexual). The use of friends' gender identity and sexual orientation as analytical categories in this research is not meant to suggest that these groupings are immutable or absolute. Adopting categories for the purpose of grouping and analysis is done provisionally as a means for uncovering patterns across transgender social perception and experience. The way analytic categories are defined for this research is consistent with an intersectional framework that makes inequality a central component where comparisons can be made across normative (cisgender/heterosexual) and non-normative (transgender/sexual minority) dimensions of gender identity and sexual orientation.

Method

Participants and recruitment procedure

Participants included 536 individuals who self-identified as transgender or gender variant. With regard to gender identity participants self-identified as 40.4% male, 33.5% female, 16.3% gender nonconforming, 7.2% bigender, and 2.6% did not identify. With regard to sexual orientation identity, participants self-identified as 35.1% queer/pansexual/fluid, 19.2% heterosexual, 19.2% lesbian/gay, 19.0% bisexual, and 7.5% questioning. In addition, 78.1% of the participants were identified as part of a larger LGBT community.

Participants represented all regions of the United States, residing in 46 states and Washington DC. Participants ranged in age from 18 to 73. . . . There was some diversity in the sample where 16.4% participants identified as racial minorities, specifically: 1.1% Native American; 1.5% Asian/Asian American; 2.6% Hispanic; 4.0% African American/Black; 7.2% other/bi-racial; and 83.6% Caucasian/White. With regard to socioeconomic status, participants self-identified as 32.6% working class; 42.3% middle class; 22.1% upper-middle class; and 3.0% upper class. In terms of educational background, 1.0% had some high school education; 6.0% had a high school diploma; 9.0% had completed vocational school; 33.9% had some college education; 30.0% had earned a bachelor's degree; and 20.1% had an advanced college degree. . . .

Measures

Data analysis focused on participants' free response answers to four open ended questions. Questions were presented in the order that follows: (1) what are the unique benefits and barriers to having friends who also identify as transgender? (2) What are the unique benefits and barriers to having friends who identify as cisgender (non-transgender)? (3) What are the unique benefits and barriers to having friends who identify as sexual minorities (lesbian, gay, bisexual, pansexual, queer, etc. as it relates to sexual orientation)? and (4) What are the unique benefits and barriers to having friends who identify as heterosexual? . . .

Results and Discussion

Although participants were asked to describe unique friendship benefits and barriers with individuals of different identities, many of their responses resonated with the way friendship has been described in the general friendship literature. General features of friendships include *having someone to talk to, emotional support, acceptance,* and *shared experiences* (Duck, 1991; Rawlings, 1992). Participants described their friendships similarly but usually transgender specific experience was central to their definitions of support, acceptance, and experiences. For example, instead of *having someone to talk to,* a benefit expressed by transgender participants was *can talk about transgender issues.* Articulation of friendship benefits and barriers made it clear that transgender identity was salient to how participants were defining "experiences."

Unique Benefits and Barriers Differed Across Normative and Non-normative Experiences

Because our focus is on documenting unique friendship experiences across friends' identities, we focus this "Results" section on findings for the 16 benefits and 10 barriers for which different patterns emerged. This analysis revealed unique benefits and barriers to friendship for both normative (cisgender and heterosexual) and non-normative (transgender and sexual minority) dimensions of identity. . . .

Unique Benefits and Barriers to Friendships with Cisgender and Heterosexual Individuals

Eight benefits and six barriers were significantly more likely to be expressed in reference to cisgender and heterosexual (normative) friends when compared to transgender and sexual minority (non-normative) friends. Unique benefits included: (1) helps me feel "normal"; (2) transgender/sexuality issues do not dominate conversation and friendship; (3) validation more powerful from someone with normative identity; (4) more opportunity for friendship due to larger population; (5) emotionally stable; (6) helps me present as identified gender ("pass"); (7) offers more diverse perspectives and interactions; and (8) opportunity to educate about transgender experience. . . .

Friendship benefits with cisgender and heterosexual individuals centered on validation and privileges associated with normative experience. One participant noted that a benefit of having cisgender friends was "I don't stand out in public and have 'normal' friends who do 'normal' things." Just being associated with and accepted by normative friends helped transgender individuals feel "normal," "pass" more readily, "fit in," "blend in," and even "melt more easily into society." This

association with larger culture can also translate into feeling more "safe" when out in public.

Friendships with cisgender and heterosexual individuals were seen as a way of being connected to mainstream society. This is illustrated in the following participant response: "These individuals are part of general society and association with them helps in acceptance and participation in society." As one participant put it, "most people are not LGBT in the world, (and) you have to learn to work with them." Normative friends were seen as living in the "real world" and served as a reminder that "there is life outside the T community" or, as another participant put it "the trans bubble." Participants also recognized that "there are a whole lot more of them. Even in the 'friendly' cities, the trans community is very small. If I restricted my friendships there I'd have very few friends."

For transgender participants, normative friends were "more emotionally stable," could be "your little voice when you start getting crazy," and were seen as "grounding." Normative friends were viewed as uniquely able to teach "how to pass as male/female," to "help navigate the way through a gender in which I was not raised," to "give advice on female issues as well as clothing, makeup, life situations," and to serve as a "role model." One participant speaks to this:

> The benefits of a (cisgender heterosexual) male friend for me are similar to that of a role model. I admire how he embraces his masculinity, processes his anger and supports the women in his life. As I navigate the world as male, I ease into my new exciting and challenging situations using his choices and character as a guide.

Often support from normative friends was seen as more validating than from a friend with a non-normative identity. One participant notes that the "approval/appraisals of my appearance mean more than these of other trans people." Sometimes these friendships were seen as more genuine because, as one participant put it, "I feel like we are friends because we like each other and not just because we are both trans."

Participants did note that friendships with normative friends provided an opportunity for education and developing allies. This was seen as particularly important being that "cisgendered people are the ones who can help trans individuals the most because it's best for others to hear from a side that supports, but isn't a part of, the community directly." Others valued the opportunity to educate because they were seen as the "expert" and normative friends would "accept what I say more easily because I am the only transperson they know."

Transgender participants also spoke to six barriers unique to friendships with cisgender and heterosexual friends: (1) not knowledgeable on issues of gender, sex, and privilege; (2) insensitive use of language in reference to identity; (3) difficult to talk about transgender/sexuality issues; (4) fosters feelings of discomfort; (5) not understanding non-normative experience; and (6) fewer shared experiences . . . As much as friendship with normative friends served to provide ways to fit into mainstream society, the barriers centered on the ways that cisgender and heterosexual friends could not fully understand or relate to their minority experience.

> There is somethings that the most well intentioned friend cannot grasp when something about my gender is explained to them, either because I don't have the words to explain it in a way that they get, or because fundamentally they will never 'get it.'

Normative friends often were described as not able to "get it," "not open to learning," and as not knowing "the full me, and they don't want to." When talking about cisgender and heterosexual friends, feelings of discomfort were often centered on feeling "tokenized."

> Some cisgender friends treated my transition process as this experiment they were eager to watch like I was the latest blockbuster film or a zoo animal. They also would try to tell me what they thought I should do like take pictures or YouTube videos to document my transition or what names they thought I should choose when I changed to my preferred name. This was not cool and I distanced myself and ended some of these relationships.

These findings reveal clear patterns in perception of friendship experience based on normative and non-normative dimensions of friends' gender identity and sexual orientation. Questions were asked to focus participants on one aspect of their friends' identity at a time; either based on gender identity (transgender/cisgender) or sexual orientation (sexual minority/heterosexual). However, because of the way normative identity is assumed unless otherwise linguistically signaled it was clear that the second identity was assumed normative. For example, the majority of answers provided by participants in response to sexual minority and heterosexual friends indicated that participants assumed a cisgender identity. In describing the benefit of having a heterosexual friend one participant responded "I don't stand out in public and have 'normal' friends who do 'normal' things." It is clear that although asked only about a friend who is heterosexual, a cisgender identity was also assumed. Likewise, the majority of answers regarding cisgender individuals assumed a heterosexual identity. Because of this, a secondary analysis was not necessary or appropriate to differentiate between the normative identities (i.e. heterosexual and cisgender). However, a secondary analysis was conducted to further differentiate unique experiences between sexual minority and transgender friendships.

Unique Benefits and Barriers to Friendships with Transgender and Sexual Minority Individuals

Eight benefits and four barriers were significantly more likely to be expressed in reference to transgender and sexual minority (non-normative) friends when compared to cisgender and heterosexual (normative) friends. Unique benefits included: (1) understanding non-normative experience; (2) knowledgeable on issues of gender, sex, and privilege; (3) shared experiences; (4) can talk about transgender issues; (5) offers support via mentoring and shared resources; (6) comfortable being myself; (7) shared community: "family" and belonging; and (8) non-judgmental/open-minded . . .

Consistent across these benefits was the way participants related benefits of transgender and sexual minority friendship to common understandings, shared experiences or knowledge in ways that made non-normative experience primary. These shared understandings were described both at the individual and community level. Duck (1991) discusses the general way in which friends can "develop their own sets of shared concerns, common interests and collective problems, as well as shared meanings, common responses to life and communal emotions" (p. 13). What makes these commonalities even more important to transgender friendship experience is the fact that they are much less likely to be present in friendships with cisgender and heterosexual friends. As one participant noted,

> Having other trans-identified friends normalizes my own trans experience for me simply by providing contact with someone who is "like me" . . . It makes me feel like less of a freak to have contact with other people who share my experience.

Similar sentiment was expressed for sexual minority friends: "Being a minority in this manner can lead to a feeling of community and a strong sense of 'us.'"

The fact that some participants viewed gender and sexual minorities through a lens of commonality was clear when considering their responses. Even when asked about friendships with sexual minorities specifically, participants often recast their responses by referencing friends in larger LGBT community:

> Having LGBTQQIA and perverted friends is like breathing air. It's like the most valuable thing there is. It's a mirror held up to yourself. It's (in a non-ableist way) up to five senses that can experience you: you are seen, you are heard, you are touched. Sometimes you're even smelled and tasted!

Participants described their friendships with gender and sexual minorities as providing support, information, a sense of "family," and a feeling of being "at home" with others who "live in the same universe" or "community" that sometimes operates as a "support group" and provides a "mirror" for their own experience—a place for "letting one's hair down" and being "fully myself." Many participants described a friendship narrative with

transgender and sexual minority individuals consistent with previous literature that views within LGBT community friendships as functioning as "family" (Nardi, 1992; Weinstock, 2000; Weston, 1991). These friendships were described as a respite from larger society, where the same level of comfort and community are not achieved. Benefits with transgender and sexual minority friends, then, were borne out of lack of support, understanding, and services not readily provided by traditional family, friends, and society. As one participant put it, "they know what it feels like to face the tyranny of the majority."

However, transgender participants also detailed four barriers unique to friendships with transgender and sexual minority friends: (1) invalidating gender identity and personal experience; (2) transgender/sexuality issues dominate conversation and friendship; (3) negative emotions, drama and instability; and (4) fear of being "out"-ed by association or disclosure. Again, these barriers underscore assumed commonality of experience among gender and sexual minorities but, in these cases, the shared or assumed similarity compromises the friendship. One participant expressed this in the following way:

> Many trans people tend to think there is one universal way of being trans, and that way usually doesn't apply to me at all. It can be annoying to have to remind people that we have different experiences and they shouldn't make assumptions.

Another participant indicated that among sexual minority friends there are "tendencies to make false equivalencies between sexual orientation and gender identity and mistakenly assume they understand trans experiences better than they do."

Participants also discussed the way the assumed similarity among gender and sexual minorities often led to too much of a focus on issues of gender and sexuality:

> Many of the LBGTQ friends that I've had, have really emphasized their sexuality; so much so that it takes on a larger presence in their lives than maybe even food, politics, or religion . . . I am often uncomfortable with sexuality being such a large focus of one's life.

Often just being associated with other gender and sexual minorities compromised participants' ability to present as desired: "If you are in a situation where you aren't out, you stand a chance of accidentally being outed because of the company you keep."

Unique Benefits and Barriers of Friendships with Other Transgender Individuals

Five benefits and four barriers were significantly more likely to be expressed in reference to transgender friends when compared to sexual minority friends. Benefits included; (1) shared experiences; (2) can talk about transgender issues; (3) offers support via mentoring and shared resources; (4) comfortable being myself; and (5) helps me present as identified gender ("pass") . . .

Even though participants saw transgender and sexual minority friends in ways that distinguished them from cisgender and heterosexual individuals, transgender friends were seen as providing a unique type of friendship beyond that of sexual minorities. The degree of shared experiences and understanding was seen as greater with transgender friends. Transgender friends were often characterized as being able to "completely understand" and were seen as being on "the same page." One participant noted "other transgender people are the ONLY ones who fully 'get it' so there is some understanding and kindred spiritedness there."

This commonality was often articulated as a type of support and understanding that went beyond understanding being a minority, and related specifically to being transgender. Participants characterized their transgender friends as able to "understand gender issues and dysphoria." Consequently, "they can offer real life advice from experience." These friends were seen, often, as "mentors" who made up a larger "support network" and "transgender community." Often this network helped connect individuals to specific resources, as one participant noted that transgender friends made it "much easier to find trans-friendly businesses/doctors, etc." Others described how it was nice to be seen as a resource or mentor to others.

Participants valued that their transgender friends were able to "talk to them about hormones," "speak specifically about 'trans-related issues,'" and discuss "passing" and "medical interventions." One participant describes:

> For those who have transitioned, specifically those who have undergone surgeries, hormone replacement therapies, or who are living as a gender different from what they were sexed at birth—all of these experiences are unique in our culture and because the trans experience is also highly stigmatized or emphasized as different, exotic, and so on that I can talk about my feelings and thoughts about my body and my daily life with other trans people. And to some extent, I can't share this sort of "mirroring" with cis people.

Overall, transgender friends were characterized as providing a unique type of understanding and support above and beyond that of sexual minority friends. In addition, transgender friends and networks were seen as providing access to information and resources in negotiating the health care system and around issues of transition, similar to Hines' (2007) findings on friendships between transgender individuals.

Participants also detailed four barriers that were more likely experienced in friendships with transgender friends: (1) transgender issues dominate conversation and friendship; (2) negative emotions, drama, and emotional instability; (3) fear of being "out"-ed by association or disclosure; and (4) fosters feelings of discomfort. . . .

Transgender friends were often seen as too focused on issues of gender identity. A challenge was seen as "keeping conversation from ALWAYS focusing on gender and identity." This was particularly true for individuals who were transitioning. One person noted "I would not make friends with a person who is in transition because that is all they want to discuss."

Participants characterized some transgender friends as focused on "drama," "trauma," and "emotional baggage." One participant remarked, "the reality of our lives means that at any given time a lot of us are really stressed or depressed and it can make being around more than one or two other trans people for a while draining." Other participants noted that this was not only draining but sometimes "their gender issues can trigger my own."

Discomfort was uniquely expressed in friendships with other transgender individuals in terms of jealousy and competition. One participant noted "occasional 'envy' which comes with seeing friends transitioning ahead of yourself." Another described "becoming jealous of my trans friends who are able to live more freely as trans, or who have been able to transition more fully." Jealousy and competition also included having "financial differences" or "more success with outside, sexual relationships." One participant touched on a number of these barriers:

> There is a weird competition between trans people I think. I think there is generally an internal or even external comparison many of us do to compare which is prettier, more passable, further along in their transition and more successful in general. Also, there is a concern that the other trans person may out you or judge you. Being around other trans people draws attention to my own trans identity which I don't always want to be reminded of.

Other participants went beyond noting barriers to transgender friendship to discussing no interest or association with LGBT or transgender communities. This sentiment was summed up by the following quotation: "I definitely do not seek out other trans people and have no interest in 'trans community' at all. Self ghettoisation is never pretty, no matter the reason. (sic)"

Unique Benefits and Barriers of Friendships with Sexual Minorities

Five benefits and two barriers were significantly more likely to be expressed in reference to sexual minority versus transgender friends. Benefits included: (1) shared community: "family" and belonging; (2) non-judgmental/open-minded; (3) offers more diverse perspectives and interactions; (4) opportunity to educate about transgender issues; and (5) opportunity for sexual partners. . . . As a group these benefits had elements that both acknowledged sexual minorities as having non-normative experiences (shared community: "family" and belonging) but also saw their experiences as outside transgender experience much like cisgender and heterosexual friends (opportunity to educate about transgender issues, offers more diverse perspectives and interactions). At times, sexual minority friends were seen as uniquely able to draw on their experiences as a sexual minority but to remain more objective and non-judgmental than transgender friends. One participant said of sexual minority friends, "they understand an extent of what I feel, but have a differing enough viewpoint to be able to offer objective advice."

Participants also detailed two barriers that were more likely experienced in friendships with sexual minority versus transgender individuals: (1) not understanding non-normative experience; and (2) fewer shared experiences. . . . The quote below includes elements of both of these barriers:

> Cisgender sexual minorities frequently feel that they understand transgender individuals better than they actually do because the T is included in LGBT. They are more likely to feel that the T is the least important part of the LGBT community, but still feel that they should be appreciated as allies. They are less likely to acknowledge their own privileges and ingrained cissexism.

Participants also noted that often sexual minorities can "make false equivalencies between sexual orientation and gender identity" and that unique experiences of transgender and sexual minority individuals become "conflated." Also noted was the "prevalence of highly gendered spaces and situations in many LGB communities"

To some degree, how participants responded to the question of sexual minority friendships often seemed to depend upon whether participants themselves identified as a sexual minority. Not surprisingly, transgender participants who were also sexual minorities tended to focus on their shared experiences with sexual minorities. For example, "having friends who identify as a sexual minority helps me to realize that I am not alone in my struggle for sexual orientation equality." And, "I'm queer as well and so they understand." Transgender participants who identified as heterosexual were more likely to discuss being misunderstood (e.g. "sometimes that they don't always understand that after my transition I am straight") and isolated (e.g. "I have identified as straight for many years, and felt like I didn't really fit in with them, and that's been slow to change.") from the larger LGBT community.

Conclusion

In thinking through the present findings it is important to note that participants were discussing friendship experiences in direct response to prompts that asked them to describe the unique benefits and barriers of friendship with transgender, cisgender, sexual minority, and heterosexual individuals. Analyses were intentionally framed to uncover transgender friendship patterns across gender identity and sexual orientation of friends. Although we do note the benefits and barriers that were similar across friendships, we elaborate on the findings that speak to the unique aspects of each friendship type. Consideration of the differences along with the similarities is necessary for a full characterization of these friendships. Three benefits and two barriers discussed by participants did not differ in across gender identity or sexual orientation of the friend.

Additionally, the findings of this research may over emphasize the role of identity in friendship. In fact, some participants questioned or rejected the framing of this research entirely. When asked about friendships with sexual minorities, one participant indicated "it depends on the person, not their sexual identity." Another responded that the benefits of having cisgender friends: "are the same as having friends period—they provide support, love, communion, and the opportunity to live in community and to grow as a human being."

Despite the limitations of a framework which disproportionately emphasizes unique friendship experiences, the present findings expand our understanding of transgender friendship in important ways. Because transgender friendship has rarely been studied, it has been discussed primarily in the context of the larger LGBT friendship literature. There were distinct ways that our findings resonate with that literature. In particular, the discussion of friends as "family" was emphasized specifically in the transgender friendship narratives with sexual minorities. In addition, the way that participants' friendship experiences were strongly influenced by the normative/non-normative dimensions of friends' identity parallels the way the LGBT friendship literature has made distinctions between friendships within and outside the LGBT community. This research also highlights the ways that the larger LGBT community is not always the ideal friendship site for transgender individuals and how the traditional LGBT framework may not always capture the diverse experiences of those who identify as transgender.

Although the focus of this work was to consider patterns of friendship experience across friends' sexual orientation and gender identity, our findings also serve as a beginning point for understanding different friendship patterns that exist among transgender individuals. For example, friendship experiences with sexual minorities varied based on whether the participants also identified as transgender. In addition, some of our participants expressed no desire to have a connection to LGBT and transgender communities. It is important to note that our recruitment strategy, which relied upon online transgender resources and referrals, likely led to an underrepresentation of such individuals. This is significant as the benefits and barriers to friendships within and outside of LGBT and transgender communities would likely be experienced differently. In addition, we intentionally recruited participants broadly and although we included both transgender and gender variant individuals, we did not seek to understand how participants may approach friendship differently based on their unique conceptualizations of gender identity. Understanding patterns of friendship experiences among transgender individuals is an important direction for future research.

Another important direction for understanding the current findings would be to explore friendship benefits and barriers in relation to transgender identity development and disclosure. Friendship, in general, is emphasized during times of transition, when individuals' identities are at odds with the norm, and during times of great social change (Weeks, 1995). Transgender friendship experiences are ideally understood in this context. Likewise, transgender identity is not static. Rather it is experienced as a developmental process (Devor, 2004; Lev, 2004) where transgender experience of friendship would likely differ with regard to where an individual is in that process. Friendship experience may also be impacted by disclosure of transgender identity or status in the context of friendship (Galupo et al., 2014). Although we did not systematically analyze data related to our participants' transgender identity development or salience of their identities it is important to recognize that some of the benefits and barriers of friendships would be experienced differently at different points in identity development. Because friendship is experienced in social context and in relation to friends' identities, identity development of friends (based on sexual orientation and gender identity, both normative and non-normative) would also be relevant. For example, the barrier "transgender issues dominate conversation and friendship" may be more likely to be an issue to an individual who is friends with someone who is more actively processing their transgender identity than themselves. Likewise, the benefit of "opportunity to educate about transgender experience" may only be a benefit if the friend is at a stage of understanding their cisgender identity and position of privilege.

Transgender Friendship, Intersectional Theory, and Cultural Constructs of Normality

The present research provides a unique contribution to the friendship literature by focusing on friendship from a transgender lens. By approaching the topic from an intersectional theoretical perspective, the analysis moves beyond strictly describing friendships with individuals of different identities to exploring how inequities are used to construct cultural conceptions of normality and ultimately shape both transgender and cisgender experience. It is important to note, however, that we primarily attended to intersections of identity for sexual orientation and gender identity of the friend. We did not differentiate experience across participants' sexual orientation, gender, or gender identity nor did we attend to race or class in our intersectional analysis. Further analysis

along these lines would be necessary to fully examine friendship experiences of transgender individuals. However, the specific focus on sexual orientation and gender identity used in the present intersectional analysis is particularly useful for understanding the larger discourse on normality in the LGBT literature.

The LGBT friendship literature, which almost exclusively focuses on sexual orientation, had previously conceptualized normative experience based explicitly on notions of heterosexuality (Galupo, 2007a, 2009; Muraco, 2012; Nardi, 1999; Shepperd et al., 2010; Weinstock, 2000). While cisgender identities and experience were assumed, they have not been previously explored as categories of analysis in the research. Thus, when reading this literature it is difficult to disentangle the way cultural constructions of normal are impacted by heterosexism and cisgenderism.

As transgender experience is problematized in society and pathologized in the psycho-medical literature it is particularly useful to attend to the discourse regarding normality expressed in transgender friendship narratives. The use of cisgender as a category of investigation had not previously been incorporated in the friendship literature and was crucial to exposing how normative identity is dually constructed upon cisgender and heterosexual assumptions. In considering friendship, some participants discussed the way being associated with, or accepted by, cisgender and heterosexual friends contributed to a felt sense of normality in their own lives. Participants themselves defined both cisgender and heterosexual friends as "emotionally stable," "grounding," and "'normal' friends who do 'normal' things." Acceptance from these friends provided a "validation" not provided by friendships from within the LGBT communities. It was clear from the narratives that heterosexual or cisgender identity alone was not enough to regard a friend as normal. Rather, it was the combination of the two.

The conceptual conflation of gender identity and sexual orientation can make it difficult to address the unique ways that transgender and cisgender individuals negotiate these two dimensions of identity across social situations. By simultaneously considering gender identity and sexual orientation, the present research makes visible the intersection between the two in the context of friendship and serves as a model for using cisgender as a category of investigation in relationship and social identity research.

References

Anzaldua G (1990) Bridge, drawbridge, sandbar or island: Lesbians-of-color hacienda alianzas. In: Albrecht L and Brewer RM (eds) *Bridges of Power: Women's Multicultural Alliances*. Philadelphia: New Society, pp. 216–231.

Berger RM (1982) *Gay and Gray: The Older Homosexual Man*. Urbana: University of Illinois Press.

Collins PH (2000) It's all in the family: Intersections of gender, race and nation. In: Narayan U and Harding S (eds) *Decentering the Center: Philosophy for a Multicultural, Postcolonial, and Feminist World*. Bloomington: Indiana University Press, pp. 156–176.

Crenshaw K (1991) Mapping the margins: Intersectionality, identity politics and violence against women of color. *Stanford Law Review* 43(6): 1241–1299.

Devor AH (2004) Witnessing and mirroring: A fourteen stage model of transsexual identity development. *Journal of Gay & Lesbian Psychotherapy* 8: 41–67.

Duck S (1991) *Understanding Relationships*. New York, NY: Guilford.

Esterberg KG (1997) *Lesbian and Bisexual Identities: Constructing Communities, Constructing Selves*. Philadelphia, PA: Temple University Press.

Fassinger RE and Arseneau JR (2007) 'I'd rather get wet than be under the umbrella': Differentiating the experiences and identities of lesbian, gay, bisexual, and transgender people. In: Biesche KJ, Perez RM and DeBord KA (eds) *Handbook of Counseling and Psychotherapy with Lesbian, Gay, Bisexual, and Transgender Clients*. Washington, DC: American Psychological Association, pp. 19–49.

Futty JT (2010) Challenges posed by transgender-passing within ambiguities and interrelations. *Graduate Journal of Social Science* 7(2): 57–75.

Galupo MP (2009) Cross-category friendship patterns: Comparison of heterosexual and sexual minority adults. *Journal of Social and Personal Relationships* 26: 811–831.

Galupo MP (2007a) Friendship patterns of sexual minority individuals in adulthood. *Journal of Social and Personal Relationships* 24(1): 139–151.

Galupo MP (2007b) Women's close friendships across sexual orientation: An analysis of lesbian-heterosexual and bisexual-heterosexual women's friendships. *Sex Roles* 56: 473–482.

Galupo MP (2011) Bisexuality: Complicating & conceptualizing sexual identity. *Journal of Bisexuality* 11: 545–549.

Galupo MP and Gonzalez KA (2013) Friendship values and cross-category friendships: Understanding adult friendship patterns across gender, sexual orientation, and race. *Sex Roles* 68: 779–790.

Galupo MP, Krum TE, Hagen DB, et al. (2014) Disclosure of transgender identity and status in the context of friendship. *Journal of LGBT Issues in Counseling* 8: 25–42.

Galupo MP, Sailer CA and St. John SC (2004) Friendships across sexual orientation: Experiences of bisexual women in early adulthood. *Journal of Bisexuality* 4: 39–53.

Galupo MP and St. John S (2001) Benefits of cross-sexual orientation friendships among adolescent females. *Journal of Adolescence* 24: 83–93.

hooks b (1984) *Feminist Theory: From Margin to Center*. Cambridge, MA: South End Press.

Hines S (2007) *TransForming Gender: Transgender Practices of Identity, Intimacy, and Care*. Bristol, UK: Policy Press.

Hines S (2010a) Sexing gender/gendering sex: Towards an intersectional analysis of transgender. In: Taylor Y, Hines S and Casey M (eds) *Theorising Intersectionality and Sexuality*. Basingstoke: Palgrave Macmillan, pp. 140–162.

Hines S (2010b) Queerly situated? Exploring negotiations of trans queer subjectivities at work and within community spaces in the UK. *Gender, Place & Culture* 17(5): 597–613.

King D (1990) Multiple jeopardy, multiple consciousness: The context of a Black feminist ideology. In: Malson M, Mudimbe-Boyi E, O'Barr JF, et al. (eds) *Black Women in America: Social Science Perspectives*. Chicago: University of Chicago Press, pp. 265–296.

Lev AI (2004) *Transgender Emergence: Therapeutic Guidelines for Working with Gender-Variant Individuals and Their Families*. New York, NY: Haworth Press.

McCall L (2005) The complexity of intersectionality. *Signs: Journal of Women in Culture and Society* 30(3): 1771–1800.

Monro S and Richardson D (2010) Intersectionality and sexuality: The case of sexuality and transgender equalities work in UK local government. In: Taylor Y, Hines S and Casey M (eds) *Theorizing Intersectionality and Sexuality*. Basingstoke: Palgrave MacMillan, pp. 99–118.

Muraco A (2006) Intentional families: Fictive kin ties between cross-gender, different sexual orientation friends. *Journal of Marriage and Family* 68: 1313–1325.

Muraco A (2012) *Odd Couples: Friendships at the Intersection of Gender and Sexual Orientation.* Durham, North Carolina: Duke University Press.

Nagoshi JL and Brzuzy S (2010) Transgender theory: Embodying research and practice. *Affilia: Journal of Women and Social Work* 25(4): 431–443.

Nardi PM (1992) That's what friends are for: Friends as family in the gay and lesbian community. In: Plummer F (ed.) *Modern Homosexualities: Fragments of Lesbian and Gay Experience.* New York, NY: Routledge, pp. 108–120.

Nardi PM (1999) *Gay Men's Friendships: Invincible communities.* Chicago: Chicago University Press.

O'Boyle CG and Thomas MD (1996) Friendships between lesbian and heterosexual women. In: Weinstock JS and Rothblum ED (eds) *Lesbian friendships.* New York: New York University Press, pp. 240–248.

Price J (1999) *Navigating Differences: Friendships Between Gay and Straight Men.* New York, NY: Harrington.

Rawlings WK (1992) *Friendship Matters: Communication, Dialectics, and the Life Course.* New York, NY: Aldine DeGruyter.

Riggle EDB, Rostosky SS, McCants LE, et al. (2011) The positive aspects of a transgender self-identification. *Psychology & Sexuality* 2(2): 147–158.

Serano J (2007) *Whipping Girl: A Transsexual Woman on Sexism and Scapegoating of Femininity.* Emeryville, CA: Seal Press.

Shepperd D, Coyle A and Hegerty P (2010) Discourses of friendship between heterosexual women and gay men: Mythical norms and an absence of desire. *Feminism & Psychology* 20: 205–224.

Stanley JL (1996) The lesbian's experience of friendship. In: Weinstock JS and Rothblum ED (eds) *Lesbian Friendships.* New York: New York University Press, pp. 39–59.

Tillman-Healy LM (2001) *Between Gay and Straight: Understanding Friendship Across Sexual Orientation.* Lanham, MD: Rowman and Littlefield Press.

Trujillo C (1991) *Chicana Lesbians: The Girls Our Mothers Warned Us About.* Berkeley, CA: Third Woman Press.

Weeks J (1995) *Invented Moralities: Sexual Values in an Age of Uncertainty.* Cambridge: Polity Press.

Weinstock JS (2000) Lesbian, gay, bisexual and transgender friendships in adulthood. In: Patterson CJ and D' Augelli AR (ed.) *Lesbian, Gay, and Bisexual Identities in Families: Psychological Perspectives.* London: Oxford University Press, pp. 122–155.

Weston K (1991) *Families We Choose: Lesbians, Gay, Kinship.* New York, NY: Columbia University Press.

Zinn, MB and Dill BT (2000) Theorizing difference from multiracial feminism. In: Zinn MB, Hindagnev-Sofelo P and Messner MA (eds) *Gender Through the Prism of Difference,* 2nd edn. Boston: Allyn & Bacon, pp. 23–29.

Affairs of the Heart: Qualities of Adolescent Romantic Relationships and Sexual Behavior

PEGGY C. GIORDANO, WENDY D. MANNING, AND MONICA A. LONGMORE

Researchers have increasingly explored the character of adolescent romantic relationships, and scholarly as well as popular interest in teen sexual behavior has continued unabated. Yet as Furman (2002) recently noted, little research connects what have developed as two rather distinct traditions in the adolescence literature (see also Rostosky, Welsh, Kawaguchi, & Galliher, 1999). It is well recognized that social dynamics influence adolescent behavior, yet more research has been conducted on family and peer influences (East, Felice, & Morgan, 1993; Longmore, Manning, & Giordano, 2001; Whitaker & Miller, 2000; Whitbeck, Conger, & Kao, 1993) than on the relationship contexts within which these intimate behaviors unfold.

The current study relies on a symbolic interactionist framework and associated measurement emphasis. This theoretical perspective suggests the need to consider adolescents' own subjective experience of romantic relationships, and develops the idea that these behaviors (as all actions) acquire meaning and significance through interaction and communication with others (Mead, 1934). Clearly, much learning with regard to issues of sexuality takes place within the confines of family and friendship. Yet adolescent dating relations are also social relationships, and such liaisons grow in salience and importance during this phase of the life course (Sullivan, 1953). Thus, it is useful to conceptualize sexual behavior as more fully situated within the particular relational contexts within which it potentially but not inevitably takes place. Consistent with a symbolic interactionist perspective, we focus heavily on *communication* and *emotion* as central to constructions of meaning, and extend the symbolic interactionist framework to encompass dynamics such as *power and influence* (see e.g., Sprey, 1999). . . .

Background

Research on adolescent sexuality has often adapted a problem behavior lens, focusing on predictors used to explain behaviors such as delinquency and drug use. For example, researchers have documented that non-traditional family structure, lack of supervision, and lower parental attachment are associated with an earlier age of sexual onset (Cohen, Farley, Taylor, Martin, & Schuster, 2002; Davis & Friel, 2001; Thomson, McLanahan, & Curtin, 1992). Aside from using similar predictors, research that actively links sexual behaviors to delinquency, drug and alcohol use, smoking and school dropout also perpetuates the problem behavior or risk perspective (Jessor, 1998; Rosenbaum & Kandel, 1990).

Numerous studies have also focused on peer influence processes, both as predictors of sexual behavior, and as influences on the meanings of this involvement. Research has documented that having sexually active friends is related positively to the onset of sexual intercourse (Bearman & Brückner, 1999; Miller et al., 1997), and ethnographic studies have also highlighted that views about romance and sexuality are heavily shaped by peer interactions. Qualitative research in particular has often focused on distinctively gendered meanings about romance and sexuality that stem from peer socialization (Martin, 1996). This research has stressed that male adolescents are frequently encouraged to think of romance as a competitive game where sex is of primary importance (Anderson, 1989; Wight, 1994), while girls are socialized to value romance and the development of intimacy (Eder, Evans, & Parker, 1995). Maccoby (1990) and other scholars have suggested that the competitive interaction style boys hone within the peer group also influences the character of male-female interactions, including inequalities of power within these relationships (see also Thorne, 1993).

Symbolic interactionist theorists have noted that all but the most habitual of actions acquire new meaning in light of the interactive contexts within which they occur (Mead, 1934). Thus, while parents may have a general interest in delaying their adolescent child's sexual involvement, and peers (especially male peers) may encourage sexual experimentation and "gamesmanship," it is not likely that couple level behaviors are completely predetermined by the preferences of these more distal reference groups. In general recognition of the importance of romantic relationships in the lives of adolescents, researchers have begun to examine these relationships more closely (Brown, Feiring, & Furman, 1999), and developmental psychologists in particular have focused on the nature and quality of early romantic ties (see e.g., Florsheim, 2003). However, studies investigating the character of these early relationships have not often examined links to sexual involvement (Furman, 2002).

Prior research has documented that dating, having a boyfriend/girlfriend or "going steady" are significant predictors of adolescent sexual debut, as this provides the concrete opportunities within which sexual behavior becomes a realistic possibility (Cavanaugh, 2004; Cooksey, Mott, & Neubauer, 2002; Halpern, Joyner, Udry, & Suchindran, 2000; Little & Rankin, 2001; Thornton, 1990). However, beyond simply entering the dating world, it is important to determine whether the adolescent's subjective experience of the relationship is related to sexual behavior choices. Cleveland (2003) relied on data from adolescents as well as their partners and found that the risk profile of the partner added to the odds that sex had occurred, even after the respondent's own risk profile had been taken into account. These findings highlight that both partners that comprise the couple are important to consider, but nevertheless focuses primarily on what each adolescent brings to the relationship, rather than on characteristics of the relationship itself. In addition, this approach sustains the conceptualization of adolescent sexual behavior as fundamentally a risky or problem outcome.

Rostosky et al. (2000) have been critical of the risk and problems approach to adolescent sexuality, and have investigated the connection between such relationship qualities as commitment and the frequency of intimate sexual behaviors within middle and late adolescent relationships. In support of this broader view of sexuality, the researchers documented that perceived commitment was related to "lighter" forms of sexual intimacy (e.g., fondling), but was not significantly related to variations in the frequency of sexual intercourse. The current study builds on this prior work by specifying multiple qualities and dynamics of adolescent romantic relationships, and assessing whether variations in these subjectively held perceptions are systematically associated with sexual behavior choices. Our objectives differ slightly from those of Rostosky et al. in that our primary interest is in whether adolescents in a dating relationship have moved to particular levels of sexual intimacy, rather than the frequency with which such behaviors occur. However, consistent with the emphases of these researchers, we preserve the distinction between what may be consider "lighter" forms of sexual intimacy and sexual intercourse itself. Below we focus on the specific dimensions that we assess in more empirical detail in our analyses.

Communication Processes

Researchers have found that as interactions proceed from a superficial to a more intimate basis, the level of *intimate self-disclosure* within the relationship serves as a "barometer" of the state of the relationship (Jourard, 1971). The opportunity to share confidences with another is a basic reward and feature of close attachments (McCall & Simmons, 1966). As such communications reflect and undoubtedly themselves heighten perceived closeness, our hypothesis is that higher levels of self-disclosure will be associated with greater odds of engaging in sexually intimate behavior, including sexual intercourse. The rationale underlying this hypothesis is straightforward: through recurrent interaction and communication, young people begin to perceive certain relationships as significant and close. Those who subjectively experience intimacy of communication with a given partner may construct a view of this relationship as especially meaningful, and in turn become more likely to move to higher levels of behavioral intimacy as well.

A related but conceptually distinct aspect of communication, particularly during adolescence, is perceived awkwardness. Almost by definition, adolescents lack an extensive backlog of experience in conducting male-female relationships, and familiarity with sexually intimate behaviors as well. Thus, a certain amount of social and communication awkwardness often accompanies involvement in this new form of relationship (Brown et al., 1999). Our hypothesis is that these feelings of awkwardness should serve as an inhibitor of sexual intimacy even where other factors such as peer norms or low parental supervision might generally predispose teens to sexual involvement.

Emotional Processes

Researchers across a number of disciplines have recently given increased attention to the role of emotions in understanding human behavior (Katz, 1999; Pacherie, 2002; Turner, 2000). Girls are typically depicted as highly invested in and responsive to interactions within romantic as well as within other social contexts (Gilligan, 1982; Thompson, 1995). Thus suggesting that girls may be influenced in their sexual decisions by feelings for their current partner is hardly a novel assertion. However, prior analysis of the TARS [Toledo Adolescent Relationship Study] data documented that boys often reported strong emotional connections to their partners and emotional engagement in these relationships. These results accord well with Rostosky's

(1999) finding that male and female respondents in their sample did not differ in reported levels of commitment, and with results of in-depth interviews described by Tolman et al. (2004). A next step is to determine whether specific forms of emotional engagement are associated with adolescent sexual behavior choices, and whether such relational features are more strongly related to girls' relative to boys' behaviors.

Intimate self-disclosure and communication awkwardness can be considered indices of closeness or intimacy, but ultimately refer to the amount of talk and comfort with it that occur within the relationship. Thus, in assessing overall feelings of intimacy, we also include attention to even more basic dimensions, including the feeling that one is *cared for* by another, along with the level of *enmeshment* or intensity that characterizes the relationship. It is also useful to consider relationship dynamics that are relatively unique to the romantic context, including feelings of *passionate love*. In general, consistent with our expectations regarding communication processes, we hypothesize that stronger emotional feelings and more positive subjective views of the relationship will be related to the likelihood of sexual intimacy, even after traditional predictors of adolescent sexual behavior have been taken into account. Based only on the ethnographic research reviewed at the outset, we might expect that these relational factors would be more strongly related to girls' than boys' sexual behavior choices. However the aggregate portrait that emerges from prior analyses of the TARS data and other researchers' recent findings (e.g., Tolman et al., 2004) provide a caution to this line of theorizing. Our provisional hypothesis is that few gender differences will emerge in the nature of the association between such factors as love and caring and the likelihood that intimate sexual behavior occurs within a particular relationship.

Influence and Power

Our discussion of relationship qualities has focused on communication processes and emotional feelings that can be considered distinct yet related dimensions of intimacy and closeness.

However, such relationships vary further in their power and influence dynamics. To the degree that the partner is viewed as a significant source of *influence* in the life of the adolescent, this should operate in a manner similar to the other dimensions of intimacy outlined above: perceiving the partner as a significant 'reference other' should be associated with higher odds of sexually intimate involvement. Consistent with prior sociological treatments, however, it is also useful to distinguish such influence processes from *power,* often defined as the ability to overcome some resistance or exercise one's will over others (Weber, 1947).

Some researchers have suggested not only that power is gendered within relationships, but that this may influence the nature of sexual decision-making. While the idea of greater male power in relationships was originally discussed in connection with adult marital relations, the notion of gendered inequalities of power has also developed as a fairly common theme within the adolescence literature (Eder et al., 1995; Thorne, 1993; Martin, 1996; Thompson, 1995). However, Galliher et al. (1999) relied on a multi-method approach, including self-reports and observations, and found that most couples described themselves and were observed as involved in egalitarian relationships. Recent analyses of aggregate trends using the TARS data yielded a generally similar portrait, in that a majority of adolescent respondents described egalitarian decision-making processes (Giordano, Longmore, & Manning, 2006). However, analyses of total scores on the power scale used indicated that male respondents scored significantly lower than their female counterparts on perceived power (items referenced who had the most "say" in those instances where the partner disagreed). These findings may reflect that adolescent males are relatively more engaged in these relationships, while being less confident than some previous characterizations would lead us to expect. In addition, structurally based sources of inequality (e.g., greater access to labor force participation, women's heavy investment in childrearing) are, during the adolescent period, still at a distance.

Risman and Schwarz (2002) posit that cohort shifts in gender and power relationships may also have occurred, and forge the link to sexual behavior patterns. They document recent declines in rates of adolescent sexual behavior, and theorize that girls may have become increasingly less dependent on their relationships with males (e.g., higher rates of college attendance and labor force participation), potentially providing more of a sense of autonomy with regard to sexual decision-making. These researchers did not measure power directly, however, suggesting the need to examine whether and how power is related to adolescents' sexual decisions.

If we assume that girls, on average, may have a somewhat stronger interest in delaying sexual intercourse (due to concerns over reputation, pregnancy, and in general a preference for having sex within a more intimate relationship context), a reasonable hypothesis is that those who believe that they have less power will be more likely to report having sex with a given partner. This would also be generally congruent with Galliher's (1999) finding that young women who perceive less decision-making power report lower psychological well-being. In turn, this could be associated with lower self-efficacy with respect to the process of negotiating comfortable levels of sexual intimacy with their partners (see Longmore, Manning, Giordano, & Rudolph, 2004). This hypothesis however, assumes young women's constant interest in delaying sex, and young men's uniform interest in moving forward. Qualitative researchers in particular have increasingly questioned the idea that girls lack "sexual desire," (Tolman, 2005), and recent research has also depicted increasingly complex views of boys' perspectives (Giordano et al., 2006; Tolman et al., 2004; Wight, 1994). Because power has been accorded such a central role in discussions of male-female relationships and sexuality, we believe that it is important to include attention to this dynamic in our examination of links between relationship qualities/processes and sexual behavior outcomes. However, our hypotheses with regard to power are more provisional than those focusing on communication and emotion, as outlined above. . . .

Results

. . . [A]mong teens who have not had sexual intercourse with their dating partner (n=364), 45%

were sexually intimate. Among the sample of teens who were dating 36% had sexual intercourse with their dating partner. Our longitudinal analyses are limited to respondents who had not had sexual intercourse at wave one with their current partner, and 24% went on to have sexual intercourse with their wave one dating partner prior to the wave two interview.

. . . [D]uration of the relationship is significantly related to sexual intimacy and sexual intercourse, while reports of sex prior to the focal relationship are related to sexual intercourse in the current relationship. Female respondents are somewhat less likely to report sexual intimacy, and age is positively related to both forms of sexual behavior. Parental monitoring and peers' sexual behaviors are related to sexual intercourse in the expected directions. . . .

In addition, results revealed that the relationship qualities are related to sexual intimacy when relationship duration is not in the model. However, a majority of the relationship quality measures were not significantly related to sexual intimacy (short of intercourse) when duration is included (exceptions include communication awkwardness, love, partner influence). . . .

Communication

The next model predicting sexual intercourse adds level of reported self-disclosure. Results indicate that, controlling for the other factors, variations in levels of self-disclosure are not significantly related to sexual intimacy, but are associated with increased odds of adolescents reporting sexual intercourse within the focal relationship. Each unit increase in self disclosure increases the odds of sexual intercourse by 10%. . . . The likelihood-ratio . . . indicates that the addition of self-disclosure adds significantly to the fit of the sexual intercourse model . . . and not the sexual intimacy model . . . To investigate whether intimate self-disclosure was similarly related to the experience of sexual behavior for girls and boys, we estimated models that included self-disclosure by gender interaction terms. These interaction terms were not statistically significant, indicating a similar association between self-disclosure and the likelihood

of reporting both levels of sexually intimate behavior for girls and boys . . .

Results . . . indicate that higher levels of perceived *communication awkwardness* with the romantic partner are associated with lower odds of sexual intercourse. Each unit increase in communication awkwardness reduced the odds of sexual intercourse by 11% . . . Communication awkwardness adds to the fit of the model . . . An interaction term added to this model is not statistically significant, indicating a generally similar effect for boys and girls. . . .

Adolescents who provided in-depth relationship history narratives frequently highlighted that ease of communication was a key aspect of feelings of closeness and with the partner's importance in their lives:

> Like, okay, with me, like, if me, if me and Jesse, if we have a problem we don't go to somebody else, I'll go straight to him! And I know, like we can, we can talk about it and talk about what had happened and talk about what, makes us mad or whatever and talk about what we can do next time . . . And like, I think I can talk to him, about anything, anything at all. I don't know he just. . . . he's probably the most important person in my life ever! [Christy]

> I'd say your girl—not only she is your girlfriend, but one of your best friends. So, you could talk, tell each other everything. We basically just talked about everything, I mean, it could be, anything from personal, to school, to what you did over the weekend. We just, discussed every different topic you could think of. [David]

Jeremy, quoted below, makes a more explicit connection to sexual intimacy, as he notes that feelings of comfort with his partner were a consideration as he contemplated having sex for the first time. His remarks appear consistent with the observed inverse association between communication awkwardness and sexual intimacy highlighted above:

> I was real cool with her, and I knew it, I wouldn't, it wouldn't be no problem, for me to be with her, because I know her, you know like that, and it wouldn't be no, kind of embarrassment if something went wrong! . . . We laughed about it, you

know, while getting into it, we laughed about it, you know, ask little questions, it be questions here and there, like that. [Jeremy]

Emotional Processes

Next we consider emotional processes. . . . perceived level of caring, feelings of enmeshment and the experience of passionate love. Each of the emotional dimensions (caring, enmeshment, and love) is associated with increased odds of reporting sexual intercourse. . . . A unit increase in caring increased the odds of sex by 129% . . . A unit increased in enmeshment increased the likelihood of sex by 48% . . . and a unit increase in love increased the odds of sexual intercourse by 12% . . . Gender and emotional processes interaction terms were not statistically significant, suggesting a similar relationship between each of these emotional dimensions of the relationship on boys' and girls' likelihood of engaging in sexually intimate behaviors with the focal partner. Similarly, age interactions were not significant, indicating that the emotional indicators have similar associations across age groups.

One set of themes in the relationship history narratives that accord well with the quantitative results concerns the element of "sorting" many respondents described. An aspect of viewing one relationship as especially close and meaningful is recognizing that not all relationships contain these positive features. Indeed, the narratives sometimes reflect elements of ambivalence about the opposite sex, and areas of gender mistrust. For example, adolescent girls may accept the societal view that boys "only want one thing," yet develop very positive feelings about a particular boy. In these cases, the young women have attempted to and apparently believe that they have separated "the wheat from the chaff" where boys are concerned. This notion of sorting is apparent in the quotes from Sarah and Ashley's narratives, as both emphasize the degree to which their own boyfriends should be viewed as different from "average boys":

He really wants a relationship . . . I mean he's really good at the relationship so . . . that makes me more like trusting guys and thinking guys are

changing, but still I know they're out there and they just want one thing . . . [Sarah]

He's not, I can't compare him to anybody else cause he acts different than those average boys that try to talk to me. He's different . . . Some guys like they'll talk to me and then, when I talk to them on the phone, like, "oh when can I have sex with you," I'm like, "excuse me, [if] that's the only reason why you wanted to get my number, then you could have just not tried to talk to me at all." [Ashley]

These views that a given partner represents a departure from the norm contribute to the likelihood of constructing the relationship as something special, a dynamic that increases the feelings of trust/closeness that in turn may make sexually intimate behavior more likely. Although it is more intuitive to envision this as a dynamic involved in girls' sexual choices, our analysis also reveals some indications of this sorting process in boys' choice-making as well:

She was like . . . moving too fast . . . Like she want to have sex with me in the car and I'm like, "No," and then she starts touching me I'm like, "I'm cool, I'm cool, I got to go." And I did that and I left . . . I was just I don't know, she wasn't the girl that I wanted to have sex with . . . She wasn't the right girl . . . [Aaron]

If more distal processes (e.g., the desire to gain status in the eyes of male peers) were the only relevant considerations, it is unlikely that Aaron would have been concerned about whether or not his companion were "the right" girl. Quotes such as the above thus accord well with the quantitative results documenting a significant relationship for both females and males between such relationship qualities as caring and the likelihood of becoming sexually intimate with a given partner.

The Issue of Causal Order

The magnitude of the associations revealed in . . . results described above likely reflects that some portion of this association stems from *effects* of sexual behavior on such features of the relationship as perceived intimacy of communication and caring. Indeed, in response to a direct question in the structured interview about the influence of sex on the relationship, over 60% of the boys and 80% of the girls reported that sex had brought them somewhat or much closer to their partner. Jordan's narrative provides an illustration of this idea of reciprocal effects, in this case on levels of intimate self-disclosure:

> Yeah, yeah it was like, I say, when we was together, we would talk, and, but we wasn't saying some of the stuff but after, we got real close, and after, you know what I'm saying, we got together, or had sex, or whatever, it was like, it was just, like you could just say whatever! Anything! She, I felt like saying something to her, and I say it . . . We, not as freely, but after that, it just changed, like we got a little bit more closer! And, for, for uh . . . and felt, like a little bit more comfortable around each other. That's how it was. [Jordan]

Jordan clearly perceived an increase in intimate self-disclosure after he and his partner had sex, highlighting that some of the positive meanings/ relationship dynamics may follow from as well as predict the likelihood of sexual intimacy. We do not believe, however, that the associations documented in the quantitative analysis are *primarily* due to after-effects of sex on these relational dynamics. If this were the case, this would require us to accept that these relationships were viewed by the young people involved as in no way special or significant, but only became so upon introducing sex into the relationship.

As a strategy for exploring the issue of temporal sequence more systematically, we focused on the current daters within the sample who had not had sex at the time of the first wave of interviews. In these models, we used wave one relationship quality reports to predict whether the respondents who had not had sex at wave one went on to have sex with that partner, as reported at the second interview wave. Thus, this subgroup is not randomly selected, since by definition it will not include couples who had experienced high levels of enmeshment, feelings of passionate love and the like and had already become sexually intimate by the time of the wave one interview. . . . [A] benefit of this approach is that sexual intercourse itself

cannot be a factor that influenced the nature of the relationship quality reports. Results of these analyses . . . reveal similar, albeit somewhat more modest associations. . . At the zero-order, intimate self-disclosure, caring, enmeshment, and love were significantly associated with odds of reporting that later intercourse occurred (communication awkwardness was not significant), and caring, feelings of enmeshment, and self-disclosure were significantly associated with sexual intercourse when models including all covariates except duration were estimated. When duration was included in the models . . . intimate self-disclosure was no longer significant, but feelings of enmeshment remained a significant predictor of later sexual intercourse; caring was marginally significant.

Power and Influence

. . . [A] set of cross-sectional analyses focused on whether perceptions of influence and power within adolescent romantic relationships are systematically linked with sexual behaviors. Perceived partner influence is not significantly related to sexual intercourse and does not add to the fit of the model. Gender and age interactions were not significant, indicating similar associations of influence of boys and girls and across age groups. However, partner influence is positively related to sexually intimacy (not sexual intercourse) and adds to the fit of the model. . . .

In the aggregate, power was not related to the odds of either form of sexually intimate behavior and does not add to the fit of the model. However, an interaction of gender and power is statistically significant in the sexual intercourse model. Specifically, girls who score higher on perceived power have lower odds of sexual intercourse. . . . Further analysis revealed that the effect of power is primarily observed among girls who were virgins prior to entering the current relationship. For girls who report having sex in a previous relationship, variations in levels of power do not influence the odds of having sex in the focal relationship. It is also important to highlight that regardless of their sexual status or histories, girls' power scores are higher than those of comparably situated boys. Further, variations in boys' own reports of the power balance in the relationship were not related to the likelihood of having sex within the context of their current/most recent relationship. The association between power and sexual behavior is similar for each age group.

These results indicate that some gendered processes may be involved, but more research is needed to fully understand the nature of adolescent couples' power dynamics, and how this affects sexual decisions. Since one of the items comprising the power scale references decision-making about sexuality specifically, we examined the distributions of responses to the question: "When the two of you disagree about how far to go sexually, who usually gets their way?" Responses include: a) the couple are in agreement; b) both partners have equal power; c) the partner has more power; or d) the respondent has more power. Adding a layer of complexity to the above interaction results, we observed that a majority of all teens, male and female, indicated either that they have not disagreed about how far to go sexually (35%), or reported equal power (31%). Further, only 8% of females and 12% of males thought that the male in the relationship had more power or 'say' in this area, and the content of many of the relationship history narratives tends to reinforce the notion that girls' perspectives are important to the decision-making process:

> So, if a girl says yes and a guy says no, it's a maybe. If a guy doesn't know and a girl says yes, it's yes. If a guy says yes, and a girl says yes, it's yes. If a girl says no and a guy says yes, it's no. If a girl doesn't know, and a guy says yes, it's no. If a girl, then, if a girl says yes and a guy says yes, it's yes. I think it's more that way, so I think the women have more control because their opinion matters more in that situation. [Brett]

Brett's narrative is instructive in simply elaborating the large number of possible combinations of interest where sexual decisions are concerned; yet the main point of his description appears to be that girls' perspectives are very important in understanding what eventually takes place. The content of Brett's comments likely incorporate what he has learned from parents, peer, and school personnel, and may also reflect the tendency for self serving biases in personal narratives (Neisser, 1994). Thus it seems unlikely that boys would develop a narrative account that reflects elements of 'pushing' or coercion, and girls may also be reluctant to admit that boyfriends' advances derive from an uneven power balance. Yet the number of narratives reflecting perceived mutuality and the detail included about this provide indications that many adolescents involved in intimate relationships do not themselves envision these dynamics in ways that outside observers might characterize them (i.e., the idea that males generally have more power in these relationships and use it to gain sexual access):

> That was something that I had been saving. I really wanted to save it for marriage, but I was curious and and um . . . she was special enough to me that I could give her this part of my life that I had been saving and um . . . she had felt the same way because she wanted to wait until marriage, but we had decided and we was both curious I guess and so it just happened. [Tim]

> Actually, it was at times, where we both wanted it, then there was that times when we both said "we think we should wait." You know, because, there were times where I'd be like "well, you know, you know I might feel at this time like, you know, we need to have sexual whatever" then she'll be like "well, no, I think we just need to wait a little longer." You know, then, she might say "okay, well I feel it's time" and I'll be like "well, no, I think we need to wait a little longer." [Kevin]

A number of other male and female respondents describe a dynamic in which girlfriends had apparently initiated the move toward sexual intimacy:

> Well she put the moves on me really you know what I'm saying, she kind of like, she actually put the moves on me, you know. [Pat]

> Actually I put the pressure on him . . . we never had sex which I wanted to just because, like, that was like my first love. I loved him so much and he wanted to wait 'cause he was a virgin actually until this year. [Caroline]

Taken together, the quantitative and qualitative results complicate the notion that on average males have greater power in adolescent relationships, and use it to achieve sexual intimacy with their generally reluctant female partners. If a coercive process were typical, girls' own reports of feelings of closeness would not be reliably associated with the odds of sexual involvement, as revealed in the analyses focused on various dimensions of intimacy reported above. This suggests that many adolescent girls involved in sexually intimate relationships do construct positive meanings about these relationships, before and subsequent to their sexual involvement. Yet the positive gender interaction reflecting lower power scores for female respondents who transitioned to first sex suggests that some distinctively gendered processes are also involved. More research is needed because in this analysis, we cannot ascertain whether such girls are influenced by an unfavorable power balance to make this transition, or whether the transition itself influences their perceptions of the balance of power in the relationship. In the longitudinal analyses focused on those who had not had intercourse with the current partner at the time of the wave one interview, power and influence were not associated with the odds of reporting later sexual intercourse at wave two. . . .

Discussion

While adolescent sexual behavior is related to such social dynamics as parenting practices and the orientations of one's peers, these results suggest that the generally positive qualities of romantic relationships we assessed are also important to a comprehensive understanding of intimate sexual behaviors. The results show that basic feelings of caring and other forms of emotional engagement are positively related to the odds of sexual behavior, and findings are particularly consistent for the models focused on sexual intercourse. The cross-sectional analyses show significant associations between all of the positive relationship qualities examined and sexual behavior, even after duration of the relationship, prior sexual experience, and other parent and peer factors had been taken into account. The results of longitudinal analyses

focused on the subset of respondents who had not yet had sex at the time of the first interview are generally similar, but results were stronger for the emotional processes relative to the communication indicators. When duration was included in these models, intimate self-disclosure was no longer significant, but the index of caring and measure of enmeshment remained significant predictors. This pattern of results suggests that perhaps some of the association between intimacy of communication and the sexual behavior reports captured in the cross-sectional examination reflect effects of the behavior itself on the assessments of the intimacy of self-disclosure. However, the results for caring and feelings of enmeshment are consistent across both sets of analyses. Similarly, power and influence were, in the aggregate, unrelated to the likelihood that sexual intercourse occurred, whether we examined these linkages cross-sectionally or longitudinally.

These results complicate the view of sexuality as but one of a roster other problem outcomes such as drinking, drug use and delinquent behavior, as they indicate that relationship dynamics that are considered good, healthy or even prosocial are important to a comprehensive understanding of adolescent sexual decision-making. Many of the relationship qualities we assessed are related but conceptually distinct dimensions of intimacy. It has been useful to consider these separately, rather than as a summary measure, however, as this highlights that the adolescent involved with a special romantic partner may experience multiple rewards of intimate involvement, including intimate self-disclosure, feelings of caring, and more passionate emotions (McCall & Simmons, 1966). The findings suggest some limitations not only of traditional risk perspectives on adolescent sexuality, but also of recent media treatments decrying the end of formal dating and romance. These media accounts have suggested that most teen sexual activity occurs within the context of casual relationships characterized by little caring or commitment (Denizet-Weis, 2004). Prior research (e.g., Manning, Longmore, & Giordano, 2005) shows that many adolescents do eventually gain sexual experience that could be considered "non-relationship" or casual sex, but this is not the most common context for sexual involvement. Within the dating world itself, our results show that qualities that generally reflect higher levels of intimacy are significantly associated with the likelihood of sexually intimate behaviors. More research is obviously needed across the range of different contexts in which sex occurs. High risk liaisons will continue to be an important research focus because of the social and health implications of involvement in short term, low commitment relationships. Nevertheless, the findings described above are also potentially important, because they highlight that many of these relationships have positive significance for the youths involved in them. These findings are thus congruent with a symbolic interactionist theoretical perspective. According to this framework, sexual behavior emerges not only due to an absence, lack or breakdown in the adolescent's life (e.g., low parental supervision), but are associated with social dynamics that have positive meanings for the adolescent. These results also have policy implications, suggesting the need to incorporate discussions of relationships into programs focused on sexual risk-taking, as an important supplement to curricula that currently emphasize the risky or potentially health compromising nature of this activity (e.g., programs focused on the "Health Beliefs Model"—see e.g., Becker, 1988).

It is also important to note that in many instances we did not find a strong pattern of gender differences in the effects of relationship qualities. This provides evidence that relationship centered processes and dynamics are associated with boys' as well as girls' decisions. These findings thus temper the view that girls develop and make choices on the basis of their connections to others, while boys are primarily interested in achieving autonomy. The idea that boys have relatively little interest in romance is not supported by previous analyses of these data (Giordano et al., 2006), and the present analysis contributes beyond this prior work by documenting that both boys' and girls' perceptions of relationship qualities/dynamics are significantly linked to sexual behavior. A potentially important exception is the finding with

regard to gendered effects of power. A majority of youth, regardless of sexual history, describe a situation of relatively equal power or one favoring girls in an unequal power balance; yet the lower scores of girls who transitioned to first intercourse with a focal partner suggest that this relational dynamic does not follow the pattern of gender similarity observed in assessments of the influence of overall closeness or intimacy. More frequent assessments are needed in order to fully understand the sequencing of power and sexual decisions as influenced by respondent gender. In this analysis, only a few age interaction terms were statistically significant, but more research is needed that could provide a more nuanced understanding of developmental changes in the impact of these and other relationship qualities.

This study is limited by our focus on youths residing in a single geographic region. And while we believe that respondents' subjective experiences are important to understand, this focus also has limitations, in that objective measures/observations (e.g., of power dynamics) might reveal a different pattern of results. Couple level data would also be a useful supplement to the individual reports we focused upon in this analysis. In future research, it will also be useful to focus more attention on problematic features of romantic relationships, such as conflict, jealousy, and cheating behaviors (see e.g., Tuval-Mashiach & Shulman, 2006). This multi-faceted approach is needed to document the specific conditions under which adolescent romance is associated with outcomes such as depression or violence, and when these relationships may foster positive emotions, identity development, and as indicated in these results, the development of sexual intimacy.

References

Anderson E. Sex codes and family life among poor inner-city youths. Ann American Academy of Political Social Science. 1989; 501:59–79.

Bearman, P.; Brückner, H. Peer effects on adolescent sexual debut and pregnancy: An analysis of a national survey of adolescent girls. The National Campaign for the Prevention of Teen Pregnancy; April 1999; 1999.

Becker MH. AIDS behavior and change. Public Health Reviews. 1988; 16:1–11. [PubMed: 3247487]

Brown, BB.; Feiring, C.; Furman, W. Missing the love boat: Why researchers have shied away from adolescent romance. In: Furman, W.; Brown, BB.; Feiring, C., editors. The Development of Romantic Relationships in Adolescence. New York: Cambridge University Press; 1999. p. 1–18.

Cavanagh SE. The sexual debut of girls in early adolescence: The intersection of race, pubertal timing, and friendship group characteristics. Society for Research on Adolescents. 2004; 14(3):285–312.

Cleveland HH. The influence of female and male risk on the occurrence of sexual intercourse within adolescent relationships. Journal of Research on Adolescence. 2003; 13:81–112.

Cohen DA, Farley TA, Taylor SN, Martin DH, Schuster MA. When and where do youths have sex? The potential role of adult supervision. Pediatrics. 2002; 110(6):e66. [PubMed: 12456933]

Cooksey EC, Mott FL, Neubauer SA. Friendships and early relationships: Links to sexual initiation among American adolescents born to young mothers. Perspectives on Sexual and Reproductive Health, 2002; 34(3):118–126. [PubMed: 12137125]

Davis EC, Friel LV. Adolescent sexuality: Disentangling the effects of family structure and family content. Journal of Marriage and Family. 2001; 63(3):669–681.

Denizet-Weis B. Friends, friends with benefits and the benefits of the local mall. New York Times. 2004 May 30;30.

East P, Felice M, Morgan M. Sisters' and girlfriends' sexual and childbearing behavior: Effects on early adolescent girls' sexual outcomes. Journal of Marriage and the Family. 1993; 55:953–963.

Eder, D.; Evans, C.; Parker, S. School Talk: Gender and Adolescent Culture. New Brunswick, NJ: Rutgers University Press; 1995.

Florsheim, P., editor. Adolescent Romantic Relations and Sexual Behavior: Theory, Research, and Practical Implications. Mahwah, NJ: Lawrence Erlbaum Associates; 2003.

Furman W. The emerging field of adolescent romantic relationships. Current Directions in Psychological Science. 2002; 11:177–180.

Galliber RV, Kawaguchi MC, Rostosky SS, Welsh DP. Power and psychological well-being in late adolescent romantic relationships. Sex Roles: A Journal of Research. 1999; 40(9–10):689–710.

Gilligan, C. In a Different Voice: Psychological Theory and Women's Development. Cambridge, MA: Harvard University Press; 1982.

Giordano PC, Longmore MA, Manning WD. Gender and the meanings of adolescent romantic relationships: A focus on boys. American Sociological Review. 2006; 71:260–287.

Halpern CT, Joyner K, Udry JR, Suchindran C. Smart teens don't have sex (or kiss much either). Journal of Adolescent Health. 2000; 26:213–225. [PubMed: 10706169]

Jessor, R. New Perspectives on Adolescent Risk Behavior. Cambridge, NY: Cambridge University Press; 1998.

Jourard, SM. Self-Disclosure: An Experimental Analysis of the Transparent Self. Oxford: John Wiley; 1971.

Katz, J. How Emotions Work. Chicago: University of Chicago Press; 1999.

Little CB, Rankin A. Why do they start it? Explaining reported early-teen sexual activity. Sociological Forum, 2001; 16(4):703–729.

Longmore MA, Manning WD, Giordano PC. Preadolescent parenting strategies and teens' dating and sexual initiation: A longitudinal analysis. Journal of Marriage and the Family. 2001; 63:322–335.

Longmore MA, Manning WD, Giordano PC, Rudolph JL. The influence of self-esteem and depression on adolescents' sexual debut. Social Psychology Quarterly, 2004; 67:279–295.

Maccoby E. Gender and relationships: A developmental account. American Psychologist. 1990; 45:513–20. [PubMed: 2186679]

Manning WD, Longmore MA, Giordano PC. Adolescents' involvement in non-romantic sexual activity. Social Science Research. 2005; 34(2):384–407.

Martin, KA, Puberty, Sexuality, and the Self: Boys and Girls at Adolescence. New York: Routledge; 1996.

McCall, GJ.; Simmons, JL. Identities and interactions. New York: Free Press; 1966.

Mead, GH. Mind, Self, and Society from the Standpoint of a Social Behaviorist. Chicago: University of Chicago Press; 1934.

Miller BC, Norton MC, Curtis T, Hill EJ, Schvaneveldt P, Young MH. The timing of sexual intercourse among adolescents: Family, peer, and other antecedents. Youth & Society. 1997; 29:54–83.

Neisser, U. Self-narratives: True and false. In: Neisser, U.; Fivush, R., editors. The Remembering Self: Construction and Accuracy in the Self-Narrative. New York: Cambridge University Press; 1994. p. 1–18.

Pacherie, E. The role of emotions in the explanation of action. In: Pacherie, E., editor. European Review of Philosophy: Emotion and Action. Vol. 5. Stanford: CSU Publications; 2002.

Risman B, Schwartz P. After the sexual revolution: Gender politics in teen dating. Contexts. 2002; 1:16–24.

Rosenbaum E, Kandel D. Early onset of adolescent sexual behavior and drug involvement. Journal of Marriage and the Family. 1990; 52:783–798.

Rostosky S, Galliher R, Welsh D, Kawaguchi M. Sexual behaviors and relationship qualities in late adolescent couples. Journal of Adolescence. 2000; 23:583–597. [PubMed: 11073699]

Rostosky, SS.; Welsh, DP.; Kawaguchi, MC.; Galliher, RV. Commitment and sexual behaviors in adolescent dating relationships. In: Adams, JM.; Jones, WH., editors. Handbook of Interpersonal Commitment and Relationship Stability. New York: Kluwer Academic Plenum Publishers; 1999. p. 323–338.

Sprey, J. Family dynamics: An essay on conflict and power. In: Sussman, MR.; Steinmetz, SK.; Peterson, GW., editors. Handbook of Marriage and the Family, Second Edition. New York: Plenum Press; 1999. p. 667–685.

Sullivan, H. The Interpersonal Theory of Psychiatry. New York: Norton; 1953.

Thomson E, McLanahan SS, Curtin RB. Family structure, gender, and parental socialization. Journal of Marriage and the Family. 1992; 54:368–378.

Thompson, S. Going All the Way: Teenage Girls' Tales of Sex, Romance, and Pregnancy. New York: Hill and Wang; 1995.

Thorne, B. Gender Play: Girls and Boys in School. New Brunswick, NJ: Rutgers University Press; 1993.

Thornton A. The courtship process and adolescent sexuality. Journal of Family Issues. 1990; 11:239–273.

Tolman, DL. Dilemmas of Desire: Teenage Girls Talk about Sexuality. Cambridge, MA: Harvard University Press; 2005.

Tolman, DL.; Spencer, R.; Harmon, T.; Rosen-Reynoso, M.; Striepe, M. Getting close, staying cool: Adolescent boys' experiences with romantic relationships. In: Way, N.; Chu, JY., editors. Adolescent Boys: Exploring Diverse Cultures of Boyhood. New York: New York University Press; 2004. p. 235–255.

Turner, JH. On the Origin of Human Emotion: A Sociological Inquiry into the Evolution of Human Affect. Stanford: Stanford University Press; 2000.

Tuval-Mashiach R, Shulman S. Resolution of disagreements between romantic partners, among adolescents, and young adults: Qualitative analysts of interaction discourses. Journal of Research on Adolescents. 2006; 16:561–588.

Weber, M. The Theory of Social and Economic Organization. Henderson, AM.; Parsons, T., translators; Parsons, T., editor. Glencoe, IL: Free Press; 1947.

Whitaker DJ, Miller KS. Parent-adolescent discussions about sex and condoms: Impact on peer influences pf sexual risk behavior. Journal of Adolescent Research. 2000; 15:251–273.

Whitbeck L, Conger R, Kao M. The influences of parental support, depressed affect, and peers on the sexual behaviors of adolescent girls. Journal of Family Issues. 1993; 14:261–278.

Wight D. Boys' thoughts and talk about sex in a working class locality of Glasgow. The Sociological Review. 1994; 42:703–738.

The Gendered Body

Perhaps nothing is more deceptive than the "naturalness" of our bodies. We experience what happens to our bodies, what happens *in* our bodies, as utterly natural, physical phenomena.

Yet to the social scientist nothing could be further from the truth. Our bodies are themselves shaped and created, and interpreted and understood by us, in entirely gendered ways. How we look, what we feel, and what we think about how our bodies look and feel are the products of the ways our society defines what bodies should look like and feel. Thus, for example, cultural standards of beauty, musculature, and aesthetics are constantly changing—and with them our feelings about how we look stacked up against those images.

Take, for example, women's notions of beauty. Feminist writer Naomi Wolf argued that "the beauty myth"—constantly shifting and unrealizable cultural ideals of beauty—traps women into endless cycles of diets, fashion, and consumer spending that render them defenseless. Fortunes are made by companies that purvey the beauty myth, reminding women that they do not measure up to these cultural standards and then provide products that will help them try. By such logic, women who experience eating disorders are not deviant nonconformists, but rather over-conformists to unrealizable norms of femininity. As Katherine Mason points out in her essay here, our bodies are social bodies, and size and gender have significant implications for understanding inequality as well as identity. And Richard Mora observes the ways that Latino boys make sense of their changing bodies.

Perhaps nowhere are our bodies more "gendered" than in our sex lives. He and she have different sexualities, different experiences of pleasure, different motivations for sex. Half of the sexual jokes we have in our stock of stupid jokes are about the differences between men's and women's sexualities. And they follow a distinct pattern: he wants sex all the time, is constantly going for it, constantly ready for it, and is sexually "organized" to have lots of sex with lots of different people with little or no emotional connection to them. She, by contrast, doesn't really like sex, requires a deep emotional commitment before she'll consent, and is far more conservative in her sexual repertoire.

This gives rise to most of the conventional Mars and Venus stereotypes about gender and sex. She trades sex to get love; he trades love to get sex. Sex is a competition, and women and men engage in a battle of the sexes, a war between the sexes even, in which he attempts to conquer, to break down her resistance, and she decides if she will surrender, capitulate. In this model, she gives, he gets. And if she gives, she loses, and he wins.

But empirically, the reality is far from that stereotypic model. And we think that's a good thing. Frankly, we think that adversarial model is also a recipe for bad sex. The real story of our sexual lives is that these stereotypic constructions have begun to erode to the point where women and men are converging—in their motivations to have sex, in what they like, and with whom they want to have it. Women's and men's sexualities are increasingly similar. Neither Martian nor Venusian, our sexualities are decidedly Earthbound (though the experience itself can send us to the moon!).

In their essay reprinted here, Michael Kimmel and Rebecca F. Plante show how gendered sexual fantasies reveal a "his" and "hers" sexualities—and how those gendered sexual worlds are converging. Raine Dozier looks at bodies and sexualities at the boundaries being crossed by transgendered people. Finally, Deborah Tolman and her colleagues explore the ways that gender ideologies are used to construct adolescent boys' and girls' sexual identities.

The Unequal Weight of Discrimination: Gender, Body Size, and Income Inequality

KATHERINE MASON

Americans are getting fatter.[1] This oft-repeated claim, usually presented as a simple statement of fact, tends to evoke a particular range of anxieties, meanings, and moral judgments, nearly all of which assert that it is bad to be fat. To public health researchers, the statistic that more than half of the adult population of the United States has been classified as "overweight" or "obese" since the mid-1980s is cause for alarm. These researchers predict that current generations will live shorter lives than their parents and that those lives will be marked by greater rates of ill health and disability. Accordingly, public policy analysts worry that such predicted health consequences will lead to increased health care costs. Former U.S. Surgeon General Richard Carmona exclaimed that "[o]besity is a terror within; it's destroying our society from within and unless we do something about it, the magnitude of the dilemma will dwarf 9/11 or any other terrorist event that you can point out" (Pace 2006). In contrast, many others, particularly those outside of the United States, view fatness as a fitting metaphor for America's culture of expansionism and overconsumption (Saguy 2008). In this article, I do not examine the claim that being fat is bad for one's health, nor do I document the range of discourses and meanings surrounding fatness in the United States (for coverage of such discourses, see Boero 2007 and Saguy and Riley 2005). I instead focus on how, as carriers of the so-called "obesity epidemic," fat people embody socially stigmatized

characteristics (Carr and Friedman 2005; Puhl and Heuer 2010) and thereby face a range of social disadvantages including—but not limited to—income discrimination. This article highlights the shortcomings of how weight-based discrimination has been measured in past research, and proposes a method for positively establishing the presence of discrimination. I then use this method to test past research's contention that women are more severely disadvantaged by weight-based inequality than are men, while updating the literature with recent data from the 1990s and late 2000s.

In taking this approach, my work joins a small but growing body of research that examines the income inequalities between fat and nonfat people. These studies step outside of typical framings of fatness and fat people as problems for society, instead analyzing how existing social arrangements are problematic for fat people. Namely, as anti-fat rhetoric (such as the perspectives described above) characterizes fatness as a stigmatized property of individuals, people with that characteristic may face discrimination and inequality due to their body size.

As a note about terminology, the convention in studies such as this is to discuss body size in terms of the four categories of the body mass index (BMI): underweight, normal weight, overweight, and obese. Some studies (e.g., Conley and Glauber 2007) also use the term "healthy weight" in place of "normal weight." In this article, I will use the BMI

Katherine Mason, "The Unequal Weight of Discrimination: Gender, Body Size, and Income Inequality," *Social Problems*, Vol. 59, No. 3 (2012), pp. 411–435. Reprinted by permission of Oxford University Press on behalf of Society for the Study of Social Problems, Inc.

categories when I am referring to body mass specifically as it is measured by height and weight: this is the metric available to me in the data I analyze. When speaking about weight-based inequality in general, however, I will use the terms "fat" and "nonfat." This language choice reflects the fact that there is considerable disagreement both within and outside of medical circles about the exact relationship between body mass and health. At the start of the twenty-first century, people who fall within the "normal" BMI range are no longer the norm—as of 2006, adult men in the United States had an average weight of 195 pounds and an average BMI of 28.8 (well into the overweight range), while women averaged weights of 165 pounds and BMIs of 28.3 (McDowell et al. 2008). Furthermore, using the term "healthy weight" to describe people with BMIs in the 18.5–25 ("normal") range may also be inaccurate. Several studies, most notably Katherine Flegal and colleagues' (2005) article, "Excess Deaths Associated with Underweight, Overweight, and Obesity," have shown that it is in fact people with BMIs in the "overweight" range, not the "normal" range, who have the lowest rates of mortality and morbidity in the United States. For this reason, when not referencing BMI in particular, I use descriptive terms—"fat" and "nonfat"—in place of the normative language of "normal" or "healthy" weight.

Previous research in this area has investigated fat people's personal experiences of discrimination and its relationship to self-esteem (Carr and Friedman 2005), the legal and ethical guidelines for dealing with anti-fat employment discrimination (Kristen 2002; Roebling 2002), and the correlation between fatness and lowered wages and rates of employment, often mediated by gender and/or occupation (Averett and Korenman 1996; Cawley 2004; Cawley and Danziger 2005; Gortmaker et al. 1993; Hamermesh and Biddle 1994; and Haskins and Ransford 1999).

While many of these studies provide quantifiable evidence of the employment inequality faced by fat people, they are nonetheless limited in what they can tell us about the nature of that inequality. Researchers may claim that the income differences between fat and nonfat people are due to discrimination, but they face countervailing arguments that fat people are lazy, undisciplined, and thus, less likely to succeed in well-paying jobs. While such arguments may strike some as being premised on inaccurate stereotypes, they nevertheless point to methodological weaknesses in the aforementioned studies. Several researchers have tried to control for confounding traits by including subjects' intelligence test scores or educational achievements in their analyses (e.g., Averett and Korenman 1996; Gortmaker et al. 1993), but so long as they determine discrimination via residual explanations—that is, by controlling for a number of variables that might explain differences in income and then taking any remaining income differences between groups as evidence of discrimination—they are always open to the critique that those differences are caused not by anti-fat discrimination, but by some other explanatory factor left out of the analysis.

The purposes of this study are twofold. First, I update the research on weight-based income inequality, most of which was published in the mid-1990s and based on data from the 1980s (such as Steven Gortmaker and colleagues' [1993] study using the 1979–1988 National Longitudinal Survey of Youth, or NLSY). My data, a comparable sample of young people born approximately two decades after the subjects of the previous wave of research (the 1997–2008 National Longitudinal Survey of Youth, hereafter NLSY97), allow me to revisit the hypotheses that earlier researchers tested while paying heed to changing social norms across the intervening years (most notably, trends in body size, marriage, and educational attainment). The second purpose of this study is to elaborate a *positive* test for a specific type of discrimination: statistical discrimination. While statistical discrimination is not the only type of discrimination that exists, this test (first described by Joseph Altonji and Rebecca Blank [1999] for studying racial/ethnic and gender inequalities) makes it possible to positively establish the presence of discrimination, simultaneously providing a more nuanced view of the different forms and degrees of discrimination that may be operating. Using the concepts of *meritocratic discrimination, statistical discrimination,* and *prejudicial discrimination* as tools for investigating the nature and severity of income disparities among obese and nonobese workers, this study provides evidence that (1) weight-based income discrimination against obese people exists, (2) its effects are especially pronounced among those who are very obese, and (3) it has more severe consequences for women than for men.

The remainder of this article is divided up as follows. First, I discuss previous work showing that the fat body is often subjected to workplace discrimination. Several of these studies have highlighted how women, especially, are the victims of anti-fat prejudice (even when anti-fat discourses do not explicitly target them). In a discussion of the particular article on which my own work is premised, Gortmaker and colleagues' (1993) "Social and Economic Consequences of Overweight in Adolescence and Young Adulthood," and the accompanying response from the editors at the *New England Journal of Medicine,* I show why a residual explanation of discrimination is insufficient, and why a positive test for discrimination is needed. Further, I elaborate a spectrum of discrimination against which to compare my findings, based on varying degrees of employer rationality and stereotyping. Subsequently, I lay out the four hypotheses to be tested, describe the methods and data used in this study, and review the findings. Finally, in the discussion, I explain the significance of these results and suggest future directions for research.

Fatness and Income Inequality: A Review

What Is the Relationship Between Fatness and Socioeconomic Inequality?

The existing studies on anti-fat discrimination in employment provide a helpful framework for thinking about the problem overall. First, by discussing the correlation between obesity and experiencing inequality in the form of lowered wages, this article asserts that fatness is often a *cause* of diminished income and life chances, not solely a consequence.

Although the association between lower socioeconomic status (SES) and fatness in the United States has been well documented, the direction of causation in that correlation remains hotly debated. Unlike characteristics such as race/ethnicity and sex, both of which are popularly seen as stable characteristics of an individual, both class and body size are viewed as being somewhat variable at the individual level (reflected in the fields of study dealing with, respectively, social mobility and weight management). Thus, whereas a correlation between, say, sex and income could be easily read as showing the effect of one's sex (the unchanging, causal variable) on one's income, causality is less apparent in the relationship between body size and class. Cawley (2004) outlined and tested three major hypotheses surrounding the correlation between obesity and low wages: (1) obesity causes lower wages (whether due to decreased productivity or to discrimination); (2) low wages cause obesity (because of the availability of cheap, bad-quality, fattening foods); and (3) some other factor (such as, for example, inherited social class) causes both obesity and lower wages. Cawley found no evidence to support hypothesis 2, but he did find evidence to support hypotheses 1 (particularly for women) and 3 (in the case of certain racial/ethnic minority groups). The connections between obesity, SES, stress, health, and nutrition (to name just a few) are, no doubt, complex and often multidirectional. What Cawley found is that the relationship between obesity and income cannot be explained completely by background factors, and the direction of causation in that relationship is from obesity to income, not the reverse.

If fatness (at least in the United States) contributes to income stratification, what does that phenomenon look like, and how does it play out? Furthermore, how does gender mediate the relationship between weight and income? In the following section, I review the three main methodological avenues through which researchers have approached these questions: (1) laboratory studies of discriminatory hiring and employment practices toward hypothetical employees; (2) self-reported experiences of stigma and discrimination; and (3) residual explanations of discrimination in large-scale multivariate statistical analyses. Thereafter, I describe how my chosen approach will build on existing studies' findings while adding a more robust measure of employment discrimination into the mix.

Laboratory Studies

Cawley's research, which looks at discrimination in real-life statistics, is rare among studies in this field; more common are experimental studies of discrimination such as those described by Rebecca Puhl and Kelly Brownell (2001):

> Studies on employment have shown hiring prejudice in laboratory studies. Subjects report being less inclined to hire an overweight person than a thin person, even with identical qualifications. Individuals make negative inferences about obese persons in the workplace, feeling that such people are lazy, lack self-discipline, and are less competent. One might expect these attributions to affect wages, promotions, and disciplinary actions, and such seems to be the case (p. 800).

While such studies provide a helpful insight into the possible workings of weight-based employment inequality, Puhl and Brownell note that they are limited by their artificiality—this type of research has tended to be based on the responses of a convenient study population, college students, making hiring judgments about hypothetical employees, not on the actual practices of seasoned employers.

In a similarly controlled laboratory experiment, Matthew Mulford and associates (1998) found that people tended to cooperate better and more frequently with coworkers they perceived to be attractive, a judgment that, at least in the U.S. context, is likely to include the evaluation of people's bodies. Likewise, Daniel Hamermesh and Jeff Biddle (1994) discovered that there were both earnings penalties for unattractiveness and earnings premiums for exceptional physical beauty, regardless of one's occupational category or gender. They did find other effects by gender, though, showing that women who were considered unattractive participated in the labor force at lower rates and married men with less human capital. In a separate study, these authors employed a four-person panel of judges to rate the matriculation photographs of lawyers for physical beauty and found

that those deemed more attractive were more often selected into private practice (i.e., higher-paying) law jobs than those who were less attractive (Biddle and Hamermesh 1998).

Self-Reports of Weight-Based Stigma and Discrimination

In addition to the aforementioned laboratory experiments that purport to measure average people's propensity to discriminate on the basis of weight or attractiveness, another type of research that has contributed to scholarly understandings of weight-based discrimination involves the use of self-reported experiences of stigmatization and inequality. Puhl, Tatiana Andreyeva, and Brownell (2008) looked at data from the 1995–96 National Study of Midlife Development in the United States (MIDUS), which asks respondents to report on any discrimination they have encountered in a range of settings. The authors found significant gender differences in the prevalence of reports of height/weight discrimination (4.9 percent of men reported being affected by height/weight discrimination, while more than double that number of women—10.3 percent—did so). They also found important gender differences in how educational background and age affected respondents' likelihood of reporting height/weight discrimination, and noted that height/weight discrimination was comparable to racial/ethnic discrimination in its prevalence. Deborah Carr and Michael Friedman (2005), who also analyzed the MIDUS 1995–96 data, add that better-educated respondents and those in higher-status occupations (professional and managerial positions) were more likely to report being victims of discrimination.

Markus Schafer and Kenneth Ferraro (2011), who used the MIDUS 1995–96 data as well, argue that whether or not the experience of discrimination that respondents report is objectively "real," its *effects* certainly are. Drawing on the sociological concept of "stigma," they suggest that respondents' understandings of their own bodies are mediated through social perceptions, such that the feeling of stigmatization may actually have a negative effect on respondents' physical well-being. Puhl and Chelsea Heuer (2010) agree, writing that the "stigmatization of obese individuals poses serious risks to their psychological and physical health, generates health disparities, and interferes with implementation of effective obesity prevention efforts" (p. 1019).

Studies based on self-reported experiences of weight-based discrimination provide an important perspective on how negative societal attitudes toward fat bodies may become the basis for stigmatization and a wealth of negative consequences that follow. In such research (Puhl and Heuer 2010; Schafer and Ferraro 2011), the *objective* experience of discrimination (as measured by, for example, material inequities) is less important than the respondents' *subjective* feeling of stigma. However, this characteristic also represents a limitation in what self-reported weight discrimination studies can tell us. In the third section of this literature, then, I turn to large-scale surveys that study the income disparities between obese and nonobese workers.

Residual Explanations of the Relationship between Fatness and Income Inequality

Baum and Ford (2004) draw on nearly two decades' worth (1981–1998) of longitudinal data from the original National Longitudinal Survey of Youth (NLSY) to look at earnings inequalities due to body size. They find that there is a robust wage penalty for being obese (significant in a variety of statistical models that they test) and, in keeping with previous findings about the effects of gender, that women consistently suffer more from this penalty than do men (p. 897). Although the authors suggest that at least some of this inequality is due to employer discrimination, they add that they did not test for it. At most, they make a convincing case for discrimination using a residual explanation (that is, attributing to discrimination residual differences between groups that remain after controlling for other likely causes in a regression model).

Susan Averett and Sanders Korenman (1996), also using data from the NLSY, found that obese women tended to reside in lower socioeconomic brackets than nonobese women (which was not the case for obese men), and that this phenomenon was due to a combination of outcomes of obesity: lowered marriage prospects (by which obese women had less chance of marrying and, if married, less chance of being married to a man with high earnings), as well as direct employment discrimination.

Gortmaker and colleagues (1993) conducted one of the most comprehensive statistical studies of body size and income inequality. They suggest a starting model for testing income inequalities in overweight and nonoverweight individuals using the NLSY, an earlier wave of the data set (NLSY97) I analyze in this project. Examining variables from the 1988 data, Gortmaker and associates found persistent, significant effects of being "overweight" in several areas of adult life: for men, lowered incomes; for women, not only lowered incomes but also lower rates of marriage and lower educational attainment. While this study did not prove conclusively that discrimination was the cause of these differences, it did rule out several competing theories. First, the authors found no support for the hypothesis that differences in economic outcomes between overweight and nonoverweight people could be explained by their class origins (a hypothesis that Cawley [2004] also examined and rejected). In other words, even though people brought up in poorer households and neighborhoods were more likely to be overweight *and* to work in low-income jobs, accounting for class of origin could not explain away the association between overweight and lower incomes. A second hypothesis this article tested was that overweight people might be less healthy than nonoverweight people, and that chronic ill health—not discrimination—might be the cause of the lower-paying jobs held by overweight respondents. This hypothesis, too, was unsupported by the evidence. Likewise, overweight people did not appear to differ markedly from nonoverweight people in their self-esteem, and so their disparate financial outcomes could not be explained by personal characteristics like confidence and self-esteem. From these findings, the authors concluded that the most likely causes of overweight people's lower incomes were stigma and discrimination.

Although Gortmaker and his colleagues rigorously ruled out several competing theories before they arrived at this conclusion, the response from the editors in the same issue of the *New England Journal of Medicine* shows why even a very well done residual account of discrimination may not be enough to convince skeptics. Albert Stunkard and Thorkild Sorensen (1993), the editors who wrote a comment on the piece by Gortmaker and associates, suggested that further research should take into account the possible influences of genetics on both SES and weight. On the face of it, this suggestion seems reasonable; previous research has found that children may inherit their biological parents' SES even when those parents do not raise them, perhaps through mechanisms like IQ. Stunkard and Sorensen noted that there is a good chance that children's weight and body types may also contain a genetic component inherited from their parents. What makes this editorial troublesome, however, is that genetics were offered as a possible explanation of not just SES or fatness, but the *connection* between the two. In other words, they seem to be suggesting that genetic determinants of SES (such as intelligence) may be tied to genetic determinants of weight, thus implying that fat people are less intelligent than nonfat people. That the editors could make this connection in spite of Gortmaker and his colleagues having controlled for intelligence (and finding that income differences between overweight and nonoverweight people persisted) shows that still more rigorous testing for discrimination may be needed.

Thus, the three aforementioned branches of research on weight and income inequality—laboratory experiments measuring test subjects' propensity to discriminate against hypothetical fat employees, subjective self-reports of discrimination and stigmatization on the basis of one's weight, and multivariate analyses using residual explanations of discrimination—all provide evidence that strongly suggests the existence of antifat discrimination. However, none employs the methodological tools to positively establish and quantify the existence of such discrimination in real-world employment settings. It is this gap that this article seeks to address.

When Do Income Differences Constitute Unlawful Forms of Discrimination?

While Stunkard and Sorensen's (1993) implication that genetics and intelligence may partially explain fat people's lowered SES is problematic, it also points to the notion that not all differences in income result from unlawful discrimination. Most employers can be said to discriminate in their employment practices, in the sense of the word meaning to distinguish (and choose) between better and worse options. What is at stake, then, is not whether employers discriminate, but how rational and lawful we perceive their discriminatory criteria to be. I argue that it is productive to think of these criteria as falling on a spectrum ranging from rational and legitimate on one side to irrational and illegitimate on the other. These assessments of each type of discrimination's legitimacy are not absolute, but are contingent on capitalist market logic (which supports merit-based hiring and wages over, for example, need-based pay) as well as on the particular requirements of a given job.

At one end of the spectrum, income differences may be due to differences in experience, skill, or effort. Here, the cause is what I am calling *meritocratic discrimination*. A classic example of this form of inequality can be found in Emile Durkheim's ([1933] 1997) discussion of the division of labor, where he writes, "Labour only divides up spontaneously if society is constituted in such a way that *social inequalities express precisely natural inequalities*" (p. 313; emphasis added). In a capitalist society, we would not consider socioeconomic differences due to productivity and skill to be illegitimate in and of themselves, even if the conscientious social scientist should be concerned with whether opportunities for people to gain the necessary experience, to identify and develop their skills, and to have their efforts recognized are distributed equitably. In the ideal-typical form of meritocratic discrimination, wage and employment differences among individual workers would neatly reflect their productivity and the demand for their labor, as given by theories about human capital and a well-functioning free market (e.g., Becker 1975; Medoff and Abraham 1981).

A second form of discrimination, which falls in the middle of this spectrum, is Lester Thurow's (1975) notion of *statistical discrimination*. In the case of statistical discrimination, employers attempt to make rational hiring and pay decisions based on spotty knowledge of an individual worker's merit. People who belong to groups believed to lack favorable work characteristics are paid less or "are not hired because of the objective characteristics of the group to which they belong, although they, themselves, are satisfactory" (p. 172). In this form of discrimination, certain groups may have a lower *average* chance of possessing some trait that an employer is looking for (e.g., one might expect that people with lower levels of education would have, on average, lower levels of reading comprehension and writing skills), but that expectation does not hold true for every member of the group. Such outstanding individuals are said to suffer discrimination as a consequence of belonging to an "objectively" less desirable group. How can statistically undesirable individuals overcome such profiling? Thurow (1975) states:

> The acceptable workers buy their way out of the group to which they belong. Individuals know whether they do or do not have the desired characteristic. If they do, they can overcome their group's characteristics by offering to work for a short period of time for a wage lower than others who are believed to have the right set of personal characteristics. Then once on the job, where they can demonstrate that they have the right characteristics, their wages will rise to the level of others with the right characteristics regardless of the groups to which they belong (p. 173).

Thurow's argument rests on the rather tenuous premise that, in many cases, "objective" statistical information about group characteristics is obtainable. It seems likely, however, that employers will inevitably substitute well-researched information with "common knowledge." In the case of fat jobseekers, many employers may imagine them to embody traits like "laziness, lack of discipline, unwillingness to conform, and absence of all those 'managerial' abilities that, according to the dominant ideology, confer upward mobility"

(Bordo [1993] 2003:195), and may also view them as "lacking self-discipline, having low supervisory potential, and having poor personal hygiene and professional appearance" (Puhl and Brownell 2001:789).

For Thurow, the problem of statistical discrimination results from employers' rational attempts to make employment decisions efficiently: they supplement their limited observable information about each applicant with statistical knowledge that they believe accurately describes a group but may be inaccurate for any individual member of the group. Statistical discrimination does not describe a situation in which members of one group systematically exploit or deny employment to members of another group. Rather, it assumes that employers are motivated by the desire to find workers who provide good value while minimizing the costs of searching for and identifying qualified job candidates. When potential employers are unable to ascertain whether an applicant has certain desired worker characteristics like dedication or intelligence (an issue that arises particularly in the case of young or inexperienced jobseekers), they fall back on observable characteristics as crude proxies.

Finally, *prejudicial discrimination* falls at the opposite end of the spectrum from meritocratic discrimination. It entails employment decisions based on characteristics that are unrelated to worker skill or productivity, and it is the form of discrimination most commonly named as such in popular and scholarly discourses. When prejudicial discrimination comes into play, it makes employers blind (or indifferent) to the qualifications of people from stereotyped groups, with the result that such job applicants will be (1) not hired or (2) placed in jobs for which they are overqualified or ill suited. As such, prejudicial discrimination represents the most blatant and irrational contributor to income inequalities among individuals in a capitalist economy.

Thinking about wage disparities in terms of a spectrum—ranging from meritocratic to statistical to prejudicial discrimination—is more helpful for developing a nuanced vision of how discrimination works than simply looking for the presence or absence of discrimination. Specifically, while these forms of discrimination may differ in their consequences for both employers and employees, all arise from employers' varying ability (or willingness) to recognize employee productivity and to match them to appropriate jobs and wages. Furthermore, the three forms of discrimination described above are given as ideal types, but in practice they are not always clear-cut or mutually exclusive. Thurow (1975:175), for example, notes that if those who seek to benefit from another group's exclusion from a workplace or occupation can manage to reduce the qualifications of enough members of that group (such as by defunding schools in regions where members of that group are concentrated), employers may inadvertently help out the exploiting group by starting to practice statistical discrimination against the exploited group. Such a situation would fall somewhere between statistical and prejudicial discrimination on the spectrum. On the other side of things, if, for example, an employer advertised a job for which punctuality was important, s/he might ask job applicants' past employers to comment on the individual's history of coming to work on time, and make a hiring decision on that basis. This would be a simple case of meritocratic discrimination. If, however, the job opening was for an entry-level position and no direct evidence about applicants' past punctuality was available, the employer might turn to whatever proxies she could find: for example, whether the employee was single or married, with or without children. Although regulations such as the U.S. federal Equal Employment Opportunity laws draw a sharp line between the first case (meritocratic discrimination) and the second (statistical discrimination, which violates the law), understanding these cases in terms of a spectrum of discrimination highlights the ways in which efforts at finding and rewarding the best workers can go wrong when employers have limited knowledge.

While one point of this spectrum model is to emphasize the continuities between different forms of discrimination, the three particular forms I have specified are helpful tools for determining the severity of inequality: not all discrimination is created equal. One difference between statistical and prejudicial discrimination is in the scope of their effects. Whereas statistical discrimination indicates unfair treatment of individuals (but the majority of group members for whom the stereotype is true are being treated fairly according to their value as workers), prejudicial discrimination has the potential to unfairly disadvantage all members of a given group. The other main difference between statistical and prejudicial discrimination becomes evident over time. Under statistical discrimination, wage deficits for low-status people should catch up to those of other comparably qualified employees as employers gain better information about them, even though their lifetime earnings will be less than those of their colleagues. On the other hand, under prejudicial discrimination, low status wages will not only *fail* to catch up to high status wages, but the effects of such discrimination will greatly accumulate over time and widen the gap. Neither of these two forms of discrimination is legally defensible, nor is it likely that workers' losses from either form will be fully recouped over time, but the magnitude of those losses differs substantially between the two types.

Developing a Positive Test for Statistical Discriminiation

Joseph Altonji and Rebecca Blank (1999) suggest a quantitative method of testing for the presence of statistical discrimination, which they recommend for studies of race and gender inequality. Many studies of discrimination, including the previously mentioned work by Gortmaker and associates (1993), look for discrimination in the residual differences in income or employment that remain after controlling for all the relevant variables available. As we have seen, the problem with this type of research is that it can never fully rule out the possibility that income differences are simply the result of some legitimate difference in workers' skill or productivity that is visible to employers, but unobserved by the researcher (in other words, meritocratic discrimination). In contrast, Altonji and Blank's model is appealing because it finds a way to *positively* test for statistical discrimination. Using an interaction term that multiplies one's years of work experience by the variable believed to be a basis for discrimination, Altonji and Blank test whether the negative effects on income due to the possession of that characteristic decrease as experience grows. If those effects lessen over time, statistical discrimination is indicated: employers gradually replace their statistical knowledge about the group to which the worker belongs with knowledge about the individual worker, and the worker is compensated accordingly. If, instead, earnings inequalities persist despite work experience, they are more likely due to prejudicial discrimination.

Hypotheses

In this article, then, I set out to determine the nature and magnitude of the income disparities faced by obese employees using Altonji and Blank's (1999) positive test of statistical discrimination. Through multivariate ordinary least squares (OLS) regression, I test the following hypotheses:

H_0: Controlling for a variety of background factors, particularly including education level and intelligence test results, will cause the relationship between obesity and reduced income to disappear. This finding would indicate the presence of *meritocratic discrimination*.

H_1: Disparities in income between obese and nonobese individuals will persist after controlling for a variety of common causes of income inequality. Furthermore, there will be a significant interaction effect between work experience and obesity, such that the income gap between obese and nonobese workers will decrease as work experience increases. This finding would indicate that *statistical discrimination* is at work.

H_2: Income disparities between obese and nonobese workers will exist, but there will be no significant interaction between obesity and work experience. This outcome would suggest that the obese worker's disadvantage in any given year neither

increases nor lessens with time. There would, nonetheless, be an accumulation of lost wages from year to year, and it would be strongly suggestive of *prejudicial discrimination*.

Finally, most existing studies in this field have tested for—and confirmed—gender differences in the degree to which fat women and men face employment inequality relative to their thinner colleagues. These findings fit with gender scholarship arguing that women and men often face different types and degrees of social scrutiny in regard to their bodies. Gendered ideals of masculine and feminine characteristics map onto bodies, creating expectations that, for example, men will be heavier and taller, and will require more space than women (Bordo [1993] 2003); men eat heartier food in greater portions while "a girl's accession to womanhood is marked by doing without" (Bourdieu [1979] 1984:195); men have the right to look at and judge women's bodies (while women do not have parallel visual access to men's bodies) (Berger [1972] 1977; Mulvey 1975); and women, freighted with historical and ideological ties to the body and nature (often evoked through associating womanhood with childbirth and maternal "instincts" or by contrasting men's supposedly innate intellectuality with feminine "nature"), are thus more likely than men to be evaluated according to their physical characteristics (Butler [1990] 2006; Ortner 1974; Wolf [1991] 2002). In light of these patterns, an additional hypothesis is needed:

H_3: Women and men may have differences in the quality and/or quantity of discrimination they face, with anti-obesity discrimination tending to be more damaging to women than to men. . . .

Results

Key Variables

For women, being obese (BMI $>$ 30) proved to be a significant predictor of lowered income. This finding indicates that the ties between income and body size continued to be important factors influencing women's life chances in the 2000s, extending into the twenty-first century the findings that Gortmaker and associates (1993) and other authors published on data from the 1980s. Holding all other variables constant at their averages, obese women earned an average of $15,220 a year while nonobese women earned an average $18,948. On the other hand, obesity was associated with smaller negative coefficients for men than for women, and male obesity had no significant effect on income....

The gender dynamics of the weight-income relationship shift when obesity is redefined as including only those with BMI scores higher than 35.... For women, the significance and magnitude of the obesity coefficient remain virtually unchanged.... For men, ... those with BMIs of 35 or greater earned an average of $16,166 per year, compared to the $25,406 earned by thinner men—in other words, lower-BMI men made 57 percent higher incomes per year. All told, these findings provide evidence that weight-based income penalties begin at lower weights for women than for men (providing partial support for H_3), but that very obese ... men are heavily penalized relative to nonobese men.

Work experience was a significant predictor of income for both women and men.... [However,] this finding suggests that incremental increases in experience during the early years of work yielded a much higher payoff per year than increased experience further down the line, whereas men in the labor force continued to increase their incomes as they gained work experience. A caveat to these work experience findings is that all of the subjects in this study were in the very early stages of their careers in 2008, and some of their past experience might have been in seasonal or temporary jobs unrelated to their career goals. If such trends continue over a longer period of time, though, it might suggest that men have an easier time getting their accomplishments and ability noticed and getting pay raises....

Interactions

Obesity and Work Experience

The interaction between obesity and work experience, which forms the basis of the test for statistical discrimination, was not significant for women or men when obesity was set at its lower cutoff point (BMI > 30) .... Likewise, the model using a higher cutoff point for obesity (BMI > 35) still showed no significant interaction effect between women's weight and their work experience... *This finding suggests that any effect of obesity on women's income was not due to statistical discrimination and may not have been helped by persistent hard work and visibility in the workplace. Thus, this finding is very suggestive of prejudicial discrimination (H_2) against obese women, although such a conclusion would appear to be based in a residual explanation of discrimination.*

In contrast, the effects of male obesity ... on income strongly indicated statistical discrimination against very obese men (H_1), due to the fact that the interaction effect between work experience and obesity was significant.... In general, nonobese men's incomes tended to lie well above women's, and obese men's incomes were either higher than all women's ... or predicted to overtake women after several years' work experience.... Figure 1 shows the different effects of work experience on income for men and women, differentiated by whether or not they were obese... while Figure 2 shows the same effects differentiated by whether or not respondents were very obese....

Obesity and Occupation

For both women and men, occupational type did not significantly interact with weight at either cutoff for obesity (BMI > 30 or BMI > 35). Although Carr and Friedman (2005) found that obese white-collar workers were more likely than their nonobese colleagues to subjectively report experiencing discrimination in some form, the current data do not support that finding when it comes to objective measures of income discrimination. Further studies looking at workers with greater labor force experience and/or at other measures of employment inequality may be needed to further substantiate Carr and Friedman's findings.

Obesity and Race/Ethnicity

Some racial/ethnic interactions with obesity were significant for women in the models I tested: Hispanic women were less likely to suffer income

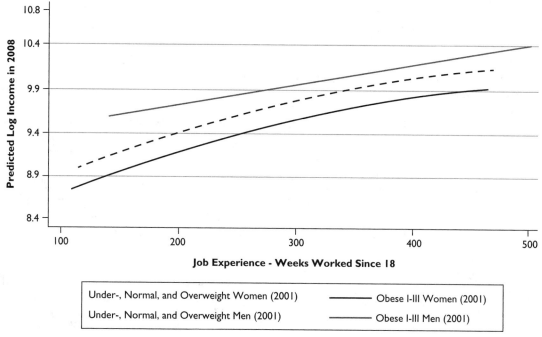

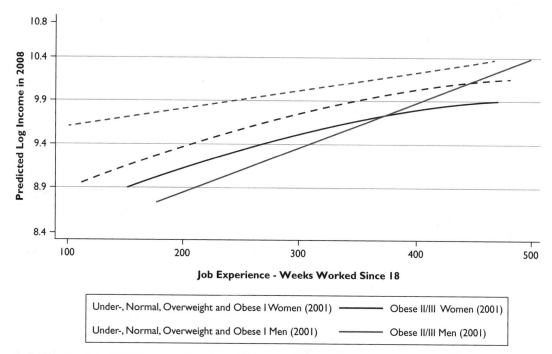

Figure 1. Predicted 2008 Incomes for Men and Women (BMI > 30)
Source: National Longitudinal Survey of Youth 97.
Note: Obese is defined as BMI > 30.

Figure 2. Predicted 2008 Incomes for Men and Women (BMI > 35)
Source: National Longitudinal Survey of Youth 97.
Note: Obese is defined as BMI > 35.

inequality due to being obese (BMI > 30) than white women, and—more ambiguously—women in the "other" racial/ethnic category were more likely than white women to face income inequality due to being very obese (BMI > 35). Men in both models showed no significant differences in the effects of obesity due to race/ethnicity. These findings align with those of other researchers, including Dalton Conley and Rebecca Glauber (2007) and Averett and Korenman (1996), who found that white women were more disadvantaged by weight-based discrimination than women of color (but that no such pattern existed for men), and with the statement by Carr and Friedman (2005) that "obesity is considered a greater normative violation among women, whites, and young persons" (p. 255).

Discussion

Past research has provided evidence for the existence of income discrimination against fat individuals. This study's findings suggest that obese women and men experience such discrimination differently, in terms of both duration and intensity. Through examination of an interaction effect between work experience and obesity, it appears that very obese men in this study were economically disadvantaged in the early years of work relative to their more normative-bodied, nonobese peers, but over time, they were able to make up the difference. This finding suggests that their early lowered wages may have been due to statistical discrimination—assumptions made by employers that eventually could be corrected with time spent on the job.

Obese women, on the other hand, earn less than their thinner female counterparts at every step of their careers, a conclusion that is supported by my own findings as well as the existing literature. For example, Conley and Glauber's (2007) study of body mass effects on later life socioeconomic status found that income penalties for obese women in 2001 persisted into their mid-fifties, but that no such effect existed for obese men. Clearly, there is a negative relationship between body mass and income for women, and it does not disappear with time on the job. Having thus ruled out H_0 (no relationship) and H_1 (statistical discrimination), the most likely explanation for obese women's income disadvantage is prejudicial discrimination. Further, this study lends support to previously suggested differences in the effects of being fat for men and for women (H_3). Specifically, there appears to be a gender gap not only in men and women's wages, but also in the degree to which they are disadvantaged by having nonnormative bodies. Women in the NLSY97 faced severe income penalties for being obese, and these effects' significance and magnitude remained robust in the presence of a wide variety of control variables. Such direct income effects represent only one of several mechanisms through which fat women have been found to suffer limited access to economic and social resources. Indirect causes of fat women's economic disadvantage include, first of all, lower levels of education, due in part to educational "cooling-out" processes that encourage them to lower their sights. Marilyn Wann (2009) describes research by C. S. Crandall (1995) showing that "[h]igh school counselors are less likely to encourage fat students to apply for college, colleges are less likely to admit equally qualified fat applicants, and parents are less likely to pay a fat daughter's college tuition" (p. xix). A second indirect cause of economic hardship for fat women is that they face worse marriage prospects, in terms of both their lower likelihood of ever marrying and the lower incomes of the men they do marry (Averett and Korenman 1996; Gortmaker et al. 1993). Thus, fat women—perhaps similar to the situation of women in other marginalized groups—are less able to rely on economic support provided by a husband, but at the same time they are less encouraged to develop the skills needed to support themselves. My findings in the realm of income inequality suggest that obese women who overcome these obstacles and find employment will be compensated less for their efforts than other women, not more. Finally, while the regression models in this study control for a variety of background factors, it is worth noting that weight-based income inequality for women may compound a number of other factors that work to further disadvantage obese women: the obese women in my sample were significantly less likely to have completed college, significantly less likely to be married, significantly more likely to have a child, and from childhood homes with significantly lower incomes than those of their nonobese female peers.

Although I found statistical discrimination (in the form of a significant interaction between weight and work experience) only for very obese men, the different patterns of weight-based wage gaps among women and men help to shed light on some of the mechanisms underlying this inequality. As noted at the beginning of this article, one popular explanation of wage gaps between fat and slender workers is that differences in pay are attributable to actual differences in productivity or ability (i.e., meritocratic discrimination). Controlling for education, experience, intellectual ability, and other factors can help make this explanation less viable, but it is still not possible to completely rule it out. There might be some as-yet-unaccounted-for variable that would explain the persistent link between higher weight and lower pay.

The finding of gender differences is instructive in this regard. For men, I have shown that statistical discrimination was taking place; very obese men were indeed disadvantaged, but they could overcome initial perceptions and close the wage gap over time. Though there was no significant interaction effect to suggest statistical discrimination for women, the men's findings can nonetheless help us understand the nature of the disadvantages women faced. If obese men, over time, were able to work hard and prove their worth, then the low pay they faced early on was due to incorrect employer perceptions, *not* to some unobserved physical or mental deficiency evidenced by their bodies.

If inferior physical or mental abilities were not the cause of obese men's disadvantages, then it seems unlikely that they would be the cause of obese women's disadvantages, either. Why would obese women suffer from some pathology affecting their ability to work, whereas obese men would not? A more likely explanation is that obese women and men both suffered from negative perceptions by employers. The gender difference, then, would result from the different degrees to which women and men continued to be judged based on their appearances. In a society where sexist attitudes still

hold sway, women are expected to demand fewer resources and take up less space—to be physically less than men (Bordo [1993] 2003). Furthermore, a pervasive cultural belief in sexual dimorphism (the notion that there are absolute, distinct physical differences between all men and all women) does more than describe the average bodily differences between women and men (e.g., that men are bigger and more muscular than women), it also disciplines those bodies in order to (re)produce sexual dimorphism. Thus, while both obese women and men experience a variety of disadvantages (in this case, income inequality) due to the stigmatization of fatness itself, obese women are further penalized for failing to do their gender properly: in short, their fatness causes them to be punished for being unfeminine. Thus, not only should studies on the social significance of fatness pay special attention to gender, but also, I argue, gender scholarship dealing with intersectionality should consider body size as a vector of inequality that, like race/ethnicity or class, interacts with and mediates gender.

Conclusion

This article contributes to the current literature in three key respects. First, previous studies attempting to statistically prove the existence of anti-fat income discrimination have often done so by pointing to residual income differences after controlling for a number of explanatory variables. Yet, one popular counter-argument to these studies claims that wage gaps between fat and slender workers are attributable to actual differences in productivity or ability (i.e., meritocratic discrimination). Controlling for education, experience, intellectual ability, and other factors can help make this explanation less viable, but can never fully eliminate it. By first theorizing a spectrum of discrimination ranging from lawful meritocratic discrimination to illegal statistical and prejudicial discrimination, then introducing Altonji and Blank's (1999) test for statistical discrimination, this article provides positive evidence for the existence of weight-based employment discrimination.

Second, most of the existing studies on weight-based income inequality draw on data from the 1980s and 1990s. To my knowledge, this article is the first to investigate income inequality and body size using the NLSY97 cohort, and one of the first to look at these trends in the late 2000s. Taken together, the present study and past work provide compelling evidence of the decades-long persistence of weight-based employment discrimination in the United States. To the extent that public policy engages with these findings, it tends to pose individual weight loss as the solution, rather than legal protections against anti-fat discrimination. However, given widespread evidence that weight-loss diets do not provide long-term weight reduction or health benefits for the majority of people (as in the 31 weight loss studies that Traci Mann and colleagues [2007] scrutinized in their meta-analysis), individual weight loss is not a viable solution to the ongoing problem of weight-based income inequality in the United States that this study illustrates.

Third, this study provides evidence of important gender differences in how women and men experience weight-based discrimination. For women, anti-obesity discrimination sets in at lower body mass levels and does not dissipate over time as they gain experience. This income penalty stacks on top of other economic disadvantages past research has found for this population, including lower average educational attainment and marriage rates, and it may be more pronounced for white women than for certain racial and ethnic minority women. For men, obesity may be linked to lowered income relative to thinner male colleagues, but only among those who are very obese (BMI > 35), a cutoff Carr and Friedman (2005) describe as the point at which "obesity may become a 'master status,' or a characteristic that overrides all other features of a person's identity" (p. 255). Yet even in this case, obese men's disadvantage is not as severe as women's. Obese men can overcome initial disadvantages with time and experience, whereas obese women will continue to face diminished wages over the course of a lifetime.

Notes

1. Throughout this article, I use the term "fat" not in the pejorative sense, but instead as it has been reclaimed by fat activists (similar to the use of the word "queer" by LGBT groups). To this end,

"fat" points to the aesthetic and normative otherness that large-bodied people experience, rather than to the medical criteria that classify them as "overweight." I use the terms "overweight" and "obese" when I am referring to body mass index designations or when they are the wording preferred by an author I am discussing.

References

Altonji, Joseph G. and Rebecca M. Blank. 1999. "Race and Gender in the Labor Market." Pp. 3143–259 in *Handbook of Labor Economics,* Vol. 3, edited by Orley Ashenfelter and David Card. Amsterdam: Elsevier Science B.V.

Averett, Susan and Sanders Korenman. 1996. "The Economic Reality of the Beauty Myth." *Journal of Human Resources* 31:304–30.

Baum, Charles and William Ford. 2004. "The Wage Effects of Obesity: A Longitudinal Study." *Health Economics* 13(9):885–99.

Becker, Gary S. 1975. *Human Capital.* 2d ed. New York: National Bureau of Economic Research.

Berger, John. [1972] 1977. *Ways of Seeing.* New York: Penguin Books.

Biddle, Jeff E. and Daniel S. Hamermesh. 1998. "Beauty, Productivity, and Discrimination: Lawyers' Looks and Lucre." *Journal of Labor Economics* 16(1):172–201.

Boero, Natalie. 2007. "All the News that's Fat to Print: The American 'Obesity Epidemic' and the News Media." *Qualitative Sociology* 30(1):41–60.

Bordo, Susan. [1993] 2003. *Unbearable Weight: Feminism, Western Culture, and the Body.* Berkeley: University of California Press.

Bourdieu, Pierre. [1979] 1984. *Distinction: A Social Critique of the Judgement of Taste.* Translated by Richard Nice. Cambridge, MA: Harvard University Press.

Butler, Judith. [1990] 2006. *Gender Trouble: Feminism and the Subversion of Identity.* New York: Routledge.

Carr, Deborah and Michael A. Friedman. 2005. "Is Obesity Stigmatizing? Body Weight, Perceived Discrimination, and Psychological Well-Being in the United States." *Journal of Health and Social Behavior* 46(3):244–59.

Cawley, John. 2004. "The Impact of Obesity on Wages." *Journal of Human Resources* 39:451–74.

Cawley, John and Sheldon Danziger. 2005. "Morbid Obesity and the Transition from Welfare to Work."

Journal of Policy Analysis and Management 24(4):727–43.

Conley, Dalton and Rebecca Glauber. 2007. "Gender, Body Mass, and Socioeconomic Status: New Evidence from the PSID." *Advances in Health Economics and Health Services Research* 17:253–75.

Crandall, C. S. 1995. "Do Parents Discriminate Against their Heavyweight Daughters?" *Personality and Social Psychology Bulletin* 21(7):742–35.

Durkheim, Emile. [1933] 1997. *The Division of Labour in Society.* Edited by Lewis Coser. New York: The Free Press.

Flegal, Katherine M., Barry I. Graubard, David F. Williamson, and Mitchell H. Gail. 2005. "Excess Deaths Associated with Underweight, Overweight, and Obesity." *Journal of the American Medical Association* 293(15):1861–67.

Gortmaker, Steven L., Aviva Must, James M. Perrin, Arthur M. Sobol, and William H. Dietz. 1993. "Social and Economic Consequences of Overweight in Adolescence and Young Adulthood." *New England Journal of Medicine* 329(14):1008–12.

Hamermesh, Daniel S. and Jeff E. Biddle. 1994. "Beauty and the Labor Market." *American Economic Review* 84(5):1174–94.

Haskins, Katherine and H. Edward Ransford. 1999. "The Relationship between Weight and Career Payoffs among Women." *Sociological Forum* 14(2):295–318.

Kristen, Elizabeth. 2002. "Addressing the Problem of Weight Discrimination in Employment." *California Law Review* 90(1):57–109.

Mann, Traci, Janet Tomiyama, Erika Westling, Ann-Marie Lew, Barbra Samuels, and Jason Chatman. 2007. "Medicare's Search for Effective Obesity Treatments: Diets Are Not the Answer." *American Psychologist* 62(3):220–33.

McDowell, Margaret A., Cheryl D. Fryar, Cynthia L. Ogden, and Katherine M. Flegal. 2008. "Anthropometric Reference Data for Children and Adults: United States, 2003–2006." *National Health Statistics Reports* 10. Retrieved February 16, 2012 (www.cdc.gov/nchs/data/nhsr/nhsr010.pdf).

Medoff, James L. and Katharine G. Abraham. 1981. "Are Those Paid More Really More Productive? The Case of Experience." *Journal of Human Resources* 16(2):186–216.

Mulford, Matthew, John Orbell, Catherine Shatto, and Jean Stockard. 1998. "Physical Attractiveness, Opportunity, and Success in Everyday Exchange." *American Journal of Sociology* 103(6):1565–92.

Mulvey, Laura. 1975. "Visual Pleasure and Narrative Cinema." *Screen* 16(3):6–18.

Ortner, Sherry. 1974. "Is Female to Male as Nature Is to Culture?" Pp. 68–87 in *Woman, Culture, and Society,* edited by Michelle Rosaldo, Louise Lamphere, and Joan Bamberger. Stanford, CA: Stanford University Press.

Pace, Gina. 2006. "Obesity Bigger Threat than Terrorism?" *Associated Press,* March 1. Retrieved August 9, 2010 (www.cbsnews.com/stories/2006/03/01/health/main1361849.shtml).

Puhl, Rebecca M. and Chelsea A. Heuer. 2010. "Obesity Stigma: Important Considerations for Public Health." *American Journal of Public Health* 100(6):1019–28.

Puhl, Rebecca M. and Kelly D. Brownell. 2001. "Bias, Discrimination, and Obesity." *Obesity Research* 9(12):788–805.

Puhl, Rebecca M., Tatiana Andreyeva, and Kelly D. Brownell. 2008. "Perceptions of Weight Discrimination: Prevalence and Comparison to Race and Gender Discrimination." *International Journal of Obesity* 32:992–1000.

Roehling, Mark V. 2002. "Weight Discrimination in the American Workplace: Ethical Issues and Analysis." *Journal of Business Ethics* 40(2):177–89.

Saguy, Abigail C. 2008. "French Women Don't Get Fat?" *Health at Every Size Journal* 19(4):219–34.

Saguy, Abigail C. and Kevin C. Riley. 2005. "Weighing Both Sides: Morality, Mortality, and Framing Contests over Obesity." *Journal of Health Politics, Policy, and Law* 30(5):869–921.

Schafer, Markus H. and Kenneth F. Ferraro. 2011. "The Stigma of Obesity: Does Perceived Weight Discrimination Affect Identity and Physical Health?" *Social Psychology Quarterly* 74(1):76–97.

Stunkard, Albert J. and Thorkild Sorensen. 1993. "Obesity and Socioeconomic Status—A Complex Relation." *New England Journal of Medicine* 329(14):1036–37.

Thurow, Lester C. 1975. *Generating Inequality: Mechanisms of Distribution in the U.S. Economy.* New York: Basic Books.

Wann, Marilyn. 2009. "Foreword—Fat Studies: An Invitation to Revolution." Pp. ix–xxv in *The Fat Studies Reader,* edited by Esther Rothblum and Sondra Solovay. New York: New York University Press.

Wolf, Naomi. [1991] 2002. *The Beauty Myth.* New York: HarperCollins.

"Do It For All Your Pubic Hairs!": Latino Boys, Masculinity, and Puberty

RICHARD MORA

Introduction

Pubescence brings about the most noticeable changes to the male body, second only to neonatal development (Martin 1996). The social meanings ascribed to these physical changes, and puberty itself, are locally situated (Janssen 2006). Hence, understanding how boys make sense of puberty, as well as how they interpret and socially construct their bodies during pubescence, may illuminate how boys' bodies figure into gender identities, given that doing gender involves bodies (Butler 1993; West and Zimmerman 1987) and that masculinity is a life-long project involving the changing physical body (Connell 2005). Yet the literature lacks thorough and sustained in situ examinations of how diverse boys employ their bodies to construct masculine identities during pubescence across a range of sociocultural contexts.

The present article seeks to contribute to the literature on masculinity by examining the gender construction of Latino boys, an understudied segment of the U.S. population. More to the point, it addresses the following research question: How do 10 sixth-grade, second-generation, immigrant Dominican and Puerto Rican boys, who publicly acknowledge that they are experiencing puberty, construct their masculine identities and employ their bodies at school? The question emerged early on in a two-and-a-half-year ethnographic study, when review of daily field notes suggested that both gender identity and puberty held social meanings within their group. Given that masculinity is

defined by peers and is constructed collectively (Swain 2003) via social interactions (West and Zimmerman 1987), peer relations were closely examined. Not assuming a priori that puberty mattered to the boys allowed for emic understandings of how the peer group influenced boys' views of their bodies and pubescence.

The data suggest that among the boys puberty was a social accomplishment connected to masculine enactments informed by the dominant gendered expectations of peers at school and in their neighborhoods, the hegemonic masculine practices espoused by commercial hip hop rappers, and the dominant gender orders in the United States and both Dominican and Puerto Rican societies. The findings contribute to our understanding of how masculinities are constructed in the United States by immigrants' children (i.e., second-generation children) who reside in low-income, working-class neighborhoods and have social ties to their nations of origin and their respective cultures. By considering the boys' situated ethnoracial identities, this article also contributes to the study of the masculine practices of diverse boys, particularly those associated with the pan-ethnic category, Latino.

The present article begins with a review of the relevant literature on masculinity. A discussion of ethnographic data collection and analysis follows. Distinct findings subsections illuminate how the boys used their changing male bodies to construct masculine identities within their social worlds. I conclude by discussing the findings in relation to

Richard Mora, "'Do It for All Your Pubic Hairs!': Latino Boys, Masculinity, and Puberty," *Gender & Society*, Vol. 26, No. 3 (June 2012), pp. 433–460. Copyright © 2012 by Richard Mora. Reprinted by permission of SAGE Publications.

observations made while the boys were in the seventh and eighth grade, and calling for further study of the social interplay between gender construction and puberty as well as the intersection of masculinity and Latino identities.

Literature

I begin by reviewing the scholarship on bodies and masculinity, followed by a brief evaluation of research on how boys experience sexual maturation that highlights the paucity of studies on how diverse boys construct their masculine identities during pubescence. Next, I review scholarship examining how boys enact their masculinities within their male peer groups at school and how schools reinforce masculinities. Finally, I focus on the intersection of masculinity and racial identity. Together, the scholarship discussed herein informs the article's theoretical framework.

The Body and Masculinity

Research shows that boys pay attention to their physical appearance for both functional and aesthetic purposes (Grogan and Richards 2002). Masculine power is ascribed to muscular male physiques. Aware that their bodies are interpreted and gendered by others, boys and men from distinct socioeconomic and racial backgrounds work on their bodies with the intent of achieving the ideal male physique attributed to high masculine status (McCabe and Ricciardelli 2004; Pope, Phillips, and Olivardia 2000). Consequently, boys and men consider a "flabby body" less manly (Lilleaas 2007, 42). British research suggests that men and boys of varying age associate fat with lack of control and weakness (Grogan and Richards 2002). While there is some evidence that Latino men may also disapprove of flabbiness (Pope, Phillips, and Olivardia 2000, 206), little research examines Latino boys' view of their bodies and masculinity.

In schools, boys of distinct ages, races, and social classes negotiate their masculine identities and social standing by demonstrating their physical dexterity, strength, and athleticism (Davison 2000; Eder, Evans, and Parker 1995; Hasbrook and Harris 1999; Walker 1988). On school campuses,

sports usually provide a venue for successful gender performances (Connell 2005). Those who use their bodies successfully during sporting activities can amass "physical capital" and gain masculine status (Swain 2000, 2003). What is more, for many low-income African American and Dominican boys (Dance 2002; Ferguson 2001; Lopez 2003), doing gender at school might involve using their bodies to fight, in spite of school rules. It is likely that physical development influences how boys use their bodies.

Presently, boys enter puberty approximately two and a half years earlier than their counterparts did at the beginning of the twentieth century (Frankel 2003). Presently, the age range for the onset of puberty in boys is nine to 14 years (compared to eight to 13 years in girls) (Katz and Misra 2011). The mean age of initial growth spurts for boys is approximately 11 years, approximately 2 years later than for girls (Abbassi 1998; Katz and Misra 2011). As a result, sixth-grade classrooms may have boys who have yet to experience pubescence and girls who look like young adult women (Eccles 1999, 38).

Boys take pride in displaying both their growing bodies and their bodily control (Davison 2000; Prendergast and Forrest 1997, 1998; Vaccaro 2011). Still, some boys experience anxiety around physiological changes, particularly those whose changes come later (Martin 1996). Boys who experience puberty later than their peers do tend to be less popular. Retrospective data based on interviews with a group of mostly white working- and middle-class high school students suggest that, compared to girls, boys tend to experience puberty alone and hardly discuss such matters with peers (Martin 1996).

While there is much scholarship documenting that doing masculinity involves the body, the literature lacks empirical studies examining how boys construct masculine identities during puberty and how class and race influence these identities. The few empirical studies that consider the relationship between puberty and masculinity are retrospective medical and psychological works that include few, if any, nonwhite participants. These studies suggest that adolescent males view masculinity as an accomplishment, with no clear connection to sexual maturation (Martin 1996; Stein and Reiser 1994). However, since the body undergoes biological and social change over the life course (Schilling 1993) and masculinity is a life-long project involving ethnoracial identities and the changing physical body (Connell 2005), it seems likely that there is some connection between boys' construction of masculinity, their ethnoracial identities, and their pubescent experiences. An in situ study of boys' enactments of masculinity during puberty could provide evidence documenting the relationship between the body and gender development.

Masculinity at School and Boy Peer Groups

Research indicates that in schools, boys' masculinity typically involves performing dominant heterosexual identities (Kehily 2001; Mac an Ghaill 1994; Martino and Pallotta-Chiarolli 2003; Renold 2005; Walker 1988), with peers regularly policing male heterosexuality (Chambers, Tincknell, and Loon 2004; Eder, Evans, and Parker 1995; Epstein, O'Flynn, and Telford 2000; Nayak and Kehily 2001). More often than not, high-status boys dictate the hegemonic masculinities that regulate and maintain the gender order (Gardiner 2000; Lopez 2003; Mac an Ghaill 1994; Martino 1999, 2000; Martino and Pallotta-Chiarolli 2003; McGuffey and Rich 1999; Pascoe 2007; Swain 2000, 2003). Though boys typically try on and test masculine identities in the presence of friends (Ferguson 2001), they nonetheless often construct their masculinities by regulating gender boundaries (Ferguson 2001; Kehily 2001; Renold 2001, 2005; Swain 2003; Witt 2000). In addition, they typically promote "compulsory heterosexuality" within their peer groups (Epstein, 2001; Epstein and Johnson 1998; Korobov 2005; Redman et al. 2002; Martino 2000).

The "panopticonic regimes of surveillance" present in peer groups normalize heterosexuality (Martino and Pallotta-Chiarolli 2003). Peers accuse those who do not live up to heteronormative expectations of being homosexuals (Dalley-Trim 2007; Eliasson, Isaksson, and Laflamme 2007; Mac an Ghaill 1994; Pascoe 2007; Renold 2003), emphasizing the importance of heterosexuality (Schrock and Schwalbe 2009). In many male peer groups, to be a boy means not being a sissy or girl (Thorne 1993), as masculinity involves the rejection of femininity and homosexuality. Hence, boys across racial and class groups typically define their gender identities against "the dual Others," namely girls and boys deemed feminine (Epstein 2001, 106; Gilbert and Gilbert 1998; Haywood and Mac an Ghaill 2001; Nilan 2000). As research makes clear, students are active agents in the making of masculinities (Connell 2000), and the ongoing gender policing within peer groups demands that boys must be vigilant about abiding by gender expectations and putting forth context-appropriate masculine performances. The consequences of not abiding by heteronormative expectations may vary in different contexts. The present study documents some of the consequences for Latino boys at an urban middle school.

Schools themselves influence gender construction among students. School staff members regularly promulgate heteronormativity with gendered school policies and activities (Connell 2005; Eder, Evans, and Parker 1995; Martino and Pallotta-Chiarolli 2003; Renold 2001, 2003, 2005; Swain 2000, 2003). Teachers and school officials, for example, influence the gender identities of Black and Latino students by ascribing deviant labels to them (Ferguson 2001; Lopez 2003). In a study examining the social mobility of Caribbean youth residing in New York City, Lopez (2003) finds that Dominican young men divested in school largely because they were singled out for more scrutiny by high school officials and security guards, and so invested in constructing their masculine identities on the streets by hanging out, dating, and making money.

Ethnoracial Identity, Class, and Masculinity

Youth from varied racial and class backgrounds construct their masculinities in different manners. For second-generation Caribbean youth, for example, proving masculinity is an experience that involves racial stigma (Lopez 2003). Furthermore, some young men of color in the United States, especially those who are working-class or poor, adopt coping mechanisms, such the "cool pose" used by African Americans males (Majors and Billson 1993) and the "masculine protest behaviors" of urban youth, including Puerto Ricans (De La Cancela 1993, 34), to deal with their marginalized position in society. Male youths from low-income neighborhoods may enact masculinities that include the use of stoic personas— "tough fronts" by Black youth (Dance 2002) and "cara de palo" (wooden club-face) by U.S.-based Puerto Ricans (Thomas 1987)—and the use of their bodies as weapons to gain status and ward off potential assailants (Majors and Billson 1993). Such presentations of self by urban youth are oftentimes part of a "code of the streets," a set of cultural ideas that dictate social expectations and conduct in urban localities, particularly those where neighborhood violence is a common occurrence (Anderson 2000).

Studies of masculine practices among U.S. Latinos and Latin American men tend to focus on machismo, or the cult of manliness (Arciniega et al. 2008; Casas et al. 1994; De La Cancela 1993; Falicov 2010; Gutmann 1996; Mirandé 1997; Torres, Solberg, and Carlstrom 2002). Early research equated machismo with behaviors attributed to working-class men and peasants from Latin America (Ramirez 1999), including male dominance, assertiveness, aggressiveness, and the valuing of physical strength and courage (Mosher 1991). However, Latin American women and individuals from various non–Latin American cultures and countries also display characteristics associated with machismo (Doyle 1995). In addition, the term carries different emic meanings in different Latin American countries (De La Cancela 1993), and some emic variants are not rooted in the dominance of women (Doyle 1995). As a result, many scholars have moved away from an overly simplified understanding of machismo (Casas et al. 1994; De La Cancela 1991; Gutmann 1996; Mirandé 1997; Torres 1998; Torres, Solberg, and Carlstrom 2002). As Torres, Solberg, and Carlstrom (2002) explain, the rearticulation of machismo has given rise to *the dialectical perspective . . . [which]* depicts machismo as both progressive and reactionary patterns of behaviors intimately related to the socioeconomic and historical elements of society" (167). Nonetheless, scholars and journalists still often equate the term with negative male attitudes and behaviors (Gutmann 1996).

The analysis of the data did not utilize the term *machismo* either as a descriptor or as an analytical term. Neither the boys nor the girls that I observed used it to describe masculine behavior. That is, the term was not emic. Furthermore, the negative connotations associated with machismo would racially bias the interpretation of the data. As a result, machismo is an inadequate descriptor. In addition, the fact that a wide range of characteristics are associated with "the cult of manliness" limits its explanatory power.

Rather than focusing on characteristics that may or may not be classified as machismo, and possibly reiterate the cultural essentializing of Latino cultures, the present study examines the influence of dominant gender norms from various gender orders on the boys' masculine performativity. Thus, let us turn to studies examining the dominant masculine expectations in both the Dominican Republic and Puerto Rico. De Moya (2004) explains that hegemonic masculinity in the Dominican Republic prescribes that men be powerful and display both physical and rhetorical dominance during interactions. Additionally, in the dominant gender order of the Dominican Republic, heteronormativity signifies masculinity. In Puerto Rico, "masculine ideology" also includes the objectification of women, stresses sexuality and heteronormativity, demands that men be providers, and emphasizes male competition (Ramírez 1999, 43–44). Males are encouraged to boast about sexual conquests, to guard against infidelity, to display courage and strength, and "to demand respect, to respond to aggressive situations, [and] to defend oneself both physically and verbally" (Ramírez 1999, 59). Research suggests that, like their Puerto Rican counterparts, Puerto Rican youth in the United States who embrace hypermasculinity typically identify highly with their ethnicity and nationality (Saez, Casado, and Wade 2009). . . .

Methods

This article is based mainly on data collected in the first four months of a two-and-a-half-year ethnographic project that followed a group of sixth-graders at Romero Elementary and Middle School, a bilingual, one-building public school in the greater metropolitan area of a Northeastern city. (All names, including the school's, have been changed.) At the time of the study, the city was majority minority, with Latinos accounting for approximately 15 percent of the population. Puerto Ricans and Dominicans are the top two ethnic groups in the city, with approximately twice as many Puerto Ricans as Dominicans. On a list of the top 20 ancestries of the city residents, Puerto Ricans were in the top three and Dominicans in the top 12 (U.S. Bureau of the Census 2000).

Romero had a total student enrollment of approximately 380, of which approximately 85 percent were Latina/Latino. The middle school had approximately 90 students, of which more than 95 percent were Latina/Latino. More than 75 percent of all students received free lunches.

Romero is located near public housing in a working-class, low-income neighborhood populated mainly by Latinas/Latinos of Dominican and Puerto Rican heritage and African Americans. This neighborhood, along with the two others in which most of the students observed resided, was one of the top five neighborhoods with the highest concentration in the city of adults for whom English is their second language (U.S. Census 2000). Youth gangs in the area marked their presence with graffiti near Romero, and some Latino and Black youths sported baseball caps associated with their respective gangs. At the end of the school day, it was common for local male youths to congregate near the school to flirt with middle school girls and meet up with friends or girlfriends.

For this article, the focus is on 10 of the boys—seven second-generation Dominicans and three second-generation Puerto Rican boys. In this article, the boys are referred to as second-generation because they are the U.S.-born children of immigrants, and the designation helps to highlight the fact that they acknowledged, enacted, and maintained their heritages . . . Along with the boys, I also observed sixth-grade peers and older students. Furthermore, to be clear, the article focuses primarily on the first four months of the study, while the students were in the sixth grade, when the boys publicly acknowledged experiencing puberty. . . .

The Latina/Latino students at Romero differentiated themselves and others of Latin American heritage from whites by referring to whites as *Americanos* (Americans). They identified themselves and other Latinas/Latinos primarily by their nation of origin. Students whose parents were born in the Dominican Republic, for example, referred to themselves as "Dominicans" and less often as "Latino," "Hispanic," or "Spanish." Many of the students publicly demonstrated their national pride by writing "DR#1" (i.e., Dominican Republic is no. 1) or "PR#1" (i.e., Puerto Rico is no. 1) on desks and inside textbooks, and by wearing accessories with their home country's national flag. The students had such strong attachment to their Caribbean countries of origin because they participated in transnationalism and, thus, sustained "multi-stranded social relations that link[ed] their societies of origin and settlement" (Basch, Glick-Schiller, and Blanc 1994, 8). The boys visited family in the Caribbean regularly. According to the students, when they visited their home countries they spent time with peers, particularly cousins and friends, many of whom looked to them for cues of what was fashionable among urban youth in the United States. Some of the boys felt the need to put forth the tough, street-smart persona often associated with the hip hop attire worn by youth and rappers in the United States, Puerto Rico, and the Dominican Republic.

Like many young men in their neighborhoods, the boys defined themselves as urban, working-class Latino males with ties to their respective countries of origin. As such, they identified with Latino and Black rappers from rough urban neighborhoods and who view the streets as "the school of hard knocks," including 50 Cent, a muscular, Black ex–drug dealer who put forth a tough persona. What the boys especially liked about rappers was that they embodied a tough, heterosexual masculinity that, along with their lyrics, displayed male dominance, a willingness to use violence, physical strength, and the ability to attract women. Conversely, the boys rejected the attributes of wholesome-seeming singers like the white Justin

Timberlake (whom the boys' female classmates found attractive) because his masculine embodiment did not reinforce their imagined future urban, ethnoracial masculinities.

In the boys' neighborhoods, fights among youths were a regular occurrence, in part because the local hypermasculinity on display encouraged physical confrontations. During the study, a handful of the boys were "jumped" (i.e., assailed) on the streets by other youths, mugged by other youths, or both. One afternoon, nearly two weeks after one of the boys was jumped and mugged, a police detective spoke with the class and tried to persuade the students to resolve their neighborhood disputes by turning to law enforcement rather than to friends and relatives. The boys were unconvinced by the detective's presentation and explained that talking to the police would make them "snitches," and that in their neighborhoods youths socially ostracized and assaulted those labeled "snitches." In addition, in line with the local "code of the streets," the boys considered fighting as both characteristic of localized masculinity and a strategic approach by which to address interpersonal conflicts. On the streets, those who did not defend themselves or seek retribution were ridiculed and called "punks," "pussies," "bitches," and/or "fags."

As part of their masculine performativity, the boys adopted tough personas and expressed their willingness to fight. Many of the boys' teachers, most of whom were supportive Latinas or bilingual white women, worried that boys' attraction to tough masculine personas would lead some of them to get involved with the local gang members or with the older middle school boys they suspected had started at least one gang while the boys were in the sixth grade. The boys, however, expressed little interest in joining the local gangs, and, in fact, made sure to avoid wearing the baseball caps associated with local gangs in order to avoid being mistaken for a gang member and assailed as a result. . . .

Findings

Representative data in the following sections illustrate how Latino boys at Romero performed masculinity within their peer group while undergoing pubescence. The first section documents how the boys referenced their bodies and puberty during playful interactions. The second section documents the boys' longing for muscular male physiques like those in their multiple social worlds. The third section examines how the boys displayed physical strength and punished their bodies to prove their manliness. The last and final section briefly discusses how the boys enacted masculinity and were perceived by others after the sixth grade.

"Puberty Is Now": Changing Bodies

While in the sixth grade, the boys were experiencing their sexual maturation—a fact they declared publicly. During a science class discussion on physical development, for example, a boy loudly interjected, "Puberty is now." In addition, the boys' exchanges regularly included references to puberty and the biological changes that come with it. When a boy appeared exceedingly "wild" (i.e., hyperactive), the other boys attributed it to hormonal changes brought on by puberty and, using language introduced by one of them, jokingly rebuked him with statements such as, "Control your hormones!" and "Let your hormones relax, c'mon. Your hormones are gonna get tired." Such commentary highlights the importance of control over one's body, an ability associated with maturity, masculinity, and adolescence, and not boyhood.

Like other boys (Dixon 1997; Martino and Pallotta-Chiarolli 2003), the boys at Romero viewed penises as appendages that distinguish boys from girls and are associated with males' manhood and dominance. They frequently brought up male genitalia to playfully disparage one another's masculine identities. One afternoon, banter about a banana resulted in the charge that Rudy, the shortest boy, had an undersized penis:

> During lunchtime, Michael holds out a peeled banana, wiggles it, and says, "Look, it's crooked." A two-inch long piece of banana breaks off and lands on the table. Michael says, "Look, Steven— he lost his manhood. It fell off."
>
> Steven smiles and says, "That's Rudy's." Cesar chimes in, "Yeah, it's like this"—Cesar holds out his pinkie and smiles.

Here, Steven and Cesar used Rudy to demarcate the low masculine status attributed to smaller male bodies. As the only boy frequently referred to as "shrimp," "small fry," or "enano [midget]," Rudy was not perceived as physically dominant, which led to the accusation that he has a small penis. The data highlight the interplay between the body and the construction of gendered identities (Butler 1993; Connell 2005).

The boys also referenced puberty to emphasize the relative nature of masculine status within their peer group's gender order. An exchange about male genitalia, for example, led Brandon to ask Steven whether he had experienced his first menstruation:

> [In class] Michael makes fun of Steven by referencing an episode of *South Park* in which a boy has a penis and scrotum growing on his chin. Michael says: "Steven got a little dicky and scrotum on his chin. And it is growing every day."
>
> Brandon joins in: "Steven, did you get your period yet?"

Brandon's depiction of Steven as a girl who is yet to experience menstruation called both Steven's gender and pubescent development into question. Here menarche, as a signifier of femininity, undermines the possibility of masculinity.

In all, I counted 43 references to secondary sex characteristics, of which nearly two dozen were during public acts of verbal one-upmanship. Participating in banter and verbal one-upmanship was a cultural, gendered expectation the boys willingly met at Romero as well as with male cousins and friends they visited in the Dominican Republic or Puerto Rico. Like other working-class Dominican (De Moya 2004) and Puerto Rican youth (Ramírez 1999), the boys constructed their masculine identities and dominance with their verbal exchanges. Contrary to the retrospective accounts of high school students (Martin 1996), the boys at Romero experienced puberty within their homosocial group, rather than alone.

The boys mentioned penises much more during the sixth grade than at any comparable period thereafter, and stopped publicly referencing puberty after the sixth grade. The stark difference from one academic year to the next likely reflects how much more willing the boys were to discuss the initial phases of their pubescence at a time when they wanted their bodies to communicate their physical development, which is not to say that they did not consider subsequent pubescent changes significant.

Bodies in Transition

The boys compared the size of their flexed biceps and the firmness of their abdomens on almost a daily basis, and by doing so assessed their bodies. With comments like, "I'm stronger," they frequently vied to carry boxes and crates for teachers. Through these verbal interactions, the boys enacted a social hierarchy based on the gender status attributed to muscular development, which was proof of a boy's physical transition beyond boyhood and of his willingness to control and transform his physique.

The boys openly shared their desire to possess the "sociocultural ideal male physique"—strong, lean, muscular, and fit (McCabe and Ricciardelli 2004). A telling example of how much they yearned for muscular bodies worthy of admiration is a portrait one of them drew of himself and his four closest friends in the class. The drawing, which according to the illustrator depicted his friends and him "in five or six years," was of five stoic young men, each wearing a tank top and baggy pants, with extremely muscular arms and chests, relatively small waists, and a weapon—either a knife, a gun, or a crowbar—in his hand. The figures are exaggerated versions of the males whose physiological aesthetic and style the boys were interested in replicating—namely, the muscular rappers they favored, the older youth at Romero, and the Black and Latino young men in the boys' neighborhoods, most of whom valued strong bodies and who, per the local "code of the street," were willing to use their bodies as weapons in a fight. Both broad and localized cultural expectations associated with masculinity and male bodies informed the boys' imaginings of future male selves during puberty.

For the boys, gladiators and other warrior types, including professional wrestlers and video game characters, also served as evidence that superior male physiques were an accomplishment, the result of physical training. Consider Michael's reference to gladiators in a fantasy replete with his aspiration to have a sculpted body and to use it in a notable manner:

> As students worked independently on an assignment on ancient Rome, Michael says to me, "Richard, I'm going to build a time machine and go back [to ancient Rome]. I'm going to work out so when I go I'm strong. I'm going to get a scar." He moves a finger along his right cheek. "I'm going to fight like the gladiators."

For both cultural and practical reasons, Michael and the rest of the boys valued tough, strong bodies skilled at fighting. Culturally, among Dominican and Puerto Rican youth at and around Romero, like among many of their peers in the Caribbean (De Moya 2004; Ramírez 1999), there was the expectation that men defend themselves. Practically, Michael and the boys were cognizant that in their neighborhoods physical fights between adolescent boys were a reality. Additionally, like marginalized, urban, African American boys (Dance 2002) and youth (Majors and Billson 1993), the Latino boys at Romero were willing to use their bodies as weapons in order to protect their physical well-being or masculine status.

Since the boys prized muscular definition, they were quite preoccupied with the amount of fat (or "flubber") on their bodies. Like other boys (James 2000), they too held fatness in low regard, equating it with a lack of bodily control. A telling incident is what transpired after the nurse had summoned the entire class for a yearly basic health examination. Rudy returned, came over to me and said, "Richard, I was nervous." I asked Rudy why he was nervous and he replied, "I don't know. My flubber. My Jell-O rolls." Then, both Pedro and Rodrigo came into the room smiling and in a celebratory tone simultaneously yelled, "I don't have no flubber!"

Aware that others scrutinized their bodies, many of the boys with flubber masked their concerns with self-deprecating humor. Michael, for example, occasionally lifted his shirt, exposing his stomach, and asked peers, "Do you think I'm fat?" Additionally, the handful of boys who had flubber

sought to communicate that they nonetheless possessed physical strength. For example, while discussing his physical appearance with a thinner, taller female classmate, a boy stated, "I don't care if I don't have a six-pack [defined abdominal muscles]. I got muscles. That's why you couldn't take the ball away from me [during a basketball game]." Similarly, consider what James says during a tense dispute with Michael over which of them could claim to possess the more "successful body" (Drummond 2003):

> Michael says James is fatter than he is. James frowns and says, "I work out with my [adult] brother. I bet you don't even work out. I am better than you in every sport, except baseball. I don't play baseball."

By highlighting his superior athleticism, James dismissed Michael's comment and communicated that his body, though fatter, was superior. As the data excerpts make clear, the boys constructed their bodies and gendered identities in relation to each other and to the gendered bodies of their female peers.

Some bodies are valued differently depending in part on the social context (Butler 1993; Connell 2005). In the boys' social world, a muscular male body was a physical representation of manliness and evidence of the physiological shift from boyhood and childhood toward male adulthood and manliness. Among their peers and the Black, Dominican, and Puerto Rican youths in their neighborhoods, muscular physiques signaled bodily control, an important trait in an urban, low-income context where the use of male bodies as weapons was common. As the next section shows, boys participated in physical activities to signal that, though their sexual maturation was not readily apparent, they were in fact transitioning beyond childhood and possessed a corporeal attribute associated with the adult men and older youth in their lives—physical strength.

Physical Strength, Toughness, and Masculine Status

At Romero, there were no school-sanctioned sports teams. Thus, unlike the boys in other studies (Eder, Evans, and Parker 1995; Martin 1996; Stein and Reiser 1994; Swain 2000, 2003), the boys at Romero lacked the opportunity to acquire masculine status by displaying their physical toughness and might on the field or court. That may explain why the boys opted to bring their masculinity "into action" through a wide array of physical activities, particularly arm wrestling matches, bloody knuckles, and slap hands, all of which the school banned to curtail verbal and physical confrontations (Swain 2003, 311). With these localized and ritualized physical enactments, the boys sought to initiate themselves into manhood, and thus punished their bodies while defining, exploring, and patrolling the boundaries of their collective masculine practices. They did this mostly in the lunch area, where it was easier to evade teachers' surveillance.

The boys eagerly engaged in various tests of strength replete with masculine performativity. For example, when Alberto refused to lend Jorge a colored pencil, their interaction turned into a physical challenge, after which Albert declared himself a man, in effect questioning Jorge's manhood:

> Albert presses his hand down on a few colored pencils on a desk. Jorge attempts briefly to get the pencils from under Albert's hand. Jorge gives up and sharpens a blue colored pencil. Albert smiles, raises his hands into the air, and yells, *"I'm a man!"*

The boys made such public declarations of manliness whenever they successfully used their bodies to best others. On average, there were six brash comments, like "I'm a man" or "I'm *the* man," per day of observation.

The boys' loud proclamations drew the attention of teachers, one of whom assured me that the boys "don't think of themselves as boys, they think of themselves as men." However, in time, I learned that when they referred to themselves as men they were simply voicing their masculine aspirations. In one another's presence, the boys readily admitted to being preadolescent boys or, as they put it, "pre-teenagers." Thus, it seems that with their declarations, the boys were attempting to make sense of their ongoing and impending physical development while also attempting to

construct tough masculine identities worthy of praise in their social worlds.

The most notable manner by which the boys publicly asserted their masculine identities was through arm wrestling matches. On average, I observed approximately a dozen arm wrestling matches per site visit. The boys used the outcomes of these challenges to rank themselves and to compare their relative physiological development. Note the following lunchtime arm wrestling session:

> Pedro, Ignacio, Bernardo, Adam, and Jason take turns arm wrestling one another.
>
> Jason beats Ignacio, looks over at me, and says nonchalantly, "Kids."
>
> Pedro points at Armando and says, "He's number one in arm wrestling." Jason nods and says, "Yeah, I don't know how he does it. I'm, like, number three." Pedro then says, "I'm, like, number four."

Jason's comment after defeating Ignacio— "Kids"—seems a playful way of associating his physically weaker peers to childlike boyhood and, by contrast, himself to adolescence, manliness, and those seventh- and eighth-grade boys that he and his classmates admired. What is more, despite being among the smallest boys in the group, Armando was the best arm wrestler in the class. As a result, he received kudos for his feat and boys from the other sixth-grade class, as well as his classmates, regularly challenged him. For the boys, arm wrestling matches were opportunities to acquire "physical capital" within their social world regardless of their physical size (Swain 2000, 2003).

The boys also sought out opportunities to arm wrestle older boys with bigger, more developed physiques. Most of the seventh- and eighth-grade boys accepted challenges only after the younger boys playfully took on a tough persona and accused them of being "scared." The older boys won every one of these matches handily. However, interactions with older, male schoolmates provided the boys opportunities to try on the stoic "cara de palo" that was central to the presentation of self embodied by many rappers and urban youth, including Dominican and Puerto Ricans that resided around Romero (Thomas 1987). Additionally, by arm wrestling seventh- and eighth-graders, the sixth-grade boys displayed their bravado to older boys who put forth the confident, tough, masculine personas the sixth-grade boys attempted to emulate both at Romero and outside of school, where being assaulted by adolescent youths was a real possibility.

Like the older boys, the sixth-grade girls also greatly influenced how the boys viewed their physicality and masculinity. Over the course of the second semester, the boys were challenged approximately two dozen times by both the girls in their class peer group and those in the other sixth-grade class. The boys rebuffed these challenges because many of their female peers were physically stronger, a fact the boys acknowledged only among themselves. For the boys to arm wrestle girls and lose would have been humiliating since they publicly claimed that males are physically stronger than females.

Their homosocial peer group offered the boys not just a refuge, but also "a performative space where heterosexuality and masculinity can be fused and displayed" (Kehily 2001, 179). The banter that punctuated arm wrestling matches was a performativity that reified their heteronormative masculine narrative. Along with grunts and laughter, all the boys regularly lobbed joking accusations of homosexuality and unmanliness at one another, for a tally of over 50 individual instances. Here is a case in point:

> Ignacio asks Albert, "You're the son of a fag?"
> Albert smiles and screams, "Do it [arm wrestle] for all your pubic hairs!"

With a homophobic slur commonly used in the boys' social worlds to stress the heteronormativity underpinning gender practices, Ignacio implied that Albert's poor performance was evidence of his father's homosexuality. Like his peers, Ignacio coupled heterosexual masculinity and physical strength—a perspective in line with the hegemonic masculinities in the boys' neighborhoods, in their respective countries of origin (De Moya 2004; Ramírez 1999), and in the United States (Connell 2000, 2005; Kimmel and Messner 1998). Albert, for his part, then associated boys' corporeal might with pubic hairs, a key signifier of puberty.

To highlight corporeal might and other masculine traits exalted in their homosocial peer group, the boys belittled any boy that did not adequately display the traits by calling him "a girl" or "a woman"—a finding echoed in Thorne (1993) and Fine (1987). Boys levied accusations like those in the following exchange over four dozen times:

> Santiago and James arm wrestle. James loses. Santiago screams to James, "You're a woman!" Santiago and James laugh. Brandon says to James, "Until you don't [sic] beat him you're a woman."

Both Santiago and Brandon insinuated that James had to display the physical might of a man during arm wrestling matches, rather than the presumed physical weakness of a woman. The boys reduced gender to a male–female binary and considered masculinity the opposite of femininity, much like the many neighborhood youths who also espoused male dominance and the patriarchal tenets of Dominican and Puerto Rican hegemonic masculinities.

Perhaps because they craved external validation, the boys were quick to praise one another for exhibiting grit during physical activities. Such public praise was sometimes a form of gender policing that reinforced the notion that manhood required the withstanding of pain in "sporting situations" (Vaccaro 2011, 71). Here is a representative instance:

> Ignacio asks me to hold out my right hand. I do. He slaps my hand hard three times with his right hand. I pull my hand away. Ignacio smiles, looks over at James and says, "C'mon, James, *you're* a man." James holds out his right hand, and Ignacio slaps it hard twice. They smile. Then, Ignacio asks Jesse to hold his hand out. Jesse does so. Ignacio slaps Jesse's hand twice and announces, "Jesse, *you're* a man." Jesse and Ignacio smile again.

Note how Ignacio declared that James and Jesse were men because, unlike me, an adult male, they displayed toughness. With his declaration, Ignacio also acknowledged his own masculinity as he too withstood pain after delivering each slap. These findings support previous research (Eder, Evans, and Parker 1995; Fine 1987) by showing that, like boys competing in sporting events, the boys at Romero valued physical toughness and sought out opportunities to demonstrate it.

Aware that their masculine status was dependent on how they utilized their bodies, the boys regularly tried to convince each other to engage in public physical challenges. For example, one afternoon, Raul held out his right clenched fist and invited another boy to play bloody knuckles with him: "C'mon, punch my knuckles. It's like a massage. It doesn't hurt me. It's like a massage. C'mon, give me a massage." When rebuffed, boys usually tried to goad their prospective competitors with statements such as "Don't be a sissy" and "Don't be a girl." More often than not, boys who declined a challenge were also met with ridicule from other peers. All this pressure and gender policing rarely failed.

As the data in this subsection have shown, the boys at Romero utilized their bodies in public displays of physical strength and toughness—attributes that they and those in their social worlds associated with manliness and relied on during physical confrontations—to gain masculine status. Participating in challenges and verbal one-upmanship is characteristic of the dominant masculinities in the Dominican Republic (De Moya 2004), Puerto Rico (Ramírez 1999), and the United States (Kimmel 2008). Consequently, via references to and enactments of their bodies, puberty became a social accomplishment connected to masculine identities influenced by multiple cultural interpretations of gender.

Little Boys, No More

Though the boys and girls were the same age, the girls were generally taller and appeared older than their actual age. As a result, the girls interpreted their own bodies as closer to adulthood and maturity than the boys' bodies. Consider what a girl asserted during a discussion in health class:

> Angelica: "The girls are growing up. They are thinking ahead. They are getting mature and the boys are not." A number of boys yell out in protest, "What?!"

The girls' reaction bothered the boys because it differed from the flirtatious interactions the girls had with many seventh-grade boys, whom the girls described as "tall" and "fine" (i.e., attractive). Throughout the observations, the girls made 26 statements in which they referred to the boys as "little boys" because of what they deemed their "childish" behavior, such as punching lockers, arm wrestling during class, and play fighting. Similarly, eighth-grade girls regularly called some of the boys "cute" and ruffled their hair, which the boys found condescending. In doing so, the girls at Romero voiced physical expectations for adolescent manliness and influenced the boys' construction of masculine identities. The data are in accordance with previous findings that girls look upon boys whose bodies demonstrate no visible signs of development as children (Dixon 1997).

Teachers also influenced the boys' perceptions of their own physical development. Their teachers mostly infantilized them with regular, public chastisements for acting "like babies" when they "whined" about one another's behavior. Less often, teachers pointed out how particular boys were physically "changing." The boys readily engaged in such assessments:

> A female teacher supervising the lunch area walks over to Pedro and Ruben, points to Ruben's face, and says, "You're starting to look sharp. Like a man."
>
> Ruben replies, "I *am* a man." The teacher smiles and says, "No, you're not. *He's* [points to researcher] a man. Do you have 36 teeth [i.e., wisdom teeth]?"
>
> Pedro interjects, "I do." He opens his mouth and counts his teeth with his right index finger: "Owan . . . tuoo . . . threa . . ." The teacher looks at Pedro and says, "No, you don't."

The boys wanted recognition for their physical development, and did not want to hear how much they physically resembled younger boys. Consequently, partly to avoid derision, the boys maintained their homosocial peer group during the sixth grade, but their female peers and teachers nonetheless influenced their masculine identities.

After the summer between the sixth and seventh grade, the boys returned to school physically transformed. All of them were taller, and most of them had shed much of the "flubber" that had occupied their minds just months earlier. Most of the boys were now taller than their female classmates. At the beginning of the seventh grade, their teachers and female peers complimented them on their physiological development, which may explain why many of them walked with more of a swagger and projected greater confidence than they had three months prior. Furthermore, from the seventh grade on, the boys rarely engaged in the physical games and challenges of "little boys." That is, they hardly made a public show of their physical strength or their ability to endure physical pain.

Instead, they turned much of their attention to public displays of acceptable heteronormative masculinity, namely flirting with and trying to woo teenage girls. The boys and girls spent a lot of time and energy flirting with one another during the seventh and eighth grade. The boys' hegemonic masculinity dictated that they had to learn to flirt in order to woo teenage girls and women. The most common form of flirting involved *piropos,* or "'amorous compliments,' often undesired by the females at whom they are directed" (Bailey 2000, 562). I documented 51 *piropos.* Among the various *piropos* used by the boys were statements used in Spanish songs as well as by older peers and relatives on the streets of their neighborhoods and of their countries of origin. For example, some of the boys regularly said something like, "*¡Oh, mami! Tu sí 'tas buena.* (Oh, baby! You *are* fine)". The boys delivered most of their *piropos* in the presence of male peers, who acknowledged particularly clever compliments.

Into the flirtatious exchanges, the boys and girls often incorporated sexual innuendos that called attention to their own developed bodies and to those of the individuals they desired. These sorts of interactions allowed the boys and girls to express their physical attraction to one another and to explore the personal and physical boundaries of potential boyfriends and girlfriends. Here is a representative observation that captures the playful manner in which the boys and girls held conversations with sexual undertones:

In class, Samuel is wearing his sweats well below his crotch. Valerie says to Samuel, "Pull 'em up."

Samuel replies, "Why don't *you* pull 'em up?" Samuel smiles, and Valerie grins. Later on, Samuel says to Valerie, "When my hair grows long you can braid it. And, the hair down here too." Samuel smiles, looking down at his crotch. Valerie smiles and says, "I'll pull it."

During these suggestive exchanges, boys displayed their compliance with compulsory heterosexuality and augmented their masculine status in the eyes of both their male and female peers by effectively flirting. Since wooing teenage girls could enhance a boy's masculine status, many of the boys claimed to have also flirted with and successfully wooed girls during their visits to Puerto Rico and/or the Dominican Republic—a claim that could not be ascertained, nor dismissed.

These findings suggest that once their physical development was apparent to others, the boys no longer felt such a pressing need to do masculinity by engaging in excessively competitive physical activities, and instead focused on enacting the heteronormative masculinity expected of males by peers at school and in their neighborhoods, as well as at home. By turning their energies toward wooing girls, the Dominican boys in the group behaved much like some of their peers in the Dominican Republic, who were expected to "show a vivid and visible erotic interest in all females that come close" by the age of 12 or 13, after the onset of puberty (De Moya 2004, 74).

Conclusion

By showing how Dominican and Puerto Rican boys collectively construct masculinity during pubescence, this article provides important insights into how diverse boys viewed their bodies and how multiple cultures inform the intersection of masculinity, ethnicity, and gender. The boys wanted height and physical musculature so that others, particularly their female peers and teachers, would no longer read them as "little boys." They yearned for muscular bodies that approximated the "socio-cultural ideal male physique" highly valued by many males, including the young Dominican and Puerto Rican men in their urban neighborhoods, and their favorite rappers and wrestlers (McCabe and Ricciardelli 2004). Thus, with their declarations, banter, and physical activities, each of the boys sought to communicate that he was on his way beyond childhood and was preparing his body for a social world wherein physical confrontations between males were commonplace. Ironically, female classmates, many of whom were taller and physically stronger, associated the boys' enactments of masculinity not with manliness but rather with childishness. Still, the boys enacted gender hierarchies based on, and espoused the male dominance of, their models of masculinity—rappers and older boys at Romero, and in their neighborhoods. They professed that male bodies were naturally strong, and considered their female classmates' greater physical strength and height a temporary fact. Together, the cultural influences to which the boys were exposed reiterated the appropriateness of both hegemonic masculinities and of those masculine practices that provided status and some level of protection in their social worlds.

The data also inform research examining masculinity and the body (Butler 1993; Connell 2000, 2005; Swain 2000, 2003), heteronormativity at schools (Dalley-Trim 2007; Eliasson, Isaksson, and Laflamme 2007; Mac an Ghaill 1994; Martino 1999, 2000; Martino and Pallotta-Chiarolli 2003; McGuffey and Rich 1999; Pascoe 2007; Renold 2003), and the intersection of racial identity and masculinity (Ferguson 2001; Lopez 2003). Much like boys observed in other studies (Kehily 2001; Mac an Ghaill 1994; Martino and Pallotta-Chiarolli 2003; Renold 2005; Swain 2000, 2003), the Dominican and Puerto Rican boys at Romero tried to embody the heteronormative masculinity present in their social worlds and to claim male supremacy and belonging. Contrary to the retrospectives of high school students (Martin 1996), the boys at Romero did not experience puberty on their own but rather within their homosocial group. Overall, the findings discussed earlier suggest that pubescence is a social process as much as a biological transformation, a social process that is interactional, collective, embodied, and situated in classed, gendered, and ethnoracialized contexts. In addition, the data contribute to the study of gender and masculinities

by explicating how the boys, as U.S.-born Dominicans and Puerto Ricans residing in low-income neighborhoods, constructed their masculine identities while seeking to abide by the dominant gender expectations in localized social worlds and the norms from their countries of origin. . . .

References

Abbassi, V. 1998. Growth and normal puberty. *Pediatrics* 102:507–11.

Anderson, E. 2000. *Code of the streets: Decency, violence and the moral life of the inner city.* New York: Norton.

Arciniega, G. M., T. C. Anderson, Z. G. Tovar-Blank, and T. J. G. Tracey. 2008. Toward a fuller conception of machismo: Development of a traditional machismo and caballerismo scale. *Journal of Counseling Psychology* 55:19–33.

Basch, N., N. Glick-Schiller, and C. S. Blanc. 1994. *Nations unbound: Transnational projects, postcolonial predicaments, and deterritorialized nation-states.* Amsterdam: Gordon and Breach.

Butler, J. 1993. *Bodies that matter: On the discursive limits of "sex."* New York: Routledge.

Casas, J. M., B. R. Wagenheim, R. Banchero, and J. Mendoza-Romero. 1994. Hispanic masculinity: Myth or psychological schema meriting clinical considerations. *Hispanic Journal of Behavioral Sciences* 16:315–31.

Chambers, D., E. Tincknell, and J. V. Loon. 2004. Peer regulation of teenage sexual identities. *Gender and Education* 16:297–315.

Connell, R. W. 2000. *The men and the boys.* Berkeley: University of California Press.

Connell, R. W. 2005. *Masculinities.* 2nd ed. Berkeley: University of California Press.

Dalley-Trim, L. 2007. "The boys" present . . . Hegemonic masculinity: A performance of multiple acts. *Gender and Education* 19:199–217.

Dance, L. J. 2002. *Tough fronts.* New York: RoutledgeFalmer.

Davison, K. G. 2000. Boys' bodies in school: Physical education. *Journal of Men's Studies* 8:255–66.

De La Cancela, V. 1991. Working affirmatively with Puerto Rican men: Professional and personal reflections. In *Feminist approaches for men in family therapy,* edited by M. Bograd. Binghamton, NY: Harrington Park Press.

De La Cancela, V. 1993. "Coolin": The psychosocial communication of African and Latino men. *Urban League Review* 16:33–44.

De Moya, A. 2004. Power games and totalitarian masculinity in the Dominican Republic. In *Interrogating Caribbean masculinities: Theoretical and empirical analyses,* edited by R. E. Reddock. Kingston: University of West Indies Press.

Dixon, C. 1997. Pete's tool: Identity and sex-play in the design and technology classroom. *Gender and Education* 9:89–104.

Doyle, J. A. 1995. *The male experience.* 3rd ed. Madison, WI: Brown & Benchmark.

Drummond, M. J. N. 2003. The meaning of boys' bodies in physical education. *Journal of Men's Studies* 11:131–43.

Eccles, J. S. 1999. The development of children ages 6 to 14. *Future of Children* 9:30–44.

Eder, D., C. C. Evans, and S. Parker. 1995. *School talk: Gender and adolescent culture.* New Brunswick: Rutgers University Press.

Eliasson, M. A., K. Isaksson, and L. Laflamme. 2007. Verbal abuse in school: Constructions of gender among 14- to 15-year-olds. *Gender and Education* 19:587–605.

Epstein, D. 2001. Boyz' own stories: Masculinities and sexualities in schools. In *What about the boys?: Issues of masculinity in schools,* edited by W. Martino and B. Meyenn. Philadelphia: Open University Press.

Epstein, D., and R. Johnson. 1998. *Schooling sexualities.* Buckingham, UK: Open University Press.

Epstein, D., S. O'Flynn, and D. Telford. 2000. "Othering" education: Sexualities, silences, and schooling. *Review of Research in Education* 25:127–79.

Falicov, C. J. 2010. Changing constructions of machismo for Latino men in therapy: "The devil never sleeps." *Family Process* 49:309–29.

Ferguson, A. A. 2001. *Bad boys: Public schools in the making of black masculinity.* Ann Arbor: University of Michigan Press.

Fine, G. A. 1987. *With the boys: Little league baseball and preadolescent culture.* Chicago: University of Chicago Press.

Frankel, L. 2003. Puberty. In *Men and masculinities: A social, cultural, and historical encyclopedia,* edited by M. Kimmel and A. Aronson. Vol. II: K–Z. Santa Barbara: ABC-CLIO.

Gardiner, J. K. 2000. Masculinity, the teening of America, and empathic targeting. *Signs* 25:1257–61.

Gilbert, R., and P. Gilbert. 1998. *Masculinity goes to school.* New York: Routledge.

Grogan, S., and H. Richards. 2002. Body image: Focus groups with boys and men. *Men and Masculinities* 4:219–32.

Gutmann, M. C. 1996. *The meanings of macho: Being a man in Mexico City.* Berkeley: University of California Press.

Hasbrook, C. A., and O. Harris. 1999. Wrestling with gender: Physicality and masculinities among inner-city first and second graders. *Men and Masculinities* 1:302–18.

Haywood, C., and M. Mac an Ghaill. 2001. The significance of teaching English boys: Exploring social change, modern schooling and the making of masculinities. In *What about the boys?: Issues of masculinity in schools,* edited by W. Martino and B. Meyenn. Philadelphia: Open University Press.

James, A. 2000. Embodied being(s): Understanding the self and the body in childhood. In *The body, childhood, and society,* edited by A. Prout. Houndmills: Macmillan.

Janssen, D. F. 2006. "Become big, and I'll give you something to eat": Thoughts and notes on boyhood sexual health. *International Journal of Men's Health* 5:19–35.

Katz, M., and M. Misra. 2011. Delayed puberty, short stature, and tall stature. In *The Mass General Hospital for Children adolescent medicine handbook,* edited by Mark A. Goldstein. New York: Springer.

Kehily, M. 2001. Bodies in school: Young men, embodiment, and heterosexual masculinities. *Men and Masculinities* 4:173–85.

Kimmel, M. 2008. *Guyland: The perilous world where boys become men.* New York: Harper Collins.

Kimmel, M., and M. Messner, eds. 1998. *Men's lives.* 4th ed. Boston: Allyn & Bacon.

Korobov, N. 2005. Ironizing masculinity: How adolescent boys negotiate heteronormative dilemmas in conversational interaction. *Journal of Men's Studies* 13:225–46.

Lilleaas, U. 2007. Masculinities, sport, and emotions. *Men and Masculinities* 10:39–53.

Mac an Ghaill, M. 1994. *The making of men: Masculinities, sexualities and schooling.* Buckingham: Open University Press.

Majors, R., and J. M. Billson. 1993. *Cool pose: The dilemmas of black manhood in America.* New York: Touchstone.

Martin, K. A. 1996. *Puberty, sexuality, and the self: Boys and girls at adolescence.* New York: Routledge.

Martino, W. 1999. "Cool boys," "party animals," "squids," and "poofters": Interrogating the dynamics and politics of adolescent masculinities in school. *British Journal of the Sociology of Education* 20:239–63.

Martino, W. 2000. Policing masculinities: Investigating the role of homophobia and heteronormativity in the lives of adolescent schoolboys. *Journal of Men's Studies* 8:213–36.

Martino, W., and M. Pallotta-Chiarolli. 2003. *So what's a boy?: Addressing issues of masculinity and schooling.* Berkshire, UK: Open University Press.

McCabe, M. P., and L. A. Ricciardelli. 2004. A longitudinal study of pubertal timing and extreme body change behaviors among adolescent boys and girls. *Adolescence* 39:145–66.

McGuffey, C. S., and B. L. Rich. 1999. Playing in the gender transgression zone. *Gender & Society* 13:608–27.

Mirandé, A. 1997. *Hombres y machos: Masculinity and Latino culture.* Boulder, CO: Westview Press.

Mosher, D. L. 1991. Macho men, machismo, and sexuality. *Annual Review of Sex Research* 2:199–247.

Nayak, A., and M. J. Kehily. 2001. "Learning to laugh": A study of schoolboy humour in the English secondary school. In *What about the boys?: Issues of masculinity in schools,* edited by W. Martino and B. Meyenn. Philadelphia: Open University Press.

Nilan, P. 2000. "You're hopeless, I swear to God": Shifting masculinities in classroom talk. *Gender and Education* 12:53–68.

Pascoe, C. J. 2007. *Dude, you're a fag: Masculinity and sexuality in high school.* Berkeley: University of California Press.

Pope, H. G., K. A. Phillips, and R. Olivardia. 2000. *The Adonis complex: The secret crisis of male body obsession.* New York: Free Press.

Prendergast, S., and S. Forrest. 1997. Gendered groups and the negotiation of heterosexuality in school. In *New sexual agendas,* edited by L. Segal. London: Macmillian.

Prendergast, S., and S. Forrest. 1998. Shorties, low-lifers, hard nuts and kings: Boys and the transformation of emotions. In *Emotions in social life: Social theories and contemporary issues,* edited by G. Bendelow and S. Williams. London: Routledge.

Ramírez, Rafael L. 1999. *What it means to be a man: Reflections on Puerto Rican masculinity,* translated by Rosa E. Casper. New Brunswick, NJ: Rutgers University Press.

Redman, P., D. Epstein, M. J. Kehily, and M. Mac an Ghaill. 2002. Boys bonding: Same-sex friendship, the unconscious and heterosexual discourse. *Discourse* 23:179–91.

Renold, E. 2001. Learning the "hard" way: Boys, hegemonic masculinity and the negotiation of learner identities in the primary school. *British Journal of Sociology of Education* 22:369–85.

Renold, E. 2003. "If you don't kiss me, you're dumped": Boys, boyfriends and heterosexualised masculinities in the primary school. *Educational Review* 55:179–94.

Renold, E. 2005. *Girls, boys and junior sexualities: Exploring children's gender and sexual relations in the primary school.* London: Routledge Falmer.

Saez, P. A., A. Casado, and J. C. Wade. 2009. Factors influencing masculinity ideology among Latino men. *Journal of Men's Studies* 17:116–28.

Schilling, C. 1993. *The body and social theory.* London: Sage.

Schrock, D., and M. Schwalbe. 2009. Men, masculinity, and manhood acts. *Annual Review of Sociology* 35:277–95.

Stein, J. H., and L. W. Reiser. 1994. A study of white middle-class adolescent boys' responses to "semerache." *Journal of Youth and Adolescence* 23:373–84.

Swain, J. 2000. "The money's good, the fame's good, the girls are good": The role of playground football in the construction of young boys' masculinity in a junior school. *British Journal of Sociology of Education* 21:95–109.

Swain, J. 2003. How young schoolboys become somebody: The role of the body in the construction of masculinity. *British Journal of Sociology of Education* 24:299–314.

Thomas. P. 1987. *Down these mean streets.* New York: Alfred A. Knopf.

Thorne, B. 1993. *Gender play: Girls and boys in school.* New Brunswick: Rutgers University Press.

Torres, J. B. 1998. Masculinity and gender roles among Puerto Rican men: Machismo on the U.S. mainland. *American Journal of Orthopsychiatry* 68:16–26.

Torres, J. B., V. S. H. Solberg, and A. H. Carlstrom. 2002. The myth of sameness among Latino men and their machismo. *American Journal of Orthopsychiatry* 72:163–81.

U.S. Bureau of the Census. 2000. *Current Population Reports.* Washington. DC: U.S. Government Printing Office.

Vaccaro, C. A. 2011. Male bodies in manhood acts: The role of body-talk and embodied practice in signifying culturally dominant notions of manhood. *Sociology Compass* 5:65–76.

Walker, J. C. 1988. *Louts and legends: Male youth culture in an inner city school.* Sydney: Allen & Unwin.

West, C., and D. H. Zimmerman. 1987. Doing gender. *Gender & Society* 1:125–51.

Witt, S. D. 2000. The influence of peers on children's socialization to gender roles. *Early Child Development and Care* 162:1–7.

The Gender of Desire: The Sexual Fantasies of Women and Men

MICHAEL S. KIMMEL AND REBECCA F. PLANTE

My sex fantasy is pretty straightforward: having sex with a porno star. All out, no holds barred, continuous sex with someone who obviously knows what she's doing. It doesn't really have to be in any specific place, and scenery isn't too important. Sorry to all of you who are into the scenery thing. [man]

It's having sex on the beach. Very romantic setting, very sweet, caring experience. The "sociological" part would be, I guess, that it includes being "the woman" i.e., being carried, not being the "aggressor," rather, being passive. [woman]

I've always had the fantasy of having sex with three or more beautiful blonde babes. It would take place on a huge waterbed in a big white room overlooking the ocean. Lesbian activity would be fine. I would try to please them at the same time (up to four) two hands, mouth, and groin and they would try to please me. One on top with the others massaging and kissing my body. Two women pleasing each other orally would be a nice enhancement. Oh yes, beforehand we would cover each other in Huskers "corn" oil and no condoms would be used. [man]

Not have a favorite fantasy "scene," more just an overwhelming feeling of tenderness and complete emotional unity between myself and my partner/husband. Loving actions that lead to sex (never really fantasize about the act), i.e., kissing (hand, arm, body), massage, being on an island (Caribbean) with no distractions. Or perhaps spontaneity in location; not in the bedroom on the bed. [woman]

These are actual sexual fantasies from a sample of nearly 350 sexual fantasies collected from undergraduates at several universities during the past decade. Gender differences are visible in every

Michael S. Kimmel and Rebecca F. Plante, "The Gender of Desire: The Sexual Fantasies of Women and Men," *Advances in Gender Research: Gendered Sexualities*, Vol. 6 (2002), pp. 55–57. Copyright © 2002, with permission from Emerald Group Publishing Limited.

aspect of these sexual fantasies—from language to sexual activities, in both content and form. Sexual fantasies can be viewed as illustrations of socially constructed gender differences and of the landscape of intrapsychic sexuality. In fantasies, we may see more about gendered conceptualizations of sexuality than if we look at actual sexual conduct, which often involves culturally expected gendered compromises.

The most basic element in the social construction of sexualities is gender. In both sexual fantasies and sexual conduct, men and women imagine and enact different sexual scripts, the culturally articulated blueprints we use to shape "appropriate" sexual conduct (Gagnon & Simon, 1973). Sexual scripts also help to confirm gender identities, consequently expressed in both fantasies and conduct.

Contrary to earlier studies of sexuality, researchers now understand fantasy to be a "normal" component of sexual experience (Kaplan, 1974; Masters & Johnson, 1966, 1970). Sexual fantasy has assumed an increasingly salient place in sexualities research, so that it is now understood that:

> Sexual fantasy is hypothesized to have links to the cognitive, affective, and behavioral systems as erotic fantasies can contain factual information, affective reactions, and lead to overt responses. Sexual fantasies can also serve as the stimulus leading to physiological arousal, the subsequent cognitive and affective evaluation, and ultimately, overt behavior. In short, sexual fantasies may be the driving force for human sexuality. (Chick & Gold, 1987, p. 62)

Some researchers even claim that sexual fantasy "provides a clearer picture of male and female sexual natures than does the study of sexual action" (Ellis & Symons, 1990, p. 551). As evidenced by their phrase "male and female sexual natures," Ellis and Symons offer a sociobiological analysis of fantasy, arguing that fantasies are rooted in evolutionary, sex-based strategies.

But how do we begin to conceptualize and operationalize possible connections between fantasies and (inter)actions? And are there sociological explanations for gender (not sex) differences?

Using respondent-written fantasies, we explore gender differences in active and passive language, sexual and sensual content, and emotional and romantic imagery. We propose some sociostructural explanations for the differences we document, and discuss some links between fantasies and behaviors.

Methods and Data Collection

For this research, we collected 340 usable responses (249 women and 91 men) to an open-ended question about sexual fantasies. Usable responses were defined as: only one fantasy mentioned, with sex of the respondent clearly indicated. We simply asked respondents to write a sexual fantasy that they consistently found arousing, perhaps the one they thought about most often. We gave no instructions about whether or how to specify details of the fantasy; respondents were free to be as descriptive or vague as they wished. Also, respondents may have provided masturbatory or coital fantasies, or daydreams, as we did not specify. The open-ended design enabled us to obtain fantasies expressed in the language, tone, and descriptive depth that each respondent chose. We collected these fantasies in seven social science classes at two colleges and one public university in suburban Long Island, New York. The lack of representation in this sample, along with other methodological considerations, is extensively discussed later.

Respondents were assured of the anonymity and confidentiality of their responses. If respondents did not wish to participate for any reason, we asked them to state something to the effect of "I do not wish to participate"; some did so and also explained why. These were collected along with the fantasies. In all, nine men (7%) and 46 women (18.5%) did not wish to participate. After analyzing the fantasies a researcher returned to each class and discussed methods, findings, and how to sociologically interpret the results.

We were particularly interested in four themes in the collected fantasies:

1. narrative description: the use of language, linguistic explicitness vs. vagueness, use of slang;

2. emotional description: relationship of affective behaviors to sexual behaviors, explicitness of emotional/intimate feelings;
3. sensual imagery: scene setting, use of props, level of nonsexual detail, geographical and temporal settings; and
4. sexual imagery; elaborateness, specificity, and vagueness of sexual activities.

In men's fantasies, we expected to find more explicit discussion of sexual conduct, vague or unspecified emotional content, little sensual imagery and romance, and diverse sexual imaginations. In women's fantasies, we expected to find vague or unspecified descriptions of sexual conduct, detailed emotional connections with partners, descriptive sensual imagery and romantic content and less diverse sexual imaginations.

We also expected to find that men's fantasies, compared with women's, employed more "active" language. For example, except when specifically describing sexual or mental submission to a partner, we expected men to use language like, "I took off her clothes." We expected women to use language like, "He took off my clothes," unless explicitly describing a fantasy of dominance.

While our primary analysis is qualitative, the fantasies were also quantitatively content analyzed using a simple coding scheme and gamma, a measure of association and order in dichotomous variables (see Table 1). We coded each fantasy

TABLE 1. Gamma and Descriptive Statistics

Variable Name	Gamma	% of men mentioning	% of women mentioning
Partner Type:			
significant other	0.6596	15.38	46.99
famous person	−0.6243	6.59	1.61
taboo person	−0.3047	12.09	6.83
multiple partners	−0.7522	40.66	8.84
"Mr. (Mrs.) right"	0.6732	3.3	14.86
Fantasy Dimensions:			
romance/romantic	0.6911	7.69	31.33
emotions/emotional	0.6208	10.99	34.54
place mentioned	0.3108	24.18	37.75
time/moment specified	0.5071	45.05	71.49
time described	0.4896	16.48	36.55
sensual props	0.031	17.58	28.51
intercourse occurred	−0.3039	78.02	65.46
fellatio occurred	−0.5714	12.09	3.61
masturbation occurred	−0.4303	7.69	3.21
lesbian acts mentioned	−0.5	13.19	4.29
Explicit Mention of:			
man as aggressor	0.4974	4.4	12.05
woman as aggressor	−0.7512	20.88	3.61
slang for "make love"	−0.5687	41.76	16.47
physical appearance	−0.6019	48.35	18.88
body type, parts, etc.	−0.549	23.08	8.03

Note: These are variables with gamma values of +/−0.30 or greater.

TABLE 2. Kappa Values for Interrater Reliability

Variable Name	Kappa	% of men mentioning	% of women mentioning
Partner Type:			
significant other	0.9104	95.7	51.99
famous person	0.7947	98.92	94.76
taboo person	1	100	86.08
multiple partners	0.9698	98.92	64.45
"Mr. (Mrs.) right"	0.8771	97.85	82.5
Fantasy Dimensions:			
romance/romantic	0.7729	92.47	66.85
emotions/emotional	0.7617	93.55	72.92
place mentioned	0.93	96.77	53.9
time/moment specified	0.6782	83.87	49.88
time described	0.5131	82.8	64.67
sensual props	0.8577	94.62	62.23
intercourse occurred	0.8656	93.55	51.99
fellatio occurred	1	100	93.76
masturbation occurred	1	100	93.76
lesbian acts mentioned	0.9275	98.92	85.17
Explicit Mention of:			
man as aggressor	0.9173	98.92	86.99
woman as aggressor	0.7543	95.7	82.5
slang for "make love"	0.8028	93.55	67.28
physical appearance	0.9723	98.92	61.19
body type, parts, etc.	0.9504	98.92	78.32

Note: These are variables with gamma values of +/−0.30 or greater. (See Table 1).
Kappa values are as follows:
0.41–0.60 moderate interrater agreement
0.61–0.80 substantial interrater agreement
0.81–1.00 almost perfect interrater agreement

based on presence or absence of 33 variables, including partner types (significant other, "Mr. [Mrs.] Right," taboo person, etc.); romantic/emotional content; sensual content (place, time described, etc.); sexual content (coitus, fellatio, cunnilingus, etc.); language (use of slang, "make love," etc.); and references to physical characteristics. Kappa, a statistic for assessing interrater reliability, yielded average interrater agreement of 96.52% for the 33 coded variables (range = 82.8% to 100%). Values for kappa ranged from 0.51 to 1, indicating substantial to "almost perfect" agreement (Table 2).

Findings

Narrative and Sexual Elements

Narrative strategics differed for women and men. Everything from length of fantasies to descriptions of sensual and sexual elements to actual language employed varied according to gender of respondent. Take, for example, these men's fantasies:

"Menage-a-trois."
"2 hot babes and myself going at it."
"To have sex [crossed out, with "make love" substituted] with an older woman 10 or so years older."
"Have sex on the beach."

These are not *excerpts* from fantasies—they are the *entire* fantasies. Overall, we found that men's fantasies were shorter than women's, word for word, largely due to amount of emotional and sensual scenery women tended to describe (discussed later). This differs from Follingstad and Kimbrell's finding that men wrote more words and longer single fantasies than did women (1986).

Other language differences appeared when considering the explicitly sexual aspects of the fantasies. Both genders used the following terms for intercourse: *make love, have intercourse, have sex, do it, fuck, and make mad passionate love.* However, there were more extensive gender differences. Some terms for intercourse in men's fantasies were *going at it, having her way with me, have, perform, inflict extreme pleasure on, knocking boots, satisfying them, penetration, and thrusting.* Women's fantasies used terms such as *get intimate, doing his dishes, jumping him, have me, be together, become one, impalement, sexual experience/situation, rolling and thrusting, it goes from there, you can guess the rest, pelvic thrust, inside me.*

The terms men used had more "active" connotations than the terms women used. Women's terms were gentler, vaguer, and less precise than men's, exemplified by "you can guess the rest" versus "inflict extreme pleasure on." Notably, not one of the 249 women in the sample referred to male genitalia as anything other than "penis." However, both men and women reserved their most creative language for coitus. Frank and Anshen (1983) noted the profusion of sex-marked verbs, particularly for the stereotypic male role in coitus (conversely, there is a dearth of terms for the stereotypic female role). They concluded that, "Women are thus assigned passive roles in sex by our language" (1983, p. 68). Richter's 1987 analysis of English language sexual slang would support this. He notes terms for women's anatomy such as *waste pipe, hole, slit,* and *teats.* Terms for men's anatomy include *tassel, prick, ladies' delight, bollocks,* and rather "active" words like *pile-driver, hair-divider,* and *live rabbit.*

Perhaps in correspondence with these differences in sexual language and slang, we found that men's descriptions of specifically sexual activities were direct, active and clear:

> "The women would wipe my cum all over themselves and lick it off one another."
>
> "She says, 'Put your cock in my ass'."
>
> "I'll be more interest[ed] if she started playing with those beautiful tits she has and starts fingering herself."
>
> "She falls down, slowly landing directly on my penis, moving in a motion I have never witnessed before. She makes me have orgasms I never had before."

In describing what *may* be sexual activities, women tended to be more vague:

> "We do not make love genitally, but whole bodily."
>
> "We begin to have intercourse."
>
> "One thing leads to another."

These differences in sexual explicitness hint at what we suggest is the underlying cultural sexual script. Women's fantasies subtly and overtly depicted the relatively standard foreplay-then-intercourse script, even when telling the reader to use the imagination to envision what happens next. Men's fantasies incorporated more description of sexual acts, particularly those that culminated in orgasm.

For these variables, qualitative analysis of differences in sexual slang and description of sexual conduct is crucial, because quantitative analysis cannot capture the extent of these differences. For example, 78% of men and 65% of women offered fantasies that implied or specified intercourse. About 12% of the men and 3% of the women described or implied fellatio. Half of the men and 56% of the women used the term "make love" in their fantasies. But simple frequencies do not show that men tended to specify, describe, and rhapsodize about intercourse, while women tended to imply and sidestep the event. We return to the sexual imagery and content of these fantasies after exploring the more emotional and sensual themes we observed.

Emotional and Romantic Elements

Our research revealed gender differences in the emotional content and tone of the sample's fantasies as well. Women often specified that the fantasy partner was a significant other, and typically used the words "boyfriend" or "husband" (47% of women), while only 15% of men referred to partners who were significant others. Moreover, 15% of the women specifically described opposite sex partners whom they called "Mr. Right," the "man of my dreams," or "wonderful in every way," while only 3% of men did so. Instead, men offered fantasies that involved a celebrity (6.5% vs. 1% of women), a taboo partner (teacher, employer), or multiple partners. Only 12% of men mentioned taboo partners (6% of women did so), but fully 40% of men's fantasies involved two or more partners. About 9% of the women's fantasies included multiple partners.

Typical women's fantasies instead included romantic and emotional ideas like these:

> "He would hold me close and cater to my every need. He would treat me like a princess."
>
> "I want this to be my honeymoon. I want this to be the first time that I make love."
>
> "Finally he comes right out and says really sensitively and emotionally how he needs me as more than a friend and we got into this huge fight and then he suddenly pins me against the wall, and starts kissing me and then stops and says he's sorry but he couldn't help it."

Women's fantasies were generally stories of love, affection, and romance. Men's fantasies involved less description of emotional or romantic themes and provided less emotional context. A few men's fantasies were, for this sample, gender-transgressive narratives, where the man described a loving, committed relationship with a significant other or "the woman of his dreams." Gender-transgressive fantasies for women in this sample described sexually active, ardent, assertive women, searching for multiple partners, who had multiple orgasms and multiple contexts for sexual expression.

Such differences conform to traditional gender stereotypes. Women learn to associate emotional commitment and affection with sexuality (Athanasiou, Shaver, & Tavris, 1970; DeLamater & MacCorquodale, 1979; DeLamater, 1987; Lott, 1992;

Simon & Gagnon, 1998). Women are often taught that sexuality should be intertwined with a "relational orientation," instead of being taught that sexuality can be viewed as a route to physical pleasure (a "recreational orientation"), as many men are (Gagnon & Simon, 1973; DeLamater, 1987). Thus, it is not surprising that women's fantasies maintain these conventions by incorporating sexual expression into committed, emotionally meaningful relationships. Men's fantasies display the learned ability to differentiate between sexual and emotional activities.

An area of quantitative difference in the fantasies in this sample involves specified or implied romantic and emotional content. Women provided more romantic fantasies with clear "emotional" content—34.5% compared to 11% of the men. This squares with what women learn about sexuality via cultural sexual scripting. Some of the women's fantasies, such as, "He would hold me close and cater to my every need. He would treat me like a princess" (cited above), were essentially romantic, emotional *non-sexual* narratives. Thirty-one percent of the women's fantasies included romantic imagery, while only 7.5% of the men's did.

One possible measure of this sample's differences in emotional and affective content could be the amount of physical description of the fantasy partner(s). We observed that elaboration of the physical attributes of the fantasy partner seemed to be present in fantasies with less emotional and romantic imagery. About 48% of the men mentioned something about the appearance of the partner(s), and 23% of the men very specifically described physical attributes of the partner(s).

This may be due to fantasy partner choice. Since fewer men fantasized a specific, "actual" partner (i.e., a significant other, spouse, lover), they may have felt more compelled to specify the distinct "pieces and parts" of the fantasy partner(s). Cultural sexual scripts also teach some men how to attach sexual attraction to specific body parts or attributes—"I'm a leg/breast/butt man" is a common expression. However, we do not often hear heterosexual women saying. "I'm a butt/penis/chest woman."

To wit, men's fantasies included very clear depictions of physical characteristics, particularly when multiple partners were mentioned:

"They must be thin with nice bubble asses and medium, upturned breasts (with nipples like pencil erasers)."

"Elle McPherson type, gorgeous looking, hot woman, straight long hair, with lots of great hot looking clothes on."

"These women are of course slim, trim and tan and obviously incredibly sexy."

"The entire Swedish bikini team—big breasts, blond, unbelievably curvy asses."

"One of the women would be blonde, the other dark haired, about 5'7" to 5'10", knock-out bodies."

Women did mention partner's physiques, but the language was more general:

"I'm out on a date with a nicely built man. . . ."
". . . tall, built, and unbelievably gorgeous. . . ."
". . . really good looking."
"Someone so gorgeous I have to have him."

Men described exactly what their fantasy partners looked like, and even mentioned celebrities who constituted visual "blueprints" of their affinities, in case the reader was unclear about exactly how gorgeous or firm the fantasy partner ought to be. When women mentioned physical characteristics, generally they stated simply that the man was attractive and fit. Another way to explore these emotional differences is to look at the differences between sensual and sexual content.

Sensual Imagery

Sensual imagery refers to narrative elements that set a scene, evoke a mood, develop a story line, provide non-sexual detail, and, especially, provide descriptions of geographical and temporal settings and the use of props (like candles, clothing, food, etc.). Descriptions of fantasy location were more common among women (38% vs. 24% of men). Women also tended to situate their fantasies temporally (e.g., morning, afternoon) and then describe the moment. Fully 71.5% of women specified a time or moment for the fantasy, while only 45% of men did so. However, only 36.5% of women

further described the temporal moment, along with 16.5% of men.

It should be noted that more often than expected, men did situate their fantasies, but rarely with the extensive description found in women's fantasies. About 64% of men specified some location, while about 74% of women did so. But this superficial numerical similarity does not fully show the gender differences in fantasy scene-setting. While many men mentioned that their fantasies occurred near water or on a beach, often this was all that they said. Most women not only mentioned the locale, but also things like the air and water temperature, the ocean surrounding the fantasized island, the number of other people in the area (if any), and various sensual props (dinner, a picnic, wine, etc.).

Women offered far more detailed descriptions of geographic location. For example, *men* offered these descriptions:

"If I had to pick a location, I guess I would choose a place a little out of the ordinary."

"My sexual fantasy involves being on an island with only sexually attractive and available females. . . .

"I like to think of dogs barking and being in an industrial setting, during lovemaking that is. Fear and discomfort are integral parts of my fantasy."

"As far as the setting goes it makes no difference, only important factor is that we are both with her at the same time."

Women's fantasies were opposite in terms of length and clarity:

". . . A tropical island. I've always dreamed about making love in a crystal blue sea, with a waterfall in the background, then moving on shore to a white, sandy beach."

"It's eveningtime [sic], the sun is setting, I'm on a tropical island, a light breeze is blowing into my balcony doors and the curtains (white) are fluttering lightly in the wind. The room is spacious and there is white everywhere, even the bed. There are flowers of all kinds and the light fragrance fills the room."

"The room would he filled with candles and soft music would fill the air, he would feed me strawberries, which we'd share, and in the morning we'd wake, bathe one another, and. . . ."

"We are out in the country. There is no one for miles around. There is an open yard in the back of the house surrounded by woods. All we can hear is the chirping of birds and the rustling of leaves. It is raining. Not a monsoon, not a drizzle, bur a warm summer afternoon shower. There is a big, beautiful, white gazebo in the middle of the yard."

Regardless of whether women were fantasizing about the beach or some other locale, they described more specific elements of the setting than did men in this sample. Women tended to emphasize romantic and aesthetic elements. Some of the fantasies included very detailed settings, replete with colors, textures, and fabrics, with no mention of anything overtly sexual. It seems that women's fantasies displayed more elaborate "sensual imaginations" than did men's.

Sexual Imagery

The specifically sexual dimensions of the fantasies revealed that women may have developed sensual imaginations, but men displayed more developed "sexual imaginations." More men than women mentioned intercourse, giving/getting fellatio, masturbatory activities, lesbian activities, and "woman as aggressor"—the woman making the first move and/or orchestrating the encounter:

Variable	Men mentioned	Women mentioned
Intercourse	78%	65%
Fellatio	12%	3%
Masturbation	7.7%	3%
Lesbian activities	13%	4%
Woman as aggressor	21%	3.6%

Women described "man as aggressor" more often than "woman as aggressor"; 12% of women described male partners this way, while 3.7% described themselves as taking the lead (see above chart).

Men's descriptions of fantasized sexual activities tended to be explicit and clear, although not necessarily verbose. For example:

"The fantasy reaches a second high point during the longest and most powerful orgasm/ejaculation ever."

"Totally uninhibited sexual activity."

"Her voice will be sincere, yet playful. She will suggest that I take a good look at her breasts. In her attitude I would find no inhibitions whatsoever."

Women described sexual scenes such as:

"He tells me I mean more to him than anything else in the world and that he's never been happier in his entire life. . . . I then look into his gorgeous eyes and say—'I do want this more than anything in the world—I love you'."

". . . Our secret, not even knowing each other's name. Like a mystery, and I'll never see him again."

"He'd get so excited that he wouldn't be able to control himself and he would grab me and make passionate love to me."

"Have my ideal man and myself together for the whole day. While we are together, we would play sports and then go home and take a shower together. Have no one else to bother us from the outside world and have it feel like eternity and never wanting to leave."

The primary difference in the moods and moments described by the respondents is that men envisioned sexual moments of wild abandon, no inhibitions, with sexually inventive, assertive women. Women rarely imagined themselves as sexual actors, aggressors or initiators, and certainly not as much as men imagined women as sexual actors.

The average man's fantasy in this sample, however, made sexual conduct clear and explicit, while providing the reader with some new slang for a vernacular collection. He tells us that he "got head" first, then she was turned onto her stomach while he entered her, and that after he came (explosively, of course), she climbed aboard him and "rode him like an angel on a bronco."

"To have sex with at least 3 women—one blond/blue eyes, brunette/brown eyes, and redhead/green eyes. All friends, 22 years old and bodies that stepped out of Penthouse. All 5'6" or shorter. Have a totally wild, uninhibited time, knocking boots all night long then start again in the A.M. I'd do it in the shower, on the hood of my caddy, and on the kitchen table. And of course I'd satisfy all of them, repeatedly."

While a scene is set, at least formally, there is no mood created by the scene-setting as in the women's fantasies. Unlike women's fantasies, we don't know whether there were any lit candles, half-drunk glasses of bubbly, and soft, gentle breezes.

Just as men's descriptions of their sexual repertoire tended to be more elaborate, that repertoire also tended to be a bit more extensive. While neither women nor men tended to mention giving or receiving cunnilingus, men did mention receiving fellatio more than women mentioned giving it. In some cases, oral sex might have been subsumed in vague, reductive narratives such as "then we messed around for a while" or "we rub and kiss each other all over."

Qualitative analysis did show that explicit language, description, and developed sexual imaginations were present in a few women's fantasies. When women wrote fantasies that included their sexual agency, multiple partners, anonymous partners, and oral sex of both types—in short, the stereotypic elements of masculine fantasies—they did so in "active," explicit language with sexual descriptiveness.

Similarities Between the Genders

We expected men to be much more likely to mention a stranger as the fantasy partner, but there was little difference between men's and women's responses (11% of men, 9% of women). There was also little difference in fantasies specifically mentioning a "friend" as a partner (12% of men, 7.6% of women). However, more men did not specify exactly who the fantasy partner was or what the relationship was (if any) to that person. For example, some men mentioned that there were two blondes, but they were further undefined. They could have both been strangers to the fantasizer, they could have been friends—it was unclear and not implied.

As for other sexual activities, such as dominance and submission, few respondents went beyond the standard cultural script (e.g., kissing, intercourse). This could be due to lack of sexual experience, age cohort effects, and/or respondent bias. Participants may have been self-conscious about presumed researcher responses to fantasy content; inhibition may have prevented respondents from including avant-garde activities and scenarios about which they actually fantasized.

In the language of the fantasies, men and women did not differ in their use of the terms *make love/have sex/have intercourse*. But there may actually be a more subtle connection between fantasized partner and/or relationship status and word chosen. Individuals of either gender may use "make love" when describing conduct with a significant other, and "have sex" with a stranger or with multiple partners. Since more women than men specify significant others, women may thus be more likely to use "make love."

Neither sex mentioned "penis/vagina" very much or used slang for genitalia, although men described *intercourse* in more ways than did women. But researchers find that men are generally more likely to improvise with language, use slang, and speak more casually (Lakoff, 1990; Coward, 1985). It has been argued that men create language and therefore feel more entitled to expand it (Spender, 1985). Further, Sanders and Robinson (1979) found that, in conversation, women use more formal and clinical terminology for genitalia and sexual activities than do men.

Limitations

The generalizability of these findings is limited in several respects. First, we used a college-based convenience sample that was intrinsically self-selecting on many levels. The students in the classes we visited were studying intimate relationships, sexuality, and gender. There were disparities between the number of women enrolled and the number of men enrolled. Additionally, the men who enroll in these classes may differ from the women who enroll. The relatively small number of men (N = 91) included in this sample may also have some bearing on the results. In addition, there was no way to guarantee that all enrolled students would be in attendance on the day of fantasy collection. Every student who was present had the option of not participating; there is no way to know how many students elected not to write a fantasy but also did not return an answer to this effect.

Another kind of respondent bias may also be present. While comfortable with participating generally, some respondents may have felt uncomfortable writing fantasies that they considered avant garde, unusual, or "kinky," fearing negative researcher responses. Some respondents may have tried to anticipate what kinds of fantasies we wanted and may have thus tried to provide especially typical responses. Clearly, respondent and sample biases must be taken into account when interpreting the results.

These results are not fully generalizable to all men and women because of other independent variables that bear on the sample. Most of the respondents were between 18 and 22, a typical college student age range. An older or younger sample would be likely to provide different fantasies, connected perhaps to different life experiences and relationships. The research occurred in a college setting; respondents of a similar age range who are not in college might answer differently.

The sample may also be overly skewed away from white, middle-class respondents also. The campuses at which data were collected are highly diverse campuses; one actually has a majority of people of color on campus and a minority white student body (49%). However, there were no overt differences among the fantasies that lead us to suspect that "race" needed to be provided by respondents (along with "sex") as an independent variable. Nonetheless, if we *had* asked for other independent variables, non-gendered differences may have become more obvious. This is especially possible given that different racial and ethnic groups vary in religiosity and subcultural sexual scripts. The different experiences of minorities and non-minorities are visible in virtually every aspect of social and mental life, and sexuality intersects with race and ethnicity along with gender, class, and sexual orientation.

Beyond the limitations on generalizability imposed by the sample, there are other considerations posed by our methodology. An open-ended question enabled respondents to write almost nothing ("menage-a-trois," for example) or to compose long essays. Future research that asks respondents to specify certain elements (such as who? where? when?, etc.) of fantasies might yield responses with more comparability, although forced-choice response options can lead to other problems. Additionally, the coding scheme we devised was developed based on what we expected to find in the fantasies. Finally, regarding descriptive excerpts, the excerpted or actual fantasies included here were chosen to highlight typical gendered differences. Gender transgressive fantasies, and the few that seemed indistinguishable as to the author's sex were not included in this discussion.

The Sociology of Sexual Fantasies

Both women and men fantasize themselves as sexually irresistible objects of desire, and both fantasize themselves as the recipients of sexual activities. Women seem to use a more passive linguistic style than do men when describing penile-vaginal intercourse. Men seem to use more active language to describe sexual activities, even when fantasizing themselves as the recipients of these activities, even when tied up (from one fantasy with bondage: "I tell her to suck me and she does").

How can this be explained? How can men use the language of *activity* to describe something during which they seem to be powerless? In heterosexual encounters, men and women often interpret the same behaviors from different sides of the power equation. For example, men experience both fellatio and cunnilingus as expressions of their power—along the lines of, "I can get her to suck me," and "When I go down on her I can make her come"—regardless of whether the man is "actually" active or passive.

Symmetrically, women experience both fellatio and cunnilingus as expressions of their lack of power—"He forces my mouth onto his penis," and, "He goes down on me and I'm helpless" (from the fantasies in this sample)—regardless of whether the woman is "actually" passive or active. Perhaps measures of activity and passivity may more accurately be cast as measures of interpersonal sexual power, in terms of who has more power in heterosexual interactions. These "false symmetries" lead us to consider the ways in which a sociological discussion reveals important dimensions of sexual fantasy that have been overlooked by previous psychological researchers.

Although our findings corroborate earlier research findings, our interpretation is different. Psychobiological research on fantasies tends to locate fantasy in sex-linked, innate mental structures. Ellis and Symons, for example, claimed that evolutionary selection was responsible for the gender differences they observed. Thus, men's penchant for new, different, and unknown female partners was explained (the need to spread "seed") and women's penchant for emotional, committed male partners was explained (the need to find one male who would be responsible for the offspring of their union).

Instead, we suggest that gender differences in fantasies are rooted in deep *social* structures. Differential sexual scripting, with the goal of reinforcing socially constructed gender role identities, is the primary axis of disparity. With socialization into a binary gender system that also assumes heterosexuality, gender is enormously powerful in the construction of the sexual self. So we would expect to see gender differences trumping sexual orientation differences, although this idea has not been fully explored.

Since our social structures also have inequities built in, we would expect to see these inequities reproduced in even the most intimate realms of individuals—in sexual fantasies, the intrapsychic level of sexual scripting. These structural gender inequalities have consequences. By casting themselves as fantasy objects of desire, with less visible sexual agency (heterosexual), women may ultimately be less able to exert sexual desires in social interactions. Meanwhile men, who cast themselves as sexual actors, filled with sexual agency, may ultimately enact a wider range of sexual behaviors without quandaries.

One possible consequence of how inequalities play themselves out in fantasies has an empirical element: in our sample, none of the men or women mentioned having safer sex. Respondents mentioned condoms (and contraception, for that matter) *only* to point out that their fantasies explicitly *did not* include latex, safety, or worries about disease/pregnancy. This superficial symmetry, however, only serves to mask the important difference. We could be concerned with these respondents' general inability to incorporate safer sex practices into their fantasies, but clearly women and men are differently affected by this inability.

Recall that when women fantasized about men, the men they fantasized about were loved, trusted, and intimate; most women fantasized about past or present significant others. When men fantasized about women, their relationships to the women were unclear, perhaps involving strangers, friends, or multiple partners. Here the potentially dangerous consequences of unsafe sexual practices are far more marked—especially for the female partners. Women's fantasized lack of sexual agency can thus translate into an inability to implement safer sex practices *and* insist on them. Men's abundant socio-structural sexual power can thus translate into an ability to avoid safer sex and to persuade partners to avoid it as well. In both cases, the women fantasizers and the anonymous women of men's fantasies are at risk.

We might also see arenas of difficulty between the sexes in the form of sexual harassment and date rape. With such visible incongruities between the ways in which heterosexual men and women *imagine* sexual encounters, it is possible that these disparities could be transformed into violent and aggressive sexual conflicts. Duncombe and Marsden (1996) describe ". . . the level of the basic discourses of sexual exchange [that] undermine women's ability and right to initiate or refuse sexual intercourse" (p. 224). We suggest that these basic exchanges and discourses are evident in the genders' fantasies. When inequitable power exchanges permeate the intrapsychic dimensions of sexual scripting, hetero-sex can be compromised in multiple ways.

The gray areas between fantasies and realities seem likely to be translated into problems for heterosexual women and men. If women translated their sexual fantasies into behaviors, then they would demand sensual intimate emotional connections with committed sexual partners. If men translated their fantasies into behaviors, then they would want highly sexual encounters with active and skilled women, without always requiring an emotional, relational context. Thus when women and men have sex with one another, each may experience a level of compromise from the ideal(ized) images expressed in fantasies. Duncombe and Marsden (1996) refer to these compromises collectively as "sex work," expanding Arlie Hochschild's concept of emotion work (1983). In heterosexual "sex work," partners interpret gendered sexual scripts in terms of necessary compromises, particularly regarding sexual needs and satisfaction. Duncombe and Marsden found, for example, that couples developed informal strategies to indicate sexual availability and prevent women from having "openly to show desire" (1996, p. 227).

This suggests that heterosexual men may believe that their sexuality would be "feminized" by demands for emotional displays of tender affection and cooperation in mood and scene setting. On the other hand, heterosexual women may feel that their sexuality would be "masculinized" by the anonymous and highly sexual interests of some men. During class discussion after data collection, one woman referred to men's more recreational fantasizing, saying. "It doesn't matter if it's me or someone else doing it to him right then. What seems more important is that it's being done right then by *someone*."

But Jayne Stake's research (1997) on how people integrate traditionally masculine and feminine characteristics suggests that successful "real-life" integrations are associated with well-being and enhanced self-esteem. When called on to be both expressive and instrumental, study subjects felt better in the work situations they described. Could sexuality be a similar "real-life" situation where the merging of traditionally gender-linked traits would benefit participants?

There are several areas of heterosexual men's and women's sexual fantasies that would benefit from a merging of interests. Women would profit by heeding the desires of their male partners, who long for ardent, aware, enthusiastic sexual mates. Men would profit from increasing their ability to be emotionally committed, passionate and sensual. Taken together, both men and women who seek each other as partners would reap the benefits of women's increased sexual agency and men's increased intimacy.

Gender differences within the most internalized aspect of sexuality—at the level of sexual fantasizing—suggest that the sociocultural structure of gender is pervasive. In heterosexual conduct, we see how fantasy and reality converge and diverge, with men looking for active, sexually experimental partners and women looking for emotional contexts and lush sexualized settings. In the "real-life" of sexuality, we see how partnered sex can involve compromises that range from the benign (e.g., choosing one position over another) to the horrible (e.g., non-consensual force). The rich internal world of sexual fantasies needs fuller exploration so that we can better understand gender and sex.

References

Athanasiou, R., Shaver, P., & Tavris, C. (1970). Sex. *Psychology Today*, (July) 39–52.

Chick, D., & Gold, S. R. (1987). A Review of Influences on Sexual Fantasy: Attitudes, Experience, Guilt and Gender. *Imagination, Cognition and Personality, 7*, 61–76.

Coward, R. (1985). *Female Desires: How They Are Sought, Bought and Packaged*. New York: Grove Press.

DeLamater, J. (1987). Gender Differences in Sexual Scenarios. In: K. Kelley (Ed.), *Females, Males, and Sexuality: Theories and Research*. Albany: State University of New York Press.

DeLamater, J., & MacCorquodale, P. (1979). *Premarital Sexuality: Attitudes, Relationships, Behavior*. Madison: University of Wisconsin Press.

Duncombe, J., & Marsden, D. (1996). Whose Orgasm is this Anyway? "Sex Work" in Long-term Heterosexual Couple Relationships. In: J. Weeks & J. Holland (Eds.), *Sexual Cultures: Communities, Values, and Intimacy*. New York: Macmillan.

Ellis, B. J., & Symons, D. (1990). Sex Differences in Sexual Fantasy: An Evolutionary Psychological Approach. *Journal of Sex Research, 27*, 527–555.

Follingstad, D. R., & Kimbrell, C. D. (1986). Sex Fantasies Revisited: An Expansion and Further Clarification of Variables Affecting Sex Fantasy Production. *Archives of Sexual Behavior, 15,* 475–486.

Frank, F., & Anshen, F. (1983). *Language and the Sexes.* Albany: State University of New York Press.

Freud, S. (1975). *Three Essays on the Theory of Sex.* New York: Basic Books.

Gagnon, J. H., & Simon, W. (1973). *Sexual Conduct: The Social Sources of Human Sexuality.* Chicago, IL: Aldine Books.

Kaplan, H. S. (1974). *The New Sex Therapy: Active Treatment of Sexual Dysfunctions.* New York: Brunner and Mazel.

Lakoff, Robin Tolmach. (1990). *Talking Power: The Politics of Language in Our Lives.* New York, NY: Basic Books.

Leitenberg, H., & Henning, K. (1995). Sexual Fantasy. *Psychological Bulletin, 117,* 469–496.

Lewis, M. (1991). What Do Women Really Want? In: *GQ.* November.

Lott, B. (1992). *Women's Lives: Themes and Variations in Gender Learning* (2e). Pacific Grove, CA: Brooks/Cole Publishing.

Masters, W. H., & Johnson, V. E. (1966). *Human Sexual Response.* Boston: Little, Brown.

Masters, W. H., & Johnson, V. E. (1970). *Human Sexual Inadequacy.* Boston: Little, Brown.

Richter, A. (1987). *The Language of Sexuality.* Jefferson, NC: McFarland and Co.

Sanders, Janet S., and William L. Robinson. (1979). Talking and Not Talking About Sex: Male and Female Vocabularies. *Journal of Communication* 29(2): 22–30.

Simon, William, and John Gagnon. 1998. Psychosexual Development. *Society* 35(2):60–67.

Spender, D. (1985). *Man Made Language.* London: Methuen.

Stake, J. (1997). Integrating Expressiveness and Instrumentality in Real-Life Settings: A New Perspective on the Benefits of Androgyny. *Sex Roles, 37,* 541–564.

Postscript 2013

The data for this article were collected through the 1990s, and it was originally published in 2002. Are there any changes?

As social scientists, we offer this hypothesis: Most of the heterosexual men reading this article will not find very big differences with the fantasies men had in the 1990s and those they have today. But many of the heterosexual women—maybe as many as 50%—will say "Huh? Mine are a lot hotter and more explicit than that!" At least that's the trend researchers have found among college-aged women as they've extended and expanded this research over the past two decades (Kim & Ward, 2012; Stewart & Szymanski, 2012; Burns & Mathes, 2011).

The convergence of "his" sexuality and "her" sexuality is reflected not only in behaviors, but also in fantasies. In short, *her* fantasies are increasingly resembling *his* fantasies; gender convergence is entirely in the direction of heterosexual women's fantasies and behaviors becoming increasingly like heterosexual men's. This "masculinization" of sex comes from several sources that shape both genders' fantasies—and still, we argue, shape them differently.

For one thing, the dramatic increase in gender equality in every arena, from boardroom to bedroom, has resulted in women's increased ability to find their sexual "voice"—to believe that they know what they want, and to feel entitled to get it or have it. Thanks to the women's movement and media like *Cosmopolitan* magazine, younger women today seem more capable of being sexually agentic and more sexually expressive than possibly any generation in our history. Women know they can like sex, want sex, and get horny—they think they are as entitled to pleasure as any guy is. There is room to explore what this really means, however, as some researchers have questioned the construction of exactly this kind of narrative (Fahs, 2011; Hawley & Hensley, 2009). Where and how do women learn about themselves sexually?

Heterosexual women's sexual voices are also shaped by the media environment in which they live, where that voice is given tone and depth and resonance. It is no accident that that emerging sexual voice perfectly fits as a complement to (heterosexual) men's. The "pornification" of American life—the ubiquity of pornographic images across all media platforms, and the ways in which those pornographic images become the foundation on which young people construct their sexualities—has a different impact on women and men (Stewart & Szymanski, 2012; Wentland, Herold, Desmarais & Milhausen, 2009).

These media—whether harder core pornography or the softer, more "feminine" variety of *50 Shades of Gray*—are the raw materials from which some women fashion their sexual agency. Prior to the porn revolution, there probably weren't massive numbers of women who thought that a man ejaculating on their face was a real turn on. The facial was "invented" to make it clear to viewers that a real orgasm happened, which authenticates the sex itself, just as women's shaving their pubic hair originated in pornography, as directors and photographers sought better and clearer camera angles (Schick, Rima, & Calabrese, 2011). And "surrender" to one's passion didn't inevitably include being tied up by a man you hardly know (Hawley & Hensley, 2009). While all this has changed for heterosexual women, we just don't know much about heterosexual men's fantasies; researchers have not explored this much, except one study that reported that men who were anxious about relationships and intimacy tended to have more *romantic* than sexual fantasies (Birnbaum, 2007).

Karl Marx famously wrote that people "make their own history," but not "just as they please . . . under circumstances chosen by themselves." Rather, he continued, we make our own history "under circumstances directly encountered." So too our sexualities. We create our own sexual selves using all the materials we encounter in our lives—movies, TV, books, conversations with friends and family, via texts, tweets, Instagram pictures and sexts. We imagine, and perhaps we experiment, before something becomes part of our sexual repertoire; we expand, explore, and eliminate. We add, we adapt, and we discard feelings, behaviors, and even identities.

Our sexual fantasies are therefore important components in the construction of our sexualities and our sexual selves, throughout our lives. Our fantasies may be places where we can retreat—to experience the erotic without negative consequences, even, perhaps, without guilt, shame, or embarrassment . . . this is the stuff of dreams.

Works Cited

Birnbaum, Gurit E. (2007). "Beyond the Borders of Reality: Attachment Orientations and Sexual Fantasies." *Personal Relationships, 14*(2): 321–342.

Burns Christopher T. and Mathes, Stefanie. (2011). "Digging in My Secret Garden: Disinhibitory Effects of the 'Hidden Observer' on Reported Sexual Fantasies." *Canadian Journal of Human Sexuality, 20*(4): 143–150.

Fahs, Breanne. (2011). *Performing Sex: The Making and Unmaking of Women's Erotic Lives.* Albany: SUNY Press.

Hawley, Patricia H. and Hensley, William A. (2009). "Social Dominance and Forceful Submission Fantasies: Feminine Pathology or Power?" *Journal of Sex Research, 46*(6): 568–585.

Kim, Janna L. and Ward, L. Monique. (2012). "Striving for Pleasure Without Fear: Short-Term Effects of Reading a Women's Magazine on Women's Sexual Attitudes." *Psychology of Women Quarterly, 36*(3): 326–336.

Schick, Vanessa, Rima, Brandi N., and Calabrese, Sarah (2011). "Evulvalution: The Portrayal of Women's External Genitalia and Physique across Time and the Current Barbie Doll Ideals." *Journal of Sex Research, 48*(1): 74–81.

Stewart, Destin and Szymanski, Dawn. (2012). "Young Adult Women's Reports of Their Male Romantic Partner's Pornography Use as a Correlate of Their Self-Esteem, Relationship Quality, and Sexual Satisfaction." *Sex Roles, 67*(Sep, 5/6): 257–271.

Wentland, Jocelyn J., Herold, Edward S., Desmarais, Serge, and Milhausen, Robin R. (2009). "Differentiating Highly Sexual Women from Less Sexual Women." *Canadian Journal of Human Sexuality, 18*(4): 169–182.

Beards, Breasts, and Bodies: Doing Sex in a Gendered World

RAINE DOZIER

Gender is ubiquitous and, along with race and class, orders most aspects of daily life. "Talking about gender for most people is the equivalent of fish talking about water" (Lorber 1994, 13). Because transsexuals, transgendered people, and others at the borders of gender and sex are fish out of water, they help illuminate strengths and weaknesses in common conceptions of gender. This project clarifies the relationship between sex, gender, and sexual orientation through interviews with female-to-male transsexuals and transgendered people.[1] The interviewees challenge the underlying assumption in much of gender literature that sex, gender, and sexual orientation align in highly correlated, relatively fixed, binary categories. Instead, these categories are a process of differentiation and constructed meaning that is bound in social context.

Sex, Gender, and Sexuality

In the United States, the term "gender" is increasingly used as a proxy for the term "sex" (Auerbach 1999). My own small rebellion against this tendency is to respond literally. When asked to indicate sex, I reply female; when asked for gender, I reply male. Perhaps I am doing little to change concepts of gender and sex,[2] but at least I am on mailing lists that target my diverse interests! At the same time that the public seems to be increasingly using "gender" as proxy for "sex," gender theorists are more clearly delineating the relationship between sex and gender. However, because gender and sex are seemingly inexplicably connected in most aspects of social life, theorists have

difficulty in retaining these delineations throughout their work.

Intellectuals have been creating, critiquing, and advancing concepts of gender for the past 30 years. Generally, gender is defined as the socially constructed correlate of sex. The concept of gender as socially constructed has been theorized extensively and illustrated in a variety of arenas from the playground to the boardroom (Fausto-Sterling 2000; Kanter 1977; Kessler 1990; Lorber 1994; Messner 2000; Thorne 1993; West and Zimmerman 1987). However, many definitions positing gender as an ongoing accomplishment rely on sex as the "master status" or "coat rack" on which gender is socially constructed (Nicholson 1994). Although there is a general consensus that gender is socially constructed, theorists have too often relied on sex as its initiating point.

Delphy (1993) critiqued the overreliance on sex in defining gender. She claimed that illustrating the social construction of gender by describing the cross-cultural variation in men's and women's behavior and social roles only reinforces the notion that gender originates in sex. The description of cross-cultural variation further entrenches the notion of "gender as the *content* with sex as the *container*" (Delphy 1993, 3). Both Nicholson (1994) and Delphy (1993) challenged the view that gender derives from sex and, in a sense, posited the opposite: That "gender is the knowledge that establishes meanings for bodily differences" (Scott 1988, 2). Gender, then, is the concept that creates and defines sex differences.

Raine Dozier, "Beards, Breasts, and Bodies: Doing Sex in a Gendered World," *Gender & Society*, Vol. 19, No. 3 (June 2005), pp. 297–316. Copyright © 2005 by Sociologists for Women in Society. Reprinted by permission of SAGE Publications.

Typically, sex is assigned based on genital inspection at birth, but biological sex is a complex constellation of chromosomes, hormones, genitalia, and reproductive organs. The study of intersexed and sex-reassigned children illustrates that social notions of sex are employed when biological sex is ambiguous (Fausto-Sterling 2000; Kessler 1990). Because sex is an organizing principle of most societies, people are forced to be one or the other, even when "only a surgical shoehorn can put them there" (Fausto-Sterling 1993, 24). Given this, sex is both a physical attribute and socially constructed.

West and Zimmerman (1987) grappled with the social aspect of sex by adding a category to the sex, gender, and sexuality framework. They defined "sex category" as socially perceived sex and claimed that "recognition of the analytical independence of sex, sex category, and gender is essential for understanding the relationships among these elements and the interactional work involved in 'being' a gendered person in society" (West and Zimmerman 1987, 127). However, the categories of sex category, gender, and sexuality are not just analytically, but also practically, distinct. West and Zimmerman ultimately identified gender as the performance one is accountable for based on sex category's leaving little room for feminine men and masculine women. "In virtually any situation, one's sex category can be relevant, and one's performance as an incumbent of that category (i.e., gender) can be subjected to evaluation" (West and Zimmerman 1987, 145). We are left with the ironic conclusion that gender is socially constructed yet is rigidly defined by sex category—an inadequate framework for the explanation of atypical gender behavior.

Lorber (1994, 1999) attempted to uncouple masculinity and femininity from sex category by developing subcategories of gender including gender status (being taken for a man or woman), gender identity (sense of self as a man or woman), and gender display (being feminine and/or masculine). Even with this delineation, Lorber, like West and Zimmerman (1987), consistently slipped into assumptions of the "natural" link between categories. For instance, she claimed transsexuals and "transvestites" do not challenge the gender order because "their goal is to be feminine women and masculine men" (Lorber 1994, 20). As well, she described socialization as a woman or man as "produce[ing] different feelings, consciousness, relationships, skills—ways of being that we call feminine or masculine" (Lorber 1994, 14). This account fails to explain the behavior and identity of trans people for two reasons. First, it assumes the intransigence between the categories man/masculine and woman/feminine, which is not the experience of transsexuals and transgendered people. Not all men, constructed or biological, are masculine or wish to be. Second, Lorber asserted that being treated as a man or woman in social interaction creates a masculine or feminine consciousness. This assertion fails to explain how people grow up to have a gender identity contrary to that expected from their socialization. Lorber's work is important in defining gender as an institution that creates and reinforces inequality, but it also illustrates how easily sex and gender (masculinity and femininity) become elided when sex is used as the initiating point for gendering individuals.

Just like sex and gender, sexuality can also be defined as socially constructed. Sexual behaviors and the meanings assigned to them vary across time and cultures. For instance, Herdt's (1981) study of same-sex fellatio in a tribe in Papua, New Guinea, found that this behavior did not constitute homosexuality or pedophilia, although it might be defined as both in the United States. In the United States, same-sex behavior is assumed to occur only in individuals with a gay or bisexual orientation, yet the AIDS epidemic forced educators and epidemiologists to acknowledge the lack of correlation between identity and behavior (Parker and Aggleton 1999). Schippers (2000) documented a lack of correlation between sexual orientation and sexual behavior in her study of alternative hard rock culture in the United States. Seeing sexual behavior and its meaning as highly reliant on social context helps explain the changing attractions and orientation of female-to-male transsexual and transgendered people (FTMs) as they transition.

Sex, gender, and sexuality, then, are all to varying degrees socially interpreted, and all contribute to an overarching concept of gender that relies on both perceived sex and behaviors and their attribution as masculine or feminine.

A growing number of scholars are writing particularly about FTMs and female masculinities. The longest-term contributor has been Devor (1989, 1997, 1998, 2004). Adding to Devor's work in recent years have been Cromwell (1999), Halberstam (1998), Prosser (1998), and Rubin (2003). Although transsexuals are increasingly represented in academic research, concepts of gender, sex, and sexuality are rarely explored. Gender theorists have often examined transsexuality through the lens of gender (Kessler and McKenna 1978; Nicholson 1994; West and Zimmerman 1987); less often have transsexual theorists interrogated gender through the lens of transsexuality. Using transsexuality as a standpoint to complicate and critique gender has been more common in nonacademic writing (Bornstein 1995; Califia 1997; Feinberg 1998).

Most work in the social sciences regarding transsexuals has focused largely on male-to-female transsexuals (Bolin 1988; Ekins 1997; Lewins 1995). Work by social scientists is important because it can help transform individual, personal experiences into broader social patterns and illuminate the role of social interaction and institutions. The limited research on FTMs offers a unique construction to social science research regarding transsexuality. Devor (1997) documented the lives of 46 FTMs using extensive quotes, allowing FTMs to speak about their lives, their upbringing, and their experiences with transitioning. Although this work is an incredibly detailed recording of the life experiences of FTMs, Devor avoids interpreting or theorizing about the experiences of FTMs and the potential meanings they have for the field of gender studies.

Prosser (1998) took to task the loss of materiality and "the body" in postmodern work regarding transsexuals. Prosser reminded theorists that gender is not simply conceptual but real, and experienced in the body (see Devor 1999). Although Prosser's critique of postmodern thought around transsexuality is extremely important, my interviews indicate that he may overemphasize the importance of the body in transsexual experience. Particular body characteristics are not important

in themselves but become important because of social interpretation.

Cromwell (1999) eloquently summarized notions of gender and sexuality and described them as being located in either essentialist or constructed frameworks. He criticized both and claimed that exclusively constructionist explanations rely on the primacy of social interaction, implying that gender identity does not exist when individuals are alone. He claimed that trans people are important to study because, through them, it is evident that even if socially constructed, there is an underlying, unwavering gender identity. Most important though, Cromwell asserted that trans people's construction of identities, bodies, and sexualities as different rather than deviant subverts the dominant gender/sex paradigm. Rubin (2003) concurred with Cromwell's view of the paradox that gender identity is socially constructed yet at the same time embodied and "absolutely real" (Cromwell 1999, 175). Prosser (1998), Cromwell, and Rubin all challenge aspects of gender theory that do not mesh with the experiences of transsexuals and transgendered people. The body is a very real aspect of the (trans)gendered experience and expression, and even though gender identity is socially constructed, it takes on a solidity and immutability that is not dependent on social interaction.

With this emerging academic work regarding transsexuality, the need to examine how transsexuality and transgenderism complicate the gender field has arisen. Questions such as the following have become increasingly compelling:

> What is the impact of changing sex on the individual's social and sexual behaviors? How does an individual's sex affect other people's interpretation of his or her behavior? As sex changes, how does social interaction change?

By investigating the changing behaviors and interactions of FTMs as they transition, this article illustrates important connections between gender and perceived sex and contributes to the social scientific understanding of transsexuality. Examining the experience of FTMs clarifies that masculinity and femininity are not inextricably linked with male and female and that perceived sex is important in interpreting behavior as masculine or feminine. This project also adds to social scientific work on transsexuality by using transsexuality as a standpoint to critique gender in a systematic, empirically based manner. As well, it supports recent academic work regarding FTMs (Cromwell 1999; Prosser 1998; Rubin 2003) by illustrating the importance of the body to gender and gender identity and helps to increase the representation of FTMs in the social scientific literature on transsexuality.

Study Design and Sample

For this project, I interviewed 18 trans-identified people, all born female, the majority residing in Seattle, Washington. . . .

Respondents ranged in age from 20 to 45 and had begun living as trans between the ages of 18 and 45 (see Table 1). I say this with some hesitation because many FTMs privately identify as trans for years before transitioning or being out about their identity. In this case, I am defining "living as trans" as being referred to as "he" consistently, publicly and/or in their subcultural network. With this definition, three of the respondents were not living as trans even though they identified as transgendered.

Fourteen of the respondents were white, one was African American, two were Latino, and one was Chinese American. Only one respondent did not previously identify as lesbian or bisexual. After transitioning, defining sexual orientation becomes more complicated since sex, and sometimes sexual preference, changes. Assigning sexual orientation requires assigning people to categories based on the sex of the sexual participants. Since many FTMs report being newly attracted to men after transitioning, it appears that their orientation has changed even though, in a sense, they remain homosexual (previously a lesbian, now gay). However, if they are still primarily involved with lesbians or with feminine women, it is difficult to say their orientation has changed when only their perceived sex is different. As well, if an individual is primarily attracted to feminine people, but after transitioning dates feminine men as well as feminine women,

his gendered sexual preference has not changed, so it is unclear whether this describes a change in sexual orientation. Because of these complexities, the table records the reported sexual preference as closely as possible without relying on usual categories of sexual orientation.

Even though they were raised in a variety of locations, the great majority of respondents currently live in urban areas. The sample is probably not representative of the trans population in the United States because it is overwhelmingly urban and emphasizes FTMs who have chosen not to assimilate into mainstream, heterosexual culture. These people, it seemed, might be better positioned to comment on changes in the trans community regarding notions of sex, gender, and sexuality because they have access to greater numbers of trans people and are more often engaged with others about trans issues.

At the time of the interviews, five of the informants were nonoperative and not taking hormones. Only one seemed certain he never wanted medical intervention, and that was due to a compromised immune system. Of these five, none have seriously considered taking hormones, but four expressed a strong desire for chest surgery that involves removal of the breasts and repositioning of the nipples if necessary. Two could not have surgery for financial reasons and one for medical reasons, and one was hesitant for family and political reasons.[3]

Grounded theory expands our understanding of qualitative research; it relies not only on documentation of interviews but also on the standpoint of the researcher and her or his intimate relationship with the topic of interest. For this reason, I reveal myself as transgendered, born female, with no immediate plans to transition. By "transition," I mean to live as a man by taking hormones and acquiring whatever surgeries necessary. This position as both transgendered and not transitioned gives me a keen interest in the relationship between sex, sex category (perceived sex), and gender and perhaps a voyeuristic interest in hearing what it is like to "cross over"—the difference between internal identity as a man and social interaction when perceived as one. I believe being trans identified gave

Table 1. Sample Characteristics

Pseudonym	Age	Race/ Ethnicity	Current Sexual Preference	Time from Beginning of Physical Transition	Transition Status
Aaron	34	White	Bio women, bio men, FTMs	1 year	Hormones
Billy	30	White	Bio men, FTMs	6 years	Hormones, chest surgery
Brandon	20	African American	FTMs, male-to-female transsexuals, bio women		Nontransitioned
Dick	27	White	Bisexual	2 years	Hormones, chest surgery
Jessica	22	White	Mainly bio women, femmes		Nontransitioned
Jay	27	Chinese American	Bio women		Nontransitioned
Joe	38	Latino	Bio women, FTMs	8 years	Hormones, chest surgery
Kyle	25	White	Bio women		Nontransitioned
Luke	25	White	Mainly bio women		Nontransitioned
Max	21	White	Bio women, femmes	1 year	Hormones, chest surgery
Mick	38	White	Lesbians	2 years	Chest surgery
Mitch	36	White	Bio women, femmes	4 years	Hormones, chest surgery
Pete	34	White	Queer, bisexual	3 years	Hormones, chest surgery
Rogelio	40	Latino/Black	Bio women	6 years living as trans, 1 year taking hormones	Hormones
Sam	30	White	Bio women, bio men, FTMs	4 years	Hormones, chest surgery
Ted	29	White	Pansexual	1 year	Hormones
Terry	45	White	Unknown because of recent transition	3 months	Hormones
Trevor	35	White	Bio women, femmes	1 year	Hormones, chest surgery

Note: Bio women = biological women; bio men = biological men; FTMs = female-to-male transsexual and transgendered people.

me easier access to trans people and made it easier for interviewees to confide in me not only because they felt more at ease but because I had familiarity with common cultural terms, customs, and issues.

Findings

The perceived sex of individuals, whether biological or not, influences the meaning assigned to behavior and the tenor of social and sexual interaction. FTMs illustrate the reliance on both sex and behavior in expressing and interpreting gender. Perceived sex and individual behavior are compensatory, and both are responsible for the performance of gender: When sex is ambiguous or less convincing, there is increased reliance on highly gendered behavior; when sex is obvious, then there is considerably more freedom in behavior. For this reason, sex is not the initiating point for gender. Instead, sex, whether biological or constructed, is an integral aspect of gender. "If the body itself is always seen through social interpretation then sex is not something that is separate from gender but is, rather, that which is subsumable under it" (Nicholson 1994, 79).

As I listened to interviewees, the tension and balance between behavior and appearance, between acting masculine and appearing male, became evident. In general, interviewees confirmed Nicholson's (1994) assertion that (perceived) sex is an important aspect of the construction of gender and that perceived sex is a lens through which behavior is interpreted. However, particular sex characteristics such as a penis or breasts are not as crucial to the perception of sex as their meanings created in both social and sexual interaction.

Generally, after taking hormones, interviewees were perceived as men regardless of behavior and regardless of other conflicting sex signifiers including breasts and, in the case of one interviewee, even when nine months pregnant.[4] The physical assertion of sex is so strong through secondary sex characteristics that gender identity is validated. Interviewees find certain sex characteristics to be particularly important to their social identity as male: "I think it's all about facial hair. It's not about my fetish for facial hair, but socially, when you have facial hair, you can pass regardless of what your body looks like. I mean, I was nine months pregnant walking around and people were like, 'Ooh, that guy's fat' " (Billy).

Another interviewee also finds facial hair to be particularly important to initial gender/sex attribution. In reply to the question, "For you, what is the most important physical change since transitioning," he responds, "Probably facial hair, because nobody even questions facial hair....I've met FTMs that have these huge hips. I mean this guy, he was [shaped] like a top, and he had a full beard. Nobody questioned that he had huge hips, so that is the one key thing. And probably secondary is a receding hairline. Even with a high voice, people accept a high voiced man" (Joe).

As the interviewees became socially recognized as men, they tended to be more comfortable expressing a variety of behaviors and engaging in stereotypically feminine activities, such as sewing or wearing nail polish. The increase in male sex characteristics creates both greater internal comfort with identity and social interactions that are increasingly congruent with sex identity. As a result, some FTMs are able to relax their hypermasculine behavior.

I went through a phase of thinking every behavior I do is going to be cued into somehow by somebody. So, I've got to be hypervigilant about how many long sentences I say, does my voice go up at the end of a sentence, how do I move my hands, am I quick to try and touch someone....And I got to a point where I said, This is who I am....There are feminine attributes and there are masculine attributes that I like and I am going to maintain in my life....If that makes people think, "Oh you're a fag," well great, all my best friends are fags....But when I was first coming out, it was all about "I've got to be perceived as male all the time, no matter what." That bone-crushing handshake and slapping people on the back and all of that silliness. I did all that. (Rogelio)

Like Rogelio, Pete finds transitioning gave him the freedom to express his feminine side: "It was very apparent how masculine a woman I was...and now it's like I've turned into this flaming queen like 90 percent of the time. And so my femininity, I had an outlet for it somehow, but it was in a kind of gay way. It wasn't in a womanly kind of way, it was just femininity. Because I don't think that female equals femininity and male equals masculinity" (Pete).

Sex category and gendered behavior, then, are compensatory; they are both responsible for the social validation of gender identity and require a particular balance. When sex is ambiguous or less convincing, there is increased reliance on highly gendered behavior. When sex category is obvious, then there is considerably more freedom in behavior, as is evident when talking to FTMs about the process of transitioning.

For two interviewees, gay men are particularly valuable role models in deconstructing traditional masculinity and learning to incorporate "feminine" behavior and expression into a male identity:

> So, those fairly feminine men that I have dated have been very undeniably male, but they haven't been a hundred percent masculine all the time, and I think I've learned from my relationships with them to sort of relax. Lighten up a little; nail polish isn't going to kill anybody. I think that I'm more able to be at peace with all of the aspects of myself.... [Now] I'm not going to go out of my way to butch it up. I'm male looking enough to get away with it, whereas when I did that kind of stuff before I transitioned people were like, "Well, you're not butch enough to be a man." (Billy)

FTMs transition for many reasons, but aligning external appearance with internal identity and changing social interaction were the chief reasons given by my interviewees. "Doing gender" (West and Zimmerman 1987) in a way that validates identity relies on both internal and external factors. Being able to look like one feels is key to the contentment of many FTMs. More than interacting with the social world as a man, comfort in one's body can be a chief motivator for FTMs, especially when seeking chest surgery. "I'd say that having a flat chest really seems right, and I really like that. I can throw a T-shirt on and feel absolutely comfortable instead of going [hunching shoulders]. And when I catch my reflection somewhere or look in the mirror, it's like, 'Oh, yeah' instead of, 'Oh, I forgot,' and that's been the most amazing thing... recognizing myself" (Trevor).

Some interviewees believed they would be content to live without any medical treatment or with chest surgery but not hormones as long as they were acknowledged as transgendered by themselves and their social circle. Even for those who were able to achieve a reasonable level of internal comfort, social interaction remained an ongoing challenge. Feeling invisible or not being treated in congruence with their gender identity motivated them to take hormones to experience broader social interaction appropriate to their gender identity. Some FTMs reported the desire to be seen as trans by other FTMs as an important factor in their decision to transition. For others, being

called "ma'am" or treated as a woman in public was particularly grating. Being "she'd" was a constant reminder of the incongruence between social identity and internal gender identity.

> And the longer I knew that I was transgendered, the harder it got to live without changing my body. It's like the acknowledgment wasn't enough for me, and it got to a point where it was no longer enough for the people who knew me intimately to see my male side. It just got to be this really discordant thing between who I knew I was and who the people in my life knew I was... because I was perceived as a woman socially. I was seen as a woman and was treated differently than how I was treated by my friends and the people that I loved.... So finally after a couple of years... I finally decided to take hormones. (Billy)

The potential impact on social interaction is key to the decision to transition. Although for some FTMs, gaining comfort in their body is the crucial element in decision making, for most interviewees, the change in social interaction is the motivating factor. Being treated as a man socially is important enough to risk many other things including loss of family, friends, and career. For other interviewees, though, not wanting to be treated as a man in all social situations motivated them not to transition. "In some ways, I wouldn't really want to give up my access to woman's space, and I think that would be a big reason why I wouldn't do it because I like being around women. I don't feel like I'm women identified, but I'm women centered. So in that sense, I wouldn't want to give up being able to spend a lot of time with women in different contexts that I might lose if I passed as a man" (Jay).

Some interviewees also worried that appearing as a biological man would make them no longer identifiable as trans or queer, making them invisible to their communities. As well, for some of those not transitioning, the potential loss of friends and family outweighed their desire to transition.

As expected, social interaction changed radically after transitioning, but sometimes in ways not anticipated. Whether these changes were positive or negative, expected or not, they still provided FTMs with social validation of their gender identity and the clear message that they were passing.

Changing Interaction

Many transmen found being perceived as a man enlightening. The most often noted changes to social interaction included being treated with more respect, being allowed more conversational space, being included in men's banter, and experiencing an increase in women's fear of them. Some FTMs realized that they would be threatening to women at night and acted accordingly while others were surprised to realize that women were afraid of them. "I remember one time walking up the hill; it was like nine o'clock, and this woman was walking in front of me, and she kept looking back, and I thought, 'What the hell is wrong with that girl?' And then I stopped in my tracks. When I looked at her face clearly under the light, she was afraid. So I crossed the street" (Joe).

For many FTMs, becoming an unquestioned member of the "boys' club" was an educational experience. The blatant expressions of sexism by many men when in the company of each other was surprising to these new men.

> I was on one of the school shuttles on campus and it was at a time when there weren't a lot of people on. There was a male bus driver, myself, and a young woman on the bus, and she had long blonde hair, a very pretty girl. She got off the bus, and there was just me and the bus driver, and the bus driver was reading me as a guy and totally being a sexist pig. I did not know how to deal with it or how to respond, let alone call him on his shit because I wasn't particularly, at this point, feeling like I wanted to get read or anything. So I basically just nodded my head and didn't say anything. (Ted)

One nontransitioned FTM who is usually taken for a man at work also feels pressure to conform and to ward off suspicion by either ignoring or contributing to sexist and homophobic comments when among coworkers. This is in direct contrast to Pete's experience, who became known as an outspoken advocate for women and minorities at his job after transitioning: "I feel like I'm one of the guys, which is really kind of odd. In some ways, it's really affirming, and in some ways, it's really unsettling. In Bellevue [his former job], it was a joke. 'Pete's here, so you better shut up.' Because they're sexist, they're homophobic, they're racist. And I would say, 'This is not something I think you should be talking about in the lunch room.' So I was constantly turning heads because I'm kind of an unusual guy" (Pete).

Acting like a "sensitive new age guy" did not challenge Pete's masculinity or essential maleness but simply defined him as "kind of an unusual guy." He was able to assume this role because his gender was established and supported through his unquestionably male appearance.

Interviewees found that their interactions with both men and women changed as they transitioned. After transitioning, a few FTMs, like the previously quoted interviewee, maintained strong feminist ideals and worked hard to change to appropriate behavior for a feminist man. This was an effort as behavioral expectations for men and butch lesbians differ radically, and what may be attributed to assertiveness in a masculine woman becomes intolerable in a man:

> I found that I had to really, really work to change my behavior. Because there were a lot of skills that I needed to survive as a butch woman in the world that made me a really obnoxious guy. There were things that I was doing that just were not okay. Like in school, talking over people. You know when women speak, they often speak at the same time with each other and that means something really different than when a guy speaks at the same time. And so it wasn't that I changed, it was that people's perceptions of me changed and that in order to maintain things that were important to me as a feminist, I had to really change my behavior. (Billy)

The perception that behavior had not really changed, but people's assignation of meaning to that behavior had, was common in the interviews. That is, what is masculine or feminine, what is assertive or obnoxious, is relative and dependent on social context. And the body—whether one appears male or female—is a key element of social context. These interviews suggest that whether a behavior is labeled masculine or feminine is highly dependent on the initial attribution of sex.

Besides gaining information as insiders, FTMs also felt they gained permission to take up more space as men. Many FTMs transition from the lesbian community, and most in this sample had been butch identified. As a result, they were used to having what they perceived to be a comfortable amount of social space even though they were women. As they transitioned, however, they were surprised at how much social privilege they gained, both conversationally and behaviorally. Terry, a previously high-profile lesbian known for her radical and outspoken politics, reported, "I am getting better service in stores and restaurants, and when I express an opinion, people listen. And that's really weird because I'm not a shy person, so having people sort of check themselves and make more conversational space than they did for me before is really kind of unsettling" (Terry).

As well as being allowed conversational space, many of these new men received special attention and greater respect from heterosexual women because their behavior was gender atypical yet highly valued. They were noticed and rewarded when confronting sexist remarks, understanding women's social position, and performing tasks usually dominated by women. Billy reports an experience in a women's studies class where he was the only man siding with the female students' point of view: "A woman came up to me after class and said, 'Wow, you know you're the most amazing feminist man I've ever met.' I just did not have the heart to ruin that for her. I was just like, you know, there are other guys out there who are capable of this, and it's not just because I'm a transsexual that I can be a feminist" (Billy). The ability to shop for clothes for their girlfriends was cited by two interviewees as a skill much admired. They reported excessive attention from saleswomen as a result of their competence in a usually female-dominated area:

One other thing I have noticed about women, and in particular saleswomen in stores, is that they're always shocked that I can pick out good clothing items either for myself or for someone else, and I don't really need help with that. And I get flirted with constantly by saleswomen, I think largely because they get that I get how to shop. So, they see this guy that's masculine and secure in himself and he's not having to posture, and he can walk up with an armload of women's clothes that he's been picking out....She [the saleswoman] says, "Wow, I want a boyfriend like you." So I get a lot of that. (Mitch)

These accounts underscore the relationship between behavior and appearance. When FTMs are perceived as men, their gender-atypical behavior is not sanctioned or suspect but admired and rewarded. Their perceived status as male allows their masculinity to remain intact even in the face of contradictory evidence. This contrasts with the experience of one FTM not taking hormones who is usually taken for a butch lesbian. Saleswomen at Victoria's Secret treated him rudely when he shopped for lingerie for his girlfriend until he made a greater effort to pass as a man. When passing as a man, he received markedly better service.

Not all FTMs gain social status by being perceived as men. It is a common assumption, bordering on urban legend, that transitioning brings with it improved status, treatment, and financial opportunities. However, having a paper trail including a previous female name and identity can severely compromise job prospects, especially in a professional position.

The reality is we are on the bottom of the economic totem pole. And it does not matter what our educational background is. We could be the most brilliant people on the planet and we're still fucked when it comes to the kinds of jobs that we've gotten or the kinds of advances that we've gotten in the job market. Here I am, I've been out of law school for nearly 10 years, and I'm barely scraping by. And if I go in and apply for a job with a firm, well yeah, they may really like me, but once they start doing any investigating on my background, my old name comes up. (Mitch)

The assumption of a rise in status after sex reassignment also rests largely on the assumption of whiteness. Through my limited sample and conversations with friends, it appears that becoming a Black man is often a step down in status. Rogelio talks about the change in his experience as he becomes more consistently taken for a man:

> I am a Black male. I'm the suspect. I'm the one you have to be afraid of. I'm the one from whom you have to get away, so you have to cross the street, you have to lock your doors. You have to clutch whatever you've got a little closer to your body....It's very difficult to get white FTMs to understand that....[As a Black person], if I go into a store, I am followed. Now I am openly followed; before it was, "Oh, let's hide behind the rack of bread or something so that she won't see us." Now it's, "Oh, it's a guy, he's probably got a gun; he's probably got a knife. We have to know where his hands are at all times." (Rogelio)

Although it is an unpleasant experience, he reports that at least he knows he is consistently passing as a man by the rude treatment he receives from other men in social situations.

Another group of FTMs also experiences being perceived as male as a liability, not a privilege. Even though FTMs can have feminine behavior without calling their maleness into question, feminine behavior does lead to an increase in gay bashing and antigay harassment. FTMs who transitioned from being very butch to being perceived as male generally experienced a radical decline in harassment. Two of these butches were even gay bashed before transitioning because they were perceived to be gay men. With additional male sex characteristics, however, they were no longer perceived to be feminine men. For these men, the transition marked a decline in public harassment and intimidation. However, for more feminine FTMs, the harassment increased after transitioning. Appearing as small, feminine men made them vulnerable to attack. This interviewee reported a marked increase in violence and harassment after transitioning:

> I get gay bashed often. That's my biggest fear right now is male-on-male violence....Once I just got over pneumonia. I was downtown and I was on my way to choir, and some guy looked at me, and I was wondering why he was staring. I looked at him and I looked away. He called me a faggot because I was staring. He said, "Stop looking at me, faggot," and he chased me seven blocks. At first I thought he was just going to run me off, but I kept running and he was running after me as fast as he could and everybody was standing around just kind of staring. And I became really panicked that no one was ever going to help if I really needed it. People yell "faggot" at me all the time. (Dick)

One interviewee experienced about the same level of violence and harassment before and after transitioning. Unfortunately, he was attacked and harassed as a gay man as often before as after transitioning. On one occasion before transitioning, he was followed home and badly beaten by two men who forced their way into his house believing that they were assaulting a gay man: "If I'm with my partner I'm read as straight so I don't have to worry about being jumped as a gay guy, but if I am at a queer event and my partner's not around or if I'm just by myself....But I've just gotten to a point where I'm like, 'Fuck it.' At least now that I am on hormones, I have a little more strength to fight back" (Ted).

In sum then, FTMs are motivated to change their physical presentations for two reasons: First, to become more comfortable with their bodies and achieve greater congruence between identity and appearance and, second, to change social interaction so that it better validates their gender identity, both subculturally and in the wider social world. This strategy to change social interaction is very effective. All FTMs who transitioned noticed a marked change in their social interactions. Not all of these changes in interaction were positive, however. First, the recognition that women are treated poorly compared to men was a shock. Second, being identified as a man was a liability when one was Black or appeared feminine. In other words, the assumption of an increase in privilege only consistently applied to masculine, non-Black men. Even then, the liabilities of being found out, especially on the job, remained.

Sexual Orientation and Gender Identity

Sexual behavior is another site that more clearly explicates the relationship between sex and gender. Sexual orientation is based not solely on the object of sexual and erotic attraction, but also on the sex category and gender performance created in the context of sexual interaction. The performance of gender is crucial in the sexual arena for two reasons: First, because sexuality is expressed through the body, which may or may not align with an individual's gender identity and, second, because heterosexual intercourse can symbolize the social inequalities between men and women. Altering the body alters the sexual relationships of FTMs by changing their gender/sex location in sexual interaction.

Many FTMs change sexual orientation after transitioning or, at the least, find that their object attraction expands to include both sexes. Devor (1997) found a large increase in the number of FTMs who, after transitioning, were sexually attracted to gay men. Why do many transmen change sexual orientation after transitioning? Even the earliest sexuality studies such as the Kinsey report (Kinsey, Pomeroy, and Martin 1948) provide evidence that individuals' attractions, fantasies, and behaviors do not always align with their professed sexual orientation. Currently, a diverse gay culture and the increased ease of living a gay lifestyle have created a wide variety of options for people with attractions to the same or both sexes (Seidman 2002). As well, coinciding with a rise in gay and lesbian cultures in the 1960s and 1970s was a heightened feminist consciousness. For some feminists, sexual relationships with men are problematic because of the power dynamic and broader cultural commentary enacted in heterosexual relations. Bisexual women sometimes find the dynamic untenable and choose to identify as lesbians. Aaron, a previously bisexual woman, confirms:

> I do have an attraction to men; however, when I was a straight woman, I totally gave up going out with men because I was a strong female person and had a lot of problems interacting with men, even in the anarchist community, the punk community. They like tough girls, this strong riot girl persona, and yet when you're in the relationship with those same people, they still have those misogynistic, sexist beliefs about how you're supposed to interact in bed, in the relationship. I just

never fit into that mold and finally said, "Fuck you guys; I'm not going there with you," and just came out as a dyke and lived happily as a dyke.... What I realize coming into the transgendered community myself was that it made so much sense to become transgendered, to become visually male, and to be able to relate to men as a man because then they would at least visually see me as part of who I am in a way that they could not see me when I was female.... That's really exciting for me.... I can still relate to femmes who are attracted to transmen. I can still relate to butches. I can still relate to straight women...but I also get back being able to relate to men, and that's definitely a gift. (Aaron)

In another example, Dick was primarily involved with men and briefly identified as a lesbian before transitioning. He found sexual orientation and gender identity to be inexplicably entangled as he struggled to clarify his identity. When he was a woman and in a long-term relationship with a man, he began to identify as queer. He assumed that his male partner was incongruent with his queer orientation. Over time, he realized that the sex of his partner was not as crucial to his queer identity as was the gender organization of the relationship. Identifying as queer was an attempt to express the desire for interaction congruent with gender identity rather than expressing the desire for a partner of a particular sex.

> [Transitioning] makes a difference because it's queer then, and it's not locating me as a straight woman, which is not going to work. The way that I came out as queer, I thought it was about sexuality but it's really about gender. I was in a relationship with a man who I had been with for a couple of years...and then I started figuring out this thing about queerness, and I could not put my finger on it and I couldn't articulate it, but I knew that I couldn't be in a relationship with him.... But what I figured out a lot later was that it wasn't about not wanting to be with a guy; it was about not wanting to be the girl. (Dick)

Heterosexuality, then, is a problem for these FTMs not because of object choice but because of the gendered meaning created in intimate and sexual interaction that situates them as women. Most of the FTMs in the sample who changed sexual orientation or attractions after transitioning did not previously identify as bisexual or heterosexual. Two key changes allowed them to entertain the idea of sexual involvement with men. First, the relationship and power dynamic between two men is very different from that between a man and a woman. Second, in heterosexual interactions previous to transitioning, the sexual arena only reinforced FTMs' social and sexual position as women, thus conflicting with their gender identity. After transitioning, sexual interaction with men can validate gender identity:

> So, it's okay for me to date men who were born men because I don't feel like they treat me weird. I couldn't stand this feminization of me, especially in the bedroom. Now I feel like I actually have a sex drive. Hormones didn't make me horny, the combination of me transitioning and taking hormones made me have maybe a normal sex drive. (Dick)

> I've never totally dismissed men as sexual partners in general, but I knew that I'm very much dyke identified. But I think being masculine and having a male recognize your masculinity is just as sexy as a woman recognizing your masculinity, as opposed to a man relating to you as a woman. (Trevor)

I do not wish to imply that many lesbians are simply repressed bisexuals or heterosexuals using sex reassignment to cope with their sexual attraction toward men. Instead, I am arguing that the sexual interaction between FTMs and men is decidedly different from heterosexual interaction. The type of male partner generally changes as well—from straight to gay. For many FTMs, their change in sexual orientation and the degree of that change were a welcome surprise. Some appreciated the opportunity to interact with men on a sexual level that felt free of the power dynamics in heterosexual relations. Others were happy to date other FTMs or biological men as a way of maintaining their queer identity. Several interviewees who transitioned from a lesbian identity did not like appearing heterosexual and identified as queer

regardless of their object choice because their body and gender status disrupted the usual sexuality paradigm. Still, they struggled with their invisibility as queer after transitioning. "Being with an FTM, we're the same, it's very queer to me....A lot of times, I'm bugged if I walk down the street with a girl and we seem straight....I think that's the worst part about transitioning is the queerness is really obliterated from you. It's taken away. I mean you're pretty queer, somebody walking down the street with a guy with a cunt is queer, but it's invisible" (Joe).

In his work with male-to-female transsexuals, Lewins (1995) discussed the relationship between gender and sexual orientation in the context of symbolic interactionism. The sexual arena is a site for creating and validating sex and gender identity because "when we desire someone and it is reciprocated, the positive nature of continuing interaction reaffirms and, possibly for some, confirms their gender identity" (Lewins 1995, 38). Sexual interaction, depending on the sexual orientation of the partner, is key to validating the male identity of FTMs. Whether that partner is a heterosexual or bisexual woman or a gay man, the interaction that involves the FTM as male confirms gender identity.

Conclusion

Trans people are in the unique position of experiencing social interaction as both women and men and illustrate the relativity of attributing behavior as masculine or feminine. Behavior labeled as assertive in a butch can be identified as oppressive in a man. And unremarkable behavior for a woman such as shopping or caring for children can be labeled extraordinary and laudable when performed by a man. Although generally these new men found increased social privilege, those without institutional privilege did not. Becoming a Black man or a feminine man was a social liability affecting interaction and increasing risk of harassment and harm. Whether for better or worse, being perceived as a man changed social interaction and relationships and validated gender identity.

In addition to illustrating the relativity of assignation of meaning to behavior, these interviews illustrate the relativity of sexual orientation. Sexual orientation is based not exclusively on object attraction but also on the gendered meanings created in sexual and romantic interaction. Sexual orientation can be seen as fluid, depending on both the perceived sex of the individuals and the gender organization of the relationship.

This study of a small group of FTMs helps clarify the relationship between sex and gender because it does not use sex as the initiating point for gender and because most respondents have experienced social interaction as both men and women. Much sociological theory regarding gender assumes that gender is the behavioral, socially constructed correlate of sex, that gender is "written on the body." Even if there are case studies involving occasional aberrations, gender is generally characterized as initiating from sex. With this study, though, the opposite relationship is apparent. Sex is a crucial aspect of gender, and the gendered meaning assigned to behavior is based on sex attribution. People are not simply held accountable for a gender performance based on their sex (see West and Zimmerman 1987); the gendered meaning of behavior is dependent on sex attribution. Whether behavior is defined as masculine or feminine, laudable or annoying, is dependent on sex category. Doing gender, then, does not simply involve performing appropriate masculinity or femininity based on sex category. Doing gender involves a balance of both doing sex and performing masculinity and femininity. When there is no confusion or ambiguity in the sex performance, individuals are able to have more diverse expressions of masculinity and femininity. This balance between behavior and appearance in expressing gender helps explain the changing behavior of FTMs as they transition as well as the presence of men and women with a diversity of gendered behaviors and display.

Notes

1. Interviewees do not necessarily identify as female-to-male transsexual and transgendered people (FTMs). There are many terms that more closely describe individuals' personal identity and experience including "trans," "boy dyke," "trannyboy," "queer," "man," "FTM," "transsexual," and "gender bender." For simplicity and clarity, I will use "FTM" and "trans" and apologize to interviewees who feel this does not adequately express their sex/gender location.

2. See Lucal (1999) for an excellent discussion regarding interpersonal strategies for disrupting the gender order.

3. Politically, some feminist FTMs express discomfort at becoming members of the most privileged economic and social class (white men).

4. After taking testosterone, an individual appears male even if he or she discontinues use. The interviewee who became pregnant discontinued hormones to ovulate and continue his pregnancy, then began hormones again after childbirth.

References

Auerbach, Judith D. 1999. From the SWS president: Gender as proxy. *Gender & Society* 13:701–703.

Bolin, Anne. 1988. *In search of Eve: Transsexual rites of passage.* South Hadley, MA: Bergin & Garvey.

Bornstein, Kate. 1995. *Gender outlaw: On men, women, and the rest of us.* New York: Vintage.

Califia, Patrick. 1997. *Sex changes: The politics of transgenderism.* San Francisco: Cleis Press.

Cromwell, Jason. 1999. *Transmen and FTMs: Identities, bodies, genders, and sexualities.* Urbana: University of Illinois Press.

Delphy, Christine. 1993. Rethinking sex and gender. *Women's Studies International Forum* 16:1–9.

Devor, Holly [Aaron Devor]. 1989. *Gender blending: Confronting the limits of duality.* Bloomington: Indiana University Press.

———. 1997. *FTM: Female-to-male transsexuals in society.* Bloomington: Indiana University Press.

———. 1998. Sexual-orientation identities, attractions, and practices of female-to-male transsexuals. In *Current concepts in transgender identity,* edited by Dallas Denny. New York: Garland.

———. 1999. Book review of "Second skins: The body narratives of transsexuality" by Jay Prosser. *Journal of Sex Research* 36:207–208.

Devor, Aaron H. 2004. Witnessing and mirroring: A fourteen stage model of transsexual identity formation. *Journal of Gay and Lesbian Psychotherapy* 8:41–67.

Ekins, Richard. 1997. *Male femaling: A grounded theory approach to cross-dressing and sex-changing.* New York: Routledge.

Fausto-Sterling, Anne. 1993. The five sexes: Why male and female are not enough. *Sciences* 33(2): 20–24.

———. 2000. *Sexing the body: gender politics and the construction of sexuality.* New York: Basic Books.

Feinberg, Leslie. 1998. *Trans liberation: Beyond pink or blue.* Boston: Beacon.

Halberstam, Judith. 1998. *Female masculinity.* Durham, NC: Duke University Press.

Herdt, Gilbert. 1981. *Guardians of the flutes: Idioms of masculinity.* New York: McGraw-Hill.

Kanter, Rosabeth Moss. 1977. *Men and women of the corporation.* New York: Basic Books.

Kessler, Suzanne J. 1990. The medical construction of gender: Case management of intersexed infants. *Signs: Journal of Women in Culture and Society* 16:3–27.

Kessler, Suzanne J., and Wendy McKenna. 1978. *Gender: An ethnomethodological approach.* New York: John Wiley.

Kinsey, Alfred C., Wardell B. Pomeroy, and Clyde E. Martin. 1948. *Sexual behavior in the human male.* Philadelphia: W. B. Saunders.

Lewins, Frank. 1995. *Transsexualism in society: A sociology of male-to-female transsexuals.* Melbourne: Macmillan Education Australia.

Lorber, Judith. 1994. *Paradoxes of gender.* New Haven, CT: Yale University Press.

———. 1999. Embattled terrain: Gender and sexuality. In *Revisioning gender*, edited by Myra Marx Ferree, Judith Lorber, and Beth Hess. Thousand Oaks, CA: Sage.

Lucal, Betsy. 1999. What it means to be gendered me: Life on the boundaries of a dichotomous gender system. *Gender & Society* 13:781–97.

Messner, Michael A. 2000. Barbie girls versus sea monsters: Children constructing gender. *Gender & Society* 14:765–84.

Nicholson, Linda. 1994. Interpreting gender. *Signs: Journal of Women in Culture and Society* 20:79–105.

Parker, Richard, and Peter Aggleton. 1999. *Culture, society and sexuality: A reader.* Los Angeles: UCLA Press.

Prosser, Jay. 1998. *Second skins: The body narratives of transsexuality.* New York: Columbia University Press.

Rubin, Henry. 2003. *Self-made men: Identity and embodiment among transsexual men.* Nashville, TN: Vanderbilt University Press.

Schippers, M. 2000. The social organization of sexuality and gender in alternative hard rock: An analysis of intersectionality. *Gender & Society* 14:747–64.

Scott, Joan. 1988. *Gender and the politics of history.* New York: Columbia University Press.

Seidman, Steven. 2002. *Beyond the closet: The transformation of gay and lesbian life.* New York: Routledge.

Thorne, Barrie. 1993. *Gender play: Girls and boys in school.* New Brunswick, NJ: Rutgers University Press.

West, Candace, and Don Zimmerman. 1987. Doing gender. *Gender & Society* 1:125–51.

"That's Just How It Is": A Gendered Analysis of Masculinity and Femininity Ideologies in Adolescent Girls' and Boys' Heterosexual Relationships

DEBORAH L. TOLMAN, BRIAN R. DAVIS, AND CHRISTIN P. BOWMAN

The goal of reaching gender equity in many dimensions of young peoples' lives has appeared ever more tangible recently, such as in education (U.S. Department of Education, 2012) and participation in sports (National Federation of High Schools, 2014). Yet adolescents' heterosexual relationships remain a conspicuous exception to this trend. Girls' emerging sexuality continues to incite panic and punishment, while girls themselves contend with stigma for suspected "inappropriate" sexual expression (Fahs, Dudy, & Stage, 2013). Conversely, boys are consistently portrayed as either acquiring sexual experience as a commodity (Kimmel, 2008) or easily provoked by girls in "provocative" attire, barely able to keep uncontrollable sexual impulses in check (Pascoe, 2011). A persistent gender hierarchy seems intransigent in the lives of all boys and girls despite periodic public sentiment and research recognizing girls as sexual beings (Levy, 2006) or boys as relational (Way, 2011).

The dominant epidemiological and behavioral paradigm for adolescent sexuality research has been rooted in a gender difference model—utilizing gender as a population parameter to identify who is engaging in what sexual and relational behaviors and/or taking what kinds of risks and suffering negative consequences. Yet this generally quantitative body of research has remained remarkably decontextualized, having neither inquired about nor explained the myriad ways in which gender is instrumental within adolescents' heterosexual relationships (Tolman & McClelland, 2011). In this mixed-methods study, we depart from the gender difference model in pursuing an approach of *gendered analysis*—an approach anchored in feminist theories of gender ideologies and institutionalized heterosexuality—to address the question, *How and why does a gender hierarchy continue to exist in adolescent heterosexual relationships and sexuality?*

Gender as Ideologies: How Gender Matters

A gendered analysis is predicated on an understanding that gender is not reducible to an embodied trait or a social role; rather, gender is understood as a socially constructed system of ideologies about masculinity and femininity (Connell, 1987; Hill Collins, 2004; Pleck, Sonenstein, & Ku, 1993; Tolman & Porche, 2000). Femininity and masculinity as ideologies describe interlocking sets of practices, norms, beliefs, and mandates that work in tandem to organize and regulate gender-appropriate emotional expressions, behaviors, bodies, and sexuality that are anchored in a politics of gender and thus possible to change (Budgeon, 2014; Schippers, 2007). Femininity ideology comprises qualities girls are to enact, including being responsive and

Deborah L. Tolman, Brian R. Davis, and Christin P. Bowman, "'That's Just How it Is': A Gendered Analysis of Masculinity and Femininity Ideologies in Adolescent Girls' and Boys' Heterosexual Relationships," *Journal of Adolescent Research* (2015): 0743558415587325. Copyright © 2015 by Deborah L. Tolman, Brian R. Davis, and Christin P. Bowman. Reprinted by permission of SAGE Publications.

caring, avoiding conflict and anger, preserving relationships, curbing hunger (for food, sex), having and maintaining a body that conforms with particular standards of beauty, and not expressing sexuality (Bartky, 1991; Bordo, 1993; Brown & Gilligan, 1992). By contrast, masculinity ideology comprises qualities boys are to enact, including being assertive and exerting power over others, protecting and providing for female partners, having irrepressible sexual desire for women, and avoiding feminine behaviors or attitudes such as emotional expressions of connection with or sexual desire for men (Connell, 1987; Kimmel, 2008).

Functioning in tandem, these ideologies create and reproduce a gender hierarchy (Rubin, 1984). Gender is constituted and organized such that characteristics of femininity are undesirable and subordinate to those of masculinity, the latter being more valued and the norm by which all humans are compared, such that men who do not comply are marginalized and women who evidence them are punished (Butler, 1990; Rich, 1980; Rubin, 1984). These unrealistic, idealized versions of femininity for girls and masculinity for boys are *hegemonic*—seemingly the only way to be an appropriate man or woman, obscuring other possibilities in adolescents' relationships and sexuality (Schippers, 2007; Tolman, 2006; Rubin, 1984). While a growing body of research continues to document a variety of expressions of masculinities and femininities among young people, such expressions are still bound to and engaged with these hegemonic injunctions even as they are resisted or "queered" (Bordini & Sperb, 2013; Renold, 2006, 2007; Ringrose, 2013; Ringrose, Harvey, Gill, & Livingstone, 2013). Throughout this article, our references are to these hegemonic forms of femininity and masculinity ideology.

Interlocking Dimensions of Institutionalized Heterosexuality

This gender hierarchy is continually reproduced, maintained, and enforced through institutionalized heterosexuality—not merely a sexual orientation but a system of beliefs, behaviors, and relationships, of which gender hierarchy is a constituent part, that is presumed to organize all aspects of society, from schools and the workplace to the State and other formal and informal institutions (Jackson, 2006). Enactments and management of gender-appropriate conduct, beliefs, norms, and other practices are expected, and surveillance to ensure compliance by individuals and institutions is constant (Bartky, 1991; Butler, 1990); violations of these mandates often result in punishment and other negative consequences that can take the form of isolation, bullying, or violence (Kimmel, 2008; Rich, 1980). While by no means a comprehensive accounting of a gender hierarchy, two particular interlocking dimensions and reproducing forces of institutionalized heterosexuality are especially salient for adolescent relationships and a focus of the present study: (a) the belief that boys can and should be coercive in their relationships (Pleck et al., 1993) and (b) a broad array of conventions for girls to enact on their own behalf and in relation to boys to ensure that heterosexual relationships are properly organized.

Expectations and, in some sense, acceptability of threatened and actual coercion by boys can be understood as complementary to the expectation that girls place high value on and work to maintain unequal heterosexual relationships (Burns, Futch, & Tolman, 2011; Hlavka, 2014; Renold, 2006; Tolman, Spencer, Rosen-Reynoso, & Porche, 2003). Undergirding these expectations are the ways gender hierarchy plays out in the realm of sexuality. While some adolescent girls may be more willing to defy or carefully navigate these expectations and explore their sexual feelings than in previous generations (Holland & Thomson, 2010; Renold & Ringrose, 2008; Roye, Tolman, & Snowden, 2013), adolescent sexuality is more generally circumscribed by a sexual double standard, such that boys are expected to be sexually demanding and out of control, while girls are to be gatekeepers whose desire for sex is minimal or relatively unimportant (Butler, 1990; Jackson, 2006; Kreager & Staff, 2009; Rich, 1980; Rubin, 1984; Schippers, 2007; Tolman, 2006; Warner, 1993). Yet male coercion and a number of feminine conventions for heterosexual relationships extend beyond the sexual double standard. Thus, while the sexual double standard constitutes one of the ways in which a gender hierarchy continues to organize adolescent heterosexual relationships, it does not represent a comprehensive account.

Adolescent Sexuality and Heterosexual Relationships

Findings from feminist research support a theoretical framework of institutionalized heterosexuality. Adolescent girls and boys continue to be socialized into gendered sexualities (Mahalik, Burns, & Syzdek, 2007; Saewyc, 2012; Striepe & Tolman, 2003). The bulk of this almost exclusively qualitative research has focused on adolescent girls' sexual subjectivity, defined as a girl's sense of herself as a sexual being and actor (e.g., Fine, 1988; Holland, Ramazanoglu, Sharpe, & Thomson, 1992; Tolman, 2002). Institutionalized heterosexuality has long been implicated also in girls' constant vigilance of themselves and other girls, as well as social ambivalence about boys, and is tempered by distress at and/or strategies for how to manage these imperatives (Bordini & Sperb, 2013; Burns et al., 2011; Renold & Ringrose, 2008; Ringrose et al., 2013; Holland & Thomson, 2010). More recently, a growing parallel literature on adolescent boys' perceptions of their own and girls' sexuality has emerged (e.g., Dworkin & O'Sullivan, 2007; Martino, 2000; Renold, 2007). These studies document that boys continue to feel pressure to act as sexual predators and to establish and maintain hegemonic masculinity in heterosexual relationships with girls, especially through coercion and possessiveness, even when they are uncomfortable about these pressures or, in rare cases, refuse to abide by them (Epstein, Calzo, Smiler, & Ward, 2009; Kimmel, 2008; Tolman et al., 2003, Way, 2011).

This gender separation in feminist research designs has produced a deeper understanding of how femininity ideology constrains girls and masculinity ideology constrains boys. Yet only a handful of studies have included *both* boys and girls to track and understand adolescent heterosexual relationships (Hird & Jackson, 2001; Holland, Ramazanoglu, Sharpe & Thomson, 1998/2004; Martin, 1996; see Renold, 2006, 2007, for a study of young children). The most significant example of

this work was conducted two decades ago in the United Kingdom by Holland et al. (1992, 1994, 1998/2004, 2000, 2003). The authors found that girls and boys described "unequal relationships in which conventional [or hegemonic] masculinity and femininity are mutually dependent," and in particular that girls "collude[ed] with their male sexual partners in . . . reproduce[ing] . . . male power" (Holland et al., 1998/2004, p. 156), dubbing this socialization process and effect "the male-in-the-head." No studies have since explored adolescent heterosexual relationships using a gendered analysis that includes both girls and boys and interrogates the roles of both masculinity and femininity ideologies.

Gender Ideologies and Adolescent Relationships: A Mixed-Methods Study

These previous studies suggest the need for a gendered analysis of the ways in which expectations about *girls'* enactments of femininity ideology and of *boys'* enactments of masculinity ideology may *each* play a role in the formation and maintenance of heterosexual relationships for *both* adolescent girls and boys. In the present mixed-methods study, we attempt to answer two distinct research questions:

Research Question 1: Do ideologies of masculinity and femininity each play a role in both adolescent girls' and boys' beliefs about relationships and sexuality? And if so,

Research Question 2: In what ways do masculinity and femininity ideologies operate in boys' and girls' lived experiences of those relationships and navigation of sexuality?

In Study 1, we establish the correlational and explanatory power of endorsement of both gender ideologies by boys and by girls in relation to gender-salient outcomes. In Study 2, we illustrate through a thematically informed narrative gendered analysis *how* hegemonic masculinity and femininity ideologies work as a gender hierarchy, generating the inequitable relationships that reproduce institutionalized heterosexuality. We conclude by discussing how both sets of findings together provide a way of explaining how the documented ongoing unequal gender hierarchy persists in adolescents' heterosexual relationships and sexual encounters.

Study I

We first explored the role of gender ideologies in heterosexual relationships and related outcome measures for both adolescent girls and boys. Consistent with an analytic framework of gendered analysis, rather than identifying gender differences in a single set of common outcomes, such as age at first intercourse or relationship status, we investigated two distinct gendered outcomes. For boys, we chose endorsement of male coercion in heterosexual relationships ("male coercion"; Epstein et al., 2009; Kimmel, 2008; Tolman et al., 2004; Way, 2011). For girls, we chose conventions that apply to girls in the heterosexual relationship script ("conventions for girls in heterosexual relationships"; Burns et al., 2011; Fine, 1988; Holland et al., 1994; Kim et al., 2007; Renold & Ringrose, 2008). Our goal in selecting only two gendered outcomes was not to achieve a comprehensive understanding of all domains of institutionalized heterosexuality but to test the hypothesis that these complementary yet distinct gendered outcomes for adolescent boys and girls will be explained by both ideologies of masculinity for boys and femininity for girls. Specifically, we anticipated that (a) both gender ideologies would predict boys' endorsement of male coercion and girls' endorsement of feminine conventions in heterosexual relationships, and (b) masculinity ideology would be a more powerful predictor for boys and femininity ideology a more powerful predictor for girls. . . .

Results and Discussion

As there were relatively few participants in any one of the various race/ethnicity groups and reducing such data to "white/non-white" results in a loss of interpretive capacity, the race/ethnicity variable was not included in this analysis. Additional demographic variables were omitted from analysis due to participant non-response in excess of 10% of the total sample; analyses of non-response data revealed no patterns in relation to other study variables for either girls or boys. . . .

Adolescent girls

As seen in Table 1, girls who highly endorsed masculinity . . . and/or femininity . . . ideologies also highly endorsed feminine heterosexual conventions . . . As predicted, both femininity and masculinity ideologies remained significant predictors for girls, with the final model accounting for 29% of girls' endorsement of feminine heterosexual conventions . . . Contrary to our second hypothesis, follow-up analyses . . . revealed that masculinity ideology . . . was a stronger predictor of feminine heterosexual conventions for girls than femininity ideology in terms of body self-objectification . . .

Adolescent boys

As also seen in Table 1, boys who endorsed higher levels of femininity . . . and/or masculinity . . . ideologies also tended to highly endorse male coercion in heterosexual relationships . . . Masculinity and femininity ideologies were each found to be significant predictors for boys, with the final model accounting for 37% of boys' endorsement of male coercion in heterosexual relationships . . . Follow-up comparison . . . found femininity ideology . . . to be a slightly stronger predictor than masculinity ideology for boys . . . however, while this difference was statistically significant, it was of low substantive significance . . .

In these analyses, we found that, as predicted, both masculinity and femininity ideologies contributed to explaining the gender-salient outcomes of both girls' endorsement of feminine heterosexual conventions and boys' endorsement of male coercion in relationships. For boys, both masculinity and femininity ideologies contributed to explaining endorsement of male coercion. Unexpectedly, however, masculinity ideology played an especially strong role over and above femininity ideology for girls. Taken together, these analyses suggest that both masculinity and femininity ideologies contribute to outcomes salient for girls and for boys in the reproduction of a gender inequality in relationships but that these gender ideologies do so in distinct and hierarchically complementary ways for girls and boys.

TABLE I. Girls' Feminine Heterosexual Conventions and Boys' Endorsement of Male Coercion in Relation to Gender Ideologies.

Girls (n = 144)

Variable	Zero-order r				Model 1		Model 2	
	AMIRS	AFIS (ORB)	AFIS (ISR)	FEMCON	b	β	b	β
AFIS (ISR)				.25**	.07	.12	.05	.10
AFIS (ORB)			.49***	.31***	.13	.25**	.09	.18*
AMIRS		.19*	.13	.49***			.51	.45***
Adjusted R^2						.10		.29
R^2 change						.11		.19
F change						8.75***		38.29***
M	2.80	1.51	1.85	2.85				
SD	0.81	0.37	0.42	0.78				

Boys (n = 106)

Variable	Zero-order r			Model 1		Model 2	
	AFIS-B	AMIRS	COERC	b	β	b	β
AMIRS			.52***	.53	.52***	.34	.34***
AFIS-B		.46***	.54***			.48	.38***
Adjusted R^2					.26		.37
R^2 change					.27		.11
F change					35.58***		18.78***
M	1.97	1.86	1.81				
SD	0.37	0.46	0.47				

Note: AFIS (ISR) = Adolescent Femininity Ideology Scale (Inauthentic-Self-in-Relationships) subscale; AFIS (ORB) = Adolescent Femininity Ideology Scale (Objectified-Relationship–With-Body) subscale; AMIRS = Adolescent Masculinity Ideology in Relationships Scale; FEMCON = Feminine Heterosexual Conventions; AFIS-B = Adolescent Femininity Ideology Scale, Boys' version; COERC = Male Coercion in Heterosexual Relationships; b = unstandardized regression coefficients; β = standardized regression coefficients.

*p < .05. **p < .01. ***p < .001.

487

Study 2

The findings that ideologies of femininity and particularly masculinity contributed significantly to distinct outcomes for girls and boys provide empirical support for our gendered analysis approach with both girls and boys. Yet these findings also point to a complexity in how gender ideologies function in tandem beyond our two previously operationalized dimensions of institutionalized heterosexuality. Thus, in Study 2, we qualitatively explored a second and broader research question: *In what ways do masculinity and femininity ideologies operate in boys' and girls' lived experiences of heterosexual relationships?*

Method

Participants and procedure

. . . A total of 35 girls (45% White, 33% Latina, 18% bi- or multi-racial, and 3% other) and 18 boys (61% White, 17% Latino, 6% Asian/Pacific Islander, 11% bi- or multi-racial, and 6% other) comprised the sample. Participants were individually interviewed in hour-long sessions conducted in private locations on campus during regular school hours. All four interviewers were female; our previous experience has demonstrated that boys are as willing as girls to narrate expressions of both physical desire and emotional connection with female as with male interviewers (Tolman et al., 2004). . . .

Results and Discussion

We report two key findings: (a) Both boys and girls recognized and/or voiced both masculinity and femininity ideologies in narrating their distinctly different observations and navigations of heterosexual relationships and sexuality, often evidencing confusion at, or in a few cases outright rejection of, these ideologies; and (b) even in cases of doubt, confusion, or rejection, these narrations illuminate how these two ideologies work in tandem to perpetuate and reproduce the gender hierarchies that anchor institutionalized heterosexuality in these adolescents' heterosexual relationships. In light of space limitations, we have chosen to present four extensive exemplars with carefully explicated interpretation of these gendered patterns: two

exemplars of each key finding, one each from a girl and a boy. Where appropriate, we have chosen "outlier" exemplars in which more overt expressions of gendered experience were evident, which serve the useful function of clarifying and amplifying normative or otherwise subtle processes (Maxwell & Miller, 2008). This approach enabled us to render key aspects of the subtle, complex, and interdependent ways in which these gender ideologies are utilized and experienced by boys and girls clearly audible as well as highlight how they operate in tandem to reify, question, or resist institutionalized heterosexuality. All names reported herein are pseudonyms chosen by participants.

Girls' and boys' discomfiting engagements with masculinity and femininity ideologies

In line with our findings in Study 1, we found that both girls and boys utilized both masculinity and femininity ideologies in describing their observations of, and in narrating their own, heterosexual relationships. In particular, their narratives reflected the deployment of these gender ideologies, often through the sexual double standard that privileged boys' sexuality while circumscribing girls' sexuality. Both girls and boys narrated denigrating characterizations of girls who did not restrict their sexuality to monogamous, heterosexual relationships—that is, girls who engaged in or showed desire for sex or who evidenced interest in sex outside of monogamous relationships. At the same time, both girls and boys naturalized boys who appeared to act as sexual aggressors, conveyed having irrepressible sexual desire, or demonstrated an absence of desire for relationships. These narratives often demonstrated that boys enacted these personas and behaviors for the approval of their male peers, while girls conversely "earned" and then had to negotiate the negative consequences of being labeled "sluts."

Yet even as both boys and girls voiced this duality in their observations and in their own experiences as a taken-for-granted reality of adolescent social life, we also noted a pervasive confusion about or questioning of these judgments. While explaining the "logic" of how the sexual double standard operates, particularly in their own experiences with it, *both* boys and girls became tongue-tied, lost their train of thought, and were unable to finish sentences. As they laid it out, they recognized the contradiction and inequity of punishment for girls perceived to be enacting sexual expression as contrasted with either admiration for boys as "players" who commodify or collect sex or admonishment for boys who do not.

Boys observed how these social rules and consequences are ubiquitous and yet also problematic, but they could not put their fingers on why:

> Some of my guy friends compete with each other to see who has more girls and who has slept with more girls . . . Like they'll make bets sayin' how much—how—how many girls in one month and they'll make bets . . . they put like 10 bucks on every other girl more that they got than they said they were gonna get . . . They have no heart for girls. Like so many—they don't really see how many girls' hearts they are actually breaking . . . I can't do that to girls . . . I mean, a lot of girls like—don't know. But then, there's also some girls—you also got the girls out there that—you know—that actually like to have sex and they don't care who they have it with and they just want to have an orgasm. You know what I'm sayin'? . . . I feel bad for some girls that are tramps 'cause they're really nice girls . . . And then like after that, all the boys know that, "Oh she's—she'll—well you know she's—she—she's easy or whatever. I'll go up to her and you know—kick G's [have sex] with her and then—you know—go to her house after and do whatever [laughs]." . . . And before you know it, you've got the reputation of bein' a tramp . . . Some girls—that's just the way—there's not a lot of girls like that. All girls, I think, like have a good heart in them and they really like—they—they don't have—I don't know. (Ryan, aged 16, White)

Ryan, who had been in a 1-year heterosexual relationship with regular sexual encounters, observed that girls are treated as objects of sexual conquest, for which his friends "compete . . . to see who has more girls and slept with more girls," going so far as to "make bets" about their counts. He recognized that girls have sexual desire and pleasure: "Some girls . . . actually like to have sex . . . and just want to have an orgasm," outside the scope of a

relationship. However, he invoked the sexual double standard, calling such girls "tramps" because "they don't care who they have it with." Ryan thereby acknowledged, if not fully recognized, the demands of femininity ideology, juxtaposing this description of appropriate enactment of femininity against the complementary—and unequal—enactment of masculinity by boys who know such girls as "easy" and available, while they themselves are socially encouraged to seek sex without commitment. He expressed doubt and confusion by bookending his explanation of how the social dynamic unfolds with the phrase, "I don't know." Narrative analysts argue that such invocation of "I don't know" suggests a tentative knowledge about the point that is made (Brown & Gilligan, 1992; Tolman, 2002; Way, 2011), which Ryan in essence took back by denying that knowledge—"I don't know"—at the end of his observation.

Many girls, along with a few boys, by contrast, narrated a recognition and frustration with an unfair sexual double standard:

> You'll see people in the hallway and you'll be like, "She's a slut." And they'll be like, "Why?" And you'll be like, "She slept with like four dudes and like she's 13," or something like that. . . . [Guys] get good reputations when they do it. . . . It's unfair. Like if I sleep with a guy, I'll get called a slut from a girl. But then like that girl will go with that guy too, and like the guy's friends are like, "Yeah, yo. You're sweet"—Something like that. You know what I mean? (Smiley, aged 17, White)

Smiley, who has had sex and boyfriends (at least one who was physically abusive), knew that if a girl "slept with four dudes," or if she herself "sleeps with a guy," she gets called "a slut," while the boy involved earns respect from his friends. She judged this gendered system "unfair" as girls are punished for sexual activity, while boys support one another in sexual conquest. If a girl breaks up with one boy to go out with another, the rejected boyfriend "will still be happy for the other guy but he'll hate you." Like Ryan, Smiley explained that guys "get good reputations" for precisely the same sexual actions for which girls get labeled "sluts" with the rhetorical question, "You know what I mean?" In this way,

Smiley referenced this inequity as shared knowledge requiring no further explanation (Brown & Gilligan, 1992; Tolman, 2002).

Both girls and boys demonstrated an array of perspectives on gender ideologies as they play out in the sexual double standard, with some uncritically embracing it, others expressing that it is somehow wrong and unfair, and a few outright naming and rejecting it. Yet virtually all the participants, girls and boys alike, expressed confusion about the origins of these gendered expectations and/or why they persist. While the sexual double standard was the firm constant against which they positioned their own experiences and observations of how heterosexual relationships and gendered sexuality are expected to "work," both girls and boys narrated conflict in attempting to make sense of it. Smiley described this gender hierarchy as "unfair" and "weird." Ryan evidenced considerable confusion, claiming that he himself "can't do that [use and collect girls for sexual purposes and 'break . . . girls' hearts']." Ryan's confusion centered on the binary of "tramps" and "really nice girls" who challenged his simultaneous assertion that "all girls . . . have a good heart." Caught in this dilemma, Ryan's recourse was to conclude, simply, "I don't know." Even girls and boys who expressed their desire for egalitarian relationships in which the thoughts, feelings, and sexual agency of both partners are recognized expressed puzzlement over the ubiquity of these gender ideologies and the subsequent inequities they produce.

Girls' and boys' different enactment and management of gender ideologies

Also mirroring the quantitative findings, we found the *balance* of these two ideologies in girls' and boys' narratives to be different. For girls, boys' enactments of masculinity ideology were at the forefront of how they navigated their relationships and sexual decisions and how they managed their own enactments of femininity ideology. That is, many of the girls' narratives included their own management of femininity ideology *in tandem with* and sometimes *subjugated to* their expectations of the boys' enactments of masculinity ideology. Coercion of varying intensity was a central

theme, pervasive in these girls' descriptions of their own and other girls' experiences with relationships and sexuality. Most of the girls described coercion that was verbal and emotional rather than physical. A handful of girls described physical coercion along a continuum from verbal threats to physical harm. The following stark example is of more overt coercion and makes very clear the process by which the co-constitutive functioning of masculinity and femininity ideologies produces and sustains inequity in heterosexual relationships:

> [My boyfriend and I] would just have fights. Like verbal fights. And I'm very like, emotional, like . . . We'd fight over silly things . . . he was just like verbally, physically, emotionally, just all mental stuff. Like he was really abusing me. And like he would sit there and comment, "Don't wear this. Don't wear that." You know. "Wha—What are you trying to do?" He would go to my work and make sure that I'm not talking to a boy, like not talking to them, but just you know, he'd want them to know that I am his. You know what I mean. And like, we'd just like rough around and stuff, but I'd end up always getting hurt . . . And we f—we fought. And I was like, "Just get out of my house." And he's like, "Why do you do this? Blah, blah, blah." And he just smacked me. And I was like, "All right you can leave now." Of course, I give into him, so he left. And then I felt bad. It's freezing out there. And I'm like, "You gotta come inside. I'm like, I'll call a ride or whatever. If you want to stay and talk about things, then we'll work things out." (Juliana, aged 16, White)

Juliana, who had a 2-year relationship inclusive of regular sexual encounters with the boy described above, voiced the interplay of masculinity and femininity ideologies to make sense of her relationship with a controlling and abusive boyfriend. She pointed out several of her boyfriend's controlling behaviors, such as his demands that she not "wear this [or] wear that" and "not talk to a boy." She narrated his coercive behavior: "He was really abusing me . . . verbally, physically, emotionally." The logic Juliana articulates is the logic of masculinity ideology: He controls and coerces her, because "he'd want them [his male peers] to know that I am his." Juliana recognized that she would "end up always getting hurt" when her boyfriend "roughs around" with her; in some cases, such as when his behavior became violent (e.g., when "he just smacked" her), she insisted that he leave. However, this moment of resistance was short-lived as Juliana enacts femininity ideology in response to his enactment of masculinity ideology. In describing her own response, she said she "felt bad" because "it's freezing out there" and she decided to take care of her abusive boyfriend by letting him back inside and "call[ing] a ride or whatever." She mobilized the femininity mandate of doing the emotion and care work in a relationship by offering to "talk about things" and "work things out," but only if he "wants to."

Although much of her behavior directly reflected femininity ideology, Juliana also had to engage with masculinity ideology, because her boyfriend's enactments thereof directly affected her. The more she understood how he negotiated masculinity ideology, the better she was able to anticipate his behaviors. In an abusive relationship, where a boyfriend's behavior is so often unpredictable, any knowledge of his thought processes is valuable. Juliana was also aware that her enactments of femininity ideology assuaged her boyfriend's masculinity-driven vulnerabilities, and so she worked diligently to perform proper femininity. She utilized these gender ideologies to articulate a logic for his controlling behavior, justifying his actions in terms of the effect on herself rather than holding him accountable ("I'd end up getting hurt."). When describing his coercive and violent behavior, brief moments of resistance ("You can leave now") ultimately gave way to a resolution to emotionally support and physically shelter him.

Also consistent with femininity ideology, any real focus on her own desires was absent from Juliana's narrative. When her boyfriend told her not to "wear this [or] wear that," she did not say or perhaps even know how that made her feel. She justified his behavior based on what she perceived *he* must be thinking, simultaneously perceiving his enactment of masculinity and enacting her own femininity. Even when he assaulted her and she told him to leave, she immediately returned to

putting herself in his frame of mind, feeling "bad" for him for being out in the cold rather than feeling angry or hurt or any other emotion for herself. For Juliana, femininity ideology dictated that she follow her boyfriend's lead, expect and tolerate his control of her behavior, and emotionally support him even at the expense of her own well-being. Juliana was continually *managing* her boyfriend's enactments of masculinity ideology, because understanding his emotions, attitudes, and behaviors enabled her to leverage the ostensible protections the mandates of femininity ideology afforded her. This example illuminates how Juliana occupied a substantially less powerful position than her boyfriend in their relationship. She did not have the luxury of ignoring his thought processes, constrained as she was in her responses to his enactments of masculinity ideology. It is because her boyfriend was abusive that it became all the more crucial for Juliana to stay precisely tuned to his enactments of masculinity to keep herself safe and to predict his behaviors as much as possible.

While girls managed both femininity and masculinity ideologies, navigating masculinity ideology was virtually the entire focus in boys' narratives, particularly in terms of demonstrating sexual conquest, constant sexual desire, and not being gay. For boys, femininity ideology among girls, when it was part of their described experiences, functioned almost exclusively as a backdrop to their negotiations of masculinity ideology. That is, boys recognized but did not feel compelled to accommodate or support girls' enactments of femininity. Boys' discussions about their expectations of girls, which arose far less frequently than girls' discussions about their expectations of boys, were highly instrumental: Rather than concern about the negative implications for girls violating conventions of femininity ideology, boys narrated how those violations complicated their own successful enactments of masculinity. In keeping with the mandate of femininity ideology that girls should resist boys' sexual advances, girls were expected to be gatekeepers—a mandate predicated on girls' own proscribed control of their own sexual feelings. A primary theme of many boys' narratives was the effort to cement their standing as appropriately masculine, which included but did not entirely comprise overcoming this gatekeeping. However, some boys evidenced discomfort with this simplistic understanding of their own sexuality and feelings about relationships, particularly how their feelings for girls may have been seen to interfere with the interplay of femininity and masculinity ideologies in regulating and maintaining constructions of girls' and boys' sexuality:

> I had an experience with a person like a couple months back who wasn't considered the ah—the cream of the crop as far as girls are concerned. And a bunch of my friends thought it was a bad idea. And like I was kinda having trouble with it for a while. But then ah—my best friend, his name's Seth, he kinda stood up and said—he kinda stood up—stood up and laid the law down. He—he expressed to them—not how I was feeling, but a way a guy should feel in general. And I was just like, "Okay." He said to all my friends— like this girl happens to be known as an easy ride. And uh—and Seth said—like they were all like rantin' on me—"I don't understand what the big deal is. Angel's with a girl. He's gonna get some. And uh—that's it. Why're you guys all buggin' on him?" And then they all stopped. I was grateful that they stopped, but I think he portrayed the wrong message, like the wrong reasons. Like, I [am] certainly not in the relationship to get some, but like that's what he told them. It did make them stop. That was good enough. And, I don't know. It's just like—like I wasn't in that relationship to get some. (Angel, aged 15, Latino)

In this situation, Angel, who dated regularly and recounted some sexual experience, described how the terms of masculinity ideology functioned to get his friends to "stop . . . buggin' on him," even as he denied that "get[ting] some" was his motivation for this relationship. This example illuminates how femininity ideology, when it did arise in the boys' interviews, functioned primarily as a context for their own navigation of masculinity ideology. It also demonstrates how masculinity and femininity ideologies are mutually constitutive and need one another to operate. Angel engaged with femininity ideology to navigate his friends' expectations of behavior compliant with masculinity

ideology. He recognized the strictures of femininity ideology in his understanding that, because his girlfriend was "known as an easy ride," she was therefore not "the cream of the crop as far as girls are concerned"—her violation of femininity ideology diminished her, and paradoxically both diminished and elevated him. Yet while Angel recognized the unfairness of the sexual double standard for his girlfriend, the consequences of femininity ideology for her are salient to him *only* as they pertain to his own enactment of appropriate masculinity. He describes his friends "rantin' on" him because they thought dating this girl was "a bad idea," and he says that he "was kinda having trouble with it for a while." Only after one of his friends pointed out that by dating this girl, Angel is "gonna get some"—enacting masculinity appropriately by having sex—do his friends think there was a "good enough" reason to date her. The primary concern of Angel's friends—getting through the gates—won out, reinforcing the expectations of masculinity ideology.

Yet, Angel himself remained conflicted. Although he was "grateful that they stopped" bothering him, he explained that his friend "portrayed the wrong message" and that he was "certainly not in the relationship to get some." He struggled to make sense of his own feelings, which did not line up with what was expected of him. He said his friend explained to the group "not how I was feeling, but a way a guy should feel in general." He was aware of his girlfriend's reputation but neither discussed how her failure to enact femininity mandates may have affected her nor stood up for her as a sexual agent and person deserving of respect. Instead, he focused only on how her reputation affected him, even as he appreciated the relationship as more than just a method of obtaining access to sex. Ultimately, Angel's situation left him flummoxed, relaying a common pattern in both boys' and girls' narratives: When recognizing that the logic of gender ideologies is unfair, they fell back on the ambivalent trope of "I don't know." Angel, in retrospect, wondered why he did not object to the inaccurate characterization of his motives or express the offense he took at the denigration of his girlfriend.

The boys' narrations of how they navigated masculinity and femininity thus stood in stark contrast to how the girls engaged with these ideologies. Whereas the girls tended to articulate expectations of femininity for themselves entangled with their attention to expectations of masculinity for boys and how that ideology affects girls directly, the boys tended to focus on expectations of femininity insofar as it provided a context for their navigations of masculinity. Angel narrated his rejection of masculinity ideology, instead positioning himself as relatively egalitarian. However, even though Angel was clear that he was not in the relationship to gain access to sex, the expectations of masculinity and femininity ideologies nevertheless protected him from ridicule; he seemed both resigned to allowing his friend to mobilize these ideologies to harness their mutual friends' harassment yet unable to see an alternative that would make it possible for him to express any emotion beyond lust without negative consequences.

General Discussion

In a departure from the lens of gender differences generally characterizing research on adolescent relationships and sexuality, we used a gendered analysis to evaluate if and how the gender ideologies of masculinity and femininity shed light on the perpetuation of gender inequity in adolescent heterosexual relationships for boys and girls. Using a theoretical framework of institutionalized heterosexuality, we suggested that gender ideologies of boys' masculinity and girls' femininity, articulated as a key structure of institutionalized heterosexuality, together produce a gendered hierarchy in relationships for *both* boys and girls. We first quantitatively tested this claim, finding contributions of both masculinity and femininity ideologies for both boys and girls to two conceptually linked and gender-salient relational and sexual domains of institutionalized heterosexuality: girls' endorsement of feminine conventions in heterosexual relationships and boys' endorsement of male coercion. In line with our first hypothesis, both gender ideologies were found to predict these gendered outcomes for both girls and boys. Contrary to our second hypothesis, however, masculinity

ideology played an especially strong role over and above femininity ideology for girls, while both masculinity and femininity ideologies contributed significantly for boys.

The second qualitative study enabled us to attend to the broader tapestry of girls' and boys' narratives of experiences with heterosexual relationships and their navigations of sexual expression. By focusing on the interweaving of masculinity and femininity ideologies, narrated by both boys and girls and inclusive but not limited to male coercion and feminine conventions of heterosexuality, we gained an understanding of how these gender ideologies function in tandem in reproducing gender inequitable relationships. These young people made sense of and managed the hegemonic mandates of these gender ideologies in complex and nuanced ways: While some participants embraced gender ideologies uncritically, others experienced them (femininity ideology in particular) as wrong and unfair, with a few girls and boys outright rejecting them. Even so, pervasive confusion about the origins of these gendered expectations and/or why they persist characterized both girls' and boys' struggles in attributing meaning to both their own and their partners' beliefs and behaviors. These findings provide insight not only into adolescents' enactments but also into how even unresolved questioning keeps these mandates in place.

Understanding the Persistence of a Gender Hierarchy

Nearly two decades after the groundbreaking work of Holland and colleagues (1992, 2000, 2003, 1998/2004), the "male-in-the-head" pattern was still audible: Girls tended to articulate not only the management of femininity *in tandem with* masculinity but also their own femininity as *subordinate* to their management of boys' masculinity. In contrast, boys acknowledged but did not manage girls' enactments of femininity ideology. Boys' only interaction with femininity ideology was in terms of girls' sexual gatekeeping to the extent that it was relevant to the management of their own masculinity. This gendered pattern was consistent with feminist and critical race theories, which describe how those in positions of less power in a hierarchical system need to understand how those with more power act and think, while those in positions of greater power are not compelled to comprehend the outcomes of their own dominating behavior (Du Bois, 1903/2007; Miller, 1976). This conclusion is buttressed by a notable absence of coercion and overt dominance in boys' narratives about their own and other boys' relationships with girls, in stark contrast to girls' narratives where coercion was a common theme.

A compelling explanation for this silence around boys' coercion is the current public discourse of rejecting dating violence, which may lead boys or girls to choose not to disclose this aspect of their relationships. Yet as our findings suggest, even as girls and boys both "move away from" gendered practices, they remain tethered to those practices. While girls found themselves consumed by conflicting expectations for their sexualities through the dual management of both their own femininity and boys' masculinity, boys noted how difficult it was to express feelings of tenderness and caring denied them by an ideology of masculinity operating on the background of a compliant and subordinated femininity (Connell, 1987). Knowledge of both masculinity and femininity ideologies is thus necessary for explaining and understanding the persistence and seeming intransigence of a gender hierarchy as it operates in the heterosexual relationships and sexual experiences of both girls and boys.

Limitations

Given the novel approach of this study, we note several important limitations. In evaluating only two discrete gender-salient outcomes of feminine heterosexual conventions for girls and male coercion for boys, we were unable to fully capture the multidimensional complexity of our participants' relationships, let alone institutionalized heterosexuality. While the follow-up narrative analysis confirmed the critical salience of these two gendered outcomes for both adolescent girls and boys, we recognize and encourage the importance of constructing more complex outcome variables, as well as potential moderators or mediators, capable

of measuring the extent of girls' and boys' acceptance of these ideologies. Given the uneven presence of coercion and feminine conventions of heterosexuality across the boys' and girls' interviews, inclusion of both these outcome measures in quantitative studies of both girls and boys may provide more insight. . . .

Praxis for Resistance: Future Directions

Research on adolescent girls in the early 1990s identified a process whereby many girls began to "lose their voices" as they entered adolescence even as others raised theirs to resist the ways that "appropriate" femininity—to be nice and kind yet not to recognize or speak about difficult or disruptive knowledge—suppresses girls (Brown & Gilligan, 1992). Yet the findings of this study suggest that vocal resistance offers only a partial analysis and praxis for enabling girls to shift the dynamics of their relationships and self-concepts; a fuller analysis must allow also for boys' experiences and navigations in the lives of both girls and boys. Replicating the "male-in-the-head" findings (Holland et al., 1992, 2000, 2003, 1998/2004), this study offers two key elements for dismantling institutionalized heterosexuality in the realm of relationships. First, while attending to the needs and feelings of one's partner is a quality of a good relationship, the importance for girls of masculinity ideology underpinning boys' behavior and experience suggests that girls need to learn to recognize how and understand *why* they attend as closely to what boys are supposed to do and feel as they do to the mandates of femininity. Second, a singular focus on girls contributes to rather than relieves the persistence of a gender hierarchy; also needed is greater recognition of the vital importance of and support for boys' listening, speaking their hearts and minds, and expressing what they feel and/or know about their own desires and hopes for relationships. Having access to an analysis of how these ideologies work in tandem can enable both boys and girls, as well as adults, to get at the heart of the perpetuation of gender inequity, which ultimately may help explain unhappiness, unmet expectations, feeling bad about oneself, and even violence.

Behaviors of dating violence, girls' self-protection, and boys' self-constraint describe only the symptoms of gender inequity; a focus on the intransigence of the gender hierarchy offers hope for a "diagnosis" that both problematizes and can provide alternatives to, and tools for, resisting and reconfiguring these gender ideologies. Consistent with recent research (Burns et al., 2011; Renold & Ringrose, 2008; Ringrose, 2013; Way, 2011), many adolescents in the current sample proved critical observers of their worlds, eager to imagine something better even as they were stymied in understanding the current gender hierarchy. Adolescents' ability to question ubiquitous, hegemonic gender ideologies constitutes a fissure in institutionalized heterosexuality—a fissure that complements the challenge to a gender hierarchy posed by same-sex and transgender relationships (e.g., Iantaffi & Bockting, 2011; Kustritz, 2003)—and an opportunity to push back against rigid and unrealistic norms that deny opportunities to be fully human. Yet if we allow for the possibility that adolescent girls can be recognized as sexual people without being thought of as "sluts," along with the possibility that adolescent boys are driven by a desire for emotional intimacy rather than just sex, then we open the door for adolescents and adults to rework relationships beyond the binaries that reproduce gender inequity and enable relationships that are a source and example of human connection.

References

Bartky, S. L. (1991). *Femininity and domination: Studies in the phenomenology of oppression.* New York, NY: Routledge.

Bordini, S., & Sperb, T. (2013). Sexual double standard: A review of the literature between 2001 and 2010. *Sexuality & Culture, 17,* 686–704. doi:10.1007/s12119012-9163-0

Bordo, S. (1993). *Unbearable weight: Feminism, western culture and the body.* Berkeley: University of California Press.

Brown, L. M., & Gilligan, C. (1992). *Meeting at the crossroads: Women's psychology and girls' development.* Cambridge, MA: Harvard University Press.

Budgeon, S. (2014). The dynamics of gender hegemony: Femininities, masculinities and social change. *Sociology, 48,* 317–334. doi:10.1177/0038038513490358

Burns, A., Futch, V., & Tolman, D. (2011). "It's like doing homework": Academic achievement discourse in adolescent girls' fellatio narratives. *Sexuality Research and Social Policy, 8,* 239–251. doi:10.1007/s13178-011-0062-1

Butler, J. (1990). *Gender trouble: Feminism and the subversion of identity.* New York, NY: Routledge.

Connell, R. (1987). *Gender and power.* Palo Alto, CA: Stanford University Press.

Du Bois, W. E. B. (2007). The souls of black folk. New York: Oxford University Press. (Original work published 1903, Chicago: A.C. McClurg & Co.).

Dworkin, S., & O'Sullivan, L. (2007). *"It's less work for us and it shows us she has good taste": Masculinity, sexual initiation, and contemporary sexual scripts.* Nashville, TN: Vanderbilt University Press.

Epstein, M., Calzo, J., Smiler, A., & Ward, L. (2009). "Anything from making out to having sex": Men's negotiations of hooking up and friends with benefits scripts. *Journal of Sex Research, 46,* 414–424. doi:10.1080/00224490902775801

Fahs, B., Dudy, M. L., & Stage, S. (Eds.). (2013). *The moral panics of sexuality.* New York, NY: Palgrave Macmillan.

Fine, M. (1988). Sexuality, schooling, and adolescent females: The missing discourse of desire. *Harvard Educational Review, 58*(1), 29–53.

Fish, S. (1980). *Is there a text in this class? The authority of interpretive communities.* Cambridge, MA: Harvard University Press.

Hill Collins, P. (2004). *Black Sexual Politics.* New York, NY: Routledge.

Hird, M. J., & Jackson, S. (2001). Where "angels" and "wusses" fear to tread: Sexual coercion in adolescent dating relationships. *Journal of Sociology, 37*(1), 27–43.

Hlavka, H. R. (2014). Normalizing sexual violence: Young women account for harassment and abuse. *Gender & Society, 28,* 337–358. doi:10.1177/0891243214526468

Holland, J., Ramazanoglu, C., Sharpe, S., & Thomson, R. (1992). Pleasure, pressure and power: Some contradictions of gendered sexuality. *The Sociological Review, 40,* 645–674.

Holland, J., Ramazanoglu, C., Sharpe, S., & Thomson, R. (1994). Power and desire: The embodiment of female sexuality. *Feminist Review, 46,* 21–38. doi:10.2307/1395415

Holland, J., Ramazanoglu, C., Sharpe, S., & Thomson, R. (2000). Deconstructing virginity-young people's accounts of first sex. *Sexual and Relationship Therapy, 15,* 221–232. doi:10.1080/14681990050109827

Holland, J., Ramazanoglu, C., Sharpe, S., & Thomson, R. (2003). When bodies come together: Power, control and desire. In J. Weeks, J. Holland, & M. Waites (Eds.), *Sexualities and society: A reader* (pp. 84–94). Oxford, UK: Polity Press.

Holland, J., Ramazanoglu, C., Sharpe, S., & Thomson, R. (2004). *The male in the head: Young people, heterosexuality and power* (2nd ed.). London, England: Tufnell Press. (Original work published 1998)

Holland, J., & Thomson, R. (2010). Revisiting youthful sexuality: Continuities and changes over two decades. *Sexual and Relationship Therapy, 25,* 342–350. doi:10.1080/14681991003767370

Iantaffi, A., & Bockting, W. (2011). Views from both sides of the bridge? Gender, sexual legitimacy and transgender people's experiences of relationships. *Culture, Health & Sexuality, 13,* 355–370. doi:10.1080/13691058.2010.537770

Jackson, S. (2006). Gender, sexuality and heterosexuality: The complexity (and limits) of heteronormativity. *Feminist Theory, 7,* 105–121. doi:10.1177/1464700106061462

Kim, J., Sorsoli, C., Collins, K., Zylbergold, B., Schooler, D., & Tolman, D. (2007). From sex to sexuality: Exposing the heterosexual script on primetime network television. *Journal of Sex Research, 44,* 145–157.

Kimmel, M. (2008). *Guyland: The perilous world where boys become men.* New York, NY: HarperCollins.

Kreager, D. A., & Staff, J. (2009). The sexual double standard and adolescent peer acceptance. *Social Psychology Quarterly, 72,* 143–164.

Kustritz, A. (2003). Slashing the romance narrative. *The Journal of American Culture, 26,* 371–384. doi:10.1111/1542-734X.00098

Levy, A. (2006). *Female chauvinist pigs: Women and the rise of raunch culture.* New York, NY: Simon & Schuster.

Mahalik, J. R., Burns, S. M., & Syzdek, M. (2007). Masculinity and perceived normative health behaviors as predictors of men's health behaviors. *Social Science & Medicine, 64,* 2201–2209. doi:10.1016/j.socscimed.2007.02.035

Martin, K. A. (1996). *Puberty, sexuality, and the self: Girls and boys at adolescence.* New York, NY: Routledge.

Martino, W. (2000). Policing masculinities: Investigating the role of homophobia and heteronormativity in the lives of adolescent school boys. *The Journal of Men's Studies, 8,* 213–236. doi:10.3149/jms.0802.213

Maxwell, J. A., & Miller, B. A. (2008). Categorizing and connecting strategies in qualitative data analysis. In P. Leavy & S. Hess-Biber (Eds.), *Handbook of emergent methods* (pp. 461–477). New York, NY: Guilford Press.

Miller, J. B. (1976). *Toward a new psychology of women.* Boston, MA: Beacon Press.

National Federation of High Schools. (2014). *High school sports' participation increases for 25th consecutive year.* Retrieved from http://www.nfbs.org/articles/high-school-participation-increases-for-25th-consecutive-year/

Pascoe, C. J. (2011). *Dude, you're a fag: Masculinity and sexuality in high school.* Berkeley: University of California Press.

Pleck, J., Sonenstein, F., & Ku, L. (1993). Masculinity ideology: Its impact on adolescent males' heterosexual relationships. *Journal of Social Issues, 49,* 11–29.

Renold, E. (2006). "They won't let us play unless you're going out with one of them": Girls, boys and Butler's "heterosexual matrix" in the primary years. *British Journal of Sociology of Education, 27,* 489–509. doi:10.1080/01425690600803111

Renold, E. (2007). Primary school "studs": (De)constructing young boys' heterosexual masculinities. *Men & Masculinities, 9,* 275–297.

Renold, E., & Ringrose, J. (2008). Regulation and rupture: Mapping tween and teenage girls' resistance to the heterosexual matrix. *Feminist Theory, 9,* 313–338.

Rich, A. (1980). Compulsory heterosexuality and lesbian existence. *Signs, 5,* 631–660.

Ringrose, J. (2013). *Postfeminist education? Girls and the sexual politics of schooling.* New York, NY: Routledge.

Ringrose, J., Harvey, L., Gill, R., & Livingstone, S. (2013). Teen girls, sexual double standards and "sexting": Gendered value in digital image exchange. *Feminist Theory, 14,* 305–323. doi:10.1177/1464700113499853

Roye, C. F., Tolman, D. L., & Snowden, F. (2013). Heterosexual anal intercourse among Black and Latino adolescents and young adults: A poorly understood high-risk behavior. *Journal of Sex*

Research, 50, 715–722. doi:10.1080/00224499.2012.719170

Rubin, G. (1984). Thinking sex: Notes for a radical theory of the politics of sexuality. In C. S. Vance (Ed.), *Pleasure and danger: Exploring female sexuality* (pp. 267–319). Boston, MA: Routledge & Kegan Paul.

Saewyc, E. M. (2012). What about the boys? The importance of including boys and young men in sexual and reproductive health research. *Journal of Adolescent Health, 51,* 1–2. doi:10.1016/j.jadohealth.2012.05.002

Schippers, M. (2007). Recovering the feminine other: Masculinity, femininity, and gender hegemony. *Theory and Society, 36,* 85–102. doi:10.1007/s11186-007-9022-4

Striepe, M. I., & Tolman, D. (2003). Mom, dad, I'm straight: The coming out of gender ideologies in adolescent sexual-identity development. *Journal of Clinical Child and Adolescent Psychology, 32,* 523–530. doi:10.1207/S15374424JCCP3204_4

Tolman, D. (2002). *Dilemmas of desire: Teenage girls talk about sexuality.* Cambridge, MA: Harvard University Press.

Tolman, D. (2006). In a different position: Conceptualizing female adolescent sexuality development within compulsory heterosexuality. *New Directions for Child and Adolescent Development, 112,* 71–89. doi:10.1002/ed.163

Tolman, D., & McClelland, S. I. (2011). Normative sexuality development in adolescence: A decade in review, 2000–2009. *Journal of Research on Adolescence, 21,* 242–255. doi:10.1111/j.1532-7795.2010.00726.x

Tolman, D., & Porche, M. V. (2000). The adolescent femininity ideology scale: Development and validation of a new measure for girls. *Psychology of Women Quarterly, 24,* 365–376.

Tolman, D. L., Spencer, R., Harmon, T., Rosen-Reynoso, M., & Striepe, M. (2004). Getting Close, Staying Cool: Early Adolescent Boys' Experiences with Romantic Relationships. In N. Way & J. Y. Chu, *Adolescent boys: Exploring diverse cultures of boyhood* (pp. 235–292). New York: New York University Press.

Tolman, D., Spencer, R., Rosen-Reynoso, M., & Porche, M. V. (2003). Sowing the seeds of violence in heterosexual relationships: Early adolescents narrate compulsory hetero-sexuality. *Journal of Social Issues, 59,* 159–178. doi:10.1111/1540-4560.t01-1-00010

U.S. Department of Education. (2012). *Gender equity in education: A data snapshot.* Retrieved from http://www2.ed.gov/about/offices/list/ocr/does/gender-equity-in-education.pdf

Warner, M. (1993). *Fear of a queer planet: Queer politics and social theory.* Minneapolis: University of Minnesota Press.

Way, N. (2011). *Deep secrets: Boys' friendships and the crisis of connection.* Cambridge, MA: Harvard University Press.

The Gender of Violence

As a nation, we fret about "teen violence," complain about "inner city crime" or fear "urban gangs." We express shock at the violence in our nation's public schools, where metal detectors crowd the doorways, and knives and guns commingle with pencils and erasers in students' backpacks. Those public school shootings leave us speechless and sick at heart. Yet when we think about these wrenching events, do we ever consider that, whether white or black, inner city or suburban, these bands of marauding "youths" or these troubled teenagers are virtually all young men?

Men constitute 97 percent of all persons arrested for rape; 88.5 percent of those arrested for murder; 86 percent of those arrested for robbery; 77 percent for aggravated assault; 72 percent of other assaults; 73 percent of all family violence; 72 percent of disorderly conduct. Men are overwhelmingly more violent than women. Nearly 90 percent of all murder victims are murdered by men, according to the United States Department of Justice (Uniform Crime Reports 2014, Table 2; Table 6).

From early childhood to old age, violence is perhaps the most obdurate, intractable gender difference we have observed. The National Academy of Sciences (cited in Gottfredson and Hirschi 1990) puts the case most starkly: "The most consistent pattern with respect to gender is the extent to which male criminal participation in serious crimes at any age greatly exceeds that of females, regardless of source of data, crime type, level of involvement, or measure of participation." "Men are always and everywhere more likely than women to commit criminal acts," write the criminologists Michael Gottfredson and Travis Hirschi (1990, 145). Yet how do we understand this obvious association between masculinity and violence? Is it a biological fact of nature, caused by something inherent in male anatomy? Is it culturally universal? And in the United States, what has been the association between gender and violence? Has that association become stronger or weaker over time? What can we, as a culture, do to prevent or at least ameliorate the problem of male violence?

Our concern throughout this book has been to observe the construction of gender difference and gender inequality at both the individual level of identity and the institutional level. The readings here reflect these concerns.

To argue that men are more prone to violence than women are does not resolve the political question of what to do about it. It would be foolish to resignedly throw up our hands in despair that "boys will be boys." Whether you believe this gender difference in violence derives from different biological predispositions (which I regard as dubious because these biological impulses do not seem to be culturally universal) or because male violence is socially sanctioned and legitimated as an expression of masculine control and domination (a far more convincing explanation), the policy question remains open. Do we organize society so as to maximize this male propensity toward violence, or do we organize society so as to minimize and constrain it? The answers to this question, like the answer to the questions about alleviating gender inequality in the family, in our educational institutions, and in the workplace, are more likely to come from the voting booth than from the laboratories of scientists. As a society, we decide how much weight to give what few gender differences there are, and how best to alleviate the pain of those who are the victims of gendered violence.

The essays included here overturn or challenge the common stereotypes in arresting ways. Angela Stroud examines men's fascination with concealed handguns and its relationship to masculinity. Journalist Nicholas Kristof shows the dangerous consequences of the "interplanetary theory" of gendered communications: he thinks it's sex, she thinks it's rape. (Hint: she's right.) And Doug Meyer looks at the violence experienced by LGBT people—a violence that is, at its heart gendered.

References

Gottfredson, Michael and Travis Hirschi, *A General Theory of Crime* (Stanford: Stanford University Press, 1990).

U.S. Department of Justice, Uniform Crime Reports, 1991. Washington, DC: Dept of Justice.

Good Guys with Guns: Hegemonic Masculinity and Concealed Handguns

ANGELA STROUD

An estimated six million people in the United States possess a concealed handgun license (Stuckey 2010), which means they have the legal right to carry a concealed firearm in most public places. Like gun use generally, the vast majority of concealed handgun license holders are men, and men are more likely than women to support concealed handgun licensing (Carroll 2005; Jones 2005). This study explores how gender dynamics shape the motives of men who are licensed to carry concealed handguns.

Previous studies have argued that guns are symbols of masculinity (Connell 1995; Gibson 1994; Melzer 2009). Stange and Oyster (2000, 22) explain, "In [men's hands], the gun has served a symbolic function that exceeds any practical utility. It has become the symbol par excellence of masculinity: of power, force, aggressiveness, decisiveness, deadly accuracy, cold rationality." Because of these associations, it seems logical that men could use them to perform masculinity. However, the only studies of how men actually use guns have focused on criminals (Kimmel and Mahler 2003; Stretesky and Pogrebin 2007). In this study, I investigate how masculinity motivates law-abiding men in their use of concealed handguns.

To understand the relationship between carrying a concealed firearm and masculinity, I conducted 20 in-depth interviews with men in Texas who currently have a concealed handgun license. Of the nearly one million licenses issued in the state between 1995 and 2009, 81 percent were to

men and 19 percent were to women (Texas Department of Public Safety [DPS] 1995–2010). Though Texas has a "Wild West" image in popular culture, its firearm laws can be considered "middle of the road." Texas' permitting process requires a person to be at least 21 years old, pass state and federal background checks, attend a licensing course, submit two sets of fingerprints, and remit a fee to the state. Moreover, the firearm must remain concealed or the license holder can be charged with a weapons crime.

In this study, I use the concept of hegemonic masculinity to examine motives of men who have a concealed handgun license. Hegemonic masculinity is Connell's (1995) term for the discursive practices and embodied dispositions that legitimize male domination. I argue that by having a license, economically privileged white men are able to define themselves in contrast to femininity and to alternative versions of masculinity that are vilified or ridiculed. In so doing, they shore up white male privilege in society.

My research suggests that some men see their gun carrying as central to what it means to be a good husband and father who is able to protect his wife and children from danger. For older men, who fear that they are losing their ability to physically dominate others, concealed firearms can act as a totem to boost their confidence in their interactions with men. Men also justify their need for a license by positioning themselves in contrast to vilified forms of masculinity. While these men see

Angela Stroud, "Good Guys with Guns: Hegemonic Masculinity and Concealed Handguns," *Gender & Society*, Vol. 26, No. 2 (April 2012), pp. 216–238. Copyright © 2012 by Angela Stroud. Reprinted by permission of SAGE Publications.

their own gun carrying as noble and just, they attribute violence and aggression to others, particularly Black and Latino men. Hegemonic masculinity provides a framework for understanding these discursive practices, and connecting the use of concealed handgun licenses to continued male domination in society.

Literature Review

The literature on firearm use and gender has focused on three main themes: how firearms contribute to cultural constructions of masculinity (Gibson 1994; Jeffords 1994); how organizations such as the National Rifle Association (NRA) utilize masculine tropes to mobilize members (Connell 1995; Melzer 2009; O'Neill 2007); and how masculinity is implicated in violent acts in which firearms are used (Kimmel and Mahler 2003; Stretesky and Pogrebin 2007). Each of these themes is important for understanding why men want to carry a concealed firearm.

The first theme in the literature on firearm use and gender explores the relationships between firearms, violence, and masculinity in fantasy life. James Gibson (1994) argues that movies celebrating war and the warrior ethos, such as the *Rambo* series, emerged on the cultural landscape as a response to the U.S. defeat in Vietnam. The warrior ethos was an extension of the larger cultural shift that linked masculinity to masculinity and physical toughness (Jeffords 1994). The body is central to how this operates because "to be fully, appropriately masculine, a male person must exhibit physical control of his space and be able to act on objects and bodies in it" (Crawley, Foley, and Shehan 2008, 59). This post-Vietnam ethos ushered in a more militarized version of masculinity that helped to popularize the use of guns for personal defense, led to a proliferation of paramilitary organizations, and contributed to the popularity of simulated war games such as paintball (Gibson 1994).

The willingness to engage in violence is central to meanings of masculinity (Messerschmidt 2000) because "real men" must show others that they are not afraid (Kimmel 2010). Yet few men have culturally legitimate occasions to express this violence, making simulated scenarios ideal settings to engage

in violence fantasies. They promote a "New War ethos" where power, force, and might are celebrated as socially necessary when used to protect "good people" from evil. In this worldview, firearms endow "good guys" with the strength, power, and moral right needed to defend the world from "bad guys."

As Gibson suggests, the fantasy of using guns to fight "bad guys" is not only an acceptable form of violence in U.S. culture, it is also celebrated. But unlike Gibson's subjects, the vast majority of people who carry a concealed firearm will never be in a position to enact this New War ethos—even as a playful performance. Furthermore, according to Connell and Messerschmidt (2005, 838), exalted versions of masculinity need not be based in reality, and might instead "express widespread ideals, fantasies, and desires" that justify masculinity's dominance over femininity. In the case of carrying a concealed firearm, an object that is particularly useful for communicating strength, it is important to ask how fantasies of domination allow men to construct masculine selves, whether or not their guns are actually fired.

The second theme in the literature on gender and firearms focuses on the gun lobby's role in linking gun use with hegemonic masculinity (Connell 1995; Melzer 2009; O'Neill 2007). Connell argues that the gun lobby is engaged in masculinity politics, "those mobilizations and struggles where the meaning of masculine gender is at issue and with it, men's position in gender relations" (1995, 205). The gun lobby has been active in producing meanings of masculinity as it works to expand gun rights, even in the face of public outcry over the danger of guns. Connell argues that the gun lobby is able to defeat opponents of gun control by explicitly appealing to discourses of masculinity. By evoking concepts like security, family values, or individual freedom, the gun lobby works to make masculinity "a principal theme, not taken for granted as background" (1995, 205).

Scott Melzer (2009) utilizes Connell's framework to analyze how the NRA exploits popular understandings of guns as masculine symbols to mobilize its members. Melzer attended NRA conventions, analyzed the history of the organization, and interviewed its members to understand how the NRA has used masculinity discourses to become the most powerful lobby in the United States. He argues that gun ownership is associated in NRA discourse with self-reliance, rugged individualism, and a strong work ethic, a constellation of traits that Melzer refers to as "frontier masculinity." He writes that "guns and masculinity have long been inseparable" (2009, 30) thanks to mythologized narratives of the American frontier. These narratives appeal to working- and middle-class white men who are threatened by the civil rights and feminist movements. According to Melzer, the predominantly white male membership of the NRA is motivated to act in defense of guns because they symbolize individual freedom.

The NRA's magazine *The American Rifleman* is the most popular of the organization's monthly publications. Kevin O'Neill (2007) examines how the magazine's section "Armed Citizen" relays stories of violent crimes thwarted by private citizens using guns. For example, the author cites one story that tells of a man whose children rushed into his room in the middle of the night to tell their father that two men were breaking into their home. The father, who was disabled, grabbed a handgun, shot one of the intruders and held him at gunpoint until the police arrived. O'Neill finds that most of the victims in these stories are women, the elderly, or in some way disabled or in failing health. He argues that these "classically vulnerable" people heighten the narrative structure of the stories, because as otherwise helpless victims, they are able to "achieve masculinity" with firearms. According to O'Neill, the NRA uses discourses that simultaneously construct masculinity and terror, and they produce an "especially vigilant kind of citizen who is distinctly masculine in character" (2007, 459). Though defensive gun uses are statistically rare events,[1] the NRA is able to use its monthly publication to circulate stories of "real-life heroes" who use guns to defend the defenseless.

The literature on the NRA illustrates how this powerful lobby links gun use with hegemonic masculinity: Gun users heroically defend the defenseless (O'Neill 2007) and they care deeply about "American virtues," particularly individual freedom (Melzer 2009) and family values (Connell 1995). These NRA discourses "provide a cultural framework that may be materialized in daily practices and interactions" and thus represent what Connell and Messerschmidt (2005, 850) call a "regional" hegemonic masculinity. Though it is important to understand how masculinities emerge in particular contexts, what Connell and Messerschmidt (2005) call the "local level," dominant culture frames and shapes the possibilities for enacting preferred versions of masculinity in everyday life. In this article, I explore how this regional discourse is materialized in the daily practices and interactions of men who are licensed to carry concealed handguns.

The third set of studies on guns and gender examine how some men actually use firearms. However, these studies have focused on the commission of violent crimes and on what Connell might label "alternative" or "marginal" masculinities (Connell 1995). Some researchers consider criminal behavior an attempt by some marginal men to accomplish masculinity when they lack alternative resources to do so (Britton 2011; Messerschmidt 1993).

In this vein, Kimmel and Mahler (2003) analyze random school shootings in the United States. All of those shootings were perpetrated by boys and young men and "all or most of the shooters had tales of being harassed—specifically gay-baited—for inadequate gender performance" (Kimmel and Mahler 2003, 1440). By using firearms to commit acts of violence, these boys attempted to move from margin to center, from being the wimp who was picked on to the aggressor who dominated and controlled others. Similarly, Stretesky and Pogrebin (2007) interviewed gang members serving prison time for violent crimes. The authors found that the reputations of both the gang and the individual gang member were determined by their willingness to defend their honor and to be seen as masculine. The primary way this was accomplished was by using firearms. The authors write, "Guns provide gang members with a sense of power" and guns "help gang members project a tough image" (Stretesky and Pogrebin 2007, 90).

Because guns are so lethal, they imbue their users with traits associated with masculinity—control and power.

Taken together, the literature on guns and masculinity reveals a gaping hole that has implications for how we understand both the way guns factor into cultural constructions of masculinity and how hegemonic masculinity operates. On the regional level, guns factor heavily in displays of masculine violence that are celebrated in action films through fantasies of "good guys" killing "bad guys" (Gibson 1994). The gun lobby taps into and expands this discourse by tying guns to American virtues (Connell 1995; Melzer 2009; O'Neill 2007). But the only analyses that examine how real men use guns to construct masculinity have focused on criminal uses by men who embody marginalized masculinities (Kimmel and Mahler 2003; Stretesky and Pogrebin 2007). Thus, while on the regional level it is clear that guns are discursively linked to hegemonic masculinity, it is unclear how men on the local level might use guns to construct versions of masculinity that are celebrated in culture.

Race and class are central to hegemonic masculinity (Connell and Messerschmidt 2005), but have been virtually ignored in the literature on guns and masculinity. This elision is significant particularly because the image of the ideal gun user constructed by the NRA emerges alongside controlling images of Black masculinity that frame Black males as "threats to white society" (Collins 2006, 75). As a symbol that at once signifies violence and protection, gun use will likely take on different meanings when analyzed at the intersection of race, class, and gender.

The men that are the focus of my study are positioned quite differently from the marginalized men in the literature: Instead of being defined as "criminals," they consider themselves law-abiding men and are licensed by the state to carry concealed guns. Furthermore, they are predominantly white and upper middle class and thus are socially privileged. To fully explore the significance of their gun carrying, it is important not only to interrogate the meanings they give the practice, but to understand the extent to which they are able to position themselves in relationship to the larger discourses around guns and hegemonic masculinity.

The following questions emerge from this literature: How do law-abiding men use concealed firearms to signify masculinity? How are race, class, and gender implicated in the production of hegemonic masculinity? This study extends the literature on masculinities and guns by examining the gendered meanings of concealed firearm carry by law-abiding men. It also extends the literature on hegemonic masculinity by utilizing a race/class/gender focus in examining dynamics of power between local and regional levels of analysis.

Methods

I conducted in-depth interviews with 20 men who are licensed to carry a concealed handgun. . . . Sixteen of the respondents identified as white, two identified as white and Hispanic/Latino, and two identified as Hispanic/Latino (see Table 1). All but two of the respondents were married, and they ranged in age from 26 to 66 with a median age of 44. . . .

Through my analysis of the interviews, three primary themes emerged in men's explanations of why they want to carry a firearm in public: (1) to protect their wives and children from violent crime; (2) to compensate for lost physical strength as they age; and (3) to make them feel more secure in places they feel vulnerable. I will argue that each of these themes is connected to fantasies of violence and heroic defense that contribute to hegemonic masculinity.

Family Defender

Defending the family is significant in men's accounts of carrying a concealed firearm. Nearly all of the men I interviewed are married, and ten have children living at home. In almost every case, the men I interviewed explained their gun use as deeply tied to defending their families. Adam, 36, says that he first bought a gun around the age of 21 because, having just finished college, he could afford to live only in "lower income neighborhoods where there's more crime and there's more

TABLE I. Demographic Characteristics of Respondents

Name[a]	Sex	Age	Race/Ethnicity	Education	Estimated Income
Adam	M	36	White	High school degree	$61–80,000
Alex	M	26	White	High school	$21–40,000
Bill	M	38	White	Technical (military)	$101,000 +
Chris	M	63	White	College degree	$41–60,000
David	M	66	White	Advanced degree	$21–40,000
George	M	40	Hispanic	College degree	$101,000 +
Gil	M	65	White	High school degree	$101,000 +
Greg	M	57	White	High school degree	$101,000 +
Jack	M	46	White	College degree	$101,000 +
Jeff	M	48	Latino and White	College degree	$81–100,000
John	M	44	White	Advanced degree	NA
Joseph	M	45	White and Hispanic	Associate's degree	$81–100,000
Larry	M	54	White	Associate's degree	NA
Leo	M	52	Hispanic	Advanced degree	$101,000 +
Mark	M	34	White	High school degree	$61–80,000
Mike	M	36	White	College degree	$101,000 +
Nick	M	46	White	Trade school	$81–100,000
Paul	M	34	White	Technical (military)	$61–80,000
Richard	M	38	White	College degree	$101,000 +
Steven	M	30	White	Advanced degree	$101,000 +

a. All names are pseudonyms.

shootings and violence." Adam described that neighborhood as "a bad part of Houston" and said he used his gun only for protection in his home and was never very serious about self-defense. All this changed when he and his wife were expecting a child. He explains his perspective: "I'm the dad. I think my role is that I have to protect my family. That's my number one duty as a dad: to provide . . . food, shelter, and protection for my wife and my child. I mean that's what being a dad is." I asked Adam if that is a role he is trying to learn or if it's one a man automatically assumes when he gets married. He responded,

> I think you automatically assume it when you get married. And, then especially when you have a kid. And I don't know if that's my belief, or it's just the way I grew up or whatever. But you know, when you get married, you're supposed to do certain things. You know, you have roles. And I know that in today's society [pause] a lot of people like

to think well, men and women, they're the same and you know, the women work and so do the men and all that stuff. Which, to some extent, I agree. But there's other certain inherent parts of being a man and being a woman that you have certain roles. I can't have a baby! You know, physically I can't have a baby and physically I'm stronger than my wife. And, it's just up to me to protect her, in every situation. And if, you know, if we were ever attacked or accosted or something then, then it's up to me to protect her until she can, you know, be safe.

Adam became very animated about what he termed "his role" in his family and seemed exasperated by the suggestion that men and women are equals in all senses. Adam sees his wife and child as dependent on him for their safety. Rooting his argument in bodily differences makes the distinction seem natural and inevitable (Connell 1995; Hollander 2001).

Like many respondents, Adam says that a gun is a superior tool for self-defense because it doesn't matter if a criminal is larger or stronger than he is; with a gun, he can defend himself. This is what is meant when guns are referred to as "equalizers." Presumably, this logic would also apply to women and would suggest that there is nothing inevitable about Adam, and the other men who made such statements, occupying the role of the family protector. Instead of stemming from a natural consequence of him being "the dad," Adam utilizes discourses that link masculinity to physicality and aggression and femininity to vulnerability (Hollander 2001) to place his wife and children in positions of dependence.

Mark, a very tall and physically imposing man, is 34 and married with two small children. Standing 6 feet 10 inches, his first jobs after college were in personal security. Mark says he never felt particularly vulnerable until he and his wife were expecting their first child. Mark describes developing a deep-seated need to ensure that his family is protected. He says, "You know, I've got a newborn child that is relying on me to not only protect him, but to protect myself and his mother." As his perspective shifted toward a focus on defending his family, Mark not only obtained a concealed handgun license, he also pursued advanced training in handgun self-defense tactics. He now carries a gun everywhere he goes—including the gym and his own home—whether it is legal or not. Like Adam, he suggests that becoming a father was a transitional moment for how he thinks about vulnerability and self-defense. Both men went from only having guns in the home to wanting to carry a gun in public because, as fathers, they feel it is their duty to protect their family.

Though Mark says that he carries a gun to protect his family, he also explains that he spends much of his time apart from them. Mark says that he would love for his wife to carry a firearm because "if something happens to me, you know, if I get shot, she can take it and use it. If I'm not there. If she's by herself." He elaborates by saying, "I can't be with [my kids] 24 hours a day. She can't be either, but you know, she's more . . . likely to be there than I am." In this explanation Mark wants

his wife to be armed not because she would also become a family defender but because he cannot always be with his family. Like Mark, many of the other married men I interviewed said that they wish their wives would carry a concealed handgun, but in contrast to how they see their role as fathers, they do not see their wives as bad mothers because they are not licensed. Moreover, their wives' refusal to be armed further emphasizes that it is a father's job to protect his family.

When I asked Mark if he is ever stressed about his wife's safety when he is not with her, he replied, "No, I mean . . . she's a good girl. She can take care of herself [laughs]. But you know, it's been in the back of my mind always. You . . . gotta kinda balance the practicality versus the, the uh [long pause] oh, what's the word? The paranoia." There is a disconnect between how Mark explains his need for a concealed firearm—because crime can happen to anyone, anywhere—and his general comfort with the fact that his wife does not carry a gun. His contradictory response underscores how, in addition to simply being a tool for self-defense, Mark's possession of a concealed handgun license signifies that he is a good father and husband.

The men I talked to consider themselves law-abiding, virtuous, and brave defenders of their families—matching the image of the ideal gun owner perpetrated by the NRA (Connell 1995; Melzer 2009; O'Neill 2007). But paradoxically, carrying a concealed firearm does not actually enable them to defend their families. Though Mark suggested that as his family's breadwinner, his defense is integral to his family's security, he nevertheless minimized the threat to his wife and children when he is away from them. In fact, the fathers I interviewed recognize that their wives are more likely than they are to be in a position to use a gun in defense of the family. This contradiction suggests that while carrying a concealed gun may symbolize their fatherly role, it may not actually translate into an ability to protect their wives and children from harm.

Though they may never be in a position to carry out heroic fantasies of masculine bravery, their concealed handgun suggests to them that they could. By signifying that their wives and children are dependent on them for protection (whether or not this is actually true), the men I interviewed are discursively positioning themselves as brave leaders of their families; thus, their concealed handgun license is very useful as a symbol that allows men to construct hegemonic masculinity. In many respects, it is an ideal symbol because it signifies to them that they are good fathers and husbands, even when they are away from their wives and children.

The Aging Male Body

Few respondents younger than 40 said that they needed a gun primarily to defend themselves; however, five of the 12 respondents 40 and older explained that age factored into why they have a concealed handgun license. For example, Jeff, 48, is an affable gun enthusiast. He regularly participates in shooting competitions and carries a firearm with him whenever he can. Like many respondents, Jeff reports that he cannot carry his gun at work. When I asked him how that makes him feel, he replied, "Vulnerable. [Laughs]. As I'm being reminded, like today at my orthopedist, trying to get my knee fixed, I'm not as young as I used to be. And [pause] I don't, I don't want to have to dance with somebody if they want to do me violence." Jeff explains that with a gun he does not have this sense of vulnerability and instead feels relaxed knowing he has "a superior ability to deal with a situation harshly if I have to." He then tells the following story:

> Years ago I was practicing martial arts regularly. And a friend of mine at the office—a good friend of mine—was just always real aggressive. And, he had his usual fifteen pots of coffee that day, and got vulgar like he always did, and I think . . . he said, "I'll kick your ass" or something like that. I just turned around and smiled at him. And he said, "Oh man, I'm sorry. I didn't mean it. I was just joking." I said, "I know. I know you were joking, don't worry about it" [laughs]. Then we laughed it off. And he was very visibly shaken. I wasn't gonna do anything to him, but he knew and I knew that I could've. No big deal.

Jeff felt proud that his officemate feared him. Though he is older now, and not able to do martial arts, carrying a firearm gives him the same sense of confidence. Jeff's firearm supplies him with a virility that his aging body has surrendered. He says he feels "calm and relaxed" when he's carrying a gun and that when he is armed, if someone threatens him, he can just smile back, rather than worrying about how to handle the situation. Without having to show his firearm to others. Jeff's gun makes him feel at ease, confident he can handle any confrontation.

Gil, 66, lives in a major metropolitan city in the Southwest. He says he carries a firearm because "I refuse to be a victim. I refuse to put myself in the position where . . . someone can exercise that kind of control over me." Gil relayed a story about a time when he felt physically threatened and did not have his firearm with him. He was coming out of a sporting arena in a major metropolitan city. "We were goin' into the parking ramp to get our vehicle. And there were a bunch of [long pause] young [pause] punks." Gil struggled to find the words to describe the group of people he was approaching. "It was pretty uncomfortable for about five minutes, until I was certain that they were goin' somewhere else and not to us." When I asked if the group of people were being hostile toward him, he replied, "Well . . . let's just say I was uncomfortable." And, after a long pause, he said, "I think we've all had that experience in a public place." Because sports arenas are gun-free zones, Gil could not carry his gun and had left it in his car. When I asked him how his behavior would have been different if he had his gun on him, Gil said he would have been more confident. "In what ways?" I asked. He replied,

> Confident in that I can take care of myself. You know, at my age, I'm not gonna win many kung fu fights with an assailant [laughs]. And, you know, 34 years ago if someone wanted to mix it up, I probably would've been okay taking my chances. But you get to a certain age and you've got some problems. You know, dealing on a physical level. And you don't run as fast [laughs]. You know what I mean?

Gil then said, "You know the old saying 'Don't piss off an old guy because he'll probably just kill ya'? [Laughs]." This joke was an abrupt response to the admission that Gil no longer sees himself as physically strong. It seemed intended to convey that, though getting older has taken its toll, if provoked, he could still defend himself.

Another example of how firearms can compensate for lost capacities as bodies age comes from Larry, 54. When we met, Larry arrived on a Harley motorcycle and was wearing a black bandanna and black leather vest. A tall, stout man, he sported a goatee. Throughout the interview Larry projected a very tough, almost threatening persona. When Larry told me he carried a gun long before he had a license to do so legally, I asked him if that was because he had experienced a violent incident or if it was because of a "generalized fear that something could happen." Larry quickly dismissed the notion that he feared violent crime. Instead, Larry says, he's realistic: "Most people have this delusion that the world's this warm happy place, and for most of them, it is. But that's only because nothing's happened to them yet." Similar to the New War ethos Gibson (1994) studied, Larry has constructed a worldview in which there is a perpetual struggle between forces of good and evil. This worldview justifies Larry's tough and aggressive, thoroughly masculine, self-presentation. Later in the interview, I asked him if he had ever felt physically threatened when he was not armed. Again, Larry dismissed the idea that he would feel threatened, attributing it to his military training in hand-to-hand combat:

> If I've got a stake or a pool cue, I will own your ass. As far as not having anything? When I was a little bit younger and in a little bit better shape, I was comfortable with up to three people. So, no, I didn't particularly feel threatened. If worse gets to worst, I can grab one person, they will scream like a little girl before it's all over with and the other two people will not want to get that close.

In this moment, and in many others during the interview, Larry seemed purposive in communicating to me that being tough and capable of violence are important attributes in a man, attributes he has always had. He is both willing to engage in violence and capable of domination, traits deeply tied to masculinity (Messerschmidt 2000; Messner 1992). However, he also admits that growing older has taken a toll on his body. Because he was so quick to dismiss suggestions that he might feel vulnerable or threatened, and because he feels like he can dominate other men without a gun, I asked Larry, "So, then, why do you carry [a gun]?" He responded, "Because you never know."

Michael Kimmel (1996, 6) has argued, "Manhood is less about the drive for domination and more about the fear of others dominating us, having power or control over us." Though men like Larry might scoff at the notion that he carries a gun because of fear, he is motivated by a desire to prevent his domination at the hands of another man. Getting older has meant that these men have begun to lose access to a fundamental aspect of masculinity: the capacity to physically dominate others (Crawley, Foley, and Shehan 2008). Carrying a gun allows them to recoup the sense of dominance that stems from having an ability to fight back. Unlike subordinate men who are unable or unwilling to fight, "real" men are able and ready to defend themselves, a position that allows them to claim dominance and assert hegemonic masculinity. It is striking how elaborate the fantasies of potential domination can be. Larry describes an imaginary fight scene with a group of three men; Gil wishes he were armed when a group of young men, who did not physically threaten him, walked by him in a parking garage; and Jeff uses a gun to essentially recapture a kung fu warrior fantasy.

Though these men say that their guns are simply tools to prevent victimization, they are also symbols of virility, and, thus, carrying one impacts how they see themselves as men. This helps to explain the appeal of concealed firearms for some men: not that they are communicating to others their ability to dominate them, but that they are reassuring themselves that they will "not be a victim." Gil makes this clear when he says, "You know, none of us want to be victims. [It's] not that any of us are cowboys or going out there looking for a fight, but nobody wants to be a victim." Rather than serving as tools of aggression, for these men, having a concealed gun means that they will never have to "scream like a little girl." The gun functions as a totem of masculinity, giving them calm assurance that they can defend themselves against attack—despite their aging bodies.

Dangerous Neighborhoods

When I asked the men I interviewed how they make decisions about whether or not to carry a gun, eleven said they carry a gun wherever it is legally allowed and nine said they make decisions based on where they are going. For example, they will carry a firearm if they go somewhere they have never been; if they are traveling out of town; or if they go to a part of town with a reputation for being dangerous. "Bad parts of town" were always marked as areas with high poverty and often, though not always explicitly, as areas that are predominantly Black or Latino. When I asked Adam if he regularly carries a gun he said no, because he now lives in a safe city. Adam sets this in contrast to his experiences growing up in Houston, parts of which he describes as a "war zone." Adam says he always carries a gun when he travels to Houston because, unlike his current city, where the "bad parts of town" are relegated to one side of the city and the "nice" parts of town are on the other, Houston isn't "zoned." Adam says his friends who live in Houston carry their firearms daily because

> the gas station right down the street is totally different than the gas station one mile down the road. I mean you can have the one that's right by your house is fine and you've got no problems, there's no people hanging out there drinkin' beer and acting crazy. But you decide not to go to that one and you just drive down the street and all of a sudden it's like, you know, Compton down there.

Adam invokes "Compton" as a euphemism for race; it is code for a space he sees as predominantly poor, Black, dangerous, and scary. Like many white Americans, Adam links blackness with criminality (Feagin 2010). Because of Houston's uncertain racial landscape, he feels compelled to be armed.

Respondents' perceptions of danger were often loaded with similarly racialized notions of criminality and vulnerability. For example, Jack, a

46-year-old licensing instructor, blames Hurricane Katrina evacuees from New Orleans for what he perceives to be a steady increase in violent crime in Texas. Jack carries at least one gun on him whenever possible. When I asked him if he has ever had the occasion to use his gun, he told the following story:

> I got lost and ended up in a predominantly Black neighborhood. [A man in] an old beat-up truck in front of me was driving around and he stops . . . in the middle of the road where I couldn't go around him. And he gets out, so I pulled my weapon out and put it right where he couldn't see it just below the door. Rolled my window down about an inch and he comes back and he asks me some stupid question about how to get to the freeway and I told him, "Don't know, can't help you." And he's like, "Thanks, God bless you," or something, gets in his truck and leaves. I don't know if that was legitimate or what, but I wasn't going to take the chance.

Explanations of threat that link perceived criminality to Black men create a "racialized fear of crime" (Davis 2007) whereby feelings of vulnerability are heightened when whites make contact with the racial Other. Jack is able to use his firearm to quell this sense of vulnerability, and to protect himself should the need arise.

When I asked Adam if he has ever had a situation where he thought he might have to use his gun, he says, "Let's say you pull up to a convenience store and there's some certain people outside that make you feel a little nervous. Then you've got your gun there." Later Adam elaborates:

> You pull up and there's, you know, three guys out there, gangster guys, just kind of hanging around at midnight in front of the convenience store. . . . So you make your decision: Do I leave? Or do I protect myself? . . . So when it's just you outside and them outside, you know, I would just kind of grab my gun and stick it in the back of my pants and pump my gas and be on my way.

The use of the term "gangster" coupled with his previous comment about "Compton" suggests that Adam is describing encountering a group of Black men. He feels threatened by this group, unsure if he should get out of his car. By putting a gun in his waistband, he does not let his fear of the criminal other restrict his behavior; he does not shirk from whatever conflict he imagines might ensue.

Another example comes from Mike, 36. We met at a café in a predominantly white, upper-middle-class part of town. Despite claims that he carries wherever he can, Mike was not carrying a firearm when we met; he had left it in his truck. As we talked he said, "I don't feel strange sitting here and not having it. I think if I did have it, it would probably make me a little bit more aware of my surroundings." I was taken aback by this comment, having assumed that the power a firearm bestows would allow a person to relax. Mike explains:

> When I have it with me, I'm paying a lot more attention to people . . . somebody walks in, looks like they're lookin' for trouble. Somebody that doesn't fit. You know, not to play the, uh, race card or anything, but there aren't too many Black people around here. So if you . . . walk into a place and you don't really fit in. Like if I went over to [a predominantly Black part of town] and walked into Martin Luther King, Jr., church on Sunday morning, I'm betting I'd be one of the few white guys. And people would probably look at me and go, well what's this white guy doing here?

Mike's explanation of how race factors into the way he imagines risk is cloaked in discourses of "color blind racism" (Bonilla-Silva 2001). Equating the experience of a Black man's being seen as a potential criminal to Mike's being seen as oddly out of place in a church minimizes racial inequality. Yet race plays a profound role in how Mike imagines risk. In this predominantly white space, Mike feels safe enough to not bother bringing his gun in; however, he suggests this safety could be disrupted if a Black man were to come into the store.

Three of the four men in my sample who identified as Hispanic/Latino did not differ dramatically from the rest of the sample in how they talked about the link between race and crime. For instance, Joseph, a 45-year-old license holder who identifies as white on forms, but says that his father is Hispanic, explained that he used his "Hispanic appearance" to intimidate others when he lived in a high-crime neighborhood that was predominantly Black and Latino. He said that looking "pure white" would have made him a target. The only person in the sample who resisted racist constructions of threat was George, a 44-year-old licensing instructor who is Mexican American and lives in a predominantly Hispanic city along the Texas–Mexico border. He says that he grew up with guys who are now involved in the drug trade and that he tries to not have a "black and white" view of who is a threat. George says, "Some of the nicest guys I know . . . have tattoos from [head to toe]. Some of the meanest guys I know are the stereotypical middle-aged . . . white male professionals [who are] hot-headed, hot-tempered, on edge, on the defense all the time." Of the 20 men I interviewed, George was the only one who did not rely on a racialized fear of crime. It is significant that George was the only person interviewed who was reared and currently lives in a region that is not predominantly white/Anglo. It seems his perceptions of criminality were not developed according to the white racial frame (Feagin 2010).

R. W. Connell (1995, 80) writes that "in a white supremacist context, Black masculinities play symbolic roles for white gender construction." In this case, many of the men I interviewed identified Black men and areas of town marked as poor and predominantly Black or Latino as threatening. Indeed, race is conflated with social class, such that Mike sees it as impossible that a Black man would have a legitimate reason to enter a café in a wealthy part of town.

It is significant that in the previous descriptions of fear-inducing events none of the respondents describe being physically confronted or overtly threatened by the Black men they encounter. Instead, they report that simply coming into contact with Black men induces a desire to be armed. The men I interviewed project violence, aggression, and criminal intent onto the Black men they encounter. These characterizations are a form of "gendered racism" that are used both to "validate inequality [and] also to contrast Black masculinity with white masculinity as a hegemonic ideal" (Harvey-Wingfield 2007, 198). The men I interviewed construct their sense of masculinity in contradistinction to what Black masculinity represents to them: They presume the men they see are criminals, thus they are armed in defense. They imagine the men they see will be violent; thus they are prepared to respond. Whiteness is critical to these dynamics not because these men see it as an evident marker of status, but because (to them) whiteness signifies nothing at all.

Discussion

Concealed handguns, by definition, are not visible to others. Moreover, the vast majority of license holders will never fire their guns in public. Despite this, concealed handguns prove profoundly meaningful in the reproduction of hegemonic masculinity. For some of the men I interviewed, carrying a concealed gun in public allows them to position themselves as defenders of their families, and as embodiments of the American virtues of self-reliance, strength, and courage (Connell 1995; Melzer 2009; O'Neill 2007). Having a license is critical to how this operates because only people without a criminal record can obtain one, and only with a license can someone carry a gun legally. Being law-abiding is the lynchpin that distinguishes "good guys" from "bad guys" (Gibson 1994).

Ironically, although men say they need a gun to defend their families, they are often away from their wives and children and thus would be unable to carry out their role of the defender should the need arise. Second, men who say it's their job to defend their families because they are physically stronger than their wives are among the same people who say that guns are needed for self-defense because as "equalizers" they reduce whatever physical differences might exist between a perpetrator of violent crime and themselves. Third, these men say that they wish their wives would be armed (a claim that is not surprising given that the threat of ever-present victimization is precisely what justifies the need for a concealed handgun license). These contradictions suggest that concealed handguns function as props for doing masculinity by asserting the "father/husband as protector." The consequence is that it heightens the extent to which women are presumed to be vulnerable, in need of protection by the men in their lives (Hollander 2001). Having a concealed handgun license is a material practice that sustains their belief in essential gender differences by enabling men to fantasize about being the defenders of their families.

The men I interviewed also have elaborate fantasies of potential violence at the hands of other men. As they age, some begin to see themselves as less capable of self-defense. Because the body's capacity for aggression and violence is central to what it means to be masculine (Crawley, Foley, and Shehan 2008), some older men feel that their masculinity is diminished. According to Kimmel (2010, 120), this gets to the root of men's fear, a fear that others might "unmask us, emasculate us, reveal to us and the world that we do not measure up, that we are not real men." With a concealed handgun, the capacity for aggression and domination is restored. As Jeff explained, this can boost a man's sense of confidence, as he is able to regain access to the muscular version of masculinity and the capacity to dominate other, weaker men that is celebrated in American culture (Gibson 1994; Jeffords 1994).

No figure makes these men feel more physically vulnerable than the specter of the Black criminal. They ascribe a violent masculinity to men of color, and construct a sense of self in contradistinction. Because they assume that the Black men they encounter are potentially armed and dangerous, they want to carry a concealed handgun. Having a gun allows them to maintain a confidence that they are capable of responding to any threat, like Adam at the gas station: Should he get out of his car or drive off? Will he stand up to the threat or shirk from it?

It has been established that gang members—and other marginal men—can brandish and shoot guns to assert control and dominance over other men (Stretesky and Pogrebin 2007). The men I interviewed use guns in a similar way, but with profoundly different implications. When gang members use guns, they may be empowered in that instance by their masculine performance of domination, but it is also a sign of their marginalization. Indeed, the men Stretesky and Pogrebin (2007) interviewed were all incarcerated. In contrast, the men

I interviewed are among the most privileged in society and already have access to culturally celebrated versions of masculinity: Most of them are white and middle- or upper-middle class, and all of them are heterosexual. Their state-issued license to carry a concealed handgun, a license that is expensive and available only to those who can afford it and who are not legally restricted, gives them an added level of privilege: It gives them a symbol around which they construct both an empowered and culturally celebrated masculinity.

This work extends the literature on guns and masculinity by illustrating how dynamics between masculinities of privilege and marginalization lead to qualitatively different meanings for the same object. Criminals use guns to do masculinity (Kimmel and Mahler 2003; Stretesky and Pogrebin 2007), and so do law-abiding men. Unlike boys who shoot their classmates in a desperate attempt to be seen as "manly" (Kimmel and Mahler 2003), or gang members, for whom masculine bravado is a valuable currency (Stretesky and Pogrebin 2007), the men I interviewed gain access to aspects of masculinity that are celebrated at the regional level of culture by media and the gun lobby (Connell 1995; Gibson 1994; Jeffords 1994; Melzer 2009; O'Neill 2007). That these men are able to tap into these discourses—to cast themselves in the light of versions of masculinity celebrated by dominant culture—reveals the extent to which they are privileged. By contrast, Black and Latino men are assigned masculine traits of dominance, aggression, and violence, but this happens in a cultural context in which their skin color makes them suspect and they are assumed to be criminals (Collins 2006).

The implications of this study suggest the need for further research. The literature on hegemonic masculinity would benefit from closer attention to how dominant culture shapes and frames the discursive strategies that men have available to construct masculinities. One topic that should be addressed is the experiences of men of color who have concealed handgun licenses. How do Black men who are legally armed deal with the assumption that they are criminals? To fully understand how gender shapes the experience of carrying a concealed handgun, the case of women license holders must be considered. Does carrying a concealed handgun give women access to dominance in the way that it does for men? I am currently conducting interviews with women who have a concealed handgun license to understand how they explain their interest in carrying a firearm in public.

The men that I interviewed explain their desire for concealed firearms in light of versions of masculinity that are celebrated in culture: They want to be good fathers and husbands, they want to be able to fight back if attacked, and, unlike dangerous criminals, they are interested only in self-defense. Thus, their concealed handguns signify to them that they are "good guys," men who will use violence if necessary, but only to fight "bad guys."

Note

1. It is impossible to determine the exact number of defensive gun uses (DGUs) that occur in a given year, and estimates vary from 600,000 to 2.5 million (Cook and Ludwig 1998). While Kleck and Gertz (1995, 180) argue that there is "little legitimate scholarly reason to doubt that defensive gun use is very common in the U.S.," many scholars provide evidence that does just that. For example, Cook and Ludwig (1998) argue that reported incidents of DGUs are wracked with methodological problems that lead to highly inflated numbers. McDowall, Loftin, and Presser (2000) argue that reported DGUs often involve scenarios where the defender had no way of knowing the motives of their alleged offenders and so could not reasonably argue that their gun stopped a criminal act. Though the overall number is debated, what is known is that the vast majority of DGUs happen at home, while DGUs in public, the type that CHLs are intended for, are rare (Cook and Ludwig 1998).

References

Bonilla-Silva, Eduardo. 2001. *White supremacy and racism in the post civil rights era.* Boulder, CO: Rienner.

Britton, Dana. 2011. *The gender of crime.* Lanham, MD: AltaMira Press.

Carroll, Joseph. 2005. Gun ownership and use in America. *Gallup Poll*, 22 November.

Collins, Patricia H. 2006. A telling difference: Dominance strength and Black masculinities. In *Progressive black masculinities?*, edited by A. Mutua. New York: Routledge.

Connell, R. W. 1995. *Masculinities*. Cambridge, UK: Polity.

Connell, R. W., and J. W. Messerschmidt. 2005. Hegemonic masculinity: Rethinking the concept. *Gender & Society* 19:829–59.

Cook, Phillip J., and Jens Ludwig. 1998. Defensive gun uses: New evidence from a national survey. *Journal of Quantitative Criminology* 14:111–31.

Crawley, Sara L., Lara J. Foley, and Constance L. Shehan. 2008. *Gendering bodies*. Lanham, MD: Rowman and Littlefield.

Davis, Angela. 2007. In *Race, ethnicity, and gender: Selected readings*, edited by Joseph F. Healey and Eileen O'Brien. Thousand Oaks, CA: Pine Forge Press.

Feagin, J. R. 2010. *Racist America: Roots, current realities, and future reparations*. Hoboken, NJ: Taylor & Francis.

Gibson, James. 1994. *Warrior dreams: Paramilitary culture in post-Vietnam America*. New York: Hill and Wang.

Harvey-Wingfield, Adia. 2007. The modern mammy and the angry Black man: African American professionals' experience with gendered racism in the workplace. *Race, Gender, and Class* 14:196–212.

Hollander, Jocelyn. 2001. Vulnerability and dangerousness: The construction of gender through conversations about violence. *Gender & Society* 15:83–109.

Jeffords, Susan. 1994. *Hard bodies: Hollywood masculinity in the Reagan era*. New Brunswick, NJ: Rutgers University Press.

Jones, Jeffrey M. 2005. Public wary about broad concealed firearm privileges. *Gallup Poll*, 14 June.

Kimmel, Michael. 1996. *Manhood in America: A cultural history*. New York: Free Press.

Kimmel, Michael. 2010. Masculinity as homophobia: Fear, shame, and silence in the construction of gender identity. In *Privilege*, edited by Michael S. Kimmel and Abby L. Ferber. Boulder, CO: Westview.

Kimmel, M., and M. Mahler. 2003. Adolescent masculinity, homophobia, and violence: Random school shootings, 1982–2001. *American Behavioral Scientist* 46:1439–58.

Kleck, Gary, and Marc Gertz. 1995. Armed resistance to crime: The prevalence and nature of self-defense with a gun. *Journal of Criminal Law and Criminology* 86:150–87.

McDowall, David, Colin Loftin, and Stanley Presser. 2000. Measuring civilian defensive firearm use: A methodological experiment. *Journal of Quantitative Criminology* 16:1–19.

Melzer, Scott. 2009. *Gun crusaders: The NRA's culture war*. New York: New York University Press.

Messerschmidt, James W. 1993. *Masculinities and crime: Critique and reconceptualization of theory*. Lanham, MD: Rowman and Littlefield.

Messerschmidt, James W. 2000. *Nine lives: Adolescent masculinities, the body, and violence*. Boulder, CO: Westview Press.

Messner, Michael. 1992. *Power at play: Sports and the problem of masculinity*. Boston: Beacon Press.

O'Neill, Kevin Lewis. 2007. Armed citizens and the stories they tell: The National Rifle Association's achievement of terror and masculinity. *Men and Masculinities* 9:457–75.

Stange, Mary Zeiss, and Carol K. Oyster. 2000. *Gun women: Firearms and feminism in contemporary America*. New York: New York University Press.

Stretesky, P.B., and M.R. Pogrebin. 2007. Gang-related gun violence: Socialization, identity, and self. *Journal of Contemporary Ethnography* 36:85–114.

Stuckey, Mike. 2010. Record numbers now licensed to pack heat. Msnbc.com, April 24, 2010, http://www.msnbc.msn.com/id/34714389/ns/us_news-life.

Texas Department of Public Safety. 1995–2010. Demographic information by race/sex: License applications: Issued (calendar year).

When the Rapist Doesn't See It as Rape

NICHOLAS KRISTOF

Brian Banks was one of America's best high school football players when, in 2002, at age 16, he was accused of rape.

The accuser, Wanetta Gibson, said that Banks had forced her into a stairway at their high school in California and raped her.

Expelled from school and then later convicted of rape, Banks served more than five years in prison. He became not a professional football star but a registered sex offender.

Then, in 2011, Gibson recanted. There was no rape (apparently she made the accusation to prevent her mom from learning that she had been sexually active). Banks was eventually exonerated and his conviction overturned, and, at 28, he played briefly for the Atlanta Falcons. But, after a decade away from football, it was too late to catch up.

That kind of nightmare is what many Americans have in mind when they fear an aggressive clampdown on sexual violence. It's a legitimate fear.

Jon Krakauer tells the story of Brian Banks in his terrific new book, "Missoula," as a cautionary reminder. Yet, in his book about acquaintance rapes in a college town, he also makes clear that what is far more common is another kind of injustice: perpetrators of rape who get away with it again and again.

One careful study found that false allegations make up between 2 percent and 10 percent of rape cases. Yet victims (mostly women and girls, but also men and boys) are routinely tarnished or blamed; Human Rights Watch reported this month that nearly two-thirds of members of the military who report sexual assaults face reprisals. Given the risks, the great majority of rape cases are never reported to the authorities.

The result is impunity. And that fosters more rape.

Scholars have found that many sexual assaults are carried out by a small number of men who strike repeatedly—often without realizing that they are rapists.

The way this research is conducted is astonishing: Men were simply surveyed and asked whether they had ever had sex with someone who didn't want to. Remarkably, men repeatedly said, yes, they had.

One of the most chilling sections of Krakauer's book quotes a fraternity brother, "Frank," describing his technique to a researcher, David Lisak:

> We'd be on the lookout for the good-looking girls, especially the freshmen, the really young ones. They were the easiest. . . . Then we'd get them drinking right away. . . . They'd be guzzling it, you know, because they were freshmen, kind of nervous.

"Frank" recounted how he targeted one young woman, plied her with alcohol-spiked punch, and then led her to a bed. "At some point, she started saying things like . . . 'I don't want to do this right away,' or something like that. I just kept working on her clothes . . . and she started squirming. But that actually helped, because her blouse came off easier. . . . She tried to push me off, so I pushed her back down. . . . I mean, she was so plastered that she probably didn't know what was going on, anyway. I don't know, maybe that's why she started pushing on me. But, you know, I just kept leaning on her, pulling off her clothes."

"Frank" said he kept his arm across her chest, by the base of her neck, to reduce her squirming as he had sex with her. When he was finished, he dressed and returned to the party.

And the woman? "She left."

There are no easy solutions, but one way to fight the epidemic is legal: Prosecute aggressively, while recognizing that sexual encounters are often complex, ambiguous, fueled by alcohol, and prone to he-said-she-said uncertainties.

Another way to fight back is cultural: Blunt conversations among men and women alike about consent, alcohol, and the need for friends to step up with what's called "bystander intervention." That means that just as you don't let a friend drive drunk, you don't let a friend take advantage of someone—or let a plastered friend get steered to a predator's bed.

One of the fundamental challenges is that the word rape conjures a mental image of a stranger jumping out of bushes. Sure, that happens. But most sexual assault happens among acquaintances. We flinch at the truth that most rapists are less likely to point a gun than to proffer a plastic cup of booze, that they charm and kiss before they menace. That's why men must be a part of these discussions, for it's a failing of all society that men like Frank are unaware that they are rapists.

I'll encourage my (college-age) kids to read "Missoula." And we need to have more open conversations among young men and women alike about the genuine risks of false accusations—but also about the far more common injustice of lax legal and social mores that allow predators to get away with rape after rape. It's time to stop flinching.

An Intersectional Analysis of Lesbian, Gay, Bisexual, and Transgender (LGBT) People's Evaluations of Anti-Queer Violence

DOUG MEYER

Most studies that have focused on violence against lesbian, gay, bisexual, and transgender (LGBT) people have overlooked the intersections among race, class, and gender (Mason 2002). Conversely, I examine LGBT, or queer, people's violent experiences through a feminist and intersectional lens, exploring the evaluations of 47 respondents interviewed in New York City. In particular, I build on studies that have examined the severity of anti-queer violence, focusing particular attention on LGBT people's evaluations of physical and verbal abuse (Herek, Gillis, and Cogan 1999; Rose and Mechanic 2002). Previous research has suggested that lesbians and gay men generally perceive homophobic physical attacks as more severe than verbal abuse or violence that is not based on their

Doug Meyer, "An Intersectional Analysis of Lesbian, Gay, Bisexual, and Transgender (LGBT) People's Evaluations of Anti-Queer Violence," *Gender & Society*, Vol. 26, No. 6 (December 2012), pp. 849–873. Copyright © 2012 by Doug Meyer. Reprinted by permission of SAGE Publications.

sexuality (D'Augelli and Grossman 2001; Dunbar 2006; Herek et al. 1997). In contrast, my results reveal significant intersectional differences, thereby dispelling the notion that LGBT people evaluate forms of anti-queer violence in uniform ways.

Scholarship examining the severity of anti-LGBT violence has typically focused on the traumatic psychological effects of hate crime—that is, physical violence rooted in bias and based on aspects of one's identity such as race, religion, or sexual orientation (Iganski 2001). Although studies of hate crime victims have drawn attention to an important research area, they have arguably led to a homogenized portrayal of LGBT people, with little attention to the differences among them (Dunbar 2006; Mason 2002). Examining these differences remains important, as homogenizing LGBT people's experiences marginalizes the concerns of queer people who are the least privileged (Cohen 1997; Ward 2008). I use an intersectional approach to examine the ways in which race, gender, and sexuality simultaneously structure respondents' evaluations of anti-queer violence. Thus, while previous research has focused primarily on the homophobic implications of anti-queer violence (see D'Augelli and Grossman 2001; Herek, Gillis, and Cogan 1999), my results indicate that multiple systems of oppression shape LGBT people's evaluations of their violent experiences.

Theoretical Framework

Intersectional theory contends that social phenomena are often best understood by examining the overlap of institutional power structures such as race, class, gender, and sexuality (Choo and Ferree 2010; Collins 2000; Crenshaw 1991). In contrast, approaches that take only one system of oppression into account sometimes provide homogenized and distorted views of marginalized groups, advancing the interests of more privileged individuals (King 1988; Zinn and Dill 1996). Much of intersectional theory, for example, has critiqued race-only or gender-only frameworks, which may ameliorate the effects of one system of oppression, while simultaneously reinforcing other power structures (Bettie 2003; Cohen 1999; Ward 2008). As a result, intersectional approaches have suggested

that attempts to redress social inequality should account for the multiple and simultaneous effects of systems of oppression, taking into consideration the experiences of individuals who are oppressed along multiple axes of inequality (McCall 2005; Zinn and Dill 1996).

Although intersectional theory has revealed some limitations of using singular frameworks for understanding social phenomena, studies of LGBT hate crime victims and social movements concerned with preventing anti-queer violence have focused overwhelmingly on homophobia and heterosexism, revealing the psychological costs of homophobic violence (Dunbar 2006; Herek, Gillis, and Cogan 1999; Jenness and Broad 1994). Anti-queer violence, however, can typically be explained not only by sexuality but also by gender, as many of its forms occur when LGBT people "do gender" inappropriately (Perry 2001; West and Zimmerman 1987). Nevertheless, with a few notable exceptions (see Mason 2001, 2002; Perry 2001), studies of LGBT hate crime victims have typically neglected the gendered implications of anti-queer violence, overlooking how gender and sexuality are simultaneously implicated in LGBT people's violent experiences (Mason 2002). Herek (1990), for example, notes that lesbians and gay men both experience violence for violating gender norms, yet conceptualizing homophobic hate crime as emanating from "cultural heterosexism" ignores the role of sexism and misogyny in shaping forms of anti-lesbian violence (see Herek et al. 1997). Concurrently, research that has accounted for gender has sometimes downplayed the role of homophobia, with one early and influential study of anti-lesbian hate crime conceptualizing "lesbianism as an extension of gender and conceptualiz[ing] anti-lesbian violence as an extension of misogynistic violence" (von Schulthess 1992, 71). This understanding of anti-queer violence as shaped primarily by gender has informed subsequent work, as Perry (2001, 110) conceptualizes "gay-bashing as a response to doing gender inappropriately," making little reference to homophobia and heterosexism.

Adopting a feminist intersectional perspective, I view gender and sexuality as overlapping rather than competing systems of inequality, not privileging one system over the other. Most studies of LGBT hate crime victims, focused on the effects of homophobic violence, have been unable to account for the ways in which LGBT people's violent experiences may be based on racism and sexism in addition to, or even instead of, homophobia and heteronormativity (Madriz 1997; Mason 2002; Moore 2011). Indeed, although hate crime research has explored race and gender differences in terms of the frequency with which LGBT people encounter violence (see Dunbar 2006), systems of oppression have typically been examined in isolation of one another (Mason 2002). Thus, we know relatively little about how forms of inequality simultaneously structure queer people's violent experiences. Meanings of gender and sexuality, for example, may be implicated differently in forms of anti-queer violence for LGBT people of color and white LGBT people, yet this dynamic has not been fully explored by hate crime scholarship. Furthermore, although meanings of race and sexuality may have different implications for lesbians and gay men, our understanding of these intersectional differences remains limited if research continues to examine heteronormativity as separate from other institutional power structures.

I argue that systems of oppression play an important role in structuring LGBT people's evaluations of anti-queer violence. Departing from my previous work focused on social class (see Meyer 2008, 2010), here I place primary emphasis on the intersections among race, gender, and sexuality. By doing so, I expand on research that has examined LGBT people of color's experiences in managing racism in white LGBT communities and homophobia in heterosexual communities of color, as well as the heterosexism and institutionalized racism in society at large (Cohen 1999; Collins 2004; Moore 2011). Studies examining racism and classism in white queer communities have emphasized the role of advocacy and service organizations in advancing the interests of white, middle-class LGBT people, particularly white and middle-class gay men, while also marginalizing low-income LGBT people of color by constructing their views as the least reputable (Smith 1999; Ward 2004, 2008). This research indicates that despite the universalizing tendencies of the mainstream gay rights movement, LGBT people do not have uniform interests along race and class lines (Cohen 1997; Moore 2006; Ward 2008). Additionally, scholarship examining homophobia in Black heterosexual communities has focused on the role of the Black church and has emphasized how homosexuality has historically been linked with whiteness (Cohen 1999; Collins 2004; Johnson 2001). The association of homosexuality and whiteness, while not unique to Black communities, has led to notions of authenticity whereby the most "authentic" racialized identities have become constructed as exclusively heterosexual (Collins 2004; Johnson 2001; Smith 1999).

Confronting heteronormativity and institutionalized racism, white LGBT communities and Black heterosexual communities have often reinforced the whitening of homosexuality to present their social group as "respectable" to mainstream society (Cohen 1999; Collins 2004; Moore 2011). Thus, LGBT people of color frequently confront a "politics of respectability," whereby they are discouraged from presenting themselves in a negative way and, therefore, confront pressures to hide their sexuality or gender identity—pressures that white LGBT people do not face because of their racial identity (Collins 2004; Moore 2011). Still, research suggests that LGBT people of color have frequently resisted a politics of respectability, challenging their invisibility in white LGBT communities and heterosexual communities of color (Cohen 1999; Moore 2011; Smith 1999). In contrast, white queer people do not typically have to contend with discourse that they have disappointed their racial communities, because the social construction of whiteness as an invisible social status allows white people to violate social norms without having their actions ascribed to their racial identity (Frankenberg 1993).

Building on work that has explored racial differences among LGBT people, I provide empirical evidence that white queer people are able to overlook the racialized implications of their violent experiences, while LGBT people of color, who do not have the advantage of white privilege, contend with discourse that they have disappointed their racial communities (Cohen 1997; Collins 2004). Furthermore, expanding on previous research that has explored Black lesbians' strategies of cultivating respectability, I examine how gay men of color may challenge discourse that they have inappropriately represented their racial communities in different ways than Black and Latina lesbians (Moore 2006, 2011). Finding significant intersectional differences, I reveal that meanings of race, gender, and sexuality intersect to structure LGBT people's evaluations.

Consistent with other intersectional work, I argue that LGBT people's violent experiences should not be categorized in dichotomous, mutually exclusive ways. As Patricia Hill Collins (1998, 923) has argued, "Within dichotomous thinking that juxtaposes actions to words, speech can never be violent. It can only provoke violence." Nevertheless, as studies of LGBT hate crime victims have suggested that "hate crimes hurt more" than other forms of violence, the cumulative effect of this research has been to imply a hierarchy of traumatic experiences, with hate-motivated physical violence placed toward the top and verbal abuse and non-bias crime placed toward the bottom (Iganski 2001, 626). Conversely, as intersectional frameworks contend that systems of oppression should not be hierarchically ranked, I argue that LGBT people's oppressive experiences should also not be classified in hierarchical ways (Crenshaw 1991; King 1988). Still, although I attempt to move away from hierarchical understandings of violence, respondents did sometimes rank their violent experiences in different ways depending on their social position. Here, I examine these intersectional differences in how respondents constructed hierarchies of violence, exploring the simultaneous effects of race, gender, and sexuality.

Despite the many contributions of intersectional theory, scholarship has increasingly problematized its emphasis on difference, arguing that intersectional approaches would be better served by examining racialized and gendered processes rather than the differences among raced or gendered bodies (Choo and Ferree 2010). Other feminist theories have problematized research that reifies socially produced differences, as such studies tend to essentialize the characteristics of social groups by ignoring the variation within these groups and exaggerating the differences between them (Epstein 1988). I focus on intersectional differences among LGBT respondents, yet to avoid essentializing these differences I emphasize the social, rather than inherent, nature of the differences described here. Indeed, the larger context in which respondents' violent experiences occurred, including race and gender norms, played a significant role in shaping their evaluations.

Intersectionality has been theorized more frequently than ethnographically explored (Bettie 2003). This gap persists in studies of hate crime, with some areas of the literature giving serious consideration to the intersection of race, class, and gender, particularly research on racist hate crime (see Blee 2002; Daniels 1997); yet LGBT people's qualitative experiences of violence have not been examined through an intersectional lens. In contrast, I use an intersectional approach to expand our understanding of anti-queer violence, revealing how systems of oppression simultaneously structure LGBT people's evaluations of their violent experiences.

Methods

The data presented in this article are drawn from a larger project that focuses on race, class, and gender differences among 47 people who experienced anti-LGBT violence (Meyer 2008, 2010). To explore these intersectional differences, I conducted semi-structured, in-depth interviews, recruiting participants from a wide range of advocacy and service organizations in New York City, many of which provide services for LGBT people of color. . . .

Respondents' demographic characteristics and experiences of violence are shown in Table 1. In total, I interviewed 20 women, 17 men, and 10 transgender people. Twenty-one participants identified as Black or African American, 16 as white, eight as Latina or Latino (five identified as Puerto Rican, two as Mexican, and one as Colombian), and two as Asian (one identified as Chinese and one as Vietnamese). Six of the 15 lesbian respondents identified as Black, five as white, and four as Latina; the sample also includes six Black transgender women. Among gay male respondents, eight identified as white, seven as Black, one as Latino, and one as Asian.

TABLE 1. Respondents' Demographic Characteristics and Experiences of Violence

Gender and Sexuality (with Pseudonyms)	Age	Race/Ethnicity	Form of Anti-Queer Violence Described
Lesbians			
Diamond	51	Black	Physical, verbal, sexual assault
Latoya	50	Black	Physical, verbal, sexual assault
Aisha	53	Black	Physical, verbal
Jasmine	44	Black	Physical, verbal
Jetta	28	Black	Physical, verbal
Tamika	53	Black	Physical, verbal
Judy	43	Latina	Physical, verbal, sexual assault
Page	45	Latina	Physical, verbal, sexual assault
Maria	26	Latina	Physical, verbal
Tina	21	Latina	Physical, verbal
Dorothy	49	White	Physical, verbal
Martha	54	White	Physical, verbal
Catherine	46	White	Verbal
Julia	28	White	Verbal
Jill	49	White	Verbal
Bisexual women			
Leslie	50	Black	Physical, verbal
Ling	29	Asian	Physical, verbal
Heterosexual women			
Anne	41	Black	Physical, verbal
Lisa	36	Latina	Physical, verbal
Emily	55	White	Verbal
Gay men			
Andre	24	Black	Physical, verbal, sexual assault
Cole	33	Black	Physical, verbal
Daniel	26	Black	Physical, verbal
Gideon	25	Black	Physical, verbal
Jayvyn	33	Black	Physical, verbal
Kevin	62	Black	Physical, verbal
Walter	24	Black	Physical, verbal
Frankie	48	Latino	Physical, verbal
Thomas	41	Asian	Physical, verbal
Bill	51	White	Physical, verbal
George	45	White	Physical, verbal
Greg	43	White	Physical, verbal
Jacob	40	White	Physical, verbal
Mark	46	White	Physical, verbal
Paul	57	White	Physical, verbal
Ted	33	White	Physical, verbal
Bob	54	White	Verbal

(continued)

TABLE I. *(continued)*

Gender and Sexuality (with Pseudonyms)	Age	Race/Ethnicity	Form of Anti-Queer Violence Described
Male-to-female transgender women			
Dominique	23	Black	Physical, verbal, sexual assault
Eva	46	Black	Physical, verbal, sexual assault
Ebony	20	Black	Physical, verbal, sexual assault
Lela	48	Black	Physical, verbal
Lakeisha	38	Black	Physical, verbal
Kayla	36	Black	Physical, verbal
Carol	39	Latina	Physical, verbal, sexual assault
Mary	47	White	Verbal
Female-to-male transgender men			
William	29	Latino	Physical, verbal
Intersexed			
Nevada	36	White	Physical, verbal

I use the phrase "LGBT people of color" to denote Black, Latino/Latina, and Asian participants. As 21 of these respondents identified as Black, eight identified as Latina or Latino, and two as Asian, this research focuses primarily on the experiences of Black LGBT people and, to a lesser extent, the experiences of Latino/Latina participants. I have combined the violent experiences of multiple groups of LGBT people of color to highlight how white respondents did not confront the same pressures as other racial and ethnic groups. Of course, as only 16 white respondents participated in this project, the results presented here should be viewed as suggestive rather than definitive. Still, there seemed to be some noteworthy racial differences, as outlined below. I sometimes refer to "lesbian and transgender women," not to collapse their violent experiences, as anti-transgender violence obviously differs in significant ways from anti-lesbian abuse (see Schilt and Westbrook 2009), but to highlight the ways that lesbian and transgender women's evaluations differed from those of gay male respondents. Here, my positionality as a white gay man undoubtedly shaped the interview data; white and gay male respondents sometimes felt comfortable sharing arguably racist or sexist thoughts with me, while LGBT people of color

focused on homophobia more than racism, classism, and sexism with a white, male academic. Although I have tried not to reinforce hierarchies based on race, class, and gender, the interview process and my analysis of the data are inevitably immersed in these power dynamics. To ensure respondents' confidentiality, I use pseudonyms throughout this article.

Findings and Discussion

LGBT people of color often viewed their violent experiences as implying that they had negatively represented their racial communities, while white respondents did not perceive forms of anti-queer violence in this way. Moreover, even though lesbian respondents confronted some similar forms of abuse across racial lines—violence for "converting" another woman into lesbianism, for example—their evaluations also differed in race-specific ways, as lesbians of color emphasized their autonomy to challenge notions that they had not contributed to their racial communities. Although gay male respondents perceived their violent experiences in some similar ways across racial lines—viewing the violence as an attempt to impose meanings of weakness onto them, for example—gay men of color, in contrast to white gay men, highlighted their emotional and physical strength to construct themselves as valuable members of their racial groups. In the following sections, I first outline these intersectional differences in how respondents viewed the racialized implications of anti-queer violence, and then I describe participants' evaluations of physical and verbal abuse, finding that lesbian and transgender women often perceived physical violence as indicating the possible onset of a sexual assault, while gay men more frequently constructed homophobic insults as severe.

The Racialized Implications and the Gendered Dynamics of Anti-Queer Violence

LGBT people of color regularly interpreted their violent experiences as attempts to punish them for not appropriately representing their racial communities. For instance, Jayvyn, a 33-year-old Black gay man, explained his reasons for believing that some Black heterosexual men have harassed him: "It's like I've let down Black men by being gay or something. That means that I've identified myself with weakness, and I'm not supposed to do that." Black lesbians made similar comments when describing the racialized implications of their violent experiences, revealing a complex intersection of race, gender, and sexuality norms. Referring to these intersections, Latoya, a 50-year-old Black lesbian, described a violent experience that had occurred on the street, when she was holding hands with her girlfriend, a Black woman whom Latoya described as "very girly." The violence involved a male stranger telling Latoya to "take that white shit home" and realize that her girlfriend "just needed a dick." The man became physically violent—punching Latoya's arm—when she told him that "no woman would touch" him, since he was "disgusting." Describing this experience, Latoya problematized its implications:

> The physical is what gets to me, that's like telling me that I have to stop doing this. . . . Like I have to stop making [my girlfriend] a lesbian. They act like I did this to her. And it's like I'm not supposed to because then I'm making Black people look bad. Like if I left her alone, she wouldn't be

gay. . . . They act like she has no control over herself. I didn't do anything to her. They don't know her. She can be who she wants.

Here, Latoya underscored her girlfriend's autonomy, while deriding sexist and heteronormative discourse whereby masculine lesbians are viewed as corrupting feminine women—the former supposedly "make" the latter lesbian. This understanding of lesbian sexuality reinforces traditional gender ideology by constructing masculine women as active (they are "doing" the changing) and feminine women as passive (they are changed), while also stereotyping lesbians as either corrupting and controlling or flighty and complicit. In this context, Black lesbians with butch gender presentations of self could then perceive homophobic violence as an attempt to punish them for "making Black people look bad," as they had supposedly converted Black feminine women into lesbianism.

Gay men, regardless of their racial identity, did not describe accusations that they had "made" another man gay. Butch lesbians, however, frequently perceived their violent experiences as attempts to punish them for "converting" a woman into lesbianism; approximately half of the lesbian respondents involved in this study perceived at least one of their experiences in this way. Gender and sexuality norms played a central role in these situations, as perpetrators appeared to undermine the sexual agency of the woman whom they perceived as feminine, while using physical violence against the more "masculine" partner. Furthermore, given the social construction of race in the United States, and given that most of the violence respondents described was intraracial, lesbians often had to confront different discourses depending on their racial identity. For instance, Jetta, a 28-year-old Black lesbian, argued that the severity of violence depends on its intention:

> It's more about what the person is trying to do. . . . [If] they're telling me that I'm a bad African American or whatever, that pisses me off. I go to church every Sunday. I live my life how I want. A good African American—I live my life how I want. I can take care of myself. I am who I am, that's not gonna change.

Rebelling against ideas that she has failed to represent Black people positively, Jetta emphasized her autonomy, stating that she represents Black people well because she lives her life as she wants. Other Black lesbians also argued that they had represented their racial communities in a positive way, although perhaps not as overtly as Jetta. In contrast, white lesbians, free from these racialized pressures, did not typically have to confront discourse that they had disappointed their racial groups. Martha, for example, a 54-year-old white lesbian, described one of her violent experiences without making reference to her racial identity: "It'd be nice to know that I can wear all the butch-y stuff I want. That it doesn't matter. I'd just like to be able to do what I want." There were several similarities between the experiences of Martha and Jetta: both identified as butch lesbians; both had experienced violence when they were with their "more feminine" girlfriends. Both respondents also thought that the violence was directed against them, rather than their partners, because they appeared masculine in their gender presentation of self and because they were viewed as a "bad influence," supposedly converting their girlfriends into lesbianism.

Despite these similarities, their evaluations placed different emphases on autonomy. Martha and Jetta focused on their independence: Martha said, "I'd just like to be able to do what I want," while Jetta declared, "I live my life how I want." Nevertheless, Jetta focused more on the ways in which she is self-sufficient, repeatedly underscoring how she lives according to her own wishes; twice she said, "I live my life how I want," connecting this autonomy to her being a "good African American." Martha explained her desire to wear the clothes she wants, but she did not employ the narratives that were more frequently used by Black and Latina women, regarding how their autonomy makes them valuable members of their racial communities. Indeed, Jetta underscored her self-sufficiency to challenge notions that she negatively represents African Americans, while Martha, speaking from a position of white privilege, did not have to contend with discourse that she had betrayed her racial group.

Since Jetta's girlfriend was Black and Martha's girlfriend was white, the meaning of "converting" a woman into lesbianism took on different forms for these respondents. While Martha did not struggle with the racialized implications of her supposed conversion of a white woman into lesbianism, Jetta thought that others might view this act as causing harm to her racial community; she thought that she was being punished for "making" her girlfriend—another Black woman—a lesbian. In this regard, Black lesbians who identify as butch may face particularly harsh sanctions, as the act of "converting" a Black woman into lesbianism may be viewed as preventing a Black woman from reproducing. As neither white lesbians nor Black gay men are likely to confront such discourse, Black lesbians with masculine gender presentations of self may confront these pressures in such a way that other social groups do not.

Whereas lesbians in this study often focused on their autonomy to challenge perpetrators' discourse, gay male respondents more frequently highlighted their emotional and physical strength. Here, the gender dynamic of respondents' violent experiences played an important role in structuring their evaluations; although some respondents described verbal harassment from women and physical violence from their mothers during childhood, the overwhelming majority of respondents described experiences of physical violence perpetrated by men. As a result, gay male respondents regularly perceived their violent experiences as a masculinity contest, with heterosexual men trying to impose notions of weakness onto them. In response, gay men frequently underscored the ways in which they were strong, both emotionally and physically. While gay men across racial lines emphasized their emotional and physical strength, these respondents interpreted the meaning of the violence differently based on race. That is, gay men of color often viewed their violent experiences as implying that they were weak for identifying as gay and, perhaps implicitly, for associating themselves with whiteness. For instance, Jayvyn, the 33-year-old Black gay man mentioned previously, constructed himself as strong to challenge notions that he was performing Blackness inappropriately:

I'm gaaaay. Everyone knows it, the second I walk out the door. That doesn't make me a bad African American or whatever. . . . I'm not a weak little thing. . . . I can defend myself. I know how to fight. I can get past things pretty quick. I can handle things emotionally, spiritually. They [people who have attacked me] aren't like that. They'll only go calling me names when their friends are around.

Black gay male respondents typically rejected notions that they had not appropriately represented their racial communities; instead, they usually suggested that their gender and sexual identities were a legitimate way of expressing themselves. Moreover, Black gay men regularly noted the importance of emotional strength, sometimes even suggesting that other men could benefit from being emotionally stronger. With the statement above, Jayvyn constructed himself as emotionally stronger than his attackers, who only insult him "when their friends are around." This type of response was one of the ways that LGBT people pointed to their perpetrators' hypocrisy. As heterosexual men used homophobic insults in groups—when their friends could protect them—gay men constructed this behavior as signifying weakness, as indicating that their perpetrators were susceptible to peer pressure and fearful of perpetrating homophobic violence without the protection of their friends. This interpretation, then, inverts the meaning of anti-gay violence by constructing perpetrators as weak-willed, and therefore hypocritical, given that they had tried to construct gay men as weak.

While white gay men who participated in this study also perceived their violent experiences as attempts to construct them as weak, they did not seem to emphasize strength to the same extent as Black and Latino men. George, for example, a 45-year-old white gay man, described his perpetrator's motivations in this way: "He was trying to say that I'm weak, which, whatever, I might be. The whole thing is just kinda stupid. It's easy to be like 'Oh, okay, you're tough, you're macho. Whatever, you can have that.'" Similar to most of the gay men whom I interviewed, George concluded that his perpetrators were trying to construct him as weak. Rather than emphasizing his strength, however, George casually dismissed its importance.

Most of the white men whom I interviewed did not necessarily reject the value of strength in this way, yet George's offhanded dismissal of meanings of weakness was more consistently expressed by white gay men than Black and Latino men. Indeed, with this statement, George suggested that the posturing of his perpetrator was "easy" to dismiss, which contrasts sharply with the more complex evaluations of LGBT people of color. Thus, constructing gay men as weak has different implications across racial lines, as Black gay men frequently emphasized their strength as a way of rejecting discourse that they were weak for having "given in" to homosexuality, which has been stereotypically linked with whiteness (Collins 2004; Johnson 2001; Moore 2011). White gay men, on the other hand, did not usually view meanings of weakness as having racialized implications and, therefore, because of their white privilege did not appear as compelled to emphasize their emotional and physical strength.

Intersectional Differences in Respondents' Evaluations of Physical and Verbal Violence

The desire on the part of lesbians of color to live an autonomous life, free of harassment, frequently led them to condemn physical violence more harshly than verbal abuse. Aisha, for example, a 53-year-old Black lesbian, described a man who kicked her shin on the subway after seeing public displays of affection between Aisha and her girlfriend. Comparing physical and verbal violence, Aisha minimized the effects of the latter: "Verbal's not as bad because I can go about my life. When someone says something to me, I can go about my life." In this study, Black lesbians regularly underscored the importance of their autonomy, constructing physical violence as a direct attack on their ability to be self-sufficient. As I asked Aisha to elaborate on her perception of physical and verbal abuse, she characterized the difference in this way:

A man says something to me, that gets under my skin, [but] touching me, that's something different. . . . Touching me is gettin' in my space. You're telling me not to be who I am. You're telling me that I should change—change to who you want me to.

For Black lesbian respondents, this understanding of physical violence as more severe than verbal abuse seemed in part to reflect what intersectional theorists have noted about the need for marginalized groups to create a safe space for themselves (Collins 2000). Lesbians of color, marginalized from both white LGBT communities and heterosexual communities of color, in addition to the more normative white, heterosexual institutions in society at large, appeared particularly likely to emphasize this need for a safe space and to highlight the ways in which physical violence violated their right to self-determination.

When respondents ranked forms of physical and verbal violence, gay men frequently emphasized the severity of homophobic insults. Frankie, for example, a 48-year-old Puerto Rican gay man, highlighted the long-term effects of homophobic insults to illustrate the pain these words have caused him: "What can hurt as much as anything is the words. The hitting hurts, don't get me wrong, but scars can heal and the words will stay with you." Most gay male respondents constructed physical and verbal abuse as approximately equal in their severity, yet a few of the gay men in this study constructed homophobic insults as more severe than a physical attack. For instance, Gideon, a 25-year-old Black gay man, downplayed the severity of physical violence in this way: "I can handle some crazy dude putting his hands on me. That's not a big deal to me. The constant comments is what gets [to] me. 'Faggot, faggot, faggot'—that's worse than someone putting their hands on me."

Rather than emphasizing the severity of homophobic insults, lesbian and transgender women more frequently described violent encounters as beginning with them "just being called names," and then escalating with the onset of physical abuse. In this regard, the comments of Carol, a 39-year-old Puerto Rican transgender woman, were characteristic:

> Like first he was just calling me names, but then it got worse when he grabbed me. . . . People have called me names in the past. That I can get over. But putting your hands on me, that's a whole new thing. That's what I can't stand.

Here, Carol referred to a violent experience in which a man approached her on the street, began making sexually harassing comments to her, and then, after questioning whether she was transgender, started using dehumanizing language ("you're an it") and calling her sexist and homophobic insults (e.g., "bitch," "faggot"), eventually pulling her by the hair. Later during the interview, Carol noted that the man's use of physical violence made her feel as if sexual assault might be imminent: "Putting his hands on me, that made me feel very unsafe. Like he could have tried to rape me." This fear of sexual assault, not typically expressed by gay men, led many lesbian and transgender women to emphasize the severity of physical violence. Physical and sexual assault, of course, are not necessarily the same, and lesbian and transgender women often differentiated between them, yet female respondents frequently viewed these forms of violence as related, constructing sexual assault as more severe than verbal abuse and perceiving physical violence as indicating the possible onset of sexual assault.

While gay male respondents suggested that perpetrators occasionally used violence to prevent an encounter from becoming sexual—accusing gay men of "hitting on" them, for example—lesbian and transgender women more frequently described violence as introducing a sexual component into the encounter. Thus, even though lesbian and transgender women did not emphasize the severity of homophobic insults as frequently as gay men, female respondents did sometimes construct verbal threats as severe, particularly when these statements implied that physical or sexual violence might be forthcoming. For instance, Jasmine, a 44-year-old Black lesbian, described an experience in an elevator when a man from her apartment building said that she "needed to be taught a lesson like a good dyke" before touching her face. Jasmine perceived the man's actions as a threat to her physical safety, as a suggestion that he could sexually assault her. Later during the interview, she argued that physical violence was worse than verbal abuse, but then immediately said, as if recalling the violent incident in the elevator:

JASMINE: That's only if [the verbal] doesn't intimidate me.

INTERVIEWER: How might it intimidate you?

JASMINE: Like is he going to tell me something that threatens me as a woman. Tell me what he's gonna do.

Confronting the possibility of a sexual assault, lesbian respondents occasionally emphasized the severity of verbal threats, noting how these statements can invoke sexualized violence.

The differences between female and male respondents must be understood in the context of gendered power dynamics. Gay men often decrease in status for identifying as feminine, and may view homophobic insults as a particularly harsh attack on their gender and sexual identities. Lesbian and transgender women are likely to construct physical and sexual violence as severe because women frequently confront the threat of sexual assault in a way that gay men do not (Madriz 1997; von Schulthess 1992). The narratives of lesbian respondents, focusing on self-sufficiency, should also be viewed in light of gender norms that encourage women to endure hardship in a stoic manner (Madriz 1997). Furthermore, gay men's repeated emphasis on strength should be understood in the context of gendered expectations and social control mechanisms that encourage men to perform masculinity through strength (Perry 2001).

Beyond Dichotomous Constructions: Anti-Queer Violence as Rooted in Multiple Systems of Oppression

Respondents' attempts to compare physical and verbal violence frequently revealed the difficulty of distinguishing between these forms of abuse, as their violent experiences often did not fit neatly into one category or another. Indeed, about half of the LGBT people in this study noted how physical and verbal violence overlapped. For instance, Judy, a 43-year-old Puerto Rican lesbian, described an attempted rape in which a man used a mix of sexist and homophobic insults while forcibly trying to remove her clothes. When asked to compare physical and verbal violence, Judy problematized the politics of making such distinctions:

It's hard to tell which is which. It goes back and forth. So, sometimes you don't know. . . . It can't be said that what happened is one or the other, because when both are happening, then I have to sit there and be like, "Ok, what was bothering me about it?" That would drive me crazy.

Emphasizing how physical and verbal violence occur alternately and simultaneously, Judy underscored the futility of distinguishing between these two types of abuse, arguing that such attempts require people who have experienced violence to engage in the psychologically taxing process of differentiating between concurrent events.

In contrast, some studies of hate crime victims have defined bias crimes with both physical and verbal violence solely as physical attacks, even though they are also verbal attacks (see D'Augelli and Grossman 2001; Rose and Mechanic 2002). As a result, by constructing physical and verbal violence as dichotomous, mutually exclusive categories, hate crime research may categorize LGBT people's violent experiences differently than some LGBT people would do. Narrow definitions of violence have already been critiqued extensively in the domestic violence literature, yet this same understanding of abuse, where all of its forms are understood as harmful, has not been incorporated into studies of hate crime victims (DeKeseredy 2000). Indeed, to suggest that "hate crimes hurt more" than other forms of violence reinforces problematic discourse that victims may confront—that some of their violent experiences are not severe (Iganski 2001, 626). Forms of violence obviously differ in terms of their severity, but constructing extremely broad categories of abuse does more to conceal these differences than to reveal them. Moving beyond hierarchies, while accepting that LGBT people may rank forms of violence on their own, I have focused on the meaning that queer people attribute to their violent experiences, without entirely discarding distinctions between physical and verbal abuse. Nevertheless, as studies of hate crime proceed, this dichotomy of physical and verbal violence may prove less useful, as research continues to examine multiple forms of anti-queer violence.

By emphasizing the effects of different types of violence (e.g., physical or verbal, bias-motivated or not motivated by bias), studies of LGBT hate crime victims have frequently overlooked other important effects, such as the role of race, class, and gender in structuring LGBT people's evaluations. As research has focused primarily on the negative consequences of homophobic attacks (see D'Augelli and Grossman 2001; Herek, Gillis, and Cogan 1999), our understanding of anti-queer violence remains limited, as the violent experiences of white lesbians, LGB people of color, and transgender people, for example, are often not structured solely, or even predominantly, by homophobia and heteronormativity (Mason 2002; Moore 2011). Thus, by focusing on homophobia at the exclusion of other forms of inequality, these studies have inadvertently reinforced the interests of LGBT people who perceive their violent experiences as predominantly rooted in homophobia—most frequently, as my other work has shown, white and middle-class gay men (Meyer 2008). Indeed, as I have outlined elsewhere, Black and Latina lesbians found it particularly difficult to determine whether their violent experiences were based on their sexuality because they often could not be certain whether racism or misogyny had also played a role, particularly when the violence was perpetrated by white men (Meyer 2008).

Although attempts to place singular emphasis on homophobia tend to reinforce the interests of LGBT people who are oppressed primarily based on their sexuality, an alternative strategy of constructing gender as competing with, or more important than, sexuality and heteronormativity also produces an inadequate understanding of anti-queer violence. Anti-lesbian violence, for example, cannot simply be understood by adding homophobia to existing frameworks of violence against women (von Schulthess 1992); indeed, homophobia does not merely amplify sexist violence, but it makes certain forms of misogynist violence possible. Still, respondents' violent experiences were undoubtedly shaped by structures of male domination, as many forms of anti-lesbian violence served to punish women for rejecting the sexual advances of heterosexual men, while perpetrators regularly used anti-gay violence to position themselves as stronger than gay male respondents. In both of these cases, homophobic violence serves as a social control mechanism designed to police gender norms and sustain the privilege of male heterosexuality. Nevertheless, in the contemporary United States, where gender nonconformity is viewed as indicative of homosexuality and where both of these identity markers are stigmatized, most forms of anti-queer violence should be understood as attempts to reinforce both gender and sexuality norms (Mason 2001).

Reactions to anti-queer violence are even implicated in this intersection of gender and sexuality, as respondents frequently mentioned how heterosexual people whom they had told about the violence implied that it had occurred because they had been "too open" or "too obvious" about their sexuality or gender identity. Respondents frequently perceived these remarks as suggestions that they should perform gender in a more traditional way (Meyer 2008, 2010). Furthermore, I have argued in this article that attempts to punish LGBT people for being "too open" about their sexuality or gender identity have different implications based on race, as Black and Latino/Latina respondents found such suggestions particularly troubling. In this sense, lesbians and gay men of color viewed criticisms of them being "too open" about their sexuality as implying that they had inappropriately represented their racial communities, while white respondents did not typically perceive such criticisms in this way.

Conclusion

In this article, I have emphasized that respondents frequently interpreted their violent experiences in different ways, even when the violence took on similar forms. Both Black and white lesbians, for instance, experienced physical violence for "converting" another woman into lesbianism, but this act had different implications for each of these groups, as Black lesbians often thought that their supposed conversion of a woman of color into lesbianism was viewed as harmful to their racial communities. Since white lesbians did not usually view their violent experiences as having racialized implications, similar forms of abuse were perceived differently depending on the respondent's racial identity. Thus, the ways in which LGBT people evaluate the severity of their violent experiences is not a straightforward process that can simply be measured by examining the type of abuse they have experienced.

Accounting for the overlap of multiple systems of oppression typically provides for the most satisfactory understanding of anti-queer violence. Indeed, examining my results through the lens of only one system of oppression would likely distort our understanding of anti-queer violence and perhaps even reinforce existing relations of domination (Collins 1998). Employing a gender-only framework, for example, to examine differences with regard to strength between gay men of color and white gay men, we might be tempted to view the gender performances of Black and Latino respondents as more traditionally masculine than those of white gay men, since the former more frequently emphasized the importance of strength. When also considering the intersection of race and sexuality, however, this difference can be viewed, more accurately, as gay men of color attempting to reject discourse that they were weak for negatively representing their racial communities—discourse that white gay male respondents did not confront.

While I examine intersections of race, gender, and sexuality in this article, I have not focused on important dimensions of oppression such as those based on religion, disability, or social class. Simultaneously analyzing all forms of inequality may be impossible, yet studies can appear incomplete or reductive when overlooking some systems of oppression (Cohen 1997). Moreover, while the number of inequalities addressed may be less important than the relevance of those inequalities, it remains imperative to explore the theoretical loss that occurs when some institutional power structures are not included in our analyses (Choo and Ferree 2010). Here, although my analysis of anti-queer violence remains imperfect by not exploring the effects of social class, I have emphasized the overlapping role of race, gender, and sexuality in structuring LGBT people's evaluations to help

facilitate a shift from the unitary effects of homophobia to the intersections among multiple systems of oppression. This intersectional shift would include taking into greater consideration social class inequality within queer communities.

Despite the potential difficulty of simultaneously accounting for multiple systems of oppression, much of sexualities scholarship would likely benefit from examining the overlap of heteronormativity with other institutional power structures. The emerging field of intersectional sexualities research has flourished recently (see Collins 2004; Moore 2011; Ward 2008), yet intersectional theory has arguably remained marginal to sexualities scholarship more generally (Cohen 1997; Moore 2011). As I have argued here, however, research that focuses exclusively on sexuality, homophobia, and heteronormativity frequently falls short of its potential, as the experiences of many groups of LGBT people are unlikely to be fully understood (Cohen 1997). Employing an intersectional approach to examine the lives of LGBT people necessitates not only including queer people who are oppressed along multiple axes of inequality, but also moving beyond frameworks that construct homophobia as the most predominant form of oppression confronting LGBT people. Such intersectional analyses include paying particular attention to the ways in which homosexuality is raced and classed, examining how these intersections may affect marginalized groups of LGBT people such as low-income women of color. Furthermore, as intersectional approaches continue to explore how privilege operates in LGBT communities, including how gender functions for men, race for white people, and social class for middle-class queer people, these analyses will help us to uncover the ways in which seemingly race-less and gender-less social positions play an important role in structuring individuals' experiences and perceptions. Future research should be particularly attentive to the effects of privilege and oppression among LGBT people, which includes expanding on my analysis to examine social class.

Given that queer people of color were usually describing intraracial violence based on their sexuality or gender identity, I have focused more attention on homophobia in heterosexual communities of color than on racism in white LGBT communities. This emphasis is also a result of the interactional context of the interviews, in which queer people of color may have felt most comfortable describing homophobia, rather than racism, with a white, gay male interviewer. Perhaps suspicious of how their descriptions of racism would be represented by a white gay man, queer people of color appeared to focus most of their attention on homophobia in their race-based communities, possibly viewing me, given my race and social class privilege, as someone who outsiders would listen to and who could bring their concerns to the outside world. The results presented in this article should be understood within this context, and caution should be taken with regard to making homophobia seem as if it is relegated to Black or Latino/Latina people, as stigmatizing homosexuality is not exclusive to these communities (Cohen 1999; Collins 2004; Smith 1999). Indeed, white, heterosexual men perpetrated most of the violence described by white respondents. Thus, as regulating homophobia to Black and Latino communities has the effect of blaming heterosexual people of color for the persistence of heteronormativity and freeing white heterosexual people of their responsibility for perpetuating heterosexism, scholarship focusing on homophobia in race-based communities should be balanced with an emphasis on the institutionalized privileging of heterosexuality.

I have focused on the particular challenges confronting LGBT people of color relative to white queer people, with the latter being able to overlook the racialized implications of their violent experiences because of their white privilege. Of course, white and middle-class gay men who are privileged within queer communities may face prejudice and discrimination in society at large and may confront relatively little privilege in comparison with white and middle-class heterosexual men, as heterosexuality remains institutionally supported in such a way that homosexuality is not. Still, as the violent experiences of many LGBT people continue to be shaped by racism and sexism as much as homophobia and heteronormativity, the effects of multiple and intersecting systems of oppression

should be taken into account. Indeed, the intersection of race, gender, and sexuality structured LGBT people's evaluations of their violent experiences. Thus, rather than focusing exclusively on homophobia, a more productive examination of anti-queer violence would explore how sexuality overlaps with race, class, and gender to structure LGBT people's experiences and perceptions of violence. More broadly, intersectional approaches are likely to aid in our understanding of sexualities to reveal how topics traditionally associated with homophobia and heterosexism are implicated not only in sexuality norms but also raced and gendered ones.

References

Bettie, Julie. 2003. *Women without class*. Berkeley: University of California Press.

Blee, Kathleen. 2002. *Inside organized racism*. Berkeley: University of California Press.

Choo, Hae Yeon, and Myra Marx Ferree, 2010. Practicing intersectionality in sociological research: A critical analysis of inclusions, interactions, and institutions in the study of inequalities. *Sociological Theory* 28:129–49.

Cohen, Cathy. 1997. Punks, bulldaggers, and welfare queens: The radical potential of queer politics? *GLO: A Journal of Lesbian and Gay Studies* 3:437–65.

Cohen, Cathy. 1999. *The boundaries of Blackness*. Chicago: University of Chicago Press.

Collins, Patricia Hill. 1998. The tie that binds: Race, gender and US violence. *Ethnic and Racial Studies* 21:917–38.

Collins, Patricia Hill. 2000. *Black feminist thought*. New York: Routledge.

Collins, Patricia Hill. 2004. *Black sexual politics*. New York: Routledge.

Crenshaw, Kimberlé. 1991. Mapping the margins: Intersectionality, identity politics, and violence against women of color. *Stanford Law Review* 43:1241–99.

Daniels, Jessie. 1997. *White lies*. New York: Routledge.

D'Augelli, Anthony R., and Arnold H. Grossman. 2001. Disclosure of sexual orientation, victimization, and mental health among lesbian, gay, and bisexual older adults. *Journal of Interpersonal Violence* 16:1008–27.

DeKeseredy, Walter. 2000. Current controversies in defining nonlethal violence against women in intimate heterosexual relationships: Empirical implications. *Violence Against Women* 6:728–46.

Dunbar, Edward. 2006. Race, gender, and sexual orientation in hate crime victimization: Identity politics or identity risk? *Violence and Victims* 21:323–37.

Epstein, Cynthia Fuchs. 1988. *Deceptive distinctions.* New York: Russell Sage Foundation.

Frankenberg, Ruth. 1993. *White women, race matters.* Minneapolis: University of Minnesota Press.

Herek, Gregory M. 1990. The context of anti-gay violence: Notes on cultural and psychological heterosexism. *Journal of Interpersonal Violence* 5:316–33.

Herek, Gregory M., J. Roy Gillis, and Jeanine C. Cogan. 1999. Psychological sequelae of hate crime victimization among lesbian, gay, and bisexual adults. *Journal of Consulting and Clinical Psychology* 67:945–51.

Herek, Gregory M., J. Roy Gillis, Jeanine C. Cogan, and Eric K. Glunt. 1997. Hate crime victimization among lesbian, gay, and bisexual adults: Prevalence, psychological correlates, and methodological issues. *Journal of Interpersonal Violence* 12:195–215.

Iganski, Paul. 2001. Hate crimes hurt more. *American Behavioral Scientist* 45:626–38.

Jenness, Valerie, and Kendal Broad. 1994. Antiviolence activism and the (in)visibility of gender in the gay/lesbian and women's movements. *Gender & Society* 8:402–23.

Johnson, Patrick. 2001. *Appropriating Blackness.* Durham, NC: Duke University Press.

King, Deborah. 1988. Multiple jeopardy, multiple consciousness: The context of a Black feminist ideology. *Signs* 14:42–72.

Madriz, Esther. 1997. *Nothing bad happens to good girls.* Berkeley: University of California Press.

Mason, Gail. 2001. Body maps: Envisaging homophobia, violence, and safety. *Social & Legal Studies* 10:23–44.

Mason, Gail. 2002. *The spectacle of violence.* New York: Routledge.

McCall, Leslie. 2005. The complexity of intersectionality. *Signs* 30:1771–1800.

Meyer, Doug. 2008. Interpreting and experiencing anti-queer violence: Race, class and gender differences among LGBT hate crime victims. *Race, Gender & Class* 15:262–82.

Meyer, Doug. 2010. Evaluating the severity of hate-motivated violence: Intersectional differences among LGBT hate crime victims. *Sociology* 44:980–95.

Moore, Mignon. 2006. Lipstick or Timberlands? Meanings of gender presentation in Black lesbian communities. *Signs* 32:113–39.

Moore, Mignon. 2011. *Invisible families.* Berkeley: University of California Press.

Perry, Barbara. 2001. *In the name of hate.* New York: Routledge.

Rose, Suzanna, and Mindy Mechanic. 2002. Psychological distress, crime features, and help-seeking behaviors related to homophobic bias incidents. *American Behavioral Scientist* 46:14–26.

Schilt, Kristen, and Laurel Westbrook. 2009. Doing gender, doing heteronormativity: "Gender normals," transgender people, and the social maintenance of heterosexuality. *Gender & Society* 23:440–64.

Smith, Barbara. 1999. Blacks and gays: Healing the great divide. In *Blacks, gays, and the struggle for equality,* edited by E. Brandt. New York: New Press.

von Schulthess, Beatrice. 1992. Violence in the streets: Anti-lesbian assault and harassment in San Francisco. In *Hate crimes,* edited by G. Herek and K. Berrill. Newbury Park, CA: Sage.

Ward, Jane. 2004. "Not all differences are created equal": Multiple jeopardy in a gendered organization. *Gender & Society* 18:82–102.

Ward, Jane. 2008. *Respectably queer.* Nashville: Vanderbilt University Press.

West, C., and D. Zimmerman. 1987. Doing gender. *Gender & Society* 1:125–51.

Zinn, Maxine Baca, and Bonnie Thornton Dill. 1996. Theorizing difference from multiracial feminism. *Feminist Studies* 22:321–32.